Patriot Pride

The 50 year rise of the New England Patriots as seen through a fan's eyes

Vin Femia

ISBN: 978-1-886284-78-4

Library of Congress Catalog Card Number: 2010930588

First Edition, First Printing

Published by

Chandler House Press
PO Box 20100, West Side Station
Worcester, MA 01602 USA
Phone/FAX 508-753-7419
www.chandlerhousebooks.com

Table of Contents

Vin Femia

Patriot Pride

This book is dedicated to my late father, Frank Femia, who loved football and taught me to love it too.

SECTION 1 – The Very Colorful Patriot Team History

Chapter 1 – Introduction

On February 3, 2008, Tom Brady led the undefeated Patriots on a late fourth quarter drive for a touchdown. The touchdown gave the New England Patriots a 14-10 lead in the Super Bowl over the New York Giants with just over two minutes left to be played in the game. Unfortunately, the defense could not stop the Giants. New York wound up scoring a touchdown of their own with 35 seconds remaining, and winning the championship of the National Football League. The Patriots had suffered their first and only defeat of the season in that year's ultimate game.

On September 7, 2008, barely over seven months later, Brady and the Patriots charged into the 2008 season looking to make up for that one notable blemish. The team's primary goal was to win the Super Bowl championship that was left as unfinished business from the preceding year. However, halfway through the first quarter of the first game of that season, Tom Brady suffered torn ACL and MCL ligaments in his left knee when being hit while trying to pass, and his season was over.

With Brady's injury, the Patriots had just lost their emotional leader, the NFL's Most Valuable Player, and a quarterback who had just had a record-breaking year in 2007. What was left to replace Brady was a quarterback who had not started a game since high school, and behind him was a rookie who had never yet played a down in a regular season NFL game. Thankfully, what was also left was an outstanding coach and a veteran core of players who knew how to win in the ultimate team game. How the Patriots handled adversity, and what the team did to try to overcome the loss of Tom Brady and try to reclaim that past glory is the main subject of this book, as we go through the Patriots' 2008 and 2009 seasons in week-by-week summaries, written as the games occurred and the season progressed. The summary will show the ups and downs of that season, as we see how the Patriots did in their quest to remain one of the NFL's elite teams.

Before we go through those seasons, it is also instructive to take a brief journey through the team's history, which began in 1960 in the fledgling American Football League. The Patriots had a very rocky, and often quirky, first four decades before achieving the dynastic success that they had in the first decade of the 21st century. The history shows how the Patriots got to where they are, and all of the bumps and laughs along the way.

Long-time fans will enjoy the decade-by-decade journey summarized in this first section of the book. It will jog your memory in many cases, and there may even be some anecdotes that are completely new to you. Many of the key games in Patriot history will be summarized, and that history is described through a fan's perspective. I hope that these personal insights will add to your enjoyment of these memories.

For those who are interested just in what transpired in 2008 and 2009 (or want to skip ahead and start with that), that roller coaster of a season begins in Chapter 7 of Section 2.

Every Patriot fan will enjoy the interviews with key contributors to Patriot history over the years. The interviews were fun to do, and the interviewees were very open and honest about their careers, their most memorable games, their toughest opponents, and other aspects of their careers.

The Patriots have a unique history, and the 2008 and 2009 seasons were themselves mysteries that unfolded over those long seasons. Whether you choose to start with the history and follow that through to the 2008 and 2009 seasons, or just read about 2008 and 2009, or just read the interviews, here's hoping that you enjoy reliving those moments, and that the Patriots continue to have success for many years to come.

Chapter 2 – 1960's: The "Foolish Club" Comes to Boston

   Although baseball and college football had been the primary team sports that America's fans had cherished in the first half of the 20th century, by the end of the 1950's the NFL had begun to come into prominence. The 1958 NFL championship game was an event that transcended sport and became legendary. The title game matched the Cinderella Baltimore Colts, with their brilliant young quarterback, Johnny Unitas, against the historic New York Giants, in a game played at Yankee Stadium in New York, the media capital of the world. It was also the first football game ever to have an overtime, as the two teams were tied 17-17 at the end of regulation and had to play OT to determine the championship. The tie had been created thanks to a tremendous two minute drill executed by Unitas that led to a game-tying field goal. Another great drive by Unitas and the Colts resulted in an Alan Ameche running touchdown and a sudden death win for the Colts. Interest in pro football was raised to another level as a result of this game.

   With the rise in prominence of pro football, a couple of very rich men decided that they wanted to be part of it. Lamar Hunt, son of Dallas oil billionaire H.L. Hunt, wanted to buy the Chicago Cardinals, one of the 12 NFL franchises in existence at the time. When the Cardinals were sold instead to the Bidwell family and moved to St. Louis, Hunt petitioned the NFL in 1959 to expand and to put a team in Dallas. The NFL refused, and told Hunt that it was not interested in expansion.

   A man like Lamar Hunt does not take no easily, and so he decided that the only way that he could get into pro football was to start his own league, and so he did.

   Hunt contacted fellow Texan Kenneth (Bud) Adams, who had similarly been interested in having an NFL team in Houston. They lined up other potential owners, including Bob Howsam in Denver, Ralph Wilson in Buffalo, hotel magnate Barron Hilton in Los Angeles, Max Winter in Minneapolis, and Harry Wismer in New York, and this group of owners agreed to create a new league, the American Football League (a.k.a. the AFL). As their plans moved forward, suddenly, the

NFL became interested in expansion and proposed adding franchises in Dallas and Minneapolis in 1960 and in Buffalo and Houston in 1961. Hunt and Adams decided not to accept this offer, however, but to honor their commitment to their fellow AFL owners and continue with the new league. Unfortunately, Max Winter did not follow suit and honor his commitment, and the Minnesota franchise withdrew from the AFL and accepted an offer to join the NFL.

When the city of Oakland, California was granted a franchise in the AFL to replace Minnesota, Wayne Valley, the club's CEO, after a particularly wild meeting of the AFL's potential owners, dubbed the group "The Foolish Club". Indeed, even without the meeting to inspire this title, any group that decided to challenge the NFL could indeed have earned a nickname such as this.

The league now had seven teams and needed an eighth. Seattle, Miami, and Atlanta all reportedly had shots at being in the AFL, but, on November 16, 1959, the eighth and final AFL franchise was awarded to Boston. The owner was Billy Sullivan, and though there were some questions about Billy's financing, he and his family were now part of the NFL, and would be for many years to come.

- - -

The team had been formed just in time for the inaugural AFL draft, which was held just days after Boston joined the league. The team drafted Ron Burton, a running back from Northwestern, as its first-ever draft pick and Syracuse running back Gerhard Schwedes became the team's first territorial pick (the AFL, like the National Basketball Association, was allowing teams to make a territorial draft of a player with some local ties, to help build fan interest in their teams). Burton had also been drafted by the NFL's Philadelphia Eagles and had a choice to play in the more established NFL, but chose to sign with the fledgling AFL and Boston (it is interesting to note that Burton is the father of current Boston TV sportscaster, Steve Burton). It was a big feather in the cap of the Boston team.

Billy Sullivan also hired Mike Holovak, the former BC football coach, to be his director of player personnel, and Lou Saban was hired in February 1960 as the team's first head coach.

The team had a public contest to have fans suggest a team nickname, and on February 20, the franchise announced that "Patriots" was the name selected, in honor of the Revolutionary War history of Boston. The team also selected red, white, and blue, naturally, as the colors for the Patriots' uniforms.

Now what was left was finding a home field and filling out the roster of players. The Red Sox refused to let the Patriots play at Fenway Park. Similarly, Boston College and Harvard did not want professional football using their fields. The Manning Bowl in Lynn was a possibility -- but imagine the irony of the 2000-era Patriots playing big games against the Indianapolis Colts and their star QB Peyton Manning at a facility called the Manning Bowl. Eventually Boston University agreed to allow the Patriots to play at their field, which, incidentally, had been the home of baseball's Boston Braves before they moved to Milwaukee in 1953 and then later to Atlanta. Drivers entering Boston on the Massachusetts Turnpike can still see three BU dorms outlined as left, center, and right field overlooking the stadium.

Players were signed. Some were castoffs of NFL teams, some were rookies. One very interesting player signed was Gino Cappelletti, who had been a player at the University of Minnesota and then had played some in the Canadian Football League. Cappelletti went on to become one of the team's all-time greats as a kicker and wide receiver, and then, after his retirement as a player, became an excellent radio broadcaster of Patriot football games, teaming for many years with play-by-play announcer Gil Santos to form a broadcasting team that has become very popular with Patriot fans.

- - -

Finally, everything was ready for the 1960 season to begin and for real football to be played. The Patriots were in the AFL Eastern Division, and the league was configured as follows:

<u>East</u>
Boston Patriots   (now New England)
Buffalo Bills
New York Titans   (now Jets)
Houston Oilers   (now Tennessee Titans)
<u>West</u>
Denver Broncos
Dallas Texans   (now Kansas City Chiefs)
Oakland Raiders
Los Angeles Chargers (now San Diego)

Interestingly, the NFL created an expansion team in Dallas for the 1960 season as well. They called it the Cowboys. The Cowboys were to go winless in that first season, and only a 31-31 tie with the Giants in the season's last game gave them anything but a loss in every game. The Cowboys have since gone on to become one of the most popular teams in all of American sport, and eventually their popularity caused Lamar Hunt to move the Texans from his beloved Dallas to Kansas City, where they became the Chiefs.

The Patriots played in both the first exhibition game for the AFL, on July 30, 1960 against the Bills in Buffalo (a 28-7 Patriot win), and in the league's first regular season game. That first game was played on Friday night, September 9, 1960 before a crowd of 21,597 at BU Field. The Patriots hosted the Denver Broncos, whose main claim to fame in that first season was being the only pro football team to wear socks with vertical stripes. Boston was favored in the game but lost it to Denver 13-10. *The Foolish Club's* league was now underway.

The team finished fourth in the AFL East with a 5-9 record. Butch Songin was the passing leader. Gino Cappelletti and receiver Jimmy Colclough were the leading scorers. The team had started 5-5 but lost its last four games, including the finale to Houston, which went on to win the AFL's first championship, beating the Chargers in the championship game.

One story that I loved from this time was about reporters meeting with billionaire H.L. Hunt, whose son, Lamar, was the owner of the Dallas Texans. One of the reporters asked the elder Hunt what he thought of his son, Lamar, losing a million dollars operating the Texans. H.L. Hunt's reply was something like "A million dollars, huh? At this rate he'll run out of money in a hundred years." It was obvious that the Hunts were willing to lose some money on their investment in pro football, and that they were in it for the long haul.

In 1961 the Patriots started 2-3 and head coach Lou Saban was fired by owner Billy Sullivan. Sullivan persuaded Mike Holovak to take over as coach. Holovak did so reluctantly but became a great leader and the team responded by finishing the season with 7 wins, 1 tie, and only 1 loss, good enough for a 9-4-1 record and a second place finish behind Houston, which went on to win the championship again.

One of Holovak's moves was to alternate quarterbacks on every play. The two quarterbacks in question were the returning veteran, Butch Songin, and newcomer Vito "Babe" Parilli, who had been obtained in a trade with Oakland before the season had begun. The tactic ended when Songin was injured with three games remaining in the season. Parilli took over and played so well in three road wins over Denver, Oakland, and San Diego that Holovak decided that he should be the starter for 1962 and traded Songin to New York. Babe would be a fixture at quarterback for Boston for years to come.

Under Holovak, Gino Cappelletti became a wide receiver as well as a kicker, and Larry Garron began to see more playing time at running back, alongside Ron Burton. Cappelletti, in fact, wound up leading the team in pass receptions, with 45.

One of the oddest plays in the sometimes-odd history of the Patriots occurred during that 1961 season, as a fan reportedly came onto the field and helped the Patriots win a game, and did this without being seen by the game officials. This happened in a game on November 3, 1961 in Boston. The Patriots were leading the Dallas Texans 28-21 with just a few seconds left in the game. Dallas QB Cotton Davidson threw a long pass to Chris Burford, and the officials ruled Burford down at the 1 yard line. Many fans thought that the game was over and charged onto the field from the stands to celebrate. The officials had to move the crowd back, however, as there was still one second left on the clock. On what would be the final play of a memorable game, Davidson dropped back and threw a pass intended again for Burford. Just then a fan wearing a trench coat or windbreaker (reports vary) came out of the crowd and ran in front of Burford, waving his arms to distract the Dallas receiver, and the pass sailed incomplete over Burford's head. None of the officials saw it (!) so the game was over and Boston had won. Some say it was Billy Sullivan in that trench coat, some say not. Some say it didn't happen. Others say it did. Gino Cappelletti is reported to have said that the team saw it on film the next day and roared in laughter. As to whether the culprit was Billy Sullivan or not, Cappelletti is quoted in Michael Felger's book "Tales from the Patriots Sideline" that he didn't think so; Cappelletti's belief was that "it was some bookmaker from East Boston trying to protect a bet." Whatever it was, it was hilarious.

- - -

The Patriots repeated at 9-4-1 and second place in 1962, and played one of their seven home games at Harvard Stadium. The Patriots were in a battle with Houston for first place in the AFL East until the final week of the season, when they lost to the Raiders in Oakland, 20-0. It was Oakland's only win of the season. It would be the first of many heart-breaking losses for the Patriots, and the first of many at the hands of the Raiders.

An agreement was reached for the Patriots to play six home games at Fenway Park in 1963, which was a big step for the team. The first home game was played at BC Alumni Stadium, so the Patriots did wind up playing games in their first three years at all three of the local colleges who had good-sized football fields.

The 1963 season was a very successful one for the Patriots. The team had really come together in all phases of the game in 1963. The offense was led by the passing of Babe Parilli, a solid running game featuring Larry Garron (750 yards rushing), and excellent receiving by Cappelletti, Colclough, and rookie Art Graham. The defense was anchored by a strong front four of Bob Dee, Larry Eisenhauer, Houston Antwine, and Jim Lee Hunt and an excellent second year middle linebacker from Notre Dame, Nick Buoniconti.

Though their record was not as good as that of the two previous years, they finished tied with Buffalo for first place in the AFL East with a record of 7-6-1. Oddly, Buffalo's coach was Lou Saban, who had been the Patriot coach in 1960 and for the first 5 games of 1961.

With the AFL East finishing in a tie, Boston and Buffalo met in a playoff game in Buffalo on December 28. There was a big snowstorm before the game, which led many to favor the Bills, who had home field advantage, and a strong running game led by Cookie Gilchrist, who had led the AFL in running yards gained during the season. However, the Patriots dominated the game, holding Gilchrist in check and getting a nice 56 yard TD run from Garron and a solid game from Babe Parilli in a 26-8 upset win that sent them to San Diego for a championship match-up with the Chargers.

"Match-up" was a misnomer, though, as the Chargers thoroughly destroyed Boston 51-10. I and other Patriot fans remember too vividly San Diego running backs Keith Lincoln and Paul Lowe running unstopped through the Boston line for long gain after long gain after long gain. Lincoln had a 67 yard touchdown run in the first quarter and 206 yards rushing on only 13 carries for the game. Lowe had a 58 yard touchdown run, also in the first quarter, and finished with 94 yards of his own, on 12 carries. The game was never a contest.

Patriot fans could soothe their disappointment with the hope that the team could come back and play for another championship in the next year or two, but little knew that they would be in for drought of many years before another Patriot appearance in the post-season playoffs.

The Patriots did start 1964 looking as if a repeat AFL East title was indeed a possibility. They started the season with four straight wins, three of which were on the road: 17-14 over the Raiders in Oakland, a revenge 33-28 win at San Diego, 26-10 over the Jets in Boston, and a 39-10 win at Denver. Buffalo had also started the season 4-0, so another season-long battle with the Bills seemed likely. San Diego broke Boston's winning streak with a 26-17 win at Fenway Park.

The team was 6-2-1 when they traveled to Buffalo to face the undefeated 9-0 Bills. They would be facing a powerful Buffalo offense led again by running back Cookie Gilchrist and the pass combination of quarterback Jack Kemp and speedy receiver Elbert Dubenion. 43,000 fans turned up for the game and the Bills' players and fans were looking for revenge of their own against Boston, but it was the Patriots who had the upper hand, winning 36-28 as Gino Cappelletti had three TD receptions and the Patriot defense had a strong game.

The Patriots won their next three games to go into the season finale with Buffalo at 10-2-1. Buffalo came into the game with a record of 11-2. The team that won the game would win the AFL East. Again a snowstorm plagued a game between these two Northern rivals. Snow covered much of the field, and the day was bitter cold. Unlike the 1963 playoff game, though, it was the Bills who overcame the elements and their opponents. Buffalo opened the scoring with a 58 yard touchdown bomb from Kemp to Dubenion and went on to win the game 24-14 and with it the Eastern title. The Bills later capped their great season by winning the AFL championship as well, with a 20-7 win over the Chargers.

There were some very interesting player additions to the AFL and to the Patriots for the 1965 season. The Jets and their owner Sonny Werblin made headlines across the country by signing Joe Namath, a quarterback from the University of Alabama, for a then unheard-of $ 400,000. Media and football experts scoffed at the money that the Jets were spending on an unproven quarterback. The Jets compounded this criticism by also signing John Huarte, the quarterback from Notre Dame who had won the 1964 Heisman Trophy after a great season with Notre Dame, to a $ 200,000 contract. The Jets had signed two rookie quarterbacks for more money than many veteran quarterbacks were making. The Patriots rookie splash, such as it was, was Jim Nance, who had modest success in 1965 but better success later.

The 1965 season was not a good one for the Patriots. They lost their first 5 games, tied San Diego, and then lost again. They had a miserable 1-8-2 record before gaining some respectability by winning their final three games. Still, their 4-8-2 record was good enough only for third place in their division.

1966 brought a new team into the AFL, the Miami Dolphins, and a peace settlement between the NFL and AFL. Part of the settlement was an agreement to match the two league champions in a World Championship game at a neutral site, beginning in January 1967. It was also agreed that two leagues would merge into one following the 1969 season, when their existing TV contracts would be expiring.

Before the 1966 season, the Patriots made history by signing Rommie Loudd as an assistant coach. Loudd thus became the first African-American assistant coach in the AFL. Loudd later moved into the front office to become Director of Player Personnel.

The Patriots rebounded from their terrible 1965 season to go 8-3-2 in their first 13 games of 1966 and head into their season finale with a chance to play for the AFL championship. The main reason for that turnaround from 1965 was the play of Jim Nance. Nance in 1966 ran for an AFL record 1,458 yards. Babe Parilli was still starring as quarterback. Interestingly, his backup was John Huarte, the former Jet. Huarte had performed well in the College All-Star game in 1965 (an annual game pitting just-graduated college players against the defending NFL champion; the game is no longer played), but missed time in training camp and, as a result, was beaten out for a quarterback job in New York.

Prior to that season finale, the biggest game of the season had been a Fenway Park showdown with Buffalo on December 4 for the AFL Eastern Division lead. Boston came into the game with a record of 6-3-2. Buffalo, at 8-3-1, was a half game ahead of Boston coming into the game.

In the first quarter, with Buffalo ahead 3-0, Boston's bruising fullback, Jim Nance, blasted through the line on a third down and 2 and raced 65 yards for a touchdown that put the Patriots ahead 7-3. Both teams were playing excellent defensive football, so the score remained 7-3 into the third quarter when the Patriots caught a break. A pass from Babe Parilli intended for Joe Bellino (the former Heisman Trophy running back from Navy) was almost intercepted but bounced off of the hands of the Buffalo defender and was hauled in by Bellino at the Buffalo 5 yard line. Parilli scored on a rollout from the three yard line, and the Patriots had a 14-3 lead and the defense held that lead to give them one of the biggest wins in the young history of the franchise. Their 7-3-2 record and .700 winning percentage now allowed them to take over the division lead from 8-4-1 Buffalo with its winning percentage of .667. A 38-14 win at Houston the following week kept the Patriots in the driver's seat for the division crown heading into the season finale at New York.

If they could then win that, they would have a chance to get to that first AFL-NFL championship game, a game which would later become glamorized as "The Super Bowl". Patriot fans were ecstatic. Could their team really be on their way to playing the mighty Green Bay Packers of the NFL for that first World Championship?

The Patriots would finish the 1966 regular season with a game at Shea Stadium against the Jets. The Jets and their new star QB, Joe Namath, upset the Patriots 38-28 to end the Patriots' chances for post-season play. Boston's record of 8-4-2 put them ½ game behind Buffalo, which finished 9-4-1. The Patriots' season thus ended in disappointment as the Bills wound up winning the division. Lamar Hunt's Kansas City Chiefs would go on to beat the Bills and play the Green Bay Packers in the first Super Bowl, and the Packers wound up as champions with a 35-10 win.

Little did anyone know that this would be the Patriots' last winning season for 9 years. They finished the decade of the 1960's with records of 3-10-1 for last place in 1967, 4-10 for fourth place in a five team division in 1968, and 4-10 and tied for third in 1969, the last year of the AFL's existence before its merger into the NFL.

The team continued to bounce around different places that they called home, playing in Fenway Park in 1967 and 1968 and Boston College Alumni Stadium in 1969. They would then move to Harvard Stadium in 1970 before moving to Foxboro in 1971, where they have remained since.

The Patriots were the true nomads of the NFL for much of the 1960's. This was never more true than for their home opener in 1968, which was moved from Fenway Park due to conflicts with the Red Sox schedule. That game, played on September 22, 1968, had to be moved. Was it moved to Harvard Stadium? No. Was it moved to BU Stadium? No. Was it moved to BC Alumni Field? No. Was it moved to the Manning Bowl in nearby Lynn, MA? No. Was it moved to Holy Cross' Fitton Field in nearby Worcester, MA? No. It wound up being played in far away Birmingham, Alabama. Aren't you glad that you did not have tickets and have to make arrangements to travel from Boston to Birmingham for that game? Then, after all of that, you would have seen a 47-31 loss to the Jets, so it would probably not have been worth the trip after all.

At this time rumors continued to fly that the Patriots would have to move out of Boston. Billy Sullivan had been trying to get a stadium built for his team, but could not. Birmingham was hoping that the Patriots might move there, and so invited them to come down for that 1968 game. Memphis, Jacksonville, Seattle, and Tampa were among the cities also courting the Patriots, but Sullivan steadfastly refused to move the team.

Mike Holovak remained as Boston's coach until 1968. He was replaced by Clive Rush. In yet another odd moment in Patriot history, Rush was nearly electrocuted at a press conference called shortly after his selection as the new head coach. When Rush was called to speak, he grabbed the microphone, but since the microphone was not grounded, electric current starting flowing through Rush's body. He was saved from electrocution only by the quick work of a Patriot official who realized what was happening and ran to unplug what was a very "live" mike. It was quite an intro for Coach Rush.

- - -

From my personal experience, 1969 was also the year in which I attended my first NFL game. I was a student at Holy Cross at the time, and my very good friend, Tom Mulligan, from New York, was interested in going to see the Jets, who had won the Super Bowl earlier in the year in a stunning upset of the powerful Baltimore Colts. I agreed to go with him and we took a bus into Boston to go to Alumni Stadium. I was somewhat awestruck not only to be seeing an actual professional football game for the first time, but also to see the defending Super Bowl champions in that game. We had end zone seats (as you might expect two unemployed college students to have) and it happened to be the end zone where the Jets were warming up, so we got to see the World Champions close up. Since they were playing the woeful Patriots, who had started the season by losing their first three games, and who were starting journeyman Mike Taliaferro at quarterback while the Jets were starting one of the all-time greats, Joe Namath, it was expected that the Jets would win easily.

In the fourth quarter, the Jets indeed had moved to a 23-7 lead, but the Patriots were driving. At the time, the AFL had the rule where a team that scored a touchdown could choose to try for a 1-point or 2-point conversion (the NFL only allowed 1-point conversions at the time). I was thinking to myself "If the Patriots score they will go for 2 points, so that they can tie the game with another touchdown and 2-point conversion."

Well the Patriots did score, and to my surprise, Coach Clive Rush sent out the kicking team to go for the 1-point conversion. The kick made the score 23-14 and absolutely guaranteed a Patriot loss. The Pats would now need two scores in little time to avoid their fourth consecutive loss, instead of one score that they would have needed had they made the two point conversion. It was an extremely bad decision by an extremely bad coach. I have always believed that one of the primary responsibilities of a professional sports team's coach or manager is to put his team in the best possible position to win. Bill Belichick certainly has done that since he has been the Patriots' coach. Rush certainly did not do that. To say that I was surprised would be an understatement. To say that I was shocked would bring back too many painful memories to the once nearly-electrocuted Coach Rush, and despite my disdain for that decision, I would not wish to do that to him.

One of the many weird things that happened under Clive Rush was his desire in 1969 to create what he called "The Black Power Defense". In essence, he wanted his defensive team to be made of black players and black players only. This was a terribly awkward idea even in an age well before political correctness. Players should be playing based on merit, black or white. In contrast, Boston Celtics' basketball coach Red Auerbach became the first NBA coach to start five black players in 1965. When he was asked about it, Auerbach was surprised, and responded that starting these five players was done to give his team the best chance to win. Auerbach did things because they were right. Rush might have been trying to create a defense with a catchy nickname such as the Dallas Cowboys' "Doomsday Defense", the Minnesota Vikings' "Purple People Eaters" (they wore purple uniforms), or the Los Angeles Rams' "Fearsome Foursome", but this was not well thought out. It was especially odd considering that he did not even *have* eleven black players on his defensive roster at the time. He tried to convert some offensive players to defense, but that did not work and this whole idea was quickly shelved.

Coach Rush's Patriots finished 4-10 in 1969, which turned out to be his only full season with the team. When the Patriots started out 1-6 in 1970, Rush was fired and replaced by John Mazur. Rush never did get another head coaching job in professional football. This did not come as a shock to any astute observer (and that will be the last reference to Clive Rush and/or that microphone in this book; I promise).

- - -

Now it was on to the 1970's and Patriot fans could hope that the new decade would bring success. Unfortunately, things would have to get worse before they would get better.

Chapter 3 – 1970's: Flashes of Glory

One of the best things to happen to the Patriots in the 1970's happened well before they played their first game of that decade. There was an agreement reached to build a new stadium for the team and the Patriots could finally put an end to their nomadic existence. On April 4, 1970 it was announced that a stadium that would house the team would be built in Foxboro, Massachusetts. The new stadium would be ready for the 1971 season.

Also, off the field, the NFL-AFL merger became official and the teams formerly part of the AFL were now absorbed into an expanded NFL. In the new league configuration, the Patriots would be part of what would now be called the American Football Conference (AFC) and would be in the AFC East along with the Baltimore Colts (who had been one of the elite teams in the NFL for years), the Miami Dolphins, and two old, traditional rivals, the Buffalo Bills and the New York Jets.

The Patriots also raised some eyebrows by signing Joe Kapp to be their quarterback for 1970. Kapp had just come off a fantastic season for the NFL's Minnesota Vikings, leading them to a 12-2 record and to their first Super Bowl (a stunning loss to the AFL's Kansas City Chiefs). Kapp had been the spiritual leader of the Vikings and one of the toughest quarterbacks to play the game. Having Kapp join the team was a real public relations win for the Patriots and a big upgrade at that position from the incumbent, Mike Taliaferro.

Clive Rush was still the coach, and the craziness continued in the season opener against Miami, which was played at Harvard Stadium. The craziness this time involved Bob Gladieux, a running back and special teams player who had been one of the last roster cuts made by Rush before the season began. Gladieux reportedly came to the game with a friend, after they had downed quite a few pre-game drinks. Before the game, and while the friend had gone under the stands to fetch another round, over the public address system came an announcement asking Gladieux to report to the Patriot locker room. Apparently Rush had just cut another player and needed someone to fill the roster spot. Meanwhile, the friend had returned to the stands and wondered where Gladieux had gone. A few minutes later he got his answer when the Pats kicked off and he heard the PA announcer say "tackle by Gladieux" and he looked down and saw Gladieux in uniform running off the field. Things like this could only happen, it seemed, with the Patriots.

The Patriots actually won that game, 27-14, but lost the next six. That led on November 12 to the firing of Clive Rush and the hiring of John Mazur as his replacement. The Patriots would finish their second half under Mazur with the same 1-6 record that they had had under Rush, and so they finished 2-12 on the season.

The Patriots' poor 1970 season had one silver lining, however, as it gave them the # 1 overall pick in the 1970 NFL draft. They used that pick wisely, drafting Stanford quarterback Jim Plunkett with the pick. Plunkett was a super college quarterback, the 1970 Heisman Trophy winner, and had come off a huge upset of previously undefeated Ohio State in the Rose Bowl. He was a definite upgrade over Joe Kapp, who had not performed nearly as well in Boston as he had for Minnesota.

The Patriots used their second pick to draft defensive end Julius Adams, another good player who would become a key contributor for the Patriots, anchoring their defensive line for many years.

- - -

The Patriots made a positive move in the front office in 1971, hiring Upton Bell as their new General Manager. Bell had previously been Director of Player Personnel for the Baltimore Colts, the team that had won the 1970 World Championship in Super Bowl V. Upton's father, Bert Bell, had been the NFL Commissioner from 1946-1959, and before that had been involved in the formation of the Philadelphia Eagles in 1933 and was a co-owner of the Pittsburgh Steelers from 1941-46, so Upton brought an excellent personal and family football heritage into this position. At 33, he was also now the youngest General Manager in the NFL.

Despite his background and knowledge, Bell wound up having run-ins with Patriot owner Billy Sullivan, most notably on the decision regarding the head coach, John Mazur, whom Upton had wanted to fire at the end of the 1971 season. Although Upton believed that he and Sullivan had agreed when Bell was hired that Bell had the right to hire and fire the head coach, Sullivan then did not hold to that agreement and retained Mazur for 1972, despite Bell's desire to replace him. Mazur was ultimately fired, after a 2-7 start in 1972.

Bell was Patriot GM for just two years, before the organization decided to go in a different direction and hired Chuck Fairbanks as Head Coach and GM, but he helped to improve the Patriots' operation in many ways, such as establishing a full-time scouting operation for the team and hiring a number of very good people to key positions in the organization. (Note: more information about all of this will be described in the section of this book that summarizes interviews with key players and contributors to the team's history.) He helped set the groundwork for the success that the team would have later in the decade.

- - -

With the completion of Schaefer Stadium in 1971, and the Patriots' move from Boston to Foxboro, the team decided that it was no longer appropriate to use "Boston" to designate the team's home. It's not clear why they decided that, since other teams have moved out of their original home cities and retained that name (the New York Giants move to New Jersey is one example, another is the Jets move to New Jersey, the Detroit Pistons playing in Auburn Hills, the Dallas Cowboys playing in Irving Texas, and so on) but decide that they did. The first name chosen was the Bay State Patriots but that name was scrapped when the realization struck that newspaper headlines about the BS Patriots would not help the team's image. On March 22 the name "New England Patriots" was chosen and has stuck since that time.

The grand opening of Schaefer Stadium was scheduled for August 15, an exhibition game with the New York Giants. The opening did not prove to be grand by any stretch of the imagination. The new stadium sits on Route 1 in Foxboro, not a high access road. This led to enormous traffic jams leading into the game, and it took hours for some fans to get their cars near the stadium. When they arrived, they found that there was not enough parking, and what was available was barely adequate – mostly dirt and gravel fields. When they finally did get into the stadium, they found that most seats were not really seats, but part of long aluminum or concrete benches. While aluminum may have been cost-effective, it is also worth noting that aluminum benches can be very hot places to sit in the summer, and very cold in the winter. Finally, during the game, the heavy use of toilets during timeouts and halftime was not something for which the stadium architects had adequately planned. Toilets overflowed, and the water pressure level in Foxboro had dropped so low that the Fire Department was concerned about whether they would be able to handle any fires that might occur in their town on game days. Once again, it seemed like these things could only happen to the Patriots.

The only positive thing about the day was that the Patriots won the game 20-14, but that only sent the fans out into jammed parking lots and major traffic jams on Route 1 heading in the opposite directions. Again it took some fans many hours to get out of the parking lot and then to get home.

The parking problems would not be easily solved but the toilet and water problem was resolved. When it was, stadium and town officials felt that they needed to confirm that the problem would no longer occur, so they enlisted the aid of hundreds of people one Saturday in what became known as "The Big Flush" test. The volunteers went into every Men's Room and Ladies' Room in the stadium, and, upon hearing a signal, simultaneously flushed every toilet and urinal and turned on every faucet in every sink in the stadium. Everything came out okay (so to speak). The Big Flush was a success, but again, this was the type of thing that seemingly could only happen with the Patriots.

Things were a little better on the field. Jim Plunkett proved to be everything that he was cracked up to be. He played every down on offense in every game of the season. Plunkett did sustain a lot of hits though, behind a weak offensive line, but he persevered and the Patriots improved from their 2-12 record in 1970 to 6-8 in 1971. Five of their losses were to teams which had been in the playoffs the previous season – AFC and Super Bowl champion Baltimore, NFC champion Dallas, Miami, Detroit, and San Francisco. Among the Patriots' highlights though were an opening day 20-6 win over the powerful Oakland Raiders, a 34-13 win over a rising Miami team on December 5, and a season-ending 21-17 win in Baltimore over the defending Super Bowl Champion Colts.

It seemed to many that with a more experienced Plunkett back to build off the improvement shown in 1971 New England's fortunes were on the upswing, but the team fell back to 3-11 in 1972. John Mazur was fired after starting the season 2-7 and was replaced by Phil Bengston, who had succeeded the legendary Vince Lombardi as coach of the Green Bay Packers. Bengston had been fired by Green Bay when they could not repeat the success they had had under Lombardi, and he had little success as New England's interim coach. The team was 1-4 under him.

In the off-season before the 1973 season, Sullivan decided to find a strong coach and to give him full power and authority over the team as both coach and general manager. With a young, developing team, hiring a successful college coach was also a consideration and Sullivan went hard and fast after Joe Paterno, the legendary, highly successful coach at Penn State. He almost landed Paterno, but Joe decided that he and his family were happy in Happy Valley and he decided to stay at Penn State. It was a good decision for Joe as he went on to coach 35+ more years at Penn State (and was still there in 2009) and would become one of the winningest coaches in college football history.

With Paterno no longer a possibility, Sullivan turned to Chuck Fairbanks, the young coach who had turned around the fortunes of the University of Oklahoma team, and had restored the Oklahoma Sooners to national prominence. Fairbanks was announced as the new Patriot head coach and GM on January 26, 1973, and, in his time with the Patriots made a very positive impact on the team.

Among Fairbanks' strengths was recognizing young talent, and the players that he drafted while at New England formed a solid backbone for success and were among the best players in the team's history. This began with his very first draft, as Fairbanks used the three selections that he had in the first round to pick Alabama guard John Hannah, Southern Cal running back Sam "Bam" Cunningham, and Purdue wide receiver Darryl Stingley. Hannah especially was a great pick, as he went on to become one of the best offensive linemen in pro football history.

The team went 5-9 in Fairbanks' first year as coach, and then he added more talent in the draft after the 1973 season, selecting linebacker Steve Nelson and running back Andy Johnson. The nucleus of a good team was starting to form.

Things really started looking up as the 1974 season started. The Patriots opened the season with a home game against the Miami Dolphins. The Dolphins were pro football's newest dynasty, having appeared in three consecutive Super Bowls, winning the last two in a row, and becoming the only team in pro football history to go undefeated in a season, 17-0 in 1972. Their most recent game was the 1974 Super Bowl in which they utterly demolished the Minnesota Vikings 24-7, a game that was effectively over in the first quarter.

On this day, however, Plunkett was great and the Patriots shocked the pro football world by upsetting the highly favored Dolphins 34-24. They followed that with a 28-20 win over the Giants, a 20-14 win over the Los Angeles Rams, a 42-3 dismantling of the Baltimore Colts, and a 24-0 road win over the New York Jets. The Patriots, long the doormats of the National Football League, were now suddenly 5-0 to begin the season. The passing attack led by quarterback Jim Plunkett, receivers Randy Vataha (a Stanford teammate of Plunkett) and Reggie Rucker, and the running back tandem of powerful Sam "Bam" Cunningham and the elusive Mack "Mini-Mack" Herron gave the team a very diversified offense. *Sports Illustrated* magazine featured a story about them entitled "Patriotic Shout". The story was led off with a picture of Jim Plunkett barking signals at the offensive line. Could the Patriots be ready to join the league's elite?

Not quite yet, as a 30-28 loss at Buffalo on October 20 gave them their first defeat. They regrouped with a 17-14 win at Miami to finish the first half of the season at 6-1. The bottom fell out after that however, as the team went 1-6 over the second half of the season. Still, the resultant 7-7 record was the team's first non-losing season since 1966. In the draft after that season the Patriots picked up two notable additions, tight end Russ Francis from Hawaii and the University of Oregon was selected in the first round. A little known quarterback from Kansas State was selected in the fifth round. His name was Steve Grogan, and he would have a huge impact on the history of the team.

- - -

The great 5-0 start of 1974 was reversed in 1975 as the team started 0-4. They would finish 3-11 after losing their last six games. More importantly, all-everything quarterback Jim Plunkett had been injured, which helped lead to the team's demise. Plunkett only started 5 games, but his replacement, the unheralded Steve Grogan, came in and impressed everyone with his passing ability, a running ability rarely seen in quarterbacks, and outstanding leadership.

As surprising as it may have seemed at any point since he was drafted in 1970, Jim Plunkett was now considered expendable, as the Patriots looked to a future that had Grogan as their starting QB. Plunkett was traded to the San Francisco 49ers in a big trade that brought the Patriots a number of players and draft picks. The years of battering that Plunkett took behind the Patriot offensive line had taken its toll. Plunkett was nowhere near the player in San Francisco that he had been previously. San Francisco let him go and his career appeared over. However, he latched on with the Raiders, and wound up resurrecting his career there, becoming a starter and winning two Super Bowls as the Raiders' QB. In any case, he will be remembered fondly by many Patriot fans as a gallant warrior who helped lift up a moribund franchise during his time with the team.

With Plunkett gone, the team was now in the hands of Steve Grogan for 1976 and beyond, and Grogan became one of the most influential players in the team's history. Many people consider the era of 1976-1978 to be the greatest in the team's history before the amazing successes that would come in 2001 and later. In fact, the Patriots in 1976 had one of the greatest seasons in the team's history, one that was spoiled with an aggravating playoff ending that left a bad taste in the mouths of many, as will be described shortly.

The 1976 team was strong on offense, with a backfield led by Steve Grogan, who would throw for 2,162 yards and run for 324 yards of his own. Fullback Sam Cunningham was a 1,000 yard rusher, finishing with 1,015. Halfback Andy Johnson ran for 699 yards and was a threat to pass out of the option and catch passes from out of the backfield also. Darryl Stingley led the receivers with 370 yards receiving, and Russ Francis and Andy Johnson added 367 and 343, respectively. The offensive line was strong, particularly on the left side, where guard John Hannah and tackle Leon Gray were a formidable duo of run and pass blockers. The defense featured a tough line with Julius Adams, and Ray "Sugar Bear" Hamilton, excellent linebackers, including Steve Nelson, George Webster, Steve Zabel, and Sam Hunt. Rookie Mike Haynes was fast becoming one of the best defensive backs in the NFL.

The team started out decently, going 5-3 in its first eight games, but then really jelled, winning its last six games, to go 11-3 for the season. One key win was a Monday night 41-7 devastation of the New York Jets on October 18 in which Steve Grogan had a great game passing and running. For the season Grogan passed for 18 touchdowns and ran for 12 more, outstanding numbers for a quarterback in the modern pass-happy NFL.

The Patriots' 11-3 record tied them with Baltimore for first place in the AFC East. By nature of the NFL tiebreaker system, Baltimore won the division, but the Patriots also made the playoffs as the AFC wildcard team, the second place team with the best record in the conference. The Patriots were red-hot going into the playoffs and were a team that other teams feared. In the first round of the playoffs, they would be going up against the Oakland Raiders, whose 13-1 record was the best in the league. The Raiders' only loss had been to these same New England Patriots. The Patriots had blasted the Raiders 48-17 on October 3, so it was very possible that New England could defeat Oakland again. It was a match-up that was highly anticipated by fans around the league.

The game was played in Oakland on Saturday night, December 18. I was in the Air Force at the time and my family and I watched the game with Tom and Pam Finnie, our friends from Ohio who for some reason were Red Sox and Patriot fans (we had gone with them to Baltimore in September 1975 to see a two game Red Sox – Orioles showdown in Memorial Stadium). We and Patriot fans everywhere were elated with the start of the game and deflated at the ending. The Patriots greatly outplayed the Raiders for most of the game but were done in by two long drives by Oakland at the end of each half, the last greatly aided by some very questionable officiating.

The Patriots entered the fourth quarter leading 21-10. Andy Johnson had run for one touchdown, Jess Phillips for another, and

Steve Grogan had thrown a 26 yard touchdown pass to Russ Francis. The Patriots had lost two other scoring opportunities due to trick plays, one of which was an ill-advised (or clever call?) end-around pass by tight end Russ Francis that was intercepted by Oakland, killing one drive.

The Patriots still had a 21-17 lead late in the game after a 1 yard touchdown run by Oakland's Mark Van Eagen, and were on a drive that could have killed the clock and ended Oakland's hopes. On a key third and six play, Grogan threw for Francis but Oakland linebacker Phil Villapiano, badly beaten on the play by Francis, clearly held Francis and prevented the big tight end from raising his arms and catching the ball. TV replays showed that the infraction by Villapiano was obvious and that a penalty call should have been made. In fact, Villapiano later admitted to Francis that he was beaten on the play and his only choice was to grab Francis and hope that the officials would not call it. They complied. Instead of a catch and first down, or an interference call against Villapiano, the Patriots were forced to try a 50 yard field goal attempt by kicker John Smith, but the kick missed.

Oakland QB Ken Stabler, one of the best ever at the two minute drill, then drove the Raiders down the field, The Patriots defense stiffened and had Stabler in a third and 18 situation. Stabler attempted a pass and threw incomplete, leading to what would be a desperation fourth down play. However, long after the play ended, a penalty flag was thrown and New England defensive lineman Sugar Bear Hamilton was called for a roughing the passer penalty. The Patriots were incredulous, and replays again showed an error by an official, in this case Ben Drieth. The phantom penalty gave Oakland a big first down, and Stabler capitalized on a one yard run with only 10 seconds to go in the game. The touchdown on that drive wound up giving Oakland a very undeserved 24-21 win.

No one on the Patriots and no Patriot fan could believe the bad officiating which had clearly cost the Patriots a win. Years later an impartial ESPN list included the Ben Drieth call as one of the worst officiating calls in history. It was no consolation to Pats fans, who then watched Oakland go on to beat the injury-riddled Pittsburgh Steelers in the AFC Championship game, and an outclassed Minnesota Viking team to win the Super Bowl. It was a championship that very well could have been theirs, given the way that they had played down the stretch and in that game. One has to wonder what Patriot history would have been like had they not suffered this defeat at the hands of both the Raiders and the game officials.

- - -

The *Sports Illustrated* pro football preview issue of September 19, 1977 had Ken Stabler on the cover and that cover highlighted three items. The third of those highlighted items said "Scouting Reports: Beware of the Patriots". The preview inside said that the 1976 Patriots "came within a referee's whistle of knocking off Super Bowl winner Oakland in the first round of the playoffs." It added that "So complete, so convincing is the Patriot turnaround that New England now rates as the principal threat to Oakland's hopes for another Super Bowl championship." Those were heady words for Patriot fans who had become accustomed to mediocrity from their NFL team.

Despite the lofty predictions, the Patriot pre-season was one of turmoil. Guard John Hannah and Tackle Leon Gray had formed a great tandem on the left side of the New England offensive line. Now they formed a tandem that threatened to derail the Patriot season before it had even started. Angered by the Patriots' refusal to renegotiate their contracts, to which reportedly Chuck Fairbanks had agreed but Billy Sullivan had rejected, the two linemen walked out of training camp. They continued their holdout into the first four games of the season. When they finally did return, the team that was held in such high regard was a very ordinary 2-2 and Hannah, Gray, and Fairbanks had become disenchanted with the Patriot ownership.

The Patriots then went 6-2 in their next eight games and, now with an 8-4 record, were in a battle with Baltimore and Miami for first place in the AFL East. The Pats played Miami in Foxboro in the next-to-last game of the season and beat them 14-10, but oddly, the win eliminated both teams from playoff contention (a function of the quirky NFL tie-breaking system), and Baltimore won the division. Playing for nothing in the season finale in Baltimore, the Patriots lost to the Colts 30-24 and finished a season that to some degree was a lost season from the very beginning. Baltimore and Miami finished the season 10-4 and New England 9-5. Baltimore was off to the AFC playoffs along with Pittsburgh, Oakland, and Denver. The Patriots were just going home for the off-season.

- - -

A new fad crept into the NFL in the late 1970's – cheerleaders. This was likely spurred by the tremendous success and popularity of the Dallas Cowboy cheerleaders, who had become famous through the frequent sideline shots of the cheerleaders in Dallas' Texas Stadium. The shots were often gratuitous, panning up from the cheerleaders' boots to their push-up tops that showed a lot of cleavage and finally to their faces. They were all young and good-looking, and the Cowboys, NFL, and Hollywood took advantage of their popularity with shows and specials about "The Dallas Cowboy Cheerleaders". To their credit, the women also did charity functions and hospital visits, but their main purpose was to generate increased interest in the sideline.

Soon, most of the NFL teams began following the lead that the Cowboys had set, and started employing cheerleaders of their own. These were not the typical high school or even college cheerleaders to which most of us had become accustomed, cheerleaders who would wear school sweaters, short skirts, and bobby socks. These cheerleaders wore skimpy and revealing halter tops (as described above), tight hot pants, and sheer pantyhose. They were meant to be sex symbols, since sex sells, even in the NFL. Apparently sexiness on the sidelines was OK, but when many of the women from a number of teams posed topless or naked for *Playboy* magazine, that was too much for the NFL. A number of the cheerleaders, including one of the Patriot cheerleaders, were fired for their *Playboy* "appearance".

Cheerleaders remained in the game, and do to this day, but there has not since been any such controversy or any such posing in *Playboy* or any other magazines such as this. Good.

- - -

Patriot football on the field in 1978 got off to a bad start, and this one was tragic. Promising young wide receiver Darryl Stingley was paralyzed by a violent hit from Oakland safety Jack Tatum in a pre-season game. The game was played in Oakland on August 12, 1978. Stingley ran a slant route over the middle and leaped for a high pass from Steve Grogan. Tatum, the Oakland safety, was generally recognized as one of the dirtiest players in the league. He saw Stingley go up and saw that he was in a vulnerable position. Most players, especially in a meaningless pre-season game, would not have hit an opposing player as Tatum did but Tatum took advantage of Stingley's vulnerability, laying a vicious and unnecessary hit on him. The blow immediately knocked Stingley down and sickened almost everyone who was watching.

Stingley wound up being paralyzed from the neck down. He was in an Oakland hospital for days before he was able to be moved back to Boston. Tatum never apologized, never went to visit Stingley in the hospital (Oakland Coach John Madden and other Oakland players did), and, according to many sources, never said a word to Stingley.

The rest of these two men's lives were a study in contrast. Stingley, the victim, went through a long recovery and rehab, although he never regained the use of his legs. He did, however, later create a charitable foundation and began working with inner city kids. He made something of his life despite the tragedy. On the other hand, Tatum, the perpetrator who never apologized, made money with a book whose title contained the word 'assassin' and he seemed to relish his 'tough guy' reputation.

They say that crises bring out the best and worst in people. Rarely is it exemplified as clearly as it was in the case of the proud Darryl Stingley and what he made of his life after the tragedy and the despicable Jack Tatum and the money that he made from his career and book after the injury that he caused so unnecessarily.

- - -

The Patriots overcame the loss of Stingley and became one of the NFL's top teams. They were 8-2 after 10 games (the league had now moved from a 14 game schedule to 16) and their offense was virtually unstoppable in many of those games. A seven game winning streak after a slow 1-2 start was highlighted by a 55-21 drubbing of the Jets on October 29. The 11th game was against Houston in Foxboro and the Patriots started out on fire, marching down the field and scoring on their first five possessions to take a 23-0 lead just before halftime. It appeared that New England was on its way to routing another opponent. Unfortunately, three of those drives had ended in field goals and when Houston scored a touchdown late in the first half the momentum had switched. Houston scored 26 unanswered points and became a shocking 26-23 winner in a game that New England had dominated early.

The Patriots went to 10-5 and clinched the AFC East with a 26-24 win over Buffalo on December 10. It was the Patriots' first-ever outright division title. Despite everything going so positively, it was at this time that the now-successful Patriots reverted to their earlier laughing-stock ways.

Rumors had been rampant that Patriot coach Chuck Fairbanks was planning to leave the Patriots at the end of the season and return to college coaching with the University of Colorado. When Billy Sullivan learned that the rumors were true, he went ballistic. He suspended Fairbanks for the final game of the season and named two co-coaches for that game, Ron Erhardt to coach the offense and Hank Bulloch to coach the defense. The turmoil of their coach leaving and the very predictable confusion that stemmed from now having two leaders destroyed Patriot preparation for that final game and they lost badly to Miami, 23-3.

The Patriots should have been preparing for their playoff opener against Houston, which would be the first home playoff game in the team's history. Instead, what they had was a circus. After the debacle in Miami, Sullivan reversed positions and agreed to allow Fairbanks to coach the playoff game.

The Patriots, who at one point were considered serious Super Bowl contenders, were never in the game. Houston ran out to a 24-0 lead behind the passing of quarterback Dan Pastorini and the running of powerful Earl Campbell. Pastorini was wearing a flak jacket to protect broken ribs suffered in a late season game against Pittsburgh. He did not seem to be affected by the jacket, though, as he started the scoring with a 71 yard touchdown bomb to receiver Ken Burrough.

With a 7-0 lead, the Oilers started their next drive at their own 1 yard line and momentum seemed to have switched to New England as the Patriots stopped the Oilers on a third down run and looked to have forced the Oilers to punt from deep within their own territory. However, well after the whistle Patriot safety Tim Fox inexplicably jumped onto the already stopped ball carrier and was correctly whistled for a late hit penalty. The penalty gave the Oilers a first down and they completed a 99 yard touchdown drive culminated with a 19 yard touchdown pass from Pastorini to Mike Barber.

A third Pastorini TD pass, and the second caught by Barber, made the score 21-0 lead at halftime. After a Houston field goal made it 24-0, the Patriots began to show some life, and scored just before the end of the third quarter on a 24 yard halfback option pass from Andy Johnson to receiver Harold Jackson. Another Patriot TD made it 24-14 in the fourth quarter but a Patriot turnover gave the ball to Houston at the Patriot 18 and Earl Campbell blasted it in on three running plays, the last from two yards out, to seal a 31-14 win.

The Patriot season, which had started with the Stingley tragedy, had built to a great record and division championship, and then was marred by the repercussions from Fairbanks' decision to leave, was now over. The Patriots were in disarray yet again. For his part, Fairbanks at Colorado was never able to duplicate the success that he had previously had as a college coach with Oklahoma and as a pro coach in building a bumbling Patriot team into a strong contender.

- - -

On a more cheerful note, by this time (1979) my family had grown to four: myself, my wife, and two sons. We had moved from Virginia, where I had been stationed as a member of the Air Force. One Saturday we were driving in the area and decided to stop and see what Schaefer Stadium looked like, since there was nothing going on at the Stadium that day. We parked the car and walked around the facility, and inadvertently walked through a gate that had somehow been left open and were in the stands. The boys wanted to go down to the field so we did. As they were running on the field and having fun I could see a Patriot official or security guard coming down the steps toward us, and assumed that he would ask us to leave. He did come and ask what we were doing, and I explained about the open gate. He saw how much fun the boys were having and saw that we were no threat to do any damage, so instead of asking us to leave, he told us to feel free to stay a short while, but then we should leave, and then he headed back up the steps away from us. We stayed for less than ten minutes and then left, and I will never forget his kindness in letting us do so.

Contrast that with an experience that my now-grown oldest son and I had in Milwaukee 19 years later. We were attending a Brewers-Twins game in May that was very sparsely attended. We had seats in the first row of the second section behind home plate. For most of the game, we were the only people in that area. We spent time talking with an usher about the game, the Brewers, and the old Milwaukee Braves, who had also played in County Stadium, where this game was being played. As the game moved into the seventh inning, I motioned to the seats in the section in front if us and asked the usher if we could move there. He said "No". Now, really, no one was there, it was the seventh inning on a chilly May night, so it was unlikely that anyone would show up at this point, and if they happened to show up and happened to have tickets for the two seats that we were in, we would have gladly moved either into other empty seats in the same section, or back those few rows to our original seats. It would not have been a big deal to let us move, but he did not. In my opinion, one of these stories shows excellent public relations (thank you, Patriots), and the other was bad public relations. We could have moved anyway in Milwaukee, easily to a couple of sections over and down, but we chose not to do so, in case this person was worried about his job if he let us move to two of the many empty seats. Oh well.

Our experience at Schaefer Stadium that day led us to buy tickets for one of the 1979 pre-season games, and so on August 19, 1979, we set out for our first game in Foxboro. What we found was a big traffic jam after we got off of Route 495 and onto Route 1, about five miles from the stadium. When we got to the parking lots, we found not paved lots, but dirt and gravel fields where people were parking. It was not the high-class NFL we had expected. We walked through two other lots to get to the paved lots where season ticket holders and the press were able to park, and finally into the stadium. We had end zone seats but had a decent view of the game from that location. Despite the traffic and parking lots, we enjoyed our day at the game, especially since the Patriots beat the rival Oakland Raiders 35-14.

- - -

Ron Erhardt was named coach for that 1979 season, after his co-coaching stint at the end of 1978. The team went a respectable 9-7 for the season but was nowhere near the powerhouse that it had become under Fairbanks. Though they would be a decent team in 1979 and again in 1980, there would be no playoff games, and, worse, a spiral downward was beginning.

Chapter 4 – 1980's: The Class of Raymond Berry

After the Patriots had achieved a modicum of success from 1976-1978 under Chuck Fairbanks, they started falling back to the pack and toward mediocrity shortly after the 1980's began. There was one final good season under Ron Erhardt in 1980, as the team finished 10-6, but with five AFC teams having 11-5 records, there was no room in the playoffs for New England.

The bottom then fell out in 1981 as the team dropped to an NFL-worst 2-14 record. The final game of the season was a game at Baltimore with the Colts who would finish with an equally horrendous 2-14 won-lost record. Reporters referred to the game as "The Stupor Bowl" as it matched the two teams with the league's worst records. The team that lost would get the #1 pick in the NFL draft. That team was the Patriots, who concluded their season with a 23-21 loss to the Colts.

For the second time in Patriot history, the team would have the #1 pick in the college draft. In 1970 they had used that pick wisely, drafting Jim Plunkett from Stanford. This time they chose Kenneth Sims, a big defensive end from the University of Texas. This pick did not work out as well as the Plunkett pick had. Though Sims would be a member of the Patriots from 1982-89, he was often injured and did not go on to have a stellar career. He certainly did not live up to the promise inherent in being the overall #1 pick. One player they could have had with that pick was Marcus Allen, who went on to have a Hall of Fame career as a running back with the Raiders and Chiefs. Ah, what might have been.

- - -

The Patriots went into the 1982 season with a new head coach. Ron Meyer, who had been a successful college coach at Southern Methodist University, was hired on January 15. Maybe the Patriots were hoping to repeat the same success with Meyer as they had had when they pulled Chuck Fairbanks up from the college coaching ranks.

It was also at this time that the Patriots began what seemed like a decade-long search for someone other than Steve Grogan to be their starting quarterback, though they usually wound up going back to Grogan. In 1981 and 1982 the heir apparent was Matt Cavanaugh, who had been drafted from the University of Pittsburgh in 1978.

As luck would have it, New England's opponent in the season opener was the Baltimore Colts, the same team which New England had played in the previous season's finale ridiculed as "The Stupor Bowl". Baltimore was also rebuilding under their new head coach, Frank Kush, who had been a very successful coach at Arizona State University. The Patriots won this game, 24-13, breaking a 10-10 halftime tie behind a good blitzing defense and a solid offensive performance. Patriot running back Tony Collins gained 137 yards rushing. Robert Weathers scored one touchdown on a 1 yard run. Matt Cavanaugh passed for another, a 30 yard TD pass to Ken Toler.

After a 31-7 loss at home to the Jets in the season's second game, The Patriots and all of the NFL had the season interrupted by a players' strike. The strike was about – what else – money, and lasted two months, from September 20, after the Monday night game between the Packers and Giants, until November 21, when the strike was settled and the season resumed.

One of the weirder games in a Patriot history (that had many more such games than most teams) occurred on December 12 at home against Miami. A major snowstorm was dumping a lot of snow on the Schaefer Stadium field during the game and conditions were treacherous. Often during the game snowplows were used during stoppages in play to plow snow from the yard lines sideline-to-sideline so that officials and players would have some idea of the location of the play. The score was 0-0 late in the fourth quarter when the Patriots were set to try a field goal. During a timeout, Coach Ron Meyer asked one of the snow plow drivers who was set to push snow off the yard line to also swerve as he crossed the field from the yard line to the spot between yard lines where the ball would be set for kicker John Smith. The snow plow driver, a convict on work-release named Mark Henderson, did so, thus clearing the kicking surface for Smith to try a 33 yard field goal. As he did immediately, and again after Smith had made the field goal, Dolphin Coach Don Shula protested. When the game ended 3-0 with that field goal being the only scoring, Shula continued his protest to the league but to no avail. The infamous "snow plow game" stayed as a 3-0 win for the Patriots.

Thanks in part to this fortuitous snow plowing, the Patriots finished with a 5-4 record in the strike-abbreviated season, but luck was on their side for once. The league had decided to expand the playoffs to include 16 teams because of the shortened season, and since the Patriots had the seventh best record in the AFC, they qualified for a spot in the playoffs.

Facing the Pats in the playoff would be the second-seeded Miami Dolphins, who had finished 7-2. The game was not very close, as Miami won 28-13. Miami was led by quarterback David Woodley, who completed 16 passes in 19 attempts for 246 yards and two touchdowns, and running back Andra Franklin who rushed for 112 yards on 26 carries. Miami had gotten its revenge on the Patriots for the December snow plow game. The Dolphins went on to the Super Bowl, but lost that game 27-17 to Washington.

Schaefer Stadium was renamed Sullivan Stadium in June, 1983 in honor of Billy Sullivan, the team founder and long-time owner.

Our family went to two regular season games in the 1983 season. My oldest son, Mike, and I went to a game against the Jets on September 18, along with my parents, sister, and brother-in-law. Steve Grogan and Richard Todd were the starting quarterbacks, and we had good seats location-wise, at about the 40 yard line, but the seating in Schaefer Stadium was on aluminum rows with just numbers painted about a body's length apart, and not individual seats, so there was frequent shifting and bumping with nearby fans. It didn't bother any of us, though, as the Patriots beat the Jets 23-13.

The next game for which we had tickets was on November 13, against the Miami Dolphins, and just Mike and I went. What is memorable about that game was that it was a windy, drizzly, and very cold day. During the first half, Mike and I agreed that, because of the cold, we would leave midway through the fourth quarter. By later in the first half, we had moved that up to the end of the third quarter. At halftime, we had moved that up even further, to the middle of the third quarter. By the end of halftime we agreed to leave after the first series of the second half. The Patriots won this one, 17-6, with us listening to most of the second half on the radio during the ride home. At least we were no longer in that freezing drizzle.

Mike and I also went to two games in 1984, a September 23 26-10 loss to Washington, and a 20-14 win over Cincinnati on October 14. Washington was a very strong team, with Joe Thiesmann at quarterback and John Riggins at running back, but what was most impressive about them was the size of their offensive line. Cincinnati's offensive line, anchored by the great Anthony Munoz, was also impressively huge. In all the games that I have seen over the years, these were the two teams that really stood out with their size. Cincinnati's was second to one, and that one was Washington's. Unlike the Miami game, in which we left early, we stayed late after the Washington game, deciding to wait inside the Stadium for the parking lots to clear out to some degree before heading out to our car. After a few minutes we were asked to leave, as they wanted to start cleaning the seating area. We left and got caught in traffic. C'est la vie.

New England finished with an 8-8 record in 1983 and was 5-3 to start 1984 when Ron Meyer was fired. Stories circulated that the players were not happy with Meyer's style and play-calling and that team management was not happy with Meyer's frequent demands for trades. When Meyer fired defensive coordinator Rod Rust after a 44-24 loss at Miami, without having discussed it with team management or ownership, it was the last straw. Meyer was fired and replaced by Raymond Berry, who finished the season 4-4 for an overall team record of 9-7, which was not good enough for the team to make the playoffs. In their continuing odd quest to find a better quarterback than Steve Grogan, the Patriots had now turned to Tony Eason, who had been drafted in 1983 from the University of Illinois.

Raymond Berry was like a godsend for the Patriot franchise. Berry was a Hall of Fame receiver who teamed with Johnny Unitas in the late 1950's and early 1960's to form one of the greatest passing combinations in pro football history. Berry overcame a number of physical issues (e.g., vision problems, one leg being shorter than the other) through a lot of hard work and effort. He and Unitas were famous for staying late after practices to work with each other to improve their timing and feel on pass plays. From such extra work came the buttonhook pass in which Berry would start downfield with the snap of the ball and then curl back; Unitas would throw a well-timed pass as Berry made the loop back and the pass would be in Berry's hands before the defender could get back to him. The extra work that Unitas and Berry had done paid great dividends for the Colts in the famous overtime championship game in 1958, as the duo completed a number of passes that helped the Colts drive down the field to tie the game late in the fourth quarter, and then drive down the field to win the game in overtime.

For the third year in a row, we went to two games in 1985. We had tickets for the September 29 game against the Raiders, and again were going to go with my parents, sister, and brother-in-law. Unfortunately, Hurricane Gloria hit the East Coast and moved dangerously up the eastern seaboard during the middle and end of the preceding week. It went through Connecticut, from where my family would be coming, and up through central and eastern Massachusetts. We were without power for a while, and rain continued for a couple of days. It looked as if we would not be able to get to the game, but then skies cleared on Saturday, so we decided they could indeed drive up and we could go. This one was a 35-20 loss to the Raiders, who had moved from their original home in Oakland to Los Angeles (they would eventually move back to Oakland). We also got to the October 20 game against the New York Jets, which had a happier ending, a 20-13 Patriot win.

Raymond Berry's work ethic, dedication, and emphasis on the team over individuality paid great dividends for the Patriots. In 1985 the Patriots improved to 11-5 and made the playoffs as a wild card team. The Patriots then shocked their fans by winning three games in the playoffs and getting to the Super Bowl. The added shockers were that the three playoff wins all came on the road (the first NFL team to accomplish that feat), and they were over three of the Patriots' old nemeses, the New York Jets, the Oakland Raiders, and the Miami Dolphins.

The first game in this outstanding playoff run was against the Jets in the Meadowlands on December 28. The 1985 Patriots had developed a swarming defense led by linebackers Andre Tippett and Steve Nelson, and a solid offense, led by runner Craig James, who had rushed for 1,227 yards during the season, and the passing of Eason and Grogan to Stanley Morgan and Irving Fryar (Fryar had been the Pats' and league's #1 overall draft pick in 1984). John Hannah, widely considered the best offensive lineman in the NFL, anchored the offensive line. All of these components came into play in combining for a 26-14 win over the Jets, aided by four Jet turnovers triggered by the strong Patriot defense. It was the first NFL playoff game that the Patriots had won.

A trip across the country brought the Pats to Los Angeles to play the Raiders, who had moved to LA from Oakland (they would subsequently move back, as noted previously). The Patriots rallied from a 17-7 deficit to defeat the Raiders 27-20. The opportunistic defense (and special team play) was the story of the game, as six LA turnovers - three interceptions and three fumble recoveries, including a big recovery of a Raider fumble of a New England kickoff - led the way to victory.

Though they now had started to achieve some success, there were still more Patriot shenanigans that fans had to weather. Near the end of the Patriot win over Oakland, some of the bad feelings that had existed for years between these teams came to the fore. Patrick Sullivan, son of Patriot owner Billy Sullivan, was on the field and for some reason began to taunt the Raiders. Huge defensive tackle Howie Long (who played high school football in Masachusetts and who was later to become a network TV studio football commentator) seemed to be a particular target of Patrick's yelling, though Patrick has said that it was not he but one of the Patriot assistants who was taunting Long. After the game Pat and Howie got into it again and a scuffle broke out. During the scuffle, Pat Sullivan was hit in the head by Raider linebacker Matt Millen (who later became the target of jokes for a long and very unsuccessful career as general manager of the Detroit Lions).

There were some very entertaining quotes from this incident, as related in Michael Felger's book, "Tales from the Patriots Sideline". Apparently, at the start of the melee, Patrick Sullivan asked Howie Long "Do you know who I am? I'm the owner of the Patriots", to which Long replied "Well, unless your old man died, you don't own anything." John Hannah is quoted as saying that he and Steve Nelson were leaving the field when they saw the skirmish begin and Hannah asked Nelson if they should help out. Nelson responded "He got himself into it. Let him get himself out." Finally, in maybe the best quote of the day, a reporter asked the Patriot team doctor if anyone had gotten hurt during the game. The doctor summed it up in one pithy statement, saying "Aside from that goof Pat Sullivan, everyone is fine."

The next week was a surprising one across New England, surprising in that there seemed to be extreme confidence in the air as the Patriots made yet another coast-to-coast trip to play the Dolphins in Miami. The confidence seemed unusual since the Patriots were playing their third straight road playoff game, they had made two grueling cross-country trips between those games, and, more to the point, New England had lost 18 straight times at the Orange Bowl to the Dolphins, a streak that began in 1967. Yet fans across New England now expected victory, and "Squish the Fish" signs were popping up all over the area.

The fans' expectations were rewarded with a resounding 31-14 win over the Dolphins on a rainy day in Miami. The defensive opportunism continued, as 24 of New England's 31 points came as the result of turnovers. The scoring started after a Miami fumble on their first play from scrimmage. Tony Franklin started things off for New England with a 23 yard field goal. After a Dan Marino TD pass had given Miami a 7-3 lead, the Patriots regained the lead with a 66 yard drive, culminated by a 4 yard TD pass from Tony Eason to Tony Collins to make it 10-7. A Marino fumble led to another New England score and a 17-7 halftime lead.

Miami fumbled away the opening kickoff of the second half, and New England capitalized on a TD pass from Eason to running back Robert Weathers.

New England then had a turnover of its own, by punt returner Roland James. That James was the player returning punts was another situation that harkened back to the Patriots' often turbulent history. Normally Irving Fryar would have been the punt returner, but he had cut a tendon in his right hand during the week before the game. Fryar claimed that he did this trying to get a knife out of a kitchen drawer. Other reports claimed that Fryar's hand was cut in a fight with his wife in a domestic dispute.

Fryar, in fact, was someone who contributed more than one odd story to Patriot history, including the time he left a game against Buffalo early after being injured, but instead of getting treatment sped away in his car and wound up wrapping it around a tree and being found by police while the game was still in progress. On other occasions he claimed to have been robbed in a jewelry store, was pulled over while driving in New Jersey on a suspended license, got into a fight with patrons outside of a bar in Providence, and was implicated with drugs on more than one occasion. Fryar eventually found religion and changed his ways, but not before adding more history such as this to Patriot lore.

The Patriot lead over the Dolphins had been cut to 24-14, but the Pats caused yet another Miami fumble, and nine consecutive running plays got the Patriots a clinching touchdown to make the final 31-14. The Patriots were on their way to a Super Bowl for the first time in the team's history!

Super Bowl XX – New England vs. Chicago Bears

Waiting for the Patriots in that Super Bowl was one of the most powerful teams in the league's history, the 17-1 Chicago Bears. The Bears were led by a brutal defense, featuring linemen Richard Dent, Dan Hampton, and William "The Refrigerator" Perry; linebackers Mike Singletary, Wilber Marshall, and Otis Wilson; defensive backs Dave Duerson and Gary Fencik; and a host of other tough defenders, all playing at the top of their games. The offense featured Walter Payton, one of the greatest running backs in NFL history. Although they did not have a great passing attack, quarterback Jim McMahon was an inspirational leader for the team. Head Coach Mike Ditka and defensive coordinator Buddy Ryan were considered among the very best in the game.

The Bears' only loss had been on a Monday night, to Dan Marino and a very emotional Dolphins team in Miami. This loss ensured that the 1972 Dolphins would remain the only undefeated team in NFL history (a refrain that would return again in 2007). They had gotten to the Super Bowl by beating two very good teams in the playoffs, and had not allowed either of those teams to score a single point. They defeated the Giants 21-0 and the Rams 24-0.

In preparation for the Super Bowl, which was to be played at the Super Dome in New Orleans, the Bears had made an MTV video called "The Super Bowl Shuffle" in which players performed lyrics such as the following:

[done by all players]
We are the Bears Shufflin' Crew

Shufflin' on down, doin' it for you.
We're so bad we know we're good.
Blowin' your mind like we knew we would.
You know we're just struttin' for fun
Struttin' our stuff for everyone.
We're not here to start no trouble.
We're just here to do the Super Bowl Shuffle.

o
o
o

[Jim McMahon]
I'm the punky QB, known as McMahon.
When I hit the turf, I've got no plan.
I just throw my body all over the field.
I can't dance, but I can throw the pill.

o

That's why you all got here on the double
To catch me doin' the Super Bowl Shuffle.

o
o
o

[Otis Wilson]
I'm mama's boy Otis, one of a kind.
The ladies all love me for my body and my mind.

o

I didn't come here lookin' for trouble,
I just came down to do The Super Bowl Shuffle.

o
o
o

[Richard Dent]
The sackman's comin', I'm your man Dent.
if the quarterback's slow, He's gonna get bent.
We stop the run, we stop the pass,
I like to dump guys on their -.
We love to play for the world's best fans,
You better start makin' your Super Bowl plans.
But don't get ready or go to any trouble
Unless you do The Super Bowl Shuffle.

o
o
o

[Gary Fencik]
It's Gary here, and I'm Mr.Clean.
They call me "hit man," Don't know what they mean.
They throw it long and watch me run,
I'm on my man, one-on-one.
Buddy's guys cover it down to the bone,
That's why they call it the 46 zone.

o
o
o

[Refrigerator Perry]

You're lookin' at the Fridge, I'm the rookie.
I may be large, but I'm no dumb cookie.
You've seen me hit, you've seen me run,
When I get the pass, we'll have more fun.
I can dance, you will see
The others, they all learn from me.
I didn't come here lookin' for trouble,
I just came here to do The Super Bowl Shuffle.

It was excellent theater and the video was shown many, many times on MTV, which is one reason that I remember the lyrics to this day (plus, remembering lyrics to songs is something that I do well, for some reason).

The Bears were heavy favorites, 10 ½ points by some oddsmakers, and some experts wondered if the Patriots would even be able to be competitive. As it turns out, they were competitive at first, but then the roof caved in on them.

On the second play of the game, the Patriots string of causing opponents' turnovers continued. Walter Payton fumbled, and the Patriots took over on the Chicago 19 yard line. With the ball that close to paydirt, the Patriots chose not to use their running game, which had helped to carry them through their playoff run, but to pass the ball in deference to the fantastic Chicago defense against the run. After three straight incomplete passes by Tony Eason (the Bears' pass defense was also outstanding), New England had to settle for a 36 yard field goal. Still, they were ahead of the vaunted Bears 3-0 after only 1:19 of play. It was the earliest score in Super Bowl history.

After that, the game was all Chicago. The Bears got a field goal to tie it on the ensuing series. The Patriots then had to punt after two incompletions and a 10 yard sack of Eason by Richard Dent and Wilber Marshall. On its third series New England finally tried a run, by Craig James, but he was stopped almost immediately. Eason then went back to pass and was hit and fumbled, leading to another Chicago field goal. Another Patriot fumble and Chicago TD made it 13-3 after the first quarter, and the game was effectively over. The Chicago defense was stopping everything that the Patriots had, and Tony Eason seemed almost shell-shocked from the pressure he was getting on every pass attempt.

It was an insurmountable 23-3 lead for Chicago at the half. With a little over five minutes to go in the first half, Raymond Berry replaced Eason with veteran Steve Grogan to try to spark the offense. Ironically, Eason had taken over for Grogan when Grogan had suffered a leg injury in an overtime loss to the Jets in late November; the roles were now being reversed. Grogan wound up as maybe the best player on the field for the over-matched Patriots, as he wound up going 17 for 30 for 177 yards and standing up to the relentless Chicago rush.

The Chicago lead ballooned up to 44-3 in the third quarter. One indignity was a 1 yard touchdown run by William Perry that made it 44-3. Coach Ditka had used the 300+ pound defensive tackle during the season on goal line plays for touchdowns, but this seemed to be a case of (a) rubbing it in and (b) not letting an all-time great, Walter Payton, have a chance to score a Super Bowl TD in favor of the theatrics of letting Perry do it. It was not a classy move by Ditka.

Grogan had been hit all day trying to pass, but he then led a 76 yard Patriot drive for a touchdown, and completed it with an 8 yard touchdown pass to Irving Fryar to make it 44-10. A fourth quarter safety, on yet another sack of Grogan, this one in the end zone, completed the scoring in a thoroughly dominating 46-10 Chicago win.

The stats showed the utter domination of the Chicago defense. Eason completed zero passes in six attempts. The Patriots had absolutely no running game, gaining only 7 yards, and it took them 11 carries to do even that. Had it not been for the valiant efforts of Steve Grogan, the game could have been even worse for the Pats. Fittingly, defensive lineman Richard Dent, the sack man Dent from "the Super Bowl Shuffle", was voted the game's Most Valuable Player.

The season was over, and the Patriots had made it to the big game. Unfortunately, what they ran into when they got there was a juggernaut.

- - -

After the Super Bowl, a new controversy reared its ugly head. *The Boston Globe* published a story that rumors were circulating about drug abuse by some of the Patriots and that some players had allegedly tested positive for drugs (reportedly cocaine). To this day it is not clear if there was a problem or not, but if there was, Raymond Berry handled it, and after that the team agreed to team-wide testing. There was no further problem.

- - -

In the year following that Super Bowl the Patriots went through a number of changes, and had some success before starting a decline. In January solid defensive lineman Julius Adams retired after 15 years with the Patriots. A bigger loss came in June with the retirement of offensive guard John Hannah. Hannah had been with the team since 1973 and had started 183 games. He was generally considered the best offensive lineman of his time, and *Sports Illustrated* had done a cover story on him (a rarity in and of itself for an offensive lineman) in

1981 in which it proclaimed Hannah as "The Best Offensive Lineman of All Time". It would be a big loss for the Patriots.

Despite the changes, the team went 11-5 in 1986 behind Tony Eason and won the AFC East. Their first round playoff game was in Denver on January 4, 1987 against the Broncos and their Hall of Fame quarterback John Elway. The game was still close at 20-17 Broncos in the fourth quarter when Tony Eason was sacked in the end zone for a safety. The resultant 22-17 score made it imperative for the Pats to go for a touchdown since a field goal would not be enough, and they could not get that TD, falling to the Broncos by that same 22-17 score. The Broncos would go on to the Super Bowl where they would lose to Bill Parcells' New York Giants 39-20.

1987 saw another strike hit the NFL after the second week of the season. The Patriots were 1-1 at the time and they, like many teams, had stocked replacement players, expecting a long strike. One such Patriot player was Doug Flutie, the best player in the history of Boston College football, and the 1984 Heisman Trophy winner. Flutie had been forced to take his career to Canada due to the short-sightedness (no pun intended) of NFL General Managers who thought that Flutie was not tall enough to succeed in the NFL. Even a biased Holy Cross graduate such as, say, I am, could see that they were wrong and that Boston College grad Flutie was a winner who should play in the NFL. Flutie did get his chance and performed well. He was kept on the team even after the strike was settled and the regular players returned.

The 1987 season was shortened by one game, with the game between the start of that strike and the readiness of the replacement players having been lost. The Patriots finished at 8-7, tied for second in the AFC East behind Indianapolis, but did not make the playoffs.

One team that definitely did not plan well for this strike was the defending champion New York Giants. The Giants fell from 14-2 in 1986 to 6-9 in 1987. The Washington Redskins won the Super Bowl, as they had in 1982, the previous year impacted by a player strike. The Redskins defeated Denver 42-10. There must be some political joke in there about Washington and union strikes, but it's not clear what it is.

Doug Flutie became the Patriots' top quarterback in 1988, starting 9 games and completing 92 of 179 passes for 1,150 yards and 8 touchdowns. The team finished at 9-7 though, and missed the playoffs for the second straight season.

That 1988 season brought a big change at the top for the Patriots. After owning the team since its inception in 1960, Billy

Sullivan sold the team in July. Allegedly Billy's son Chuck, also an official with the team, had lost a lot of money trying to promote a Michael Jackson concert tour, and that was a contributing factor to the Sullivans having to sell their beloved Patriots. The new owner was Victor Kiam, the CEO of Remington, most famous for its razors. Interestingly, a couple of months later, on November 23, Sullivan Stadium was also sold. This sale was to a long-time Patriot fan and season-ticket owner named Robert Kraft, who would years later, as we shall see, turn the Patriot franchise into one of the most successful in all of professional sports.

   With new ownership in place in 1989 the Patriots began what seemed to be their typical end of the decade decline, going just 5-11 that year. It would prove to be the last year for the very honorable Raymond Berry, and when Berry was gone, the team would again nose-dive to become again bottom-feeders looking from the depths of the standings up at the rest of the NFL.

Chapter 5 – 1990's: A New Attitude

The decade of the 1990s saw things start to turn around toward the positive for the Patriots, but not before they had to suffer through some more adversity on and off the field.

With the transfer of ownership from Billy Sullivan to Victor Kiam, Sullivan Stadium was renamed again in January 1990, this time to Foxboro Stadium.

A change with much more impact to the team's fortunes took place on February 26, however, as respected coach Raymond Berry was relieved of duties (read: fired). Former defensive coordinator Rod Rust was named the new head coach of the team. Ostensibly, the reason for this change was that Berry did not go along with changes that Kiam proposed (e.g., to the coaching staff). This was not a good move for New England, as Berry could have provided some much-needed stability among the changes that were occurring. Berry had not only been successful on the field, having gotten the team to its first Super Bowl, but had also helped steer the team through what could have been a catastrophic problem with drug abuse in 1985, not hiding the problem, but dealing with it before it became worse.

With the change from Berry to Rust, the team hit rock-bottom in 1990, going 1-15. The only win came in the second game of the season, against the Colts in Indianapolis. They then proceeded to lose their last 14 games. The Patriots had the #1 pick in the draft yet again, this time with Notre Dame's outstanding Raghib "Rocket" Ismail available. Ismail was a dynamic player in college, a receiver with great catching and running skills and a kick returner to be feared. It is interesting to speculate how Ismail would have done being paired with Steve Grogan now, and especially with the rocket arm of Drew Bledsoe later in the 1990s, but that would just have to remain speculation, as the Patriots decided to trade that #1 pick to Dallas and "move down" in the draft (a typical New England move in that era). Ismail wound up going to the Canadian Football League.

As it turns out, Steve Grogan also played his last game in the NFL in 1990, having thrown 92 passes, completing 50, for 615 yards, and turning the quarterback job over to Marc Wilson, a retread from the Oakland Raiders. Grogan retired, ending his valiant career as the player with the longest tenure with the Patriots, 16 years. He is a player who gave it his all every time out there.

Rod Rust did not survive the 1-15 record. He was fired in January of 1991, and replaced by Dick MacPherson, who had been the head coach at Syracuse University for 10 years. MacPherson came in brimming with energy and enthusiasm (and in fact reacting to a question about that at an early press conference by asking reporters something along the lines of "Wouldn't your wife like it if you were enthusiastic?").

MacPherson replaced journeyman Marc Wilson at quarterback with journeyman Hugh Millen. The Patriots did show some improvement in 1991, going 6-10, but there were maybe only two really good things that happened in 1991. One was that the artificial turf of Foxboro Stadium was replaced with natural grass. The other was that one of the wins in 1991 was a thrilling overtime win in October against the Minnesota Vikings.

We happened to be at the Minnesota game, our first game in person since 1985; Mike, my son, and I went with, my sister Carol and brother-in-law Dennis. Since Dennis was a long-time Viking fan we got tickets behind the Viking bench from where we could watch Minny coach Jerry Burns, a particular favorite of Dennis. We decided to get to the game early and do some light tailgating, with sandwiches and all. As we settled back in the gravel parking lot, a truck parked near us and a bunch of guys jumped out and unloaded their grill and cases of beer. One of them loudly yelled "ooo-ee, that's what it's all about." I drew laughs all around us by immediately stating "I always thought it was the hokey pokey." It was not one of my most clever lines ever (if there have been any clever ones), but it sure got one of the best responses.

The game went into overtime at 23-23. The Patriots won it with no time remaining on the clock, on a 42 yard field goal by Jason Staurovsky. The 26-23 win boosted New England's record to 3-4, but there was no follow-up momentum, as the team lost its next four games.

Everything else in the Kiam era was negative. While the 1-15 record in 1990 was the low point on the field, the Lisa Olson incident was the embarrassingly low point off the field. Olson was a female reporter for *The Boston Herald*. After one game in the 1990 season, Olson was interviewing Patriot player Maurice Hurst when the mess started. A number of naked Patriot players gathered around her and started taunting her. They later claimed that Olson, unlike other female reporters, was not acting professionally and was regularly ogling them as they moved through the locker room naked or in various stages of undress. Whether their story is true or not, there would have been better ways to deal with their complaints than this. Olson wanted an apology from the team and claimed that she wanted it not to come out in the papers, but there was no apology and the story did come out. That made it even worse for everyone, as NFL Commissioner stepped in and had the incident investigated, leading to fines, and Olson eventually had to leave her position not only in covering the Patriots for the newspaper, but wound up leaving her job at the *Herald* due to the constant harassment that she was receiving from players and some fans. It was a tremendous public relations embarrassment for the Patriots, let alone being just plain stupid and wrong.

Kiam sold the team in May of 1992 to James B. Orthwein, a Saint Louis businessman. Rumors circulated for a while that Orthwein might be interested in moving the team to St. Louis, which at the time did not have a team of its own, but he did not. The team suffered through another bad season in 1992, finishing 2-14. We were at one of the games, a 31-14 loss to New Orleans in a game that the Saints thoroughly dominated. After the season Orthwein fired MacPherson as coach and made the personnel move that had one of the most positive impacts on the team in its history.

Enter Bill Parcells.

Parcells had been the highly successful coach of the New York Giants, winning the Super Bowl twice, in 1987 and 1991. He coached great players in Lawrence Taylor, Phil Simms, and others, and seemed to make his players better. He was sometimes caustic in dealing with players and reporters (sometimes? That's an understatement) but he was smart and his post-game press conferences were always interesting and informative, and often very clever and amusing.

The hiring of Parcells brought instant credibility to the Patriots, who had had very little of it in the team's first 33 years of existence. Fans loved the move, and initial reports indicated that the team office was besieged with requests for season tickets immediately. They would not be disappointed.

The team also changed uniforms, giving up the traditional red shirts and also the white helmets with the logo of a Patriot hiking the ball. They now had modern metallic blue shirts and a Patriot with zoom streaks behind it (a Flying Elvis as some critics called it). It was a new look to match a new attitude for a new team.

Parcells looked at the returning quarterbacks and was not very happy with what he saw in starter Hugh Millen and reserve Scott Zolak. In his book "Finding a Way to Win", Parcells described Zolak as someone without necessarily starting quarterback talent, but who was a hard worker. Millen, on the other hand, was described as someone who seemed to feel that he was the starter and entitled to preferential treatment, and so did not work hard.

What Parcells did have was the # 1 overall pick in the NFL draft, and there were two quarterbacks in the draft who were considered exceptional – Drew Bledsoe of Washington State and Rick Mirer of Notre Dame. Parcells was debating which to make the # 1 pick. Though I have been a lifetime Notre Dame fan (thanks to my father), I had seen Mirer play a lot on TV and felt that his talent was overrated. I was hoping that Parcells would go for Bledsoe, and he did. Bledsoe went # 1 to New England, Mirer # 2 to Seattle. Mirer never really made it in the NFL. Bledsoe became a star with the Patriots.

In training camp Parcells made an extraordinary move. He issued an edict to the team of what he expected and that he expected them to work hard, or they would be gone. In years past being gone from the Patriots might have seemed a blessing to some players, but not any more. Parcells' presence in and of itself had made the team credible.

Parcell's inaugural season in New England in 1993 started out 1-11 with the only win being a 23-21 win over the Cardinals in Arizona in Game # 5. However, the Patriots were competitive in most games, and had in fact lost 8 of those games by a total of 26 points. They then won their last 4 games, 7-2 over Cincinnati, 20-17 at Cleveland, 38-0 over Indianapolis, and 33-27 in overtime against Miami. Bledsoe hit receiver Michael Timpson with a 36 yard TD pass to win that Miami game in overtime. The win knocked the Dolphins out of the playoffs. The four game winning streak to end the season showcased the improvements the team had made under Parcells, and enthusiasm was high for 1994.

In his first pro season Bledsoe completed a respectable 214 passes in 429 attempts for 2,424 yards. He had 15 touchdown passes and was intercepted 15 times. One thing that concerned me and some other fans was that Bledsoe rarely seemed to pump fake before he threw. Once he pulled his arm back to pass, pass he would. We could only hope that he would learn to do this as his career progressed; unfortunately, he did not seem to do so.

- - -

1994 began with news that would ultimately change the Patriots future for the better. Bob Kraft was purchasing the team from James Orthwein. Kraft had been a long-time fan of the Patriots and a season ticket holder. He also owned the Stadium. He had a passion for the game, a very good business sense, and a lot of class. Fans instantly sensed that this would be good for the organization, and responded with their checkbooks. The announcement of Kraft taking over the team was met by another big spike in season ticket sales, including a one day record of 5,958 tickets sold the day after the announcement. The fans were pleased to have Kraft, and Kraft would go on to become one of the most beloved team owners in New England sports history, and an icon in the NFL.

On the field in 1994 the Patriots again started slowly, losing their first two games to Miami and Buffalo, then winning three in a row then losing four in a row to stand at 3-6 going into a November 13 game at home against Minnesota. The Vikings were coming into the game with a 7-2 record and were seen as one of the elite teams in the league.

The Patriots played a bad first half and came into the locker room trailing 20-3. Parcells was irate. He let his team know exactly how he felt. In his book "Finding a Way to Win", Parcells recounts that he looked into the eyes of some of the team's veteran leaders, like offensive tackle Bruce Armstrong, and said "How long are you going to take this around here? … if you want to take this for the rest of the season, just let me know, and that's fine with me. But don't call yourself professional football players. If you are willing to take this stuff, this isn't a team and this isn't professional football."

He reminded the team that they would get the ball to start the second half and told them that they would use the two minute offense to start the second half. He then finished by saying "We still have time to win this game."

The speech must have really hit home with the Patriots and the fired-up players played a completely different second half. Playing in the two minute offense caused the team to play aggressively, and always be on the attack. Bledsoe wound up throwing a phenomenal 70 passes in the game, 53 of them after halftime. Bledsoe's last pass was a 14 yard touchdown pass to a diving Kevin Turner in the left corner of the end zone 4:10 into overtime. It gave the Patriots an astounding 26-20 win, one of the greatest comebacks in team history.

Interestingly, the Patriots had driven to a first down at the 14 yard line before the pass to Turner. Parcells stated in his recount of the game that in the previous year, with Bledsoe as a rookie, he would have run the ball twice and gone for the field goal. Now, with Bledsoe in his second year and with the second half momentum clearly on his side, he called for a play action pass and it worked perfectly. The win, and the way that they won, was a great confidence builder for the team, and a big key to its success that would follow not only that season, but beyond.

The Patriots then rode that momentum to win five games in a row going into the last game of the season, a Christmas Eve battle with the Bears in Chicago. A win would put the Patriots into the playoffs. The Pats led 6-3 in the third quarter, made a big block on an attempt at a tying 38 yard field goal by Chicago, and held on for a 13-3 win. They were in the playoffs.

The playoff game was on New Year's Day in Cleveland against the Browns. The Browns head coach was Bill Belichick, a once and future assistant to Parcells, and later to become the best head coach in Patriot history. The quarterback match-up was young Drew Bledsoe against veteran Vinny Testaverde, himself a former overall # 1 pick as Bledsoe had been. Both played well. Testaverde played better.

The teams were tied 10-10 at halftime, the Patriots having scored on a 13 yard TD pass by Bledsoe. The Browns then dominated the time of possession with two long third quarter drives and 10 points to take a 20-10 lead. The Patriots got a field goal with 1:30 left to make it 20-13, and recovered the ensuing on-side kick, but could not get the tying TD and the game ended 20-13. Bledsoe had completed 21 of 50 passes for 235 yards, but had also been intercepted three times. Testaverde was 20 of 30 for 268 yards and had no interceptions. Each threw a touchdown pass.

The playoff loss to Cleveland was clearly disappointing, but it was also obvious that New England was a team on the rise.

That rising would be delayed by one year, as the Patriots fell back to a 6-10 record in 1995. The season opened fine with a 17-14 win over the same Browns who had ended the 1994 season. It was New England's first opening day win in four years. The game was a thriller, with New England winning on a 1 yard touchdown run by rookie running back Curtis Martin with just 19 seconds left in the game. This capped an excellent 14 play 85 yard drive by the Patriots, including a big conversion on fourth and one on a Bledsoe run just two plays before Martin's TD. Dave Meggett, the Patriots' versatile receiver/kick returner, ran in the two point conversion for the 17-14 final.

A five game losing streak followed that opening day win, and the Pats' chances for the playoffs were pretty much gone. A win over Buffalo was followed by an overtime 20-17 loss to the expansion Carolina Panthers, and the season wound down to its 6-10 conclusion. Curtis Martin was a very bright spot for New England, rushing for 1,487 yards in his rookie season. It now seemed that the Patriots had a running game to balance the Bledsoe aerial attack.

Indeed all of the pieces, not just Bledsoe and Martin, were in place for a successful season in 1996.

Wide receiver Terry Glenn was the rookie addition to the team in 1996, the team's # 1 pick, from Ohio State. The # 2 pick was defensive back Lawyer Milloy from Washington and # 3 was Tedy Bruschi a defensive lineman from Arizona that the Patriots saw as a linebacker in the NFL. The pick of Glenn was later learned to be controversial, as Parcells wanted to draft a defensive player (lineman Vonnie Holliday was high on his list) but Bob Kraft and others were more interested in having the team acquire Glenn, and that was the choice made. Being overruled on this pick was probably a contributing factor to Parcells leaving the team after this season, and citing then the metaphor that "if they want you to cook the dinner, they should at least let you shop for some of the groceries." The Patriots also selected Nebraska defensive tackle Christian Peter with a later pick, but released him shortly after the draft when it was learned that Peter had a history of violence against women. Bob Kraft and the Patriots did not want a player of such questionable character on the team, and they should be commended for acting on those beliefs.

Terry Glenn's career got off to a slow start in training camp, and when Parcells was asked at one point by a reporter how Glenn was doing his response was something along the lines of "she's coming along", an attempt to motivate Glenn to act like a man and get on the field. Glenn responded with a fine season, catching 90 passes for 1,132 yards.

The other receiving star was tight end Ben Coates, who wound up with 62 catches for 682 yards. With Glenn, Coates, Shawn Jefferson, and Dave Meggett to catch his passes, Drew Bledsoe had an outstanding year, completing 323 passes in 623 attempts for over 4,000 yards (4,086 to be exact), and made the Pro Bowl as an AFC All-Star.

Curtis Martin had another fine year running, topping the 1,000 yard rushing mark for the second straight season with 1,152, and scoring 17 touchdowns – 14 running and three on pass receptions. His running mate in the backfield was Sam Gash, a bruising blocker who, along with an offensive line led by Pro Bowler Bruce Armstrong, helped spring Martin for many of his yards.

On defense, Willie McGinest, the team's # 1 draft pick from USC in 1994, anchored the line. The linebacking core was outstanding with Chris Slade (drafted from Virginia in the second round in 1993, the same draft that brought in Bledsoe), Todd Collins, and Ted Johnson. The defensive backfield came into its own, led by cornerback Ty Law, the team's # 1 draft pick in 1995, Lawyer Milloy, Otis Smith, and "Big Play" Willie Clay.

Special teams also had a couple of special players, rookie kicker Adam Vinatieri and veteran Dave Meggett, who had been a key special team player on Parcells' championship Giants.

The team had obviously been very well-built through the draft and free agent additions. They were ready for greatness.

The team stormed through the season with an 11-5 record, second only to Denver's 13-3 record in the AFC. All of the team's key players responded with excellent seasons, as noted above. All year I had waited for Dave Meggett to return a punt for a touchdown as he seemed ready to bust a return for one many times during the season. He finally did so in the last game of the season, a Saturday game on National TV against the Giants at the Meadowlands on December 21. This led to a 23-22 win to cap the regular season.

By nature of the Broncos and Patriots having the two best records in the AFC, both teams had first round byes in the playoffs. When Denver was upset by Jacksonville, 30-27, on Saturday of the second week of the playoffs, the Pats went into their Sunday playoff game with Pittsburgh knowing that a win would allow them to host the AFC Championship game the following week.

That Sunday game with Pittsburgh, played on January 5, was played in a very soupy fog that enveloped Foxboro Stadium. I wasn't at the game, but my son Mike was, and he said that you could barely see the field from the higher seats.

What he and the rest of the fans, as well as those of us watching on TV, saw was the Patriots get off to a great start. With the Pittsburgh defense known for its aggressive play, Bledsoe executed a perfect play action fake to Curtis Martin and when the Pittsburgh defenders fell for the fake and came up to stop the run, Bledsoe threw a perfect bomb over their heads to a streaking Terry Glenn. Glenn grabbed the ball and his momentum took him out of bounds, but not before he had completed a 53 yard pass play on the Patriots' first play from scrimmage. That set up a 2 yard touchdown run by Martin.

Pittsburgh was the defending AFC champion (they had lost to the Dallas Cowboys in the Super Bowl). Neil O'Donnell had been the quarterback the preceding year, but he was replaced this year by a combination of Mike Tomczak and speedy Kordell (Slash) Stewart. Stewart was called Slash since he was used as a quarterback/ running back/ wide receiver in Coach Bill Cowher's offense, and was always a running threat at QB. The two QBs, the running of Jerome Bettis, and that aggressive defense, nicknamed Blitzburgh for its 51 sacks during the season, were the strengths of the Steelers.

On this day, however, all of Pittsburgh's strengths were blunted. Tomczak was only 16 of 29 for 110 yards, and Stewart was 0 for 10 throwing. Bettis was injured and only totaled 43 yards rushing on 13 carries. The Patriots' versatile offense kept Pittsburgh off-balance all day. Curtis Martin gained 166 yards rushing on just 19 carries, the biggest of which was a 78 yard touchdown run where he burst through the right side of the line and ran untouched into the end zone to give New England a 21-0 halftime lead. The final was 28-3 and the Patriots would indeed be hosting the AFC championship game.

Opposing New England in that championship game would be the Jacksonville Jaguars. The Pats and Jags had met in week 4 of the regular season. It was a topsy-turvy game for both teams. New England started strongly and led 22-0 but then gave up a Hail Mary pass at the end of the first half that gave Jacksonville a score and some momentum. Three TD passes including yet *another* successful Hail Mary pass by lefty QB Mark Brunell gave the Jaguars a tie at the end of regulation and sent the game into overtime. The Patriots won it 28-25 on a 40 yard field goal by rookie kicker Adam Vinatieri, his fifth field goal of the game.

This January AFC Championship game was nothing like that September regular season game, but it had its moments too. It was a cold day in Foxboro, and maybe the cold had something to do with the high snap two minutes into the game that let the Patriots sack Jacksonville punter Bryan Baker at the Jaguars' 4 yard line. This led to an early TD and a 7-0 New England lead.

Then, with Adam Vinatieri lining up for a 29 yard field goal attempt, the odd history of the old Patriots made an appearance, perhaps to remind everyone that it still was the Patriots out there. The lights in the Stadium went out. After an 11 minute delay before power was restored, Vinatieri made the kick, and the Pats had a 10-3 lead.

Late in the first half, the Patriots faced a fourth and three at the Jacksonville 45. There were 29 seconds to go in the half. Conventional wisdom would argue for a punt to avoid the chance of the other team getting the ball in good field position and scoring before the half. However, Parcells (and Belichick later) were known to go against conventional wisdom and go on fourth down. I have always liked that aggressive mentality. It means that you have confidence in your team to get the yardage, and a good team, a Super Bowl team, should to be able to get three yards when they need it. Plus, who would want to give Jacksonville a shot at yet another Hail Mary to end the half? The

Patriots got the first down on a five yard pass from Bledsoe to Ben Coates. A long bomb from Bledsoe to Shawn Jefferson then put the Patriots inside the five yard line and a Vinatieri field goal made it 13-3 at the half.

The Jaguars did make it tense in the fourth quarter, getting a field goal to make it 13-6, and then driving to the New England 5 yard line with less than four minutes to go. Brunell fired into the end zone looking for the tying touchdown, but Big Play Willie Clay made the interception to preserve the Patriots' lead.

Still Jacksonville was not done. A Patriot punt gave the Jaguars the ball on their own 42. The first play called was a running play by James Stewart, but Stewart fumbled and the ball bounced nicely and neatly into the hands of New England DB Otis Smith. Smith grabbed it and raced 47 yards for the touchdown that clinched a 20-6 New England win. The Patriots were going to the Super Bowl.

- - -

Unfortunately, Bill Parcells, a coach who hated having his team have any distractions, was in the middle of creating a huge one of his own. Parcells was in the final year of his contract, and rumors were rampant that he was unhappy in New England (with not having full control as GM as well as coach), and, in addition, rumors were hot that Parcells had already been talking to the New York Jets and had agreed to become their coach in 1997. This was a very unprofessional thing for a coach to be doing as his team was preparing for a championship game and possible Super Bowl berth. But that was Parcells.

In the on-field presentation of the AFC Championship Trophy, owner Robert Kraft, a very classy man, praised Parcells as "the greatest coach in the history of the game in modern times". Parcells declined to acknowledge Kraft, though he did add a touch of class to the proceedings himself. Sam Gash had been a key part of the team, but an injury had kept Gash out of this game and hospitalized. At one point Parcells made mention of a guy in a hospital who also was a big part of this, lifted the trophy, and said "This one is for you too, Sam Gash."

Super Bowl XXXI – New England vs. Green Bay Packers

Super Bowl XXXI in 1997 matched the two teams from the league's smallest venues, Green Bay, Wisconsin, and Foxboro, Massachusetts. Like the Patriots, the Packers had gotten in by beating a second year expansion team, the Carolina Panthers.

Super Bowl week, which should have been a great and fun week for Patriots' fans, was ruined to some degree by all the hoopla and distraction surrounding Bill Parcells. Would he stay? Would he go? Had he already signed with the Jets?

This Parcells-created distraction also took away from the Packers, who were making their first appearance in the Super Bowl since winning Super Bowls I and II in 1967 and 1968 with Bart Starr leading the Packer dynasty to its fourth and fifth titles in seven years (the first three coming before the Super Bowl was created).

It was all so unnecessary, and it was ludicrous. Day after day the top stories revolved around Parcells. Not Bledsoe. Not Green Bay star QB Brett Favre. Not Curtis Martin. Not anything but Parcells. Sure, there were stories about Bledsoe, Favre, Martin, and others, but the spotlight was brightest on Parcells and his potential departure. *Sports Illustrated* reported that the Packers had gotten so sick and tired of hearing about Parcells that their coach, Mike Holmgren, had to warn them not to lose their focus.

Happily, after two weeks, it was finally time to play the game and it was a good one.

Green Bay started the scoring with a 54 yard touchdown pass from Favre to Andre Rison on their second play from scrimmage. A field goal followed and the Packers had a 10-0 lead and a rout was possible.

Just then the Patriots regrouped. Using screens and play action passes, the Patriots roared back with two touchdowns to take a 14-10 lead of their own after the first quarter. The first TD was a 1 yard pass from Bledsoe to Keith Byars, the second a 4 yard TD pass to Ben Coates. The Coates touchdown had been set up by a big 44 yard pass play from Bledsoe to Terry Glenn.

Surprisingly, the Patriots were eschewing the running game that everyone expected them to use, and the game was being placed in the hands and talented throwing arm of Drew Bledsoe. After the second TD pass by Bledsoe, the shot of him on the sidelines was one I will never forget. He was talking in the earphones to the coaches upstairs and he looked extremely confident and focused. It was reminiscent of Joe Namath in Super Bowl III.

Bledsoe broke the Super Bowl record for passes in the first quarter, with 15. At the half, New England had made 30 passes and had only seven runs. Unfortunately, they were trailing 27-14 as Green Bay had come back on an 81 yard touchdown pass from Favre to Antonio Freeman and a 2 yard TD run by Favre, and had also begun clamping down on Bledsoe.

Still, there was a question of whether Bledsoe's talent could get the Patriots a comeback win. He engineered a 53 yard, 7 play drive in the third quarter that cut the lead to only 6, at 27-21. The TD was scored on an 18 yard run by Curtis Martin. It now seemed to be a game, as the Patriots were only a touchdown and extra point conversion away from taking the lead.

That joy was short-lived, however, as Green Bay's Desmond Howard, a dangerous kick returner, took the ensuing kickoff on his 1 yard line and raced 99 yards for the backbreaking touchdown that decided the game. Many people wondered if Parcells would order a squib kick to try to keep the ball out of Howard's hands, but he elected to kick it to him and try to pin the Packers back deep. In this case, it worked to Green Bay's advantage.

A two point conversion put Green Bay up by two touchdowns, 35-21, and that's the way the game ended. It was a valiant try by New England, but they were now 0-2 in Super Bowls.

The carnage continued after the game, as Parcells decided not to accompany the team back on its flight from New Orleans to Boston. This was a decidedly classless move by the team's head coach, who had previously been noted for his class.

At his farewell press conference, with owner Bob Kraft standing nearby, Parcells made an equally classless statement; this is when he made that comment that "If they want you to cook the dinner, they should at least let you shop for some of the groceries." It was an obvious attempt by Parcells to criticize the team for not having him be both Coach and General Manager, and for not letting him decide what players the team should take in the college draft. It was also an uncalled-for cheap shot by Parcells toward his boss.

Days later it was announced that Parcells was signing with the Jets to be their head coach, and taking many of his coaches with him. A year later, Curtis Martin would join him in New York as a free agent. The NFL investigated and found the Jets guilty of illegal tampering with Parcells and awarded the Patriots a number of draft picks as compensation. The whole affair left a bad taste in the mouths of many Patriot fans, and ramped up a Patriots-Jets rivalry that has remained hot to this day.

- - -

The new Patriot head coach was Pete Carroll. It had been thought that Robert Kraft would turn to Bill Belichick as his head coach, as Kraft thought highly of Belichick, but perhaps to move the team away from Parcells' influence, Kraft chose instead to go with Pete

Carroll. Kraft is quoted in Jim Donaldson's book "Stadium Stories: New England Patriots" as saying of Belichick, "He impressed me a great deal. Maybe I should have hired him right then. But Parcells had driven us so crazy during the Super Bowl that I felt anyone who could work with him wasn't right for my system. I wanted a clean break." So Belichick was not made head coach in 1997; the choice was Carroll.

Carroll had had a brief and unsuccessful stint as an NFL head coach, ironically with the Jets in 1994 where he had gone 6-10, and had most recently been a defensive coordinator for the San Francisco 49ers. Carroll would remain at New England for three years, with the team declining in each year. He always appeared to me as someone who was out of his element, and often had that deer-in-the-headlights look about him. He went on to be a very successful college coach at Southern Cal, but one wonders if the enormous talent that Southern Cal usually has is more of a key to their success than is Pete Carroll.

Perhaps as a carry-over from the Super Bowl, the Patriots started out 4-0 in 1997, beating San Diego, Indianapolis, the Jets, and Chicago. The first sign of cracks in the armor came in that Jets' game. It was expected that Carroll and the Patriots would be highly motivated in the game against Parcells and the Jets, called "The Tuna Bowl" in reference to Parcells' nickname. Instead it was the Jets who carried the play, and had a chance for a game-winning 29 yard field goal at the end of regulation. The Pats averted what would have been an embarrassing loss by blocking the field goal. They then won the game in overtime, 27-24, on a 34 yard field goal by Vinatieri.

The Patriots could only manage to split their next ten games and took a 9-5 record into a big match-up at home against the Pittsburgh Steelers in the next-to-last week of the regular season. It appeared at the time that the two teams would be heading to the playoffs, and the winner of this game would most likely have a first round bye in the playoffs and home field advantage in any playoff game between the two teams.

New England was coming off a big 26-20 road win at Jacksonville. This game with Pittsburgh was a Saturday match-up, broadcast nationally. It would turn out to be a disaster for New England.

New England took a 14-7 lead at halftime, thanks to an 18 yard TD pass from Bledsoe to Ben Coates and a 1 yard TD pass from Bledsoe to Sam Gash. Kordell Stewart had scored a TD for Pittsburgh on a 1 yard run.

Two Steeler field goals made it 14-13 in the 4th quarter, and then Dave Meggett made a great pass off of a deflection and turned it into a 49 yard touchdown. New England was up 21-13 and in control. Then came the key sequence in the game.

The Patriots had the ball on a third and seven near midfield with just over two minutes left in the game; the Steelers had no timeouts remaining. At this point, while a first down would definitely ice the game, a running play was what should have been called. Even if the Patriots did not make the first down, they would have run a lot of time off the clock, and then they could punt and look to pin the Steelers deep in their own territory. Instead, they made what can charitably be considered either a bad play call, a bad play execution, or both.

The last thing a good team would do at this point would be to throw a pass to the sideline and risk an interception. What the Patriots did was throw a pass to the sideline and what they got was an interception. Kevin Henry intercepted the ball for Pittsburgh and ran it back 36 yards. The ball was now inside the Patriot 20 yard line and fans like me were fuming. A touchdown and two point conversion later, the score was tied 21-21 and heading into an overtime that should not have been necessary if the Patriots had played smarter football.

The Steelers won the coin toss to get the ball first in OT and marched down the field for the winning field goal. A key play was a screen pass that looked as if it might get a few yards but wound up getting 41 (was the defense demoralized by the bad play calling of the offense?) to set up the field goal. Pittsburgh won 24-21.

Both teams won their divisions, but because of that frustratingly bad play, the Steelers would have a first round bye and the Patriots would have to play a wild card game. They defeated Miami 17-3 to set up a rematch with the Steelers, this time in Pittsburgh. That game was almost as aggravating as the regular season game with the Steelers.

A 40 yard run by Kordell Stewart gave Pittsburgh a 7-0 first quarter lead, but the Patriots got two field goals by Vinatieri, and the score was 7-6 Pittsburgh late in the game. The Patriots were driving, and a field goal could win the game for them, but Drew Bledsoe was sacked on a blitz by Pittsburgh linebacker (and future Patriot) Mike Vrabel. Bledsoe fumbled the ball; Pittsburgh recovered and ran out the clock. The Patriots' season was over.

After the season, Curtis Martin defected to the Jets. He had again run for over 1,000 yards, so this was a big loss. The Patriots also squandered the compensatory draft picks they had gotten from the Jets, so the slide downhill was underway. The players drafted with the four picks acquired from the Jets as compensation for New York signing Parcells were running back Cedric Shaw, receiver Tony

Simmons, linebacker Andy Katzenmoyer, and offensive lineman Damon Denson, none of whom was a big contributor for New England.

The Patriots dropped from 11-5 in the last year under Parcells to 10-6 in Pete Carroll's first year with the team to 9-7 in his second year, 1998. They dropped from first in the AFC East to fourth, narrowly making the playoffs as the final wild card team. Their one playoff game was a resounding 25-10 loss to Jacksonville.

The 1998 season did feature a courageous performance by Drew Bledsoe. Playing despite a broken index finger on his throwing hand, Bledsoe led the team to two dramatic victories. The first was a Monday night home game against Miami on November 23. Trailing 23-19 with less than three minutes to go, Bledsoe led the Patriots on an 80 yard drive, converting two fourth downs and two third and long yardage situations before hitting Shawn Jefferson with a 25 yard TD pass to win the game 26-23. The following Sunday, also at home, Bledsoe led the Patriots on another game-winning fourth quarter drive. This was an 82 yard drive engineered with Buffalo leading 21-17. Bledsoe hit Jefferson for 10 yards and a big first down on a fourth and nine play and then got the ball to the one on a pass interference call against Buffalo on a throw intended for Terry Glenn. Bledsoe hit Ben Coates for the touchdown that gave the Patriots a thrilling 25-21 victory.

Bledsoe's injury worsened though, and Scott Zolak wound up starting against San Francisco on December 20, and then starting the playoff game against Jacksonville on January 3.

Bad luck also returned to the Patriots after the 1998 season. To replace Curtis Martin, they had drafted running back Robert Edwards from Georgia. Edwards rewarded them by rushing for 1,115 yards, and he and the team looked forward to many good years as a runner for the Patriots and a lot of success in his future. Instead, Edwards suffered a freakish and devastating injury in a beach flag football game for rookies sponsored by the NFL as part of its Pro Bowl festivities. In fact, the injury to his knee was so bad that Edwards almost had to have a leg amputated. He would never be the same. He was out of football until 2002 when he made a brief and unsuccessful attempt at a comeback with Miami.

The steady decline under Pete Carroll continued as the team's record dropped again in 1999, this time to 8-8 and there were no playoffs for the Pats.

On the bright side, my son Mike surprised me with tickets to the Patriot pre-season game with the Dallas Cowboys on August 21. This was special for a couple of reasons. First of all, the Cowboys were my other favorite football team besides the Patriots. Like the Patriots, they started in 1960, the first year in which I was interested in football. As a young boy and fan of cowboy shows on TV, their name made me an immediate fan, and I fell in love with them even more when they finished the season winless. They lost the first 11 games of the 12 game season before tying the New York Giants 31-31 on the last day of the season. As a constant fan of the underdog, I was won over by that, and they immediately became my NFL team. A couple of gallant near-miss losses to the Green Bay Packers in the 1966 and 1967 NFL Championship games solidified that, as the frequent dismissal of the Cowboys as 'always the bridesmaid never the bride' rankled me. When the great and classy Roger Staubach, one of my favorite college and pro football players of all time, became their quarterback, I was definitely hooked.

The second reason that made his getting these tickets special was a family reason. When I was in the Air Force and stationed in Wichita Falls, Texas in the summer of 1973, I had gotten tickets for a pre-season game between the Cowboys (then quarterbacked by the afore-mentioned Roger Staubach) and Kansas City Chiefs. As it turns out, this was the time that my wife and I learned that our first child was on the way, and my wife was not feeling all that well, so we did not go to the game. That first child was Mike, and now, 26 years later, he said that he wanted to make up for making me miss that Cowboy game by getting tickets to this one. What a really nice thing to do for his old dad.

Our seats were in the end zone, which was fine with me. The Cowboys had been the dominant team of the 1990s and still had some of their top stars, including quarterback Troy Aikman, and running back Emmitt Smith. Smith was another of my all-time favorite players, and is not only one of the greatest running backs in NFL history, but the one who during his career rushed for 18,355 yards, the highest career total in league history.

The game was played on a Friday night in August that had a cold rain falling throughout. We saw some very good plays by both teams, but more by New England in a game won by the Patriots 34-14.

1999 also saw Kraft and the Patriots flirting with a potential move to Hartford, Connecticut, when Massachusetts state congressmen seemed to be putting obstacles in the team's hopes to build a new stadium. Kraft had initially wanted to invest his own money in a stadium complex in South Boston, but was rebuffed. He did reach a deal with Connecticut in which the state agreed to put up $300 million for the facility and another $100 million for road and infrastructure changes. Kraft accepted the deal and appeared in a press conference with Connecticut governor John Rowland, Drew Bledsoe, and others. Kraft did not seem happy moving out of the Boston area, however, and

Rowland came under a lot of criticism in Connecticut for giving Kraft and the Patriots too good a deal. The Krafts had negotiated a termination clause in the contract that called for no contractual penalties if the deal were terminated before May 2, 1999. The Patriots, citing reports that the Stadium would not be completed by the 2002 season, backed out of the deal on April 30, 1999. Eventually, agreement was reached with Massachusetts on a new stadium to be built in Foxboro, adjacent to the current stadium. That stadium was completed for the 2002 season, but it turned out to be mostly Kraft's money that would build what would be Gillette Stadium.

A bigger and much better change occurred after the 1999 season. Pete Carroll wanted more power on personnel decision making as head coach of the Patriots. Kraft may have agreed with the idea in general, but he decided on a different person to be in charge.

It just so happened that Bill Belichick was now available. He had been the designated successor to Bill Parcells as head coach of the Jets, but when Parcells retired (again) and Belichick was named Jets' head coach it fell apart. It lasted one day before Belichick realized that Parcells looking over his shoulder was not a good situation and he resigned as head coach of the Jets (or as "HC of the NYJ" as he described it in a press conference for which the New York media roundly criticized him).

In any case, Belichick was available, and Kraft wanted him, and he got him. On January 27, 2000, the Patriots named Bill Belichick the 14th head coach in the team's history. He would turn out to be the best.

Chapter 6 – 2000's: Dynasty - "We're All Patriots"

There is an interesting consistency in the recent history of the NFL, that a team of the decade has been a team that ended the preceding decade at or near the bottom of the standings.

In 1958 the Green Bay Packers were 1-10-1. Two years later they were in the NFL Championship game and in 1961 began a string of seven years in which they won five championships, including the first two Super Bowls. New Coach Vince Lombardi and star players like Bart Starr, Paul Hornung, Jim Taylor, Herb Adderley, Ray Nitschke, and Willie Wood helped turn around the Packers.

In 1969 the Pittsburgh Steelers were 1-13. They then began a dynasty that would lead to four Super Bowl Championships in the 1970s behind new Coach Chuck Noll and a group of stars that included Terry Bradshaw, Franco Harris, Mean Joe Greene, and the famed Steel Curtain defense. The Cowboys of Tom Landry, Roger Staubach, and Bob Lilly, and the Dolphins of Don Shula, Bob Griese, and Larry Csonka were also good in the 70s but the Steelers were the best.

In 1979 the San Francisco 49ers were 2-14. Then in came head coach Bill Walsh, quarterback Joe Montana, Steve Young, receiver Jerry Rice, and others, and the 49ers would win five Super Bowls between 1982 and 1995.

In 1989 the Dallas Cowboys were 1-15, before they would go on to win three Super Bowls in the 1990s, behind Troy Aikman, Emmitt Smith, and Michael Irvin, an outstanding offensive line, and a speedy, opportunistic defense. The Cowboys won their championships under two coaches, though Jimmy Johnson, who won two, had put the pieces in place for a third under Barry Switzer.

The Patriots under Peter Carroll had regressed in the late 1990s and the 2000 Patriots fell to a record of 5-11. However, with new head coach Bill Belichick, a defense that now featured veterans Willie McGinest, Tedy Bruschi, Ty Law, Lawyer Milloy, and offense and kick returning threat Troy Brown, the Patriots were just one player away from creating dynastic magic of their own. They just needed a quarterback of their own like the quarterbacks of past dynasties, to match their successes.

The only highlights of the 2000 season may have been the fact that New England and Buffalo played twice and both games went into overtime. Their last game in 1999 also went into OT, so this was three times in a row for these long-time rivals. Buffalo won the first of 2000 16-13 and New England won the second 13-10 in snowy Buffalo.

The lowlight may have been the ending of the last game of the season, at home against Miami. A Drew Bledsoe pass at the end of regulation was ruled an illegal forward pass, and so the game ended, with the Dolphins winning 27-24. About fifteen minutes after the players had trudged into their locker rooms, the officials called them back onto the field, saying that the pass was really incomplete and that there were still three seconds to be played. The officials then sent them back without running in a play, claiming that they would not run that play for safety reasons, and that the game was over. However, they called them back onto the field again, since the NFL had chimed in and stated that the game had to be played to its completion. Michael Bishop was put in at quarterback for the Patriots for that last play. He threw a desperation bomb that fell incomplete, thus officially, and finally, ending the season.

After the 2000 season Bill Belichick stated, "We'll be more competitive. We'll have more depth." He and Director of Player Personnel Scott Pioli immediately delivered on that latter promise, drafting Richard Seymour of Georgia and Matt Light of Purdue in the NFL draft. They also added a number of veteran free agents who would prove to be cornerstones of the team's future success. This included linebackers Mike Vrabel, Roman Phifer, and Bryan Cox; defensive back Terrell Buckley; wide receiver David Patten; and running back Antowain Smith. Going into the 2001 season, there would be 24 new faces on the team's 53 man roster. One of the roster returnees was Drew Bledsoe, the face of the franchise, who on March 7 was signed to a new 10 year, $103 million contract.

Opening day of 2001 was September 9 in Cincinnati. Troy Brown was the star for New England, with 7 catches for 126 yards; he was on his way to a then-record 101 catches for the season. Unfortunately, the Patriot defense could not stop Cincinnati's Corey Dillon, who rushed for 86 yards in the first half, and 104 on 24 carries for the game, as Cincinnati won 23-17.

The Tuesday following Opening Day was September 11, 2001, and it was a day that all Americans will remember. The country was hit with terrorist attacks, with two planes crashing into and destroying the Twin Towers of the World Trade Center in New York, a third crashing into the Pentagon, and a fourth brought down in a Pennsylvania field thanks to the courage of the brave passengers, before it could also do more damage in Washington. Many innocent Americans lost their lives in the attacks. Many brave Americans, policemen, firemen, and ordinary people, prevented many others from losing theirs. The attacks cannot either adequately or appropriately be described in a book about football such as this. Suffice to say that the scars from this will linger forever in the memories of anyone alive at the time.

The NFL decided to cancel the games of the following Sunday, September 16, to let the nation continue to grieve, and to let the workers in New York, Washington, and Pennsylvania continue their rescue and recovery efforts. This was a wise decision, in contrast with the decision that the NFL made to play its games on November 24, 1963, two days after the assassination of President John Kennedy. The American Football League did cancel its games on that fateful November weekend in 1963. Legendary NFL Commissioner Pete Rozelle would later describe the decision to play those games in 1963 to be the biggest mistake that he made as Commissioner.

When play resumed on September 23, there were moments of silence before all NFL games, and many ceremonies honoring the heroes and in remembrance of the victims. The Patriots were playing a home game against the New York Jets, and, to bring things back to football, it would prove to be one of the most momentous days in Patriot history.

Late in the game, with the Patriots trailing 10-3, Drew Bledsoe had to take off and run while being chased on a pass attempt. He ran to the right for the sideline and just before he could get out of bounds, he took a vicious hit from Jet linebacker Mo Lewis.

When the Patriots got the ball again later in the game, fans were surprised to see a new quarterback run onto the field. The new quarterback was Tom Brady, who had been drafted in the sixth round of the 2000 NFL draft. Brady had had a so-so career at the University of Michigan, sharing time/platooning with Drew Henson, who later played baseball in the New York Yankee farm system and football for the Dallas Cowboys.

Up until this point in his career, Brady had thrown exactly three NFL passes, completing one. However, he had impressed the Patriot staff with his hard work and willingness to do anything to help the team. He was especially good at being the scout team quarterback, running the opposition's offense against the Patriots' defense in the practice week preceding games.

As Brady came into the game against the Jets, some fans thought the move had been made due to Bledsoe's inability to generate much offense in the first two games of the season. Sitting at home, I thought this was a move made for that reason, meant to try to shake up the team and generate some offense. This was seemingly confirmed when TV sideline reports identified the reason they had gotten from the Patriot sideline was that the change had been made because of a "coach's decision".

As it turned out, that coach's decision was made because Bledsoe seemed to be really dazed and somewhat incoherent on the sideline. He was obviously injured, more injured, in fact, than had been originally thought. Later, he had to be rushed to the hospital and it was determined that Lewis' hit had sheared a blood vessel in Bledsoe's lung. Bledsoe had lost a lot of blood, was not in good shape, and would be lost to the Patriots for weeks. Brady finished the game in that 10-3 loss to New York, and it now was the case that he would be the Patriots' starting quarterback for the next few weeks, at least.

The first start of Brady's career was the following Sunday against the Colts and their superstar quarterback Peyton Manning. Brady led his team to a stunning 44-13 victory with a very efficient and error-free performance, hitting 13 of 23 passes for 168 yards and no turnovers.

When a team's star goes down, as Bledsoe did, other players need to step up their games and make big plays. The Patriots did that all season. In this game, the first such step-up was by linebacker Bryan Cox, who set an early tone for the team by blasting an Indianapolis receiver with a big hit on a pass reception early in the game. The message was that these Patriots were going to play hard, hit hard, and not let the loss of Bledsoe ruin their season. Bledsoe was on the sideline talking to and helping Brady, as he would be all season. The Patriots were taking the first steps to becoming a real TEAM.

Brady and the Patriots had a letdown in the season's fourth game, losing to Miami 30-10 and falling to 1-3 on the season. Brady was not good in this game, fumbling twice and hitting only 12 passes for a meager 86 yards. This, and one other game later in the season, may have been the last bad games that Brady played for many years.

The Patriots bounced back from the Miami loss with wins over San Diego and Indianapolis the next two weeks. The San Diego win was a coming-of-age game for Brady, who showed flashes of the great quarterback that he would very soon become, as he rallied the team from a 26-16 deficit with 8:38 to go to beat the Chargers and their QB, Doug Flutie. He first led the team on a 69 yard, 15 play drive to a field goal by Adam Vinatieri; Brady was 5 for 8 passing on that drive. He was also 5 for 8 passing on the next drive, the last pass being a 3 yard touchdown pass to tight end Jerome Wiggins to tie the game with only

40 seconds left in regulation. An overtime drive that led to a 23 yard Vinatieri field goal gave the Pats a very satisfying 29-26 win.

The Indianapolis game was a career highlight game for David Patten, as the Patriot receiver accounted for four touchdowns in a 38-17 win over the Colts. Patten caught two passes for touchdowns, including a Patriot record 91 yard touchdown pass from Brady. He ran for another touchdown on a tricky end-around play. He passed for a fourth touchdown on another gadget play, hitting fellow receiver Troy Brown for a 60 yard touchdown pass. Tom Brady was 16 for 20 for 202 yards, but the day belonged to David Patten.

As shown with his clever use of David Patten, Patriot offensive coordinator Charlie Weis was using a very imaginative offense. There were end-arounds, halfback options, receivers throwing passes, and even a play where Brady handed off and then sprinted to the outside to catch a pass himself. Opponents preparing for games against the Patriots had to prepare for anything and everything that this great offensive mind could create.

Game 7 at Denver was the other bad game in Brady's maiden season as starting QB. He threw four interceptions in the fourth quarter as the Patriots suffered a 31-20 loss. The Patriots evened their record back to .500 at 4-4 with a 24-10 win the following week against the Atlanta Falcons. Brady was back on track with a 21 for 31 passing day for 250 yards. He had three touchdown passes and no interceptions.

Game 9 with Buffalo was a revenge game for Antowain Smith, who had been a Bill the previous season. The Patriots took a 7-0 lead in the first quarter on a 6 yard touchdown pass from Brady to Kevin Faulk. The lead was 14-11 late in the fourth quarter when Smith blasted through the line on a short yardage play, broke tackles, and scored on a 42 yard run with 1:52 to go that put the game away as a 21-11 New England win. I believe that this was the game in which Smith came into the past-game press conference and began his comments by singing the theme from The Brady Bunch TV show. It was clear that the Patriots were all starting to believe they had something really special in their young quarterback.

New England's next game was against the powerful St. Louis Rams in Foxboro. The Rams had been Super Bowl champions in 2000, and had one of the most powerful offenses the league had seen in years. Their nickname "The Greatest Show on Turf" was a testimony to the great passing attack led by quarterback Kurt Warner (who would win the league's MVP award that season), and three very speedy and very good receivers, bolstered by a running attack that featured Marshall Faulk, one of the best players in the league. Just as Patriot coach Bill Belichick had long been considered a defensive genius, Ram coach Mike Martz was considered an offensive genius.

The game was a Sunday night game and it was a good one. The Rams won, 24-17, but, despite the loss, New England gained a lot of confidence with their strong performances on both offense and defense. Their play so impressed Mike Martz that the Ram coach flatly predicted that the Patriots would represent the AFC in the Super Bowl. This was surprising considering the Patriots' 5-5 record this season, and spotty history, but it proved to be accurate as the Patriots would not lose another game all season.

The St. Louis game was the first game for which Drew Bledsoe had been cleared to play after his devastating injury. He and Brady shared time at QB during practice the week before the game, and Belichick thought this sharing did not allow Brady to be as prepared for the game as he otherwise would have been. Bledsoe was now ready to play, and assumed he would get back the starting job that had been his. Belichick had a big decision to face – stay with Brady, the hot young quarterback, or go back to Bledsoe, the team's star for so many years.

The Bledsoe controversy continued for the next few days. Bledsoe had been the starter before the injury and he expected to be again now that he was healed. He was the face of the franchise, and it was a franchise that was building a new stadium for 2002 and needed a star (like Bledsoe) to help draw fans. But Belichick felt that the team had not played well with Bledsoe at QB early in the season and that the team was playing better under Brady. He also felt that Brady had outstanding leadership qualities to go along with a great work ethic. So Belichick told both players, and then announced that Brady would remain the team's starting quarterback.

Bledsoe was angry at first. He felt betrayed. He felt that he had not lost the job, but had had it taken away from him. To his credit, after his initial reaction, Bledsoe buried the anger and disappointment and was a tremendous help to Brady and the team for the rest of the season. He showed himself to be a very classy athlete and classy person.

At the other end of the spectrum of controversy and how to handle it was wide receiver Terry Glenn. Glenn had started the season inactive. He had been suspended for four games by the NFL for substance abuse. When he did rejoin the team, he was continually an on-again, off-again distraction, and was later suspended again by the team for his attitude problems.

Unlike Bledsoe, Glenn did not handle himself well. In an interview on Channel 4 TV with Bob Lobel and Steve Burton, Glenn made a complete fool of himself. In an answer to a question "Do you want to play for the Patriots?", Glenn responded "I did. That is d-i-d did" and went on to say that he was "not getting paid and my hamstring hurt" implying that he was faking injury because he was not happy with his pay. That is not a way to ingratiate yourself with hard-working fans. So we had one veteran (Bledsoe) handling his situation like a professional, another like a spoiled brat. When Bledsoe was traded after the season, he took out a full page ad to thank fans for supporting him during his time with the Patriots. When Glenn left, no one cared.

With the Patriots at 5-5 after the St. Louis game and with Brady now established as the team's starting quarterback, a new era in Patriot history started with a game against the New Orleans Saints. Brady threw for 258 yards and 4 touchdowns with no interceptions as he led the Pats to a 20-0 halftime lead and a 34-17 win. A new trick play proved successful, a direct snap from center to running back/receiver Kevin Faulk, which the team ran at least twice, gaining 7 yards and 24 with the gadget play. The team was now 6-5, trailing the first place Jets and Dolphins who were at 7-3, but the Patriots were getting hot.

A showdown with the Jets followed, and it was before that game that Terry Glenn was suspended for conduct detrimental to the team and had that pathetic interview with Channel 4. This included refusing to practice or play after being cleared by the medical staff. The Patriots without Glenn came back from a 13-0 halftime deficit to beat the Jets 17-16.

It was a dramatic game. Mike Vrabel got the Patriot comeback started with an interception. The Patriots drove for their first touchdown, scored on a run by Antowain Smith. The biggest play in the drive was a 46 yard pass on a slant route from Brady to little-used receiver Fred Coleman (it was one of only two pass receptions for the season by Coleman). It was now 13-7 Jets and they extended it to 16-7 with a field goal. A Marc Edwards 4 yard touchdown run made it 16-14 in the third quarter, and a Vinatieri field goal in the fourth quarter put the Patriots ahead 17-16.

There was one last big play to help preserve that lead. The Patriots had a 3rd and 2 at the New England 41 with 1:46 left in the game. A timeout was called and Brady went to the sideline to confer with Belichick on the critical call. A quarterback keeper was called which Brady questioned. At this point, Drew Bledsoe, who had become a mentor to Brady, told the young quarterback "Just run the ball, get the first down, and win the game." Brady went back on the field, ran the ball, got the first down, and won the game.

A 27-16 win over Cleveland gave the Patriots an 8-5 record and a three game winning streak. They carried these to Buffalo where a key play, and a very lucky break, gave them a win in yet another overtime game with the Bills.

The game was tied 9-9 going into OT. Brady threw a completion to David Patten at the Buffalo 41. Patten made the catch, but was knocked unconscious on a hard hit by the Buffalo tackler. Patten fell and was out cold from the blow. His head hit out of bounds, his body landed in bounds, and he fumbled the ball. Buffalo recovered. But wait, it was not a fumble. After the officials reviewed the replay it was ruled that the ball had been in contact with Patten's leg when his head hit out of bounds. By rule, since his head hit out of bounds, he was out of bounds, and the ball was out of bounds since it was in contact with a player who was out of bounds. The Patriots retained possession. Then power runner Antowain Smith ran for 38 yards, once again breaking away from a jam-up at the line scrimmage, and set up a game-winning 23 yard field goal by Vinatieri. The Patten play showed that even the freaky plays were going the Patriots' way during this streak.

The next game was a Saturday night game against Miami on December 22, a cold night in Foxboro. Antowain Smith rambled for 156 yards on 26 carries and opportunistic defensive back Tebucky Jones forced two fumbles as the Patriots moved their record to 10-5 with a 20-13 win over the Dolphins. Another great trick play call led to New England's first touchdown. This one was a direct snap to Kevin Faulk, but in this variation, Brady was a wide receiver. He ran a pass pattern to the left and Faulk, instead of running, threw a pass to Brady. Brady grabbed it and ran out of bounds at the Miami 20 after a 23 yard gain. Smith then completed the drive with a touchdown run for a 7-0 lead and the Pats were on their way.

A bye week and a 38-6 destruction of the Panthers in Carolina finished the Patriots regular season. They had won their final six games to compile an 11-5 record and win the AFC East. They would have a first round bye in the playoffs with the second-best record in the AFC. Only the Steelers at 13-3 were better.

The Oakland Raiders 38-24 win over the Jets in the first round meant that the Raiders would be coming to Foxboro for that playoff game. It would be the last game ever played at Schaefer/Sullivan/ Foxboro Stadium and it would be one of the most memorable in NFL history.

The success of the night game telecasts had resulted in this game, on Saturday, January 19, being played at night. It was risky to play a night game in New England in the winter, but the networks hoped that a game in the cold and maybe even snow would be dramatic. They got much more than they ever expected from both the weather and the game.

A major snow storm hit the area that day. The game was an 8:00 start and the snow was falling heavily by the afternoon and blizzard-like conditions continued before and during the game. Snow covered the field; game time temperature started at 25 degrees and dropped. Getting traction was difficult for both teams. It was clear that this could very well be a low-scoring game, perhaps a 7-0 or 3-0 game (Patriot fans could remember that the famous 'snow plow game' against Miami had ended at 3-0 in conditions that were not quite as bad as they were for this Oakland game).

Oakland scored first and carried a 7-0 lead into halftime, as the players went into the locker room to get some much-needed heat and relief from the snow and cold.

The Patriots made adjustments at halftime, including a decision to go more with the passing game. Brady drove the team down the field after the half, hitting David Patten on two big pass plays for 44 yards, setting up a 23 yard field goal by Vinatieri midway through the third quarter. The Patriots were a little frustrated to have not gotten a touchdown, but at least they were finally on the scoreboard.

Two field goals from the powerful kicking leg of Oakland's Sebastian Janikowski gave the Raiders a 13-3 lead going into the fourth quarter, a big 10 point lead made bigger by the wintry conditions. At that point the Patriots went with a lot of no huddle offense, and the maneuver paid off as Brady led the team on a long drive that resulted in a game-changing touchdown. Brady got the score himself, scrambling on a busted pass play for six yards and the TD. Brady dove into the snowy end zone, got up, and emphatically spiked the ball in triumph. I will never forget that look of joy and almost-boyish enthusiasm on his face after he scored the touchdown. The Oakland lead was down to three, at 13-10.

The Patriots then got the ball with time remaining for one last drive to tie or win the game. On the most crucial and controversial play of the game, the season, and maybe Patriot history, Brady dropped back to throw and was blitzed by Oakland defensive back Charles Woodson. Brady's arm came forward to throw but as he did, he noticed Woodson bearing down on him (Patriot coaches reportedly loved Brady's feel for pass rushes in the pocket and ability to avoid them). Instead of throwing, he brought the ball down to his waist and tried to cover it with his left hand, but Woodson stripped the ball from his hands, and Oakland recovered the fumble. The Raider offense started onto the field to run out the clock for the win.

However, referee Walt Coleman went over to review the replay and what he saw made him overturn the fumble call. Since Brady's arm had been going forward, it was, by rule, an incomplete pass. The Patriots still had the ball.

The Raiders yelled and screamed about the ruling after the game. They did so in the off-season too, claiming that this now-famous "Tuck Rule" needed to be changed; it was not. The officials had indeed made the correct call. Since Brady had never secured the ball to his body, the forward arm motion, by rule, did mean that the play should have been called an incomplete pass, as it was with the replay override. (For anyone who is interested, a summary of the Tuck Rule can be found in Appendix B of this book.)

With new life, Brady marched the team down closer, and with 27 seconds to go in the game, Adam Vinatieri set up for what would be a very difficult 45 yard field goal attempt with the snow still falling hard. The ball was snapped and Vinatieri's kick was something of a spinning line drive that never got too far above the players. It was, to the delight of the snow-covered fans in the Stadium and Patriot fans everywhere, long enough and just high enough to get over the cross bar. The game was tied at 13-13 and would head into overtime.

The Patriots got the ball first in overtime and Brady once again marched them down the field, this time for 61 yards in 15 plays. Brady was superb on that drive, completing his first six passes, and then converting a critical fourth and four pass from the Oakland 27 to David Patten. Patten caught the ball on his knees at the 22 for the first down. After a couple of plays took the ball down to about the 5 yard line, in came the field goal unit for another field goal attempt by Adam Vinatieri, this time from 23 yards away.

Vinatieri's kick was higher and truer than the one that had tied the game, and just as good. The Patriots had won 16-13. Snapper Lonie Paxton raced into the end zone and fell on his back waving his arms and legs to make snow angels in celebration of the victory.

Playing in horrible weather conditions, Brady was fantastic. He was 32 of 52 passing for 312 yards. He led his team on three clutch drives in the fourth quarter and overtime for three scores. He and Adam Vinatieri really started building their reputations as outstanding clutch performers in this game.

Post-game talk centered on the Tuck Rule call. Interestingly, many Patriot fans felt that the NFL had finally evened things up for the Patriots after they were robbed of victory in the 1976 Playoff game versus the Raiders (described earlier in this book). Even more interestingly, replays showed that Woodson may have slammed his right arm into Brady's helmet before the fumble. That could have been called a roughing the passer penalty and would definitely have conjured up memories of the crucial and controversial roughing the passer call that went against the Patriots in that 1976 game. Maybe somewhere Sugar Bear Hamilton was smiling.

- - -

The Steelers won their playoff game the next day, 27-10 over the Baltimore Ravens (the transplanted Cleveland Browns), so the AFC Championship Game would be in Pittsburgh the following Sunday.

The Steelers were 9 point favorites, and they, and all of Pittsburgh, seemed to assume that they would easily beat the Patriots. In fact, Coach Bill Cowher had told Steeler players to get their Super Bowl plans out of the way before the game, so as not to be distracted during Super Bowl week. What happened to winning the game first, Coach?

Pittsburgh's versatile quarterback Kordell Stewart and bruising running back Jerome Bettis were still the Patriots' biggest worries on defense. The Pittsburgh defense was big and strong and dirty (more on that shortly). But it was two old pros for the Patriots who were the stars on this day.

Troy Brown got the Patriots started with a beautiful punt return for touchdown. Fielding a long punt from Pittsburgh's Josh Miller, Brown shot through the middle of the field and didn't stop until he had outraced everyone into the end zone for 55 yards and a touchdown.

As alluded to above, I have always believed that the Steelers were one of the dirtiest teams in the league, often using illegal or late hits, and seemingly wanting to hurt opposing players (for evidence that goes beyond the Patriots, see the hit made right on the knee of Bengal quarterback Carson Palmer in a 2005 wild card playoff game that knocked Palmer out of the game, or Jack Lambert picking up Cowboy player Cliff Harris and body-slamming him to the ground in Pittsburgh's win in Super Bowl XII, or numerous other examples). Pittsburgh's dirty play entered into this game late in the first half, and the victim this time was Tom Brady.

Brady had started well, going 12 for 18 for 115 yards, and with the score 7-3 Patriots, he dropped back to pass again. Pittsburgh's

Lee Flowers came blitzing from the right side, and rolled into Brady's legs. Brady fell to the ground in pain. The hit had caused an ankle injury and it sent Brady to the sidelines for the rest of the game. It was an unnecessary hit, but it accomplished what Pittsburgh had wanted, knocking the Patriot star out of the game for good.

Into the game came veteran Drew Bledsoe, and the classy veteran made what would be his last game on the field for the Patriots a shining moment in his career. Bledsoe completed his first pass, hitting David Patten for a 15 yard gain, and drove the team to the Pittsburgh 11 yard line. He then lofted a pass to Patten in the back right corner of the end zone with less than a minute to go in the first half. Touchdown Patriots! The Patriots went into halftime ahead 14-3.

The Steelers started the second half with a drive to the New England 16 and set up for a field goal attempt. The kick was blocked by the Patriots, and Mr. Versatile, Troy Brown, scooped it up on the run and headed for the Pittsburgh end zone. After running a short while, Brown was in danger of being tackled when he alertly lateraled the ball to teammate Antwan Harris, who raced it the rest of the way for a touchdown and a 21-3 Patriot lead.

The Patriots survived an odd and scary "don't do that play", an ill-advised pass thrown by Bledsoe as he was falling down, and managed to hang on for a 24-17 win.

Bledsoe and Brown were the stars of the game. When Bledsoe went to the post-game press conference, he kidded the press with a comment about how nice it was to see them again. As for the teams, the Steelers now had a whole off-season to prepare for their next game; the Patriots were on their way to the Super Bowl.

Super Bowl XXXVI – New England vs. St. Louis Rams

Awaiting the Patriots in the Super Bowl was "The Greatest Show on Turf", the St. Louis Rams. The Rams had gone 14-2 and had a sparkling offense, one of the best in NFL history.

The game was played on February 3, 2002 in New Orleans, the site of both previous New England Super Bowls. The stories and mild controversy in the week leading up to the Super Bowl was about whether the Patriot quarterback for the game would be the veteran Drew Bledsoe or the young star, Tom Brady. Brady's injury and Bledsoe's solid play in the Pittsburgh game led to the conjecture, but Belichick made it clear that Brady was healthy enough to start and that he would indeed be the starter.

My son Mike and I were at the Celtics' game against the Clippers earlier in the day (we are big Celtics' fans). The Celtics won

104-91, but we left early to get back to watch the Super Bowl. You could tell that we were impatient (and strangely confident too, by the way) about the Patriots' chances, as we were slightly annoyed that the Clippers starting lineup included many long, multi-syllabic names such as Michael Olowakandi and Eric Piantowski, so the intros took a few seconds longer than they could have had the team consisted of a lot of Joe Smith's or Mike Bibby's, and longer than we would have liked on Super Bowl Sunday. Were we ready for some football, or what?

As the Patriot players gathered in the runway leading to the field before the pre-game introductions, the video scenes were memorable. There was Brady knocking helmets with his teammates. He was clearly hyped up for the game. When Brady knocked helmets with Bledsoe, Bledsoe had an amused smile on his face as a parent might have with an exuberant child jumping all over the house on Christmas Eve. Bledsoe was heard in the film saying "you're the man, 12" to the very motivated # 12, Tom Brady.

The St. Louis offense was announced first, and there were cheers as star QB Kurt Warner, RB Marshall Faulk, and others were introduced. When it was time for the Patriots' introductions, fans were pleasantly surprised to hear a clearly exasperated TV broadcaster, Pat Summeral, say that the Patriots had decided to be introduced as a team, not as individuals. And so the entire team charged onto the field together. It was a great display of teamwork. Later it was learned that the Patriots had rejected numerous requests from the network and from the NFL to have the players be introduced individually, as had been the case in all previous Super Bowls, and almost every other pro football game in history. Some fans later wrote in to their newspapers, or to *Sports Illustrated* or other publications to say that this was the moment that they knew the Patriots would win. Perhaps they were right.

The Patriot game plan was to focus on stopping the versatile Marshall Faulk and not blitz as much against Kurt Warner as they had in their regular season game with St. Louis. They intended to hit Faulk every time he ran the ball and every time he went out on a pass pattern, and they executed that plan very well.

Saint Louis was ahead 3-0 in the second quarter when the Pats ran a rare blitz and linebacker Mike Vrabel put pressure on Warner coming in from Warner's right. As a result of that pressure, Warner hurried his throw and the pass was intercepted by Patriot defensive back Ty Law, who raced 47 yards down the sideline into the end zone. New England had a shocking 7-3 lead over the mighty Rams.

Just before the two minute warning Warner completed a slant pass around midfield to receiver Ricky Proehl. The Rams had a 15 yard gain, but a big hit by the Patriots jarred the ball loose from Proehl, and it was recovered by New England at the Ram 40 yard line. Brady hit Troy Brown for 16 yards, Jerome Wiggins for 9, and Kevin Faulk for 7. With the ball on the 8 yard line, Brady threw an easy toss high into the end zone and David Patten made an acrobatic catch, reaching up back and over his head to catch it before falling onto his back in the end zone. Touchdown, Patriots!

The play had been run perfectly by Patten, after an adjustment had been made to this pattern by the Patriot coaches during the practice week to take advantage of St. Louis tendencies. Instead of the normal route of doing a square out turn toward the sideline, Patten was told to do the square out but then turn back downfield, or in this case, toward the back of the end zone. He ran it the new way, the St. Louis defender went for the move to the outside to try to get an interception, and Patten was open when he made the second cut to the back of the end zone. It was a great practice adjustment by the Patriots that paid off in a big score. With 31 seconds left in the first half the Patriots had taken an improbable 14-3 lead. They went into halftime sky-high with momentum.

A third quarter interception by Otis Smith set New England up for a 37 yard Vinatieri field goal, extending the lead to 17-3, but St. Louis wasn't through yet. In the fourth quarter the Rams marched down the field before the Patriot defense stiffened and had the Rams in a 4th down and goal at the three. Warner scrambled and fumbled, and New England defensive back Tebucky Jones picked up the loose ball, and ran 97 yards for an apparent touchdown that would have put the game out of reach. New England fans were going crazy, but then everyone saw that there was a penalty flag on the play. Willie McGinest had been caught holding Marshall Faulk as Faulk went out on a pass pattern. It was a good call, and it nullified the Patriot TD and gave the ball back to St. Louis. A quarterback sneak by Kurt Warner brought the Rams back within a touchdown, 17-10. Momentum now seemed to have moved over to the Ram sideline.

New England fans, used to late game misery of Red Sox and Patriots in past years, must have thought that this was a turning point. It was like the roughing the passer penalty against Sugar Bear Hamilton in Oakland in 1976, the unnecessary late hit by Tim Fox against Houston in 1978, the baseball going through Bill Buckner's legs in 1986, Bucky Dent, and numerous other such turns of fate that most readers would probably just as soon not read any more about, so we will leave it at that.

This misery looked even more possible as the Rams got the ball at their own 45 with just 1:51 left in the game. It took St. Louis only three pass plays to go 55 yards and tie the score: Warner for 18 yards to Az-Zahir Hakim, Warner for 11 yards to Yo Murphy, and Warner 26 yards for a touchdown to Ricky Proehl. It was now 17-17 and it looked as if momentum had now taken up permanent residence on the Ram sideline.

I was ranting and raving at this point, about how I didn't want to read once again about how a team from New England had battled hard and well and had almost done it, but lost at the end, like the Red Sox and Reds in the classic 1975 World Series. It was time to win one of these I thought (and ranted about, to be honest).

The Patriot coaches had similar thoughts. The Patriots took over after the Ram kickoff at their own 17 yard line. There was 1:21 left in the game and neither the Patriots nor Rams had any timeouts remaining. The conventional wisdom was that New England should just have Brady 'take a knee' and have the clock run out, sending a Super Bowl into overtime for the first time ever. TV analyst John Madden stated that was what the Patriots would do. However, Bill Belichick and Charlie Weis had other thoughts on the sideline. Belichick was concerned that the Rams had momentum and could carry that to an overtime win. He and Weis conferred and agreed to go for it. It was a bold decision that would reverse the sports' fortunes of New England forever. Belichick and Weis were showing extreme confidence in Brady. *Sports Illustrated* later quoted Belichick as saying "With a quarterback like Brady, going for the win is not that dangerous, because he is not going to make a mistake." That is supreme confidence.

Brady was surprised at the decision, but excited. Then he made it happen. He dropped back three times and with his deep receivers covered, three times looked off his primary receivers and completed drop-off passes to J.R. Redmond for 5 yards, 8 yards, and then, after two incompletions, for 11 yards, and two first downs. Belichick and Weis had agreed that if they had not gotten those quick first downs they would have killed the clock and gone into overtime. Now they were on the march.

With second and ten on the New England 41 Brady hit Troy Brown over the middle and Brown gained 23 yards to the St. Louis 36 before racing out of bounds to stop the clock. The Patriots still wanted to get a little closer, so Brady threw one more pass and one more completion, this one in the middle of the field to Jerome Wiggins down to the 30. With time running down, Brady coolly brought the team to the line of scrimmage and spiked the ball, stopping the clock with 7 seconds left in regulation. How cool was Brady? He nonchalantly caught the ball as it was bouncing back down after the spike and handed it to the referee.

After watching Brady's execution on this drive, announcer John Madden, who had earlier felt that the Patriots should play for overtime, said "What Tom Brady just did gives me goose bumps." It was another indication that the Patriots had something really special with this young quarterback.

Brady trotted to the sidelines and in came New England's other Mr. Clutch, kicker Adam Vinatieri, for a 48 yard field goal attempt. Vinatieri's kick sailed high and true; it split the uprights almost perfectly down the middle. Long-time Patriot radio announcer Gil Santos screamed "The kick is up. It's good! It's good! And the game is over. The Patriots have won the Super Bowl." Santos later added, a little more calmly, but with a lot of happiness and pride coming through in his voice, "Well, New England, your Patriots are the best team in the National Football League." He and his long-time radio partner, Gino Cappelletti, started singing the Queen song "We are the Champions", on the air

> *We are the champions, my friends*
> *And we'll keep on fighting till the end*
> *We are the champions*
> *We are the champions*
> *No time for losers*
> *Cause we are the champions*

It may not have been as melodious as the Chicago Bears Super Bowl Shuffle had been in 1986, but for long-suffering Patriot fans it was much sweeter.

It looked as if the clock had 3 seconds on it as the kick sailed through the uprights, but time ran out on the play. I kept waiting for the officials to bring the teams back onto the field and for some disaster to befall New England (a kickoff return for touchdown?) but it did not happen. The Patriots were champions of the world. As the song goes, We are the champions … (and so on)

In the ceremony on the field after the game, with red, white, and blue confetti flying all around and a beaming Tom Brady holding his Super Bowl MVP trophy, owner Bob Kraft summed it up best: "The fans of New England have been waiting for 42 years. We are the World Champions. At this time in our country, we are all Patriots, and tonight the Patriots are champions." New England fans everywhere could nod their heads in agreement with everything he said.

One Super Bowl post-script that I particularly enjoyed was written in *Sports Illustrated.* A few hours after the game, Brady went to Belichick's hotel room where Bill was celebrating with family and friends. Belichick handed Brady a beer. According to the story, Brady grinned sheepishly. He had been offered the opportunity to go to Orlando, Florida and film the "I'm going to Disneyworld" commercials that Championship MVP's had been doing in recent years.

According to team rules, Brady had to get the coach's permission to miss the team flight home. There was a long pause before Belichick smiled and said "Of course you can go. How many times do you win the Super Bowl?" Happily, once was not enough for either of them.

- - -

The final line score was:

	1	2	3	4		Total
Saint Louis	3	0	0	14	-	17
New England	0	14	3	3	-	20

The Patriots were champions. The team and its fans were on top of the world. Being announced as a team before the game was inspiring to many.

Tom Brady was an overnight sensation. His cool, calm demeanor, burning intensity, and great clutch play had made him a star. He had thrown only three passes as a rookie. Early in his career he was fourth on the quarterback depth chart, behind Drew Bledsoe, Damon Huard, and Michael Bishop. Now he was the MVP of the Super Bowl. It was a great story.

Speaking of stories and Brady, there was a great one which was recounted by Nick Cafardo in his book "The Impossible Team" about the 2001 Patriots. Shortly after Brady was drafted in the sixth round in April 2000, he and owner Bob Kraft passed each other in the stairs at the New England practice facility. Brady, carrying a pizza, introduced himself to Kraft. As they started back, Brady apparently turned and said "Mr. Kraft, I'm the best decision your organization ever made." It was bold, it was confident … and it was also right.

- - -

Success is never final, but failure can be. That, or words to that effect, is a quote that I remember from Bill Parcells.

Belichick may have remembered these words too, as he always seemed to have the right idea of how to inspire the team at the start of each season. One time, he had Bill Russell, the Celtic great, winner of 11 NBA championships in 13 years (or 14 in 15 if you add in two NCAA titles and an Olympic Gold Medal), come and give a motivational talk in training camp. If you cannot be motivated by the greatest winner in the history of American sports, it's not clear what can motivate you.

- - -

2002 was a year of almost, and a year of change, for the Patriots. They had a new, beautiful stadium, Gillette Stadium, to play in. They had a brand new Championship banner to hang there. And they had said goodbye to long-time favorite Drew Bledsoe, who had been traded to Buffalo for a first round draft pick. Bledsoe had handled his demotion from starting QB with a lot of class. He had, very professionally, assumed the role of Brady's backup and advisor. Patriot fans appreciated the class Bledsoe had shown in what had to have been a tough situation for him. After he was traded, Bledsoe took out a full page ad in the Boston papers thanking the fans for all the support they had shown him. It was a final display of class by a very classy individual.

The Patriots opened the 2002 season at home, on Monday night, September 9. It was the first regular season game at the new Gillette Stadium. Opposing them were the Pittsburgh Steelers, looking for some revenge for their loss to New England in the AFC Championship Game. It was no contest. The Patriots brilliantly used a no-huddle offense to give the Steelers little chance for defensive adjustments, and utterly demolished Pittsburgh 30-14. New receivers Deion Branch and David Givens, rookies from Louisville and Notre Dame, respectively, and tight end Christian Fauria fit right into the attack led by a very confident Tom Brady.

Two more wins followed, a 44-7 blasting of the Jets at the Meadowlands followed by a 41-38 overtime win over Kansas City. The Kansas City win showed some cracks in the New England armor, as the Chiefs scored the last 14 points to tie the game and only a 53 yard drive to an Adam Vinatieri game-winning 35 yard field goal in OT salvaged the win.

Four losses in a row followed, to San Diego, Miami, Green Bay, and then, after a bye week, to Denver. The Patriots now had a 3-4 record. The Green Bay loss was particularly galling. The final score was 28-10, and the Patriots played badly. Packer running back Ahman Green gained 136 yards as the Patriot defense was not good at all in stopping the run. The worst play though came on offense. It was a screen pass that Brady attempted to Kevin Faulk deep in Patriot territory. The ball fell to the ground, but since Faulk was behind Brady, it was a live ball, a fumble, not an incompletion. No Patriot was alert enough to run after the ball. The Packers did, and got a touchdown out of it. I was furious. I'll bet that Belichick was even more so.

Despite the losses, I looked at the remaining schedule as of November 1, and felt that the Patriots could win all but one and finish 11-5. The only game that I thought would be a sure loss was the November 17 game at Oakland, where the Raiders would be sky high looking for revenge for their loss in the snow in Foxboro in January.

The first game was in Buffalo against the Bills and their new quarterback, old friend Drew Bledsoe. Bledsoe was no match for the Patriots as New England won easily 38-7. A 33-30 win at Chicago, the almost obligatory loss to Oakland, 27-20, and a 24-17 win over Minnesota sent the Patriots into a rare Thanksgiving Day game with a 6-5 record. I felt they could and should have won all of their remaining games.

The Patriots rarely play on Thanksgiving, which I always felt was odd, given that Thanksgiving really started with the Pilgrims and Indians in New England. It seems more appropriate to play a Thanksgiving game in New England than Detroit or Dallas, but NFL traditions are NFL traditions. New England went into Detroit for this Thanksgiving Day game and came out a winner, 20-12. A big Tedy Bruschi interception was a key play for the Pats in this game.

A 27-17 win over Buffalo followed. I believe that this may have been the game in which Belichick introduced a very innovative defensive concept. With Bledsoe having to pass late in the game, the Patriots lined up with no down linemen, and 7 players standing up in linebacker positions. The intent was to confuse the Bills offensive linemen and Bledsoe, as they would not know from where the pass rush would be coming. It worked and was very effective (I wondered in the 2008 Super Bowl if the Patriots would employ that same tactic against Eli Manning on the last fateful drive by the Giants but, alas, they did not; I have often wondered since what would have happened had they tried).

Now at 8-5 and with three games left, at Tennessee, and with the Jets and Miami at home, the Patriots' fate was in their own hands.

The Tennessee game was a Monday nighter and turned into a big upset loss to the Titans, 24-7. That set up a big showdown game for the 8-6 Patriots against the 7-7 Jets. First place was on the line. Poor play by the Patriots, especially by the defense, and a great 11 for 11 start by Jet QB Chad Pennington (a regular thorn in the Patriots' side) propelled the Jets to a 30-17 lead that put the Jets in the driver's seat for the AFC East. The Patriots would play an early game on

Sunday, December 29, against the Dolphins, with the loser being eliminated. The Jets were playing a late game against Green Bay. The Patriots needed a win and a Jet loss to win the AFC East.

Inexplicably, in a game as big as this, the Patriots came out flat. They trailed 21-10 at the half, and Dolphin running back Ricky Williams had already gained 120 yards rushing against a sluggish Patriot defense.

With about 5 minutes to go, and Miami leading 24-13, the Patriots finally showed some life. A long pass from Brady to David Givens resulted in a pass interference call against Miami, and a first and goal at the Miami 3. A TD pass from Brady to Troy Brown and a 2 point conversion pass from Brady to Fauria made it 24-21. The Dolphins expected an on-side kick, but the Patriots crossed them up by kicking deep and pinning Miami back at their own 4 yard line. After three plays and a punt, the Patriots took over and drove to the tying field goal. In overtime, the Patriots won the toss and elected to receive. Miami kicker Olindo Mare kicked the ball out of bounds, a big blunder that gave the Patriots the ball at their 40. With great field position to start, Brady then drove the Patriots 43 yards on 7 plays, and Adam Vinatieri booted a 43 yard field goal to win the game 27-24.

All attention now shifted to the Jets game with Green Bay, but not for long. Green Bay and its quarterback, Brett Favre, were playing horribly. Romeo Crennel noted early that the Green Bay players didn't seem to want to play that day at all, and Belichick stopped watching early since he seemed to sense the same thing. They were right. The Packers rolled over and played dead for the Jets and the Jets just rolled, to a 42-17 win. The Jets had won the AFC East, and one year removed from a triumphant Super Bowl win, the Patriots were not even in the playoffs.

- - -

Interestingly, the Boston TV stations were reporting after the game and in subsequent days that Brady had a shoulder injury and that, had the Patriots made the playoffs, it was entirely possible that Brady could not have played and Damon Huard would have been the Patriot quarterback for the playoffs. I have never heard that story confirmed by Brady, Belichick, or the Patriots, but some writers were convinced that this was indeed the situation. In any case, there would be no playoff games for the 2002 season, so the point was moot. It was time to look forward to 2003.

- - -

The Patriots went undefeated in the 2003 pre-season games, and looked like a powerhouse going into the 2003 season. Then, the players were jolted in the week before the season opener when team leader Lawyer Milloy was cut from the team's roster. Milloy and the team were in a contract dispute, and the Patriots felt that Milloy's play was declining and did not want to pay a huge contract. Milloy was too proud to accept what the Patriots were offering, and so the Patriots made the decision to release Milloy.

Once again, a coach known for eliminating distractions for his team had found a big one on his hands, as Parcells did before the 1997 Super Bowl. The release of Milloy was received very bitterly by the team. Even Tom Brady, normally very positive in his praise of the organization, was critical of that decision. Even worse, Milloy, now a free agent, had signed with Buffalo, the very team that New England would be playing in its season opener. The Patriots were very distracted and very demotivated. Almost anyone could see that a big loss was probably coming. It came.

The Bills opened the season with a 31-0 blowout of the Patriots. Lawyer Milloy played very well, and even made a big play with a deflection of a Tom Brady pass into the hands of a Buffalo teammate for a big interception. Milloy had gotten his revenge on New England.

The Patriots' next game was a late afternoon game in Philadelphia against the Eagles. The Eagles, like the Patriots, were expected to be among the best teams in their conference but had lost their opener as well. This would be a big test for both teams. Before the game, more controversy reared its head, thanks to the ESPN pre-game show. On that show, in discussing the Patriots loss to Buffalo and the associated discontent about Lawyer Milloy, ESPN studio analyst Tom Jackson said of the Patriot players, "Let me be very clear about this. They hate their coach." It's not clear where Jackson had gotten his information, since that did not appear to be the case. Whether the Patriots heard this or not, they came through with a big 30-15 win over Philadelphia that put their season back on course.

The only thing bad about the Philly win was an injury to strong and fast Patriot linebacker Rosevelt Colvin. Colvin had been signed as a free agent and was expected to be a big addition to the Patriot pass rush and pass coverage. A hip injury suffered on the Philadelphia turf had knocked Colvin out for the season. It was a big loss for the Patriots in the midst of a big win.

After a 23-16 win over the Jets and a 20-17 loss to Washington, the Patriots went off on a winning streak unparalleled in

NFL history. They won their next 15 games that season, including the Super Bowl, and the first six games of their next season. The 21 straight wins was an all-time NFL record. The Patriots were at the peak of their game and at the peak of their sport.

There were a number of highlight-reel games in the streak. After starting the streak with 38-30 and 17-6 wins over the Titans and Giants, the Patriots took their third in a row with a thrilling 19-13 overtime win in Miami. Richard Seymour blocked a 35 yard field goal attempt by Olindo Mare with two minutes to go to preserve the tie, and then the game was won in spectacular fashion in OT. After Mare missed another field goal attempt and a Tyrone Poole interception at the 18 thwarted another Miami drive, Tom Brady fired a bomb to the left that hit Troy Brown in stride for a game-winning 82 yard touchdown.

After a 9-3 win over Cleveland, the next highlight was a Monday night game on November 3 against the Broncos in Denver that greatly enhanced Belichick's growing reputation as a football genius. The Broncos were leading the game 24-23 with less than 3:00 to go. The Patriots had been backed up to their own 1 yard line and had to punt. The Broncos would get good field position and would probably win the game. Belichick saw an opening, however, that few others saw. He ordered long snapper Lonie Paxton to snap the ball out of the end zone. This would give Denver 2 points on a safety, but the Patriots would then get a free kick from their 20 that would drive Denver further back and give New England at least a chance for a win. Paxton snapped the ball way over the punter's head (and in fact hit the goal post), so the ploy worked. It was now 26-23 Denver. The subsequent free kick, followed by a hold of Denver by the defense, and a Denver punt gave Brady and New England the ball at their own 42 with one more chance to tie or win. Everyone expected the Pats to move into position for a tying field goal, but Brady marched them all the way into the end zone. The touchdown came on an 18 yard pass to David Givens, perfectly placed by Brady into Givens' hands in the left side of the end zone. It gave the Patriots a 30-26 win going into a bye week, which gave sportswriters and reporters a lot of time to praise the brilliance of Bill Belichick's decision. The praise went on for days, as it rightfully should have.

From my personal viewpoint, this was an interesting time. I was in the hospital recovering from surgery after a regular colonoscopy that went bad (that can be the subject of some other writing) so I watched the next game from my hospital bed at UMass Memorial Hospital in Worcester (not where the colonoscopy took place), in the ward on 3 West, where I was receiving outstanding care from the nurses and doctors. It was a Sunday night game, which I watched with the TV volume on low, to keep from disturbing my roommate. I did want to see that game, though, because it was a biggie: the Patriots and Bill Belichick, coming in at 7-2, and the Cowboys and Belichick's former boss, Bill Parcells, now un-retired (again) and coaching the Cowboys, also coming in to the game with a 7-2 record. This was the first match-up of the two former partners since their split in 2000 when Belichick left the New York Jets to come to New England.

Belichick told the team during the week preceding the game not to let themselves get distracted by the hype surrounding the Belichick-Parcells story or, as he dubbed it, the irrelevant aspects of the game. Then, as if to give them a final demonstration of where their focus should be, Belichick ignored Parcells as the two were on the field during pre-game warm-ups.

The Patriots dominated the game, winning 12-0. The only touchdown of the game was a 2 yard TD run by Antowain Smith, which was set up by a 57 yard pass from Brady to David Givens. The extra point was missed, so the score was 9-0 at halftime and a second half field goal accounted for the final margin. Parcells gave Belichick an awkward hug at midfield after the game, and the hype ended shortly after their respective post-game press conferences.

Win number seven in the streak should have been a loss. New England was trailing the Houston Texans 20-13 late when a Brady to Graham 4 yard touchdown pass on a fourth and 1 tied the game with 40 seconds left in regulation. A Vinatieri 28 yard field goal won it in overtime.

The Patriots won their 8th in a row at Indianapolis on November 30, but it was a real nail-biter. It was the first time the Patriots and Colts had met since expansion and realignment had taken the Colts out of the AFC East and into the AFC South. (It is odd that Indianapolis is considered a southern team, but geographical correctness is apparently not a requirement for the NFL). Both teams came in at 9-2 and were viewed as two of the top teams in the league. The Patriots went ahead 17-0 on a Vinatieri field goal, a rushing TD from interim running back Mike Cloud, and a 31 yard TD pass from Tom Brady to Dedric Ward. The Colts came back to make it 17-10 with 12 seconds left in the first half, but the Colts kickoff went deep (announcers expected a squib kick to keep the Patriots from any scoring chance), and the very speedy Bethel Johnson ran it back 92 yards for a New England touchdown. When asked after halftime what his team would do differently in the second half, Colt Coach Tony Dungy wryly said that they would not kick it again to Johnson.

The Patriots had a 31-10 lead when two Brady interceptions and three Peyton Manning TD passes had the game tied at 31-31. Another good kickoff return by Bethel Johnson after the third Colt TD set up a Patriot TD on a 13 yard Brady pass to Deion Branch. It was now 38-31 Pats, but a Kevin Faulk fumble set up a 29 yard field goal by Mike Vanderjagt that brought the Colts back to within four points, at 38-34.

The Patriots were forced to punt on their next series, and punter Ken Walters' kick was very short, giving Indy the ball at the 50 yard line. The Colts drove to the 2 yard line, but the Patriots made an outstanding goal line defense that prevented Indianapolis from scoring. On first down the Patriots stopped Indianapolis' excellent running back, Edgerrin James, at the 1 yard line. They stopped him again on second down and Manning called timeout. The Colts now had no timeouts left. On third down Manning threw an incompletion to the left side of the end zone. It was now fourth and 1 from the 1 and Manning handed the ball again to Edgerrin James. Patriot linebacker Willie McGinest had anticipated the play and flew in from James' right, grabbed James' leg and hauled him down short of the end zone. The Patriots had held, Indianapolis had not scored, and the Pats left with a thrilling victory that had them at 10-2 for the season.

New England finished off the season by winning its last four games, 12-0 over Miami, 27-13 over Jacksonville, 21-16 over the Jets, and 31-0 over Buffalo.

The win over Miami on December 7 was played the day following a blizzard that had dropped about two feet of snow on Gillette Stadium. Workers shoveled snow out of the seating areas and down conveyor belts to the field, where plows moved it to the sidelines and dump trucks carted some of it away. The win was clinched when Tedy Bruschi ran back an interception for a touchdown, which sparked off a spontaneous celebration by fans that had never before been seen in Foxboro. As the PA system played the Gary Glitter song "Rock and Roll, Part Two", with its repeated line of "da-da-da-da-da-da-DUH-hey", fans responded by simultaneously throwing handfuls of snow up in the air on every "hey". It was really something to see.

The win over Buffalo gave them sweet revenge over the Bills and provided mirror bookends to the season – they had lost in Buffalo 31-0 on the first day of the season and had now beaten Buffalo by the same 31-0 score at Foxboro on the last day of the season. The win gave New England a 12 game winning streak and a 14-2 record for the season.

The league had co-MVP's that season, Tennessee quarterback Steve McNair and Indianapolis quarterback Peyton Manning. The Patriots would now have to face both of them in successive weeks in the playoffs. They faced them both, and defeated them both. First was Tennessee, in a game played on January 10, a bitter cold Saturday night in Foxboro. The temperature was 4 degrees Fahrenheit with the wind chill factor making it 10 below. We were at a birthday party that night, but checked the score on enough occasions to know that the Patriots won a hard-fought contest, 17-14, with an Adam Vinatieri field goal in the fourth quarter being the difference.

Indianapolis then came to Foxboro for the AFC Championship on January 18. The Patriot defensive backs hammered the Colt wide receivers all day and took Indianapolis out of its vaunted passing game. Peyton Manning was sacked four times, and had four interceptions as well. The star of the game was Patriot cornerback Ty Law, who accounted for three of those interceptions. The Patriot defense shut the Colts down. The team led 15-0 at the half and won 24-14 to send them to their second Super Bowl in three years.

Super Bowl XXXVIII – New England vs. Carolina Panthers

Super Bowl XXXVIII was played at Reliant Stadium in Houston on February 1, 2004. The Patriots were playing the upstart Carolina Panthers, who had upset the Eagles in Philadelphia in the NFC Championship Game, 14-3. It was another tight Super Bowl that would be decided by three points, and by more clutch fourth quarter heroics from Tom Brady and Adam Vinatieri. Brady led the Patriots on two dramatic drives in the last seven minutes of the game and Vinatieri once again kicked the game-winner in the Super Bowl as if it were a practice kick with no pressure riding on it at all.

The game was scoreless after the first quarter and in fact was still scoreless with 3:05 left in the first half. The Patriots had had two field goal attempts to this point, one no good and the other blocked. The Patriots had the ball thanks to a great play by linebacker Mike Vrabel. Vrabel had blitzed Carolina QB Jake Delhomme with 5:22 left in the half and swatted the ball away from Delhomme. New England recovered the fumble at the Carolina 20 yard line. With 3:05 to play, the Patriots scored on a 5 yard pass from Tom Brady to Deion Branch, and suddenly the floodgates opened. Delhomme hit Steve Smith for a 39 yard TD to tie it 7-7. Brady hit Givens with a 5 yard touchdown pass to put New England ahead 14-7. Carolina countered with a booming 50 yard field goal by kicker John Kasay, and the half ended with New England ahead 14-10.

Halftime at this Super Bowl was one of the most memorable, if not THE most memorable, in football history. Singers Janet Jackson and Justin Timberlake were performing, and when Timberlake finished one song with the regrettable line "gonna have you naked by the end of this song" he grabbed a piece of Jackson's top that was supposed to come off, but more of Janet Jackson's top came off than had been planned. Janet Jackson's right breast was now exposed for all the world to see. I saw this on TV and was certainly surprised; it was one of those "did I see what I think I just saw" moments. Yes, Jackson had shown one more body part than either she, the NFL, the CBS Network, the Federal Communications Commission (FCC), or most women anywhere would have liked. The controversy surrounding "nipplegate", as it was called by some (or the 'wardrobe malfunction' as Timberlake called it), raged for days after the game, CBS was fined by the FCC, and this exposure caused some TV censorship laws to be changed.

So much for fashion and clothing -- or in this case, the lack thereof -- and TV history, let's get back to football.

The second half was like the first. Neither team scored in the third quarter, and then there was a scoring explosion in the fourth quarter. A two yard touchdown run at the start of the 4th quarter by New England's Antowain Smith started the flurry. It was 21-10 Patriots.

Delhomme led Carolina downfield for 81 yards, the touchdown scoring on a 33 yard run by DeShaun Foster. Carolina went for a two point conversion (a little early in the game for that according to some critics), but missed, so the score was now Patriots 21 Panthers 16.

Brady then drove New England to the Carolina 9 but then made an uncharacteristic mistake, an interception in the end zone.

Delhomme, three plays later, threw to Mushin Muhammad for a shocking 85 yard touchdown. Again the 2 point conversion attempt failed, but Carolina led 22-21 with only 6:53 remaining. Could New England be primed for an upset?

Brady then marched the Patriots downfield and the team had a second and goal from the Carolina one yard line. Into the Patriot offensive huddle came linebacker Mike Vrabel as an extra tight end and blocker, and he wound up catching a touchdown pass from Brady to put New England back into the lead. The Patriots attempted a two point conversion to extend the lead to seven, and succeeded, as Kevin Faulk took a direct snap while Brady jumped and faked that the ball had been hiked over his head. Faulk ran it in and it was 29-22 Patriots.

Back in this seesaw match came Carolina.

Delhomme led the Panthers 80 yards in 7 plays, culminated in a 12 yard touchdown pass to Ricky Proehl to tie the game 29-29. This was the same Ricky Proehl, then with the Rams, who had also tied the Patriots late in Super Bowl XXXVI on a 26 yard pass from Kurt Warner. Maybe if they ever see him in a future Super Bowl the Pats should triple cover him late in the game.

John Kasay's kickoff after the Proehl TD went out of bounds, giving Brady and the Patriots good starting field position, at their 40. The Patriots moved to a third and three at the Carolina 40, when Brady hit Deion Branch for 17 yards to set up the game winning 41 yard field goal by Adam Vinatieri with four seconds left. The Patriots and their fans could now breathe a sigh of relief. The game was over and the Patriots had won their second Super Bowl 32-29.

The final line score was:

	1	2	3	4		Total
Carolina	0	10	0	19	-	29
New England	0	14	0	18	-	32

Tom Brady was the Super Bowl MVP for the second time, and had a marvelous game, going 32 for 48 for 354 and 3 touchdowns. Jake Delhomme also had a great game for Carolina, going 16 for 33 for 323 yards and three TD's of his own. Deion Branch was the receiving star with 10 catches for 143 yards. By the end of the game injuries had decimated the Patriot defensive backfield and Delhomme's passing nearly finished the job. However, the Patriots held on and won the shootout to claim their second Super Bowl Trophy. Whew!

- - -

By nature of their Super Bowl win, the Patriots were given a new honor. They started the 2004 season with a Thursday night game preceding the normal Sunday starts. It was on national TV, against the Colts. This was a new concept for the NFL, and a good one. I had often thought over the years that the NFL should start its season with one game, on the Saturday night before the opening Sunday. The league took that idea one better, avoiding the high school and college games on Friday and Saturday night, and started on Thursday. They also went into this in typical NFL flash, with a one hour pre-game featuring musical performers such as Mary J. Blige, remote reports from Jacksonville where the next Super Bowl would be played, and other attractions. It could have been a distraction, but Bill Belichick and the Patriots did not let it become so.

This Thursday opener matched the two teams that many believed were the two best teams in the league. The one that many conceded to be the best, the Patriots, came out of it with a 27-24 win, their 16th win in a row. A missed 48 yard field goal in the final minute of the game by Indianapolis' Mike Vanderjagt was the key. Vanderjagt had not endeared himself to Colts' fans during the off-season with his criticism of Indy QB Peyton Manning, and this would not help his popularity anywhere in Indiana.

The big addition to the Patriot roster for 2004 was powerful running back Corey Dillon. The Patriot running attack had ranked a lowly 27th in the league in 2003, and the Pats felt that they needed a good running game to balance Tom Brady's aerial attack. They acquired Dillon from Cincinnati for a second round pick. Dillon had rushed for over 1,000 yards in the first six of his seven seasons in the NFL, but had earned a reputation as a malcontent in Cincinnati, where a string of losing seasons had made the Bengals one of the league's doormat teams. Dillon was not a problem at all in New England either on the field or off, as he gained 1,635 yards in his first season with the team for a new team rushing record, and was a team leader for his three years in New England, helping to mentor rookie running back Laurence Maroney in Dillon's last and Maroney's first seasons in the NFL.

The streak continued with consecutive win # 17, 23-12 at Arizona, and, after a bye week, # 18, 31-17 at Buffalo. The Pats won at Buffalo but Coach Bill Belichick surprised reporters at the press conference the next day by completely berating his special team's play. He had some reason to do that, since the team had given up a 34 run on a dropped snap and run by the Bills' punter, had surrendered a 98 yard kickoff return, had accounted for zero punt return yards of their own, and had also fumbled a punt. New England was ahead only 24-17 when Tedy Bruschi blitzed and sacked old friend Drew Bledsoe, the Buffalo QB, and caused a fumble. Richard Seymour recovered the fumble and ran 68 yards for the clinching touchdown.

The special teams were much improved the next week, a 24-10 win over Miami on October 10 that let the Patriots set an all-time pro football record with their 19th win in a row. The Dolphins defense battered Tom Brady, but Corey Dillon rambled for 94 yards on 18 carries for the win.

The Patriots' streak continued to 21 with wins of 30-20 on October 17 and 13-7 on October 24 over the Seahawks and Jets, respectively, but news of the streak was relegated to secondary status in the press and on TV, and was almost lost in the hubbub (no pun intended) surrounding the Hub's other big outdoor team, the Red Sox. The Red Sox in late October were in the midst of a heroic streak of their own, a great comeback from being down 0-3 in the 7 game

American League Championship Series showdown with the New York Yankees. The Red Sox would come back to win the final four games of that series and go on to win their first World Series in 86 years.

The streak was finally stopped by a very fired-up Pittsburgh Steelers team in Pittsburgh, 34-20, on Halloween. The Steelers would go on to post a 15-1 record for the season, finishing ahead of New England's 14-2 in the AFC.

The Patriots followed the loss at Pittsburgh with another mini-streak of 6 wins in a row: 40-22 at St. Louis, 29-6 over Buffalo, 27-19 in a Monday night game at Kansas City, 24-3 over the Baltimore Ravens, 42-15 at Cleveland, and 35-28 against Cincinnati, Corey Dillon's former team.

They suffered their second loss on December 20, on a Monday night in Miami. This loss was a shocking upset to a Miami team that would finish 4-12 for the season. What made it even more shocking was that the loss stemmed from a rare bad play by Tom Brady. Brady made a Bledsoe-esque throw as he was falling down. Brady threw instead of hanging onto the ball and taking the sack. This resulted in a Miami interception that was the key play in a 29-28 win for the Dolphins.

The Patriots finished the season with a 23-7 road win over the Jets and a 21-7 win over the hapless 2-14 San Francisco 49ers.

After a bye week in the first of the playoffs, the Patriots would be facing their old nemesis, Indianapolis, in their first playoff game. Led by outstanding QB Peyton Manning, runner Edgerrin James, and wide receiver Marvin Harrison, the Colts had one of the strongest offenses in NFL history, but they were completely shut down by New England in the game. The Patriots controlled the ball for 38 minutes, led by a 144 yard rushing day by Corey Dillon, and knocked the Colts out of the playoffs for the second straight year, with a 20-3 victory that was not as close as the score might indicate. The result gave Peyton Manning an 0-7 record in Foxboro. Conversely, it gave Tom Brady a 7-0 record in post-season games.

The New England defense held James to just 39 yards rushing, and frustrated Manning who finished with 238 yards on 27-for-42 passing. Manning had led the league in passing and had set an NFL record with 49 touchdown passes over the season. He accounted for no touchdowns in this game. Meanwhile, the Patriots had a number of time-consuming drives that ate clock time and kept Manning and his offense off the field. The first long drive lasted 9:07 and 16 plays that gained New England 78 yards and led to a 24 yard field goal by Adam Vinatieri. A six play 49 yard drive made it 6-0 Pats, before Manning led his team to its only points in the game, an 11 play, 67 yard drive that resulted in a 23 yard field goal for Mike Vanderjagt on the last play of the first half, and a 6-3 New England lead at halftime.

A 15 play, 8:16 third quarter drive by Brady and the Pats gave New England the game's first touchdown, a 5 yard TD pass from Brady to David Givens. A 94 yard, 7:24 drive in the fourth quarter, capped by a 1 yard TD run by Tom Brady, made the final 20-3 for New England.

New England once again had injuries deplete their defensive secondary, with starting cornerbacks Ty Law and Tyrone Poole out for the game and season, but still held Indianapolis, the fifth-highest scoring team in NFL history, to a measly three points.

The challenge in New England's second playoff game, the AFC Championship game at Pittsburgh, was completely different. Instead of the offensive powerhouse they had faced in the Colts, the Patriots would now be facing the NFL's top defensive team, the Steelers. Pittsburgh had gone 15-1 for the season, with rookie QB Ben Roethlisberger having gone 14-0 since stepping in as the starting quarterback.

Just as they made a shambles of the Indianapolis offense, holding them to 3 points, the Patriots made a shambles of the Pittsburgh defense, blasting them for 41 points in a 41-27 victory. Both the way that the Patriots held down Indy's offense and exploited Pitt's defense had caused jaws to drop or eyebrows to rise all over the country among NFL fans.

It was a cold day in Pittsburgh for this game, 11 degrees at the start of the game and the Patriots made it colder for Steeler fans. Patriot defensive back Eugene Wilson intercepted Roethlisberger's first pass of the game to set up a 48 yard field goal by Adam Vinatieri. The defense set up the next score too, as Mike Vrabel recovered a rare fumble by Pittsburgh's running back Jerome Bettis, whose nickname, "The Bus", described his powerful running style. The Patriots recovered at the 40 yard line and scored immediately as Brady threw a 60 yard touchdown bomb to Deion Branch on the first play after the fumble.

A Steeler field goal cut the New England lead to 10-3, but Brady hit Branch with a 45 yard pass that set up a 9 yard touchdown pass from Brady to David Givens, and Rodney Harrison returned another Roethlisberger interception 87 yards for a touchdown. That gave New England an astounding 24-3 halftime lead.

The second half started with a New England punt on its first series that was followed by three consecutive touchdowns. Jerome

Bettis scored on a five yard run to make the score 24-10, but New England stormed back with a 69 yard drive in 7 plays to make it 31-10 on a 25 yard touchdown run by Corey Dillon. Pittsburgh responded with a 60 yard drive, the last 30 of which were covered on a TD pass to Hines Ward to make it 31-17, and the Steelers cut the lead further to 31-20 with 13:32 left in the fourth quarter.

There was still time for a Steeler comeback, but the Patriots methodically put the game away. A 49 yard drive that took 5:26 ended with a field goal to increase the lead to 34-20. Another interception by Eugene Wilson stopped Pittsburgh, and Brady took another 5:06 off the clock with a 55 yard drive that ended with Deion Branch taking the ball on a reverse and running 23 yards to make it 41-20. The Steelers scored again with 1:31 left, but it only made the final score closer, at 41-27. The Patriots were off to their third Super Bowl in 4 years.

Super Bowl XXXIX – New England vs. Philadelphia Eagles

It was another Super Bowl, and it would be another three point win for New England, but this was not won on a field goal at the end of the game.

The Philadelphia Eagles were the opponent, and Philly was one of the NFL's best teams, having appeared in four consecutive NFC title games. Their star quarterback, Donovan McNabb, was considered one of the best in the game, though not on the same level as Peyton Manning or Tom Brady. However, McNabb's style was completely different, as he was a scrambling QB who decided games both with his legs, as a runner, and his arm, as a strong, accurate passer.

Most of the pre-game hype centered on the Eagles and their loud and controversial wide receivers. Terrell Owens ("T.O.") was one of the loudest and most obnoxious players in the league. He had previously been with the 49ers, where he wore out his welcome with his antics and complaints about his own quarterback. He had an injured right ankle, but was expected to play. The other wide receiver was the lesser-known and less-talented Freddie Mitchell, who disparaged New England's defensive backfield with his remarks during the week preceding the game.

The game between these two NFL powers from the northeastern corridor was played on February 6, 2005 in Alltel Stadium in Jacksonville, Florida.

The Patriots felt that they had to control the running and scrambling of Donovan McNabb, and so played a 4-3 defense with 4 down linemen and 3 linebackers, as opposed to their usual 3-4 alignment.

It was a tough game, well-played by both teams.

After a scoreless first quarter, Philadelphia opened the scoring with a 6 yard touchdown pass from McNabb to his tight end, L.J. Smith, with 10:02 left in the second quarter.

The Patriots then drove to the Eagle 4 yard line but lost the ball when Brady fumbled after bumping into running back Kevin Faulk on a play fake. The Patriots held and then made it a 7-7 tie at the half on a 4 yard touchdown pass from Tom Brady to David Givens.

Halftime for this Super Bowl was much calmer than it had been the previous year. Thankfully, there was no bare-breasted Janet Jackson and no wardrobe malfunction as there had been for that Super Bowl. The two teams just made their adjustments and fans settled back for a big second half.

The Patriots took their first lead with 11:09 left in the third quarter on a 2 yard touchdown pass by Tom Brady. The TD-catching receiver was none other than Mike Vrabel, the linebacker who had carried the novel idea of coming into the game as an extra tight end into another dimension. This was the second straight Super Bowl in which Vrabel had caught a TD pass from Brady, as this had become a staple play in the Patriot goal line offense.

The Eagles came back though to tie the game at 14-14 on a 10 yard pass from McNabb to Philadelphia's all-purpose player, receiver/ running back/ kick returner Brian Westbrook. The score came with 3:39 to go in the third quarter and sent the two teams into the fourth quarter with that tie score.

Brady, as calm and determined as ever, led his team on a 9 play 66 yard drive, coolly completing 4 passes in 4 attempts. Corey Dillon put the Pats ahead 21-14 with a two yard touchdown run. When New England got the ball back, Brady and Deion Branch completed a highlight play, a 19 yard completion over the middle with Branch making an acrobatic catch over the back of the Philly defender. That set up a field goal by Adam Vinatieri that pushed the New England lead to 24-14.

What followed was one of the most perplexing sequences in Super Bowl history. Although trailing by 10 points with 5 minutes remaining, the Eagles did not seem to be in any rush. Whereas most teams would be in the two minute, no huddle offense to try to get two scores, Philadelphia slowly and methodically went into a huddle after every play. They did march down the field -- though march sounds quicker than it actually was; make that "moved" down the field – on a 79 yard "travel" (not drive) that ended with a perfect 30 yard TD strike from McNabb to receiver Greg Lewis. The Eagles' "stroll" down the field left them with only 1:48 left in the game. They tried an on-side kick but New England's Christian Fauria recovered it near midfield. That meant that when the Patriots had to punt, they did it from great field position, and punter Josh Miller used that to pin Philadelphia at its own 4 yard line with 46 seconds remaining. It was still nail-biting time for nervous Patriot fans, but safety Rodney Harrison made a diving interception of a McNabb pass that clinched the victory for New England with 9 seconds to go.

The final line score was:

	1	2	3	4		Total
New England	0	7	7	10	-	24
Philadelphia	0	7	7	7	-	21

The end of the game was very emotional on the Patriot sideline. Belichick's 86 year old father, Steve, a former coach and great football strategist himself, joined his son on the sideline, and wound up joining him in being doused with Gatorade in the now-ceremonial action that ended many a game. Even better was the scene involving Belichick and his two top assistants, offensive coordinator Charlie Weis and defensive coordinator Romeo Crennel. The three had been together for many years, and now for three Super Bowl wins, and they knew that they would be separated the following year.

Weis had been hired to coach at the University of Notre Dame, his alma mater, and Crennel would be hired as the new head coach of the Cleveland Browns. As the game ended, these three men gathered in a big group hug that lasted for quite a few seconds. It was obvious that the three men really respected one another and enjoyed working together. It would have been great to know what they talked about. Belichick was not forthcoming about it, but, according to the account of the encounter in *Sports Illustrated,* Charlie Weis indicated that "We said we'd been together a long time. We'd had some good times, some bad, but these are moments we'd always had together. And it wouldn't matter that we wouldn't be together anymore. You can be the richest man in the world and not be able to buy moments like this." Well said, Charlie, and well done, Bill, Romeo, and Charlie. You and your team played and won with class and now were back on top of the world.

- - -

Deion Branch, with 11 catches for 133 yards, was named the Super Bowl MVP, although the choice could have just as easily been Tom Brady (23 for 33 for 236 yards, 2 touchdowns and no interceptions) or Rodney Harrison, who did a great job anchoring the depleted New England secondary.

After the Super Bowl, there was a very interesting column written by Rick Reilly in *Sports Illustrated* about Deion Branch. The column started by describing how some other players from other teams had gotten in trouble in the days, or sometimes even hours, before playing in a Super Bowl. It went on to describe what Deion Branch did, and the description is awesome. It said that Deion Branch

> "picked up his cell phone and called every coach in his life who meant something to him. He called Pee Wee coaches. He called his high school receivers coach. He called his junior college offensive coordinator. He called his college head coach. He called 13 coaches in all.
>
> And do you know what he told them? Thank you.
>
> Thank you for caring about me ... Thank you for believing I could do this."

The article went on to quote Vernorris Bradley, Branch's high school receivers' coach, as saying that Branch told him "Thanks for all the ways that you influenced me. I just want you to know how much I appreciate all that you did." Bradley went on to say that when he got the call, "I was just floored ... A guy that famous and successful can think about a guy who coached him that long ago? On the day of the Super Bowl? Man, that's somebody who hasn't forgotten where he came from."

That is also someone who has a lot of class. Good job, Mr. Branch.

- - -

Three Super Bowl wins in four years is a feat accomplished only once previously, by the 1992, 1993, and 1995 Dallas Cowboys. The Patriots were viewed positively by all of the NFL and all of sports everywhere. Theirs was now the model franchise that all other organizations tried to emulate. In fact, *Forbes* magazine in an issue published the following September, named the Patriots "The Best Team in Sports" and had a picture of team owner Robert Kraft on its cover, a rare, if not unique, honor for a sports team.

The accolades continued, as Tom Brady was named Sportsman of the Year by *Sports Illustrated* in its end of year issue. With that honor, Brady joined such sports greats as Tiger Woods, Stan Musial, Bill Russell, Bobby Orr, Chris Evert, Jack Nicklaus, Cal Ripken Jr., and Joe Montana. Although he had won two Super Bowl MVP awards and was one of the most popular players in all of sports, Brady was still a down-to-earth guy who was acknowledged as one of the hardest working members of the team. He personified the classy style of the Patriots. Perhaps the highest praise that Brady ever received came a couple of years later from his normally stoic coach, Bill Belichick. When Belichick was recruiting free agent wide receiver Jabar Gaffney to the team in 2006, he explained the Patriot team-first approach and overall Patriot style to Gaffney. He explained that everything revolves around the team, not individual statistics or glory. He described a scenario where no one takes credit, and everyone is part of the whole team effort. He concluded his comments to Gaffney by stating "Just listen to Tom." It would be hard to find any higher praise than that which is conveyed in those four words from Belichick about his hard-working star whose only goal is team success.

- - -

It was Brady, though, who had to carry the team on his shoulders quite a bit in the 2005 season, as injuries kept mounting up on the team. The biggest medical condition of all though was a stroke suffered by linebacker Tedy Bruschi shortly after the 2004 season. This life-threatening condition hit Bruschi suddenly and hard. He recovered, but his career seemed to be over, and the films of him leaving the hospital showed a very shaky walker. Happily, he would return during the season, but that did not appear to be possible early on.

Injuries at one point caused the team to be playing without five offensive starters in the first 12 games, including center Dan Koppen, who was lost for the season in November. Luckily, the team still had Brady and that helped overcome a lot of these player losses.

The team made one very interesting draft pick, choosing Southern Cal quarterback Matt Cassel in the seventh round of the draft. What was surprising about this was that Cassel had not started a game at Southern Cal; he was the backup to Carson Palmer and then Matt Leinart. Palmer and Leinart had both won the Heisman Trophy while in college, but to draft a quarterback who had never started a game in college was almost shocking. It was a tribute to the Patriots scouting and willingness to take a chance. Cassel would now back up superstar Tom Brady in New England, but would get his chance in 2008.

The Super Bowl win over Philadelphia gave the Patriots another Thursday night opener, and the Patriots responded with a relatively easy 30-20 win over the Oakland Raiders. Their next game was at Carolina, a game that we watched in airports on our way back from visiting family in New Mexico, so we only saw portions of a Panther 27-17 win over New England.

The pattern of win-one, lose-win continued for the next few weeks. New England went to Pittsburgh and defeated the Steelers again, this time 23-20 on a late drive by Tom Brady that led to a game-winning field goal by Adam Vinatieri. They then were blown out by San Diego 41-17 with San Diego's star running back LaDanian Tomlinson dominating the action. Then it was down to Atlanta where another late drive by Brady led to another game-winning field goal by Adam Vinatieri, as the Patriots won 31-28. Brady and Vinatieri had been great clutch players throughout their careers and seemed to have perfected the art of the late drive and winning field goal, never more so than in 2005. Fans could only wonder where the team would be without them. A 28-20 loss to Denver put the team's record at 3-3 going into the bye week.

The next game was a home game on Sunday night, October 30, against Buffalo. Thanks to being given tickets by a friend, it was also the first time that my son Mike and I would get to see a game in person at Gillette Stadium. We actually drove to the game separately and met at the gate. What we saw when we went inside was impressive. My feeling before Gillette was that a football stadium was a football stadium – 100 yards of green playing field, deep sidelines, a lot of concrete and that's about it, nothing like baseball with different distances, corners, walls, and nuances. What I saw was a state-of-the art facility, clean, with wide concourses that had a large variety of food choices and easy movement without bumping into a lot of people as you walked to your seats (nothing like the Patriot home locales of the past). The extra touches like the New England lighthouse with a blinking light at one end, and the walkway that fans could cross and briefly watch the game from a different angle, were extremely well done. When we next went back, in 2008, we also saw Patriot Place, a shopping and eating mall, which would also include a Patriot Hall of Fame and a CBS-themed dining and visual experience called "The CBS Scene" that would be attractions to non-football fans as well. All credit for this goes to the Kraft family for their vision in creating a very good environment for football and family activities.

Our seats were on the 45 yard line, just a few rows up from the field behind the Buffalo bench, the best seats that we have ever had for a football game. We had a bird's-eye view then of the story of the night, the return to the playing field of Tedy Bruschi, now fully recovered from his stroke. The crowd gave him a thunderous ovation when he came out onto the field for warm-ups, when he was introduced before the game, and when he made his first tackle of the game.

Bruschi in fact played every down of Buffalo's first drive, a drive that lasted over eight minutes. Bruschi made a great read and stop of a reverse run by receiver Roscoe Parrish and helped turn the play into a loss of yardage for the Bills. Buffalo got no points on the drive, however, thanks to a missed field goal. New England had the ball only once in the entire first quarter, but two holding calls prevented them from getting anything going.

In the second quarter, Patriot running back Patrick Pass ran for 12 yards and 9 yards on successive plays, but then was involved in a weird play not far from our seats. He ran to the sideline and seemed to just drop the ball as he grabbed the back of his leg. It was officially a fumble (although it looked as if he just dropped the ball in order to grab his leg) and Buffalo recovered. Pass left the game with an injury and did not return. Corey Dillon, who had previously been injured, replaced him.

Buffalo runner Willis McGahee was the star of the next drive which got to a first and goal and led to a field goal and a 3-0 Buffalo lead. New England had a chance to tie it before the end of the half, and appeared to have done so on a 39 yard field goal by Adam Vinatieri, but the Patriots were penalized for delay of game (argghh), so the points came off the scoreboard. Vinatieri had to try again, this time from 44 yards, and the kick was wide left. The score stayed 3-0 Bills at halftime.

New England received the kickoff to start the second half and seemed inspired. Corey Dillon's running helped get the team to the Buffalo 33 where Brady threw deep to Deion Branch who caught the ball and ran it in for a touchdown and a 7-3 New England lead.

Buffalo came right back with a long TD pass of their own, 55 yards from Kelly Holcombe to Eric Moulds, and the Bills were back in the lead at 10-7. Two field goals then made it 16-7 Buffalo. The second field goal came after a Buffalo defender hit Brady's arm as he was about to pass, causing a fumble that Buffalo recovered at about the New England 30. There was just over ten minutes left to play, and with the Patriots needing two scores to win, there was a lot of nervous murmuring (to say the least) in the crowd.

Brady got the Patriots back on the comeback trail by hitting Branch on a big 37 yard pass play. Buffalo challenged the call of a complete pass, bringing the official to the replay area right in front of our seats. The play stood as called, and the Patriots continued their drive, with Corey Dillon running in for the TD from the one yard line. The drive only took three minutes and the Pats had now pulled to within 16-14.

On the second play of the Bills' next series, Patriot linebacker Rosevelt Colvin made the play of the game. He sacked Kelly Holcomb, stripped the ball from his grasp, and recovered the fumble. Brady hit Branch for 22 yards and then Corey Dillon ran it in from the one to give the Patriots the lead at 21-16.

The Bills had two more chances with the ball but the Patriots held on for the win.

This was a close one that was won by a nice comeback by New England. Tom Brady finished 14 of 21 passing for 199 yards and a touchdown. Corey Dillon wound up carrying 18 times for 72 yards and 2 touchdowns. Willis McGahee led Buffalo with 136 yards on 31 carries. Mike Vrabel led the defense with 14 tackles, but Bruschi, in his return, also contributed 7 tackles and a lot of inspiration, as the Patriots escaped with a win in this one.

That brought the Indianapolis Colts to New England for the next game, a Monday nighter between these two elite teams. Peyton Manning finally got his first win at Foxboro as he threw for 321 yards and 3 touchdowns in a 41-20 win.

The Pats were now 4-4 and were still in their win-one, lose-one pattern. The next game fit the pattern, as the Patriots won 23-16 in Miami, but the Patriots finally broke the pattern by winning their second in a row, 24-17 over New Orleans. The Saints came in at 2-7 and quickly went down 7-0 as the Patriots went 98 yards on their first series, scoring on a Brady TD pass to Deion Branch. The Patriots converted three 3rd down and one 4th down play on the drive. New England still needed an interception in the end zone by Eugene Wilson on the last play of the game to escape with this win, 24-17. It was clear that the 2005 Patriots were not the powerhouse that the 2003 and 2004 team had been.

A 26-16 loss at Kansas City in which Tom Brady threw four interceptions brought the team's record to 6-5. They then reeled off four wins in a row, 16-3 over the Jets (another snowy day, another win in the snow for NE), 35-7 at Buffalo, 28-0 over Tampa Bay to clinch the team's third straight AFC East championship, and 31-21 over the Jets at the Meadowlands. A 28-26 loss to Miami gave the Patriots a 10-6 record for the season, and sent them into the playoffs as the fourth ranked team in the AFC, with the rankings as follows:

Indianapolis	14-2	Division Champion
Denver	13-3	Division Champion
Cincinnati	11-5	Division Champion
New England	10-6	Division Champion
Jacksonville	12-4	Wild Card

Pittsburgh   11-5   Wild Card

Brady had had a spectacular season, completing 334 of 530 passes for 4,110 yards and 26 touchdowns, with only 14 interceptions.

New England blasted Jacksonville 28-3 in the wild card playoff game, making the Patriots a perfect 10-0 in the post-season under Belichick and Brady. Tom Brady threw three touchdown passes in the game and Asante Samuel capped the scoring with a 73 yard interception return for a touchdown. On the same weekend Pittsburgh defeated Cincinnati 31-17 with the key play being a cheap shot hit by the Steelers on the knee of Cincinnati quarterback Carson Palmer on the second play from scrimmage in the game. That knocked Cincinnati's star quarterback out of the game. Some things never change, and the Steeler style of play is one of those things.

This brought the Patriots to Denver for the second round on January 14, 2006, and the Broncos handed Brady his first playoff loss ever, 27-13. After having committed only six turnovers total in their first ten playoff games under Brady, the Patriots committed five turnovers in this one game. The biggest came on a Patriot drive late in the third quarter. The Patriots were trailing 10-6, but had driven down to the Denver five yard line. A score here could give the Patriots the lead and momentum that could carry them to a big win. That is what I thought, and I'll bet there were many others who felt the same way.

Brady went back to pass, and, faced with a strong blitz from Denver, he threw the ball to his right into the end zone. Unfortunately for New England, Denver defensive back Champ Bailey made the interception and raced 100 yards down the sideline toward a TD. Only a great hustle play by Patriot tight end Benjamin Watson prevented the touchdown. Watson was on the other side of the field when Bailey made the interception but raced diagonally across the field as fast as he could and finally caught Bailey, tackling him at the New England 1 yard line. It was moot, however, as Denver scored on the next play, but announcers, writers, and fans praised the big tight end for his never-say-die attitude that typified the Patriots of the 2000 era and for his hustle in saving the TD.

Instead of a 13-10 lead and momentum, the Patriots now trailed 17-6 and pretty much that was that. The Patriots out-gained Denver 420 yards to 286 for the game, but an interception by Denver safety John Lynch with 2:56 to go iced the 27-13 win for the Broncos, and ended the Patriots' 2005 season.

- - -

As noted above, this was the first loss in a playoff game for the team in the Belichick-Brady era. There were two big personnel losses before the next season, however. All-time great kicker Adam Vinatieri left as a free agent, and signed with – of all teams – the Patriots' biggest rival, the Indianapolis Colts. The other big loss was of Tom Brady's favorite receiver, Deion Branch, who held out in a contract dispute with the team, and wound up being traded to Seattle.

The departure of Branch was really felt in the locker room. He had come to be very respected and well-liked by his teammates. Tom Brady, Richard Seymour, and others spoke about their admiration for Branch, saying that Branch embodied everything they wanted in a football player. Branch had seemed to have become Brady's favorite receiver, so his departure would definitely hamper the Patriot passing attack. Indeed, the loss of Branch would come to haunt the Patriots in the 2006 playoffs.

In the 2006 draft, New England selected running back Laurence Maroney of Minnesota with their first round pick. They later drafted Stephen Gostkowski, a kicker from Memphis, with their second pick in the fourth round of the draft. Gostkowski would have big shoes to fill as Adam Vinatieri's replacement. Maroney would have a season to work with Corey Dillon before stepping in as the Patriots' primary running back.

New England had a solid year in 2006, finishing with a 12-4 record. They started out 4-1 before reaching their bye week, defeating Buffalo 19-17 and the Jets 24-17 before losing a rematch with Denver 17-7. They then defeated Cincinnati 38-13 and Miami 20-10.

After the bye week, the Patriots picked up where they had left off, winning road games at Buffalo 28-6 and at Minnesota 31-7. The Minnesota game was a Monday nighter in which the Patriots thoroughly dominated the Vikings.

The next game was at home, against the Jets, and a soaking rain made the field muddy, sloppy, and just plain bad for football. The Jets slogged to a 17-14 upset win, but much ado was made over the next few days about the brisk post-game congratulatory handshake that Bill Belichick gave Eric Mangini, his former assistant who was now the Jets' coach. It was a non-story that blew up into a bigger story than it should have been, given that it was a somewhat acrimonious departure by Mangini from New England and the rivalry between the two teams was still hot.

The next game was at Green Bay and the Patriots utterly destroyed the Packers, 35-0, making Green Bay's legendary quarterback Brett Favre look old and ineffective.

New England continued its success against the NFC North Division teams by beating Chicago 17-13 and Detroit 28-21, with both games played in Foxboro. A 21-0 loss at Miami was followed by three season ending wins, 40-7 over the Houston Texans, 24-21 at Jacksonville on Christmas Eve, and 40-23 at Tennessee on New Year's Eve.

The Patriots again were the fourth ranked team in the AFC for the second successive year, with the rankings as follows:

San Diego	14-2	Division Champion
Baltimore	13-3	Division Champion
Indianapolis	12-4	Division Champion
New England	12-4	Division Champion
New York	10-6	Wild Card
Kansas City	9-7	Wild Card

New England blasted the Jets 37-16 in the wild card playoff game in Foxboro, though the game was close early.

New England received the opening kickoff and immediately started out with a no-huddle offense and a series of completions from Tom Brady to Jabar Gaffney led to a 10 yard TD run by Corey Dillon. A Jet field goal after a Dillon fumble cut the lead to 7-3 and the Jets took the lead on a 77 yard pass from Patriot nemesis Chad Pennington to Jerricho Cotchery. The pass was short, about 10 yards, but a missed tackle sprung Cotchery loose for the 77 yard TD that shocked and temporarily silenced the Patriot crowd.

A Gostkowski field goal tied the game and a 1 yard Brady to Daniel Graham TD pass put New England ahead 17-10 at the half.

The Jets took the second half kickoff and went on a 13 play drive. They would only wind up with a field goal, however, so the Patriots retained the lead 17-13.

Two field goals and a nice, 13-play 63 yard scoring drive, with a Jet field goal sandwiched within those scores made it 30-16 New England. The touchdown came after a big 10 yard pass over the middle from Brady to Troy Brown on a third and 8 with Brown going down to the ground to make the catch. This set up a later 7 yard TD pass from Brady to Kevin Faulk.

A desperation pass by Chad Pennington was intercepted by Asante Samuel and returned 36 yards for a touchdown that made the final 37-16. TV cameras followed Belichick as he went to midfield to shake hands with Eric Mangini. Belichick greeted Mangini with a hearty handshake and grasp of his arm, to put at least a temporary end to the non-story about their icy relationship and put a definite end to the Jets' season.

The win sent the Patriots to San Diego to meet the top-ranked 14-2 Chargers. Coach Marty Schottenheimer had a very talented team led by super running back LaDanian Tomlinson, outstanding receiver Antonio Gates, quarterback Philip Rivers, and a defense led by Shawne Merriman, who loved to do his celebratory and almost taunting "Lights Out" sack dance after recording a quarterback sack.

LaDanian Tomlinson ran for 123 yards on 23 carries and 2 touchdowns and caught two passes for another 64 yards, but it wasn't enough, as the Patriots made a thrilling comeback for a 24-21 win.

Trailing 21-13 with 8:35 to go after a Tomlinson TD, the Patriots began their comeback. Brady hit Jabar Gaffney for 17 yards and a first down at the San Diego 46 yard line and then hit Kevin Faulk for 5 yards. Facing a fourth down and 5 at the San Diego 41, Brady threw a pass down the middle but it was intercepted by Charger defensive back Morton McCree. However, once again the never-say-die Patriots got a great hustle play as Troy Brown tackled McCree and knocked the ball away from him. Brown's fellow wide receiver Reche Caldwell recovered the fumble at the Charger 32 yard line. The Patriots regained possession and had a key first down.

They moved the ball to the four yard line where Brady ran a great play-action fake to Corey Dillon and straightened up and tossed an easy pass to the wide open Caldwell for a touchdown. The play-action had completely fooled the Chargers. A direct snap to Kevin Faulk was run into the end zone for a two point conversion and the game was tied 21-21.

When the Chargers could not get a first down, they had to punt and New England had the ball again with 3:30 left to play. Brady hit Daniel Graham for 19 yards to the New England 34 and then, a couple of plays later, threw a beautiful spiral to Reche Caldwell who was racing down the sideline. It was a 49 yard completion that put the ball on the Charger 17 yard line. Stephen Gostkowski then hit a 31 yard field goal to put the Pats out front 24-21 and when the Chargers missed a desperation 54 yard field goal attempt as the clock ran out, the Patriots had a shocking upset over San Diego.

Patriot players danced on the field in celebration, some mocking the "Lights Out" sack dance of Shawne Merriman. The Chargers, and especially LaDanian Tomlinson, took exception to this and there was some pushing and shoving before cooler heads prevailed. In his post-game comments, Tomlinson called the Patriots classless and said that this stemmed from their head coach. I guess that means that it is somehow all right with Tomlinson for San Diego to have a "Lights Out" sack dance and celebrate wins and big plays but not all right for their opponent to do so. What's good for the goose is good for the gander, Tomlinson, so if you can't take it, don't dish it out.

The loss also brought to an end the coaching career of Schottenheimer at San Diego. Schottenheimer was a very good coach whose teams at Cleveland, Kansas City, and now San Diego could just not get over the hump and win a big game. Schottenheimer wound up paying the price by being fired, and Norv Turner took over as San Diego coach. He also would play a part in the on-going New England-San Diego rivalry the following season.

This win then sent the Patriots to Indianapolis for the AFC Championship Game. The Colts and Pats had both finished 12-4, but the Colts had the home field advantage by virtue of their regular season win over New England. The home field advantage would loom large, as the Colts wound up with a 38-34 win in a real thriller of a ball game.

At first, this game had the makings of a New England rout and another big win for Brady and the Patriots over Manning and the Colts, as New England jumped off to an early 21-3 lead. The Patriots got their first touchdown on a lucky play. Brady and Laurence Maroney mishandled a handoff at the Colt 4 yard line and the ball bounced into the end zone. Patriot offensive lineman Logan Mankins jumped on the ball and it was a Patriot TD. Corey Dillon had a 7 yard run for the second touchdown, and then, two plays later, Asante Samuel intercepted a Peyton Manning pass intended for Marvin Harrison and returned the interception 39 yards for a touchdown. It was now a 21-3 Patriot lead 6 minutes into the second quarter. Manning walked to the sideline dejectedly and it looked as if he and the Colts were on their way to another crushing defeat at the hands of New England.

An Adam Vinatieri field goal – *for the Colts* – made the halftime score 21-6, but gave the Colts a little life. At halftime Colt Coach Tony Dungy encouraged his team by saying "This is our game. It's our time." As if to back him up, Manning led the Colts on a 14 play, 76 yard drive, scoring himself on a quarterback sneak to get the Colts back into the game at 21-13.

After the Pats had to punt, Manning again drove the Colts to a score. This one was a one yard pass to defensive lineman and former Patriot Dan Klecko, who had come into the game as an extra blocker as the Patriots often had done with Mike Vrabel, and then caught a TD pass, also as the Patriots often had done with Mike Vrabel. Manning hit

Harrison for the two point conversion and suddenly the game was tied 21-21.

What followed next was alternating heroics by two fantastic quarterbacks, Tom Brady and Peyton Manning.

Brady threw a 6 yard TD pass to Jabar Gaffney to make it 28-21 Patriots.

Manning then drove Indianapolis to the Patriot 2 yard line, but running back Dominic Rhodes fumbled the ball. In a play eerily reminiscent of Patriot luck earlier in the game, Colt offensive lineman Jeff Saturday jumped on the ball in the end zone. Just as Logan Mankins had done earlier for New England, Saturday's play gave the Colts a touchdown on a lucky play and the game was again tied, 28-28.

A field goal by New England, one by Indianapolis, and another by New England (a 43 yard field goal by Gostkowski after a nice drive engineered by Tom Brady) gave the Patriots a 34-31 lead with under 4:00 to go. In the biggest play of the game, however, a Brady pass to the right to a wide open wide receiver, Reche Caldwell, was dropped. It would have been a sure first down and perhaps a drive that would have resulted in a touchdown. Instead the Pats had to settle for a field goal. The Patriots certainly could have used Deion Branch in this game and on this series in particular, but unfortunately, Branch was no longer with the team, having been traded to Seattle earlier in the season.

After two punts, Indianapolis had the ball on their own 20 yard line, with 2:17 to go in the game. The Colts needed to go 80 yards to score a touchdown and win the game.

All the Patriot defense had to do was hold for one more series and they would be bound for the Super Bowl, and most likely another Super Bowl win (since it would be against the offensively-challenged Chicago Bears).

But the defense could not hold. Indianapolis drove down to the 11 yard line, and two runs by Joseph Addai made it 3rd and 2 at the New England three. Expecting Manning to pass, the Patriots instead got another run by Joseph Addai. This one went for the touchdown and now the Colts led 38-34.

There was still one minute to play in the game, so the Patriots and Brady had time for one last heroic effort.

Brady started moving New England down the field, getting them to the Indianapolis 45 with 24 seconds to go, when a pass over the middle intended for Benjamin Watson was intercepted by Marlin

Jackson. The Patriots' last chance had been thwarted. It would be Indianapolis going to the Super Bowl.

I will never forget the look on Peyton Manning's face as he grabbed his helmet to go back onto the field. There was a small grin on his face that seemed to have a combination of relief, happiness, and pride. It was easy to feel good to see a great player finally win the big one, even though it came at the expense of the Patriots. He was going to his first Super Bowl (and he and his team would win it over the Bears 29-17).

While I of course wanted New England to win, I was happy both for Manning and his equally much-maligned coach, Tony Dungy. Both had shown a lot of class over the years and both deserved a win.

I was hoping that Bill Belichick would acknowledge Manning and Dungy. I hoped he would spend time with them on the field to offer his congratulations but he only gave each a cursory handshake. I was then hoping he would mention them in his post-game press conference with some comment such as "while I am disappointed in the loss, I am happy that Tony Dungy and Peyton Manning will finally get a chance to play for a championship, and I wish them well in the Super Bowl." He did not, instead talking about how his team needed to improve.

While I understand the focus on his team, this was one of the very few times in his career with the Patriots that I was disappointed in Belichick. It brought to mind Bill Russell and the Boston Celtics in 1967. The Celtics had won a phenomenal eight straight Championships between 1959 and 1966, and now in 1967 had lost the NBA Eastern Division Championship to Wilt Chamberlain and the powerful Philadelphia 76ers. Bill Russell had just taken over as player-coach of the Celtics that season after the retirement of legendary coach Red Auerbach, so his first coaching experience saw the end of that great championship run. A newcomer to the team, Wayne Embry, wondered how the Celtics would react now that they had lost. What happened pleasantly surprised him. After a few minutes in the locker room, Russell simply said "OK, guys, let's go congratulate the winners." And so they did. It was an extremely classy move by an extremely classy man, and team. Whether connected or not, the Celtics then went on to win championships again the next two seasons.

- - -

Between the 2006 and 2007 seasons, Tom Brady became a father for the first time. It had been revealed in February that Brady and his former girlfriend, actress Bridget Moynahan, were going to become parents. Moynahan, whom Brady had dated from 2004 until the end of 2006, confirmed in *People* magazine in February that she was pregnant with her and Brady's child. The baby, named John Edward Thomas Moynahan, was born on August 22 in California, and, happily, Brady was able to be there for his son's birth. The baby's middle names are the reverse of Tom's (Thomas Edward Brady). Reports are that Brady spends a lot of time with his son and is a big part of his life, which is the way that it should be. Everything else about this is, and should be, private, and so it will remain. Brady went back to preparing for the 2007 season and it would be a remarkable season for him and his team.

The Undefeated 16-0 2007 season

The biggest need for the Patriots for the 2007 was getting better receivers for Tom Brady. Brady clearly missed Deion Branch in 2006 after Branch was traded to Seattle. The Patriots not only filled that need, but filled it with two great additions, Randy Moss and Wes Welker. Moss was a very talented wide receiver who had languished in Oakland for two seasons after many excellent, and often-controversial, seasons with Minnesota. Welker was a great possession receiver who had most recently been with Miami, after starting his career with San Diego. Welker was obtained for second and seventh round draft picks. Moss was acquired on draft day for a fourth round pick. Both trades were steals, as the two players went on to have career years with New England. The Patriots also added another weapon to Tom Brady's offense, signing free agent Sammy Morris, a very good runner/receiver, who had also previously played for the Dolphins.

One notable loss was Corey Dillon, whose contract was not renewed. The running game was now primarily anchored by Laurence Maroney, who had shown flashes of good play in 2006, but was not the ball-control running back that Dillon was.

- - -

The 2007 season opened with a game against the arch-rival Jets at the Meadowlands (a.k.a. Giants' Stadium). It was a spectacular opening act for New England as they pounded the Jets 38-14. Tom Brady, Randy Moss, and Wes Welker unveiled a passing attack that would break a number of records over the course of the season.

Statistically, Brady threw for 297 yards and three touchdowns. He had 22 completions to 7 different receivers. Moss had 9 catches for an astounding 183 yards. Welker had 6 catches for 61 yards.

Artistically, there was nothing better executed than a 51 yard touchdown pass from Brady to Moss. Moss ran a crossing pattern right-to-left and beat three defenders to make the catch going into the end zone. It was a perfectly executed play.

Another of the day's highlights was provided by Ellis Hobbs, who returned the second half kickoff 108 yards for a touchdown. It was the longest kickoff return for a touchdown in NFL history. It also equaled the longest scoring play ever in NFL history (if I am not mistaken, Erich Barnes of the New York Giants had a 108 yard interception return for a touchdown in the early 1960s, in a game that I watched on TV).

The cover of *Sports Illustrated* the next week was of Randy Moss catching a pass. The headline read "Scary" with the sub-title "Randy Moss Explodes and the Patriots Send a Shiver Throughout the NFL". They certainly got that one right.

In the week after the Jets' game, controversy found a huge target in New England. Jet coach Eric Mangini accused the Patriots of spying. The claim was that the Patriots had a cameraman on the field filming the defensive signals being sent in from the sideline to the Jet defense and were using that to know what the Jets would be doing on defense in future plays. Belichick and the Patriots denied this, saying that they were not using these films in this game but for future games, and claiming that doing this was legal.

As we later learned, it is not legal to film the opposing sideline from your sideline. This is all somewhat strange, since apparently it is OK to film from the press box or up in the stands, but not from the sideline, which seems inconsistent to me. Nevertheless, a rule is a rule and what the Patriots did was a violation of the NFL rule, and I felt that they should be punished for it. They were. NFL Commissioner Roger Goodell fined Belichick a half million dollars and the Patriots another $250,000, and ruled that the team would forfeit its first round draft pick the following spring. The Patriots and Belichick agreed that they were wrong, and Belichick took responsibility for not knowing the rule, and the team moved on with its preparations for the San Diego game on Sunday.

That should have been it, but in these days of (a) almost non-stop TV talk show time that has to be filled and (b) trying to bring down anyone who is at the top, it was not. This became cannon fodder for sports talk shows and newspaper reports for weeks and became known, infamously, as "SpyGate". (For anyone who is interested, a summary of the relevant rules and provisions related to in-game filming can be found in Appendix B of this book.)

Belichick was skewered, being called a liar, a cheater, and I'm sure a host of other names. One New York paper, the *New York Post* I believe, began listing New England in the standings with an asterisk, with the asterisk footnoted as "Caught Cheating". One wonders if the

Post was forthright enough to do the same thing when listing the AL East and World Series championships of the New York Yankees whose team was riddled with illegal steroid users Roger Clemens, Chuck Knoblauch, Andy Pettitte, Jason Giambi, Gary Sheffield, Alex Rodriguez, and perhaps others during their stretch of success between 1996 and 2004. They did not. I guess it is OK for a lot of the key players on your city's team to use illegal substances to enhance their performance but not OK for a cameraman to film the other team in a football game. If the roles had been reversed, and the Jets had been caught doing what the Patriots had been, would the Post have been listing the Jets that way? I doubt it. In contrast, the Boston papers were also highly critical of Belichick and the Patriots for this filming, and many suggested that Belichick be suspended for a game. I thought that suspending him for the next Jets' game might be appropriate myself, even though I am a big fan of Belichick. I guess I can never be a sports reporter for the *New York Post* then, since I would be more of a reporter and less of a homer than that publisher wants.

Even later in the season, there were rumors that a cameraman associated with the Patriots had filmed the Rams' walk-through the day before the 2002 Super Bowl. That controversy lasted long enough that Roger Goodell brought the cameraman into his office for questioning, and investigated. Goodell's investigations showed that the story was false.

The story became even more absurd when Senator Arlen Specter of Pennsylvania wanted a Congressional investigation into Spygate. Specter was apparently upset that the Patriots had defeated the Eagles in the 2005 Super Bowl and now felt that it was cheating that helped the Patriots win. It is worth noting that Senator Specter was an investigator for the Warren Commission investigating the assassination of President John F. Kennedy, and it was he who came up with the "Single Bullet" or "Magic Bullet" theory. This is the theory that is the cornerstone on which rested the Commission's findings that Lee Harvey Oswald was the lone assassin. It requires a suspension of physical law that a bullet shot from above, specifically the sixth floor of the Texas School Book Depository, went through Kennedy's neck and throat, and then went through Texas Governor John Connally's shoulder, chest, and wrist at a near-impossible angle by the laws of physics. According to Wikipedia, "if so, this bullet traversed 15 layers of clothing, 7 layers of skin, and approximately 15 inches of tissue, struck a necktie knot, removed 4 inches of rib, and shattered a radius bone. The bullet that is supposed to have done all this damage was found on a stretcher in the corridor at the Parkland Memorial Hospital, in Dallas, after the assassination." Not only that, but the bullet that did all of this damage and was later allegedly found on the cot that brought

Connolly to the hospital in Dallas was in remarkably pristine condition when it was found, as if it had been left there by a passer-by. Conspiracy theorists who claim that Lee Harvey Oswald did not act alone pounce on this theory as erroneous. Why does this tie in to Spygate? If Arlen Specter believes the single bullet theory, then he will believe anything.

Beyond the above, it is also my opinion that the United States Congress has a lot more important things to worry about than whether one football team filmed another one in a way that violated NFL rules.

- - -

Getting away from the constant hounding of reports about Spygate and getting back onto the field against San Diego must have felt good for both Belichick and the team. These were two of the three top teams in the NFL (along with the Colts). *Sports Illustrated*, for example, had predicted that the Chargers would win the AFC, while *The Sporting News* predicted that the Patriots would, in their pre-season previews and predictions.

It was another annihilation by the Patriots, interestingly by the same 38-14 score by which they had defeated the Jets in Week 1.

As they did against the Jets, the Pats started off with a very efficient drive down the field for a touchdown on their first possession, scoring on a 7 yard TD pass from Brady to Benjamin Watson in the right corner. The TV announcers informed us that the new Charger coach, Norv Turner had scripted the first set of plays for San Diego (I don't remember whether it was the first 15 or the first 20), writing them down on paper. If so, the script needs rewrite. Apparently, for example, play #1 in Turner's script was for Philip Rivers to throw an interception. The next sets of plays were no more successful for San Diego, and the Patriots raced off to a 24-0 halftime lead. A Brady to Moss touchdown pass got New England its second touchdown, and Adalius Thomas returned an interception 65 yards down the left sideline for another TD.

San Diego received the second half kickoff and marched 72 yards on 16 plays to score on a Rivers 1 yard TD pass, but Brady returned the favor with a drive of his own and his second TD pass of the day to Randy Moss. There was a brief flurry of hope for San Diego after they scored again in the fourth quarter and Ellis Hobbs fumbled the ensuing kickoff, but two great defensive plays by Mike Vrabel and Rosevelt Colvin pushed the Chargers back ten yards on two of the next three plays. They punted, and the Patriots got a final TD on a run by Sammy Morris. The game was complete and the domination was thorough.

After the game, the Patriot players surrounded their coach and celebrated the win with him. With the Spygate fiasco plaguing Belichick during the week before the game, this was a great show of support by the team for its coach. In his post-game comments, Belichick thanked the players for staying focused, thanked the fans for their support, and thanked owner Bob Kraft, about whom he said "He's been awesome all week in a tough situation." Perhaps Tom Brady (who was 25-for-31 for 279 yards and 3 TDs in another brilliant game) summed it up best in his post-game comments by saying "After everything that went on this week, we wanted to do our best for him." They certainly did that.

- - -

Things were somewhat back to normal for the third game of the season, against old rival Buffalo. For the third week in a row the Patriots lit up the scoreboard for exactly 38 points. This time they held their opponent to seven in an easy 38-7 win over the Bills. Brady started the scoring with an eight yard touchdown pass to Benjamin Watson, then hit Jabar Gaffney for another TD, and Randy Moss for two more. The four touchdown passes represented a new career high for Brady, who finished with 311 yards passing on 23 completions in 29 attempts. In one of those obscure statistics that seem prevalent in all sports today, Randy Moss became the first player to have 100 yards receiving in each of his first three games with a new team. In a more obvious statistic, after three weeks, the NFL had only five unbeaten teams remaining: the Patriots, Colts, Steelers, Packers, and Cowboys.

Game 4 was a Monday nighter on the first of October in Cincinnati. It was another easy win for the Patriots, 34-13 over the Bengals. Brady added three more touchdown passes to his growing total. Sammy Morris had begun to be the Patriots' best running back, accounting for 117 yards rushing. The Steelers lost, so only four teams remained unbeaten after four weeks. The Patriots, at 4-0, had a three game lead in the AFC East after only four games had been played. They were four games ahead of the winless Miami Dolphins, who appeared to be the worst team in the league.

A 34-17 win over the Browns gave the Patriots a sweep of Ohio that any Presidential candidate would love. It was the fifth straight game in which the Patriots had scored 34 or more points. It was the fifth straight game in which the Patriots had won by a margin of 17 or more points. Brady had yet another 3 touchdown passes. Linebacker Junior Seau had two interceptions, but the 18 year veteran gave Coach Bill Belichick something to complain about by holding the ball high up in the air while running back one of his interceptions, thereby risking a fumble. Seau later said that he had no idea why he did it.

Randy Moss was double-teamed for most of the game and had only 3 catches for 46 yards, but Brady found other receivers, throwing TD passes to Benjamin Watson and Donte Stallworth.

The Red Sox were in another post-season run that would lead to their second World Series title in four years, but even the buzz about the Red Sox could not diminish the hype for the Patriots' next game, a battle with the unbeaten Dallas Cowboys down in Texas Stadium.

Wade Phillips had replaced the retired (again) Bill Parcells as head coach of the Cowboys. His 'deer in the headlights' look at the end of this game was a classic, as the Patriots pulled away and turned a close game into another rout. Tony Romo had settled in as the Cowboy quarterback, having replaced former Patriot Drew Bledsoe in 2006, and the Cowboy receiving corps included Former Eagle Terrell Owens and former Patriot Terry Glenn. The Cowboys were considered the best team in the NFC.

The game was close early on, and in fact the Cowboys took a 24-21 lead on an 8 yard TD pass by Romo with 10:20 to go in the third quarter. It was the first time that the Patriots had trailed in the second half of any of their games in 2007. The Patriots had no running game, as Sammy Morris had suffered a chest injury in the game that would turn into a season-ending injury. The story of the game was Tom Brady. Brady had already thrown a 6 yard touchdown pass to Randy Moss and a 35 yard touchdown pass to Wes Welker in the first quarter and a 12 yard touchdown pass up the middle to Welker to make the score 21-17 at halftime, before the Cowboys took the lead on the pass from Romo.

After falling behind 24-21, the Patriots took the kickoff and Brady methodically drove the team downfield, hitting tight end and namesake Kyle Brady for a 1 yard TD pass. On their next possession, Brady unloaded a bomb to Randy Moss that was seemingly another TD as Moss caught the ball in the end zone on the sideline. Replay review showed that Moss did not have complete possession of the ball, so the Patriots had to settle for a Gostkowski field goal and a 31-21 lead, which they took into the fourth quarter. After three running plays on their next possession, Brady threw a deep post pattern to Donte Stallworth and it turned into a 69 yard touchdown. It was Brady's fifth touchdown pass of the day, a new career high for him, and tying him with Babe Parilli and Steve Grogan for most TD passes in a game in team history. The Patriots cruised on to a 48-27 victory.

Brady was 31 of 46 passing for 388 yards and those 5 touchdowns. More importantly, the Patriots were now 6-0 for the first time since they won the Super Bowl in the 2004 season, and everyone seemed to feel that this team was something special. They were again *Sports Illustrated* cover boys (Brady this time, with the headline "Yes, That Good") and an article entitled "The Winning Machine". The feeling was that the Colts had a chance to beat them, but it was not clear if any other team could.

Next to try was the team with the worst chance to beat them, the winless Miami Dolphins. It was no contest. Brady did himself one better than the Dallas game by throwing for a franchise record 6 touchdowns, including 5 in a first half that ended with the Patriots ahead 42-7. The Patriots went on to defeat the Dolphins 49-28 in a game that was not as close as the score might indicate. Brady was 21 for 25 for 354 yards, and had a quarterback rating of 158.3, the first perfect rating in team history (quarterback rating is one of the weirdest stats in all of sports; for anyone who is interested in the details of how this is computed, a description can be found in Appendix B of this book). Wes Welker and Randy Moss had two touchdown receptions each. One of Moss' TD catches was almost laughable as he was double covered in the right side of the end zone, but out-jumped both defenders, both of whom fell as the three players came back down. There was Moss standing alone amidst the fallen defenders, with another touchdown reception on a perfectly thrown pass by his quarterback, Tom Brady. It was almost like a play from the movies.

The Patriots were now a perfect 7-0. The Indianapolis Colts defeated Jacksonville 29-7 on Monday night, so the two juggernauts continued unbeaten on the road to their November 4 match-up in Indianapolis.

Both teams won again the following week. Indianapolis went to 7-0, beating Carolina 31-7. Peyton Manning threw for two touchdowns, and Joseph Addai ran for two and caught a third, as he amassed 100 yards rushing on 23 carries.

Meanwhile, the Patriots were destroying the Washington Redskins by a 52-7 score, meaning that they had totaled 101 points in their last two games. Tom Brady had three touchdown passes and scored two more running. One of those touchdown passes was to linebacker Mike Vrabel, who, on defense, collected a nice line of 13 tackles, 3 sacks, and 3 forced fumbles. The Patriots set another team record in a season full of them, by getting 34 first downs.

Oh, and later that same evening, the Red Sox defeated the Colorado Rockies to win the World Series in a four game sweep. The Celtics were also about to start their season with new acquisitions Kevin Garnett and Ray Allen, a season that would conclude with them winning the NBA Championship. It was a great time to be in Boston.

- - -

It was time for one of the most eagerly anticipated regular season games in NFL history, the undefeated (7-0) Indianapolis Colts against the undefeated (8-0) New England Patriots. With the game being played on November 4, it was the latest calendar date match-up of two undefeated teams in NFL history. It matched New England's brilliant quarterback, Tom Brady against Indianapolis' brilliant quarterback, Peyton Manning. The two were considered almost universally to be the two best quarterbacks in the game and two of the best in history. The game also matched two of the most respected coaches in the game, Bill Belichick and Tony Dungy. It was the defending Super Champion Colts against the three-time Super Bowl Champion Patriots. In short (if it's not too late to be short), this game had it all.

The Colts were playing without star receiver Marvin Harrison, but had a 20-10 lead with ten minutes remaining in the game thanks to the heroics of Peyton Manning (16 completions for 225 yards) and Joseph Addai (112 yards rushing and 114 yards receiving). The Colts had made the score 20-10 on a 1 yard run by Manning. At this point in the game, Brady had thrown two interceptions (matching his combined total for the previous seven games) and the high-powered Patriots had only scored one touchdown, on a 4 yard pass from Brady to Randy Moss. Also at this point of the game, Brady took over and once again came through in the clutch.

The comeback began with Brady throwing a 55 yard bomb to Moss. That set up a 3 yard touchdown throw from Brady to Wes Welker that made it 20-17. When New England got the ball back, it took Brady all of 47 seconds to put his team in the lead, with the score coming on a 13 yard pass from Brady to the versatile Kevin Faulk. Brady had set up the score with a 33 yard pass to Donte Stallworth. With the Colts scrambling to score, Patriot defensive tackle Jarvis Green sacked Manning and caused a fumble. Rosevelt Colvin recovered the fumble at midfield to end that final threat, and the Patriots had a thrilling 24-20 win.

Brady finished with 21 completions for 255 yards and three touchdowns. Moss had nine receptions for 145 yards and one touchdown. Brady now had 33 touchdown passes for the season. More importantly, the Patriots had remained undefeated through eight games, and had a bye week coming to rest up after the tough game with the Colts.

- - -

The Patriots returned from the bye week and blasted the Bills at Buffalo 56-10.

One of our friends, Randy Cumming, had noticed that our town was planning to run a bus to Buffalo for the game, and asked if we and another couple, Fred and Pat Link, would be interested in going to the game with him and his wife, Pat. We thought about it, but decided that a November 18 game in Buffalo was too much of a risk weather-wise. When the game was switched from a 1:00 start to a Sunday night game to capitalize on the public's interest, the six of us were even happier with that decision, since not only would we have been even colder during the game, but the return trip would also not have us coming back until mid-morning on Monday.

What we missed seeing in person was an offensive show by New England. The Patriots scored on their first seven possessions of the game, led 35-7 at the half, amassed 30 first downs, and cruised to an easy win. Tom Brady was 31 of 39 for 373 yards and another 5 touchdowns, before being replaced by Matt Cassell with 10:57 still remaining in the game. Randy Moss had four touchdown catches. Ellis Hobbs accounted for the final score by returning a Buffalo fumble 35 yards for a touchdown in the fourth quarter.

- - -

With a 9-0 record, suddenly things began to get tighter for the Patriots. Their next game was a Sunday night encounter with the Philadelphia Eagles, and it was a tough battle, one of a handful of games that the Patriots could have lost in the unbeaten streak.

Things started out well for the Patriots. Before they even came onto the field, Buffalo had lost, making the Patriots AFC East Champions. Asante Samuel had a 40 yard interception return for a touchdown on the game's first series, but the Eagles tied it on a jump over the line and into the end zone by Brian Westbrook that ended a 14 play, 77 yard drive. It was a 7-7 game before Tom Brady and the offense had even come out onto the field. One key play call in this series was a 4th and 1 for Philly from the New England 15. Instead of settling for the field goal as most teams (but not the Patriots) would have done, the Eagles went for it, which is just the kind of risk that an underdog playing an undefeated team should take. They got the first down and ultimately the Westbrook touchdown.

Brady made his first offensive series a successful one, marching his team to a 1 yard touchdown run by Heath Evans, but the Eagles came back again on a 28 yard touchdown pass by A.J. Feeley (substituting at quarterback for the injured Donovan McNabb) to tie the game at 14-14.

As noted above, underdogs playing an undefeated team should pull out all the stops to try to win, and the Eagles did just that, trying an on-side kick after that touchdown, and recovering it. The Patriot defense held though, so the Eagles did not convert that cleverness into points.

A 23 yard field goal by Gostkowski made it 17-14, but then Feeley threw an 18 yard touchdown pass that gave the Eagles their first lead of the day. But an Ellis Hobbs 41 yard kickoff return led to a 19 yard Brady to Jabar Gaffney TD pass to the back of the end zone that gave New England a breathless 24-21 lead at halftime.

The Eagles scored again with 1:34 to go into the third quarter on another Feeley TD pass, and the Patriots were suddenly staring at a 28-24 deficit as the fourth quarter began.

After a Philadelphia punt, New England took over at its 32 yard line. Brady threw for three straight first downs, 13 yards to Stallworth, 12 yards to Faulk, and 13 yards to Welker. Brady continued to move the team on passes and three completions to the amazing Wes Welker got the ball down to the 4 yard line, from where Laurence Maroney ran it in for the go-ahead score.

The Eagles did not quit, however, and Feeley was moving them again toward a potential tying field goal or winning touchdown when Asante Samuel intercepted a pass to end the Philly drive. The Eagles got the ball back one more time, with 19 seconds left, but James Sanders intercepted another Feeley pass, and the Patriots escaped another nail-biter with a 31-28 win.

- - -

Now at 10-0, the Patriots followed the Sunday night game with Philadelphia with a Monday night game against the Baltimore Ravens. This one was even closer to a defeat than the Eagle game had been.

Running back Willis McGahee was the offensive star for Baltimore, gaining 138 yards on 30 carries, many of them difficult runs through the stingy Pat defense. McGahee's running gave the Ravens an early 10-3 lead, as Baltimore came back from an early Gostkowski field goal with 10 straight points. The Baltimore TD had come thanks to a 53 yard pass from Kyle Boller to Devard Darling, with Boller narrowly escaping a potential sack by Jarvis Green and Adalius Thomas, and four McGahee runs from the 18 that set up a Boller touchdown pass to Derrick Mason.

Tom Brady and the Patriot offense employed the no huddle offense to tie the game at 10 at halftime. Two big completions to Donte

Stallworth, and two big penalty calls on Raven players defending Randy Moss led to a 1 yard run by Heath Evans for the score.

Baltimore took the second half kickoff and Willis McGahee almost single-handedly gave them a touchdown. He ran 6 times for 50 yards, including a 17 yard run for the touchdown. The Patriots were again trailing in the second half, 17-10.

New England tied it on a Brady to Moss touchdown pass that was greatly helped by a Brady to Maroney pass for 36 yards, but the Ravens offense continued its new-found mastery of the New England defense by running the ball down to the 1 yard line, where Boller threw another touchdown pass to make it 24-17 Baltimore early in the fourth quarter.

Two sacks of Brady led to a New England punt and Baltimore took over at the Patriot 26 after a long runback and a 5 yard penalty on New England for having an ineligible man downfield on the punt. The Ravens had a chance to score and ice the game, but James Sanders intercepted a Boller pass and returned it to the Patriot 43. An offensive pass interference call on Patriot tight end Kyle Brady moved the ball back to the 33, but a play action fake to Maroney led to a pass to Maroney from Brady that gained 43 yards and set up a field goal by Gostkowski to cut the Raven lead to 24-20.

After punts by Baltimore, New England, and Baltimore again, the Patriots got the ball back with 3:30 to play in the game. Brady went to work to get his team a victory. He hit Benjamin Watson for 23 yards, and Kevin Faulk for 9. A Brady keeper gave New England a first down, but three plays later they faced a 4th down and 1 at the 30. Brady tried another quarterback sneak but the play was stuffed by Baltimore for no gain. It looked as if the drive had stalled and the Ravens would have the ball and a big upset win that would have ended the Patriots' run at an undefeated season.

But wait. Baltimore Coach Brian Billick had called a timeout just before the ball had been snapped that the officials saw and granted. The stop of Brady was not a play at all. Given a reprieve thanks to the Baltimore timeout call, the Patriots had another try. Brady brought his team to the line and tried a run but the play had been whistled dead. A false start penalty was called on offensive lineman Russ Hochstein. That made it 4th and 6, and Brady had to try to pass for the first down. He dropped back but could find no one open, so he ran the ball and wasn't stopped until he had gained 12 yards and a first down.

Three plays later it was another fourth down deep in Baltimore territory, and the Patriots caught another lucky break. Brady tried a pass over the middle to Benjamin Watson in the end zone, but the pass fell incomplete. Again it looked as if Baltimore had won, but as the pass was falling, a flag was thrown. Baltimore was called for holding Watson as he attempted to run into the end zone to try to catch the pass, and the penalty call gave New England a first down. Baltimore protested that there was no penalty, and that there was a late call, but replays showed that it was close but that there was indeed a penalty. Brady then hit Jabar Gaffney in the end zone and Gaffney appeared to have both feet in bounds as he caught the ball for a touchdown. The officials checked the TV replay and confirmed that it was indeed a good catch and a touchdown.

Baltimore had one more chance and almost converted it. They completed a Hail Mary pass down to the one yard line but time expired before they could run a play.

New England had won 27-24, but it was by a razor-thin margin against a very motivated opponent. This one could have easily been a loss, and maybe even would have been except for some very lucky plays. Sometimes it is better to be lucky then good, though thankfully the Patriots were both on this Monday night in Baltimore.

- - -

After two very tight wins against Philadelphia and Baltimore, the Patriots now would be facing another tough opponent from the Eastern Seaboard states, but this one on December 9 would be the toughest of all – the Pittsburgh Steelers were coming to town. Many experts felt that the Steelers were the biggest threat to a perfect regular season that was remaining on the Patriots' schedule.

During the week preceding the game, Steeler defensive back Anthony Smith made headlines by claiming that the Patriots had to be ready for the Steelers, not the other way around, and Smith guaranteed a Steeler win. Now that was foolish. Here he was, about to have his team play an undefeated and very strong team, and he was giving that team bulletin board material that would provide even more motivation. The Patriots were looking forward to making Smith pay for and regret his remarks, and they would definitely do so in the game.

As a sidelight, in a ceremony before the game, Patriot owner Bob Kraft and the CBS Corporation announced plans to build and open The CBS Scene Restaurant and state-of-the-art entertainment center at Patriot Place, adjacent to Gillette Stadium. It would make the Patriot Place complex even more attractive to New Englanders than it already had been.

As the game began, New England was stopped on its first series and Pittsburgh moved down the field to open the scoring with a field goal. The Patriots responded with a touchdown on a 7 yard pass from Brady to Moss, and then, on their next series, began to make Anthony Smith pay for his taunting pre-game remarks. Starting at their own 37, Brady faked to Maroney and caused Smith to move up to stop what he thought would be a running play. Meanwhile Randy Moss raced by him and Brady, after completing the fake, laid a perfect throw right into Moss' hands for 63 yards and a touchdown. It was now 14-3 and the rout, as well as the embarrassment of Smith, was underway. Pittsburgh fought back to make it a game at halftime 17-13, but the Steeler scoring was over for the day.

On the Patriots' first series of the second half, they had the ball on their own 44, when they went to some trickery. Brady dropped back and threw the ball behind him and to the other side of the field; it was a lateral to Randy Moss. Moss dropped the ball, but picked it up and threw it back to Brady, another lateral. Brady calmly waited for Jabar Gaffney to get open downfield and then threw it to Gaffney for a 56 yard touchdown pass over Anthony Smith. To be honest, it almost looked as if Brady was waiting patiently for Smith to get back near the play before making the throw to Gaffney, to embarrass the mouthy Smith. Whether or not that was the actual intent, the patience of Brady resulted in Smith getting back in the TV range as Gaffney made the catch, so viewers could definitely see that Smith had been fooled on this play as well.

The Patriots rolled on to a 34-13 win over the Steelers to raise their record to 13-0. Brady was 32 of 46 passing against Anthony Smith and the vaunted Steeler defense, for a total of 399 yards and four touchdowns. He now had 45 touchdown passes for the year, only 4 short of Peyton Manning's league record of 49, and Brady still had three games remaining to be played to try to break that record.

Randy Moss had 135 yards and two touchdowns on seven receptions, Wes Welker had nine receptions for 78 yards and one touchdown, and Jabar Gaffney added 122 yards and one touchdown on seven catches of his own.

Patriot Coach Bill Belichick was more light-hearted than usual in the post-game press conference, perhaps buoyed by the Patriots making Anthony Smith eat his words. When asked about the flea-flicker, double lateral play, Belichick joked that Moss fumbling the ball had "sold the play", as if the fumble was a planned part of the trickery. When asked about Anthony Smith, Belichick, who rarely criticized other players, could not resist in this case. "We've played better safeties than that," said Belichick, dismissively. It was clear that Belichick and the team had really enjoyed this win.

- - -

Next up were the New York Jets and everyone looked forward to this game. Some expected the Patriots to light up the scoreboard to get revenge on the 3-10 Jets and their coach, Eric Mangini, for instigating the whole Spygate controversy. However, weather played a key role in controlling the score, as snow, rain, and heavy winds hit Gillette Stadium. The Patriots controlled the game, with their defense starting the scoring less than six minutes into the game. The Jets were backed up near their own goal line and quarterback Kellen Clemens, who had taken over the starting role from Patriot nemesis Chad Pennington, threw a pass in the flat to his right that was intercepted at the 5 yard line by Ellis Hobbs. Hobbs ran it in for one of the easiest touchdowns possible.

The Patriots finally rediscovered a running game in this one, perhaps aided by the weather conditions, as Laurence Maroney ran for 104 yards on 26 carries. One of those was a 1 yard run in the second quarter for New England's second touchdown. Stephen Gostkowski added field goals of 26 and 34 yards, and the Patriot defense kept the Jets out of the end zone. New York's only touchdown came on a blocked punt that was returned 26 yards for the score. New England won the game 20-10 and the team was now 14-0 on the season.

The hapless Dolphins were next. Miami had been winless for much of the season, and they would not get a win on this day. Tom Brady threw for three touchdowns and Laurence Maroney continued the strong running that he had been showing recently, gaining 156 yards, including a 59 yard touchdown run. The Patriots won the game 28-7 and took their perfect 15-0 record into Christmas.

The *Sports Illustrated* double issue of December 31, 2007 – January 7, 2008 had a surprise for Patriot fans. On the cover was a picture of a stoic Bill Belichick, wearing a Santa Claus suit and hat. The caption under the picture read "Perfect Season Greetings" with the sub-title "Bill Belichick and the Patriots are 15-0" and under that "Happy (?) Holidays". It wasn't clear why there was a question mark in the last line, or for that matter how SI convinced Belichick to appear on the cover that way, but there was the normally reserved Belichick dressed up in his finest Santa gear. The issue was a summary of the year in sports, and had some interesting comments about the Patriots, finishing poetically and most notably with "In an age of narcissism, the Pats have embraced the sweet old concept of playing as one ... if they should win the championship in Arizona and stand beneath a shower of confetti falling from the night sky, perfect in every way, all the game will be better for having witnessed their journey".

Many sports fans were rooting for the Patriots to complete an undefeated season. There were others who were not. Among those that were not were players and fans whose teams would be competing in the playoffs against the Patriots, but that was natural competition. However, it also included those who would grumpily hold onto Spygate as a repudiation of all the good that the Patriots had symbolized during this decade, Senator Arlen Specter, and the members of the 1972 Miami Dolphins, the only team in NFL history to go through an entire season unbeaten, including the championship game. Those Dolphins, whom I liked, respected, and rooted for as they were trying to go through their season unbeaten, had become curmudgeonly about it, sadly clinging to their past glories and getting together to celebrate with champagne each season when the last undefeated team finally lost a game. Even their venerable coach, Don Shula, took a pot shot at the Patriots, saying that if they did go undefeated, their undefeated season should be listed with an asterisk, due to Spygate. Once again, I think of Bill Russell, John Havlicek, and the Boston Celtic teams that both won and lost with class and grace, and just shake my head at the way that Shula, Specter, and others were acting.

Before the Patriots could complete the regular season undefeated, they had one more game to play, a Saturday night, nationally televised game against the New York Giants at the Meadowlands in New Jersey. There was some speculation as to whether the Giants would play all of their regulars in this game, since they had clinched a wild card berth and would be starting the playoffs the following week, but to their credit, Coach Tom Coughlin and the Giants played the game as if it were as meaningful to them as it was to the Patriots. They played hard, were even inspirational in how they approached the game, and may have even used their play in this game as a springboard for what would be a successful run through the playoffs.

This was another very tight game that the Patriots could easily have lost. The Giants set the tone early with a 52 yard pass play from Eli Manning, Peyton's younger brother, to Plaxico Burress on the second play of the game, and scored on their opening drive on a touchdown pass from Manning to Brandon Jacobs. The Patriots answered with a field goal, and then Brady moved the team inside the New York 10 as the first quarter ended. At this point, just about every fan everywhere expected Brady to look to throw a touchdown pass to Randy Moss, since both were one TD pass and catch away from tying the NFL records set by Indianapolis' Peyton Manning and San

Francisco's Jerry Rice. Even with everyone expecting this, the Patriots tried it, and it was successful. Brady threw the ball high, Moss came down with it over two defenders, and the Patriots had a touchdown and the lead, at 10-7.

Moss was called for an unsportsmanlike conduct penalty for spiking the ball after his record-tying TD catch, so the Patriots were penalized on the ensuing kickoff. Partly as a result of that, the Giants immediately took back the lead at 14-10 after a 74 yard kickoff return for a touchdown by Domenik Hixon. It was one of the few times all season that the Patriots' special teams allowed a big play.

After two Patriot field goals, the Giants extended their lead to 21-16 at the half as their two minute offense produced a late touchdown on a three yard touchdown pass from Manning to Kevin Boss. The Giants increased their lead to 28-16 in the third quarter, after a 19 yard touchdown pass from Eli Manning to Plaxico Burress.

As had been the case in the Indianapolis, Philadelphia, and Baltimore games, the Patriots were seemingly on the ropes, when Tom Brady led them on a comeback. A 6 yard touchdown run by Laurence Maroney brought them closer, and left the score at New York 28 New England 23 heading into the fourth quarter.

When the Patriots got the ball back after a New York punt they were at their own 35 with less than 12 minutes remaining in the regular season. Brady dropped back and threw a long bomb down the right sideline to a streaking Randy Moss. The ball hit Moss perfectly, and the defender had fallen, but Moss dropped the ball. Undaunted, on the next play, Brady dropped back again, and threw another long bomb down the right sideline to Moss. Again it was a perfectly thrown pass and this time Moss caught it, and carried it into the end zone for a touchdown that gave the Patriots a lead. The pass was historic for many reasons. It gave Brady 50 touchdown passes for the season, a new NFL record. It gave Moss 23 touchdown catches, a new NFL record. Maroney ran for the two point conversion and the Patriots were now ahead 31-28.

An interception by Ellis Hobbs led to a 5 yard touchdown run by Maroney, upping New England's lead to a seemingly safe 38-28, but, to their credit, the Giants were still not about to give up. Another Manning to Burress touchdown cut the lead to just three points with 1:04 left to play.

New York went for the onside kick in a last ditch effort to make their own kind of history but one of the Patriots' most reliable players, Mike Vrabel, came up with the ball at the Patriots 41. The play clinched a 38-35 win that gave the Patriots the first 16-0 season in NFL history.

The offensive stars of this game for New England were numerous. Brady had a typically great day, finishing 32 of 42 for 356 yards and those 2 touchdowns to Randy Moss. Wes Welker had 11 catches for 122 yards, and Moss had 6 catches for 100 yards.

The Patriots finished the season with 589 points, a new NFL record, and 75 touchdowns, also a new NFL record. Wes Welker finished the season with 112 receptions, a new Patriot team record, easily breaking the old mark of 101 which had been set by Troy Brown in 2001, the Patriots' first Super Bowl winning season.

The Patriots had become the fourth team in NFL history to finish a regular season unbeaten, following the 11-0 Chicago Bears of 1942, the 13-0 Bears of 1934, and the 14-0 Miami Dolphins of 1972. The Bears had lost in the Championship game both of their seasons, so the Patriots would go into the playoffs trying to win all of those games and duplicate a feat accomplished only by those 1972 Dolphins, who had defeated the Washington Redskins in the Super Bowl to cap an absolutely perfect 17-0 season.

A lot was written about the Patriots, their perfect regular season, what it meant and what it would mean if the Patriots did not win the Super Bowl as well. The summary that to me seemed to hit the nail on the head was provided by Matt Crossman of *The Sporting News*, who wrote,

> "For weeks there had been talk about the relevance of 16-0. Conventional wisdom says 16-0 doesn't mean anything if it doesn't become 19-0. That takes 'what have you done for me lately' to such an extreme it's silly. Sixteen-and-Oh is so ripe with greatness it should be considered the most amazing regular season in team sports history. Losing in the playoffs will not diminish the righteousness of 16-0. Think of it this way: Some team wins the Super Bowl every year. But no team has ever gone 16-0.
>
> It should be celebrated no matter what happens next."

- - -

The first team that the Patriots would face in the playoffs would be the Jacksonville Jaguars, who had finished 11-5 in 2007. Many experts thought that Jacksonville's strong defense and excellent running game would provide problems for New England and could lead to an upset. They were right – for the first half. The score at halftime was 14-14, with the Jaguars scoring the first and last touchdowns of the half on short touchdown passes from David Garrard for eight yards to Matt Jones and six yards to Ernest Wilford. Sandwiched between those Jacksonville scores were two Patriot touchdown drives engineered by Tom Brady. One resulted in a three yard Brady touchdown pass to Benjamin Watson, the other in a one yard run by Laurence Maroney that had been set up by the recovery of a Garrard fumble by the defense's Mr. Clutch, Mike Vrabel.

Brady was on his way to a spectacular day. He would finish the day completing a jaw-dropping 26 of 28 passes (I believe that one of the incompletions was a drop), for an NFL one game accuracy record of 92.9%. Even CBS announcer Phil Simms, the former Giants quarterback who had gone 22 for 25 in a Super Bowl win in 1987 marveled at Brady's accuracy. Brady completed his first 16 pass attempts, and did not have an incompletion until the third quarter, when he was incomplete on a throw to Ben Watson on his 17th pass attempt.

Brady took the Patriots 82 yards on the opening drive of the second half, getting the touchdown on a 6 yard pass to the very dependable Wes Welker. After a Jacksonville field goal, Brady did it again on a 76 yard drive that ended with a 9 yard touchdown toss from Brady to Watson. The teams exchanged field goals in the fourth quarter, and any realistic Jacksonville hope ended when Rodney Harrison intercepted a Garrard pass with 4:34 to go, to ice a 31-20 win that sent the Patriots into the AFC Championship Game.

While everyone expected to see the Indianapolis Colts coming to Foxboro for that AFC Championship game and a rematch between these two outstanding teams, that was not the case. On the same weekend in which the Patriots eliminated Jacksonville, San Diego had upset the Colts 28-24, so it would be the Chargers who would be trying to keep the Patriots from getting to the Super Bowl, and not the Colts.

- - -

The Chargers were still a very talented team with offensive stars Philip Rivers, LaDanian Tomlinson, and Antonio Gates, and defensive stalwarts Antonio Cromartie and Shawne Merriman. The Chargers were hurting though, due to injuries, the most serious of which were a knee injury to quarterback Philip Rivers and a dislocated toe for receiver Antonio Gates that made it questionable if either player would play in Foxboro. LaDanian Tomlinson was also injured, but appeared to be the player of this big three that was most likely to play.

As it turned out, Rivers, the player least likely to play, played the entire game, and gallantly, while Tomlinson, the player previously thought to be the most likely to play, sat out much of the first half and all of the second half after only two carries and one pass reception. Gates played, but was clearly hampered by his injury. Tomlinson sat on the bench for most of the game, wearing his helmet with its reflective visor that made him look as if he were a Star Wars Storm Trooper.

Although they were banged up, the Chargers took advantage of a Quentin Jammer interception of a Tom Brady pass to take a 3-0 first quarter lead on a field goal by Nate Kaeding.

New England countered with a touchdown early in the second quarter, a 1 yard run by Laurence Maroney that was set up by a 14 yard end around run by Randy Moss, a Brady to Faulk pass for 14 yards, a run by Maroney for 8 yards and a Brady to Faulk pass for 7.

The Chargers moved right back down to the Patriot 9, thanks to Rivers' passing but without LaDanian Tomlinson to bang it in, had to settle for another field goal.

An interception off of a Rivers' pass by Asante Samuel led to a 12 yard Brady touchdown pass to Jabar Gaffney, but a third San Diego field goal made it 14-9 Patriots at halftime.

The Patriots received the second half kickoff, but instead of a big drive to open the half, as had been the case for New England often during the season, the Patriots lost the ball on another interception, a pass from Brady that hit Donte Stallworth but bounced off of the receiver into the hands of Charger defender Drayton Florence. Another Charger field goal cut New England's lead to a very nervous 14-12, which became even more nerve-wracking for Patriot fans when a Brady throw resulted in another interception on the next drive, Brady's third interception of the day. This one was particularly frustrating, because it came with the Patriots having a third and goal at the San Diego 2 yard line. Brady had good protection, but his pass to the back of the end zone that was intended for Benjamin Watson was instead intercepted by San Diego's star defensive back Antonio Cromartie.

The Patriots finally put the game away on a 15 play 65 yard drive that lasted for most of the last nine minutes of the fourth quarter. A diving catch by Kevin Faulk on a third and 11 got the Patriots a much-needed first down, and Laurence Maroney cashed it in for the touchdown from 5 yards out that made the final 21-12.

Tom Brady had suffered a foot injury during the game, though it was not known until the off-time before the Super Bowl. That may have accounted for what was a lackluster game for the NFL MVP; he wound up with only 209 yards passing for two touchdowns against three interceptions (I still believe that the Brady injury was a big factor in the Super Bowl loss to New York). Laurence Maroney took up some of the slack, with 122 yards on 25 carries and 1 TD, but Kevin Faulk may have been the star of the game for New England, with 8 catches for 82 yards, many of them clutch plays such as that diving catch for first down on the Patriots' final TD drive.

Patriot players and staff interviewed after the game seem to be expressing relief. After weeks of not answering questions about the potential undefeated season, and instead telling reporters that they were just focusing on the next game that was to be played, they finally seemed willing to talk about it. Belichick was still somewhat reserved though, with a "I'm not unaware of it" answer to one question about the potential for an undefeated season right after the game, but he did later in the week finally give an enthusiastic response to a question during a radio interview with WEEI when he said that he finally could say one thing that they had been waiting for all season. When asked what that was, Belichick's smile could almost come through the radio as he said "See you in Arizona" (the site of the Super Bowl).

One player response that particularly stuck with me well was that of veteran linebacker Junior Seau, who pointed out in his post-game press conference how meaningful this upcoming game would be. Seau's comment was "It's not often that you get to be a part of 'ever' " .

The Patriots indeed had a chance for a win that would complete a perfect 19-0 season and which could cause them to be considered as perhaps the greatest team ever.

Super Bowl XLII – New England vs. New York Giants

The only thing that put a damper on the games on that Sunday that identified the two Super Bowl teams and the only thing which really worried me (at least before we learned more about Tom Brady's foot injury), was that the Giants would be the Patriots' opponent in the Super Bowl. I felt that the Giants were the team that had the best chance to beat the Patriots. This was not only because of the tight game that the Giants and Patriots had played in the last game of the regular season on December 29, but also because I expected the hype about it being a New York team would be overwhelming. I fully anticipated (and we all got) mounds of newspaper type and long TV commentaries about how great the Giants were, and how great it would be if they knocked off the undefeated Patriots, how it would be the biggest upset in football history (Jets over Colts in Super Bowl III would really never be topped as the biggest upset in football history, in my opinion). It would again be a Manning going up against the Patriots, this time it was Eli, though, and not his more celebrated brother Peyton. It would also be yet another Boston-New York battle for supremacy, like many a Red Sox-Yankee series in the recent past, and Celtics-Knicks, Bruins-Rangers, of previous decades.

It is not that the Giants did not deserve to be in the Super Bowl; they did. They had won three road games to get to the Super Bowl, beating Tampa Bay 24-14, Dallas 21-17, and then Green Bay 23-20 in overtime. The game in Green Bay was played in bitter cold temperatures that should have favored the home town Packers, but it was the Giants who prevailed in a game in which the teams alternated having the lead. The game was tied 20-20 by a Green Bay field goal in the fourth quarter. New York kicker Lawrence Tynes missed two field goal attempts in the last seven minutes of regulation, from 43 and 36 yards, the last with 4 seconds left on the clock, so the game went into overtime.

Green Bay won the coin toss to start overtime and elected to receive. Many felt there was a good chance that future Hall of Famer Brett Favre would now shake off a bad game and lead the Packers to the winning score. But Favre is sometimes as bullheaded and erratic as he is good, and he threw an absolutely horrible pass toward Donald Driver who was running an out pattern. The very poorly thrown ball was intercepted by the Giants and Tynes hit a 47 yard field goal that sent the Giants, and not the Packers, to Arizona to face the Patriots.

The Giants thus became the first NFC team to win three road games to get into the Super Bowl. It was a feat first accomplished by the 1985 Patriots, who became the AFC Super Bowl representative after road wins at New York, Oakland, and Miami.

One of the first big signs of trouble for New England in the two weeks leading up to the Super Bowl was a newspaper photo of Tom Brady. The photo was of Brady walking in New York City to the apartment of his girlfriend, Brazilian supermodel Gisele Bundchen. What made it a big news item was that Brady was wearing a cast on his foot. Brady and the team shrugged it off then and in all pre-game questions about it, but he clearly was hurt more than he or anyone had let on.

The injury, in my opinion, played a big part in the game. The Giants had a strong defense and outstanding pass rush to begin with, but Brady had shown throughout his career that he had a great knack for sensing pressure and stepping away from it to give himself time to complete a pass. He did not have the same knack in this game, in which he faced relentless pressure from the Giant pass-rushers. The Giant pressure may have had the same effect even without a Brady injury, but Brady did not appear to be his usual self during the game.

The second bad sign of trouble was that the Patriots seemed to be straying from their usual focus during the two week period leading up to the game. Even Tom Brady, who usually did not react to such things, did react when Giant receiver Plaxico Burress predicted a 23-17 Giant win. Instead of the expected comment about waiting to see what would happen on the field, Brady responded by expressing surprise that Burress had predicted only 17 points for the Patriot offense. Other than the pass attempt made while falling down in a loss years ago to the Dolphins, this may have been the only uncharacteristic mistake of Brady's career.

The pre-game introductions also brought a third surprise, as the Patriot players came out to individual introductions. This was a far cry from the Patriots refusing to do that before their first Super Bowl win, and insisting that they be announced and come out as a team. Did it mean anything? Who knows? But I did notice the difference.

The next bad sign was the Giants winning the opening coin toss. I had hoped that the Patriots would win the toss, go right down the field and score, and establish dominance immediately. Instead, the Giants got the ball and ate up most of the first quarter clock on a 16 play drive that lasted an amazing ten minutes. It resulted in a field goal and a 3-0 New York lead. This ten minute opening drive may also have started the Patriot defense down the path of a tiring day in the hot Arizona climate.

Laurence Maroney returned the ensuing kickoff 43 yards to the New England 44, and Brady then led the Patriots right down the field for a touchdown. Maroney got one first down on a 5 yard run. Brady then hit Welker (who would go on to have a great day with a record-tying 11 catches) for an 8 yarder for another first down. The first quarter ended with the Patriots still on their first drive of the game, and Maroney finally ended the drive with a 1 yard scoring run on the first play of the second quarter.

Both teams then settled down and played great defensive football and the score after three quarters was a Super Bowl low 7-3.

The Patriots had two big chances to score but could not. The first came on a play that looked like a Patriot recovery of a New York fumble in Giants' territory in the second quarter. It appeared that Patriot linebacker Pierre Woods had recovered the fumble. It then appeared that the Giants had grabbed it back in the pile after the play, which should have been after the play and after the Patriots had gained possession, but the officials ruled otherwise and New York retained the ball. An opportunity for New England to have the ball deep in New York territory had been lost.

The next lost opportunity was a huge one. New England got the ball to start the second half and took off on a 14 play drive, but did not get any points out of this drive. It was perhaps another bad omen.

The Patriots had often scored on their first possession of the second half during the season to swing momentum their way; this time they had not done so. The Patriots started at their 21 and moved to the New York 47 yard line. It looked as if the Patriots would have to punt after a Brady pass to Kevin Faulk was short of a first down, but Bill Belichick had thrown the red flag for a replay review, claiming that the Giants had 12 men on the field. Replays showed that a Giant player had indeed not gotten off the field in time before the snap, so New York had indeed had 12 men on the field. The resultant penalty gave New England a first down. The Patriots then continued down to the New York 31 and had a 4th down and 13 to go. If Adam Vinatieri had still been on the team, the Patriots may very well have attempted a 48 yard field goal, but Belichick had noticed Stephen Gostkowski having trouble from long distances during warm-ups, and so decided to go for it. It was a decision that would be debated in the days following the game. Even more debatable may have been the play call. Instead of looking to get the first down, perhaps on a pass to Welker who seemed to be thriving on these, the Patriots went deep and Brady's pass sailed out of the end zone. Instead of seven points, or three, the Patriots had none, and New York took over. The third quarter was scoreless and the game was still tense at 7-3 New England heading into the final quarter of the season.

The fourth quarter was filled with tension and excitement. Eli Manning threw a five yard touchdown pass to David Tyree to give the Giants a 10-7 lead with 11:05 to play.

The lead was still 10-7 New York when the Patriots took over three series later at their own 20. With only 7:54 left in the season, and despite a day when he was not at his best, and during which the Giants had belted him on almost every pass play, Brady led the Patriots on an absolutely great, clutch drive for a touchdown. He hit Welker for 5 yards and Moss for 10. After a Maroney run, he hit Welker again for 13 yards and Welker again for 10 more. Moss caught a pass for 11 to the 18 yard line. It was at about this point that my son Mike wondered aloud if the Patriots might be better off to use up as much of the clock as they could before scoring; I suggested that they should get the score whenever they could and rely on the defense to hold them (it turns out that Mike may have had the better idea, as scoring early may have been wrong for this edition of the Patriots).

Faulk ran for 12 yards down to the 6 yard line, and it was first and goal for the Patriots. Two incompletions later it was third and goal for the Patriots. Then came the storybook play that should have been the final story of the season. Moss was lined up to the right and raced into the end zone past Giant defender Corey Webster. Brady hit him with a perfect bullet pass for a touchdown. The Patriots now had a 14-10 lead with 2:42 to go.

This should have been the perfect ending to a perfect season. It would have been Brady, the league's MVP, and the hero of three previous Super Bowl wins, coming off the mat where he had been knocked all day by the Giant defense, to lead this team on a winning drive. It would have been Brady in yet another late drive to win a game, as he had done so many times in his career (28 times having led his team to game-winning drives from a fourth quarter deficit or tie game). It would have been Brady, capping his perfect season with his record-breaking 50 TD passes, hitting Moss to cap his perfect season with his record-breaking 23 TD receptions. It would have given the Patriots a thrilling way to end a perfect 19-0 season. What would have been better than this? Hollywood couldn't even have written a script this good.

On the sideline, the Patriot defense seemed juiced for one final stop. Linebackers Tedy Bruschi and Junior Seau did a jumping chest bump as the touchdown was scored. The game was now in their hands.

The kickoff after this touchdown was big, and it was another big play for the Patriots. The Giants received the kick and started running it out when – boom! A Patriot defender in kick coverage, Ray Ventrone, just smashed the runner down at the New York 17 yard line. It was a great tackle. This should have been a sign of good things to come.

When Eli Manning came onto the field, he had what looked to me like a real deer-in-the-headlights look (if you don't remember it that way, look at the film of the game and see what you think). My thought was that a good play, or an early sack, would be all that was needed. But Manning got a quick pass completion to Amani Toomer for 11 yards, and after two incompletions, got another big completion for 9 yards after the two minute warning on a third down pass that set up a fourth and one run for a first down. That earlier look disappeared from Manning's face, and began to be replaced by one of confidence.

The Patriots missed a couple of chances for interceptions during this drive, including one that seemed to go right through the hands of a leaping Asante Samuel on the right sideline that would have sealed the victory for New England.

I commented to Mike during this drive that the Patriots should go back to the defensive alignment with no down linemen and 7 men positioned as linebackers that they had used against Buffalo years earlier. I thought that, as it had in that Buffalo game, it would disrupt the Giant offense as they would not know from where the pass rush would be coming and the Patriots could get a sack. Or the Patriots could disguise their pass coverage and drop more men into the passing lanes from different angles. But not having used that defense during the year would have probably made New England reluctant to try it now, though I have often wondered what would have happened if they had.

Faced with another big third down a few plays later, what followed was the biggest play of the game, and maybe the biggest of Eli Manning's career, no matter how long that career will run. Manning took the snap in the shotgun and was trapped by three Patriot defenders, Richard Seymour, Adalius Thomas, and Jarvis Green. It looked like the whistle should have been blown for an in-the-grasp sack, but it wasn't and the Patriots could not bring Manning down. He scrambled free and threw it long down the field. David Tyree, a backup receiver, then made what will almost definitely be the best play of his career, as he jumped up and trapped the ball against his helmet while being defended by Rodney Harrison, but came down still holding the ball. It was a first down for the Giants at the New England 24 yard line. It now seemed to me that luck was on the side of the Giants and that it was just a matter of time before they would score.

A pass from Manning to rookie Steve Smith gave the Giants a first down at the Patriot 13 yard line. There were just 39 seconds remaining.

The Giants lined up three receivers to the right and only one to the left. The Patriots did not roll over any defenders to that side, which was unfortunate, as it left the 5'9" Ellis Hobbs in single coverage against the much taller Plaxico Burress. Burress went by Hobbs and caught a perfectly thrown pass from Manning for the touchdown. The Giants now led 17-14.

The Patriots still had 35 seconds to try to score, and needed only a field goal to tie the game. The Patriots decided not to try to move the ball downfield with sideline passes to Welker or Faulk, but to go deep for Randy Moss. They did on first down and it was incomplete. They did on second down and it was incomplete. On third down a Giant defender came in seemingly untouched up the middle and blasted Brady down for a sack that looked like it could have torn Brady in two at the midsection. A fourth down incompletion sealed the big upset win for the Giants.

The final line score was

	1	2	3	4		Total
New York	3	0	0	14	-	17
New England	0	7	0	7	-	14

Eli Manning was the Game MVP. Had the Patriots won, it could have been receiver Wes Welker, who had a great day with 11 catches for 103 yards. But it was not to be.

While it was disappointing that the Patriots had lost, it was a win that the Giants greatly deserved. The Patriots had been the best team in the NFL in September, October, November, and December. Unfortunately, the Giants had turned out to be the best team in January and February.

SECTION 2 – 2008:
Battle Torn - The Year
Without Brady

Chapter 7– Tom Brady is Hurt. What Do We Do Now?

	1	2	3	4		TOTAL
Sunday, September 7, 2008:						
Kansas City Chiefs	0	3	0	7	-	10
New England Patriots	0	7	7	3	-	17

With 7:27 to play in the first quarter of the first game of the 2008 season for the New England Patriots, tragedy struck. For seven years the biggest fear that Patriots' fans had was of a season-ending injury to Tom Brady. Unfortunately, those fears became reality on the first Sunday of September.

Brady had not played a single down in any of the Patriots' four pre-season games. An injury to his foot kept him sidelined. The injury worried many Patriot fans, a number of whom had felt that Brady may have been more injured than either he or the team would admit in the Super Bowl loss to the Giants. Oddly, he was injured in the first game for which he had been left off the team's injury report submitted before the game; this was the first time that had happened in four years.

Brady had started strongly. He had already completed 7 of 11 passes for 76 yards midway through the first quarter and seemed on his way to another big game. The first drive ended after a completion to Wes Welker who fumbled, and the Patriots were now on their second drive. On New England's 15th play on offense, Brady dropped back and fired a long pass to Randy Moss. Moss caught it inside the Kansas City 20 but he also fumbled and Kansas City recovered, but as that happened, the CBS announcers said that all eyes were back on Tom Brady who was on the ground clutching his left knee. The replay showed that the injury had come on a hit from Kansas City defender Bernard Pollard. Pollard had been blocked to the ground by Patriot running back Sammy Morris, but had dived and accidentally (as it seemed) made a desperation dive attempting to sack Brady and bent Brady's knee back with his shoulder. According to reports, Brady immediately screamed and grabbed his knee. Gillette Stadium went as silent as some observers had ever heard it as all eyes were glued on Brady.

The Patriot medical staff came onto the field and attended to Brady. After a few minutes, he stood up under his own power, which was a positive sign for the fans (falsely positive as it turned out), and walked with the medical staff off the field.

The replay was shown multiple times and the question was raised as to whether that was a legal hit or dirty play. It was decided that it was legal, and it definitely appeared to be, but it unfortunately had knocked the NFL's reigning Most Valuable Player out of the lineup.

From that point on, many eyes in the stadium would look toward the tunnel after every play on the field to see if Brady was coming back. It was reminiscent of the Celtics' fans watching Larry Bird or Paul Pierce come back from the locker room after suffering injuries and roaring when they saw the players return. That good luck would not happen in this case, however, as the Patriots quarterback was pronounced out for the game during halftime.

Back on the field, the game was still scoreless, and a Kansas City punt had just backed New England up to its own 2 yard line. Into the game as Brady's replacement came Matt Cassel, a fourth year player on the roster, who had never started a game in the NFL. Even more oddly, Cassel had never started a game in college, as he was a backup quarterback at the University of Southern California for two other quarterbacks, Carson Palmer and Matt Leinart, both of whom had won the Heisman Trophy, thought by some to be symbolic of being college football's top player. Cassel's last start had been in his last game in high school, in November of 1999. The Patriots looked to be in deep trouble.

The first two plays with Cassel in the game were running plays, meant to get the Patriots out of the proverbial shadow of their own end zone. Unfortunately, the runs wound up losing yardage and moving the New England offense even deeper into those shadows. With a third and 11+, and the line of scrimmage being inside the New England 1 yard line, Cassel dropped back to pass. It was a play action pass, with Cassel faking a handoff for a running play to try to slow down the defensive rush. Wide receiver Randy Moss had broken off his planned route because of the KC pass coverage and was racing down the right sideline. Cassel saw that and fired a pass that fell perfectly into Moss' arms for a 51 yard gain and a big New England first down. It was the longest pass completion of Cassel's career, and brought a very loud and appreciative cheer from the nervous crowd. That play was the last play of the first quarter and the cheers carried into the break between quarters.

The drive continued, and Cassel completed it by throwing a 10 yard touchdown pass to Randy Moss to give the Patriots a 7-0 lead. The pass fluttered more than a Tom Brady pass might have in this situation, but it did get the job done.

A Kansas City field goal made the score 7-3 at the half, and halftime brought the news that Brady would not be returning for the second half.

After a KC punt on their opening drive of the second half, New England took over on its own 20, and Cassel led the team 80 yards for a second touchdown. Sammy Morris scored the TD on a 5 yard run to give New England a 14-3 lead.

Kansas City had also lost its starting quarterback, Brandon Coyne, to injury, though not one as severe as Brady's, and was using former Patriot Damon Huard as its quarterback. Huard hit wide receiver Dwayne Bowe for a 13 yard touchdown pass with 14:06 to go in the 4th quarter, to get the Chiefs back to 14-10 and give KC some hope of coming up with an upset win.

The teams exchanged punts on the next three series, and then Patriot cornerback Ellis Hobbs intercepted a Huard pass at the Kansas City 41 yard line. The Patriots moved into position for a big field goal and a one touchdown lead, 17-10, with 2:26 to go in the game. It was now up to the Patriot defense to hold that lead.

Holding the lead became shaky on Kansas City's second play, a second and 16 from the KC 27 yard line. Huard fired a pass to a streaking Devard Darling, who grabbed it and continued racing downfield until he was caught from behind by new Patriot cornerback Deltha O'Neal. The Chiefs had a first and goal at the New England 5 yard line. A tying touchdown and overtime seemed very likely, but the New England defense stepped up and made a stand, denying the Chiefs the score. The fourth down pass was defended well by O'Neal and the pass fell incomplete out of the end zone on the right side of the field. The Patriots had escaped with a narrow victory.

Matt Cassel had performed solidly, if not spectacularly. His final statistics were 13 completions in 18 attempts, for 152 yards, but there was no bigger play than his 51 yard completion to Randy Moss from out of his own end zone that set up the first NE touchdown.

Coach Bill Belichick started his post-game press conference by saluting his team for its efforts, and making a sardonic comment that he had no news about Tom if anyone was interested. Everyone definitely was interested.

- - -

The next day brought the results of the MRI on Tom Brady's knee. In a late afternoon press conference, Coach Belichick confirmed the news everyone had feared. Brady would be out for the year.

While Belichick is not one to deal in hyperbole, or to gush about any one player, he did say "I feel badly for Tom. Nobody has worked harder and meant more to this team than Tom has since I have been here."

It was later revealed that Brady had torn both the ACL and MCL ligaments in his knee and would undergo season-ending surgery.

This was a deep, deep blow to the Patriots. What they had lost was the man who was the NFL MVP in 2007, having thrown an NFL record 50 touchdown passes, and a man who was one of the hardest working players on the team and a well-respected leader, not only of the offense, but of the entire team. It was as if they had lost their heart.

The Patriots, however, have always been a team that has handled adversity as professionals, and handled it well. Belichick said in his press conference that the Patriots would have to overcome this and that they would do so by everyone doing their jobs. While lauding Tom, he responded to repeated questions about what the loss would mean by saying that Brady "played one position. He played it well. There will be someone else playing that position now." Belichick also expressed confidence that Matt Cassel could do the job.

In ensuing days, that sentiment would be echoed by any player interviewed by the press. They all expressed respect for Tom, but also indicated that they had confidence in Cassel, and indicated that if they all did their jobs, the team could still be successful.

Belichick was asked about reports that veteran NFL quarterbacks Chris Simms and Tim Rattay had worked out for the team. Belichick said the reports were not true, that the Patriots had not worked out any other QB, though he added with a half-smile that the Patriots had been contacted by a number of people. Belichick added that the team had confidence in Cassel. Offensive tackle Matt Light may have summed it up best for all team members when he pointed out in an interview, "There is nobody on the team that we don't have confidence in. If we don't have confidence in them, and more importantly, if the coaching staff did not have confidence in them, then they wouldn't be here."

So Matt Cassel, who had not started a football game since high school, was now the starting quarterback for New England. Kevin O'Connell, a rookie from San Diego State, would be his backup. Before the end of the week, the Patriots would re-sign quarterback Matt Guttierez, who had been on the roster in training camp, as their third QB. Belichick's position was that there was no desire to bring in a veteran quarterback who would be unfamiliar with the Patriots' complex system and have to spend time learning it. He was content going with the trio of Cassel, O'Connell, and Guttierez, who, though unproven, knew the Patriot system.

Other teams in past years had suffered key injuries to their starting quarterbacks and had overcome them. All-time great Johnny Unitas of the Baltimore Colts was injured and replaced by Earl Morrall in 1968. Morrall led the Colts to a 13-1 record and a spot in the Super Bowl. The undefeated 1972 Dolphins had lost Bob Griese to a broken leg. Ironically, it was that same Earl Morrall who stepped in for Griese. He won every game that he started in Griese's absence, before Griese returned during the playoffs. Jeff Hostetler replaced an injured Phil Simms in 1990 and led the Giants to a Super Bowl win over Buffalo. Kurt Warner replaced the injured Trent Green and led the St. Louis Rams to a Super Bowl win in 2000 (though it is clear that Trent Green and Phil Simms were not in the same class as Griese, Unitas, or Brady). And so on. It was on situations like these that Patriot fans could hang their hopes for 2008.

Now it was the Patriots' turn to try to overcome their loss. It was on to preparations for the Jets, without Tom Brady, the man who, as has been pointed out previously, was either THE best quarterback in football, or, at worst, one of the two best along with Peyton Manning of the Indianapolis Colts. Belichick would be challenged as he had not been for some time. Strangely, I and a number of fans with whom I spoke, were eerily confident in the team's abilities to win on Sunday, and also in its ability to have a good and successful year despite the loss of Brady. Only time and 15 more regular season games would prove whether or not that sentiment was correct.

Chapter 8 – Facing the Enemy: Matt Cassel vs. Brett Favre

Sunday, September 14, 2008:	1	2	3	4		TOTAL
New England Patriots	3	3	10	3	-	19
New York Jets	0	3	0	7	-	10

In the days preceding the Patriots' second game of the season, a battle in Giants' Stadium with their bitter rivals, the New York Jets, the storylines seemed to be about the changing of the guard. The New York Jets were now the hot story. The general consensus outside of New England, and especially in the New York papers, was that the New York Jets were now the team to beat in the AFC East and top contenders to get to the Super Bowl.

How could they not be? That was the thought of many football experts and fans. The Patriots had now lost Tom Brady and, in Matt Cassel, would be playing a quarterback who had not started a game either in college or the pros. In contrast, the Jets had obtained future Hall of Fame quarterback Brett Favre from Green Bay during the off-season, after Green Bay had tired of Favre's year-after-year flirtation with retirement. The Jets had improved in other areas as well. The previews of the game in the New York papers indicated that this would be a statement game for both Favre and the Jets.

However better the Jets might have appeared on paper, games are not won by experts determining beforehand which team is better. In the immortal words of Boston Celtic great Bill Russell, "That's why they play the games." As it turned out, the Patriots sure came to play this game, and to prove all the skeptics wrong.

- - -

In his pre-game preparations, Coach Bill Belichick did what any good coach or manager should do: he put his team in position to win. He set up a game plan suited to the talents of Matt Cassel, not one suitable for Tom Brady. The idea was to have Cassel manage the game, not make mistakes, and help his team win. Brady had been a key reason why the Patriots had won in the past, and had been a major contributor to making sure they won or driving them to a late score to win a game; Cassel instead would be put in position not to lose the game.

This positioning continued even with the opening coin flip. The Patriots won the toss, but elected to defer their choice to the second half (a new NFL rule for 2008 allowed this). This meant that the Patriots would be kicking off to the Jets, presumably putting them back near their goal line to start, and letting the Pats' defense make the first statement. If all went well, the Jets would run three plays and then punt, giving New England and Matt Cassel good field position for their own opening drive.

The strategy worked on the first play as Stephen Gostkowski's kickoff sailed out of the end zone, making the Jets start from their own 20 yard line. Things did not work out after that, however, as the Jets marched methodically down the field, reaching the Patriots' 14 yard line before the drive stalled. Luckily for New England, Jet kicker Jay Feeley badly missed a 31 yard field goal attempt, wide right, and so the game was still scoreless when Matt Cassel led the offense onto the field.

Cassel coolly led the Patriots back down the field, including hitting Kevin Faulk for a 14 yard gain on his first pass as a starter, and also hitting Wes Welker on a couple of key passes. Cassel in fact completed 4 of his first 5 passes in getting the Pats to the 2 yard line, before settling on a field goal and an early 3-0 lead.

The score was still 3-0 in the second quarter as New England was moving on its second drive. On a key third and four play, Cassel threw towards Kevin Faulk. The pass was deflected high into the air by a Jets' lineman, but Faulk stayed with it and made a nice play, coming down with the catch for a 9 yard gain and a first down. The drive ended with another Gostkowski field goal and a 6-0 lead for New England.

The Jets then made another long drive, moving to a first and goal on the Patriot three yard line. The first play was a run for one yard to the two. Another run gained another yard, and the ball was at the one yard line. Although they had Brett Favre as QB, the Jets refused to pass and went on the ground again on third down, but Richard Seymour burst through the middle of the New York line to stop the runner for a two yard loss. The Jets had to settle for a field goal, and the Pats remained in the lead, at 6-3.

This was an intriguing turn of events. With all the hoopla surrounding their acquisition of Favre, the Jets raised a few eyebrows by not throwing on any of these goal line plays. Interestingly, in an interview the next day on radio station WEEI, New England linebacker Ted Bruschi was asked if he was surprised that the Jets had called three running plays at this point. Bruschi said he wasn't and explained that the Jets had felt in recent years they had had problems with the front seven of New England's defense, the defensive linemen and linebackers. Bruschi went on to say the Jets had tried to address that with the addition of some veteran offensive linemen during the season, and that this was one of those times in a game when one team "draws a line in the sand" and says that they are going to do it and another draws their own line and says no you are not. The Patriots held and Bruschi responded to another question on this by saying that this did seem to impact the Jets' players as they went back to the sideline. It was interesting insight from one of the Patriots' key players, and one of the many smart players on the team.

Just before the end of the first half, with 2:12 to go, Cassel took a hard hit on a pass attempt from a Jet pass rusher coming from Cassel's left side and went down hard. Cassel came up holding his right knee, and moved gingerly after that. As the half ended and the teams moved to the locker rooms, New England fans were worried that the Patriots' backup quarterback was going to be sidelined as well.

The 6-3 score meant that the Patriots had been held without a first half touchdown for the first time since December 10, 2006, against the Miami Dolphins.

There was also one very interesting and amusing (for Patriot fans) sequence that occurred late in the first half. On fourth down near midfield, with the Jets out of timeouts, the Patriots had the offense on the field. Suddenly, with seconds to go before the snap, the punting team raced on and the offense raced off. The Jets could not get their defense off the field and could not call time out, so the Patriots punted with no Jet returner back to catch the punt. This should have resulted in a punt that would pin the Jets very deep in their own territory, but Chris Hanson's punt sailed into the end zone, and the Jets got the ball at the 20. Nevertheless, it was a very clever move by Bill Belichick.

- - -

The CBS announcers covering the game, Jim Nantz and Phil Simms, noted that the Patriots' third-string quarterback, rookie Kevin O'Connell, was warming up on the sideline before the second half started. However, Matt Cassel came back onto the field to start the third quarter as the Pats returned the opening kickoff of the second half to their own 21. There was one injury of note, though – running back Laurence Maroney had suffered a shoulder injury and his return to the game was doubtful.

New England went three and out on this opening drive with Cassel being sacked twice while attempting to pass. The Jets then started a drive that was reminiscent of their opening drive of the game, but three big penalties kept pushing them back. Then Brett Favre threw an interception to Brandon Meriweather and the Patriots were back in business. Cassel drove them to the game's first touchdown, hitting Kevin Faulk for a key 22 yard completion, and hitting Welker for a pass to get them to the 1 yard line (which looked to me as though it should have been a touchdown as Welker fell into the end zone on the tackle). Sammy Morris catapulted the line for the touchdown which gave New England a 13-3 lead.

After holding the Jets and forcing a punt, New England got another drive started. Faulk returned the punt 24 yards to the Jet 38. Then good running by Faulk and by former Jet and former Raider Lamont Jordan led to another Gostkowski field goal and a 16-3 lead. The drive was 8 plays, 7 of which were running plays. Again, Belichick was making sure that Cassel was managing the game, not calling on him to win it.

As the fourth quarter began, the Jets roused the crowd with an 80 yard drive for a touchdown, the score coming on a one yard pass from Favre to Stuckey. With 10:18 left, a long time in football terms, the Patriots' lead had now been cut to 16-10. Another Jet TD could give them the lead, and possibly a big come-from-behind win.

This is where good quarterbacks and good teams take over and march the ball down the field themselves, taking a lot of time off the clock and scoring again to give themselves a lead of greater than 1 touchdown.

This is also where Matt Cassel and the 2008 Patriot team took over, marched the ball down the field, killed a lot of time off the clock, and gave themselves a 9 point lead.

It was a classic drive, 11 plays and 5 minutes. Play-by-play it was:

1. Cassel to Randy Moss for 14 yards and a first down at the NE 34
2. Cassel to Dave Thomas for 14 yards and a first down at the NE 48
3. Cassel long pass to Randy Moss (Cassel's only long pass of the day), dropped at the 10 yard line; second down
4. Lamont Jordan 8 yard run to NY 44 yard line; third and 2
5. Cassel to Sammy Morris for a first down, coupled with a 15 yard roughing the passer penalty against New York, moving the ball to the Jet 25 yard line
6. Cassel to Wes Welker for 4 yards to the NY 21
7. Lamont Jordan for 8 yards and a first down at the NY 13

8. Lamont Jordan for 3 yards to the NY 10; second down
9. Lamont Jordan for 1 yard to the NY 9; third down
10. Cassel pass to Dave Thomas deflected incomplete; fourth down
11. Gostkowski 27 yard field goal with 5:18 to go

New England had a 19-10 lead and New York had the ball at the 20 yard line after the kickoff. The Jets started with a six yard completion from Favre to Stuckey. On second and 4, Patriot linebacker Adalius Thomas blew through the New York blocker assigned to him and grabbed Favre, pulling both Favre and the blocker down inside the 10 yard line for a 20 yard loss. Cornerback Ellis Hobbs knocked down Favre's third down pass attempt, and the Jets were forced to punt.

The Patriots then ran out the clock, thanks to a great play by Wes Welker. On 4th down from the Jet 31 with just under 2:00 to go, Cassel hit Welker on a flanker screen. Welker caught the ball behind the line of scrimmage, and, as he has done so many times, he maneuvered the ball past the first down marker and sealed the win for New England.

Kevin Faulk, Sammy Morris, Wes Welker, and newcomer Lamont Jordan had exceptional games for New England. Matt Cassel and the New England defense played solid games. The Patriots also showed great discipline, being called for only two penalties in the game, illegal formation on a punt, and a false start on a kneel down in the fourth quarter.

The Patriots were now 2-0 on the season, they had won their 21st consecutive regular season game (an NFL record), and Matt Cassel was 1-0 as New England's starting quarterback. Cassel had gone 16 for 23 for 165 yards and no turnovers in his first NFL start. In his post-game press conference, Coach Bill Belichick summed it up perfectly, saying, "Matt took care of the ball."

Chapter 9 – Defenseless Against the Dolphins

Sunday, September 21, 2008:	1	2	3	4		TOTAL
Miami Dolphins	7	14	7	10	-	38
New England Patriots	0	6	7	0	-	13

Joey Porter is a linebacker with the Miami Dolphins with a lot of talent and a mouth that may be as big as his talent. In the week preceding the Patriots-Dolphins game in week 3 of the NFL season, Joey made a number of comments about how Matt Cassel was no Tom Brady, how the Dolphins would be throwing everything at Cassel, and how nice it would be for the Dolphins to pick up their first win of the season. Many Patriot fans were looking forward to Porter having to eat his words after the game, but, unfortunately, it was Porter who had the last laugh.

The Patriots came into the game riding a streak of regular season wins that had grown to 21-0. In that same span of 21 games, while the Patriots were winning all of their games, Miami was winning only 1 and losing 20. They were coming off a 2007 season in which they were 1-15.

Yet, in a shocking reversal of form, Miami looked invincible, and the Patriots looked very bad. The Dolphins utterly destroyed the Patriots 38-13 to win their first game of the season and to give the Patriots their first defeat.

Perhaps the headline on the "Sports Redux" posting on the popular blog site Bostonist.com said it best: "Flat and Flattened". The Patriots came out very flat and they paid the price for doing so. Miami came out motivated, with a good game plan, and they executed that plan extremely well.

With the exception of a couple of good kickoff returns by Ellis Hobbs, no facet of the Patriot team played well. The biggest culprit was the Patriot defense, which was unable to stop Miami at all.

The biggest plays for the Dolphins were made out of an unusual formation in which running back Ronnie Brown would line up a few yards behind center and take a direct snap. Often quarterback Chad Pennington, who had had many good games against the Patriots while he was a member of the Jets, would line up in a wide receiver spot. The Dolphins ran that play numerous times and the Patriots defense never made adjustments to stop it. Ronnie Brown had a field day running that play, and the Patriots made him look like an All-Pro, a combination of Jim Brown, Walter Payton, and Paul Hornung.

- - -

The day began with Ellis Hobbs returning the opening kickoff 50 yards to the Miami 49 yard line. Even with that great starting field position, the Patriot offense was unable to generate anything and had to punt after three unsuccessful plays. Miami also had to punt on their first possession and the Patriots were able to drive to the Miami 12 yard line. Matt Cassel then dropped back to pass and was rushed hard (a recurring theme of the day was the pressure the Miami defense put on the Patriot QB). Cassel got away from the rush and scrambled into the end zone, but was the victim of a very quick whistle and a ruling that Cassel was in the grasp and therefore sacked. The replay showed Cassel was barely in the grasp of anyone before he got away. Surely many Patriot fans were wondering where that "in the grasp" call was against Eli Manning in the waning moments of the 2008 Super Bowl? In any case, the play was called back and Cassel wound up throwing an interception on the next play, so the drive resulted in no points for New England.

Chad Pennington led the Dolphins down the field on a drive of their own, connecting with Anthony Fasano, his tight end on two big pass plays and rookie Ted Ginn on another. Ronnie Brown then got the game's first score by lining up in the shotgun formation, taking the direct snap, and scoring on a 2 yard touchdown run. The Dolphins were ahead 7-0.

A Patriot drive spanning the end of the first quarter and the beginning of the second netted them a field goal to make it 7-3, but Chad Pennington followed with another Miami TD drive to make it 14-3. TheTD was scored by Ronnie Brown, this time on a conventional handoff from Pennington and a 15 yard run for the score.

The Patriots then benefited from a good bounce as a Matt Cassel pass was hit into the air by Dolphin defender Renaldo Hill, but Wes Welker made a great catch of the tipped ball at the 28 yard line and the Patriots were able to get a second Gostkowski field goal, this time from 44 yards out, to cut the Miami lead to 14-6. They were back within striking distance, but a 9 play, 77 yard drive by Pennington led to another score. Again it was Ronnie Brown, and again it was the direct snap to Brown who was behind center in the shotgun formation. This time it was for a 5 yard touchdown run with :59 to play in the first half. A jubilant Miami team went into the clubhouse at halftime with a surprising 21-6 lead over New England.

Miami started out the second half by going three plays and out, as the Patriots defense displayed its most inspired play of the game. However, the next time the Dolphins had the ball they had another long march, this time 10 plays and 79 yards. Again it was Ronnie Brown taking the direct snap for the fourth time in the game and again it was successful. This time Brown drifted out to the left and threw a left-handed pass to Fasano for a 19 yard touchdown to extend the Miami lead to 28-6.

Ellis Hobbs provided the fans some spark by returning the ensuing kickoff from out of his own end zone 81 yards to the Miami 22 yard line. This led to a 5 yard TD pass from Cassel to Gaffney, cutting the lead to 28-13 with 3:20 to go in the third quarter.

The hope was only short-lived, though, as the Dolphins began a drive from their own 15 to the 38 yard line as the third quarter expired. As the fourth quarter began, the Dolphins again lined up in shotgun formation with Brown taking the snap. This time he raced through the Patriot line and didn't stop until he was in the end zone 62 yards later. He was barely touched at all on his journey, and with 14:49 to go, the lead was 35-13. Fans started streaming out of Gillette Stadium. The game was effectively over.

Rookie Kevin O'Connell got his first action at quarterback, and looked decent, but it was hard to gauge how effective he was, given that the game was a rout. It ended with a 38-13 Miami win.

Cassel finished this day 13 for 21 for 131 yards. O'Connell was 3 for 4 for 25 yards in his NFL debut. On the other side, Chad Pennington had a typical Chad Pennington day against New England, good but not flashy, showing not a lot of arm strength but exceptional accuracy, as he was 17 of 20 for 226 yards.

Ronnie Brown was the star of the game, rushing 17 times for 113 yards, and throwing once for 19 yards and a touchdown. His partner at running back, Ricky Williams, added another 98 yards rushing.

Coach Bill Belichick was understandably terse at the press conference after the game, stating that the Patriots "couldn't move the ball on offense, couldn't stop them on defense."

With a bye week next on the schedule, Patriot defenders would probably be having nightmares about Ronnie Brown and that direct snap play for the next two weeks. Hopefully someone would come up with some way to stop it before these two teams would meet again in late November.

Chapter 10 – The Bye Week Blues

For some reason, the National Football League feels that some teams should have their only week off during the season after playing just three games on their sixteen game schedule. It makes no sense. They could easily schedule the bye weeks for weeks 7-11 and accommodate every team. In the not-so-distant past there was no bye week, so having one after just three games seems very odd indeed.

Nevertheless, the Patriots and Dolphins were among six teams who were scheduled for a bye week on September 28 for a season that would last until January.

This was the first time since week four of the 2005 season that the Patriots were not in at least a tie for first place in the AFC East. The Buffalo Bills were leading the division with a 3-0 record and were one of six undefeated teams heading into week 4, along with Tennessee, Baltimore, Denver, Dallas, and the New York Giants. The Giants, defending Super Bowl Champions, were getting little of the respect which is usually given to Super Bowl champs. This is especially hard to believe for a team from New York. They were hardly anyone's pre-season pick to repeat and rarely mentioned among the lists of contenders. In fact, they were playing second fiddle to the Jets, the other team from New York that plays in the same stadium as the Giants. The Giants were just quietly going about winning.

On the other side, there were surprising teams with losing records. The Indianapolis Colts and San Diego Chargers, both viewed as co-favorites in the AFC along with New England, were both struggling at 1-2. The Colts had Peyton Manning recovering from off-season surgery. The Chargers were the victims of a loss on a last second touchdown pass against Carolina, and a bad call by staunch NFL referee Ed Hochuli that led to a late winning TD by Denver. Also at 1-2 were the much-ballyhooed New York Jets and their new quarterback Brett Favre. It was early in the season, but these results were still surprising.

The Patriots' bye week began with two players, defensive back Ellis Hobbs and tight end Ben Watson, castigating the fans for booing the team and leaving early during the loss to Miami. As soon as I heard the teaser on the evening news, my thought was that this was not a good idea. While I don't condone fans booing, especially in one game that ends in loss after 21 straight regular season victories, the player reaction should not have been what it was. If they said anything it should have been along the lines of "We didn't play well and I can understand the fans leaving early and being disappointed; we will have to play better and turn those boos into cheers the next time that we play at home." It seems to me that such a response would have been what many of the Celtic champions of old, such as John Havlicek, Dave Cowens, Larry Bird, and Paul Silas would have said.

- - -

Thursday of the bye week saw the official retirement of one of the all-time great players and beloved Patriots, Troy Brown. Brown retired after 15 seasons with the Patriots, second in longevity only to Steve Grogan's 16. Statistically, he was great, with 192 games played (fourth in team history), 20 playoff games (second only to Tedy Bruschi's 22), more catches (557, for 6,366 yards) than any other Patriot receiver, and the top receiving game in Patriot history – 16 catches for 176 yards against Kansas City in 2002.

Qualitatively, Brown had many big plays, smart plays, and game-turning plays. He did everything that the Patriots asked of him, and did everything well. That included pass receiving, kickoff and punt returning, playing defensive back, and even being a potential stand-in quarterback. He was a true professional, and, as owner Bob Kraft described, "the consummate Patriot". He will be greatly missed.

(Note: there will be much more about Troy Brown and his retirement in the section of this book that summarizes interviews with key players and contributors to the team's history.)

Chapter 11 – California Dreaming

Sunday, October 5, 2008:	1	2	3	4	TOTAL
New England Patriots	7	10	7	6 -	30
San Francisco 49ers	14	0	0	7 -	21

The Patriots had never defeated the San Francisco 49ers in San Francisco, having lost away games to the 49ers in 1971, 1980, 1989, and 1995. The 1989 game was actually played on October 22 in Palo Alto, as a result of the earthquakes which had rocked the San Francisco area just days earlier, and which caused postponement of the World Series between the Giants and A's. The Patriots had rarely played a quarterback with as little experience as Matt Cassel. Nevertheless, with a bye week to prepare, and a not-so-great 49er team to face, the Patriots were able to prevail 30-21 in their first of two straight games in California.

One of the key elements of the game was time of possession. The Patriots had the ball for just under 40 minutes (39:52) while San Francisco had it for 20:08. More importantly, the Patriots defense held San Francisco to just 48 plays to New England's 80 (making the 49ers perhaps "the 48ers" for the day?).

That this was done against an offense whose coordinator was offensive genius Mike Martz was also an accomplishment. The defense and Matt Cassel were the stories, as Cassel had his best game yet as Brady's replacement, completing 22 passes for 259 yards in 32 attempts and one long touchdown, a 66 yard bomb to Randy Moss in the first quarter. It was the first big play pass to Moss thus far in the season.

The 49ers had a 14-7 lead after the first period, having scored two touchdowns around that Cassel-to-Moss TD, both on passes from 49er QB J.T. O'Sullivan, a former Patriot camp QB. The second and third quarters belonged to New England. A Stephen Gostkowski 35 yard field goal and a Kevin Faulk 6 yard TD run made the Pats 17-14 leaders at halftime. Randy Moss had already gained more yards in the first half than he had in the first three games combined.

Halftime ceremonies saw the 49ers retire the uniform number of their great lefty quarterback, Steve Young. Young had been a backup behind Joe Montana who, after Montana's career with San

Francisco was over, won a Super Bowl of his own and formed a great passing combination with the outstanding wide receiver Jerry Rice. Patriot fans could look forward to the retirement of Tom Brady's number somewhere in the distant future (far distant, one hopes), as Brady has often been compared to Joe Montana both in style and in coolness under pressure.

The Patriots extended the lead to 24-14 with a 2 yard run by Kevin Faulk in the third quarter. The play was an old trick play, a direct snap to Faulk, with Cassel jumping and pretending that the ball was snapped over his head, as Brady had done in the past. The Patriots, who had been burned by Miami's direct snaps to Ronnie Brown in their last game before the bye week, had now burned San Francisco on a similar play.

The Patriots extended the lead to 27-14 on a Gostkowski 40 yard field goal 7 seconds into the fourth quarter. Time of possession was over 32 minutes for New England and slightly over 12 for San Francisco.

An O'Sullivan TD pass to former Ram Isaac Bruce cut the New England lead to less than a touchdown, 27-21, with 10:22 left to play, but New England responded with a long drive of its own. The Pats went 5:40 with a 10 play 41 yard drive that set up a clinching field goal by Gostkowski. Wes Welker continued to make a habit of short catches and then good runs after the catch for first down with a 12 yard beauty on this drive. The key play on the drive though was a referee's challenge called by Belichick. The play was a third down pass on the right sideline to Kevin Faulk. Faulk made a nifty move and seemed to elude a tackle and get past the first down marker, but the officials spotted it back a few feet and called for a measurement. The measurement showed the Patriots short of the first down by inches. A punt seemed necessary until Belichick pulled the red flag from his sock and tossed it onto the field. He requested a replay review to determine whether the ball was spotted correctly. The replay showed that it had not been spotted correctly, and the corrected spotting of the ball did give the Patriots a first down, and allowed them to move into field goal range.

The 49ers had one more shot for a score, an on-side kick, and another score, but those hopes ended when Rodney Harrison deflected a pass from O'Sullivan into the arms of Patriot DB Deltha O'Neal with 2:45 left. One more San Francisco possession ended with a fourth down throwaway by O'Sullivan, and the Patriots had their first road win ever over the 49ers. The team was now 3-1 on the young season, ½ game behind the 4-1 Buffalo Bills who had fallen from the undefeated ranks with a thud, losing to Arizona 41-17.

The Patriots now would be spending a week practicing in California, at San Diego State University, preparing for their Sunday match-up with San Diego. The Chargers would be looking for revenge after their defeats to the Patriots in 2006 and 2007.

Chapter 12 – Reversal of Fortune

	1	2	3	4		TOTAL
Sunday, October 12, 2008:						
New England Patriots	0	3	0	7	-	10
San Diego Chargers	10	7	10	3	-	30

The script was familiar, but the results were not. Patriot fans had gotten accustomed to seeing long passes from Brady to his receivers, most notably Randy Moss, just about every week in the 2007 season. In this fifth game of the 2008 season, it was the San Diego Chargers who were completing the long bombs.

This was a game that I and many others expected to be a loss, for the reasons noted at the end of the previous chapter. San Diego would be looking for revenge for the playoff losses to the Patriots in 2007 and 2006, and also would be highly motivated for a win after their loss in the preceding week to Miami. It was also a Sunday night game, so the Chargers would have the extra motivation of having a national TV audience watching their quest for revenge.

The Chargers would be playing without their star linebacker, Shawne Merriman, who was injured and out for the season. The Patriots would be playing without running backs Laurence Maroney and Lamont Jordan. Jordan had been injured in the 49er game. Maroney had a shoulder injury and also described himself as having undisclosed "issues", so he was in street clothes on the sideline. Fans were beginning to be disenchanted with Maroney, who seemed to be often-injured and in the 49er game had run out of bounds short of a first down to avoid contact with a potential tackler.

The biggest injury-related news was that Tom Brady had had the first of his surgeries to repair the knee damage he suffered on opening day. The surgery was successful and Bob Kraft led all Patriot officials and fans in wishing Tom a quick recovery and looking forward to his getting back on the field in 2009.

After the opening kickoff by Stephen Gostkowski was downed in the end zone, the Chargers took over and took command early. The first play from scrimmage set the tone for the game. It was a 48 yard bomb from Charger quarterback Philip Rivers to wide receiver Vincent Jackson, taking San Diego from its own 20 to the New England 32. The Chargers would exploit the New England defensive secondary all day. They marched easily down to the New England 7 and settled for a Nate Kaeding field goal and an early 3-0 lead.

The Patriots then had an answering drive of their own down to the San Diego 31, but missed a field goal that would have tied the score. It was the first miss of the season on a field goal attempt by Gostkowski.

It was back to the San Diego aerial attack after that, as a Rivers 49 yard pass to Malcom Floyd was caught at the 1. Floyd fell into the end zone for the touchdown after making the catch of a beautifully thrown pass by Rivers. San Diego led 10-0 after the first quarter.

The Patriots countered with a field goal in the second quarter, after Randy Moss narrowly missed what would have been a great catch on the right sideline inside the 5 yard line. Moss juggled the ball as he went out of bounds; the officials correctly ruled it an incompletion since Moss never had possession in-bounds.

After an exchange of possessions, San Diego took over in great field position with 2:22 to go in the first half at the New England 31 thanks to a 22 yard punt return to the 46 and a face mask penalty on New England rookie Jerod Mayo. Philip Rivers hit Vincent Jackson for a TD from inside the 10 to make the halftime score 17-3 in favor of San Diego. As the teams ran to the locker room for halftime, Patriot offensive coordinator Josh McDaniels was seen having an animated talk with Coach Bill Belichick. John Madden seemed to think that it was a big deal, though we never learned during the TV broadcast what the discussion was about. Bill Belichick was asked about it during the week after the game and indicated that they were just discussing what to say to the team during halftime and what adjustments to make and had to speak loudly over the crowd noise. It turned out to be a non-controversy.

The Patriots started the second half fired up and took off on a 12 play 76 yard march. A 28 yard pass and run from Matt Cassel to Sammy Morris gave New England a first and goal at the San Diego 1. Then came the key sequence of the game. Cassel threw incomplete way over everyone's heads on a play action pass call on first down. A second down run play was stopped for a loss of a yard; San Diego lineman Jamal Williams blasted center Dan Koppen and knocked him back into Sammy Morris to end that play. A third down pass was thrown into the dirt by Cassel. The Patriots went for the TD on fourth down (a good call in my opinion), and Cassel dropped back to pass. He scrambled due to the rush and good coverage, but missed seeing an open Benjamin Watson who had shaken free. In Cassel's defense, he was scrambling to avoid a sack and had a big defender between him and Watson, so Cassel tried to run it in and was stopped. San Diego took over at the 2 yard line.

Instead of a New England TD that would have made it a game at 17-10, it became 24-3 San Diego as Rivers fired yet another long bomb on second down, this one 59 yards to Vincent Jackson that took the ball to the New England 35 yard line. The play was effortless for San Diego. 'Where was the defense?' Patriot fans must have been wondering again and again. Another Rivers to Jackson pass attempt resulted in a pass interference call on Ellis Hobbs at the goal line and a San Diego first down at the 1. Rivers then threw a 1 yard TD pass to Antonio Gates to cap the 98 yard drive on just 4 plays (4 plays to go 98 yards! Where *was* the defense?). It proved to be the back-breaker for New England. The game was effectively over after that San Diego goal line stand and subsequent 98 yard drive (98 yard stroll might be a more accurate description).

New England finally got into the end zone on a 2 yard run by Sammy Morris with 5:18 to play, making the final 30-10, but this one was out of control early.

The biggest concern to me seemed to be the defense. The defensive line never seemed to pressure Rivers, and the few times that their names were called seemed to be for penalties. The linebackers also did not seem to be making plays, and the defensive backfield had an atrocious game. Belichick and the team would have a lot to work on before their next game, a Monday nighter in Foxboro against the 4-2 Denver Broncos.

Chapter 13 – Bronco Busters

Monday, October 20, 2008:	1	2	3	4		TOTAL
Denver Broncos	0	0	0	7	-	7
New England Patriots	6	14	14	7	-	41

There was plenty of cause for concern going into the Monday night game with Denver. First, Tom Brady had to have a second operation on his knee, this time to remove infection that had set in after the first surgery. Secondly, there was Denver. The Broncos had won 16 of the 19 games played against New England since 1980. Denver coach Mike Shanahan had been a personal nemesis for New England coach Bill Belichick; Shanahan had a 5-2 record against Belichick's Patriots, and Belichick himself, in the week before the game stated, "I don't think there is anyone better than Shanahan is as an offensive game-planner. He creates a lot of problems for any defense."

Denver was coming in with an explosive offense that was the fourth best in the league, led by quarterback Jay Cutler. Denver had scored 166 points in six games, and had the type of long passing game that had caused the Patriots problems against San Diego. Thirdly, there were the Patriots themselves. Their defensive problems had been clear against Miami and San Diego, and their offense had been erratic. Also, Randy Moss had been the subject of some controversy, as some observers and critics claimed that he had been giving less than his best efforts in trying to catch some of Matt Cassel's passes, and that he was giving up on some balls that could have been caught.

It was the 600th Monday Night Football Game, according to ESPN. I remember the first, which paired Joe Namath and the Jets against the Cleveland Browns in 1970, with Keith Jackson, Howard Cosell, and Don Meredith announcing. I remember also the Patriots not being able to host Monday night games for many years, after some rowdiness that occurred after one Monday nighter in Foxboro in 1980. For this Monday night game, the Patriots badly needed a loud and positive home crowd that would stir them to a big win.

A win would also be good for the psyche of New England sports fans, as the Red Sox had been eliminated from their post-season the previous night, with a 3-1 loss in the seventh game of the ALCS. That result sent the Tampa Bay Rays to the World Series and not the defending champion Red Sox. The Red Sox had looked dead earlier in that series, trailing three games to one and trailing 7-0 in the seventh inning of Game 5 before rallying for an 8-7 win. A 4-2 win in Game 6 set up the Game 7 showdown, but it was not to be. New England sports fans turned their hopes to Foxboro and the Patriots' game against the Broncos.

Interestingly, this weekend saw all eight original AFL teams playing each other. On Sunday the Buffalo Bills had beaten the San Diego Chargers 23-14, the Oakland Raiders had defeated the New York Jets in overtime 16-13, and the Tennessee Titans (formerly the Houston Oilers) had defeated the Kansas City Chiefs 34-10. With that win, Tennessee remained the NFL's only unbeaten team in 2008, at 6-0. Now it was time for Broncos-Patriots, the teams that had played the first-ever AFL game back in 1960.

The Patriots suffered another setback before the game when it was announced that running back Laurence Maroney would be out for the season with a shoulder injury. With Lamont Jordan also out with an injury, the running game now consisted of Sammy Morris, Kevin Faulk, and an undrafted rookie from Mississippi with an unusual name, BenJarvus Green-Ellis.

Denver received the opening kickoff and quarterback Jay Cutler injured himself on the first play, a passing play in which his follow-through caused him to hit his right index finger on the helmet of the onrushing Vince Wilfork. The injury plagued him throughout the game. Nevertheless, the Broncos marched down the field with a mixture of passes and running plays. They got one first down on third down pass at the 45, another on a run by Michael Pittman, and were moving effortlessly down the field. It looked as if it would be a long night for New England, but then Denver runner Andre Hall fumbled the ball and New England recovered at their own 32 yard line.

Sammy Morris set the tone for the running game immediately, gaining 8 yards on his first run, 10 on his second, and 5 on his third, bringing the ball to the Denver 45. Cassel then hit a check-down pass to secondary receiver Benjamin Watson for 16 yards down to the 29. Morris gained another 2 yards, but then Matt Cassel was sacked trying to pass. ESPN analyst Tony Kornheiser told us that this was the 20th time that Cassel had been sacked in 2008 already, whereas Tom Brady had been sacked only 20 times in all of 2007. The ESPN announcers felt this was due to Cassel taking longer to look for secondary receivers than Brady, who was particularly skillful in doing so. A Cassel to Wes Welker pass set up a 31 yard field goal by Stephen Gostkowski, so the Patriots had converted the Denver turnover into a 3-0 lead.

Denver drove for two more easy first downs after receiving the next kickoff, but then Hall fumbled again while trying to run down the right sideline. Two Patriots tried to pick up the ball and run in the same motion but were unable to do so. Rookie linebacker Jerod Mayo then fell on the ball and the Patriots had it at the Denver 22. The stare that Mike Shanahan gave Hall as he came to the Denver bench was priceless. If the NFL ever puts on a sketch that requires someone to look like a maniacal killer, Shanahan could easily play the part. A run for no gain and two incompletions led to another field goal by Gostkowski, and the Patriots had a 6-0 lead after one quarter, thanks to those two Denver fumbles.

The Patriots' strong running attack was in play again as the second quarter started. Sammy Morris made three big runs and a short pass from Cassel to Welker got New England to the Bronco 36. However, another sack of Cassel, Denver's third sack of this game thus far, pushed New England out of field goal range and they had to punt.

When New England got the ball back, they drove for a touchdown. Sammy Morris continued his big day with a 33 yard run that gave him 100 yards for the day already, with 8:45 still to go in the first half. With a 4th and 1 from the Denver 4 yard line New England went for it; Sammy Morris ran it in for the game's first touchdown, and a 13-0 New England lead. It was a 56 yard drive in 6 plays and only took 2:35. By the end of this drive Sammy Morris had already accumulated 106 yards rushing on 11 carries. It was the first time in his nine year career with the Bills, Dolphins, and Patriots that Morris had ever run for 100 or more yards in a half.

A deep pass by Cutler was intercepted by Brandon Meriweather and the Patriots had the ball back at their own 16 yard line, but Cassel was sacked again on a play action pass when he was looking for Randy Moss deep. Benjamin Watson was open on a crossing pattern underneath, but Cassel did not see him, accentuating a criticism of Cassel that he does not always see his underneath receivers on a play such as this.

The Patriots did move to the Denver 42 where they had a 4th down and 1. Conventional wisdom would have them punting, but the Patriots have never been one to fall back on conventional wisdom. They went for it, which was a very gutsy call by Belichick. The play was another running play to Sammy Morris to the left side and Morris burst through for 29 yards down to the Denver 13. On the next play Cassel fired a bullet into the end zone to Randy Moss for a touchdown to cap a 9 play, 84 yard drive that took 4:25. The Patriot lead would be 20-0 at halftime.

Just before the half, Patrick Ramsey came in for Cutler, who was still hurting from hitting his finger into Wilfork's helmet on the game's first play from scrimmage. Ramsey completed one pass, and a roughing the passer call against Rodney Harrison – an unnecessary hit after the throw – moved the ball to the New England 42. Ramsey's arm was hit on the next play as he tried to pass, and the ball was intercepted by the Patriots in the Denver backfield, at the 50 yard line. It was the fourth Denver turnover of the first half, and with just seconds remaining, that old conventional wisdom would have the Patriots just take a knee and go into halftime twenty points ahead. But the Patriots wanted more. Cassel went back to pass but was sacked for the fifth time in the game, and the half ended at 20-0.

Halftime ceremonies honored former Patriot linebacker Andre Tippett, who had been inducted earlier in the year into the Pro Football Hall of Fame in Canton, Ohio. Tippett had a very good eleven year career with the Patriots, where, in my opinion, the only linebacker better than him in his time in the league was the incomparable Lawrence Taylor, who revolutionized the game from that position. It was nice to see Tippett's career be acknowledged by the fans.

After halftime, we learned that Sammy Morris had suffered a knee injury and would not return. Morris ended the game with 138 yards rushing on just 16 carries, but the hope was that he would be able to come back and play more this season. His loss to injury in 2007 was a big loss for the Patriots and it would be again if he were lost for any significant time again in 2008.

Wes Welker returned a Denver punt 44 yards to the Bronco 28 yard line, setting up another Patriot TD two plays later. This one was on a nice play call, a wide receiver screen to the left to Randy Moss who was hardly touched as he ran it in from 27 yards out. Moss then did what the announcers called "The Gillette Jump" running to the stands and jumping up to be caught by, and congratulated by, the end zone fans. Moss explained later he decided to do this when he saw a man wearing Vikings' gear including a horned hat and who seemed to have some arm tattoos of Moss from when Randy was with Minnesota. The Gillette Jump was reminiscent of The Lambeau Leap that Packer players often do when scoring a touchdown in Green Bay.

The next Bronco drive was also halted by a turnover, an interception by James Sanders of a pass by Jay Cutler, who had returned to the game for the second half. 80 yards later, after pass completions to Moss of 11 yards, a beautiful pass catch and run by Wes Welker for 27, and a run for 15 by BenJarvus Green-Ellis, the Patriots had another touchdown on a 6 yard TD pass from Cassel to Welker.

The Patriots had a 34-0 lead and were riding high, but on the last play of the third quarter, Rodney Harrison went down with an injury to his right leg. He was down on the ground for a while. In a very poignant scene, teammate and friend Tedy Bruschi came over to talk with him, and when Bruschi went to the sideline, he was seen talking to Belichick in a way that seemed to indicate that the injury was serious. Harrison was eventually taken off on a cart. He almost seemed to be waving goodbye to the fans as he left, and shrugged as if he knew his season, and perhaps his career, may be over, and there was nothing he could do about it. It did not look good.

The fourth quarter was just run-out-the-string time. The Patriot running game continued to be strong as a tough 15 yard run by Kevin Faulk set up a 1 yard TD by Green-Ellis, to complete the scoring in a 41-7 Patriot rout.

The next day we learned that Sammy Morris was day-to-day but that indeed Rodney Harrison would be lost for the season. He had suffered a torn quadriceps muscle in his right leg. Harrison suffered injuries in 2005 and 2006 that had ended those seasons prematurely. The veteran of 15 NFL seasons, who was the only player in NFL history to record both 30 sacks and 30 interceptions in his career, would be facing a long rehab from this injury, so many felt he would retire rather than attempt another comeback. I have felt ambivalent about Harrison, as he seemed often to come in with a late hit on a play (he was, in fact, three times voted the dirtiest player in the league), but he was a team leader, and provided stability in a young defensive secondary. He would definitely be missed.

Chapter 14 – Slamming the Rams

	1	2	3	4	TOTAL
Sunday, October 26, 2008:					
St. Louis Rams	3	7	3	3 -	16
New England Patriots	7	6	0	10 -	23

The St. Louis Rams followed Denver into Foxboro for a second consecutive Patriot home game following the two games in California. St. Louis had lost its first four games of the season, fired Coach Scott Linehan after the fourth loss, and then won their next two games under new head coach Jim Haslett.

The Rams were coming to Foxboro after a big 34-14 win over Dallas. Running back Stephen Jackson had shredded Dallas for 160 yards and three touchdowns before leaving the game with a pulled quadriceps muscle. It was not as bad as the Rodney Harrison injury, so Jackson did expect to play against New England. Quarterback Marc Bulger led a St. Louis passing attack that was still formidable, though not to the extent that the Kurt Warner team had been earlier in the decade.

With Rodney Harrison out, and with the Rams and their vaunted passing attack coming in, the burden fell on Brandon Meriweather and James Sanders to pick up the slack at the safety position.

As if the most recent injuries weren't enough to worry Patriot fans, there were reports that Tom Brady's knee was not healing properly after surgery. The reports indicated that Brady had needed more follow-up procedures than had been previously reported. It was also stated that the surgery may have to be redone. I first learned of this by reading Sports Redux in boston.com, which cited a story by Boston Herald reporter Karen Guregian that Brady had to have three procedures to deal with the infection in the knee from his October 6 surgery. The only light touch on this came from the Sports Redux observation that if Tom Brady was indeed about to propose to Gisele Bundchen, as recent rumors had been indicating, he was just going to have to do it without going down on one knee.

On the Wednesday before the game, the NFL announced that Matt Cassel had been named the AFC Offensive Player of the Week for his work against the Broncos and Stephen Jackson of the Rams had been named NFC Offensive Player of the week for his work against the Cowboys. Jackson, as it turned out, did not play for the Rams in the game against the Patriots because of the injury he had sustained in the Dallas game. On the other side of the field, the Patriots would be starting a makeshift defensive backfield of Deltha O'Neal, Ellis Hobbs, James Sanders, and Brandon Meriweather. On offense, they would have Kevin Faulk and BenJarvus Green-Ellis as their running backs and, of course, Matt Cassel in at quarterback, due to injuries to the expected starters.

The Patriots won the coin toss and deferred their choice to the second half, so the Rams received the opening kick. This move almost backfired immediately for New England, as Ram kick returner Donte Hall took the kickoff back 75 yards to the New England 25 yard line. Luckily, the play was called back due to holding, but that only slightly slowed St. Louis down. The Rams moved effortlessly down the field, even converting a fourth and one at their own 41 yard line (a bold move, but why not for the 2-4 Rams?). A long pass from quarterback Marc Bulger to receiver Donnie Avery put the ball on the New England 9 yard line. Deltha O'Neal was hurt on that play, so the Patriots had to go deeper into their bench and now had Mike Richardson playing defensive back. The drive ended with a 19 yard field goal by Josh Brown, giving St. Louis the early lead.

The Patriots came back quickly. Matt Cassel came out looking very good and very confident. He hit a big 20 yard pass to Wes Welker on a third and 8 on the third New England play from scrimmage, then Welker again on the sixth play, for another big third down conversion. Completions to Moss and Gaffney and two runs by Kevin Faulk set up a 2 yard TD run by Green-Ellis for a 7-3 New England lead at the end of the first quarter.

A 69 yard touchdown bomb from Marc Bulger to Donnie Avery gave the lead back to St. Louis in the second quarter. On the play, Bulger hit Avery deep, and the two Patriot defenders, Ellis Hobbs and James Sanders, collided and knocked each other down at the 25 yard line. With both defenders down, Avery ran untouched the rest of the way to complete the touchdown play.

New England responded with field goals from 30 and 27 yards by Stephen Gostkowski to take a 13-10 lead into halftime. The last field goal was set up by a 30 yard pass from Cassel to Randy Moss. This actually set up one final try for touchdown, but a pass from Cassel into the end zone was knocked out of the hands of Moss (a good play by the Ram defender) with 1 second left in the half. The Patriots had to settle for Gostkowski's field goal as the half ended.

Since the Patriots had deferred the choice after winning the opening coin toss, they were set to receive the kickoff to start the second half. The Rams crossed them up, however, with an on-side kick. It was another gutsy call by the Rams, and it worked. St. Louis recovered the ball. They did not get any points off the maneuver, and had to punt, but quickly got more chances, as the Rams picked off two of Matt Cassel's first six passes of the second half. The first was a long pass intended for Randy Moss that was deflected by either Moss or Ram defender Fakhir Brown into the hands of Ram safety Oshiomogho Atogwe. This set up a tying 44 yard field goal by St. Louis. The second interception came on a pass intended for Wes Welker. Welker fell down, and the ball flew over him into the arms of the same Ram defender, Fakhir Brown, who had contributed to the deflection for the first interception.

On their next possession, the Patriots had a third down and one at the St. Louis 36 yard line, but failed to convert, as Green-Ellis was stopped twice attempting to run for the first down. Bulger immediately went deep for a 44 yard pass to Avery to the New England 20 that set up another Josh Brown field goal. This one, in the fourth quarter, put the Rams back into the lead at 16-13.

Ellis Hobbs returned the St. Louis kickoff from the one yard line to the 50, but the Patriots could not get further and had to punt. On their next series, the Patriots moved to the tying field goal behind a 13 yard run by Kevin Faulk, and a 12 yard pass to Randy Moss. Cassel then tried a pass into the end zone to Randy Moss, and the well-thrown ball did hit Moss in the hands, but Moss dropped it. That set up the field goal from Gostkowski that tied the game at 16 with 8:22 remaining.

Ellis Hobbs hurt his shoulder on the next St. Louis possession. Mike Richardson had also been hurt on a kickoff in the second half, so Deltha O'Neal, who had left the game with his own injury earlier, was pressed back into service in the Patriot defensive backfield.

The Patriots got the ball back at their own 47 yard line with 6:57 to go. After Cassel was sacked for an eight yard loss, he connected with Moss on a big 23 yard gain to get the ball to the St. Louis 38. There were two notable things about that catch: (1) Matt Cassel avoided the St. Louis rush by stepping up into the pocket to make the throw, as we have often seen Tom Brady do, and (2) Moss made the catch over the middle and ran for a few more yards after making the catch, as we had seen Troy Brown do often during his career. The Patriots moved the ball to the 15 yard line, and scored on a nice play from Cassel to Kevin Faulk. As the Patriots came up to the line on that play, Faulk was split out wide to the left. On the snap he faked running a turn-in pattern then cut outside and ran to the left side of the end zone. Cassel threw the pass and Faulk had to turn to his right as he jumped to make the catch, and then turned back around and came down with the ball in the end zone. It was a touchdown and the Patriots now had a 23-16 lead.

There was just 3:13 left on the clock as the Rams got the ball, but they drove to the New England 33 where a Bulger pass down the right sideline was picked off by Deltha O'Neal at the 16 yard line. O'Neal ran it back inside the Ram 40 yard line. Three kneel-downs by the Patriots and three timeouts by the Rams resulted in a New England punt with 19 seconds to go. The punt went deep into the end zone, but Ram returner Donte Hall inexplicably caught it and ran around for a few seconds in the end zone, before running out of the back of the end zone. This error by Hall left Bulger and the Rams with only 5 seconds left, and when a last, desperation pass-lateral play failed before it even became worrisome for New England fans, the Pats had escaped with a 23-16 win. With Buffalo losing to Miami, the Patriots had now tied the Bills at the top of the AFC East with 5-2 records.

The stars of the game for New England were Matt Cassel, who was 21 of 33 for 267 yards, receivers Randy Moss and Wes Welker who each caught 7 passes (Moss for 102 yards, Welker for 79), and all-purpose runner/receiver/returner Kevin Faulk, who gained 60 yards rushing on 13 carries, and also caught 4 passes for 47 yards. Bill Belichick praised Faulk in his post-game comments, saying "It seems like you can always count on Kevin, no matter what phase of the game it is in."

Chapter 15 – A Rough One to Drop

Sunday, November 2, 2008:	1	2	3	4		TOTAL
New England Patriots	0	6	6	3	-	15
Indianapolis Colts	7	0	8	3	-	18

The words "rough" and "drop" in the title above are parts of key phrases that describe this loss to Indianapolis. The primary turning points were a key unnecessary roughness penalty against the Patriots that killed one drive and a big dropped pass that turned what should have been a go-ahead touchdown into a tying field goal. It was a good game to watch, but a tough loss to swallow.

- - -

In the week preceding the game, a game that should have been a big showdown with the Indianapolis Colts, a couple of interesting things happened:

- The Colts lost to the Titans, dropping their record to a surprising 3-4; it was as if the Colts, and not the Patriots, had lost their All-Everything quarterback.

- Vince Wilfork was summoned to New York to meet with Commissioner Roger Goodell to discuss what a league spokesman said was a "pattern of dirty play". This stemmed from an elbow that Wilfork was said to have thrown into the head of Denver quarterback Jay Cutler two weeks previously. However, there had been enough other incidents in the past that warranted this summons. One that sticks in my mind was an elbow to the knee of Buffalo QB J.P. Losman in Game 1 of the 2007 season that knocked Losman out of the game and really did look like a cheap shot. He was fined for that, and also for poking the eye of Giants' running back Brandon Jacobs, a late hit on Cowboy tight end Jason Witten, and other infractions. He was fined a reported $ 35,000 for this latest infraction.

- A number of Patriot players and officials were in attendance on the opening night of the Boston Celtics' season on Tuesday, October 28, as the Celtics raised their 2008 championship banner and received their rings. Among the Patriots reported to have attended were Bob and Myra Kraft, Matt Cassel, Kevin Faulk, Sammy Morris, Adalius Thomas, Heath Evans, Benjamin Watson, and Ty Warren. It continues to be nice to see players and officials from the Red Sox, Patriots, and Celtics attending each other's events and supporting one another.

- The Philadelphia Phillies won the World Series over the Tampa Bay Rays. The deciding game was started on Monday, suspended by rain, and then concluded on Wednesday. It was an odd way to end the World Series.

The Patriots-Colts game on this Sunday night did not have the same feel of previous games between these two teams. For one thing, they were not the same powerhouses they had been in preceding years. The Colts were 3-4 and the Patriots were 5-2, not the undefeated records that they had brought into their battle one year earlier. For another, this was the first time the teams would play in the Colts' new home, Lucas Oil Stadium. They would play with an open roof, so the sound that had so often been a factor against the Patriots in the old Hoosier Dome (also known as the RCA Dome), would not be so in this game. Lastly, with Tom Brady out, the usual Brady-Manning showdown would not be part of the game. It was as if Bill Russell were injured and unavailable for a game in which the Celtics would be facing Wilt Chamberlain.

The Colts still had Peyton Manning, though, so they were still a very dangerous team. The Brady-Manning battles had been epics, with the Patriots winning 7 of the 10 games in which these two matched up:

9/30/01	H	New England	44-13	
10/21/01	A	New England	38-17	
11/30/03	A	New England	38-34	
1/18/04	H	New England	24-14	playoffs
9/9/04	H	New England	27-24	
1/16/05	H	New England	20-3	playoffs
11/7/05	H	Indianapolis	40-21	
11/5/06	H	Indianapolis	27-20	
1/21/07	A	Indianapolis	38-34	playoffs
11/4/07	A	New England	24-20	

This would be the first Matt Cassel - Peyton Manning battle.

- - -

Earlier in the day the Tennessee Titans had remained undefeated at 8-0 with a 19-16 win over Green Bay in overtime. The Jets had also defeated the Bills, so a Patriot win would put them alone in first place in the AFC East. A Colt win would put them back at .500 at 4-4 and in the playoff chase.

The Colts won the opening coin toss and received the kickoff, but went three and out and punted, as did the Patriots on their first possession of the game. The New England punt by Chris Hanson was a booming 64 yarder that pinned the Colts back to their own 9 yard line. The Colts then proceeded on a 91 yard drive to a touchdown. They looked like the Colts of old, not the ones with a 3-4 record this season. The drive lasted 9 minutes and 2 seconds and ended with a 12 yard touchdown pass from Manning to Anthony Gonzalez.

The drive highlighted one positive for the Patriots and one very huge negative. The positive was that they stopped the Colt running game cold. The negative was that they were putting absolutely no pressure on Manning whenever he dropped back to throw. It was a pattern that would last the entire game.

The 9:02 drive ate up much of a fast-moving first quarter. The Patriots got the ball back with 2:18 left in the quarter and started a long drive of their own. This one lasted 6:58 and resulted in a Stephen Gostkowski field goal from 29 yards out to cut the Colt lead to 7-3.

Rookie cornerback Terrence Wheatley became the latest casualty in the Patriot secondary on the very first play on the next Indianapolis drive. Manning threw a pass 30 yards downfield to Marvin Harrison, but Wheatley and Harrison jumped up and the pass was deflected incomplete. As Wheatley came down, he landed hard on his hand, and left the field and headed into the locker room. Deltha O'Neal replaced him. Two good tackles by the always-reliable Mike Vrabel led to an Indy punt, and the Patriots converted that into another Gostkowski field goal, from 32 yards, that made it a one point game at 7-6. During the Patriots' drive to the field goal, NBC announcer Al Michaels commented on the unusual name of Patriot rookie runner BenJarvus Green-Ellis, saying that the team calls him "Law Firm". It is the first time I had heard the nickname, but it is a clever one.

The first half had an unusual ending. Manning had the Colts moving down the field and, with 19 seconds left on the clock and no timeouts remaining for Indianapolis, completed a pass to the sideline to Marvin Harrison. However, Harrison did not get out of bounds so the clock kept running. At least it should have. It did not. The clock on the field and on the TV screen still showed 19 seconds as Manning got his team to the line and tried to spike the ball to stop the clock. The clock still showed 19 seconds. Luckily the official who keeps the official clock had it right, and the Colts were also called for a false start, so by rule, 10 seconds were run off the clock and the half was over. Citing the clock not starting when it should have, Al Michaels said of the penalty and run off of the last 10 seconds "that's justice", and he was right.

Interestingly, the penalty on the last play of the first half was the only penalty of the half, as both teams were playing very good, clean, and disciplined football.

The Patriots had the ball to start the second half, and, just as they did so often in 2007, got a great drive to a score to open the half. This was a 72 yard, 7:48 drive that lasted 15 plays and, obviously, took more than half the time off the third quarter clock. The key play on the drive was a third down draw play to Kevin Faulk that gained a first down. Matt Cassel also completed third down passes to Moss and Welker for first downs, and ran for a first down himself on another third down play. Green-Ellis got the touchdown on a 6 yard run.

With a 12-7 lead in a fast-moving game, Belichick also opted to try for two points and a full one touchdown, seven point, lead. The handoff went to Faulk who appeared to get the ball over the end line for the two points as he was tackled, but officials ruled that it had not crossed the end line, so the score remained 12-7.

A key decision on the touchdown drive, and a big one for the game, was Bill Belichick challenging a ruling. Belichick felt that the Colts had 12 men on the field on one play, a first and ten, claiming that a Colt player was trying to get off the field but did not do so before the snap. The replay did not prove that to be the case, so the Patriots forfeited one timeout. Matt Cassel called another, so the Patriots were very quickly down to only one timeout early in the second half. Challenging this call on a first and ten seemed a little unnecessary to me (and NBC announcers Al Michaels and John Madden said the same thing). Losing this timeout would come back to haunt the Patriots.

Once again, after the kickoff to Indianapolis, the Patriots were not able to generate any pressure on Peyton Manning, so Manning easily marched the Colts down the field for a 9 yard touchdown pass to Gonzalez. Indianapolis tried for the two point conversion to go up by a field goal and they did convert it on a Manning pass to Reggie Wayne, so the Colts had a 15-12 lead.

The Patriots took off on what would be another time-consuming drive that started in the third quarter and ended in the fourth. Late in the third quarter, with the ball on the Colts' 40 yard line, Matt Cassel tried one of the few long passes the Pats would attempt in the game. The play worked perfectly, with Cassel hitting a wide open Jabar Gaffney as Gaffney streaked down the left sideline past two Colt defenders, but Gaffney dropped the ball. Replays showed that it went right through Gaffney's hands. It was a "perfect pass", as John Madden indicated on the telecast. It should have been caught. Instead a sure touchdown was lost.

As the fourth quarter began, New England got a first down after the Gaffney miscue, thanks to a third down slant-in throw from Cassel to Randy Moss that took the ball to the Indianapolis 26. The drive continued to a 4th down and one at the seven. The Patriots lined up to go for the first down. As they were set to snap, Bill Belichick came running down the sideline to call timeout. The play was run, and Cassel appeared to have gotten the first down on a quarterback sneak, but officials ruled that the play had been stopped before the snap to grant Belichick the timeout.

When the telecast returned from commercial, I, Al Michaels, John Madden, and others were surprised to see the Patriots lining up for a field goal and not to go for the first down. The others who were surprised included Dale Arnold and Scott Zolak, the hosts of a WEEI radio show the next morning, and other fans with whom I spoke. The field goal by Gostkowski was good, and the score was now tied at 15, but it seemed that a golden opportunity had been lost. It would have been nice to have had the confidence shown in the offense to go for the first down and it would have been very nice to have had that 15 play drive conclude in a touchdown, but it was not to be.

Additionally, the timeout by Belichick was New England's last timeout of the second half. With 11:33 left to go in the game, the Pats were out of timeouts, and could not challenge any call. It was a huge loss that would become even more so as the game wound to the final gun.

In what seemed like no time at all, but actually took 3:28, Manning moved the Colts down for a long field goal attempt by former Patriot Adam Vinatieri. It would be a 52 yard attempt. An NBC graphic informed us that Vinatieri had not made a field goal of over 50 yards in 91 games, or about 5 ½ seasons (which would have meant that his last one had come when he was kicking for the Patriots). He had missed 7 field goals of 50+ yards in those 91 games. However, Vinatieri is still Mr. Clutch when it comes to kicking, so he drilled the kick high over the crossbar and right down the middle to give the Colts an 18-15 lead.

Matt Cassel moved the Patriots back down the field, when the key play of the game happened. On a third and two, the Patriots gave it to Green-Ellis who got it close to a first down. After the whistle blew, Patriot tight end David Thomas inexplicably ran a few yards and knocked down a Colt defender. He was called for an unnecessary roughness penalty. Since the penalty occurred after the play, officials had to measure to see whether Green-Ellis had made the first down. If he had, it would be a first and 25. If not, it would be a third and 16. He had not made a first down. The Patriots got nothing on third down, and so were faced with a 4th and 16. Since they had used up all their timeouts, and since the penalty had moved the ball back out of field goal range, the Patriots were forced to go for it. A pass from Cassel was intercepted at the 25 yard line, so the Colts had the ball.

Three running plays by the Colts ate up a lot of time, since with no timeouts the Patriots could not stop the clock. When Indianapolis punted, the Patriots took over, but there were only 21 seconds left in the game. Cassel threw deep for Moss but it was incomplete; 14 seconds now remained. Cassel threw deep for Gaffney but it was incomplete; 9 seconds now remained. Cassel then threw short to Moss who ran it to the Indianapolis 39 yard line, and then tried unsuccessfully to lateral the ball to another Patriot to try to keep the play going, but it did not work. The game was over.

- - -

This was a game that ended in a disappointing fashion. The Colts played well, but the Patriots had made too many mistakes to win it. In recent years it had been the Patriots who had forced other teams to make mistakes that determined the outcome of games; tonight the Patriots did it to themselves. In descending order of importance, the keys to this game were

1. The unnecessary roughness penalty on Dave Thomas
2. The dropped pass by Gaffney that would have been a TD
3. No pressure on Manning by the defensive line
4. The Patriots' use of timeouts in the 2nd half
5. No deep passing game for New England

with #1 and #2 being the most important factors.

The Patriots were now in a three-way tie with the Bills and Jets for the AFC East lead at 5-3, with the Dolphins 1 game behind at 4-4.

It was a game that could have been won, or maybe one that should not have been lost, at least not lost the way it was.

Chapter 16 – Controlling Those Bills

Sunday, November 9, 2008:	1	2	3	4		TOTAL
Buffalo Bills	0	3	0	7	-	10
New England Patriots	7	3	3	7	-	20

Two days after the Patriots-Colts game was an extremely significant event in U.S. history. On November 4, 2008, Senator Barack Obama was elected President of the United States. Whether you voted for Obama, John McCain, Ralph Nader, Bob Barr, or any other candidate, it was an interesting and historical outcome. Obama became the first person of African-American descent to be elected President, and the news reverberated not just around the country, but around the world.

A huge crowd showed up at Grant Park in Chicago for the victory celebration and for the post-election speech by President-Elect Obama. The TV pictures showed Oprah Winfrey and Jesse Jackson with tears in their eyes. A later shot of Oprah showed her with tears in her eyes leaning her head on the shoulder of a Caucasian man next to her. I do not usually watch her show, but I did the next day to see if it was about the election and stayed with it when it was. Oprah said she had gotten e-mails from around the country asking her who the man was, and she said "I don't know." Apparently, she was so overwhelmed that she just instinctively leaned on this man's shoulder. She did say "Thank you, Mr. Man" to him on her show.

The Oprah story is iconic of the overall awesome sight of the diversity in the crowds at Grant Park - white and black, young and old, men and women - all there to celebrate a great victory and a new beginning. The diversity was great to see. THAT is America.

- - -

In Foxboro, the Patriots were continuing their preparations for a three week period in which they would play all of their AFC East rivals. The Buffalo Bills would be first. The Patriots had an overall 55-40-1 record against Buffalo, had won the last nine meetings between the two teams, and 14 of the last 15. The only loss in that stretch was the 31-0 season opener in 2003, the Sunday following the release of Lawyer Milloy, as described earlier in this book. However, the 2008 Buffalo team was a far better one than the teams which had faced the Patriots in recent years.

- - -

Since all NFL teams had played at least eight games, there were a number of mid-season NFL reports, with some interesting opinions. On Comcast Sportsnet, reporters picked the first half MVP's for the Patriots. The player selected as offensive MVP was Kevin Faulk. The player selected as defensive MVP was Richard Seymour. I agreed with the Kevin Faulk choice, and while Seymour was having his best season in a while, the lack of pressure that the defense has been putting on any quarterback, and the patchwork defensive backfield made it hard to choose a defensive player.

The mid-season predictions of *Sports Illustrated* included the Patriots winning the AFC East and being the third seed in the AFC playoffs, behind the Titans and Steelers. It went on to predict a Patriot win over the Colts in the first round and a loss to the Steelers in the second round. It predicted the Giants over the Titans in the Super Bowl. Of the Patriots, *Sports Illustrated* said, "The Brady-less Patriots play solid on defense and avoid mistakes on offense. Still, they're going to need more from Matt Cassel down the stretch. He's thrown only one TD pass in four road starts."

The *Sporting News* summary of the Patriots at mid-season stated, "Matt Cassel is playing better at quarterback, but the aging linebackers and makeshift secondary are big concerns."

- - -

New England controlled this game almost from the start. Once again they won the opening toss, deferred the choice to the second half and kicked off. After a touchback on the opening kick, Buffalo gained 7 yards on a first down run, but then had to punt after pressure from the Patriots on Bills' quarterback Trent Edwards resulted in an incompletion and a sack. It was good to see the Pats pressure a quarterback, especially after Peyton Manning had not been pressured at all in the previous game. It was even better to see that pressure continue throughout the entire game. The Bills wound up with only 168 yards of offense and had the ball for only 22:20, running 43 plays to New England's 78.

The Patriots took over the ball at their own 28 and drove it downfield for the only touchdown of the first half. New England caught a break on a key pass to Wes Welker that took the ball down to the Buffalo 17. It appeared that Welker had come down with the toe of his second foot stepping out of bounds, which would have made the pass incomplete, but the pass was called complete by the officials on the field. Buffalo did not call for a replay review in time, though, so the play stood as a completion, as called on the field. A couple of plays later, Matt Cassel dropped back to pass from the 13 yard line, but then saw an opening and ran straight up the middle and into the end zone standing up for the touchdown.

Three series later, the Patriots intercepted a pass from Edwards to Lee Evans that was overthrown over Evans' head, and the Patriots took over at the Buffalo 34. A play later the first quarter ended, but the Patriots were able to convert the turnover into points in the second quarter on a 32 yard field goal by Stephen Gostkowski.

Buffalo came back with their only sustained drive of the day, moving on 10 plays to a first and goal at the Patriot 10. The drive stopped there, and the Bills had to settle for a 25 yard field goal by Rian Lindell. There was no more scoring in the first half, so the teams headed to the locker room with New England holding a 10-3 lead.

As has so often been the case in recent years, the Patriots took the opening kickoff of the second half and took it for a lengthy drive for a score. This was a 13 play drive that ended with a 37 yard field goal by Gostkowski to push the lead to 13-3. This was the 21st drive of 10 plays or more by the Patriots this season, tops in the NFL. Also on this drive, Wes Welker caught his 6th pass of the game, thus becoming the first player in NFL history with 6 or more catches in each of his first 9 games of a season. The sixth catch in this game was a big 12 yard reception on a third and 1 that kept the drive alive.

A Deltha O'Neal interception with :35 to go in the third quarter thwarted another Buffalo drive. BenJarvus Green-Ellis raced for over 10 yards on the first play after the turnover, but as the fourth quarter began, the Patriots lost a chance to convert the turnover into more points. A pass from Cassel to Jabar Gaffney bounced off Gaffney's arms into the air, but disaster was averted as the ball luckily fell incomplete. The turnover was averted for only one play, however, as Cassel fumbled the ball on the next play and Buffalo recovered.

A Buffalo punt five plays later pinned the Patriots back to their 7 yard line, with 11:05 to go. This was when the Patriots took complete control of the game. Buffalo did not get the ball back until after the two minute warning, as the Patriots went on a beautiful 9:08 drive that took 19 plays (plus a 20th that was a penalty). It was almost a lesson in how to close out a game. The drive's plays consisted of:

1. Kevin Faulk 1 yard run

2. Cassel long pass to Moss overthrown/incomplete (at this point in the game, the Patriots had called a perfectly balanced game, with 29 running plays and 29 passing plays)
3. Cassel 28 yard completion to Sam Aiken for a first down
4. Green-Ellis 5 yard run with a nice block by pulling guard Logan Mankins
5. Flanker screen from Cassel to Welker for 9 yards and a first down at the 42 (Welker's 9th catch of the game, accounting for 96 yards)
6. Green-Ellis 1 yard run
7. Cassel to Gaffney for 8 yards to make it 3rd and 1; timeout New England with exactly 7:00 to go in the game
8. Heath Evans 3 yard run to the 46 for a first down
9. Green-Ellis 13 yard run down to the 33 (95 yards rushing for Green-Ellis thus far in the game)
10. Cassel pass to Green-Ellis incomplete
11. Cassel to Welker for 12 yards to the 21 and another first down
12. Green-Ellis 1 yard run to the 20; Buffalo timeout with 5:01 to go in the game
13. Green-Ellis 1 yard run to the 19; Buffalo timeout with 4:56 left
14. Cassel to Gaffney for 11 yards and a first down at the 8 (the drive thus far had been 7 runs and 7 passes)
15. Green-Ellis 1 yard run; Buffalo timeout with 4:02 remaining
16. Green-Ellis 3 yard run to the 4 yard line; it was his 25th carry of the game for 104 yards, the first 100 yard rushing game of his career
17. Green-Ellis 3 yard run to the 1, setting up what could have been a 4th and goal, but Buffalo was called for holding so it was an automatic first down for New England
18. Quarterback sneak by Cassel, not enough, 2nd down
19. Quarterback sneak by Cassel, not enough, 3rd down, two minute warning. CBS announcers Dick Enberg and Randy Cross were wondering if New England was more interested in running the plays into the line to keep the clock running than in scoring.
20. Green-Ellis 1 yard run through the left side of the line for a touchdown and a 20-3 lead with 1:57 to go

It was an outstanding drive that effectively ended the game. Buffalo got a quick touchdown afterward thanks to an 85 yard kickoff return (Jonathan Wilhite preventing the touchdown with a nice tackle at the 14 yard line) followed by a 14 yard TD pass from Edwards to James Hardy, but it was too little too late, and the Patriots walked off the field with a 20-10 win.

Matt Cassel wound up completing 23 passes in 34 attempts for 234 yards. BenJarvus Green-Ellis wound up with 26 carries for 105 yards. We learned during this game that Green-Ellis' mother calls him "Benny", as we continued to learn more and more about this undrafted rookie who had become the Patriots' running game. One big down note was an injury to Adalius Thomas. It was reported later to be a broken arm that would end his season, yet another big blow to a season that already had had too many season-ending injuries to too many key players.

The Patriots now had a very short week to prepare for a Thursday night battle in Foxboro with the New York Jets. It would be a battle for first place in the AFC East, as the Jets and Dolphins both won on Sunday, the Jets blasting the Rams 47-3, the biggest blowout in Jets' history, and the Dolphins defeating Seattle 21-19. Another winner on this weekend was undefeated Tennessee, which raised its record to 9-0 with a 21-14 win over the Bears in Chicago. The Patriots and Jets were now tied for the AFC East lead with 6-3 records, with the Bills and Dolphins one game behind at 5-4. Every team in the division had a winning record.

- - -

Even though it was a very short week before the Thursday night game, there were still a number of things to report.

Damien Woody had been with the Patriots from 1999 to 2003 and had played on two Super Bowl winning teams. After the 2003 season, he signed as a free agent with the Detroit Lions. This was the type of move that is hard to understand. The Patriots were defending Super Bowl champions and had a chance not only to repeat the following year (they did), but be a contender for years to come. The Lions had been a bad team for many years, and the outlook was not at all promising for the future.

Most players say that they want to play for championships and for the possibility of going to the Hall of Fame when their careers are over. Being a starter on a Super Bowl contender like the Patriots, as Woody was, could fulfill both goals. Playing on the Lions would make both unlikely. Money must have been an issue, but when you are making what professional athletes are making these days, you would think the chance to play for a championship while earning X amount of dollars would be more important than earning a relatively little more than X at a place with no playoff hopes.

The move was similar to another baffling one made by another player in the 1990s. Alvin Harper had been a starting receiver on the Dallas Cowboys team that would win three Super Bowls in that decade. It was a team with Troy Aikman, Emmitt Smith, Michael Irvin, and a host of good players. Yet Harper, a starter, opted to sign as a free agent in 1994 with the Tampa Bay Buccaneers, a team going nowhere.

I felt at the time that Harper was making a bad move, that he would be hardly heard from again, and that indeed was the case.

After four years in Detroit, in which the Lions posted records of 6-10, 5-11, 3-13, and 7-9, Woody signed with the New York Jets in March 2008 for a chance to play for a contender again. After the Jets' lopsided 47-3 win over the Rams on the Sunday before their Thursday night showdown with the Patriots, Woody was finally heard from again. He was quoted as saying the Jets needed "to get that swagger where we play this kind of football every week". If he had stayed with the Patriots, he would have been with a team that did play with that level of confidence every week.

The Jets also made a move in the three days preceding the Thursday night game, signing former Patriot defensive back Ty Law to a contract. This continued a pattern in which the Jets continually signed players and coaches who had previously been with the Patriots (Woody, Law, Curtis Martin, Tom Tupa, Ray Lucas, Hank Poteat, Bill Parcells, Bill Belichick, Al Groh, Eric Mangini, and so on), hoping both to tweak the Patriots and to try to have some of New England's success rub off on them. It was what the Red Sox used to do in signing former Yankee players and managers (like Joe McCarthy in the 1940s, Mike Torrez in the 1970s, and others), until they finally built their own team in the 21st century. It was odd to see it go the other way in the NFL.

The big win by the Jets against the Rams allowed them to rest many of their starters in the second half of that game, in preparation for the short week leading into the Thursday game. When Bill Belichick was asked at his post-game press conference after the 20-10 win over Buffalo about not being able to rest his starters, Belichick, a coach's coach, seemed very annoyed to be asked the question. He responded very pointedly, saying, "We are trying to win the game. We are trying to beat the Buffalo Bills. They are a good football team. They are 5-3. We are trying to win the game. We are not trying to rest anybody. It is the Buffalo Bills. They are 5-3. We are playing for first place. You don't rest when you are playing for first place."

He was right of course. In contrast, in a key game in the AL pennant race in September 2008, the second place Boston Red Sox were playing the first place Tampa Bay Rays with first place on the line; the Tampa Bay lead in the division had been cut to ½ game, and the Red Sox had a chance to take over the division lead with a win. Nevertheless, Red Sox manager Terry Francona decided not to play David Ortiz in that game. While it is true that the Red Sox would be facing a tough lefthanded pitcher, Scott Kazmir, this was a game against the team that the Red Sox were trailing and trying to catch, in a battle for first place. Francona explained that he wanted to rest Ortiz, but then wound up using Ortiz as a pinch-hitter in the seventh inning, after Kazmir left, and Ortiz wound up with two at bats for the game, instead of the four or five he would normally have had. The Red Sox lost this game by one run, never got back to first place, and wound up losing to Tampa Bay in seven games in the ALCS, where Tampa Bay had home field advantage, in part due to the win in that September game. Baseball is obviously a different game than football, but I doubt that Belichick would have made any kind of similar move in a game that his team was playing with first place on the line.

Of course, with the way his offense dominated the fourth quarter against Buffalo, most of Belichick's defensive starters did get a lot of time to rest in the fourth quarter anyway.

Chapter 17 – No D in OT = Missed Opportunity

Thursday, November 13, 2008: **1** **2** **3** **4** **OT** **TOTAL**
New York Jets   **10** **14** **0** **7**   **3 - 34**
New England Patriots   **3** **10** **8** **10** ***** - **31**
*** - never got the ball in overtime*

It was a battle for first place in the AFC East that the Jets won in overtime, 34-31.

It was also a roller coaster of a game with many highs and lows for both teams, but especially for New England, for whom the loss was a heart-breaker.

However, the loss was a well-deserved one, as, by my count, the Patriots only played well for 23 of the game's 68 minutes, the last two minutes of the first half, the fifteen minutes of the third quarter, the first five minutes of the fourth quarter, and the last minute of regulation. Having played well for less than half of the game, the Patriots didn't deserve to win, but they could have and almost did.

The defense especially played badly. With the exception of rookie linebacker Jerod Mayo, who played a great game from start to finish, the Patriot defense as a whole played only one good quarter, the third. They could not stop the Jets in the first quarter, second quarter, fourth quarter, or overtime.

Perhaps the biggest play of the game came on the Jets' third play in overtime. It was a third and 15 from the Jet 15 yard line. So a stop on this play would result in a Jet punt, and most likely good field position for the offense. But on the third and 15, the Patriot defense did not put pressure on Brett Favre and left tight end Dustin Keller wide open for a 16 yard reception and a first down. The Jets were able to keep the ball and in fact kept it for nearly eight minutes, as they continued an easy march to the game-winning field goal.

This failure to stop the Jets on a big third down and 15 continued a maddening pattern for the Patriots' defense. Even though the team had been very successful over the years, they had shown an alarming tendency to give up first downs on plays like this. For you math-inclined fans, it seems on big third and X yards to go plays the Patriots give up X+Y yards, where Y < 5, more than a good team should. For more evidence of that, refer to the Eli Manning drive in the

Super Bowl, or the Peyton Manning drive in the 2006 AFC championship.

Also, as was the case in those Peyton and Eli Manning references, Brett Favre looked like a beaten quarterback when the Patriots tied the score with only a second to go in regulation and the game went into OT. As was also the case, the Patriot defense could not get the stop they needed to win the game (the 2006 AFC Championship or the Super Bowl) or to give the offense the ball and a chance to win (this game).

But, we get ahead of ourselves. Let's look back on what happened earlier in the game.

New England kicked off. Unlike many of his kickoffs in the 2008 season, the kick was not deep into the end zone, and the Jets returned it to the 38 yard line.

The first play was a 13 yard run by Thomas Jones, and the tone was set. The Jets kept the ball for 10 plays on a 62 yard march to an opening touchdown and a 7-0 lead, as the Patriot defense could not stop the Jets. A big play on this drive was a pass to Lavernius Coles that was originally ruled incomplete but the call was overturned after a challenge by Jets' coach Eric Mangini. It was on one of those third and X plays in which the Jets got X+Y yards, as referenced above. So instead of getting the ball on a punt, the Patriots wound up giving up seven points.

The Patriots returned the next kickoff to their 31 and got a nice catch by Benjamin Watson for a first down at the 49 on a third and 1. A long pass by Cassel was way overthrown, but a third and 9 bullet pass to Jabar Gaffney got the ball to the Jet 31, and the drive ended with a 42 yard field goal by Stephen Gostkowski.

Again the Jets took the kickoff out past the 30 and again marched effortlessly down the field, at one point getting 12 on a third and 6 (OK, Y was > 5 on this play, but you know what I mean). They also successfully ran that gadget "wildcat" play that the Dolphins had run so successfully against the Patriots where Favre lined up left and Brad Smith took the snap and ran for 17 yards from the New England 22 to a first and goal at the five. Two incomplete passes by the Jets, with no pressure being applied by the Patriot defensive line (one incompletion was a dropped pass in the end zone by the New York receiver) led to a field goal and a 10-3 Jets' lead. After the series, the TV cameras showed Jerod Mayo being taken to the locker room. It looked as if he had been injured too.

The Patriots responded with a nice drive for a field goal to open the second quarter. Matt Cassel scrambled for one first down, Heath Evans bulled his way to another on a third and one, and Cassel hit Faulk for 19 yards to the Jet 13 before the drive fizzled and New England had to settle for three points. A graphic shown on the NFL Network which was broadcasting the game let us know that Matt Cassel had the lowest percentage of TD passes from the red zone in the NFL.

The Patriots immediately gave back those points and more as Gostkowski's kickoff was fielded by Leon Washington at the 8 yard line and he ran untouched 92 yards for a touchdown. It was 17-6 Jets and things looked bleak for New England.

They looked even bleaker after the next Jet drive. Though Jerod Mayo was back in the game, the Patriot defense again could not stop the Jets, as Favre hit receiver Jericho Cotchery on three big passes of 18, 46, and 15 yards, the last for a touchdown and a 24-6 New York lead. It looked like a rout was on.

The Jets hit a looping kick for the ensuing kickoff, and the ball bounced past several Patriots before one of them jumped back onto it at the 14 yard line. The Patriots were able to move the ball, as Cassel hit Watson with a pass to the 27 and then hit Sam Aiken on a screen that Aiken ran for 43 yards to the New York 30 yard line. Aiken then dropped a pass, and Cassel scrambled for 9 yards, setting up a third and 1. A Heath Evans run was stuffed for a two yard loss, and Patriot center Dan Koppen was hurt on the play as Evans ran into his elbow. Koppen had to leave and he too went into the locker room for treatment. The Patriots went for it on fourth and three but Cassel was sacked back at the 30, so the Jets took over.

The Patriot defense held the Jets (finally!), so New York punted with 1:51 to go in the half and the Patriots took over at their 32. Cassel completed two passes to Gaffney for 11 and 8 yards, and then scrambled for 19 yards down to the Jet 30. Cassel then hit Watson to the 21 and got a first down on a quarterback sneak on 4th and one, and then hit Gaffney with a 19 yard touchdown pass with 15 seconds to go in the half. It was a nice read by Cassel, as the Jets had double coverage on Moss on the left and also had Welker double covered in the slot, leaving single coverage on Gaffney. The TD at least made it a game at 24-13 going into halftime.

The Patriots dominated the third quarter, but critical mistakes kept them from taking the lead. They got the second half kickoff at the 21, and Dan Koppen was back in the game as they started the drive. They did so by going into the no-huddle offense, and it worked with three completions and a good run by Kevin Faulk, but Benjamin Watson fumbled the ball at the Jets' 20 after a completion, and the Jets recovered to end that drive.

At this point the Patriot defense showed some signs of life and sacked Favre twice, so the Patriots took over at their 35. The Patriots blew their second chance to get back into the game as a ball snapped from shotgun formation sailed right past Matt Cassel. The ball bounced well back and by the time the play ended, the Patriots had lost 23 yards, effectively ending that drive. TV announcer Bob Papa stated, "the Patriots keep shooting themselves in the foot." He was right.

The mistakes continued on the next drive, as Gaffney dropped a pass on third and 1 so the Patriots had to punt.

The Patriots finally converted on their next possession, with Cassel scrambling (a recurring theme for this game) behind the line before firing a pass to Wes Welker for a 29 yard completion. A 10 yard touchdown pass to Benjamin Watson on the last play of the third quarter, followed by a Cassel to Gaffney pass for the two point conversion, made the score 24-21 Jets as the fourth quarter began.

Ellis Hobbs was shaken up on the kickoff return and had to sit out one play. A Jet fumble gave the ball back to New England at the New England 40 yard line. Matt Cassel scrambled for one first down at the Jet 37 but then badly overthrew an open Randy Moss on a deep pass to the left, so Stephen Gostkowski tied the game on a 47 yard field goal.

The Patriot defense had been good in the third quarter, but now gave up another long drive to the Jets. This one lasted 7:06 and 14 plays. The Jets marched easily to the seven yard line, and did not make a first down or TD as a third down pass was incomplete. However, a holding penalty was called on Mike Vrabel and that gave the Jets a first and goal at the three. The holding call was questionable, as unbiased NFL Network broadcast analyst Chris Collinsworth pointed out as the replay was shown. Another defensive holding penalty on the Patriots, this one called on James Sanders, gave the Jets another first down at the 1, and Thomas Jones ran in for a gift TD that put the Jets back up 31-24 with 3:10 to go.

The Patriots got the ball but two incompletions sandwiched around a sack forced them to punt. They got the ball back on their own 38 with 1:04 left after a Jets punt, and Matt Cassel led them on a big clutch drive to the tying touchdown. He hit Watson for nine yards and then hit him again for another nine, before spiking it to stop the clock. He then completed a pass to Wes Welker down to the New York 25 and spiked it again to stop the clock. A false start penalty moved New

England back to the 30, but then Cassel completed another pass to Welker down to the 16 and spiked the ball to stop the clock with only eight seconds left in the game. It was fourth and one so this was a big play, possibly the last play in the game. Cassel came out again in the shotgun, as he had for most of the night. The Jets had been lining up on the line against Randy Moss for most of the game, but this time Ty Law was defending him, and backed away from Moss at the line. The ball was snapped, and Cassel had to scramble again to avoid an on-rushing Jet defender. He scrambled to his right and fired a tight spiral to the right front corner of the end zone, near the pylon, toward Randy Moss. Moss was practically being mugged by Ty Law on the play, but he dove to his left and caught the ball for the touchdown with only 1 second remaining on the clock. The play was reviewed to see if Moss had possession and both feet in bounds. Replays showed that he had! The extra point tied the game and sent it into overtime.

It was a great comeback by New England. They had been 18 points down in the first half and looked as if they were going to be soundly beaten. They were 7 points down with just over a minute to go, and Cassel engineered a clutch drive to tie it. Favre and the Jets looked shocked on the sidelines, as if they didn't know what hit them.

As the captains came out for the overtime coin toss, I had the feeling that the toss could determine the game. I had no faith in the Patriot defense at this point, so thought that if the Jets won the toss, they could easily win the game without the Patriots ever getting the ball. The Jets won the toss.

Stephen Gostkowski finally boomed a kickoff in this game deep into the end zone, so the Jets took over at their 20. Favre was sacked for a five yard loss on the first play from scrimmage and then faced that critical third and 15 a play later. Favre hit his tight end Keller for 16 yards and a first down, and it was all downhill from there. Favre hit Keller again for 12 and then again for four on a third and one for another big first down on a third down conversion. A 16 yard pass from Favre to Coles set up the game-winning 34 yard field goal by Jay Feeley.

The Jets had taken the overtime kickoff and held the ball for 7:50, 14 plays, and 64 yards. Once they converted that 3rd and 15, you had a feeling they could have had the ball forever. The Patriots had the momentum after the tying TD, but the defense could not sustain it or get the offense the ball back. It was a very tough loss for New England.

As noted previously, this was the same scenario as the Super Bowl loss to the Giants, and the AFC Championship loss to the Colts the preceding year. All the Patriots needed was a big stop to win the game or have a chance to do so, and they didn't get it done. Over 400 years ago, William Shakespeare, in "Richard III", described a scene in which King Richard has lost his horse and exclaims "A Horse. A Horse. My Kingdom for a Horse." Bill Belichick could be excused if he yelled "A Stop. A Stop. My Kingdom for a Stop." My guess is that was not exactly what he was yelling on that last drive.

The stars of the game for the Patriots were Matt Cassel and Jerod Mayo. The Patriots had no running game, as Green-Ellis, Morris, Faulk, and Evans combined for only 63 yards. As it turned out, Cassel himself almost outgained them all, as he scrambled for 62 yards. Cassel also had his first 400 yard passing game, getting 400 on the nose on 31 completions in 50 attempts, with 3 touchdowns and no interceptions. Mayo was credited with 16 tackles and 4 assisted tackles and he was all over the field for New England. His 20 tackles were the most for any Patriot since Roman Phifer had 19 in a game against the Giants in October 2003.

With the win, the Jets moved into sole possession of first place in the AFC East with a 7-3 record. The Patriots were one game behind at 6-4. They would have to play well to make the playoffs, and certainly the defense had to tighten up if they were to have even a chance to do so. At least they had 9 days to rest and prepare for the next AFC East battle, down in Miami against the Dolphins.

Chapter 18 – 9 Days 'til Sunday

     With the Patriots having played on Thursday, there were nine days between games for them. There were still a number of items about the Patriots and around the NFL that were of interest to Patriot fans.

- - -

     On the Sunday morning ESPN show "The Sports Reporters", in a segment about the Thursday Patriots-Jets game, ESPN reporter Howard Bryant stated, "The dirty little secret about what's going on up in New England is their defense." He went on to cite the Indianapolis AFC Championship Game in 2006-07, the Super Bowl against the Giants in 2007-08, and the game against the Jets the preceding week as showing that the Patriot defense was not as strong as many thought it to be. Yes – that is exactly the point that I have tried to make and wrote about the day after the Jets' game for the previous chapter. It was nice to see someone in the national media had the same view of one of the Patriots' problem areas as I did, since the local media did not seem to be focusing much on that concern.

- - -

     After Matt Cassel's excellent performance in the Jets' game, and with his continuing improvement over the season, stories started to be written about Cassel being in the final year of his contract. The gist of these articles was that Cassel would probably be with another team in 2009. There were certainly enough NFL teams that needed a quarterback – the Lions, Vikings, Bears, and 49ers among them – but it was definitely deflating to have been rooting for Cassel to do well and then see stories like this. Having seen the Patriots draft him and keep him for four years despite his not having started a game in college, it did not seem right to have him be lost to the team after he did play in 2008 (after almost being cut in pre-season according to some reports) because of his new success.

     That is the way it is in professional sports these days. In the old days, Gary Cuozzo could be a backup for Johnny Unitas for many years or Zeke Bratkowski for Bart Starr, or even Steve Young for Joe Montana in more recent years, but not any more. As soon as someone plays for any length of time, they are ready to go somewhere else to be a starter. Or, as noted previously about players such as Damien Woody and Alvin Harper, leave a successful team where they are doing well to go to a lesser team and into obscurity.

The stories about Cassel's potential departure made me dig up the *Sports Illustrated* issue from the week before the Patriots-Giants Super Bowl in 2008. That issue had a one page profile of Matt Cassel, which headlined, "He threw only 5 passes this year, but Tom Brady's understudy is always a play away from being the leading man." The format was a Q&A with the SI reporter. On the issue of being a backup, Cassel responded with "There's stress. You never know when you are going to get on the field. But I haven't suffered many bumps and bruises. And the advantage of a rested arm is that it's ready to rock and roll." On the issue of his wearing a helmet on the sideline, Cassel responded, "What I do is listen to the play call [through a helmet headset]. Then I say the call aloud as if I were in the huddle. When I watch the play, I go through the mental reps. This way, if I'm called on, it won't feel like the first time I'm in the huddle." He also mentioned that he used to call Tom Brady "Mr. Brady" until midway through his rookie season, and that Brady had mentored him about football, about his demeanor, and how to respond in the huddle. Cassel sounds like a prototypical Patriots' player. It is too bad that 2008 was to be his last season as a Patriot (Cassel was traded to Kansas City after the season).

- - -

There were some interesting developments in games that were played on the Sunday after the Pats-Jets Thursday night meeting.

The New York Giants, who many believed to be the best team in the league (I am one of those who believed that) looked very impressive in a 30-10 win over the Baltimore Ravens. The Raven run defense had been outstanding all year, but the Giants had no trouble blasting holes in the line for big gains by running backs Brandon Jacobs and Ahmad Bradshaw. The Giants wound up gaining 207 yards rushing against a defense that had not given up more than 76 in any other game in 2008. The Giants were proving that their Super Bowl win against the Patriots had certainly not been a fluke.

The NFL's other 2008 powerhouse, the Tennessee Titans, raised their record to 10-0 and continued their hopes for an undefeated season with a 24-14 win over Jacksonville. This one required a comeback from Tennessee, as the Jaguars led 14-3 at halftime. Three second half TD passes by Kerry Collins, still doing well subbing for Vince Young, led the Titans to the comeback win. Tennessee's next game would be against the New York Jets in Nashville.

Miami won again, defeating the Raiders 17-15 on a field goal with 38 seconds left. The Dolphins thus improved their record to 6-4 and moved into a second place tie with the Patriots going into their upcoming rematch in Miami. The Patriot defense would definitely need to be ready for the Dolphins and their wildcat plays with running back Ronnie Brown.

The Steelers defeated the Chargers 11-10 thanks to three field goals and a safety. According to reports, it was the first 11-10 final score in the league's history. The game was played in falling snow, but the Steelers showed that they were still the same old Steelers. The only touchdown of the game was a three yard touchdown run by San Diego's LaDanian Tomlinson in the first quarter. After Tomlinson had clearly crossed into the end zone for the score, Steeler defender Troy Polamalu hit him with an unnecessary cheap shot to knock him down for no good reason. Same old Steelers.

There was also some controversy at the end of the Steeler-Charger game. San Diego completed a pass on the last play of the game and was attempting a series of desperation laterals to free someone for a long touchdown run. Troy Polamalu of the Steelers deflected one such lateral, grabbed it, and ran it into the end zone. It was originally ruled a touchdown for Pittsburgh, but that call was later reversed. It was explained that one of the laterals was an illegal forward lateral, which made the play dead at that point. There was some dispute about whether or not there had been a forward lateral, and the league later said that the reversal was incorrect and that the play should have been a touchdown. While the bad call did not affect the outcome of the game, there was a small chance it could affect one of those many NFL tiebreakers should Pittsburgh wind up in a tie for a playoff spot at the end of the regular season. More interesting was the fact that betting locations in Las Vegas had made the Steelers a 4 point favorite for this game, so those people who had placed a bet on the Steelers and could have won had the call been made correctly, now had lost, while those who had bet on the Chargers had now won.

In Cincinnati, the Bengals and Philadelphia Eagles played to a 13-13 tie, as Cincinnati missed a 47 yard field goal attempt with seven seconds left in overtime. It was the first tie game in the league since 2002, when Pittsburgh and Atlanta played to a 34-34 tie. Eagle quarterback Donovan McNabb said after the game that he didn't know that NFL games could end in a tie. That a veteran such as McNabb did not know this rule, which just about every fan does, was a big surprise.

On Monday night, the Buffalo Bills lost at home to Cleveland, and so fell to last place in the AFC East with a 5-5 record. It was some comedown from their 4-0 start.

Chapter 19 – Beached Dolphins

Sunday, November 23, 2008:	1	2	3	4		TOTAL
New England Patriots	3	14	14	17	-	48
Miami Dolphins	7	7	7	7	-	28

"It's hard to put into words how much the Patriots have been looking forward to this game after being embarrassed in Week 3. They are anxious. They are excited. And they are glad it's finally here."

So said CBS football analyst Dan Dierdorf as he and his partner Greg Gumbel began the telecast of the Patriots – Dolphins game on November 23. It was a good lead-in to what was a very competitive game – for three quarters anyway.

New England received the opening kickoff, a short kick by Miami that the Patriots returned to their own 40 yard line, and went to work immediately from the shotgun formation. The first play was a screen pass from Matt Cassel to Kevin Faulk that went for 15 yards. The second play showed Cassel's increasing maturity as a starting quarterback, as he started to scramble, stopped, and threw a drop-off pass to Wes Welker that gained 14 more yards. Cassel then hit Moss for 9 yards on the third play, and Sammy Morris ran for 2 yards and another first down at the 20 yard line on play # 4. A holding penalty on the next play moved the ball back to the 30, and effectively stalled the drive. New England had to settle for a 30 yard field goal and a 3-0 lead. The disappointment in not getting a touchdown was tempered somewhat by a CBS graphic which showed that the Patriots had won the last 22 games in which they scored first.

After a Miami punt and a first down run by Morris, Cassel hit Jabar Gaffney in stride with a pass right into Gaffney's hands. Gaffney dropped it, continuing a disturbing recent trend. That was followed by a long throw to a leaping Randy Moss that bounced off of his hands and up into the air where it was picked off by Miami. This was the third interception by Miami of a Matt Cassel pass in the last six quarters of play between the two teams (though 1 of those came in limited time as Cassel replaced Tom Brady in a blowout last season). This one though was not Cassel's fault, as even Dan Dierdorf admitted that the ball, although high, was thrown into Moss' hands. In any case, Miami converted the turnover into points on a 2 yard TD pass from Chad Pennington and the Dolphins had a 7-3 lead.

New England started its next drive on the 26 and got a leaping one-handed catch from Moss on a pass similar to the one that had been intercepted to get out to the 48. The Patriots converted a fourth and one play on the drive, with Matt Cassel getting the yardage on a quarterback sneak. Cassel was hit hard on the play, but bulled it forward for six yards and the first down. On the next play, Cassel flipped it to Wes Welker, who caught it and got 2 yards but was hammered on the play, and stayed down. Thankfully, he only had the wind knocked out of him, so he was back after one play on the sideline, and immediately caught a flanker screen for 8 yards down to the 12.

Matt Cassel scrambled up the middle and into the end zone for a touchdown on the first play of the second quarter to put New England back on top 10-7.

A Miami punt after two unsuccessful wildcat plays gave the ball back to the Patriots again at their 41. The Patriots started driving again and were dominating the game statistics, but the ball was ripped away from Sammy Morris and Miami recovered the fumble, as penalties and turnovers continued to plague the Patriots. As Greg Gumbel told us, "It's what's keeping Miami in the game thus far."

What followed then was another of the Patriots' season-long bugaboos – third down conversions by the other team. On a third and 10 Miami got 12. On a third and 12 Miami got 20. On a third and 4 Miami got 10. Then Miami had a touchdown and a 14-10 lead thanks to a 7 yard run by Chad Pennington.

The Patriots took a 17-14 lead into halftime thanks to a 25 yard touchdown pass from Cassel to Moss. On the play, Moss caught the ball at the 20, eluded one Miami tackler, and then "lowered his shoulder," as Dan Dierdorf put it, and carried another defender into the end zone for the score.

The third quarter was a seesaw battle between the two teams. A 46 yard pass from Chad Pennington to Ted Ginn set up a 2 yard TD pass from Pennington that put Miami back into the lead at 21-17.

Cassel then led New England on an 11 play drive to reclaim the lead at 24-21. A big play on this drive was a nice 3rd and 10 conversion on a pass from Cassel to Moss. Cassel came up hobbling but stayed in the game and hit Benjamin Watson to get the ball down to the 8 and then hit Moss on a beautifully thrown looping pass over the defender in the end zone for the touchdown. It was the sixth lead change of the day.

A third and 20 sack of Pennington prevented a seventh lead change, and Miami had to punt again, and they got a good one, driving the Patriots back to their own 13. The Pats got a touchdown only four plays later, thanks mostly to a 64 yard gain on a pass from Cassel to Welker. Welker caught the ball on his 20 for the first 5 yards of the gain and then tightroped his way along the sideline to the Miami 21 yard line for the remaining 59 yards of the play. Kevin Faulk raced in from 21 yards out for the touchdown on the last play of the third quarter, and New England suddenly had a two possession lead.

Miami came back quickly, going 69 yards in 5 plays in only 1:49, scoring on a 13 yard TD pass from Pennington to Ricky Williams. That cut New England's lead to 31-28, but it would turn out to be all the scoring Miami would do on this day.

Matt Cassel got that touchdown back on a 29 yard TD pass to Randy Moss, with Moss again leaping to make the catch. This time he came down at the one and fell into the end zone for a score, his third of the day.

With the TD pass to Moss, Matt Cassel had accumulated over 400 yards passing for the day, the second consecutive week in which he had reached that milestone. That was significant for many reasons:

- It was the first time in Patriot history that a quarterback had had back-to-back 400 yard passing days

- It was Cassel's second 400 yard passing day; Tom Brady had only one 400 yard passing day in his career

- Only four other quarterbacks had thrown back-to-back 400 yard games in NFL history: Dan Fouts, Dan Marino, Phil Simms, and Billy Volek.

When asked about this in the post-game press conference, Cassel said "That's pretty cool." When he was informed of the other players who had accomplished the feat, Cassel seemed wowed, saying "That's a good crew to be with." It was a nice feather in his cap for this young QB.

Brandon Merriweather had an interception on Miami's first play after the kickoff, bringing it back to the Miami 18 yard line, where the Patriots upped the lead to 41-28 on another 30 yard field goal by Stephen Gostkowski.

On the field goal, a fight broke out between Miami linebacker Channing Crowder and Patriot blocker Matt Light. Punches were thrown, and Light also grabbed the long hair locks of Crowder. Both players were ejected. Crowder, who apparently had been jabbering all day, walked off the field with a big self-satisfied smile on his face.

Wonder if he looked at the scoreboard on his way out and saw that his team was losing badly in the game.

Miami's other big talker, Joey Porter, was flagged later in the game for an unnecessary roughness penalty and an unsportsmanlike conduct penalty within three plays, as he continued to mouth off. Miami Coach Tony Sparano sent a replacement player out for Porter and wanted to get him off the field before he could do more damage to Miami's cause, but Porter refused to leave and sent the replacement back. Nice of you to disrespect your coach and teammates, Porter. Miami reporters later reported that Porter refused to speak with them in the locker room after the game, causing the Miami broadcaster to comment sarcastically "Way to be a stand-up guy, Joey." I guess that losing the game badly caused Porter, a classic bully, to lose his loudmouth voice as well.

The Porter penalties helped the Patriots to a final touchdown on a 2 yard run by BenJarvus Green-Ellis, making the final score 48-28.

The win gave the Patriots a 7-4 record, but they were still one game behind the Jets who raised their record to 8-3 by stunning the previously unbeaten Tennessee Titans 34-13 in Nashville. At least Mercury Morris and the old 1972 Dolphins got to celebrate again as another season would go by without another team going undefeated.

It was a great day for New England's passing game. Randy Moss had 125 yards, Wes Welker 120, Jabar Gaffney 88, and Kevin Faulk 52, all season highs. Welker had eight catches and had caught six or more passes in each of his team's first 11 games, a new NFL record. Cassel had 415 yards passing, and the team accumulated 530 total yards, the most since 1979 and second most in team history.

Alice Cook of Boston's Channel 4 Sports Team provided the perfect bookend to Dan Dierdorf's comment introducing the game by reporting after the game outside the Patriot locker room that she "heard the team going by. They are so excited." She described the game as "like a heavyweight bout, trading blows right to the end." The Patriots had gotten their revenge on Miami.

Chapter 20 – Same Old Steelers

Sunday, November 30, 2008:	1	2	3	4		TOTAL
Pittsburgh Steelers	3	7	13	10	-	33
New England Patriots	7	3	0	0	-	10

The first game after Thanksgiving found the Patriots still in a giving mode. A fumbled kickoff led to one Steeler touchdown. A fumble by Matt Cassel led to a Steeler field goal. Two interceptions of Matt Cassel passes led to another touchdown and field goal. The Patriots also gave away opportunities with a number of dropped passes. It was a winnable game, but it was given away.

These were the same old Steelers that we have seen for a number of years. They had an excellent defense, which was the top-rated defense in the league. They had an efficient offense that was not flashy, but did not beat itself. Those were the good points. On the negative side, they still were also the same old Steelers in their rough, borderline dirty style of play (and maybe crossed that border in some cases, as were described earlier). With that style of play, I would not have been surprised to see Matt Cassel injured and knocked out of the game. Cassel was not, but Wes Welker was, on a typical Steeler dirty play. They were indeed the same old Steelers.

The weather before and during the game was bad. There was a wintry mix as the game started at 4:15, and a steady rain throughout the game. As the game started, Patriot fans were already aware that the Indianapolis Colts had won again, beating Cleveland 10-6 for their fifth straight win, to raise their record to 8-4. Miami had beaten St. Louis to raise their record to 7-5. The Patriots would need to win to keep pace with the Colts and stay ahead of the Dolphins.

The Giants raised their record to 11-1 by beating Washington 23-7, but the big news from the Giants was that wide receiver Plaxico Burress had shot himself in the leg with a handgun in a nightclub on the Friday night before the game. The injuries to Burress were not life-threatening, but he did face a charge of criminal possession of a weapon and possible jail sentence. This followed weeks of fines and suspensions for Burress for violating team rules. The man who had caught the touchdown pass in the Super Bowl that had ended the dreams of a perfect season for New England was now looking at the possibility of his Giant career and possibly his NFL career being ended by this latest incident.

The beginning of the Patriot-Steeler game looked promising for New England. The opening kickoff was to Pittsburgh, and it was fumbled at the 20, although Pittsburgh retained possession. Typically, there was an unnecessary roughness call against the Steelers on the play. Same old Steelers.

The Patriots got a big early break when Mike Vrabel intercepted a pass by Steeler Quarterback Ben Roethlisberger. The pass was intended to be a short throw to the right. Vrabel was just standing to the side, awaiting the play and only had to jump in the air to make the interception. On the second Patriot play from scrimmage, Cassel hit Welker on a pass underneath the Steeler coverage, and Welker took it down to the 2 yard line. Sammy Morris ran it in on the next play for a 7-0 New England lead with less than three minutes played in the game.

Cassel hit Randy Moss for 27 yards on the first play on New England's next possession, but the Patriots were forced to punt, and the Steelers wound up with a 20 yard field goal to cut the lead to 7-3. On the drive, which covered 11 plays and 62 yards, Pittsburgh faced a third and 7 and got 15 to the New England 25, faced a third and 12 and got 15 to the New England 12. The Patriots were finally able to stop a running play on third and 1, so Pittsburgh had to settle for the field goal.

The final three minutes of the first quarter and the first seven minutes of the second saw the game get bogged down (no pun intended) into a punting contest. The Patriots were able to move to a 29 yard field goal with 6:48 to go in the half to up the lead to 10-3. The most interesting play on this drive was a fourth and one that the Patriots converted. It was really fourth and an inch, as the measurement was really close. Referee Ed Hochuli had to kneel down to get a close look on the measurement, and it appeared that the ball was short by one link of the chain. Sammy Morris made the measurement moot by jumping through the line for two yards and a first down at the 19, setting up the Gostkowski three-pointer.

Pittsburgh responded with their best drive of the day, going 63 yards to tie it on a 19 yard TD pass from Roethlisberger to Santonio Holmes. Again, the Patriots were not able to stop the opposition on second and 17 and third and two plays, the Steelers predictably getting four yards on that third and two to keep the drive alive.

The CBS announcing team pointed out that the Patriots had now allowed points on 32 straight trips into the red zone (inside the 20) by the opposing team, an appalling stat. Analyst Dan Dierdorf said that he had asked Bill Belichick the night before the game what he thought of that and said that Belichick responded "What do you think? That's terrible." The stat would only get worse in the second half.

The Pats had a chance to regain the lead before the half. A 41 yard run by Kevin Faulk took the ball to the Steeler 26, and Sammy Morris followed a couple of plays later with a 13 yard run on a delay to take the ball to the 9 yard line. Cassel hit Randy Moss in the hands in the back of the end zone on second down, but Moss dropped it, his second drop of the day. Earlier he had had a ball hit his hands and face mask as he was open on a crossing pattern and he dropped that ball. It was not to be a good day for Moss. Stephen Gostkowski added to New England's woes by pushing a 26 yard field goal attempt wide right, thus keeping the score tied at 10 at the half.

As the second half began, a score from New York showed that the Jets were losing to Denver 27-14 at halftime of their game, so the Patriots could move back into a tie for first in the AFC East if they could win this game and the Jets lose theirs.

Unfortunately, the second half was one of horrors for New England. They took the opening kickoff of the half out to the 24 and then got a pass interference penalty to take the ball to the 47. Steeler defender Ike Taylor was interfering with intended receiver Randy Moss for at least 10-15 yards, impeding Moss from catching the ball or even making progress. This drive then bogged down and the Patriots punted it away to the Steelers, who took over on their own 13 yard line. The Steelers got 21 yards and a first down on the first play. They got 12 yards and a first down on a pass on the second play. They later got nine yards to convert a third and three, nine yards on a third and one to convert that into a first and goal at the nine, and wound up with a 25 yard field goal by Jeff Reed that gave them their first lead of the game at 13-10. It was the 33rd straight successful trip into the red zone by a Patriot opponent.

Ellis Hobbs had cramps and could not return the ensuing kickoff, so Matthew Slater was back to receive for New England. It was a disaster. Slater could not handle the kickoff. It bounced off of his hands, he kicked it away while trying to pick it up, and Pittsburgh recovered at the New England eight yard line. It only took two plays for Pittsburgh to score, on a TD pass from Roethlisberger to Hines Ward. The Steelers had now scored 10 points in 35 seconds and the Patriots had given up points on 34 consecutive incursions into the red zone.

It was Kevin Faulk back to receive the next kickoff (too bad it had not been Faulk instead of Slater on the previous kick). Faulk had no trouble catching the kick and he returned it to the 28. A Pittsburgh blitz then got to Matt Cassel and knocked the ball out of his hands. Pittsburgh recovered at the 26 and got a 20 yard field goal to up the lead to 23-10. It was 13 points in 2:45 and 35 consecutive... well, you get the drift.

Ellis Hobbs was back to receive the next kickoff and he returned it to the 50, but a holding penalty on Sam Aiken, the second time in this game that he had been called for a penalty on a kick return, moved it back to the 35. The Patriots failed to convert on third down, as a Matt Cassel pass was incomplete, but the Patriots got a first down on a Steeler penalty. It was a vicious hit by Steeler defender Ryan Clark on Wes Welker. As Referee Ed Hochuli described, it was a 15 yard penalty for an "unnecessary hit on a defenseless receiver". Welker was going up for a possible catch of a ball that was tipped high over his head. It was not really catchable. Clark lowered his shoulder, and left his feet to slam into Welker. It was a play that was eerily reminiscent of the hit by Jack Tatum that had paralyzed Darryl Stingley in 1978. Clark was correctly flagged for the play, and it was a dirty play, as Hochuli described in more formal terms. Same old Steelers. Welker, New England's best receiver all season, would not return to the game. His streak of games with 6 or more receptions had ended, as he had 4 catches for 30 yards in this game.

Another third down and another blitz led to another fumble by Matt Cassel as the ball was knocked out of his hands. Pittsburgh recovered. It was New England's third fumble in their last 9 touches. The third quarter ended with Pittsburgh ahead 23-10. New England had gained a total of 2 yards in the quarter.

Pittsburgh missed on a field goal attempt with 11:29 to go, but did get a 45 yard field goal on their next possession, which was set up by an interception of a Matt Cassel pass by Troy Polamalu, who we learned had been Cassel's college roommate at USC.

The first play on the next Patriot possession was a dropped pass by Jabar Gaffney inside the Pittsburgh 25. It was another lost opportunity for the Patriots.

An unsportsmanlike conduct penalty against the (same old) Steelers kept the drive alive, and the Patriots had another fourth down and one where the 'one' was incredibly one link on the chain for the second time in the game. A quarterback sneak got the first down, but the next play turned out to be another interception of a Matt Cassel pass. This one was run back 89 yards by Lawrence Timmons to the Patriot one, where only a saving tackle by a hustling Benjamin Watson prevented the touchdown. It was reminiscent of the Watson saving tackle against Champ Bailey and Denver in the playoff game in 2005.

Pittsburgh got the TD on the second play, and took a 33-10 lead that would hold up as the final score.

The 30 unanswered points by Pittsburgh were the most against New England since the 31-0 loss to Buffalo on September 7, 2003, the opening day game after the release of Lawyer Milloy.

The Patriots had surrendered 20 points on turnovers. They did not convert a third down until the fourth quarter, and only converted one time in 13 chances.

Matt Cassel wound up with only 169 yards passing after the two consecutive 400 yard games. When a reporter asked him after the game if he was worried about his free agent stock plummeting, Cassel correctly and pointedly responded "To be completely honest, I'm not going to read anything that you guys write. We've got to go as a team and get better. It's not about Matt Cassel. It's about eleven guys on offense trying to get better, our team trying to get better. It's not about one guy's performance or Matt Cassel's stock rising or dropping. I could care less about that. I care about winning ballgames."

Cassel may have come close to saying more words in that one response than Bill Belichick did in his entire post-game press conference. Belichick said that his team "had a lot of opportunities … the difference in the game was the turnovers … we played hard, just didn't play well."

Randy Moss also came to the podium for post-game interviews, and said, "I am very disappointed in my play. Bill says time and time again 'do your job.' I always say as a wide receiver that your job is to get open, catch the ball, score the touchdown ... I put a lot of blame on myself because I think this team really looks to me to do my job … I don't want to blame the weather. The balls were there. They just weren't caught."

The Patriots had five first half penalties, gave up five sacks, and had five second half turnovers. It all added up to loss number five for the season.

The Jets did lose to Denver, 34-17, so the Patriots did miss an opportunity to move back into a first place tie. At 7-5, New England was tied with Miami for second in the AFC East, and behind both 8-4 Indianapolis and 8-4 Baltimore for the two AFC Wild Card spots. They would pretty much have to win all of their four remaining games to have a chance for the playoffs, and hope for one of these teams to falter. It did not look promising.

Chapter 21 – Playoffs in Peril

The Patriots were on the playoff precipice in the week before their second two week excursion of the season to the west coast, and they were close to falling off. A look at the standings and tie-breakers showed the Patriots to be in dire shape indeed. Of the six playoff spots available in the AFC, four would go to division winners, who, at the moment were:

Tennessee	11-1
Pittsburgh	9-3
NY Jets	8-4
Denver	7-5

The leaders for the two AFC wildcard spots were:

Indianapolis	8-4
Baltimore	8-4

On the outside looking in and hoping to move up were:

Miami	7-5
New England	7-5
Buffalo	6-6

The Jets held the AFC East tie-breaker over New England, should those two teams wind up tied, since they had a better record within the division, 3-1 versus 3-2. The Jets had division games remaining with Buffalo and Miami, while the Patriots had only the season finale with Buffalo as a division game. This meant that the Patriots would most likely have to finish a game ahead of the Jets to win the division. Since the Jets had a relatively weak schedule of games remaining – San Francisco, Buffalo, Seattle, and Miami – such a finish appeared to be unlikely.

The top tie-breaker for the wildcard would be head-to head play, and there Indianapolis had an edge over the Patriots, given their 18-15 win over New England during the season. The Patriots and Baltimore did not meet during the season, so their first tie-breaker would be records in the AFC Conference. In that regard, since Baltimore was 7-3 and New England 5-5, the tie-breakers were all lining up against New England.

The best hopes for the Patriots would be for them to win all of their remaining games and hope that either the Jets or Ravens would lose twice. The Jets' schedule made that unlikely, but the Ravens schedule kept open a glimmer of hope. Baltimore had three difficult games remaining, with Washington, Pittsburgh, and Dallas, and their other game was another possibly tough one, versus Jacksonville. If they could lose two of those and the Patriots win their final four, New England would pass them by with an 11-5 record versus what would then be a 10-6 record for Baltimore. Of course, there was the matter of holding off Miami and Buffalo as well.

It was not a good scenario for New England, but at least the possibilities were there.

- - -

Wes Welker did practice with the team during the week, so, thankfully, he did not seem to have been knocked out for more than the rest of the Steeler game by that shot he received from Ryan Clark.

- - -

Earlier in the season, when Adalius Thomas was injured, there was speculation that the Patriots might try to re-sign Rosevelt Colvin, which many thought was a good idea; I was one of those. The Patriots did not sign Colvin then though. However, now, with Pierre Woods having suffered a jaw injury against the Steelers, the linebacking corps was further depleted, so the Patriots did re-sign Colvin on the Tuesday after the Steelers' game.

Colvin had been with the Patriots from 2003-2007. He had been signed with the idea that he was an excellent defender and fierce pass rusher. He did have a number of big moments for the team, but injuries cut short two of his seasons with New England. The team had released him after the 2007 season and he had signed with Houston, but the Texans released him before the season started, so Colvin had spent the season living in Houston and spending time with his family.

When Colvin was asked by a reporter if he was in good enough shape to play, Colvin kiddingly responded, "I am in great shape to wake up in the morning, to do my daughters' hair … get their clothes and prep them for school … I guess I was in good enough shape that they felt comfortable bringing me in."

Colvin's former and future teammate, Richard Seymour, said of Colvin, "We're delighted to have him back. We need him. He'll have to get into playing shape but if Ty Law can do it, he can."

Bill Belichick added, "Rosie's been here before. He certainly knows what we're doing, knows the defense. There's a smaller learning curve with him." It was a similar theme to that which Belichick echoed when the clamor was to bring in a veteran quarterback when Tom Brady went down. Belichick went with Matt Cassel in large part because Cassel knew the system. He was now doing the same with Rosevelt Colvin. The hope was that Colvin could have the same amount of success stepping into the defense as Cassel had had with the offense.

- - -

Speaking of Matt Cassel, his difficult game against Pittsburgh had one impact on talk show callers. A number of callers in the week preceding that game suggested the Patriots trade Tom Brady and turn over the quarterbacking to Matt Cassel. I definitely like Matt Cassel and appreciated the job that he had done, but trade Tom Brady? Were these people crazy? Most of the radio hosts also were asking if these callers really believed what they were saying.

Not surprisingly, those calls to the talk shows stopped when Cassel had a bad game. Ron Borges graded him at a D+ for that game in his weekly "Patriots Report Card" in *The Boston Herald*. Some fans have very short memories.

- - -

The 2009 season would bring another first for New England. It was announced on December 1 that the Patriots and Tampa Bay Buccaneers would be playing a regular season game in London, England in 2009, on October 25, 2009 at London's Wembley Stadium.

The Buccaneers seemed to be a natural choice for this game since the Tampa Bay owners are also owners of the famed English soccer team, Manchester United (a.k.a. "Man U"), one of the most famous soccer teams in the world. The Patriots are a more curious choice, since the very name of the team connotes the Revolutionary War and America winning its independence from Great Britain.

Patriot owner Bob Kraft was reported to have said, "We're really excited that the league chose us to play in London. We're interested in the globalization of the sport."

When asked what Bill Belichick thought of this, Kraft kiddingly (I believe) said that Bill was the biggest cheerleader about going over to play this game. With Bill being one of the top NFL coaches who likes to keep distractions to a minimum, it is doubtful that he would welcome the distraction of a game in a foreign country, but he will undoubtedly make the best of it.

Players were not as enthused, at least not as yet. Logan Mankins was quoted as saying "I don't really want to go to London ... but I guess if we have to, we have to."

Perhaps the best example of the Patriots' traditional response to something like this came from Mike Vrabel, who was quoted as saying "I'm worried about Seattle. I don't give a [expletive deleted] about going to London ... right now we've got to lick our wounds and head out to Seattle." Bill Belichick must have been proud – his players' focus was on the next game, not the trip to England.

In any case, it would be interesting to see New England in Old England in 2009.

- - -

On the good news front in Boston sports, the week after the Pittsburgh game also saw the defending World Champion Boston Celtics raise their record to 20-2 in the 2008-09 NBA season, and the Boston Red Sox sign 2007 American League MVP Dustin Pedroia to a new six year contract. The Bruins were also in first place in their NHL division, and had the third highest total of points in the league. These were heady days in Boston sports.

- - -

Just before the Patriots headed out to the West Coast, they brought another old linebacker out of retirement, re-signing Junior Seau to the roster. Seau flew to Boston from California Thursday, signed on Friday, and flew to Seattle with the team on Saturday.

- - -

With four games to go in the season, the Patriots top players for the season seemed to be Matt Cassel, Wes Welker, Kevin Faulk, Logan Mankins, Matt Light, and Dan Koppen on offense, Jerod Mayo, Richard Seymour, and Gary Guyton on defense, and Stephen Gostkowski on special teams. The biggest positive play in the season thus far was the Cassel to Moss bullet that tied the second Jets' game at the end of regulation, a great play by both Cassel and Moss. The most significant play, however, may have been the 3rd and 15 conversion by the Jets in overtime of that game from their own 15 yard line. Had the Patriots stopped them they would have had a good chance to get good field position, win that game, and would be sitting in first place in the AFC East.

Chapter 22 – Escape from Seattle, led by Wes Welker

Sunday, December 7, 2008:	1	2	3	4	TOTAL
New England Patriots	3	7	3	11 -	24
Seattle Seahawks	7	7	7	0 -	21

The rain often expected in Seattle started during the second quarter of the Patriots-Seahawks game. By then the Patriots' playoff drive had almost ended on two Seattle drives in the first 18 minutes of the game, but the Patriots put together a clutch drive in the fourth quarter to save their season. In between the first 18 minutes and the last 8 was a game that was a lot tighter and much more nerve-wracking than had been expected. There were also more Patriot injuries that had to be overcome.

Seattle had an injury of its own to worry them before the start of the game. Matt Hasselbeck, Seattle's starting quarterback, would be out, and backup Seneca Wallace would be running the Seahawk offense. It hardly seemed to matter as the Seahawks took the ball at their own 13 yard line after an opening three-and-out sequence by New England and marched easily down the field for a touchdown. Wallace hit former Patriot Deion Branch with a 14 yard touchdown pass for the score. It was Branch's first TD catch of the season, and only his 14th catch total for the year.

The Patriots came back with a 50 yard field goal by Stephen Gostkowski, getting first downs on a 20 yard pass from Matt Cassel to Wes Welker and a holding penalty on Seattle, but a flea-flicker failed as Cassel badly overthrew a wide open Randy Moss, so New England had to settle for three and trailed 7-3 at the end of one quarter.

It was 2 drives and 2 touchdowns for the 2-10 Seahawks as they drove another 74 yards to score on a 10 yard pass from Wallace to tight end John Carlson, and Seattle had a 14-3 lead with 12:30 to go in the second quarter. Tedy Bruschi was injured on the second Seahawk drive, suffering a bruised knee that would sideline him for the rest of the game. Nose Tackle Vince Wilfork had also suffered a shoulder injury, and defensive back James Sanders left the game with a rib injury, so the Patriots' defense was down to very few regulars who had started the season. Mike Vrabel was also injured in the second quarter, but was back after missing just one play.

Ellis Hobbs returned the kickoff after Seattle's second score for 55 yards to the Seattle 42. That set up a 2 yard touchdown pass from Cassel to Benjamin Watson. Watson was called for a 15 yard penalty for unsportsmanlike conduct after the play for "using the football as a prop" in his touchdown celebration. Why would he do this? The team had just scored and had regained some momentum. Now they would be giving Seattle good field position. Watson later exclaimed that he got the penalty for sticking the football up under his uniform shirt as a "shout out" to his pregnant wife, Kristen. Again though, why do this and risk a penalty? Why not just literally shout out to her from the sidelines to the TV camera? Luckily Seattle did not convert any points despite the good field position, so the Seattle lead was still 14-10 at halftime.

Both teams treaded water in the third quarter until a 42 yard field goal by Gostkowski cut the Seahawk lead to 14-13 with 2:40 left in the quarter. Seattle fumbled the ensuing kickoff but was able to recover. Two spectacular catches by Deion Branch then increased the Seattle lead to 21-13 before the quarter ended. On the first, Branch took a short pass from Wallace along the right sideline. He then juked Junior Seau completely, faking a move that sent Seau running out of bounds past him and completely out of the play. Branch then criss-crossed across the field and avoided tacklers until he had run 63 yards and taken the ball to the New England 9. Branch's second great catch gave Seattle a touchdown. On that one he was crossing right-to-left in the end zone, reached up with his right hand and tipped the throw back to himself to complete the catch and get the score.

The fourth quarter saw New England start to roll a little. A 32 yard pass from Cassel to Randy Moss gave New England a first down at the Seattle 13, but once again the Patriots had to settle for a field goal, not a touchdown, and the lead was now 21-16 in favor of Seattle.

When New England got the ball back again, they were on their own 29 with only 8:47 to go in the game, needing a touchdown to take the lead and keep their playoff hopes alive. What they got was a clutch drive, which, play-by-play went:

1. Cassel sacked at the 25. 2nd and 14
2. Cassel scrambles for 9 to the 34. 3rd and 5.
3. Cassel to Kevin Faulk for 11 yards to the 45. 1st down.
4. Incomplete pass. 2nd and 10.
5. Cassel to Welker for 6 to the Seattle 49. 3rd and 4.
6. Cassel to Gaffney for 5 to the 44. 1st down.
7. Incomplete pass. 2nd and 10.
8. Incomplete pass. 3rd and 10.
9. Cassel for Welker for 13 yards to the 31. 1st down.

10. Cassel to Welker for 25 yards to the 6, as Welker stiff-arms one would-be tackler and dances down the left sideline before running out of bounds. 1st down. It was Welker's 12th catch of the day.
11. Cassel rushed, forced to scramble, loses one yard. 2nd and goal.
12. Faulk runs for 6 yards to the 1. 3rd down.
13. Sammy Morris stopped on a run up the middle. 4th down.
14. Sammy Morris dives in – just barely – for the touchdown. 22-21 Patriots.

New England went for the two point conversion, and were successful on a pass from Matt Cassel to (naturally) Wes Welker. The Patriots were ahead 24-21, their first lead of the game, with 2:44 to go in the game. The only worry was whether the Patriot defense could hold that lead.

Seattle brought the kickoff out to the 34 yard line. Wallace scrambled out to his right and raced 23 yards to the New England 43 before he was stopped. What was particularly frustrating was that rookie Patriot defensive back Jonathan Wilhite seemed to stop on the play, expecting Wallace to run out of bounds at about the Seattle 42. But Wallace didn't run out of bounds. He turned up the field and raced right past Wilhite for another 15 yards before finally being tackled by Deltha O'Neal.

Seattle then had a second and eleven from the 44 as the teams lined up after the two minute warning. Safety Brandon Merriweather blitzed on the play and not only sacked Wallace but also knocked the ball out of his hands. Richard Seymour recovered the fumble, and the Patriots had escaped with a 24-21 win over lowly Seattle.

The news got even better as the Jets were upset by San Francisco 24-14, so New England, Miami, and New York were in a three-way tie for first in the AFC East with records of 8-5. The Patriots would spend the next week in San Jose, preparing for their game against the 3-10 Oakland Raiders. They still needed to win them all and get some help from other teams, but at least their playoff hopes were still alive.

Chapter 23 – What Was Buffalo Thinking?

Sunday, December 14, 2008: The 1:00 games
(Patriots vs. Oakland was a 4:00 start)

The Buffalo Bills had always been a likeable team … until this day in 2008.

The two unbiased TV commentators on ESPN's "Pardon the Interruption" show may have described it best. Here was their commentary the following day:

Michael Wilbon: The Jets were two minutes and six seconds from losing both their game and their season when they received what's being called the Miracle of the Meadowlands … The Bills had been running over the Jets and running down the clock when head coach Dick Jauron called for a J.P. Losman rollout pass. Hit, fumble, recovery, touchdown. Jets win.

Tony Kornheiser: It was a terrible call. It's an unbelievably terrible call because you have run through the Jets. Just go forward, get a first down, kneel down three times, then you're out of it. The Jets were incredibly lucky.

Michael Wilbon: The Jets benefited from this inexplicable thing. It's one of those deals when you cannot believe they made this call.

The commentators were right. It was an incredibly bad call by the Bills that prevented them from winning and allowed the Jets to escape with an undeserved victory that might cost the Patriots a playoff spot. We'll go into all of this in more detail shortly.

- - -

Going into the early games of December 14, the Patriots needed any or all of three teams to lose to improve their playoff chances. Those were the Jets and Dolphins with whom the Patriots were battling for the AFC East, and the Ravens, with whom the Pats were battling for a wild card berth.

At 3:40 that Sunday, things were looking promising. The Jets were losing to Buffalo. Miami had a slim 14-9 lead over San Francisco but the 49ers were driving for a potential game-winning touchdown. Baltimore was playing late, as were the Patriots, but the Ravens had a tough match-up with Pittsburgh. The Patriots, meanwhile, had a late game with a very bad Oakland team.

That was at 3:40. By 3:55, everything had turned from promising to grim for New England.

The most egregious situation occurred in the Jets-Bills game at The Meadowlands. The Jets had an early 14-3 lead, but Buffalo had come back to take a 17-14 lead just before halftime. It looked like the Bills would take that lead into the half, but they allowed a long run for a touchdown to Jet running back Leon Washington with less than a minute to go in the half. Instead of New York trailing at the half, they had a 21-17 lead going into the locker room. That was still not the worst of it.

Trailing 24-20 in the fourth quarter, Buffalo seemingly took the lead on a long kick return for touchdown. Only they did not. A big holding penalty negated that score. That was still not the worst of it.

Late in the game, the Bills took a 27-24 lead behind the bruising running of Marshawn Lynch and Fred Jackson who were just carrying Jet tacklers who could not bring them down. The Jet fans were booing their defense. They booed it even more when Jackson carried a pile into the end zone for the score that gave the Bills the 27-24 lead.

When Brett Favre, who was having a mediocre game, misfired on three pass attempts, the Jets had to punt the ball away and again the New York fans were raining boos down on the Jets. The Bills took over at their 20. Only they did not. Another holding penalty on the kick moved the ball back to the 10 yard line. Still, the Bills only had to run out the clock to win the game, and with their strong running attack, that looked very possible.

Three running plays got one first down. Another running play got about another 5 yards. With 2:06 to go, it looked like a certain win for the Bills and a certain loss for the Jets.

Then, incredibly, head coach Dick Jauron called a rollout pass play. I was yelling and screaming as the play developed and I'm sure Patriot fans and Bill fans everywhere were doing the same thing. Quarterback J.P. Losman rolled out to his right, was hit, and fumbled. A Jet defender picked the ball up and ran it in for a touchdown with 1:54 to go.

It was the worst play call I had seen in years – maybe calling it the stupidest play call in years is the better way to describe it. All Buffalo had to do was what had been working well all afternoon, run the football. They would have continued to move the ball and take time off the clock. At worst, if they were stopped, they would have punted and caused the ineffective Favre to have to go a long way to tie or win the game. Instead they handed the game to the Jets on a silver platter. The worst thing they could have done was to call a pass play that might have succeeded, but had an equal or better chance of having a turnover, or stopping the clock and setting up a third and long, either of which is what the Jets would have wanted. It was terrible.

In my long history of watching football, this ranks at or near the top of bad (stupid) play calls. The top (or is it bottom?) five are as follows:

1. The first play of the first game in Bart Starr's coaching career in Green Bay. With all of the off-season to prepare for this play, and all of the week before to set up the game plan, and all Sunday to consider it (since they were playing on Monday night), and then all day Monday until the 9:00 kickoff to refine it, the Packers were called for delay of game. On the first play of the season!

2. This play call by Buffalo

3. The 1997 Patriots game with Pittsburgh described in Chapter 5, where all the Patriots had to do was run out the clock and get a win and Drew Bledsoe threw an ill-advised pass to the sideline that was picked off and set up a Steeler touchdown, overtime, and a Patriot loss that cost them the home field advantage in the playoffs.

4. The 1969 Patriots-Jets game where Patriot coach Clive Rush decided to go for a 1 point conversion with his team trailing by 10 late in the game. A 2 point conversion would have put them within one touchdown of tying the game rather than losing it. He denied his team even a chance at a win.

5. A Giants-Eagles game in 1978 when the Giants had a lead and instead of quarterback Joe Pisarcik taking a knee to run out the clock, the Giants called a running play and Pisarcik and running back Larry Csonka collided, the ball was fumbled and Eagle DB Herman Edwards ran it in for the winning score.

The Associated Press story of this Bills game stated the following:

The Jets were surprised the Bills were passing in that situation, expecting Buffalo to try to run out the clock. After all, Marshawn Lynch gained 127 yards on 21 carries and New York was struggling to stop him. Instead, coach Dick Jauron overruled offensive coordinator Turk Schonert.

"Clearly the responsibility for the last call, the play-action pass, that was mine", Jauron said. "That goes right on me. It backfired clearly and caused us to lose the game."

Jauron refused to blame Losman ...

"It's on my shoulders to protect him, to keep him from that situation and I didn't do it," Jauron said.

The CBS announcers covering the game could not believe it either. They referred to it as snatching defeat from the jaws of victory. It surely was.

The Buffalo newspaper stated, "Just 11 days before Christmas, the Bills gift wrapped a victory for the Jets on a call that might haunt Dick Jauron for years." It quoted Jets' receiver Jericho Cotchery as saying "I couldn't believe what was happening, a lot of mixed emotions because the game was looking dark, and he tried to drop back to pass. I'm thankful for that. It was looking darker than dark. Whoa. I can't even explain the emotions after that play happened." It also quoted Brett Favre as saying "I, probably like most people, was thinking they were going to run the clock out, and we were going to be saying "What if?' All I could say was 'Wow.' There were several things on that play that makes you scratch your head, but I'm just glad it was in our favor." On the Buffalo side, Bills' owner Ralph Wilson was asked what he thought of the play. Wilson quipped that he should go back to the insurance business. The last word goes to Bill's defensive end Chris Kelsay, who said "It's sickening. You have a sick feeling in your stomach. I think I speak for the entire team because this game meant so much to many of us. You give yourself a chance like that and lose it like that in the last couple minutes is always tough."

- - -

Meanwhile, in Miami, a late sack of 49er quarterback Shaun Hill by Joey Porter saved the Dolphins. Their 14-9 win kept them at 9-5 and even with the Jets. If the Jets and Dolphins were both to win their next games, the Patriots would not be able to win the AFC East. This is because the Jets and Dolphins were scheduled to play each other in the season's final week. One of those teams would finish 11-5 and each held the tie-breaker over the Patriots.

- - -

That left it to Pittsburgh and Baltimore, and the Ravens were winning 9-6 with time running out. Pittsburgh rallied, however, to get a touchdown in the final minute of the game on a pass from Ben

Roethlisberger to Santonio Holmes at the goal line. The play was ruled a touchdown, though it was unclear whether the ball had actually crossed the goal line or not. Replays were inconclusive, and there was some controversy about it, but the touchdown counted, and the Steelers held on for a 13-9 win. That meant that another Raven loss would open up the possibility for the Patriots to get into the playoffs if they could win their remaining games with Oakland, Arizona, and Buffalo.

So a day that began with some promise, and had misery in the middle, ended with the Patriots still having a chance.

No thanks to Dick Jauron and the Buffalo Bills.

Chapter 24 – Over Early in Oakland

Sunday, December 14, 2008:	1	2	3	4		TOTAL
New England Patriots	21	14	7	7	-	49
Oakland Raiders	7	7	6	6	-	26

At his post-game press conference after the Patriots game with Oakland, Coach Bill Belichick said, "I just can't say enough about Matt Cassel … he did a great job in his preparation and his focus … he showed a lot of commitment to the team. He carried us a long way today."

It had indeed been a very difficult week for Cassel. His father, Greg, a screenwriter, had been found dead on Monday in his home in a trailer park in San Bernadino, California. Matt Cassel was away from the team for the first part of the week, and it was unclear whether or not he would return for the game. For their part, the Patriots were completely supportive, leaving it up to Matt to decide what he wanted to do, and being willing to go into this big game without him, if that is what their quarterback wanted. No one complained. They all showed class in supporting their teammate and friend. Cassel did return for practice, and the funeral was set for the following Tuesday, so he would play in the game.

Before the game it was learned that the Patriots would be without linebackers Pierre Woods and Tedy Bruschi. Woods had suffered a broken jaw and would become the latest Patriot to be put on injured reserve, ending his season. Bruschi had suffered a knee injury against Seattle, and was back in Boston having the knee examined. During the Oakland game offensive tackle Matt Light would be forced to leave early with a shoulder injury, as the team's injuries continued to mount up.

Luckily, the Patriots were playing Oakland, one of the worst teams in the league. This one was over early.

The Patriots kicked off and Oakland returned it out of the end zone but only to the seven yard line. Two plays later they faced a third down and the announcers told us that the Raiders had been terrible on third down conversions all year, and were one of the worst teams in the league in such situations. Given the Patriots' defense and its propensity to give up third down conversions, this was like a case of the resistible force against the movable object. In this case the movable object prevailed, as the Patriots forced an Oakland punt and took over on the Raider 40 yard line.

On third down, Cassel completed a 15 yard pass to Wes Welker to get the ball down to the 20. On a third and seven, Cassel again hit Walker for a first down at the 10. On third and goal, Cassel threw a short pass to Kevin Faulk and Faulk raced untouched to the left into the end zone, thanks to a great block by Wes Welker.

Another Oakland three and out and a short punt gave New England good field position again at the Raider 35 yard line, and Cassel hit Randy Moss for a 21 yard touchdown, with Moss taking the ball on the left right at the goal line and taking it in for the score. For former Raider Randy Moss it was sweet revenge on the team that had given up on him two years earlier. For Cassel it was a nicely executed play as he stepped up into the pocket to avoid the rush and hit Moss perfectly for the touchdown and an early 14-0 lead.

The Patriots then made it three touchdowns in three possessions with an 83 yard drive capped by a 29 yard touchdown run by Sammy Morris. Oakland got one score back on a 56 yard TD pass from quarterback Jamarcus Russell to receiver Johnny Lee Higgins, so the score at the end of one quarter was New England 21 Oakland 7.

New England's fourth possession resulted in their fourth touchdown as they continued to march easily through the Oakland defense. A 31 yard pass from Cassel to Welker set up a 13 yard touchdown from the same combination and a 28-7 New England lead. The TD catch was Welker's 100th reception of the season. It was Cassel's third touchdown toss of the day, each to a different receiver.

Justin Miller returned Stephen Gostkowski's kickoff 91 yards for a touchdown to make it 28-14. The announcers then made the unusual comment that special teams were the Raiders' best chance to score (really? What does that say about the Oakland offense?). Ellis Hobbs then countered by returning a kickoff for a touchdown for New England on the very next play. This one went for 95 yards, Hobbs' third career kickoff return TD, and the lead was quickly back up to 21 points, 35-14.

The Patriots' fifth possession did not result in a touchdown. Instead a deflection off Benjamin Watson was intercepted by Oakland at the Raider 26, but Patriot DB Jonathan Wilhite returned that favor too by intercepting a Raider pass at the Patriot 2 yard line and running it out to the 17. The Patriots got a 23 yard run on a draw play by Faulk, then 30 yards on two screen passes to Faulk, but the half ended at 35-14 when the Patriots could not get a snap off to try a field goal before the clock expired.

The Patriots took the second half kickoff and marched 68 yards in 7 plays for yet another touchdown. The drive was highlighted by a 35 yard run by Sammy Morris, and culminated by a 9 yard touchdown pass from Cassel to Moss. This gave Cassel a career-high 4 touchdown passes for the day.

Oakland got a touchdown on an 11 yard pass from Jamarcus Russell that he looped over Ellis Hobbs to Ronald Curry for the score, but the extra point was blocked, so the score was 42-20 in favor of New England after three quarters.

Just as Randy Moss had gotten his revenge against his former team, the Raiders, so too did Lamont Jordan, now back in the lineup for New England and playing solidly. Jordan got a fourth quarter touchdown on a 49 yard run, just bursting through the line and outrunning the Oakland defense. It was the longest run from scrimmage by the Patriots all season. Jordan later told reporters that he really wanted to score in this game since the Oakland coaches had not wanted him and the fans had booed him when he was with the Raiders. He told them that, as he burst into the open on this run, he kept telling himself "Please don't get caught. Please don't get caught." The Raiders never came close to catching him, so Jordan had a very satisfying touchdown.

A late Oakland TD made the final score 49-26 but this one was over early and never in doubt.

- - -

There had been a lot of talk by sports reporter about there not being a clear-cut choice for the league's MVP in 2008, as there had been in 2007 (Tom Brady) or in previous seasons (e.g., Peyton Manning). However, there seemed to me to be a logical candidate – Matt Cassel. Cassel clearly stepped into the giant void that was left when Brady was injured and played extremely well. With the Patriots' defense being shaky all year, and with the team not having much of a running game (despite a good running attack against Oakland), it was Cassel, Belichick, Faulk, and Welker who kept the team alive and in the playoff hunt. Where would the Patriots have been without Cassel? It was not clear, but it was clear that he was a major force in helping them overcome the Brady injury and still be one of the best teams in the league. Without his performance and contributions, the team might not have been able to do so. If that is not the quintessential definition of what an MVP should be, I don't know what is. As it turned out, he did not get the award, but he certainly deserved a lot more consideration than he was given.

Chapter 25 – Destroying Arizona

Sunday, December 21, 2008:	1	2	3	4		TOTAL
Arizona Cardinals	0	0	0	7	-	7
New England Patriots	14	17	13	3	-	47

By the time New England's game with Arizona started at 1:00 on Sunday, the Patriots' playoff chances already had two new strikes against it. Indianapolis had beaten Jacksonville on Thursday to clinch one of the two AFC wild card spots. Baltimore had beaten an underachieving Dallas team on Saturday to stay ahead in the race for the second and last wild card spot. Things continued to look bleak for the Patriots' post-season hopes.

The New England area was in the midst of the third of three major winter storms as the game started. An ice storm on December 11 had knocked out power to a lot of communities and a number of homes were still without power ten days later. Eight to ten inches of snow had fallen in a Friday-Saturday storm preceding this game, and snow was falling heavily as the game began. Another six to nine inches would fall in many places in New England before the day ended.

Luckily for New England, their opponents were the Arizona Cardinals, and rarely has an NFL team looked like it did not want to be playing more than the Cardinals did on this December Sunday. Arizona had already clinched the NFC Western Division. They would leave after the game with a mediocre 8-7 record and a guaranteed spot in the playoffs, while the Patriots were looking at the possibility of finishing 11-5 and not making the playoffs.

Despite a high-powered offense led by MVP candidate Kurt Warner, Arizona went three plays and out seven times in their first eight possessions, as New England was building up a 47-0 lead. Only a meaningless late touchdown by Arizona prevented New England from shutting them out.

As was the case in the Oakland game, this one was over early. New England won the toss, deferred the choice, and so kicked off. Arizona, known for their passing attack, ran the ball three times in the snowy conditions and then punted. Wes Welker returned the kick 29 yards from the New England 39 to the Arizona 32. New England fans were happy to see Matt Light come out onto the field to play left tackle.

After his injury in the Oakland game and limited practice time, it was not clear if he would be playing at all in the game. Happily, he was.

Just as Arizona's offense looked as if they just wanted to be home, so too did Arizona's defense. New England went right through them with four runs by Sammy Morris, two by Lamont Jordan, and one pass. Jordan scored the touchdown on a one yard run with Mike Vrabel in as an extra blocker and New England had the early 7-0 lead.

Another three runs and punt by Arizona gave New England the ball in good field position for a second time, this time at the New England 45. New England got their second score quickly. A 42 yard screen pass from Matt Cassel to Morris on the second play of the possession set up a three yard touchdown run by Jordan and the Patriots had a 14-0 lead.

They had a chance for another score before the first quarter ended, thanks to another three and out series by the Cardinals, but could not convert. A long pass attempt by Cassel bounced off of the fingertips of Randy Moss and the Patriots punted to the Arizona nine yard line.

As the second quarter began, the Cardinals had their fourth consecutive three and out series, and New England started at midfield. A 37 yard pass from Cassel to Jabar Gaffney set up a touchdown on a 15 yard screen pass from Cassel to Faulk, and the Patriots were ahead 21-0. The game was essentially over at that point (as if it had not already been).

The Cardinals then mounted their only drive of the first half, but it stalled as they went for a pass on fourth and one at the New England 31 and the pass fell incomplete. New England took over on downs. Another long pass to Moss was dropped and a long pass to Benjamin Watson bounced off of his hands, but Cassel hit Gaffney for 19 yards and a first down to keep the drive alive. With a fourth down and 10 at the Arizona 29, New England went for it, and Cassel scrambled for 13 yards to the 16 for a first down. Cassel then hit Wes Welker for an 11 yard touchdown. The Pats were ahead 28-0 with 1:52 to go in the first half. Welker fell into the snow at the back of the end zone after the play and started making snow angels in celebration. The officials flagged him for unsportsmanlike conduct that would be assessed on the kickoff.

At this point, a coach would be concerned about kicking from 15 yards further back and maybe letting the downtrodden team build some momentum and get back into the game, but that would be a coach playing a team other than the Cardinals on this day. Yet another three and out and a punt gave New England the ball for one last drive before the end of the half. The Patriots made it count, as Cassel hit

Gaffney for 14, Gaffney again for 16 after an incompletion, and Welker for 20 to set up a 38 yard field goal by Stephen Gostkowski that made the halftime lead for New England 31-0.

The Patriots received the opening kickoff of the second half and returned it to the 24. The first play from scrimmage was a screen pass to Randy Moss on the left. Moss caught it and ran 76 yards down the sideline for a touchdown that made it 38-0. It was the longest pass play of the season for New England.

Surprisingly, Kurt Warner was back out at quarterback for Arizona as the Cardinals got the ball. Both Warner and New England defensive end Richard Seymour had been shaken up on Arizona's last offensive play of the first half, and it was thought with the score and weather conditions, both would be held out for the second half. This was especially true for Warner, since his team had already clinched a playoff spot. However, there he was, and he still could not get the Cardinals going. The sixth Cardinals' three and out possession and punt set up New England for another score. This was a 35 yard field goal by Gostkowski set up by a 26 yard screen play from Cassel to Heath Evans, an 11 yard pass from Cassel to Moss, and a 10 yard run by Morris.

Another three and out by Arizona, their seventh in eight possessions, and another Gostkowski field goal made it 44-0. Gostkowski's 24 yard field goal was his 33rd of the season, a new Patriot team record.

Matt Leinart took over at quarterback for Arizona with 3:26 to go in the third quarter after the kickoff. Ironically, Leinart was one of the quarterbacks at the University of Southern California who played while Matt Cassel did not. In the topsy-turvy 2008 season, Cassel was a starter and star in the NFL and Leinart was a backup now coming in for mop-up duty. Leinart was sacked and hit by Brandon Meriweather, fumbled and New England recovered. This led to a field goal early in the fourth quarter to make the score 47-0.

Leinart was also intercepted by Ellis Hobbs with 14:01 to go, and rookie Kevin O'Connell came in at quarterback to replace Matt Cassel. So Cassel had the luxury of watching O'Connell battle Leinart for the rest of the game.

Leinart did connect with Arizona's outstanding wide receiver, Larry Fitzgerald, for a long, though meaningless, 78 yard touchdown pass with 6:17 to go, but the game ended in a 47-7 New England rout.

Midway through the fourth quarter, some male fan came out of the stands and for some unknown reason (too much beer would be the logical suspect) tackled Patriot linebacker Junior Seau as Seau was standing on the sideline. Seau was unhurt, but the fan was removed from the the Stadium by security personnel and arrested by Foxboro police. The Patriots also were planning to revoke the season tickets of whoever owned those seats (thanks to information on the ticket stub), whether they belonged to the attacker or not.

- - -

It was another good day for Matt Cassel. He finished 20 of 36 for 345 yards and 3 touhdowns. Had he played in the fourth quarter he might have had another 400 yard passing day, but there was no reason to keep him in this one any longer than he played.

Wes Welker had 7 catches for 68 yards, the 14th time in 15 games in which he had 6 or more catches. The only game in which he did not was when he was knocked out of the Pittsburgh game by that unnecessary hit on an incomplete pass play.

- - -

Miami had some trouble with Kansas City, but won 38-31 to improve their record to 10-5 and remain tied with the Pats for the AFC East lead.

The Patriots finally did get some good news later on Sunday, though, as the New York Jets lost their late game to Seattle 13-3. It was the Jets' third loss in four games, with their only win being the gift win from Buffalo the preceding week. The Patriots still needed help to get into the playoffs, but the Jets now had even longer odds. For New England, the case was clear. They needed to win their game at Buffalo and then hope for one of two things to happen:

- Miami to lose to the Jets, or tie the Jets, which would give New England the AFC East championship and the third seed in the AFC playoff positioning.

- Baltimore to lose to Jacksonville, or tie them, which would give New England the second wild card position and the sixth seed in the AFC playoff positioning.

At least the Patriots would have a shot going into the final weekend of the season. For a team that had lost its MVP quarterback in the first quarter of the first game of the season, that was quite an accomplishment.

Chapter 26 – Shut Out

Sunday, December 28, 2008:	1	2	3	4	TOTAL
New England Patriots	3	0	7	3 -	13
Buffalo Bills	0	0	0	0 -	0

Seven hours before the Patriot season would come to a premature end, or roughly at noon, the Patriots were out on the field at Buffalo warming up to prepare for their regular season finale against the Bills. For the fifth week in a row, the weather would not be good for the game. This time it was not rain or snow that they would face, but howling wind. The wind was reported to be 40 MPH with gusts up to 60 MPH. It made for an interesting sight. Looking out from the concourse leading to the Patriot locker room, the players could see the nearside goalpost leaning to the left and the goalpost at the other end leaning to the right. This was a result of the swirling wind inside Ralph Wilson Stadium. It was clear the wind was going to play a significant role in the game.

Six hours before the Patriots would be shut out of the playoffs by a Miami victory over the Jets and a Baltimore win over Jacksonville, the Patriots won the coin toss and elected to take the wind at their back. It was a gutsy move by Patriot Coach Bill Belichick, but after the game he talked about Bill Parcells making a similar call in the 1986 NFC Championship game between the Giants and Redskins, another game with very strong winds just as this one was. Parcells chose to take the wind at his back and the Giants got 17 points in the first quarter. They were the only 17 points in the game. Belichick said "Coach Parcells elected to take the wind at the start of that game ... I'll never forget that game and I'll never forget that decision ... That was a big decision by Bill." It was also a big decision by this Bill, Mr. Bill Belichick, against these Buffalo Bills.

The Patriots would only get three points in the first quarter, but it would be enough, as they shut out the Bills 13-0. The Buffalo Bills did not throw a pass at all while they were going into the wind in the first quarter (right to left on the TV broadcast). The Patriots did not throw a pass at all while they were going into the wind in the second quarter. That is how bad conditions were. In fact, Matt Cassel threw only 8 passes all day, completing 6, for 78 yards. However, in keeping with his remarkable season, Cassel made the passes when they counted, and helped the Patriots win.

Richard Seymour was out for the game, due to a back injury suffered against Arizona, and Tedy Bruschi was also still out, so the battered Patriots were down even more defensive starters as they came out for Buffalo's opening plays. The Bills took the opening kickoff but could only get one first down on six running plays before having to punt. The Patriots regularly had 7-9 defenders lined up near the line of scrimmage, as they did not expect Buffalo to pass.

New England went three and out and punted and so did Buffalo. The Patriots had an opportunity to score on their punt, however, as the kick was muffed by the Buffalo returner, but Matthew Slater, who had a shot at grabbing it and scoring a touchdown for New England, could not, and Buffalo recovered.

The Patriots did score on their next possession, on a 33 yard field goal by Stephen Gostkowski. This was set up by a 9 play 48 yard drive that featured the first pass of the day. It came on the 14th play of the game, and it was a swing pass from Cassel to Heath Evans that went for 19 yards to the Buffalo 44 yard line. Another pass from Cassel to Evans, this one for 12 yards, took the ball to the 20 and set up the field goal. It was the only score of the first half, as the Pats led 3-0.

Buffalo had two chances to score in the first half. The first came on a field goal attempt that started out being kicked to the left and then suddenly took off and flew past the goalposts and in front of them to go wide right. It was as if the ball went up into a jet stream. The Bills' second opportunity to score came near the end of the first half. They marched from their 20 to the New England 9 yard line behind the running of Fred Jackson, and looked ready to either tie the game or take the lead. However, bad clock management and decision-making cost the Bills that chance. They ran the ball on third down instead of spiking it or throwing it (bad clock management) and with 17 seconds left, tried to rush their field goal unit onto the field as the clock was ticking down. However, Buffalo center Duke Preston and other Buffalo players got into a skirmish with some Patriots (bad decision-making), so the clock ran out. Instead of having a chance for a field goal, the Bills squandered the opportunity with a good deal of foolishness. Given the way they had given away their game against the Jets two weeks earlier, it was fair to wonder: what is it with this Buffalo team?

The Patriots got the only touchdown of the game on an 11 play, 43 yard, 6 minute drive in the third quarter. It started with Mike Vrabel recovering a Buffalo fumble, thanks to a sack and strip of quarterback Trent Edwards by Jarvis Green. New England converted two big fourth down plays on the drive. The first was a controlled six yard rollout run by Cassel on fourth and two from the Buffalo 25 yard line. The second was a Cassel pass to Wes Welker for twelve yards on fourth and five that took the ball to the two yard line. The Patriots were going into the wind at the time, so Cassel fired the pass on a low trajectory and hard to avoid the wind making it sail. It was a nice pass that Belichick complimented in his post-game press conference. Cassel again had done his job and done it well. So too did Welker, who took the pass on the thirteen and ran it to the two, on the only pass play on the drive. Lamont Jordan ran it in from two yards out, running easily through the right side of the line.

The point after touchdown was also a thrill, as the ball went through the uprights cleanly, but then the wind blew it back through the other way, back toward the players on the field. In fact, when it landed, some Buffalo fans thought the kick was no good, but since it had gone through cleanly, it did count, and New England led 10-0.

With Buffalo having the wind at its back, TV commentator Dan Dierdorf wondered aloud why Buffalo was taking its time between plays. His thought was that the Bills should have been running a hurry-up offense to get as many plays run as they could while they had the wind advantage. Buffalo Coach Dick Jauron apparently did not agree as the Bills took as much time between plays as they would on a balmy day in September. It sure is nice for New England to have a coach like Bill Belichick who plans for and adjusts to game conditions, unlike a number of other NFL coaches.

A drive by New England that straddled the third and fourth quarters led to a field goal and the final points of the day, a 23 yard field goal by Stephen Gostkowski with 10:15 left in the game.

There was one more big play before the end of the game, again showing how Bill Belichick is at least a step above most other coaches in strategy. With a third and 8 from their own 41 in the fourth quarter, Belichick had Cassel line up in the shotgun and then quick kick as soon as he got the ball. Cassel's punt bounced deep into Buffalo territory, and the wind kept blowing it until New England finally downed it at the Buffalo two yard line. It was a 57 yard punt by Matt Cassel, and a great play call by Belichick.

As the play was being run, the TV commentators were providing high praise. As Cassel kicked, Dierdorf could be heard saying "You've got to love Bill Belichick". After the play was over, play-by-play announcer Greg Gumbel called it "a terrific coaching decision".

After the game, Belichick explained that Buffalo had rushed 10 men on a previous punt, and he did not want to take the chance of them doing so again on fourth down and maybe blocking the punt and getting good field position and a chance to score. It was a great call by Belichick, and perfect execution by Cassel.

When Belichick came out for his final regular season post-game press conference, he was more talkative than usual. It may have been that he was really pleased with the 11-5 season his team completed. Belichick described himself as "really proud of our team today … the players gave us all they had … I respect this group of guys immensely. They've worked hard. They've put up with me all year and they fought through a lot of adversity … They proved to me and anyone else who's watching that mentally and physically they're a tough football team."

Now it was left to see if other teams could help in the late games. For the Patriots to win a wild card spot, Jacksonville would have to beat Baltimore. For the Patriots to win the AFC East, the New York Jets would have to beat Miami.

It was widely felt that Baltimore would win their game against Jacksonville, and they took an early lead and coasted to a 27-7 victory. Now it was left to the Patriots hoping that the Jets could win at home against Miami.

- - -

Since the Belichick-Brady era began in 2001, the Patriots wound up making the playoffs in 6 of those 8 years. In the other two years, 2002 and 2008, the Patriots' post-season chances came down to a late Sunday New York Jets game at the Meadowlands. Brett Favre was involved in both games.

In 2002, Favre and Green Bay came into the Meadowlands to play New York, and "stunk up the joint", as they say. This was the game (described in Chapter 6) in which New England defensive coach Romeo Crennel noted early that the Green Bay players didn't seem to want to play that day at all, and Bill Belichick stopped watching early since he seemed to sense the same thing. Favre and the Packers were blown out 42-17, giving the Jets the AFC East title, and keeping the Patriots out of the playoffs.

In 2008 the Patriots needed Favre, now with the Jets, to defeat Miami. Favre instead threw three interceptions, all bad throws, and the Dolphins won 24-17 to win the AFC East and keep the Patriots out of the playoffs. The first interception was a long, "just throw it up in the air and see what happens" type of pass that Favre had thrown far too often in his career. The second came one play after the Dolphins had scored to take a 7-6 lead. Favre dropped back, looked left, and threw right, directly into the hands of a Miami defender who ran it in for 25 yards and a touchdown, a mere 15 seconds after the previous Miami score. The pass from Favre was nowhere near a Jet receiver.

The third interception came late in the game, with the Jets trailing 24-17 and driving for what looked like a potential tying touchdown. Once again Favre threw it right into the hands of a Miami defender and nowhere near a Jet receiver. The Boston Globe called it the ugliest of the three interceptions. Really, though, it was hard to choose which of three was ugliest. They all were bad.

Still Favre was not through screwing up. With time running out, the Jets got the ball back at their own one yard line. At first Favre did not even come out for the play; Brad Smith was sent in to play quarterback (what a comedown for Favre, the potential Hall of Famer). However, after a delay for a replay review of the punt, Favre did come back out onto the field. He threw a short pass that was not intercepted, and the Jets tried a series of laterals to try to get the tying touchdown. Favre was the recipient of one lateral down the field, but then promptly lateraled it forward, which, as most players and fans know, is illegal. The Jets were penalized half the distance to the goal, but still had time for one play. Favre was taken out, and the play went for naught. The Jets and Favre had not beaten Miami, so the Dolphins won the AFC East with the same 11-5 record New England had, winning because of a better conference record. The Jets, who at one point had been 8-3 and had triggered talk of a Subway Super Bowl against the Giants, had lost 4 of their last 5 to finish 9-7. Their only win was the game handed to them by Buffalo.

To add another chapter to these pitiful Favre efforts in 2002 and 2008, it was Favre who threw a horrible interception in the 2007 NFC Championship game that sent the Giants and not the Packers into the Super Bowl against the undefeated Patriots. I felt then and still do that the Patriots would have easily beaten the Packers in the Super Bowl and that the Giants were the team that had the best chance to beat the Patriots (as described in Chaper 6). The game in Green Bay was played in bitter cold temperatures that should have favored the home town Packers, but it was the Giants who prevailed. The key play came in overtime. Green Bay won the coin toss to start overtime and elected to receive. Favre had been having a bad game, but many felt that he would now shake off a bad game and lead the Packers to the winning score. But Favre is reckless and he threw an absolutely horrible pass toward a receiver who was running an out pattern. The very poorly thrown ball was easily intercepted by the Giants, setting up a game-winning field goal that sent the Giants, and not the Packers, to Arizona to face the Patriots. The Patriots would be happy never to have their fate in the reckless hands of Brett Favre again.

- - -

So, the Patriots became only the fifth team in NFL history to win 11 games and not make the playoffs. The others were the 1962 Detroit Lions, the 1963 Green Bay Packers, the 1967 Baltimore Colts, and the 1985 Denver Broncos.

- - -

New England's season had thus ended early. It was too bad that it did, since the Patriots were playing good football in December. They would have been a tough match-up for any team in the playoffs. Instead, it was unfinished business. Wait 'til next year.

SECTION 3 – Aftermath of 2008

Chapter 27 – The Case for Matt Cassel as NFL MVP

Matt Cassel should have been the NFL MVP for 2008.

This is said with no disrespect to Peyton Manning, who did win the award, and who is second on my list of favorite players in the NFL both for his work ethic and results. Peyton is clearly the main reason that the Indianapolis Colts have been Super Bowl contenders since he entered the league, and may very well be the league's best player, but being the best player does not necessarily mean that you are the MVP, as we will see shortly.

This is also said with no disrespect to Tom Brady, who was the Patriot starting quarterback ahead of Cassel when the season started, and who is first on my list of favorite players in the NFL. Brady is the man who put the Patriots over the hump to their first Super Bowl title, and two since, was the MVP in 2007, and Patriot fans want to see him back at quarterback in 2009 and beyond. Brady was the MVP in 2007. Cassel should have been in 2008.

The MVP Award should be based on impact to the team during that particular season, not on statistics or history within the league. While Peyton Manning did have great impact on Indianapolis, so too did Matt Cassel have great impact on New England. As noted in earlier chapters, Cassel stepped into the giant void that was left when Brady was injured and has played extremely well. Without Cassel, the Patriots would not have been 11-5 and playoff contenders. Without Manning, the Colts still might have been contenders.

One of the reasons that the Colts still could have been contenders was that they had a better defense and better running game than did the Patriots. The Patriot defense was not as good in 2008 as had been expected, and was especially shaky on stopping their opponents on key third down plays. While the Patriot running game was solid for the last four weeks of the season, it was not in the first twelve. Most of what the Patriots accomplished in 2008 was due to the passing of Matt Cassel, the pass-catching of Kevin Faulk and Wes Welker, and the coaching of Bill Belichick.

With regard to the MVP not having to be the best player, there is no better argument than the choices of Charles Barkley as NBA MVP in 1993 and Karl Malone in 1997 over Michael Jordan. Jordan was the best player on the planet and the reason why the Bulls won six championships in the 1990's. He could just as easily have been chosen as MVP again in 1993 and 1997, just as Peyton Manning could have (and was) chosen in 2008. However, it was Charles Barkley who made the Phoenix Suns a contender in 1993 and Karl Malone who did the same for Utah in 1997, and each was a fitting MVP choice. Matt Cassel would have been a fitting choice in 2008 for the same reasons.

In baseball in 1987, Andre Dawson of the Chicago Cubs was named MVP, although his Cubs finished in last place. Having a player whose team finished in last place be MVP could itself be questioned, but this also may have been based on statistics and Dawson's career history than performance for that particular season. A more fitting choice for MVP in 1987 would have been Jack Clark of the pennant-winning St. Louis Cardinals. St. Louis was a light-hitting team that season that did not have much power without Clark. With him they had enough to finish first ahead of the defending World Champion and highly regarded New York Mets, the best team of the 1980s. Clark should have been MVP.

There is precedence in NFL history for a choice of Cassel as MVP as well. For example, the NFL MVP in 1967 was Johnny Unitas, the star quarterback of the Baltimore Colts, and one of the all-time great quarterbacks in NFL history. The NFL MVP in 2007 was Tom Brady, the star quarterback of the New England Patriots, and one of the all-time great quarterbacks in NFL history. Unitas was injured in 1968, just as Brady was in 2008. Unitas' replacement was a lightly regarded quarterback named Earl Morrall, just as Brady's replacement was the very lightly regarded Matt Cassel. In fact, it could be said that Morrall, an NFL veteran, would be considered a much better replacement for Unitas than Cassel would be for Brady, given that Cassel had not started a game since high school. Sportswriters and fans wondered in 1968 and 2008 how the Colts and Patriots would do without their star quarterbacks and MVP's. Morrall stepped in for Unitas and the Colts remained one of the league's best teams. Morrall succeeded his teammate as NFL MVP for 1968. Cassel stepped in for Brady, and the Patriots remained one of the league's best teams. Cassel should have succeeded his teammate as NFL MVP in 2008.

Unfortunately, there are a number of cases in sports history where a player who should have been elected MVP based on impact to his team was not. Larry Bird joined the Celtics as a rookie for the 1979-1980 season and turned that franchise around. The Celtics had won 29 games in 1978-1979 without Bird and 61 in 1979-80 with him. Yet the MVP was Kareem Abdul-Jabbar, a great player with a great career for sure, but not one who had as much impact on his team in 1979-80 as Larry Bird did on his.

Similarly, the addition of Kevin Garnett to the Celtics for the 2007-08 season made that franchise NBA Champions. From 24 wins in 2006-07, the Celtics had 66 in 2007-08 (an amazing 42 more wins from one season to the next) in winning that championship. The main reason for that improvement was generally conceded to be the addition of Garnett, for his inspirational play, for his intensity, and for his teamwork and leadership. Yet the MVP was Kobe Bryant, mainly because sports commentators felt that it was his turn to be MVP. While Kobe has been a good player for years, his 2007-08 season was not much better than his other seasons, and the Lakers, perennial contenders, were not that much better in 2007-08 than they had been previously and certainly not as much better as the presence of Kevin Garnett made the Boston Celtics that season.

Lest anyone think that this is Boston-based bias, I will give you an example where a Boston athlete was given an MVP award that maybe should have gone to an opponent. Jim Rice had a great year in 1978, and in any other year may have been a good MVP choice. But 1978 was the year that Ron Guidry carried the New York Yankees with a 25-3 record as a starting pitcher, and a win the AL East playoff game versus Boston. Guidry's team won. Rice's team did not. It can be said that Red Sox of 1978 could have finished second without Rice, but the Yankees of 1978 would not have finished first without Guidry. No offense to the great season by Jim Rice, an excellent ballplayer, but Guidry should have been the MVP that season.

On December 29, the TV show "New England Sports Tonight" broadcast on the Comcast Sports Net cable network had an interesting comparison of Matt Cassel's 2008 season versus an average season for Tom Brady from 2001-2007. The numbers shown were:

	Brady Average	Cassel 2008
Completion %	63.0	63.4
Passing yards	3,766	3,693
Yards/Attempt	7.28	7.16
Touchdowns	28	21
Interceptions	12	11
QB Rating	92.9	89.4

This got me to wondering how Cassel's 2008 season, the first in which he saw considerable action, compared with Brady's 2001 season, the first in which he saw considerable action and also how Cassel's 2008 season compared with Brady's 2007 season. Thanks to information in the Patriot media guide, those comparisons are:

	Brady 2001	Cassel 2008
Completion %	63.9	63.4
Passing yards	2,843	3,693
Yards/Attempt	6.88	7.16
Touchdowns	18	21
Interceptions	12	11
QB Rating	86.5	89.4

	Brady 2007	Cassel 2008
Completion %	68.9	63.4
Passing yards	4,806	3,693
Yards/Attempt	8.31	7.16
Touchdowns	50	21
Interceptions	8	11
QB Rating	117.2	89.4

What does all of this mean? First of all, let's dive a little deeper into some of the numbers. The Patriots had a better running attack in 2001 than they did in 2007 or 2008, so some of Brady's numbers in 2001 (such as passing yards) would be lower than his in 2007 or Cassel's in 2008. These charts also show what a phenomenal season Brady had in 2007. They also show that Cassel's numbers in 2008 were not that far off from those of an average Brady season.

What it does mean, however, is that the Patriots did not suffer as severe a drop off with Matt Cassel in 2008 as could have been expected when Brady went down. He stepped in and did a very good job.

Again, this is no knock on Brady, one of the all-time greats. While Cassel's 2008 season compares favorably to Brady's first and average seasons, it does not compare favorably to Brady's 2007 season. In fact, it would be difficult to find any quarterback in any year who had a season to compare with Brady's in 2007. Yet Cassel far exceeded expectations and kept the Patriots from falling too far after the loss of Brady. He should be commended for his 2008 season.

It is also interesting to speculate what a healthy Tom Brady would have accomplished in 2008, and whether his numbers would have been similar to 2007. I suspect that they would have.

In any case, Cassel had a great season in 2008, and one worthy of being MVP. He should at least have gotten consideration and some votes from among the 50 sportswriters and broadcasters who cover the NFL. He did not get a single vote. Peyton Manning was chosen MVP overwhelmingly, getting 32 of the 50 votes. The voting breakdown was as follows:

Peyton Manning, Indianapolis QB	32 votes
Chad Pennington, Miami QB	4
Michael Turner, Atlanta RB	4
James Harrison, Pittsburgh LB	3
Adrian Peterson, Minnesota RB	3
Philip Rivers, San Diego QB	2
Kurt Warner, Arizona QB	1
Chris Johnson, Tennessee RB	1

Without undermining the hard work of any of these players, I do believe that Matt Cassel deserved more MVP consideration than Philip Rivers of the 8-8 and underachieving San Diego Chargers, Michael Turner of Atlanta which also had a star QB in Matt Ryan, or Chris Johnson of Tennessee which was really led by QB Kerry Collins and a strong defense. He certainly deserved at least one vote.

Matt Cassel was a very fitting successor to Tom Brady. He should also have been MVP.

- - -

The most interesting question going into the Patriots' off-season concerned the future of Matt Cassel, who was to be a free agent after the 2008 season. Had he been a free agent after 2007, he would have been lucky to get interest from any other team. However, coming off his excellent 2008 season, Cassel was sure to be a quarterback highly sought by many other teams. There was speculation that the Patriots might apply the "franchise tag" on Cassel, thereby keeping him as insurance in case Tom Brady's recuperation did not go as expected (and there were rumors that was indeed the case). That would allow the Patriots to keep him. In that case, Cassel for 2009 would get the average salary of the five top players at his position, a number thought to be in the neighborhood of $ 14 million. This would also give the Patriots the flexibility of trading Cassel later if Brady was healthy and getting something in return for him, instead of letting him go to another team and getting nothing for him.

Cassel was asked about these possibilities (free agency, having the Patriots apply the franchise tag to him) after New England's season-ending win over Buffalo. His reply was very Brady-like, as he said, "If it works out that I come back here, there's no doubt in my mind that I'd be a happy guy. I love the Patriots organization. I love the Krafts. I love Coach Belichick and Coach McDaniels and what I've been able to do here. They gave me an opportunity to be a pro quarterback in the NFL."

Well said by Mr. Cassel. It would have been nice to have had both him and Brady back for 2009 if there was any way to work that out to both players' and the team's satisfaction. Regardless, Patriot fans will always wish for the best of luck and success for Matt Cassel. He gave us everything he had in 2008 and had a great season. It was fun to watch him improve from week to week and to see him keep the Patriots in contention all season. It was an MVP-like performance from a real team player and classy person, as shown in the comments quoted in the preceding paragraph. Regardless of whatever you may do in the future, thank you, Matt Cassel, for a great 2008.

Chapter 28 – 2008-09 Season Wrapup

The day after the 2008 regular season ended three head coaches were fired: Romeo Crennel of Cleveland, Rod Marinelli of Detroit, and Eric Mangini of the New York Jets. None of these firings were unexpected. Marinelli's Lions had become the first NFL team ever to go 0-16 for the season. The Browns had been looked at as a rising team after 2007 but fell back to the pack in 2008. They were also shut out in their last two games of 2008. Mangini's Jets had collapsed at the end of the 2008 season, losing four of their last five. Their only win should have been a loss had Buffalo run out the clock and protected their lead.

Two days after the regular season ended, there was another coach fired, and this one was a shocker. Denver fired Mike Shanahan. Shanahan had been Denver's coach for 14 years and had two Super Bowl wins to his credit, but it was apparently not enough to offset a collapse by the Broncos in 2008. The Broncos led the AFC West by three games with three games to play but lost them all as San Diego was winning, so the Chargers won the division. The final straw may have been a 52-21 loss by Denver to San Diego on the final Sunday night game of the season. That loss put San Diego and Denver into a tie for the AFC West, but San Diego won the division on a tie-breaker, thanks to a better record within their division.

San Diego thus proceeded to the playoffs with a very mediocre 8-8 record, while the Patriots were not with a much better 11-5 record. That's the way that it goes in the NFL.

There was another surprising head coach firing in January, as Tampa Bay fired Jon Gruden, who had won a Super Bowl with the team in 2003. Like Denver, Tampa Bay had collapsed down the stretch, turning a 9-3 record into a 9-7 record and missing the playoffs.

The Patriots were tied with Miami for first in the AFC East with 11-5 records, but the Dolphins won the tiebreaker thanks to a better record in the AFC (8-4, versus 7-5 for New England). New England's losses were to Miami, the Jets, San Diego, Pittsburgh, and Indianapolis. Miami's losses were to New England, the Jets, Baltimore, Houston, and the NFC's Arizona Cardinals.

The Patriots were also tied with Baltimore for the final AFC wild card spot with 11-5 records, but the Ravens won the tiebreaker thanks to a better record in the AFC (8-4, versus 7-5 for New England). Baltimore's losses were to Pittsburgh (twice, once in overtime), Indianapolis, Tennessee, and the NFC's New York Giants.

The NFL's final standings for 2008 were:

AFC

East		South	
Miami	11-5	Tennessee	13-3
New England	11-5	Indianapolis	12-4
New York	9-7	Houston	8-8
Buffalo	7-9	Jacksonville	5-11

North		West	
Pittsburgh	12-4	San Diego	8-8
Baltimore	11-5	Denver	8-8
Cincinnati	4-11-1	Oakland	5-11
Cleveland	4-12	Kansas City	2-14

NFC

East		South	
New York	12-4	Carolina	12-4
Philadelphia	9-6-1	Atlanta	11-5
Dallas	9-7	Tampa Bay	9-7
Washington	8-8	New Orleans	8-8

North		West	
Minnesota	10-6	Arizona	9-7
Chicago	9-7	San Francisco	7-9
Green Bay	6-10	Seattle	4-12
Detroit	0-16	St. Louis	2-14

The Playoff seedings were as follows:

AFC	NFC
Tennessee Titans	New York Giants
Pittsburgh Steelers	Carolina Panthers
Miami Dolphins	Minnesota Vikings
San Diego Chargers	Arizona Cardinals
Indianapolis Colts	Atlanta Falcons
Baltimore Ravens	Philadelphia Eagles

The first round match-ups were Atlanta-Arizona and Philadelphia-Minnesota in the NFC and Indianapolis-San Diego and Baltimore-Miami (the two teams that beat out the Patriots in tie-breakers for the playoffs) in the AFC.

The Patriots had a better record than four of the playoff teams.

- - -

There were a handful of plays that made the difference in the Patriots missing the playoffs instead of being the AFC East champions. One example was the fumble by Matthew Slater in the Pittsburgh game that opened the floodgates for the Steelers and broke open what had been a tight 13-10 game before then (as described in Chapter 20). Another was the dropped pass by Jabar Gaffney in the Indianapolis game that turned a sure touchdown into a field goal in an 18-15 loss to the Colts. That game also saw the Patriots out of timeouts when they could have used them at the end of the game to give themselves a chance for a win (see Chapter 15 for details).

However, THE key play of the season was the Patriots unable to stop the Jets on a third and 15 from the Jets' 15 yard line in overtime of the game on November 13. Had the Patriots stopped the Jets on that play, the Jets would have punted, the Patriots would have had good field position, and a short drive could have positioned New England for a game-winning field goal. It also would have kept the Patriots in first place, and, if everything else went as it did, they would have been there for the remainder of the season, and they would have been in the playoffs. In reflecting on the season, if the Patriots had one play to do over again, it would have been that one. Stop the Jets then and they would have been in the playoffs. Oh well. It is what it is.

- - -

Jerod Mayo was named the NFL's defensive rookie of the year for 2008. It was a well-deserved honor, as Mayo played well all season, participating in more snaps than any defensive player, and being an impact player throughout the season. Belichick does not usually like playing rookies unless he has to because of injury, but Mayo was so good that he won a starting job for the first game of the season and kept it. It will be interesting to see how much better Mayo becomes in coming seasons.

- - -

In sharp contrast to the teamwork and camaraderie of the Patriots, the New York Jets were having a turbulent off-season from the start. In addition to the firing of Head Coach Eric Mangini, the man hailed as "Mangenius" after his first season and gone after his third, the Jets approached Bill Cowher about taking over that position, but Cowher was not interested.

It was reported that Brett Favre, who had thrown three interceptions during the Miami game, and who had a bad last month of the season, was going to take several weeks to decide whether to retire or return for another season. It seemed as if this was the same scenario that Favre had followed for many, many years – keep his current team on the string while he decides whether to come back or not. Green Bay got tired of it after having had that happen to them for many years. Now it would be the Jets who needed to wait for Favre to decide before making their plans for their next season. Then they will have to wait to see if Favre sticks to that decision once he has made it. He did not stick to his decision to retire from Green Bay in 2007.

Even worse, in the week following the end of the regular season, Jet running back Thomas Jones suggested that quarterback Brett Favre should maybe have been benched during the Miami game as a result of his poor performance. In an interview on New York radio on December 30, Jones reportedly said, "If somebody is not playing well, they need to come out of the game. You're jeopardizing the whole team because you're having a bad day. To me, that's not fair to everybody else."

On February 11, 2009, Brett Favre and the Jets did announce that Favre was retiring from football. (He did not stick to that decision this time either, coming out of retirement once again to play with the Minnesota Vikings in 2009.)

- - -

A number of the members of the Patriot organization were being sought by other teams to fill spots in their organization.

Offensive coordinator Josh McDaniels was on a number of teams' short lists as a potential head coach. McDaniels' work with the high-powered Patriot offense in 2007 and in helping to develop Matt Cassel in 2008 made him an attractive candidate for other teams. On January 12, 2009, he signed on to replace Mike Shanahan as Head Coach of the Denver Broncos. The Broncos described McDaniels as reminding them of "a young Mike Shanahan". It makes you wonder what then was wrong with the old Mike Shanahan, but we still wish McDaniels all the best. Bill Belichick issued a very nice and highly complimentary statement about McDaniels that day, saying

"Josh McDaniels is one of the finest people and brightest, most talented coaches I have ever worked with. Since joining us eight years ago, Josh performed a variety of roles and excelled in every one of them. Between his work on defense, in scouting, player evaluation and coordinating the offense, Josh is a very well-rounded coach whose outstanding body of work speaks for itself. He is the product of a pure football environment which is evident in his approach to the game. On behalf of the entire Patriots organization, we thank Josh for tremendous success in New England and congratulate him and the McDaniels family for this most deserving opportunity for advancement."

Scott Pioli, Patriot Vice President of Player Personnel, who had just finished his ninth season with the Patriots, was being sought out as a General Manager by other teams. He reportedly interviewed with the Cleveland Browns around New Years Day, although he may have been put off by Cleveland hiring Eric Mangini as their next head coach. Given the acrimony between Mangini and the Patriots, that is not unexpected. Also, Cleveland, if you are hiring a new General Manager, shouldn't that new GM be able to hire the next coach?

On January 13, the day after Josh McDaniels became the Broncos' Head Coach, Pioli also left, agreeing to become the new GM of the Kansas City Chiefs (and, unlike the situation in Cleveland, Pioli, the Chiefs' new GM, was able to hire the next coach at Kansas City, Todd Haley). Again, the Patriots were very supportive and complimentary of Pioli in their statements after the announcement of his signing with the Chiefs. Bob Kraft commented that

> "Scott Pioli was an integral part of the many championships the New England Patriots have celebrated this decade and I would like to thank him for his countless contributions throughout the past nine seasons. Scott is a great evaluator of talent. He is thorough in his evaluations, extremely organized and has done a tremendous job mining all possible resources to help Coach Belichick and his staff field the players needed to win consistently. He has played an important role in building a championship tradition with players that I am proud to call Patriots. On behalf of the entire Patriots organization, I wish Scott continued success in his new role and offer best wishes to his wonderful wife Dallas, and their beautiful daughter Mia. I think Clark Hunt and the Kansas City Chiefs have made a very wise hire."

And Bill Belichick also issued a statement in which he said

> "To sum up in words everything Scott Pioli has meant to this organization and to me personally would be difficult, if not impossible. From the day I met him, he has demonstrated a passion for football and respect for the game that is second to none. It has been extremely gratifying for me to follow Scott's career ascension from the bottom of the totem pole in Cleveland to his place as a pillar of championship teams in New England. Now with the opportunity to steer his own ship and a vision of building a winner, there is no more capable, hardworking, loyal, team-oriented person than Scott Pioli.
>
> On a personal level, the Belichick-Pioli bond runs far deeper than our workplace, as we and our families have shared countless

memories away from football. Working side by side with one of my best friends for almost two decades is special enough in itself. But to help each other achieve success beyond our dreams is a blessing and something I will always remember and appreciate."

It was clear that there was a mutual respect between the Patriots and both McDaniels and Pioli (and makes you wonder what Eric Mangini did when he left the team and what the feeling was then). Pioli and Belichick have established a great relationship, so it is sad to see him go.

Brad Seely, the Special Teams Coach, also left at about the same time. Seely was moving on to become assistant head coach/special teams coach for the Cleveland Browns. Dom Capers, who was a Patriots' special assistant and secondary coach, left to become the defensive coordinator at Green Bay. There were a number of big holes that the Patriots would have to fill during this off-season. Director of Player Personnel Nick Caserio was identified as Pioli's replacement; Caserio had started as a personnel assistant in the scouting department in 2001. Bill O'Brien, who had been Receivers Coach, was set to fill in for Josh McDaniels as Quarterback Coach, though not necessarily as Offensive Coordinator.

- - -

The weekly publication "Patriots Football Weekly" had a couple of very interesting observations in its issue of December 31, 2008 following the end of the regular season. In an Editor's Note, Editor-in-Chief and Publisher Fred Kirsch started by saying "Hold your heads up high, Patriot Nation. When it comes to the 2008 season there's absolutely nothing to be ashamed of and a whole lot of which to be proud." After talking about the team and what he described as "an incredible display of teamwork, coaching, and fortitude", Kirsch went on to say, "When it comes to individuals, the 2008 success stories begin with Matt Cassel ... it was Cassel who stepped up to oftentimes make up for the losses – and yes, shortcomings - on the defensive side of the ball." He went on to praise Jerod Mayo, Vince Wilfork, Wes Welker, Randy Moss, Mike Vrabel, and Kevin Faulk individually and compliment the players, coaches, scouting staff and front office, for making the 11-5 season possible.

In that same issue, noted football guru Ron Jaworski, a former quarterback with Youngstown State and the Philadelphia Eagles, and currently an analyst on Monday Night Football, was very complimentary about Matt Cassel as well. Jaworski said of Cassel that "Every week he seems to do something else that impresses me ... he's improved in so many ways ... he is very prepared and very professional ... Matt is a player."

- - -

The first round of the NFL playoffs, unfortunately without the Patriots participating, took place on the weekend of January 3-4, 2009. The first game pitted the Atlanta Falcons and Arizona Cardinals. It was the first home playoff game for the Cardinals since 1947, when they were the Chicago Cardinals. They had no home playoff games when they were in St. Louis, and none, until this season, in Arizona. Behind the passing of Kurt Warner and running of Edgerrin James, the Cardinals took this one 30-24. A key play was a flea-flicker in which Warner handed off to James who ran to the line, turned back, and lateraled it back to Warner, who threw a perfect bomb to Larry Fitzgerald in the end zone for the touchdown.

The second game on this "wild card weekend" was an overtime game between Indianapolis and San Diego. There were two key players in this game for San Diego. One was punter Mike Scifres who three times pinned Indianapolis back inside the 10 yard line on punts. The last time resulted in a Colt punt that set up San Diego for the tying field goal that sent the game into OT. The Chargers won the coin toss and the Colts never saw the ball in overtime.

San Diego running back Darren Sproles, subbing for the injured LaDanian Tomlinson, was the other key player in this game. Sproles capped a great game by running for the winning touchdown from 22 yards out for a 23-17 San Diego win. Sproles had 328 yards rushing, receiving, and on kick returns. This was the third highest total in NFL playoff history. His total trailed only Ed Podolak of Kansas City in a 1971 double overtime loss to Miami, and Keith Lincoln of San Diego in their 51-10 AFL championship win over the Patriots in 1963.

Baltimore beat Miami 27-9 in the game that featured the two teams that beat out the Patriots for playoff spots based on tiebreakers. Miami had five turnovers in the game (versus a total of only 13 during the regular season) as the Baltimore defense was rock-solid throughout the game. Ed Reed had two of the interceptions for the Ravens, returning one of them 64 yards for the game's first touchdown.

The Philadelphia Eagles defeated Minnesota 26-14, with former Patriot Asante Samuel returning an interception 44 yards for a touchdown in the second quarter (why couldn't he have held on to that potential interception against Eli Manning in the last minutes of the Super Bowl? It would have preserved the Patriots' undefeated season.). Donovan McNabb connected with Brian Westbrook for a 71 yard touchdown midway through the fourth quarter to put that game out of reach.

- - -

This second round of the playoffs on January 10-11 turned out to be full of surprises, as three visiting teams wound up winning games.

Baltimore beat Tennessee 13-10 in a titanic defensive struggle, won on a Baltimore field goal with only 53 seconds left in the game. Tennessee dominated the statistics, but three turnovers, including a fumble at the one yard line in the fourth quarter when they were trailing 10-7, were enough to eliminate Tennessee, the AFC's top team.

Pittsburgh earned the right to host Baltimore for the AFC title with a convincing 35-24 win over San Diego. Pittsburgh was the only home team to win in this playoff round. This game was decided in the third quarter. Pittsburgh started it with a long drive for a touchdown, and then got an interception on a deflection on San Diego's first play from scrimmage. That pass would turn out to be the only play run by the San Diego offense in the third quarter. The only other time that the Charger offense had a chance to have the ball was blown when a Pittsburgh punt bounced off of the helmet of a Charger. Pittsburgh recovered the ball and San Diego wound up running only one play in the entire third quarter.

The NFC featured two major upsets. On Saturday night, the surprising Arizona Cardinals stunned the Carolina Panthers 33-13. It was another good performance by Kurt Warner for Arizona, while his counterpart, Carolina QB Jake Delhomme, had an awful day (on his birthday no less). Delhomme threw five interceptions and fumbled once to really hurt the Carolina cause.

The second big upset occurred in the early Sunday game as the Philadelphia Eagles defeated the New York Giants 23-11 on a windy day in Giants' Stadium. The Eagles' first touchdown was set up by an interception by former Patriot Asante Samuel (again! why couldn't he have held on to that potential interception against Eli Manning in the last minutes of the Super Bowl in February?). It was a bad day by Giants' QB Eli Manning (why couldn't he have had such a day in the Super Bowl?), who could not master the wind and never could get the Giants into the end zone. Three field goals (out of five attempts) and a safety were all the scoring that the Giants could muster on this day. Manning finished 15 for 29 with two interceptions.

So the Giants, thought by many to be the best team in the NFL this season, were now eliminated, just as the 2007 Patriots, the best team in the NFL that season, had been. It was a crushing defeat for the Giants and their fans, who had expected a second consecutive

Super Bowl win. Giant center Shaun O'Hara was quoted in the New York Daily News as saying "I think shock would be an understatement. When you look at the season we had, the number of games we won, the way we won them, I can't even fathom not continuing to play. To have it taken away now, it's the worst feeling ever." Try going 18-0 and then losing in the Super Bowl, Shaun.

Instead, the Arizona Cardinals would host Philadelphia for the NFC championship. Ironically, it was the Cardinals' third time in a Championship game and the third time that their opponent in that game would be the Philadelphia Eagles. This was not that big a deal, since the first two times were in 1947 and 1948, but what was a big deal was that this was the fifth time in eight years that the Eagles had made it to the NFC Championship behind Coach Andy Reid and QB Donovan McNabb.

Oddly, the top three seeds in the NFC had been eliminated, as had the number 1, 3, and 4 seeds in the AFC. If only the Patriots could have had this group with which to contend in 2007.

In the Conference Championship games, Arizona and Pittsburgh won the right to meet in the Super Bowl. Arizona's win meant that there were only five franchises which had never been in the Super Bowl – the Jacksonville Jaguars, New Orleans Saints, Detroit Lions, Cleveland Browns, and Houston Texans (the Saints reduced that number to four a year later as they made their first Super Bowl appearance in 2010). The Cardinals had the second longest championship drought in America's four major sports, having gone 61 years since their last championship. Only the Chicago Cubs' 100 years without a World Series win tops that.

Arizona's defeat of Philadelphia was a surprise, as had been their other playoff wins leading into this game. The Cardinals took a 24-6 lead in the first half behind three touchdown passes from Kurt Warner to Larry Fitzgerald. One of these was on a flea-flicker designed especially for this game by Arizona offensive coordinator Todd Haley. In the play, called 'Philly Special' according to *Sports Illustrated*, Warner took the snap and tossed the ball to running back J.J. Arrington. Arrington started to run right on what looked like an end run, but stopped, and threw the ball back to Warner. Warner lofted a perfect pass downfield to Fitzgerald for a 62 yard touchdown.

In keeping with the Cardinals' history, they fell behind 25-24 as Philadelphia dominated the third quarter and early fourth. Then, with less than 11 minutes to go in the game, Warner led Arizona on a 14 play, 72 yard march to the touchdown that sent them to the Super Bowl. The Cardinals got the score on a screen pass from Warner to running back Tim Hightower. The Cardinals got a two point conversion and held on for a 32-25 win. Warner, who was the star for the St. Louis Rams in their two Super Bowl runs, would thus become only the second man to be the starting quarterback for two different franchises in the Super Bowl. The other was Craig Morton of the 1970 Dallas Cowboys and 1977 Denver Broncos.

The Pittsburgh-Baltimore game was a study in defense. The Steelers seemed to be dominating, but had just a 16-14 lead late in the fourth quarter. Then Troy Polamalu intercepted a Joe Flacco pass and ran it back 40 yards for the score that clinched a 23-14 Pittsburgh win.

In a typical Steeler play, late in the game, there was a vicious hit on Baltimore running back Willis McGahee. The perpetrator of the hit was Ryan Clark. Astute readers will remember Clark as the Steeler defender who knocked Patriot receiver Wes Welker out of their game on November 30. At that time Clark blasted Welker as he went up for a throw and was penalized for an "unnecessary hit on a defenseless receiver". Welker was knocked out of the game. This shot by Clark to McGahee was even worse. Clark hit him helmet-to-helmet and McGahee lay motionless of the ground for some time. Players on both teams gathered around him and some knelt in prayer. McGahee eventually was taken off on a stretcher and later reports indicated that he did have movement in his arms and legs, so what looked like a potentially paralyzing hit thankfully turned out not to be.

Clark was not penalized on the play, and in the ensuing days the NFL issued a statement that Clark would not be fined for the hit. It was similar to the statement issued in December that Clark would not be fined for his hit on Welker. Maybe both hits were legal by the letter of the law, but both were just plain wrong. If you have to keep issuing statements that a player is not going to be fined for his injury-inducing hits, maybe there is a problem that needs to be dealt with before someone does get paralyzed.

What made this even worse is that as McGahee was motionless on the ground, the operators running the sound system at Heinz Field started playing music over the PA system. Watching on TV you could hear the song "Down on the Corner" by Creedence Clearwater Revival playing. My first thought was 'Why would they do this? This guy may be lying there paralyzed, and they are playing this music?" It seemed more a time for silence, but then, when you are used to this kind of thing, as the Steelers are, maybe it is not as big a deal as it is to other football fans. Interestingly, there were criticisms of this from some newspapers, magazines, and on-line web sites. The si.com web site posted a criticism that ended with the comment "Look, it's a tough situation to be in for whoever is running the tunes -- you don't want to let the crowd become completely passive and ruin the celebration of the home team headed to Super Bowl, but at the same time, there's a guy lying on the field and no one's sure if he can even talk or move his fingers. So, for future reference music guys: just do the Paul Simon thing and let silence be the sound." I could not agree more. Maybe next time the Steelers will at least consider the situation before playing music when there is a serious injury being tended to on the field.

- - -

Super Bowl XLIII – Pittsburgh 27 Arizona 23

	1	2	3	4		Total
Pittsburgh	3	14	3	7	-	27
Arizona	0	7	0	16	-	23

In Super Bowl XLII in 2008, the New England Patriots scored with 2:42 left in the game to take the lead, but lost on a touchdown pass with 35 seconds to go. In an eerie parallel, one year later, in Super Bowl XLIII in 2009, the Arizona Cardinals scored with 2:37 to go to take the lead, only to lose on a touchdown pass with 35 seconds to go.

This Super Bowl between Pittsburgh and Arizona was a so-so game for three quarters and then an explosion of excitement in the fourth quarter.

For the 12th straight year, the NFC team uncannily won the coin flip. For the first time ever (thanks to a new rule instituted in 2008), the team winning the Super Bowl coin toss deferred, so Pittsburgh got the ball first. The Steelers marched down the field for a field goal and a 3-0 lead.

The lead was extended to 10-7 in the second quarter, but Arizona was driving toward a potential score as the half began to draw to a close. With the ball on the Pittsburgh two yard line, Kurt Warner tried to throw a slant pass on an in route, but the ball was intercepted at the goal line by Pittsburgh's James Harrison. With the half running out, Harrison ran the ball back 100 yards for a touchdown. Time expired on his runback. It was a big swing on the scoreboard. Instead of Arizona being ahead 14-10 or tied 10-10, the interception had given Pittsburgh a 17-7 lead at the half.

It was the longest play in Super Bowl history. There also maybe should have been a penalty on it, since a Steeler blocked a would-be Cardinal tackler in the back. That is illegal and often is a penalty called in a runback of a kick or interception, but the Steelers got away with it in this case and had the halftime lead.

- - -

The Super Bowl commercials are supposedly a highlight of the day, and people get paid a lot of money to come up with the commercials. In previous decades, we had been treated to such great commercials as Mean Joe Greene tossing a young boy his game shirt after drinking the boy's offered soft drink or Larry Bird and Michael Jordan engaging in a clever game of basketball H-O-R-S-E. However, cleverness in advertising doesn't seem to exist in the 21st century. Thus we were treated to a number of terrible commercials. Many probably made parents cringe as they were watching with their young children. Doritos had two commercials, the first showing a man throwing a snow globe into another man's crotch (and hasn't that cliché been overdone by now on shows like *America's Funniest Videos*?), the second showing a man crunching a Doritos chip so loudly on the street that an attractive woman's dress flies off, leaving her in her underwear. Is that supposed to be clever? Later godaddy.com had two commercials involving female race car driver Danica Patrick. One had her taking her fifth shower of the day under the control of some computer geeks watching her on a computer screen. The other had her and other woman testifying before Congress in an enhancement hearing, a takeoff on the baseball steroid hearings. That one ended with one woman reaching to pull down the collar on her shirt while saying "I'll show you enhancements." Is this really what companies pay ad executives to come up with? It's odd when the beer commercials, which are usually the worst, wind up being the best of the day.

- - -

Down 20-7 in the fourth quarter, the Cardinals came to life. Kurt Warner led them on an 8 play, 87 yard drive to a TD. The score which came on a 1 yard pass from Warner to a leaping Larry Fitzgerald in the end zone cut the Steeler lead to 20-14 with 7:33 left in the game.

The next Cardinal possession netted nothing, but a punt was downed at the Pittsburgh one. During the punt, Steeler James Harrison was called for a personal foul penalty, and replays showed him pushing down and punching a Cardinal player in the back. TV analyst John Madden called for Harrison to be ejected, but he was not. Same old Steelers. The penalty moved the ball back half the distance to the goal line, so really just a few inches, thanks to the great punt coverage by Arizona. This led to a safety as the Steelers were called for holding in the end zone on a pass play. The score was now 20-16 and Pittsburgh was kicking it back to Arizona, with 2:58 remaining.

Suddenly, the Cardinals took the lead as Warner hit Fitzgerald on a slant over the middle and Fitzgerald ran straight down the middle to complete a 64 yard touchdown play that made the score 23-20 in favor of Arizona with only 2:37 left on the clock.

The Steelers took over and Roethlisberger led them on a spectacular drive to a touchdown, connecting with receiver Santonio Holmes for most of the yardage. With a first and goal from the 6, Holmes narrowly missed a pass for TD, letting it go through his hands in the left corner of the end zone. On second down, Holmes went to the right corner, was covered by three defenders, but made a great catch on a pass from Roethlisberger, narrowly keeping both feet in bounds. The Steelers had the lead back at 27-23, and recovered a Cardinal fumble to preserve the game and the win.

After the play Holmes used the football as a prop in a celebratory move. This in the NFL today is supposed to result in an "excessive celebration" penalty. It did not in this case. Randy Moss had been called for such a penalty for simply spiking the ball after his record-setting 23rd touchdown reception in the final regular season game in 2007. Benjamin Watson was called for such a penalty for pretending to put the ball under his shirt in the December 7, 2008 game against Seattle. Wes Welker was flagged for this penalty for making snow bunnies after a touchdown in the December 21, 2008 game against Arizona. Players on almost every team got called for this numerous times during the season. However, although Holmes did this right in front of an official in the Super Bowl watched by millions, the Steelers got away with this and did not get a 15 yard penalty for the ensuing kickoff, as most teams would have.

On the Thursday following the Super Bowl, the NFL announced that Santonio Holmes should have been penalized for using the ball as a prop in celebrating his touchdown. The league also announced that there should have been a replay review by the on-field officials of the fumble call against Kurt Warner that effectively ended the game. Interestingly, it has seemed to be an all too frequent occurrence that calls that could have gone against the Steelers but didn't are revealed and acknowledged by the league in the days after a big game, or fines for late hits by Steeler players that weren't called as penalties during the game are announced in the following week. Oh well, it is what it is.

Penalty calls and non-penalty calls might have given Arizona a chance to win, but this is to take nothing away from the Steelers, who made that late, clutch drive to win the game. Roethlisberger was terrific in running his team, eluding tacklers to extend plays, and then making the throws. The Steelers did what they had to do to win the game, and thus became the first team to win six Super Bowls.

Chapter 29 – On to 2009

February 5, 2009 was the first day that NFL teams could apply the franchise tag on one of their pending free agents. In the previous years in which the Patriots have used that tag, they waited until the two week period to do so was almost over before applying that tag to a player. This occurred with Adam Vinatieri, Tebucky Jones, and Asante Samuel. However, the Patriots wasted zero time in 2009, as they applied the franchise tag to Matt Cassel on the first day that they could do so.

Cassel, who had reportedly earned a salary of $520,000 in 2008, would now be receiving an offer of $14,650,000 for 2009. This meant that he would have a nice little pay raise of over 14 million dollars. This is determined by averaging the salaries of the top 5 players at the position of the franchised player. The move was ostensibly made to provide the team insurance in case Tom Brady would not be ready for the 2009 season. If Brady was okay, this would also allow the Patriots to trade Cassel and get value in return, rather than lose him to a free agent signing with another team and get nothing in return for him.

The Patriots and Cassel both expressed satisfaction with the deal, and Cassel reiterated that he would be happy returning to the Patriots to back up Tom Brady if that is how things turned out. He accepted the tendered offer, and talked about the possibility of being Brady's backup, saying "If that's the case, I'll do what I've done my entire career, which is continue to work hard, and be ready if another opportunity comes up."

For their part, the Patriots were happy to be able to hold onto Matt Cassel, and Bill Belichick issued a statement praising Cassel, saying "Matt has been a pleasure to coach his entire career, and last season in particular, when his years of hard work and commitment resulted in a most impressive performance. We look forward to working with Matt again in 2009."

- - -

The next big day on the 2009 calendar was February 27, the first day that teams can sign free agents from other teams. The Patriots were the team making the most headlines that day and the next. First they signed veteran running back Fred Taylor, a free agent from Jacksonville and tight end Chris Baker from the Jets. Taylor's acquisition was a big one. He had gained 11,271 yards on 2,428 carries over his 11 year career with the Jaguars, for an average of 4.6 yards per carry. He had gained over 1,000 yards 7 times in those 11 years. It was clear that the Patriots would now have a much stronger running game to pair with their vaunted passing attack.

The Patriots lost two players to free agency, as both long snapper Lonie Paxton and wide receiver Jabar Gaffney signed with the Denver Broncos and their new head coach, former New England assistant Josh McDaniels.

As I was driving to Boston for the Celtics' game that night, I heard a stunner over the radio. The story was that Patriots had traded veteran linebacker Mike Vrabel to Kansas City for what was then an undisclosed draft choice. Vrabel had been a stalwart for New England for eight seasons, as one of the best players in their defense, a player with a nose for the ball and for making the big play. It was Vrabel's blitz of Kurt Warner in the 2002 Super Bowl that led to Ty Law's interception and the Patriots' first score in their first Super Bowl victory. It was Vrabel who often stripped the ball from quarterbacks to set up big turnovers for the Patriots. It was Vrabel who became reknowned for catching touchdown passes from Tom Brady in goal line situations; Vrabel caught ten passes in his career with New England, all ten for touchdowns, including two in Super Bowls. He made the Pro Bowl in 2007.

However, as *Boston Globe* writer Christopher L. Gasper so correctly put it the next day, "Vrabel's contributions can't be measured in numbers. He was the quintessential Patriot, the embodiment of the tough, smart, disciplined, and versatile football player [that] coach Bill Belichick and Pioli used as their blueprint for building the team into the NFL's model franchise. He was also one of the most underrated and undervalued pillars of the Patriots' dynasty."

The other shoe didn't fall until the following day, however. We were in New York, and, as we are wont to do on occasion in New York, we went to the ESPN Zone in Times Square to get some of their great nachos (what can I tell you, they are very good). As we were waiting to be seated, my wife told me that she saw on one of their dozens of TV screens that Matt Cassel had been traded to Kansas City. After we had gotten to our table, I checked the crawl on one screen, and, sure enough, Cassel had been traded to the Chiefs. What was extremely surprising though was that both Vrabel and Cassel had been traded in the one deal, and all that the Patriots received was one draft pick, and it was only KC's second round pick (pick # 34 overall in the draft).

That the Patriots were only able to get one second round pick for two starters astounded most fans. Over the next few days, however, the explanations seemed many. The Patriots may have wanted to trade Cassel to use his $14M to sign their own pending free agents, and did not find much of a market for him. A *Boston Globe* story on March 1 reported that "the price of moving Cassel was that they had to part with Vrabel." There was also conjecture by the *Globe* that part of the reason that the Patriots were willing to trade Vrabel was that Vrabel would be entering the last year of his contract in 2009, and was due to receive $2.2 million in base salary, but count $4.3 million against the salary cap; he may have been traded to give the Patriots more cap space freedom. The other rumor was that the Patriots would use that # 34 pick to acquire pass-rusher Julius Peppers from Carolina. While that would definitely strengthen the Patriots' defense and shore up a weakness from 2008, many observors felt that Peppers' enormous salary may have made that unlikely.

In any case, the Patriots had lost two players who were very classy performers, one for 8 years (Vrabel) and the other who stepped in admirably for Tom Brady after Brady's season ended in an injury against, ironically, the same Kansas City Chiefs to whom Cassel would now be reporting. Both players would be missed.

In announcing the trade, Bill Belichick praised Vrabel greatly, saying "When Mike arrived in 2001 we knew we were adding a solid outside linebaker. But where Mike took it from there exceeded our highest hopes. Mike Vrabel epitomizes everything a coach could seek in a professional football player: toughness, intelligence, playmaking, leadership, versatility, and consistency at the highest level. Behind the scenes, Mike's wit and personality is one of the things that we have all enjoyed about coming to work every day … Of all the players I have coached in my career, there is nobody I enjoyed working with more than Mike. In the same way people recognize guys like Troy Brown, we appreciate and thank Mike Vrabel. He is one of the very special Patriots champions."

The trade became even more intriguing when rumors began circulating that just before the Patriots completed the deal with Kansas City, Denver and Tampa Bay were discussing a three-way deal that would have sent Cassel to Denver and Bronco starting QB Jay Cutler to Tampa Bay. It was not clear what the Patriots would receive but it was more than a second round pick. The rumor speculated that this offer was made after Belichick had already agreed to the deal with KC, and that, as such, Belichick would not back out of a deal already made (if so, good for him for staying true to his word). Cutler, who reportedly is a player with an over-inflated sense of his worth, apparently was insulted that the Broncos might have considered trading him, and began feuding with Josh McDaniels and demanding a trade. It was not a good situation in Denver.

Meanwhile, in Kansas City, the acquisition of Cassel and Vrabel resulted in the team selling more than 100 new season tickets on the first business day after the trade was announced. The Kansas City Star also reported that

> "New England's motivations in the trade aren't that hard to figure out. The Patriots dealt two players from positions of depth on their roster, brought back a first-day draft choice and cleared up $18 million of cap space ... Without the trade, New England was basically out of cap space, so the Patriots didn't just bring back the 34th pick in the upcoming draft, they also brought back the free agents they are surely to add later this week.
>
> The jettisoning of Vrabel is a signature, and very smart, Patriots maneuver. Belichick does not get sentimental over football players ... New England has maintained its place atop the NFL perch this decade by knowing when to fold'em on a player. Vrabel is still a solid performer that can help the Chiefs for a year or two, but he turns 34 in August and the Patriots have rising linebacker Shawn Crable to step into his position. Crable is younger and cheaper ...
>
> For his part, Cassel didn't seem to mind. Despite his designation as New England's franchise player and his lucrative new contract, he wasn't going to get the chance to compete with the Patriots as long as Tom Brady is around.
>
> "I was resolved to the fact I was going to get traded somewhere," Cassel said Monday. "I knew there probably would be some kind of talks and transactions that would take place. I didn't know when."
>
> The Chiefs became a favored landing spot when they hired general manager Scott Pioli away from New England in January. Sure, the Chiefs were 2-14 last season, with plenty of work to do before they are again competitive...
>
> A reunion with Pioli was also a factor for Cassel.
>
> "I have a great relationship with Scott Pioli," Cassel said. "He was one of my biggest supporters throughout the year. He was always very encouraging and anytime I needed some advice, I'd usually go to him as one of the guys who was always willing to open his office door.
>
> "I was hoping there was some interest (from the Chiefs) and obviously there was."
>
> Cassel started 15 games for the Patriots last season, but only after the Chiefs knocked Brady out of the season opener with a knee injury. The Patriots wound up winning 10 of those games, with Cassel throwing for 21 touchdowns and almost 3,700 yards...

Haley spent time last year watching Cassel on video. "Matt's a young player in the league with a good year under his belt starting," Haley said. "He was able to win 11 games last year. He's the type of guy we'd like to have on the Kansas City Chiefs as we go forward. We're trying to accumulate as many good players as we can.

"He's coming from a very good system and a place where they've done a good job of winning games in the NFL. Anytime you can get a player that's been around winning, I think that's a good thing."

- - -

The Patriots added other free agent signings to strengthen the defense and backup receiver corps, signing defensive backs Sean Springs and Leigh Bodden and wide receivers Joey Galloway and Greg Lewis. They also later signed offensive lineman Damane Duckett to add depth to that area as well.

On March 24, the Patriots announced that Bob Kraft had decided to add Billy Sullivan, the team's original owner, to the Patriot Hall of Fame. It was a classy move by Kraft, who was quoted as saying "Billy Sullivan made professional football a reality in New England … without Billy Sullivan the Patriots would not exist. I hope this recognition will ensure that Patriot fans never forget his contributions."

On that same day the NFL announced that the Patriots and Bills would be playing the first Monday night game of the 2009 season, in honor of the 50th anniversary of the founding of the American Football League. To add to the occasion, the teams would wear throwback uniforms. It was a nice touch by the NFL.

More importantly, the league announced that late hits such as that made by Pittsburgh's Ryan Clark against Wes Welker, well after the throw to Welker had sailed far over his head (Clark lowered his shoulder and rammed it into the helmet of Welker, knocking him out of the game) would now be illegal. Good – this is one more wrong that has been righted.

- - -

The NFL Draft of college players has becomes a staple of ESPN. They talk about it for weeks before it happens, and they cover it for hours on the weekend that it occurs. I honestly think that it gets more coverage than it should – how many mock drafts is too many mock drafts after all? – and the start of the 2009 draft on April 25 was moved from its usual noon to 4:00 so that it could extend into prime time.

The 0-16 Detroit Lions made Georgia quarterback Matt Stafford the first pick. Besides that, the other big news in the early rounds was made by the New York Jets, who traded up from pick # 17 to pick # 5 and drafted Southern Cal quarterback Mark Sanchez. The Jet PR people immediately started comparing him to Joe Namath. Maybe he's got potential, but let's at least wait and see how he does in his first couple of seasons, people. Interestingly, this means that over the last three years the Jets have tried three completely different approaches at QB. In 2007 it was the steady but unspectacular Chad Pennington, though they benched him for Kellen Clemens. In 2008 it was the much experienced but now old and erratic Brett Favre and now for 2009 it would be the lightly experienced Mark Sanchez. Talk about going from one extreme to another experience-wise from Favre to Sanchez. The guy that I feared the most in that group was Pennington, who didn't have a great arm but had a good head for the game.

The Patriots had the # 23 pick in the draft. The player that I had hoped that they would draft was Southern Cal linebacker Rey Maualuga, pairing him with Jerod Mayo for the next X years in what could be an excellent linebacker corps. We had been out on the day of the draft (it was too nice an April day to stay inside), but did get in shortly before the # 23 pick came up, and Maualuga was still available, so I stayed tuned to ESPN to see whom the Patriots would pick. When it came time to announce the pick, we were disappointed to learn that they traded the pick to Baltimore for the # 26 pick and a pick in the fifth round (# 162).

After turning to something else, I turned back to ESPN in time for the # 26 pick. Maualuga was still available, so I was hoping that he would still be the Patriots' choice. When it came time to announce the pick, we learned that they had now traded that pick as well. This time the trade was to Green Bay, along with the # 162 pick that they had gotten from Baltimore, for a second round pick (# 41) and two third round picks (# 73 and # 83).

This meant that New England's first selection in this draft would be the second round, # 34 pick that they had gotten from Kansas City for Matt Cassel and Mike Vrabel. When that pick came up, Maualuga was still available. However, the Patriots chose defensive back Patrick Chung of Oregon. Maualuga was ultimately taken by Cincinnati with the # 38 pick in the draft.

After much more wheeling and dealing, including a trade that sent defensive back and kick returner Ellis Hobbs to Philadelphia in exchange for more draft picks, the Patriots wound up selecting 12 players in the 2009 draft. They were

Round	Overall pick	Player	Position	College
2	34	Patrick Chung	DB	Oregon
2	40	Ron Brace	DT	Boston College
2	41	Darius Butler	DB	Connecticut
2	58	Sebastian Vollmer	OT	Houston
3	83	Brandon Tate	WR	North Carolina
3	97	Tyrone McKenzie	LB	South Florida
4	123	Rich Ohrnberger	G	Penn State
5	170	George Bussey	OT	Louisville
6	198	Jake Ingram	S	Hawaii
6	207	Myron Pryor	DT	Kentucky
7	232	Julian Edelman	WR	Kent State
7	234	Darryl Richard	DT	Georgia Tech

After the draft the team also signed undrafted quarterback Brian Hoyer from Michigan State. He would become Tom Brady's backup in 2009.

SECTION 4 – 2009:
Unfinished Business

Chapter 30 – Amazing Comeback(s)

Monday, September 14, 2009:	1	2	3	4		TOTAL
Buffalo Bills	7	7	3	7	-	24
New England Patriots	0	10	0	15	-	25

The Patriots began the 2009 season with a number of very familiar faces gone from the defensive team that they had had in recent years. Rodney Harrison had retired after the 2008 season. Mike Vrabel had been traded to Kansas City along with Matt Cassel. Ellis Hobbs had been traded on draft day. Tedy Bruschi had retired during the pre-season. Then, in a very surprising move, Richard Seymour had been traded to Oakland the week before the season opener in exchange for Oakland's # 1 draft pick in two years. It was felt that Seymour, who was in the last year of his contract, would not re-sign with New England, and he had been involved in a heated contract dispute with the Patriots in his last negotiation, so the team decided to get something for him while they could, instead of losing him to free agency and getting nothing in return.

While the moves were surprising to some degree, the Patriot defense had been somewhat shaky for the previous few seasons, and had not been pressuring the quarterback as much as they had in their Super Bowl years earlier in the decade, so it may have been good to move to a younger, faster defense for 2009 and beyond.

There was a new face on the offensive side of the ball, running back Fred Taylor, and a new third receiver, Joey Galloway, but the best addition to the team was the return of Tom Brady from the injury that he had suffered on Opening Day of the 2008 season. It was a good thing for New England that he was back for this game.

- - -

The Patriots' opening game was against one of their long-time rivals, the Buffalo Bills. With 2009 being the 50th anniversary of the AFL, the NFL had designated four games for each of the original AFL teams as throwback games. This was one of them. The Patriots were wearing their old red uniforms and the helmets with "Pat Patriot" on them. The Bills were in their old style away uniforms. The officials were wearing the red-orange shirts and hats of their old AFL ancestors and had the oddest uniforms by far. This was also the 40th anniversary of the beginning of Monday Night Football.

The Faces of the NFL's first 21st Century Dynasty

Owner Bob Kraft accepts an AFC Championship Trophy from CBS Announcer Jim Nantz (Courtesy of the Telegram and Gazette)

Head Coach Bill Belichick on the sideline (Courtesy of the Telegram and Gazette)

Quarterback Tom Brady is a leader on the field (Courtesy of the Telegram and Gazette)

Players Interviewed for This Book
Gino Cappelletti, Wide receiver and Placekicker
Patriot Career: 1960-1970

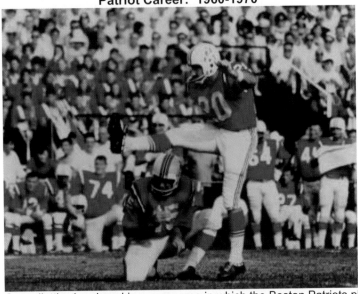

Gino Cappelletti, who played in every game in which the Boston Patriots played in the AFL, kicking from the hold of quarterback Babe Parilli (photo courtesy of Gino Cappelletti)

Gino Cappelletti at Gillette Stadium in Foxboro, MA, after our interview on Patriots' Day, April 20, 2009 (Vin Femia)

Jon Morris, Center
Patriot Career: 1964-1974

Jon Morris was an AFL All-Star 1964-1969 and was the AFC Pro Bowl Center in 1970, the first Patriot to be selected for the Pro Bowl (courtesy Jon Morris)

Jon and his wife Gail at Gillette Stadium (courtesy Jon Morris)

Bob Gladieux, Running Back, Receiver, Special teams
1969 - 1972

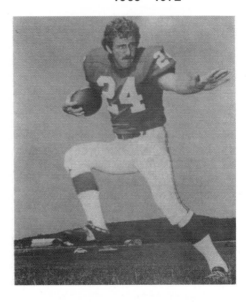

Bob Gladieux, nicknamed "Harpo" for his curly hair style, had some interesting stories about his playing days at Notre Dame and with the Patriots, including being called down from the stands to participate in the opening kickoff of a game (courtesy Bob Gladieux)

Two former Patriots, Jim "Bo" Nance and Bob "Harpo" Gladieux, seen here on opposing teams for a 1970s game in the short-lived World Football League (courtesy Bob Gladieux)

Randy Vataha, Wide Receiver
Patriot Career: 1971-76

Randy Vataha and Jim Plunkett were an outstanding passing combination in college, at Stanford, and with the Patriots. He is seen here catching a pass against the Los Angeles Rams, the team that originally drafted him. (courtesy Randy Vataha)

Upton Bell, General Manager 1971-72

Upton Bell was General Manager of the Patriots 1971 – 1972 and really helped to build a strong organization. He now hosts a radio program and posts a blog that touches on many topics. He is seen here presenting a football to former President George Bush, whom he had interviewed, an interview that is posted on his web site, www.uptonbell.com. (Photo courtesy of Upton Bell)

Upton Bell, General Manager 1971-72 and
Bob Lobel, TV Sportscaster 1978-2008

My son and I met Upton Bell, former Patriot GM, and current radio talk show host, for lunch on September 26, 2009 to thank him for the interview and his help with other interviews for this book (photo by author)

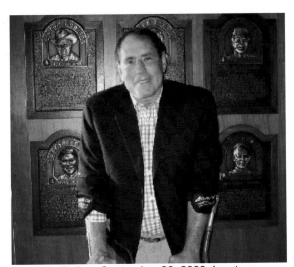

After lunch with Upton Bell on September 26, 2009, I met up with famed Boston TV Sports Anchor Bob Lobel who was attending a charity event at Fenway Park and is seen here setting up in front of plaques of Red Sox legends, including fellow broadcasters Curt Gowdy and Ned Martin (photo by author)

Upton Bell in discussion with two of the greats in sports broadcasting history: Howard Cosell (left), the bombastic, nasal-voiced analyst who helped popularize Monday Night Football, and Curt Gowdy (right), former Red Sox and NBC broadcaster who broadcast the last game of Ted Williams' career, the first game of Carl Yastrzemski's, Super Bowl I and Super Bowl III and many other of the milestone games in sports history (Photo courtesy of Upton Bell)

Lawyer Milloy poses with my daughter Christine and her friend Sarah in June 1997 (Photo courtesy of Christine Femia)

John Hannah, Left Guard
Patriot Career: 1973-1985

On the August 3, 1981 issue of *Sports Illustrated* 18, 2009, Patriot Guard John Hannah was proclaimed "The Best Offensive Lineman of All Time" (Frank White/*Sports Illustrated*)   On March NFL Hall of Famer John Hannah was kind enough to be interviewed for this book at the Patriots' offices at Gillette Stadium in Foxboro, MA (Vin Femia)

Len St. Jean, Right Guard   Patriot Career: 1964-1973

Len St. Jean, at his house in July 2009, when we did the Interview for this book (Vin Femia)

Len St. Jean in his playing days with Boston (courtesy Len St. Jean)

Steve Grogan, Quarterback   Patriot Career: 1975-1990

Steve Grogan prepares to handoff in Divisional Playoff game versus the Oakland Raiders at the Oakland-Alameda County Coliseum, December 18, 1976; Oakland won 24-21 amidst much controversy about officials' calls and non-calls (photo by Darryl Norenberg/NFL/Getty Images)

On April 10, 2009 I had the opportunity to talk with retired Patriot quarterback Steve Grogan at his office at Grogan Marciano Sporting Goods in Mansfield, MA. In the photo on the left, Steve is standing in front of some of the merchandise carried by the store. The picture on the right shows Steve standing in front of a framed poster of Super Bowl XX, in which Steve, John Hannah, and the 1985 Patriots faced the powerful Chicago Bears (Vin Femia)

Troy Brown, Wide Receiver and Kick Returner
(and occasional defensive back)
Patriot Career: 1993-2007

Troy Brown eludes Philadelphia Eagles defense in Patriots 24-21 victory in Super Bowl XXXIX at Alltel Stadium in Jacksonville, Florida, February 6, 2005 (photo by David Drapkin/Getty Images Sport/Getty Images)

Troy Brown, after our interview for this book on May 21, 2009 (Vin Femia)

Raymond Berry,
Assistant Coach 1978-1981, Head Coach 1984-1989

Raymond Berry was one of the greatest pass receivers of all time with the Baltimore Colts and then had a successful career as a coach with the New England Patriots, taking the team to its first Super Bowl in 1986 (all photos on this page courtesy of Raymond Berry)

Drew Bledsoe, Quarterback, 1993 - 2001

Drew Bledsoe hands off to Curtis Martin during a 1997 playoff game against Pittsburgh at foggy Foxboro Stadium; New England won 28-3 and went on to the Super Bowl (photo by Al Bello/Getty Images Sport/Getty Images)

Drew Bledsoe and his family in October 2009 at the family's newly planted orchard. As described in the interview with Drew, the new winery is one of the many activities with which Drew has been involved since retiring from the NFL. The winery is called Doubleback, and it is making a Cabernet Sauvignon in the Walla Walla Valley. The first release is a 2007 vintage available Spring 2010. Their website is www.doubleback.com. (Photo courtesy of Drew Bledsoe)

At Gillette Stadium, Before the Game

Patriots gather in inflated helmet before introductions (Victoria Welch)

The Lighthouse at Gillette Stadium (Victoria Welch)

The Stadium as fans begin arriving (Mike Femia)

Three Championship Banners (Mike Femia)

The Minutemen march to their positions (Mike Femia)

Cheerleaders (and Buffalo kicker) prepare for game (Mike Femia)

December 13, 2009, before Patriots-Panthers game (Photos by author)

Tom Brady warms up his
arm (Victoria Welch)

Pat Patriot warms up
the crowd (Mike Femia)

Final Huddle (Victoria Welch)

The Patriot Sideline (Victoria Welch)

Patriot Cheerleaders, December 13, 2009 (Photos by author)

Tom Brady and Stephen Gostowski warm up before the Patriots-Titans game on October 18, 2009. This was before the snow and sleet started that would last throughout the game. Both teams were wearing throwback uniforms in honor of the 50th anniversary of the AFL. The "Boston Patriots", as they were called that day, utterly destroyed the "Houston Oilers" as the Titans were called that day, 59-0, behind six touchdown passes by Tom Brady. (Photos by author)

Game Action

The Patriots kickoff to Buffalo October 30, 2005   (Mike Femia)

The offense comes onto the field (Victoria Welch)

Brady hands off to Laurence Maroney January 20, 2008 (Victoria Welch)

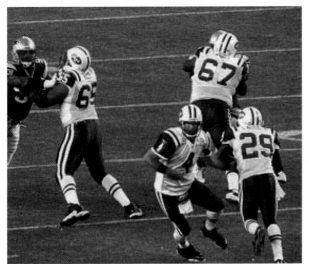

Brett Favre hands off November 13, 2008 (Victoria Welch)

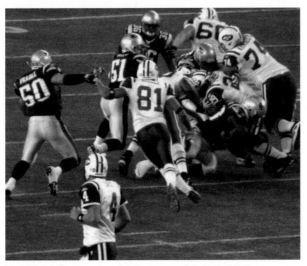

The Patriots stop the Jets' runner (Victoria Welch)

Jerod Mayo (51) was 2008
Defensive Rookie of the Year
(Victoria Welch)

Wes Welker awaits a punt
(Victoria Welch)

The line gives Cassel time to
throw (Victoria Welch)

Gostkowski attempts a field goal
(Victoria Welch)

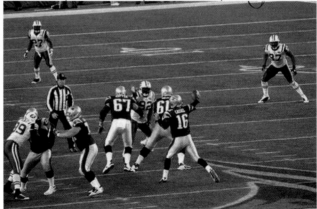

Matt Cassel marches the Patriots to a score (Victoria Welch)

Patriots on the attack against Carolina, Dec 13. 2009 (photos by author)

Stadium Scenes

The view from the 45 yard line, 2nd row (Mike Femia)

The officials sometimes have to check a replay (Mike Femia)

The Patriots go 16-0 in 2007 (Victoria Welch)

Playoff Action

Patriots-Jaguars in playoffs, January 12, 2008 (all photos on this page by Victoria Welch)

Patriots-Chargers in AFC Championship, January 20, 2008 (all photos on this page by Victoria Welch)

Patriots Celebrate winning the AFC Championship, January 20, 2008 (all photos on this page by Victoria Welch)

Patriot Difference-Makers and Key Moments

Tom Brady leads the Patriots to a big 16-13 playoff win over Oakland in the snow and cold of the last game ever played in Foxboro Stadium, January 19, 2002 (Mark Bolton/Sporting News/ZUMA)

Two weeks' later, in Super Bowl XXXVI in New Orleans, Troy Brown makes a key 23 yard catch and alertly races out of bounds to stop the clock on the Patriots' drive that set up the winning field goal (Sporting News/ZUMA)

Adam Vinatieri was a vital contributor to the Patriot dynasty. Here he celebrates after kicking the game-winning field on the last play of the 2002 Super Bowl against the St. Louis Rams. The kick gave New England a 20-17 victory and their first championship. (photo by Al Bello/Getty Images Sport//Getty Images)

Tom Brady leads New England to a 34-13 win over Pittsburgh at Gillette Stadium on December 9, 2007, embarrassing Steeler defensive back Anthony Smith, who had boldly predicted a Pittsburgh win over undefeated New England (photo by David Drapkin/Getty Images Sport/Getty Images)

Tom Brady celebrates after scoring a big touchdown in the 16-13 playoff win over Oakland, Jan 19, 2002, in the snow (Courtesy of the Telegram & Gazette)

Tedy Bruschi was a defensive leader for the Patriots from 1996--2008 (Courtesy of the Telegram & Gazette

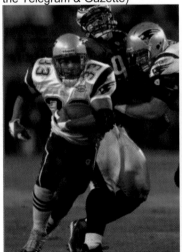

Kevin Faulk has been a mainstay for the Patriots since 1999 as an all-purpose runner, receiver, and returner (Courtesy of the Telegram & Gazette)

Tom Brady and Deion Branch were both Super Bowl MVPs for the Pats (Courtesy of Jason Chayut - kick Sportstars, Inc.)

Two of the best head coaches in Patriot history, Bill Belichick and Bill Parcells, though thought by some to be bitter rivals, watch a Senior Bowl practice together in Mobile, AL in January 2009, to scout players for their respective teams, the Patriots and Dolphins (Bob Leverone/Sporting News/ZUMA)

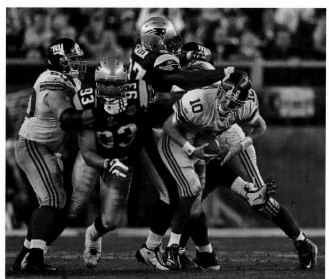

In THE key play in Super Bowl XLII, the Patriots almost had a sack of Eli Manning, but Manning eluded the tacklers and converted a key pass to David Tyree (which Tyree caught by trapping the ball against his helmet) to keep alive the drive that would give the Giants the game-winning touchdown and end the dream of a perfect 19-0 season in 2007 (Jay Drowns/Sporting News/ZUMA)

Gone (from New England) but not Forgotten

Matt Cassel stepped in for the injured Tom Brady in 2008 and had an outstanding year. He could have, and maybe should have, been NFL MVP in 2008 (see Chapter 27 for details). He now looks to bring that same success to Kansas City (Photo courtesy of the Kansas City Chiefs)

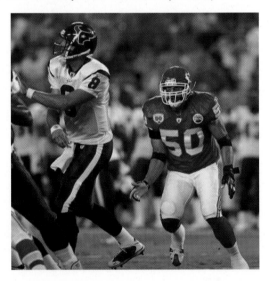

Mike Vrabel made many big plays on defense, and also caught 10 TD passes, including 2 in Super Bowls, for the Patriots, and is now bringing his experience and intelligence to the Kansas City Chiefs (Photo courtesy of the Kansas City Chiefs)

Deion Branch was a Patriot from 2002-05. He was the MVP of Super Bowl XXXIX with 11 catches for 133 yards against the Eagles. He also showed tremendous class with thank you calls to his former high school and college coaches before that game, as described in Chapter 6. He was traded to Seattle in 2006. (All photos on this page courtesy of Jason Chayut - Sportstars, Inc.)

Upton Bell, Steve Grogan, and the author discuss football in a broadcast of Upton's radio program in October 2009 (Photo courtesy of Upton Bell and Joanne O'Neill)

The Dynasty

Three Championship Banners

Three Championship Trophies

One Memorable Season

For most of the night, the Patriots actually resembled the team that had worn those red uniforms in many unsuccessful AFL (and NFL) seasons in the 20th century. Their first two drives actually went reasonably well but resulted in no points. They received the opening kickoff and Laurence Maroney returned it 52 yards to the Buffalo 49 to set New England up with good field position. However that drive stalled and the next lasted 11 plays and got them to the Buffalo 24, but the usually reliable Stephen Gostkowski missed a 41 yard field goal.

The Bills then followed with a 68 yard drive to the game's first touchdown and a 7-0 lead. This was not a good sign. Buffalo's new no-huddle offense had not scored a touchdown in pre-season, and already had one in the first quarter against the New England defense. Even worse, the Patriots lost linebacker Jerod Mayo to a knee injury on that drive, and he was lost for the rest of the game (and, as it turned out, for 4 weeks beyond that with a sprained knee). The Bills dominated the first quarter thanks in part to the Patriots' missed opportunities on those first two drives, and the teams exchanged ends of the field at the end of the quarter with Buffalo holding a 7-0 lead.

The Patriot offense showed a spark with a 14 play, 72 yard drive to open the second quarter. Fred Taylor scored New England's first points of the season on a one yard run, set up by Kevin Faulk getting two big first downs to keep the drive alive (a 16 yard pass reception on a third and nine play and a four yard run on a third and three play). There was one interesting sequence during that drive. Brady and Wes Welker failed to connect on a quick pass to the right side, and neither looked happy. The explanation later was that Brady expected Welker to come back toward the quarterback, but he did not. Welker just stayed spread out, so the pass fell short. Brady seemed to be telling Welker that he had not done what he was supposed to have done. So, what happened on the very next play? Brady came right back to Welker with a 13 yard pass that got the ball down near the goal line and set up Taylor's TD run. It was reminiscent of the key play in the last regular season game against the Giants in the 2007 season, where Brady hit Randy Moss with a long pass that Moss dropped, and Brady came right back to him again with a bomb on the next play. It resulted in a big fourth quarter TD that kept the Patriots' hopes alive for an undefeated season. It was a great move then and now by a great quarterback to show that he still had a lot of confidence in his receiver, despite the error made on the previous play.

Brady had five completions in seven attempts on that drive, but on the next he threw an interception on a bad pass attempting a screen, and Buffalo defender Aaron Schobel returned it 26 yards for an easy touchdown. The Patriots then drove to the two yard line but had to settle for a 20 yard field goal that left the score 14-10 in Buffalo's favor at the end of the first half.

The third quarter was more of the same. The Patriots drove from the two yard line to the Buffalo 36 on 13 plays after a punt by the Bills, but again failed to convert on fourth down. Brady was really firing the ball and looking sharper on this drive, but the running game was doing nothing to help the cause. The Bills got a field goal to make it 17-10 after three quarters and keep things uncomfortable for the Patriots and their fans.

Another Patriot drive stalled to open the fourth quarter, but Gostkowski hit a field goal to cut the Buffalo lead to 17-13. My game notes at this point said simply "* no running game! *" as I, and probably many others, realized that it would be up to Tom Brady to win this game for New England.

The Bills then began to drive again, and another old Patriot demon surfaced. On a third down and five, the Bills got eight yards. However, a questionable offensive interference penalty on Bills' receiver Terrell Owens (an old face now in a new place) set them back to a third and 15. So the Bills got 18 yards and a first down. On a third and eight from the 19, the Bills got 10 yards and another first down. A screen pass gave Buffalo a touchdown and a 24-13 with 5:32 to go.

It all looked hopeless.

Fortunately, the Patriots still had two things in their favor: (1) they still had Tom Brady and (2) they were playing the Buffalo Bills (see Chapter 23, the chapter entitled "What Was Buffalo Thinking?" for more details on why this was a Patriot advantage, even at this late stage of the game).

Brady came through by leading the Patriots on an 81 yard march in 3:26 to a touchdown, hitting tight end Benjamin Watson on an 18 yard TD pass for the score. The Patriots tried a two point conversion but it failed, making the score Buffalo 24 New England 19 with just over two minutes to play.

The Patriots kicked off to Buffalo, and the general feeling was that they would use their three timeouts to stop the clock while on defense, and hope to give the ball back to Tom Brady with about 90 seconds to play. However, they were given a huge gift by the questionable Bills, as kick returner Leodis McKelvin inexplicably decided to run the kickoff out of the end zone, though his blocking was not in place (Buffalo had lined up expecting an on-side kick). He got it out to the 31 yard line where he should have just fallen on the ball, but instead, again inexplicably, he decided to fight for additional yardage, which was meaningless at this point in the game. The Patriots, specifically Brandon Meriweather and Pierre Woods, were able to strip the ball out of his hands. A scramble for the fumble ensued, and it was Patriot kicker Stephen Gostkowski who came up with it.

Three plays later, the Patriots had the lead. Brady completed a pass to Randy Moss. Brady completed a pass to Wes Welker. Brady completed a pass to Benjamin Watson for 16 yards and a touchdown. With 50 seconds to play, New England now led 25-24!

A missed two point conversion, and a Buffalo desperation lateral-the-ball-all-over-the-place-and-hope-for-a-miracle play that did not work, ended the game. The Patriots had escaped (and it really felt like an escape) with a 25-24 win.

The pass to Watson for the winning TD was a beauty. There were two defenders on Watson, and if Brady had thrown it to try to lead the receiver, there was a good chance for a Buffalo interception. Instead he threaded the needle to some degree and threw it a little behind Watson so Benjamin had to make a backward grab of it for the TD. It was a great throw by a great quarterback.

The Patriots' passing statistics for the game were excellent. Brady completed 39 passes in 53 attempts for 378 yards and two touchdowns (welcome back!). Randy Moss and Wes Welker each had 12 receptions for the game, for 141 and 93 yards, respectively. However, the running game was practically non-existent, with 73 yards on 23 carries – and it seemed worse than that – and the defense was shaky again, as it had been often in the recent past. There would be plenty for Coach Bill Belichick and his staff to work on with the team before its next game.

The radio broadcast of Gil Santos at the end of the game was a gem. As Brady completed the winning touchdown pass to Watson, an exuberant Santos excitedly proclaimed "Tom Brady, you ARE Tom Terrific!"

Nice comeback, Tom, and nice comeback, team.

Phew!

Chapter 31 – Jets Swagger, Pats Stagger

Sunday, September 20, 2009:	1	2	3	4		TOTAL
New England Patriots	3	6	0	0	-	9
New York Jets	0	3	10	3	-	16

You have to give the Jets credit, however reluctantly you may choose to do so. They ran their mouths off more than a professional team should, but then they backed up the trash talk that they did off the field before the game with their play on the field during this game.

- - -

The Patriots and Jets had had a bitter rivalry in recent years. It looked like Rex Ryan, the new Jets' Head Coach, wanted to make it even more bitter.

In a press conference shortly after taking the job with the Jets, Ryan made headlines by talking about the fact that he was not going to "kiss Belichick's rings". In the week leading up to this game, Ryan sent a recorded phone message to New York's season ticket holders telling them to come to the game prepared to be loud. His defensive back, Kerry Rhodes, took things even a step further, being quoted in the week leading up to the game as saying, "You go out from the first play and try to embarrass them … we don't want to just beat them, we want to send a message."

All of this, in past years, would have been fodder that the Patriots used to motivate them to play at a high level and cause the big mouths to clamp shut. Anthony Smith and Pittsburgh certainly got that treatment in 2007, as did Freddie Mitchell of the Eagles before Super Bowl XXXIX. Unfortunately, in 2009, the Patriots did not come through and the Jets did. The Jets did not embarrass the Patriots, but they did beat them 16-9. It was a bad day for New England and a good day for New York.

Rex Ryan continued to thumb his nose at the Patriots as the game started, sending out three former Patriots as his captains for the opening coin toss – Kevin O'Connell, Damien Woody, and Larry Izzo. All of this was very high school-ish, but it worked.

- - -

The Patriots started well, looking sharp on the opening drive before stalling and punting. Then, on New York's first play, a sack and strip of Jet rookie QB Mark Sanchez resulted in the Jets being backed up to their own three yard line for a second and 27. Eventually the Jets had to punt and the war of attrition that was the first half began. The Patriots had three drives into the New York red zone inside the 20 yard line, but had to settle for three field goals. Stephen Gostkowski hit field goals of 45, 25, and 29 yards to give the Patriots a 9-3 lead at halftime.

The second half was all New York. A 44 yard kickoff return by Leon Washington got the Jets started. Sanchez hit Jericho Cotchery for 45 yards and, two plays later, Dustin Keller for 9 yards and a touchdown. The lead and the momentum were now all in New York's favor.

Midway through the third quarter, the Patriots were penalized on two consecutive plays for delay of game for letting the play clock expire. It was very unlike the Patriots. They also wound up the day with 11 penalties for 89 yards. That was also uncharacteristic.

The Patriots had two chances late in the game for a game-saving drive, but could not make it happen. The game ended with Sanchez taking a knee in front of an appreciative New Jersey crowd.

"We believe that we are the better team today," Ryan said. "We went out and showed it. I think our fans are huge in this victory ... I thought they were the difference."

On the other side, Bill Belichick said, "Give the Jets credit. They just did a better job than we did today and I don't think there's really a while lot more to say about it." He was right.

Perhaps the only bright spot for New England was the play of rookie receiver Julian Edelman, who replaced the injured Wes Welker. Edelman had eight catches for 98 yards. Brady was 23 of 47 passing, meaning that he has thrown a total of 100 passes in the season's first two games. The team needed a running attack.

They may need more too, as the Jets outplayed them in all three phases, and outcoached them as well.

So the Jets had their much-sought win over New England, their first ever over Tom Brady at home, and the first over the Patriots at the Meadowlands since September 11, 2000. They had gotten their wish.

It will be interesting to see what happens next -- for both teams.

Chapter 32 – One Step Forward

Sunday, September 27, 2009:	1	2	3	4	TOTAL
Atlanta Falcons.	3	7	0	0	- 10
New England Patriots	3	10	3	10	- 26

After staggering and being embarrassed against one Ryan in the previous week, the Patriots turned it around against another Ryan this week. In this case it was former BC and current Atlanta Falcon quarterback Matt Ryan (not related to Rex Ryan). The Falcons came into the game undefeated in their first two games of 2009, and the pick of the reporters on the pre-game broadcast to win this game.

At the start of the game, it looked like those reporters and prognosticators were correct. Atlanta got the ball at the 20 yard line on the opening kickoff, and proceeded to march down the field with little resistance from the Patriots. It looked like the start of a long day for New England. However, after getting to the Patriot eight yard line, the Falcon drive stalled, and they had to settle for a 26 yard field goal. It felt as if momentum changed when they wound up with three points instead of seven.

The Patriots then returned the favor, driving to the Atlanta three yard line, before having to settle for a field goal of their own to tie the game at 3-3. Some of the old woes of the early season continued to plague the team in the first quarter. Tom Brady overthrew Joey Galloway on one play, and then overthrew Randy Moss who was wide open on a play that could have been a touchdown. It would have been a TD in 2007; it was not to be in 2009. Then, on another play, Brady hit Galloway with a pass in the end zone, but Galloway had stepped out of bounds before making the catch, so it turned into a frustrating incompletion. It was clear that Brady could have used the services of Wes Welker, who was missing his second straight game due to injury.

New England started a drive in the second quarter at their own 49, thanks to a poor punt by Atlanta. Brady attempted a bomb to Moss that was on-target, but deflected at the last second for an incompletion. One pass and four good runs by Fred Taylor later they had a touchdown and a 10-3 lead. It was Taylor getting the TD on an eight yard run. Taylor would go on to have a very good game, with 105 yards on 21 carries.

More of those early season woes, and actually some carried over from previous seasons, showed their ugly faces on the next

Atlanta possession. At one point, the Falcons had a fourth down and three at the New England 34. A defensive stop would have been big, but the Falcons got seven yards and a big first down (that old X+Y yards surrendered by the Patriot defense that was described earlier). A touchdown run by Michael Turner knotted the game at 10-10. Worse for the Patriots, Vince Wilfork injured his ankle on the drive and did not return. With Jerod Mayo still out, and now Wilfork sidelined, things looked bleak for the New England defense, but they did not allow Atlanta another point after this drive.

A 33 yard Patriot field goal gave New England a 13-10 halftime lead, but it should have been more. Brady hit Galloway with a pass at the five yard line, but Galloway let it bounce off of his hands for an incompletion. Brady then threw to Sam Aiken, but Aiken stopped running his route for some reason, so the pass sailed in front of him for an incompletion. A visibly frustrated Brady was seen talking in what we will call a very animated fashion (he was mad) to his receivers on the plays and again on the sidelines as the field goal unit came on. "Another misfire in the red zone for the Patriots," was how the TV broadcaster described it. He was right.

The second half started with New England on their own 17, but a good running attack led by Fred Taylor led them down the field. Tom Brady overthrew Ben Watson on one play, but later hit Watson at the six yard line to get the Patriots close. It was their fourth trip into the red zone, but again they wound up with only a field goal after a near interception and an overthrow of Moss. It was 16-10 but still shaky, for a number of reasons.

On their next drive, New England had a fourth down and inches at their own 24 yard line. Surprisingly to some, Bill Belichick decided to go for it, although failing to make the first down would have left Atlanta in great position to get a go-ahead touchdown. When asked about it after the game, Belichick said, "We felt like we could get a yard." That may have been understated, but it was a great move by the coach both to motivate his team and show confidence in them. They got two yards and a first down at the 26. Brady then threw a 19 yard pass on the mark to Moss to get the team to the 45, and then a bullet to Moss for a first down at the Atlanta 44. Then, facing a fourth and three at the Atlanta 37, threw a nice pass to Moss for 21 yards and a first down at the 16. A pass to the one bounced off the hands of Watson, though, so it was yet another field goal, raising the Patriot lead to 19-10.

The fourth quarter saw another dropped pass, this one by rookie Julian Edelman, Wes Welker's replacement, but then Brady hit tight end Chris Baker in stride down the right sideline for a 56 yard touchdown pass to put the game out of reach at 26-10. It was Brady's

200th career touchdown pass. It was also a score that came from beyond the red zone, so those red zone woes were not yet put to bed.

Statistically, things looked good for the Patriots. Brady finished with 25 completions in 42 attempts for 277 yards and one TD. Taylor had those 105 yards on 21 carries as noted previously. Moss had 10 catches for 116 yards. While the statistics were good, there was obviously still plenty to work on and worry about, with the very tough Baltimore Raven defense coming to Foxboro for New England's next game.

Chapter 33 – Another Close Call with Baltimore

Sunday, October 4, 2009:	1	2	3	4	TOTAL
Baltimore Ravens	7	0	7	7	- 21
New England Patriots	3	14	7	3	- 27

For the second straight week, the Patriots were facing one of the NFL's undefeated teams. This time it was the Baltimore Ravens, the last AFC team to qualify for the playoffs in 2008, and thus the team that beat out the Patriots for the AFC's last playoff slot. The Ravens had always had a very strong defense, one of the best in the league. Now, for the first time in years, they had a strong offense to go with it, led by second year quarterback Joe Flacco.

One plus for the Patriots going into the game was that Wes Welker was back on the active roster for the first time since opening night. Interestingly, the Patriots decided to put Joey Galloway on the inactive list for this game. This was not due to injury; Galloway was healthy. It was due to the fact that Galloway had not yet seemed to fit into the offense. Rookie Julian Edelman, a quarterback in college, would be eligible for this game as a receiver, while Galloway, a 15 year veteran, would not be. It was not a good sign for Galloway's future with the team.

The game started out on a high note for New England. Baltimore fumbled the opening kickoff and the Patriots recovered at the Baltimore 12 yard line. They were in great position to cash in an early touchdown. Unfortunately the red zone blues continued for the Patriots as they had to settle for a 32 yard field goal by Stephen Gostkowski after three very unsuccessful plays from scrimmage: an incompletion out of an empty backfield on first down, a one yard run by Laurence Maroney out of the I formation on second down (fans must have been wondering why Fred Taylor was not in the game for that run), and a sack on third down.

Baltimore took over on their own 19 after the next kickoff, and had little trouble marching 81 yards for a touchdown. What little trouble they did have came on their first two plays, which were both incomplete passes. A Patriot offside penalty gave the Ravens a third and five, and they got 17 yards and a first down to keep the drive alive. Two more third down conversions got Baltimore to the New England seven yard line. An incomplete pass, a loss of eight on a play in which the ball was stripped out of Flacco's hand and caught in the air by an offensive lineman, and a delay of game penalty pushed the ball back to the twenty, but that did not matter to Baltimore. Flacco hit Derrick Mason on the right side of the end zone for a 20 yard touchdown pass and a 7-3 Baltimore lead. It was Mason's sixth catch on this drive, four of which were for Raven first downs. It was easier for Baltimore to go 81 yards than it had been for New England to go 12.

New England got the ball on the 24 to start their next possession, and the offense suddenly heated up. Tom Brady hit Wes Welker for 11 yards and a first down on the first play. Then, after negative yardage by Maroney (where was Fred Taylor?), Brady hit Edelman for another first down. A key roughing the passer penalty on a Baltimore third down play moved the ball to the Raven 22 and kept this drive alive for New England. Kevin Faulk ran for eight yards and Fred Taylor for two to give New England another first down. They were back on the 12 yard line again, for the second time in two possessions. Would they cash in this time or have to settle for another field goal? After an incompletion, Fred Taylor, now in the game and getting the ball, ran for eight yards and one yard on the next two plays to set up and fourth and one at the three. To his credit, Bill Belichick decided to go for it, and Sammy Morris blasted through the line for two yards and a first down at the one as the first quarter ended.

A false start penalty (sigh!) set the Patriots back five yards to the six. Brady was looking to pass but had to scramble and ran to the right. Baltimore's All-Pro linebacker, the very tough Ray Lewis, was set to blast Brady on the tackle, but, luckily, Brady saw what was coming and dove down at the two, avoiding the big hit that Lewis was in position to make. A quarterback sneak by Brady on the next play got the two yards and a touchdown. The Patriots were back in the lead at 10-7.

As Baltimore got possession after the kickoff, Brady raced into the locker room. The Gillette Stadium crowd was holding its collective breath wondering what was happening. Meanwhile, on the field, backup quarterback Brian Hoyer was warming up feverishly. As CBS Analyst Phil Simms described it, "Hoyer threw about a hundred passes in one minute" to get warmed up since "you never know if there will be a turnover and you'll have to go in." Luckily for the crowd and the fans watching, and maybe even for Brian Hoyer, Brady came back out and was ready to play on the next series.

After a couple of exchanges of possession with no score, there was a very long and very scary delay in the game due to an injury to Baltimore left offensive tackle Jared Gaither. Gaither, a 23 year old from the University of Maryland, hit the crown of his helmet on the back of Joe Flacco as he was pass blocking, and laid on the field for a long while as both teams' medical teams attended to him. He was taken off on a stretcher board after about ten minutes. Happily, reports from the hospital were positive in that Gaither was conscious and moving his arms and legs, but it was certainly very worrisome watching the activity on the field by the medical personnel.

When play resumed, Baltimore was forced to punt, and the Patriots drove to another touchdown that was aided by a roughing the passer penalty against Baltimore. In this case, Baltimore's Terrell Suggs was called for the infraction, for going low on Brady, diving at his knees. Suggs either missed or barely grazed Brady, but the call was made. There was a lot of controversy about that over the next few days by TV and radio talk shows, including former teammate Rodney Harrison, now a TV commentator, jokingly saying that Brady should start wearing pants and not a skirt, but I think the call was correct. If the intention of the new rules is to protect a vulnerable quarterback from having his season ended by a late or low hit, then this type of penalty needs to be called.

Two big passes to Randy Moss before the penalty and a 13 yard pass to Wes Welker after it set up a 13 yard touchdown run by Sammy Morris on the old Statue of Liberty play, as Brady faked the throw and then brought his arm down for the handoff to Morris. The TD sent the Patriots into the locker room with a 17-7 halftime lead,

The third quarter saw an exchange of punts on each team's opening series and then a defensive touchdown scored by the Ravens as Terrell Suggs stripped the ball from Brady as Brady attempted to pass from a play from his own 14 yard line. Baltimore recovered the fumble for a touchdown, cutting the Patriot lead to 17-14.

The Patriots started looking more like the Patriots of two years ago after they got the kickoff and started a drive at their own 21. Brady hit Sam Aiken down the middle for a 26 yard completion to the Baltimore 40 and then hit Moss perfectly over the middle again to bring the ball down to the Baltimore 20. Two running plays set up a third and four and Brady, being pressured, lofted a nice pass to Randy Moss at the one yard line and Moss trotted in for his first touchdown of the season, extending the New England lead to 24-14 at the end of three quarters. There was also some criticism of the pass by commentators and others called it lucky, but it looked like a case of Brady doing what he had to do to make the play and throwing the right kind of pass in that situation.

Joe Flacco led Baltimore 80 yards in seven plays to a touchdown early in the fourth quarter. The touchdown came on a 13 yard pass from Flacco to running back Willis McGahee, but the score was really set up on a 50 yard run through the line by Ray Rice that brought the Ravens to the New England 27.

The Patriots drove back for a field goal on a long drive of their own, featuring a clutch 12 yard pass from Brady to Welker to convert a third and eight (it was sure nice to have Wes Welker back), and some nice plays by the very reliable Kevin Faulk and Sammy Morris. On the other hand, Laurence Maroney heard some boos from the crowd as he took a loss on one play, and Phil Simms commented that the crowd was booing due to Maroney's reputation of trying to finesse runs when he needs to blast straight ahead. As Simms put it, "don't dance in the hole."

The Patriots actually tried a fake field goal and punter and placekick holder Chris Hanson completed a pass that looked like it got a first down on the left sideline, but the receiver was called for illegal motion. Baltimore actually challenged the call and asked for a review by the officials as they claimed that the pass was not complete for the first down. Replays showed that it was, however, so Baltimore accepted the penalty and moved New England back five yards. Stephen Gostkowski then hit a 33 yard field goal to make the score 27-21 but a touchdown would sure have been a lot better for everyone's nerves.

Baltimore had two more shots at a go-ahead or winning touchdown. The first ended when the Patriot defense stopped Willis McGahee short on a fourth and one run from the Baltimore 45. It was a great stop by Gary Guyton and Brandon McGowan. However, Baltimore's last possession, starting from their own 20 with 3:32 left in the game, had all Patriot fans worried.

Flacco quickly completed a 12 yard pass for one first down, and another for 11 yards and another first down. After a Patriot blitz sandwiched Flacco and forced an incompletion, he completed another pass for nine yards and then got a first down on a quarterback sneak. The Baltimore offense was driving. The New England defense was bending.

A pass completion for nine yards took the Ravens to the New England 37 at the 2:00 warning. Ray Rice ran for five to the 32 for another first down. A 12 yard screen pass to the 20 preceded an incompletion in the end zone, and then a pass to the 13 set up a crucial third and three. A Flacco pass intended for Derrick Mason was knocked down by rookie defensive back Darius Butler, putting the game on the line with an even more crucial fourth and three. Flacco again went back to pass and threw to Mark Clayton on the right. The ball hit Clayton perfectly (right on the 9 of his #89 as one reporter put it), but Clayton had the ball bounce off of him for an incompletion. That was it. The game was over. The Patriots had escaped with a 27-21 win.

This was a great game. It was Baltimore that had given the Patriots their closest call to a loss in their undefeated regular season in 2007, and had come close to beating them again in this game. Still, the Patriots were able to hold on.

With the win and a loss by the Jets to the New Orleans Saints, the Patriots and Jets were now in a tie at the top of the AFC East with 3-1 records.

At the end of the weekend there were five unbeaten teams in the NFL: the Saints, Vikings, Colts, Giants, and Broncos.

Interestingly, the Patriots had played an undefeated team in each of their first four games, beating the 0-0 Buffalo Bills, losing to the 1-0 Jets, and then beating the 2-0 Falcons and 3-0 Ravens. They were now on to Denver to play yet another undefeated team, the 4-0 Broncos. It would be nice to see them continue the streak.

Chapter 34 – A Mile High Low

Sunday, October 11, 2009:	1	2	3	4	OT	TOTAL
New England Patriots	10	7	0	0	** -	17
Denver Broncos	0	7	3	7	3 -	20

*** - never got the ball in overtime*

They did not continue the streak.

The Patriots and Broncos played the first regular season game in AFL history in 1960, and the Broncos surprised the Patriots with a win in that game. They did the same on this cold Sunday in Denver, beating New England 20-17 in overtime.

This was another one of the AFL-retro games in which both of these original AFL teams wore their original uniforms, and the Patriots were referred to as the Boston Patriots. This was the first time that I had gotten to see the Broncos' brown and gold uniforms (or 'seal brown and mustard gold' as the announcers told us) with socks that had vertical stripes. They were indeed as hideous as they have always been described.

The good news for New England was that Jerod Mayo would be back in the lineup. The bad news was that Fred Taylor had injured his ankle late in the game against Baltimore and would be out for many weeks, maybe even for the season. The worse news for fans in general was that the Red Sox had been eliminated from their playoff run earlier in the day, losing to the Angels to get swept 3-0 in their ALDS matchup. New England and Boston fans were looking to the Patriots to provide something positive for their sports viewing.

The Patriots kicked off to start the game and Denver began at their 20. The first play was a bad omen as the Broncos started out with the wildcat play (called 'wild horses' in the Denver playbook) and got 12 yards on a run by Knowshon Moreno. Moreno broke two tackles to get those yards, a pattern that would be repeated often during the day. The Patriots defense offered little resistance as Denver marched 50 yards in 9 plays before missing a 48 yard field goal attempt.

New England's offense then carried out a nice drive of their own, going 62 yards in 7 plays capped by an eight yard touchdown pass from Tom Brady to Wes Welker. Along the way there were a couple of very big plays. One was a third and four pass to Julian Edelman for six yards and a first down at midfield. Another was a screen pass to Sammy Morris for 35 yards taking them down to the Denver 15. Morris would finish the day with 68 yards rushing on 17 carries.

Jerod Mayo made his presence felt in a big way by forcing a fumble from Moreno on the next possession, with the Pats taking over at the Denver 43. New England had to settle for a 53 yard field goal after getting only 8 yards in 5 plays, but the biggest play was an overthrow by Brady of a wide open Randy Moss at the goal line on a play from the Denver 35. The Patriot offense was still not in synch.

Kyle Orton threw an 11 yard TD pass to Brandon Marshall to get Denver back within a field goal, but New England responded with a 10 play 74 yard drive to a touchdown that made the score 17-7 at the half. Wes Welker was a star on this drive, catching passes of 13, 17, and 11 yards. The last one brought the ball to the 10 yard line but Welker was shaken up on the play, having been speared in the back by a player leading with his helmet. Brady hit Benjamin Watson with a seven yard pass for the touchdown with :05 left in the half.

A squib kick gave Denver one chance for a desperation bomb before the half. Orton's pass was intercepted at the two yard line by Randy Moss, inserted in the game in the 'prevent defense'. It was Orton's first interception of the year. Oddly, it was the only pass that Moss caught in the first half, and it was not even from Brady, or anyone on his own team. Now that is unusual.

The third quarter saw New England punt twice and miss a 40 yard field goal. Denver got a 24 yard field goal from Matt Prater after a 12 play, 66 yard drive on their first possession of the second half, with former Patriots Jabar Gaffney and Daniel Graham getting key receptions on the drive, so the score was 17-10 in New England's favor as the teams moved to the fourth quarter.

The Patriots drove 44 yards from their own four yard line on a drive that bridged the third and fourth quarters. They were aided by a running into the kicker penalty on a punt that gave them a first down, and later by a Denver neutral zone infraction, but could not keep the drive going. Worse, Matt Light went out with an injury on the second play of the fourth quarter, injured when teammate Dan Koppen was knocked back into his leg. He left the game and did not return.

Denver tied the game with a 98 yard drive on 12 plays, aided by some questionable calls. A Denver fumble after a pass catch was ruled not a fumble since the officials ruled that the receiver's forward momentum had been stopped. Replays showed otherwise, but this is one of the judgement calls which is not reviewable by instant replay. A 27 yard screen to Moreno kept things moving, as again an opponent moved easily down the field against the Patriot defense. A pass by Orton from the 22 sailed incomplete and out of bounds at the 5, but the officials called Brandon Meriwether for taunting, and the penalty moved the Broncos to the 11. The announcers first thought that it might have been a late hit, but then seemed surprised that it was taunting. The surprise was due to the fact that the replay showed the official throwing his flag before the taunting occurred. As the flag was in the air, you could see Meriwether throw his arm and say something to the receiver. CBS analyst Phil Simms commented, "He threw the flag before he made the move." Perhaps the official's name was Claire Voyant and he knew that Meriwether would taunt the receiver? Hmmm…

In any case the ball moved half the distance to the goal, to the 11 yard line, and Orton hit Brandon Marshall for the tying touchdown on the next play.

The Patriots got the ball twice more with chances to regain the lead but could not. The second possession looked like a typical drive engineered by Brady to a game-winning field goal, but it was not to be. Brady was stripped of the ball on a pass play by Denver's Vonnie Holliday and Denver recovered to end that drive. Replays seemed to indicate that Brady's arm was coming forward, so it could have been ruled an incomplete pass, but it was not, and the game went into overtime.

Denver won the coin toss and the game. They started at their own 20 and went 58 yards on 11 plays to set up a game-winning 41 yard field goal by Prater. It was an easy drive by Denver as on successive plays they passed for 11, passed for 7, passed for 4, ran for 9, ran for no gain, passed for 8, ran for 11 (through more missed tackles by New England), ran for two, threw two incomplete passes (the second negated by but a neutral zone infraction on New England as Tully Banta-Cain inexplicably lined up offside), incomplete, field goal, game over. It was like a hot knife going through soft butter.

So the Broncos stayed unbeaten at 5-0 and New England fell to 3-2. Luckily, the Jets lost to Miami on Monday night, so the two teams remained tied atop the AFC East, but the Patriots would have a lot of work to do to get themselves, and particularly their offense, back in synch.

One odd statistic shown at the end of the game was that Tom Brady's record against Denver was 1-6, by far his worst record against any opponent.

All in all it was a real low in the mile high city for the Patriots and their fans.

Chapter 35 – 59-0!

Sunday, October 18, 2009:	1	2	3	4	TOTAL
Tennessee Titans	0	0	0	0 -	0
New England Patriots	10	35	14	0 -	59

After five weeks of playing undefeated teams, the Patriots were facing one of 2009's winless (0-5) teams. However, it was the Tennessee Titans, who actually had had the best record in the NFL in 2008 at 13-3 and had won their first ten games that season. It was surprising how far they had fallen in one year with essentially the same players. It would have been less surprising had this happened in 2008 to New England after the loss of Tom Brady.

It was a miserable day weather-wise in Foxboro. I know, since I was there. It was the wettest that I have ever been that I can remember. It started with the drive to Foxboro which was made in steady rain, and sitting and eating in the car as it was pouring. The car was parked about 1/4 mile from the Stadium, which is pretty good for Gillette Stadium parking. As we started walking to the stadium I wound up getting soaked by the time we were only halfway to the place. It looked like it was going to be a long and wet afternoon.

It was still about an hour before the game, so I went and sat under the overhang that is over the last two rows in the lower section. As I was watching I thought 'Is that snow falling?' And sure enough it was. Then it was snowing harder. Then, about 20 minutes before the game I went out to take some pictures for this book and realized that it was sleeting. So I slogged my way up to the top level, where our seats were. I even bought a yellow poncho to cover my winter coat. My gloves got all wet so I could not take them off to take more pictures. But sitting in snow at the top level was better than sitting in pouring rain would have been.

Then the game started and it was amazing. The Patriots dominated the Titans. New England's first drive started at the Tennessee 29 yard line after a nice punt return by Julian Edelman. The Patriots moved into the red zone but could not convert a touchdown, and then Stephen Gostkowski missed a field goal.

After that miss, the Patriots scored on their next nine possessions as they absolutely destroyed the Titans. It started with a 45 yard run through the middle by Laurence Maroney. Maybe running in the snow is good for this former University of Minnesota player as it did not seem that he was 'dancing sideways' as he got to the line but kept running straight ahead. He would finish the day with 123 yards rushing on 16 attempts.

Maroney's touchdown and another red zone incursion that resulted in a field goal instead of a touchdown gave the Patriots a 10-0 lead at the end of the first quarter.

The second quarter belonged to Tom Brady.

All Brady did in the fifteen minutes of the second quarter was throw five touchdown passes, an NFL record for one quarter. He threw another on the first drive of the third quarter before sitting out the rest of the game. The six TD passes tied Brady's own team record for touchdown passes in a game. The touchdowns came as follows:

- Brady handing off to BenJarvus Green-Ellis who ran to the line, turned, and flipped the ball back to Tom Brady for a flea-flicker pass. Brady threw a perfect bomb to Randy Moss who caught it in stride as he raced into the end zone for a 40 yard TD.

- Brady scrambling to his left and throwing a 28 yard TD pass to Randy Moss running left to right in the back of the end zone after eluding two Titan defenders.

- Brady throwing a screen pass to the right to Kevin Faulk who threaded the Titan defense for 38 yards and a touchdown.

- Brady hitting Wes Welker down the right sideline for a 30 yard completion and a touchdown.

- Brady hitting Welker on the right side of the end zone for a 5 yard touchdown pass with 12 seconds left in the first half.

- Brady hitting Randy Moss on the left side of the end zone for 9 yards and a touchdown 4:47 into the third quarter.

It was annihilation. From our seats in the upper level we could see Moss and Welker breaking free on their patterns and Brady seemed to hit them at just the perfect time. On the pass where Brady scrambled, Moss did a great job of working to get himself free and Brady was equally great at eluding the rush until he could find Moss.

The 45-0 halftime score gave the Patriots the biggest halftime margin in NFL history. The 59-0 score tied a record for the biggest shutout since the AFL-NFL merger (though it was less that the 73-0

Chicago victory over Washington in the 1940 NFL championship game). The Patriots had left 11 points on the table with two red zone drives in the first quarter that resulted in one field goal and a field goal miss instead of two touchdowns. So if everything else went as it did it could have been 70-0!

While the Patriots were doing this, the Titans were doing nothing. Titan QB Kerry Collins completed exactly one pass in eleven attempts in the first half, and finished two for twelve in the game. He also fumbled once and had one pass intercepted. Vince Young replaced him in the second half and threw an interception of his own as he threw two passes with no completions. With all of that and another first half fumble, Tennessee wound up with five turnovers in the game.

This was one of the games scheduled to commemorate the 50th anniversary of the founding of the AFL, so the teams wore throwback uniforms. The Patriots wore their old red uniform shirts. The Titans wore the uniforms of the old Houston Oilers, including the helmets with oil derricks on them. Maybe the best thing that Tennessee can do is to try to assign this loss to the Houston Oilers and not claim any responsibility for it in their record books.

- - -

The sixth Brady TD made the score 52-0 early in the third quarter, which was the score when I left. I'm kind of glad for that decision given the miserable weather conditions and potential traffic problems at the end of the game. Traffic was still slow on Route 1 and we could see the aftermath of one accident there and another on 495.

- - -

There were a couple of interesting personnel moves for this game and in the week following.

Linebacker Adalius Thomas was made inactive for the game, which was a surprise to many since there was no indication that he was injured. It turns out that he was not injured enough to keep him from playing, this was just a Belichick decision. Thomas had not been having the kind of year that people expected from him, so there was some speculation that this was a move intended to light a fire under Thomas. When asked about it a number of times on Wednesday, Thomas continually responded by saying that it was the coach's decision and referring the questioner to Belichick for more information. That was a good way to keep this from exploding into more headlines and controversy.

Replacing Thomas for the set of linebackers available for this game was Junior Seau, who had been signed the previous week.

Interestingly, when all of the players for both teams came out for pre-game warm-ups in the snow, Junior Seau was the only one who continually took his helmet off. That made it clear to the fans that he was there and active for the game. Or was it because Junior was not yet used to having a helmet on after being retired again for a while? Before this game, the last time that Seau was seen on film was for a TV show in which he did different jobs. One was being a rodeo hand and the film showed a rodeo bull knocking down Seau. Seau was not hurt but maybe that convinced Seau that facing Coach Bill was better than facing Rodeo Bull.

Joey Galloway was inactive for the third straight game and then the Patriots released him the following week. That was too bad. A Galloway in his prime would have been a great third receiver option to go along with Welker and Moss. However, there were continuing reports that Galloway was not doing well learning the Patriot offense, which, combined with a number of key dropped passes in the first three games of the season, spelled doom for Joey's career in New England.

- - -

The Patriots set a number of NFL and team records in this rout, including:

Patriot records:
- Most points in a game – 59
- Most points in a half – 45
- Most points in a quarter – 35
- Most total yards in a game – 619
- Most passing yards in a half – 345 (Tom Brady)
- Most TD passes in one quarter – 5 (Tom Brady)
- Most TD passes in one half – 5 (Tom Brady)
- Most TD passes in one game – 6 (Tom Brady, ties his own record)
- Most touchdowns in a game – 8 (tie)
- Most passing yards in a game – 426 (tie)

NFL records:
- Most TD passes in one quarter – 5 (Tom Brady)
- Largest halftime lead – 45 points

Statistically, and not surprisingly, a number of Patriots had great days. Brady completed 29 passes in 34 attempts for 380 yards and those six TDs. Welker had 10 catches for 150 yards and two TDs. Moss had 8 catches for 129 yards and three TDs.

- - -

The post-game press conferences after this 59-0 were also interesting.

Bill Belichick started his press conference in the usual low-key fashion that he has after a victory, saying, "OK. Well that was, I thought, a really good effort by our team today all across the board. I'm really proud of them ... I thought we executed at a pretty good level and hit some really big plays both in the running game and in the passing game, turned the ball over on defense, played pretty solid in the kicking game, so it was a good, solid, all-around effort. The team had a good week of practice and that was reflected in the way they played and the players did a good job under the conditions ... a good win." If that isn't understatement, it is hard to know what is.

He was later asked a question about the overwhelming win, and did admit, "You never go into a game thinking it'll be like this."

Tom Brady added a touch of humor in is press conference, as he commented, "Coach Belichick was on us pretty tough, being the only team to not hit a 40 yard pass play or have a 20 yard run all season, so hopefully it will keep him quiet for a week or two." Maybe. Of course, since one of those weeks is the team's bye week, it is possible.

- - -

After playing undefeated teams in their first five games, the Titans were the first of two winless teams that the Patriots would play next. This Tennessee game was in snowy New England. Now it was off to merry old England for their next game against the Tampa Bay Buccaneers in London.

Chapter 36 – Jolly Good

Sunday, October 25, 2009:	1	2	3	4	TOTAL
New England Patriots	14	7	7	7 -	35
Tampa Bay Buccaneers	0	7	0	0 -	7

"It's the only team that has the word 'England' in it," joked Alastair Kirkwood, the managing director of NFL UK (and as quoted in bostonist.com on October 23). He was talking about the Patriots coming to London for this game against Tampa Bay. King George III might be turning over in his grave at the phrase "the Patriots coming to London" after the events leading up to the Declaration of Independence. He may have felt that way even more strongly after the Patriots left Merry Old England with a 35-7 win over the Buccaneers.

Regardless of what King George would have said, what Coach Bill did say was a nice summary, as he described this game as "a great way to end this week for our football team."

- - -

The 21st century Patriots went into the game minus a key player. Julian Edelman had broken his arm in the Tennessee game and was out. Rookie Brandon Tate was added to the roster to fill Edelman's roles on kick returns and as backup receiver, but Edelman had really been playing well, so his loss would be felt – maybe not so much against the winless Bucs, but in weeks to come.

- - -

Tampa Bay fell into a hole just 2:34 into the game, when, on the fifth play of the game, Brandon Meriweather intercepted a pass by Tampa Bay quarterback Josh Johnson and ran it in for a 39 yard touchdown and a very early 7-0 lead for New England. Johnson was making his fourth career start and would wind up completing only nine of his 26 passes before being replaced.

Meriweather intercepted Johnson again on Tampa Bay's next possession, returning it 31 yards to the Tampa Bay 46. With 9:00 to go in the first quarter Meriweather had 70 yards of interception returns versus 59 yards of total offense for the Buccaneers.

The Patriots had to punt on the possession after that interception, but got a touchdown on their next possession, a 67 yard, five play drive. An end-around run by Brandon Tate on the first play of that drive got a first down. Another came on a 37 yard pass from Brady to Randy Moss. On the fifth play, from the 14 yard line, Brady hit Wes

Welker on a wide receiver screen, and Welker weaved his way through Tampa Bay to an end zone pay day and a 14-0 lead.

Welker started the next drive off well with a 24 yard punt return to the Tampa Bay 30 yard line, but that drive fizzled after reaching the 11 yard line as a scrambling Tom Brady looped a pass into the end zone that was intercepted.

New England struck quickly for a touchdown the next time they had the ball, scoring on a 54 yard pass from Brady to Sam Aiken. It was a short crossing pattern to Aiken who caught it at the 50 yard line and ran it the rest of the way for the score. The play was set up nicely by Brady, who deftly moved up into the pocket to avoid pressure before seeing Aiken come open and hitting him with that crossing pass.

Tampa Bay did get on the scoreboard just before halftime, as Josh Johnson hit Antonio Bryant with a 33 yard touchdown pass with 1:14 left in the half, to make the halftime score 21-7, but that would end the scoring for the day for the Bucs.

The Patriots opened the third quarter with a 10 play, 73 yard drive (ah, that was nice to see), capped by a 35 yard TD pass from Brady to Benjamin Watson. Brady hit Watson in stride between the right hash mark and right sideline. Brady was continuing to look more and more like his old self.

A one yard TD run by Laurence Maroney in the fourth quarter ended the scoring for the day. This ended yet another long drive by New England, covering 89 yards on 10 plays.

- - -

The 35-7 win sent the Patriots into their bye week with a 5-2 record and in first place in the AFC East. Around the NFL there were three undefeated teams remaining: the Colts, Broncos, and Saints. There were also three winless teams: the Buccaneers, Rams, and Titans. The Colts were coming up on the Patriot schedule, but first, after the bye week, was a date in Foxboro with the 2-4 Miami Dolphins.

- - -

It was another great day for Brady and Welker. Welker had 10 catches for 107 yards. Brady was 23 of 32 for 308 yards and three touchdowns. The end zone interception in the second quarter was Brady's first INT in 183 passes. It was a new franchise record, breaking the old mark of 179 by Brady's predecessor, Drew Bledsoe. Brady tied another of Drew Bledsoe's record with the 26th 300 yard passing day of his career … so far.

In his post-game press conference, Bill Belichick talked about the game and some of the things that he had done in England. Visiting Churchill's war bunkers was a highlight for him, "something that I'm sure I'll remember," said the coach. Then one of the questioners mentioned, "You haven't touched upon Tom Brady very much," and said something inaudible to us about Brady being comfortable in the offense. Belichick's reply was almost effusive in praising Brady:

> "Tom's comfortable running our offense. He's been doing it for nine years. Tom's a guy that just works hard and every week he's such a positive player on our football team, both for himself, our team, and the younger players, particularly in a week like this with Sam [Aiken], Brandon [Tate], and even Matt Slater jumping in there and taking a few plays. Nobody prepares harder than Tom. Nobody works harder than Tom. And all the success that he gets on the field he really deserves, because he puts so much into it and he gives so much of himself for this football team. He's a great leader. He's a great worker. And I'm glad he's our quarterback. There's nobody I'd rather have than Tom Brady."

Me too.

Chapter 37 – Taming the Wildcat

Sunday, November 8, 2009:	1	2	3	4		TOTAL
Miami Dolphins	3	7	7	0	-	17
New England Patriots	7	9	8	3	-	27

A year earlier, when Miami played at New England in Game 3 of the 2008 season, Miami's use of the wildcat formation played havoc with the Patriot defense and gave New England its first loss of that season (see Chapter 9 for details). That was not the case in 2009.

During the week, as always, Miami linebacker Joey Porter had a lot to say, complaining in particular that Tom Brady gets too protected and even tells the officials when to call a roughing the passer penalty. After the game, as is often the case, Joey Porter didn't have much to say. For one thing, since he had not been credited with any sacks or tackles, there was not much that he could say after this game.

There were some tense moments, but New England controlled the wildcat, controlled Porter, and, after a scintillating touchdown pass from Brady to Randy Moss, controlled the game.

Brady was intercepted on the third play from scrimmage, trying to throw deep to Randy Moss. It was a very nice defensive play by Miami Defensive Back Vontae Davis, who was right behind Moss and leaped up to make the interception.

New England got a touchdown later in the first quarter on a one yard run by Laurence Maroney. Three Patriot field goals and a Miami touchdown made it 16-10 Patriots at halftime.

The game turned in a very contrasting third quarter.

Miami took the second half kickoff and marched 66 yards on 16 plays, taking a whopping 10:09 off the clock in doing so. They converted a fourth and one from the New England 44 along the way. They ran the wildcat or direct snap often, using Ronnie Brown (New England's tormentor in 2008) and reserve quarterback Pat White in relief of Chad Henne to run the direct snap. With a first down at the New England three, they ran the wildcat and Brown did not get in. They ran it again and did not get in. They ran it again and this time scored on a one yard pass by Ronnie Brown. They now had the lead at 17-16.

It looked like momentum was with Miami, but it was not.

Three plays after the long, grueling Miami TD drive, the Patriots struck quickly and went back into the lead. Maroney ran for five yards, Brady hit Welker for four, and then came the play of the game. On a third and one from his own 29, Brady hit Moss with a 71 yard touchdown pass. Moss caught it at the 40 as he crossed from right to left. He gave a beautiful stiff arm to Vontae Davis at the 50 and then he was "off to the races" as CBS commentator Greg Gumbel described. The stiff arm was an open right hand to Davis' face mask which reminded CBS analyst Dan Dierdorf of Jimmy Brown. It was a great play. A Brady to Moss pass on the two point conversion gave New England a 24-17 lead.

A fourth quarter 40 yard field goal by Stephen Gostkowski ended the scoring and the Patriots had a 27-17 win.

The Dolphins ran the wildcat 16 times on 70 plays. Their primary backs doing this were Brown and White (Ronnie and Pat, respectively). On their third quarter TD drive, they ran it nine times and had little to show for it. They got only 12 yards on seven runs, had one incompletion, and had the one yard TD pass.

"They were embarrassed a year ago," by the wildcat, according to Greg Gumbel. They were not this year. Steve Grogan said the next day that he felt that Miami ran that formation too often, and should have used Ricky Williams and their powerful running game more than this trickery, but happily they tried it again, and even more happily, the Patriots were ready for it.

The win put New England two games ahead in the AFC East with a 6-2 record, as they prepared to head to Indianapolis and a showdown with Peyton Manning and the undefeated Indianapolis Colts.

Chapter 38 – Fourth and Two

Sunday Night, November 15, 2009:	1	2	3	4	TOTAL
New England Patriots	7	17	0	10	- 34
Indianapolis Colts	7	7	0	21	- 35

It was the renewal of the best rivalry the NFL has had to offer since the Dallas-San Francisco battles of the 1990s. It was a matchup of the two players generally considered the two best players in the NFL, Tom Brady and Peyton Manning. It was a battle for playoff positioning, and for the Patriots to try to prevent the Colts from challenging New England's record for most consecutive regular season games won.

And it was all overshadowed by one decision.

With 2:08 to go in the game, leading 34-28, and facing a fourth and two at his own 28 yard line, Patriot Head Coach Bill Belichick decided to go for a first down. While most coaches would have punted in the same situation, or would try to draw the defensive team off-side with a hard snap count fake, Belichick did not do either of those things. He had Brady try a pass to get the first down, and when the play failed to do so, it gave Peyton Manning and the Colts the ball just 29 yards away from a game winning touchdown. Manning and the Colts proceeded to move those 29 yards easily, on just four plays, and scored with just 13 seconds left in the game. After that, there was not enough time for Brady to lead the Patriots to a miracle comeback of their own.

Why did Belichick make this decision? In the post-game press conference he mentioned a couple of times that he thought that they could get a yard. Someone finally pointed out to him that it was fourth and two and he needed two yards and he acknowledged that he knew that. He still said he felt that they could get it and that would win the game.

I watched the whole Belichick decision in disbelief. As you can tell from previous chapters, I did not have much faith in the Patriot defense, which too often this decade has given up the long game-winning drive that turns what could have been a great win into a devastating loss (see the Super Bowl vs. Giants in February 2008, the AFC Championship vs. Colts in January 2007 and others), but still. Maybe this decision would have looked ingenious if they had gotten a first down, but still this was an odd decision to make. This is when you punt the ball and make the other team at least work to get the game-winning TD. By work I mean going maybe 65 or 70 yards instead of 29.

In Belichick's defense (and defense is a key word here), he had just seen his defense give up two touchdown drives that were long in yards, short in time, and much, much too easy in execution. He may have felt more confidence in his offense and with the ball in Tom Brady's hands to try to make a first down on fourth down, rather than rely on that defense. If so, I kind of wish that they had gone on a quick count and try to catch the Colts just laying back trying not to be drawn off-side.

Of course, if the Pats had been able to avoid an end zone interception and an end zone fumble in the third quarter, which they dominated, or could have gotten a TD instead of yet another FG in the 4Q to go up 38-21 instead of 34-21 then it all would not have mattered. There was certainly a lot of ranting and raving in our living room at ~ 11:45 that night, much of it at Laurence Maroney (a waste), the NE defense (porous), the NE running game and pass rush (both practically non-existent), the Patriot mis-use of timeouts in the second half, which they did against Indy last year as well, and this shall-we-say-questionable decision.

Admittedly, the play looked closer to working than the officials gave New England credit for. The pass from Brady was caught by Kevin Faulk, and it looked like he had gotten to, or just beyond, the 30 yard line, which would have given New England a first down. However, the official responsible for spotting the ball came in from the sideline and had his foot positioned at the 29 yard line. He was making an up-and-down gesture with his two hands in front of him, indicating that he felt that Faulk was bobbling the ball as he was hit at the 30 and then driven back to the 29, so he did not give him forward progress to the 30. I'm not sure if his call was correct. The replays seemed to show that Faulk had possession at the 30. It also makes you wonder. If this play had occurred at the two yard line and Faulk was bobbling it, then was driven back into the end zone and tackled, would it have been a safety, or would they have awarded him forward progress to the two? I'm pretty sure from all of my years of watching football that the ball would have been placed at the two. So why not award forward progress here? On the other hand, no one from New England argued the case too vociferously, so maybe they did not disagree with the spot.

Maybe no one from New England complained because they could not challenge the ruling on the field. Since New England had used all of its allotted timeouts, the team did not have one in reserve to challenge the ruling have the officials review the replay. Also, had this play been run after the two minute warning, the booth officials could call for a replay. However, the play had started before the two minute warning, and though it ended after it, this did not allow for the booth replay. The frustrating thing about this was that New England had wasted at least one of those timeouts.

Let's set this up. Indianapolis had just scored a touchdown to cut New England's lead to 34-28. It was an easy march downfield for 79 yards that took only 1:52 (!) When New England received the kickoff after the touchdown, they had a first and ten at the twenty. As they came out for first down, Tom Brady noticed that they did not have the right personnel on the field for the play that was called, so he had to call a timeout. This is crazy. Why weren't the right people ready to come out onto the field? If this had happened when the Patriots came out for their last drive against the Rams in the 2002 Super Bowl, maybe the dynasty would never have happened.

In any case, this was a very much unnecessary and wasted timeout, and it came back to haunt them. A running play gained no yards (no surprise). A pass to Wes Welker gained eight to the 28 and set up a third and two. Brady threw again to Welker and the pass was broken up, and nearly intercepted, at the right sideline. That set up the fourth down play. The Patriots took their final timeout to discuss it, and decided to go for it. What happened next is described above.

A surprised and probably very grateful Peyton Manning led the Colts back onto the field and once again easily marched through the Patriot defense, using four plays to waltz the 29 yards to the game-winning touchdown. In typical dagger-to-the heart cruelty, the touchdown came on the same kind of play that Peyton's brother Eli ran to get the game-winner in the 2008 Super Bowl. The Colt receiver, Reggie Wayne, had single coverage by Jonathan Wilhite on the left, just as Giant receiver Plaxico Burress had against Ellis Hobbs in that Super Bowl. With no one to help Wilhite cover Wayne, Manning drilled the ball into Wayne's hands and the Colts had a 34-34 tie. The extra point then put them ahead 35-34.

With 13 seconds to go, Brady tried a pass over the middle to Wes Welker for nine yards. This was another head-scratcher. In that Giants' Super Bowl game, with more time on the clock, the Patriots tried four long bombs to Randy Moss, where some shorter passes, like this one to Welker, could have moved them into position for a tying field goal. With 13 seconds to go in this one, and with no timeouts, this was the time for the long bomb, especially against a set of inexperienced Colt defensive backs who had given up long pass completions earlier. Maybe it all makes sense, but it certainly "is a puzzlement", to quote the King in "The King and I". In any case, on this night in Indianapolis, it was the Colts who were the King.

- - -

For much of this game, prior to these last 2 ½ minutes, it was the Patriots who were in control. The Colts only led twice, once early, at 7-0, and then late, with the 35-34 win.

Peyton Manning led Indianapolis on a 90 yard drive on the team's second possession. The drive was highlighted by a great pass from Manning to Reggie Wayne on the sideline. The play was defended well, but Manning put it perfectly in Wayne's hands on the right sideline at the 26 yard line. The touchdown was another great play by Manning, who faked right, faked left, and settled underneath for a 15 yard pass on third and ten to Joseph Addai for the TD.

After that, it was all Patriots. Brady completed a pass to Randy Moss for 55 yards from the New England 39 to the Indy six yard line. Moss raced up field and caught the perfectly thrown ball in stride between two defenders. This set up a one yard TD run by Laurence Maroney to tie the score at 7-7 after one quarter.

On New England's next possession, a 29 yard run by Kevin Faulk on a draw play took New England to the 42. A pass by Brady to Moss on the left sideline gained 20 yards to the 21. After a holding call moved the Patriots back to the 31, a slant pass to Wes Welker gained 15 yards and put the Patriots in the red zone. As was the case too often in 2009, the red zone incursion could only result in a field goal, not a touchdown. An 11 play drive had ended in three points instead of ten. New England ranked 26th in the NFL in red zone efficiency – a horrible stat for such a good team – and that red zone problem would definitely haunt them in this game.

After getting the ball back for New England's next series, Brady threw a perfect bomb on a fly pattern to Randy Moss, who lined up on the right and raced straight down the field. Brady hit Moss in stride and it turned into a 63 yard touchdown and a 17-7 New England lead. This was a beautiful pass by Brady, who was putting on a brilliant show of great quarterback play with his Indy counterpart, Peyton Manning.

New England took a 24-7 lead on a 57 yard drive on five plays on its next possession. This one was set up by a 36 yard Brady completion to Benjamin Watson, and was scored on a nine yard pass from Brady to Julian Edelman. Brady did a great job of eluding the Colt rush before throwing the pass, stepping out of the grasp of one defender and stepping away from another. It was Edelman's first NFL touchdown. It was also Edelman's first game back after breaking his arm in the Tennessee snow game that I had attended. He still had a cast on his right arm, so he used his left arm to spike the ball in celebration.

As the game moved toward the end of the first half, I had the feeling, "Don't let them score. Don't let them get any momentum." I'd seen the defense give up too many of these late half scores that gave the other team momentum (or lost games) and the last thing that I wanted was for Peyton Manning and the Colts to get some momentum.

However, a 20 yard touchdown pass from Manning to Wayne over Jonathan Wilhite cut the lead to 24-14 and gave Indianapolis some much-needed momentum. Wilhite actually played the pass well, but was just beaten by an excellent pass-catch combination in Manning and Wayne. Then, when New England had three incompletions and had to punt with 4:02 to go in the half, I was even more worried that the score would be 24-21 at the half. Luckily Indianapolis had a dropped pass and a penalty that kept them from scoring on that drive, and on the last drive of the half they moved to the 40 but could not score. It was 24-14 at the half.

The third quarter was completely dominated by the Patriots. They should have scored at least twice and put the game away, but they did not score at all. They got the ball to start the half, and started at their 27. A 15 yard run by Kevin Faulk and a 14 yard pass to Wes Welker (all the yards gained came after the catch) went for naught, as a Brady pass from the 33 yard line to Moss in the end zone was intercepted by the Colts.

Manning then gave the ball back on an interception of his own, this one by Leigh Bodden on a ball thrown by Manning from his 38 that Bodden intercepted at the New England 24. This set the Patriots up at their own 12 yard line (after an unsportsmanlike conduct penalty) and they began a long, time-consuming drive down to the Colt three yard line. But they lost this opportunity when Laurence Maroney fumbled the ball away. Indianapolis recovered in the end zone, and the Patriots had squandered not only yet another red zone opportunity, but an opportunity to take complete command of the game.

Both Upton Bell and Steve Grogan, on Upton's Monday night radio program, blamed Maroney for the fumble, saying that he did not protect the ball with both hands as he should on this type of play. Replays showed them to be right.

They got one more chance as the third quarter ended as a 69 yard punt return by Welker set them up with a first and goal at the Colt seven yard line as the third quarter ended. They did cash in this time on two plays. After a 2 yard run by Kevin Faulk, Brady fired a bullet to

Moss in the end zone for a five yard TD pass. The Patriots were up 17, 31-14, and they seemingly were now in control.

That control did not last long, however, as Manning led the Colts back immediately on a too-easy 79 yard drive to a touchdown that cut the lead to 10, at 31-21. The score came on a 29 yard pass from Manning to Pierre Garcon, who put a nice double-move on Bodden to free himself for the TD. It took Manning only 2:04 and five plays to go those 79 yards, and he got very little resistance from the Patriot defense. He certainly did not get any pressure from the pass rush. Manning was hardly touched in the fourth quarter.

The Patriots were forced to punt on their next possession, and then had another opportunity to break the game open as Manning, from his own 18 yard line, just lofted a pass that was easily intercepted by Wilhite at the 46 and returned to the 31. Handed another golden opportunity, the Patriots could only get a 36 yard field goal by Stephen Gostkowski, so the lead which could have been back to a somewhat comfortable 17 points, was instead a somewhat shaky 13 points, 34-21. Two Manning touchdowns could still give the Colts the win.

One of those touchdowns came much too easily (this is a recording), as Manning marched the Colts another 79 yards to another touchdown, this time in only 1:52, on a four yard run by Joseph Addai. So, with 2:23 to go, the lead was down to less than a touchdown, 34-28. The rest of what happened is described above, and, for the sake of Patriot fans, won't be repeated.

- - -

The Belichick decision stole headlines and fed radio and TV talk shows for days. Unfortunately, it overshadowed what had been a great match-up of the top two players in pro football, Brady and Manning.

The Brady-Manning match-up is one of the best in all of sports. It involves two great athletes who both carry themselves with a lot of class. It is reminiscent of Larry Bird-Magic Johnson, Muhammed Ali-Joe Frazier, Sandy Koufax-Juan Marichal, Johnny Unitas–Bart Starr, Chris Evert–Martina Navratilova, and the ultimate rivalry: Bill Russell – Wilt Chamberlain. It is great to watch these two battle each other in these Patriot-Colt games.

Further, the Patriot-Colt rivalry of this decade matches other great rivalries in other decades: Cowboys-49ers in the 1990s, Redskins-Giants in the 1980s, Steelers-Raiders in the 1970s, Packers-Colts in the 1960s, and Browns-Lions in the 1950s (yes, the Bowns and Lions were both actually very good once).

Before the game, NBC polled 20 living Hall of Fame quarterbacks on who they thought was best, Brady or Manning. The results showed 13.5 votes for Manning and 2.5 votes for Brady, with four abstentions. It is probably right, but Tom does have those three Super Bowl rings to Manning's one, so maybe everything evens out.

- - -

It was a frustrating week for Patriot fans.

The Patriots and those fans could only hope that the team gets another shot at the Colts in the AFC Championship Game. In the meantime, the Patriots should work on their pass rush, running game, time and timeout management, and ability to score touchdowns and not field goals when they get the ball inside their opponent's 20 yard line.

Chapter 39 – Crying Time Again

Sunday, November 22, 2009:	1	2	3	4		TOTAL
New York Jets	0	7	7	0	-	14
New England Patriots	14	10	0	7	-	31

The week began with a real contrast in head coaching style.

The Patriots had just come off a very tough loss against the Colts. Bill Belichick was not receptive to complaints and criticisms about his decision to go for it on fourth down in his own territory late in that game. When reporters asked if he would make that decision again, Belichick brushed them off by saying that you only get one chance. He said that his team needed to focus on the Jets, their next opponent. After the game, a 31-14 Patriot victory over the Jets, Belichick talked about how he saw on Wednesday that the team had put the Colts loss behind them and were focused on the Jets. "They were ready to play this afternoon," was how Belichick complimented his team in the post-game press conference.

The Jets had just come off a very tough loss against the Jaguars, losing on a field goal as time ran out. Rex Ryan stood before his players to talk about that game and the upcoming game against the Patriots and cried. He then chided his own performance by bringing a box of Kleenex to his press conference the next day. I wonder what some other head coaches would think about a coach crying in front of his players. I think that Vince Lombardi, George Halas, Bill Parcells, Bill Belichick, Chuck Noll, Jimmy Johnson, or any of the other great coaches would scoff at the idea. A coach crying in front of his players? They would wonder what the team would think about their coach, among other things.

Of course, Ryan might have been crying about the way that the Jets season had started to collapse around him. After a 3-0 start that had New York fans and reporters talking Super Bowl, the Jets had lost five of their last six, and so came into the game with a 4-5 record. They would leave the game with a 4-6 record after the Patriots routed them by that 31-14 score.

It was a 'Tale of Two Cities' contrast during the game as well.

The key performers on the positive side for New England were Tom Brady, Wes Welker, and defensive back Leigh Bodden. Brady completed 28 passes in 41 attempts for 310 yards. It was the fifth straight game in which Brady had thrown for more than 300 yards. Welker was phenomenal, catching 15 passes for 192 yards. He also ran once, and end-around on which he gained 11 yards. Bodden intercepted three passes by Jets quarterback Mark Sanchez, returning the first for the first touchdown of the game.

The key performer on the negative side for New York was Mark Sanchez, who threw four interceptions, and fumbled the ball away another time. The Patriots helped make Sanchez look like the rookie quarterback that he is, rather than the Joe Namath clone that many Jets fans saw after the season's first three games.

A decent performer for the Jets was defensive back Darrelle Revis, who covered Randy Moss for most of the game and did a very competent job. He got some help from other defenders, which helped open things up for Welker, but he also should be given credit for keeping Moss from dominating the game as he can, and as he did against the Colts for much of the preceding game.Bodden got the scoring started for the Patriots with 5:47 to go in the first quarter by stepping in front of a Sanchez pass intended for Jericho Cotchery and returning it 53 yards down the right sideline for a touchdown.

The Jets then failed to convert on a third and two when Sanchez hit receiver Braylon Edwards right between the numbers for what would have been a first down, but the ball bounced off of Edwards and fell incomplete. The Patriots then took over and drove 76 yards on nine plays to another touchdown. This one was scored on a play from the four yard line that oddly started with no time on the clock at the end of the first quarter. The Jets had just been called for defensive holding as the quarter ended, but, since a quarter cannot end on a defensive penalty, one more play would need to be run before the teams switched ends. This seemed to surprise both teams and the CBS announcers. In any case, Brady made it worthwhile by fooling Revis with a quick throw to Moss to the left right on the goal line, and Moss spun in for the TD. It was a great timing pass play by Brady and Moss. With another combo this might have been dangerous, as had Revis stepped into the play he would have had nothing but 100 yards of open space between him and a TD. With Brady and Moss, it went exactly as planned.

The Patriots made it 21-0 early in the second quarter. On a third and seven from the New York 46 yard line, with 11:54 to go in the first half, Brady hit Welker on a deep pattern down the right seam for 43 yards to set up a first and goal at the three yard line. It was a beautiful play. Welker does not usually run a deep pattern, but he did on this play, and he caught the Jets by surprise. Brady's pass hit Welker in stride at the 20 yard line, and there was no defender within five yards of Welker when he made the reception, though one did have an angle on him and was able to tackle him before he could reach the end zone. After the game, when asked about the play, Welker responded, "I think they got confused. I noticed it and Tom did too. So we just took off down the field." Laurence Maroney carried it in for the touchdown.

Another Bodden interception set the Patriots up for another score. On a third and eight from the 43, Sanchez threw a pass to his left that Bodden caught at the New England 40 with one knee on the ground. He returned it for eight yards, and at that point had more yards in interception returns (61) than the Jets had for total yards in the game (26). The Patriots could not get a fourth TD after the interception, but did extend the lead to 24-0 on a 26 yard field goal by Stephen Gostkowski.

About the only thing that could hurt New England at this point was a big turnover that would give the Jets some hope and momentum at halftime. It almost happened when the ball was knocked out of Tom Brady's hands as he attempted to pass on a third down, but the Patriots recovered the fumble. CBS analyst Phil Simms commented, "big mistake by Tom Brady ... don't give them a chance." Unfortunately, it did happen, and they did give the Jets a chance as New England's punt was blocked and run in for a touchdown from the four yard line that cut the lead to 24-7. The Jets had only 34 total yards in the first half, but did now have that blasted hope and momentum.

When the third quarter started with an 80 yard New York touchdown drive on 11 plays, it was suddenly 24-14, and the Jets had some life and the Patriots and their fans had some worries. Three times already this year the Patriots had given up leads in the second half. These were against the Jets, Broncos, and Colts, and they had accounted for their three losses. CBS showed a graphic that the Patriots had a 66-1 record from 2002-2008 when leading at the half, but were only 5-3 in 2009. All of those three 2009 losses were on the road, could it happen now at home?

The answer was no. After three punts ended the third quarter with that 24-14 score, Leigh Bodden made his third interception of the game on the first play in the fourth quarter by the Jets, at the New England 26 yard line. While that did not lead to a Patriot score, another interception off Sanchez, this one by Brandon Meriweather, did. This interception came as a result of the Patriots pressuring Sanchez out of the pocket to his left, and forced Sanchez to throw as he was backing up to avoid the sack. This set New England up at the Jets' 25 yard line, and eight plays later a one yard TD run by Maroney gave the Patriots a 31-14 lead.

One more turnover by Sanchez, a fumble at the New England 29 on a ball knocked out of his hands by a rushing Tully Banta-Cain, put the finishing touches on a big win for the Patriots.

- - -

Across the NFL, two teams, Indianapolis and New Orleans, remained undefeated with 10-0 records. The next opponent for New Orleans was New England, in a Monday night game after Thanksgiving. It would be yet another battle with yet another undefeated team for New England in 2009, their seventh in the season's eleven games.

- - -

At his press conference after the game, Rex Ryan complained about a late pass attempt from Brady toward Moss, saying that he "felt disrespected". This is the same Rex Ryan who made a point to say that he was not going to "kiss Belichick's rings" when he took the job with the Jets. This is the same Rex Ryan who had sent a recorded phone message to New York's season ticket holders before the first Patriot-Jet game in 2009 telling fans to come to the game prepared to be loud. This is the same Rex Ryan who had sent out three former Patriots as his captains for the opening coin toss in that game, Kevin O'Connell, Damien Woody, and Larry Izzo. And this is the same Rex Ryan who presumably was happy when his defensive back, Kerry Rhodes, said before that game with the Patriots, "We don't want to just beat them, we want to send a message." Rex, if you can't take it, don't give it out.

As the New York Post put it the day after the game, "If the Jets' waste of potential brought tears to coach Rex Ryan's eyes during the impassioned speech he delivered to his team last week, he needed a whole case of Kleenex to blot his disbelieving eyes after this pathetic performance."

Crying before the game, whining after it – it was a perfect set of weepy bookends for a nice revenge win.

Chapter 40 – Down in New Orleans

Monday Night, November 30, 2009:	1	2	3	4		TOTAL
New England Patriots	7	3	7	0	-	17
New Orleans Saints	3	21	7	7	-	38

In a pre-game show before their game with the undefeated (10-0) New Orleans Saints, Coach Bill Belichick said that one key to the game would be the Patriots not turning the ball over on offense. The other, he said, was that the defense would be giving up yards to the powerful Saints' offense, but that they can't give them all up on one play.

Unfortunately for the Patriots, they did just what Belichick did not want them to do, with two big turnovers (and almost a third) and many, many big plays for the New Orleans offense.

This was a real beat-down, the kind of which the Patriots have not experienced since before the Tom Brady era started in 2001. It was a 38-17 win for New Orleans and it seemed like the defeat was more than that.

The commentators in the pre-game show mentioned how interesting it is how often the game of the year involves the Patriots. They also showed Belichick walking around the Superdome before the game with a camera crew, apparently reliving memories of the 2002 Super Bowl, the last game that the Patriots had played in New Orleans and their first Super Bowl win ever.

New Orleans received the opening kickoff and got the blowout started immediately. On the first play from scrimmage, quarterback Drew Brees, quite possibly the third best quarterback in the NFL behind Brady and Peyton Manning, hit Devery Henderson for a 33 yard pass completion. The Saints continued down the field but had to settle for a field goal from John Carney and a 3-0 lead.

The Patriots came back with a drive of their own, for 80 yards and a touchdown. They converted two fourth down plays on the drive, the second a fourth and one from the four yard line that resulted in Laurence Maroney running it in for a touchdown. The drive took 7:40 which seemed like a great situation for the Patriots, keeping the ball out of the hands of Brees.

After forcing New Orleans to punt on its next possession, the Patriots wound up in great field position when Wes Welker returned the punt 41 yards from his 13 to the New Orleans 46 yard line. It looked like the Patriots were in position to score another TD, take a 14-3 lead, and put some pressure on the shoulders of the Saints. However, this was the high point of the game for New England. Tom Brady was forced out of the pocket on New England's first play and threw a bad pass that was intercepted by New Orleans at their 40. New England led 7-3 at the end of one quarter, but then the floodgates opened (uh, maybe not a good metaphor for New Orleans, but it certainly describes the game that night).

New Orleans marched down the field and scored on an 18 yard screen pass from Brees to Pierre Thomas.

After a New England punt put them on their own 25, Brees immediately threw a 75 yard touchdown pass to a wide open Henderson. "Don't give it all up on one play," is what Belichick had said before the game, but that is exactly what happened. No one was within 10 yards of Henderson in any direction. He caught it at the 50 and ran it in easily for the score. It was now 17-7 New Orleans.

A 36 yard field goal by Gostkowski made it 17-10, but that close score did not hold for long, as New Orleans score again on a 38 yard bomb from Brees to Robert Meachem to the middle of the field for a catch at the goal line. The New Orleans lead was now 24-10, and for the first time in nearly a decade I found myself thinking 'don't let them score again before halftime.' Luckily they didn't, but only because the Saints decided to take a knee to end the half. It was their only possession in what would be a six possession sequence in which they did not score. As I said to my son at halftime, this team is scary good.

Laurence Maroney fumbled on the first play from scrimmage in the second half, but thankfully the New Orleans defender fumbled it right back before the New Orleans offense could get back onto the field. From the New Orleans 49, Brady eluded the Saints rush by sliding to his left and completed a bomb to Randy Moss at the two yard line. Maroney carried it in and the Patriots had some hope at 24-17.

It turned out to be false hope, though, as Brees connected with a 69 yard pass play on New Orleans' first play and two plays later the lead was back to 14 at 31-17.

The game was a contrast in line play. Brady was under pressure throughout the game. Meanwhile, the only handprints that Brees had on his uniform were from his teammates slapping him on the back after another good throw. The Patriot defense was putting absolutely zero pressure on Brees.

A 9 play, 75 yard drive by New Orleans in the fourth quarter ended in a 20 yard bullet by Brees right down the middle for his fifth touchdown pass of the game. It was 38-17 New Orleans, and the Monday Night Football announcers were left to say things on that drive such as "it's easy", or "it's just pass and catch here." It was astonishing. Belichick took Brady out and put Brian Hoyer in with about five minutes left in the game. When is the last time Brady came out in a blowout loss?

Bill Belichick started his post-game press conference by saying "Uh …," and then paused and sighed. That pretty well summed up how all of us watching the game felt as well. He went on after the pause to say "You've got to give New Orleans credit. They were obviously the better team tonight. It really wasn't as competitive a game as we hoped it would be or as we needed it to be. … They were a better team tonight … That's a good football team." Yes. At the risk of repeating myself, they are scary good.

Tom Brady added when he got to the podium, "There's a reason why they're 11-0 … We didn't play to their level."

Earlier, as the game was nearing its end, the TV cameras showed a few minutes of Belichick and Brady talking on the sideline as the play on the field continued. It was clear that it had been a long night for both of them. Sadly, it almost looked like the end of an era. The Patriots would need to make a long climb back out of the hole of this game.

Chapter 41 – Even Further Down in Miami

Sunday, December 6, 2009:	1	2	3	4		TOTAL
New England Patriots	7	7	7	0	-	21
Miami Dolphins.	0	10	9	3	-	22

Instead of climbing out of that hole in Miami, the hole got even bigger. The Patriots lost 22-21 after taking an early 14-0 lead, and it was the same old problems that still have not been fixed, specifically:

1. No pass rush
2. No running game
3. Inability to score in the red zone (related to #2)
4. Inability to stop the other team on third down (related to #1)

The most frustrating thing was the lack of a pass rush. Miami was playing a quarterback, Chad Henne, who had only become a starter when Chad Pennington was injured (the Dolphins seemed to have a penchant for quarterbacks named Chad, but then, as my wife pointed out, it is the state famous for the hanging chads on election ballots). He had all the time in the world to check off from one receiver to another, survey the field, and make his throws. He was sacked once, and hardly touched any other time. He completed 29 of 52 passes for 335 yards and two touchdowns. He also led a 51 yard drive to the game winning field goal. He did this even though overthrowing or underthrowing his receivers a number of times. In other words, it could have been worse.

The lack of a running game hurt badly at the end of the game. The Patriots got the ball with 4:44 to go. Miami had only one time out remaining. A running game which could get two first downs could have helped salt the game away. They could muster nothing on the ground.

The end result was a second consecutive loss for New England, the first time that has happened in over three years. The last time that it happened was November 12, 2006.

It all started out so well, too. Tom Brady hit Randy Moss with a beautiful 58 yard touchdown pass on the first Patriot possession of the game. It was play action followed by a fake reverse. Brady unloaded and hit Moss at the 15 yard line in stride with what Phil Simms described as a pass with a "perfect arc" and Randy just ran right in for the score.

Brady was hit by two defenders as he threw, and as soon as the play was over, he ran off the field and into the locker room. We were told by the TV announcers that Brady had hurt his arm, but when asked about it after the game, Brady wouldn't say anything about the injury. He came back quickly though, and did not miss a play. He led New England on a 13 play, 80 yard drive to another touchdown and a 14-0 lead on a six yard run by Kevin Faulk. That TD run was enabled by great blocking by the Patriot offensive line, particularly Matt Light. Faulk had a clear lane to run through to paydirt.

After a Miami 88 yard drive for a touchdown and a New England punt (on fourth down with less than one yard to go), Brandon Meriweather intercepted a Henne pass to set up New England again. Another long bomb by Brady, this one for 58 yards to Wes Welker, brought the Patriots to the Miami 15 yard line. This was another beauty, Brady hitting Welker in stride at the 50, but Welker was caught from behind. It looked like another touchdown was coming, or at least a field goal, but it turned into nothing, as the Patriots went for it on fourth and one from the six yard line but Sammy Morris was stopped by a wall of defenders and Miami took over. Instead of a 17-7 lead, it was only 14-7. Make that 14-10 as Miami drove almost effortlessly from its own six yard line to the Patriot eleven for a field goal.

New England struck again on its first possession of the second half. It was another long Brady pass that did it. This one was to Sam Aiken for an 81 yard touchdown down the right sideline. Aiken made a great play on this one, batting the ball and grabbing it away from the Miami defender, Sean Smith, at midfield. Smith fell down. Aiken stepped over him and ran untouched to the end zone. It was 21-10 New England with 12:02 to go in the third quarter.

But that was it for New England. They would not score again.

At 21-19 with 9:39 to go the Patriots had a chance to salt it away. They had a second and goal at the Miami four, but Brady was intercepted in the end zone by Vontae Davis as he tried to get it to Moss in the back right corner of the end zone. It was another red zone opportunity squandered in a year full of them for New England.

Then, as noted previously, they got the ball with 4:44 to go and could not get a first down. After a three and out, Miami got the ball with 3:44 to go and drove for the winning score. A critical play was a fourth and six conversion in which Henne, with no pressure whatsoever from the Patriot line (this is a recording), hit Greg Camarillo for 13 yards and a first down at the 29. Dan Carpenter hit a 41 yard field goal with 1:02 left and Miami had its first lead of the game at 22-21.

That became the final score when Miami intercepted Brady to end the Patriots' last hope. This was particularly galling as the interception came thanks to Brady being harassed and having to throw as he was falling down. What was galling was that Miami was only rushing three men! The contrast was striking. Miami got to Brady with only a three man rush, whereas New England could not put any pressure on Henne no matter how many men they were rushing. Just as had been the case against New Orleans, the Patriots did sack Henne once, but for most of the day, no Patriot defender seemed to be in same zip code as Henne.

Brady and Wes Welker were the only Patriots about whom you could say "they had a good game." Brady was 19 of 29 passing for 352 yards and two touchdowns. This included going 13 for 14 in the first half for 196 of those yards – and his only incompletion was a throwaway to avoid a sack when all of his receivers were covered. Welker had 10 catches for 167 yards. But two men can't do it all.

Elsewhere, Indianapolis and New Orleans both won, to stay undefeated at 12-0. Indianapolis' win was its 21st regular season victory in a row. That tied the NFL record held by the Patriots. That made it a bad day all around for New England.

So, to sum up, no offensive or defensive adjustments at halftime (maybe Belichick misses experienced coordinators like Charlie Weis and Romeo Crennel), absolutely no pass rush, no running game, no red zone efficiency, no stopping the other team on third down all added up to no happy time for New England in South Florida.

Chapter 42 – Brady to Welker, Brady to Welker

Sunday, December 13, 2009:

	1	2	3	4	TOTAL
Carolina Panthers	*7*	*0*	*0*	*3*	*- 10*
New England Patriots	*0*	*7*	*7*	*6*	*- 20*

Tumultuous. That may be the best way to describe the week of the Patriots' 13th game of the season, against the Carolina Panthers.

What made it tumultuous was the start of the week and the excruciating loss to Miami followed by the middle of the week, when Bill Belichick sent four players home from practice. This happened on Wednesday, the day of a morning rush hour snowstorm in New England. Roads were not plowed and traffic was slow everywhere (it took me an hour for what is normally a 20 minute ride to work, for example). Four players were late for a team meeting scheduled for 8 AM: Adalius Thomas, Gary Guyton, Derrick Burgess, and Randy Moss. Since they were late, Belichick sent them home.

The reaction from the four players was very different. Randy Moss was silent (though some reporters and Carolina defenders said that he took it out on the team by not giving a good effort in the game against the Panthers on Sunday, adding to the tumultuous nature of the week). Derrick Burgess blamed himself. Adalius Thomas was defiant. Thomas, who had not been happy earlier in the year when he was made inactive for the Tennessee game, seemed even more unhappy with this. He explained that he had been caught in a weather-caused traffic delay and had called in. He was therefore surprised to be sent home. "I can't figure out what Bill thinks or knows," he said, adding, "There's nothing to really apologize about." He said that he arrived at "8:09 or something like that," and was surprised when Belichick told him to leave the facility for the rest of the day.

Thomas explained, "There's one thing about Mother Nature. You can't control that … You can't run people over getting to work ... You leave home. There are people there, cars sitting in the road. You're sitting there. What are you going to do? It's not The Jetsons. I can't jump up and fly."

Belichick was apparently not amused by either the cartoon references or the comments. On Wednesday, at the end of practice, he reportedly gathered the team and told them, "It's not summer any more. It's New England in December. Plan accordingly. An 8 AM meeting is still an 8 AM meeting." On Saturday he made Thomas inactive for the Carolina game.

Meanwhile, Tom Brady became a father for the second time on Tuesday night and still was there in time for the meeting on Wednesday. He had also been listed as questionable for the Carolina game due to shoulder, finger, and rib injuries, the latter suffered while being hit on that long TD pass to Randy Moss in the Miami game. He did play, however.

Against this backdrop, happily it was the Carolina Panthers who were coming to Foxboro (as was I, for my second game of 2009). It was Carolina's first-ever visit to Gillette Stadium. Carolina was 5-7 and would be missing starting quarterback Jake Delhomme and starting little-used Matt Moore in his place. It was the recipe for a big New England win, right?

Right. But not by much. The Patriots had a lackluster first half and were trailing 7-0 as the half wore down. The Panther TD was scored on a 41 yard TD on a post pattern from Moore to Steve Smith that Smith caught at the goal line. New England's best two plays in the first half were a punt by Chris Hansen that pinned Carolina back at the seven in the second quarter, and a pass interference penalty on Carolina on a Brady pass from the Patriot 49 yard line that set up New England at the Panther 21 yard line. The Patriots converted that to a score on a three yard touchdown run by Kevin Faulk, who ran untouched into the end zone through a huge hole on the right side. The TD was set up by a big Brady to Wes Welker pass for eight yards and a first down at the ten. It was New England's first score in almost 56 minutes of play, since the Sam Aiken TD just after halftime in the Miami game. It was 7-7 at the half.

The Patriot offense did come out strong in the second half. They took the second half kickoff and marched down the field, but a fumble by Sammy Morris ended that opportunity. New England was not to be denied on its next possession, however, as they marched 96 yards for the go-ahead touchdown. The drive was highlighted by the combination of Brady to Welker, who connected five times for 65 yards (by my count) on the drive. This included

- On the second play, a Brady to Welker pass from the 6 to the 12, on which Welker was slammed to the ground immediately after catching the pass, but bounced right up and ran back to the huddle. It was Welker's 100 path reception of the season.

- On the third play, a Brady to Welker pass from the 12 to the 25 on a crossing pattern for a first down.

- On the sixth play, a Brady to Welker pass from the 35 to the 48 for a first down.

- On the ninth play, a Brady to Welker pass from the Carolina 41 to the 32.

- On the tenth play, a Brady to Welker pass from 32 to the 9, for a first down.

It seemed like every time Brady needed a key conversion, he looked to Welker. Randy Moss was not having a good day, with only one reception (which he fumbled), two dropped passes, and another pass that was intercepted when it looked like Moss either ran the wrong route or did not pursue the ball as he might have. This is what fueled the complaints from some reporters that he did not put out the effort and criticism from the Carolina defenders that he was quitting on plays. I couldn't see it, so I won't comment on it any further.

In any case, the 13th play of this drive was a five yard TD pass from Brady to Benjamin Watson, and the Patriots were now in the lead for the first time at 14-7.

Two Stephen Gostkowski field goals, of 48 and 47 yards, following a Panther field goal made the final score 20-10.

Indianapolis and New Orleans both won to improve their undefeated records to 13-0. The win by Indianapolis was their 22nd regular season win in a row, breaking the record previously held by New England and tied a week earlier by the Colts.

Miami and the Jets both won to stay one game behind the Patriots.

The New England win was in a grinder of a game, but the Patriots were able to get this one primarily due to one factor:

Brady to Welker.

Chapter 43 – Shufflin' D in Buffalo

Sunday, December 20, 2009	1	2	3	4	Total
New England Patriots	0	14	3	0	- 17
Buffalo Bills	3	0	0	7	- 10

The primary stories during the week before the Patriots' game in Buffalo revolved around whether Randy Moss quit on the team in the Carolina game. Opinions varied but Patriot players and coaches were staunch in their defense of Moss.

The major story during the *day* preceding the game was about a massive snowstorm that hit the East Coast, dropping 20 inches of snow in parts of North Carolina, Virginia, Washington D.C., Baltimore, and Philadelphia, and 15 inches in New York and Boston. Oddly, the weather was great in Buffalo.

The big story in the *hours* before the game was the unavailability of two of the starters in the Patriot defensive line. Vince Wilfork and Ty Warren.

The Patriots compensated for the Moss stories by going to him early and often. Moss wound up with 5 catches for 70 yards and a touchdown.

The Patriots compensated for the loss of Wilfork and Warren by going to their little-used formation in which they have one down lineman and a number of players upright and shuffling around so that Buffalo would not know who would be rushing the passer and who would be dropping back in coverage. It was the formation I had hoped that they would use on the Giants' last drive in the 2008 Super Bowl, when one key stop on that drive could have meant an undefeated season. Would it have worked? Who knows? But it did work in Buffalo as the Patriots finally – *finally* – showed a decent pass rush, sacking Buffalo quarterbacks 6 times. It was a big factor in a grinding 17-10 win over Buffalo.

The early signs were not positive, as Buffalo took the opening kickoff and marched down to the Patriot two yard line. They got little resistance from the Patriot defense, and the drive stalled only due to a motion penalty on Buffalo on a third and goal. The Bills had to settle for a field goal, despite taking 9:24 off the clock and driving to what looked like a sure touchdown.

The Bills kept racking up penalties at bad times, including two pass interference penalties that set up New England's only two touchdowns of the game, both in the second quarter. The first touchdown came on a "laser" from Tom Brady to Randy Moss for 13 yards and a score. The description of "laser" came from CBS analyst Dan Dierdorff. Oddly, it was Tom Brady's first completion of the game, and he would only have five in the first half. Nevertheless, he hit this one when the Patriots needed it. The second TD came after a Buffalo pass interference penalty put the ball on the one yard line. Laurence Maroney ran it in for a 14-3 New England lead at the half.

Once again the Patriots did not do much in the second half, but they were able to hang on for a 17-10 win and their first real road win of the season (they had beaten Tampa Bay in London, but that was on a neutral field; this was their first win in an opponent's stadium).

Miami lost in overtime to Tennessee, 27-24, and the Jets lost to the Falcons 10-7 thanks to a TD in the last two minutes by the Falcons. That opened New England's lead in the division to two games with two games to go. New England improved their record to 9-5 while the Dolphins and Jets dropped to 7-7.

Elsewhere, the Saints lost to Dallas 24-17 to end their hopes for an undefeated season, but the Colts improved their unbeaten record to 14-0 with a comeback win over the Jaguars. The Colts thus became only the third team in NFL history to start a season 14-0, joining the 1972 Dolphins and the 2007 Patriots.

Chapter 44 – More Touchdown Passes Than Incompletions

Sunday, December 27, 2009:	1	2	3	4		TOTAL
Jacksonville Jaguars	0	0	0	7	-	7
New England Patriots	7	21	0	7	-	35

Tom Brady must love playing against the Jacksonville Jaguars.

He had a brilliant game on the Sunday after Christmas, completing 23 of his 26 passes for 267 yards and four touchdowns. This almost matched his previous game against the Jaguars, the 2007 playoff game in which he completed 26 of 28 passes for 262 yards and three touchdowns. In that 2007 game, one of his incompletions was a dropped pass. In this 2009 game, one of his incompletions was a dropped pass and another was a pass deliberately thrown away when his receivers were covered. What that means is that in his most recent two games against Jacksonville Brady misfired on only two of 54 passes. That is accuracy. That is also phenomenal.

Brady's outstanding performance also led to big games for his two receivers. Wes Welker had yet another game in which he caught 10 or more passes, as he was on the receiving end of 13 passes from Brady for 138 yards. It was the seventh game of 2009 in which Welker had double figures in receptions, tying an NFL record. It also raised his total number of receptions for the year to 122, a new Patriot record. Considering that he had missed two full games early in the season, this is amazing.

Randy Moss was on the receiving end of three of Brady's touchdown passes, making it a much different game and post-game for him than his last appearance in Foxboro, in which he was accused of quitting on the team. The mood was much more positive on this Sunday, and Moss was involved in a highlight that had nothing to do with the game on the field. At one point the scoreboard showed a picture of a fan in the stands wearing a Randy Moss mask and a frizzy hair wig. The players on the sideline seemed to really enjoy seeing that and it got big laughs from Moss and Brady. After the game, Brady commented that he should try to get one of those masks on E-Bay.

More important than all of this, however, was the fact that this win clinched the AFC East Title for New England, a spot in the playoffs, and a home game in the first round of those playoffs. Whereas in 2008 an 11-5 record was not good enough for the playoffs, the Patriots' 10-5 record in 2009 not only qualified them for the playoffs but won the division with a week to spare in the regular season. What a difference a year makes.

The only real negative in the game was a fumble at the goal line by Laurence Maroney that ended the first drive of the day for New England. It was a very nicely engineered 10 play, 82 yard drive by Brady and the Patriots. Maroney took the handoff on a play from the one yard line, barreled into the line, and lost the ball. The officials called it a fumble, but it looked as if the ball had dropped straight down and hit the goal line, which would have meant that the ball had crossed the plane of the end zone for a touchdown before the fumble. The Patriots challenged the call, as they should have, but the replays were inconclusive, so the ball went over to Jacksonville.

It was the second time this season that Maroney had fumbled the ball away at the goal line. The first such fumble may have cost them a game against the Colts. The fumble in this game against the Jaguars cost Maroney playing time as he was relegated to the bench for the rest of the game.

The Patriot defense rose to the challenge, stopping Jacksonville on fourth down in their own territory, setting up a two yard TD pass from Brady to Moss. The defense actually had a good day all around, and made another big play to set up the Patriots' second score. That was an interception by Brandon Meriweather that set up a 26 yard TD pass from Brady to tight end Chris Baker.

Sammy Morris took on the bulk of the running chores from the benched Maroney and set up the third Patriot TD of the game with a 55 yard run to the Jacksonville 11 yard line midway through the second quarter. Morris got the TD himself on a one yard run. Another touchdown -- a six yard TD pass on a bullet throw from Brady to a wide open Moss in the end zone -- made it 28-0 at the half. By this time Brady was 14 of 16 passing. He was 7 for 7 to start the game, threw two incompletions, and then hit his next 14 passes.

The third quarter consisted of only two drives. The first, by Jacksonville, consumed 8:34 and consisted of 16 plays, but an interception by New England inside the five ended that drive. New England then ran 10 plays and got the ball to the Jacksonville 12 as the quarter ended. Movement by the offensive line moved the ball back to the 17, but it was no problem, as Brady hit Moss on the right inside the five and Moss stretched the ball into the end zone before he hit the ground for his third touchdown catch of the day. A late Jaguar TD made the final 35-7.

- - -

Elsewhere, the Indianapolis Colts had their bid for an undefeated season end with a 29-15 loss to the New York Jets. I have always liked the Colts – until this week. This loss was disgusting. The Colts pulled their starters in the third quarter of a close game as if they didn't care to win. Perhaps they didn't. They were more interested in resting their starters for the playoffs than trying to win this game and go undefeated. However, there have been a number of times this decade in which the Colts have started a season 10-0, 11-0, or 13-0 (and now 14-0), then rested their starters and lost their edge. A team that could have, and maybe should have, won multiple Super Bowls had won only one.

Before this decade the Colts had similar seasons (1964, 1967, 1968) in which they were nearly undefeated but wound up losing when they shouldn't have. In 1964, for example, they lost their first game, won the next 12, and then essentially gave up and lost the last game of the season and were hammered in their one and only playoff game. Resting their starters at the end of a season has never worked for them. When will they ever learn?

More importantly, on this Sunday there were a number of AFC teams still in the running for a playoff berth. One of these was the team that the Colts were playing, the New York Jets. By giving up and not caring, the Colts essentially gave this game away to the Jets and put them in the driver's seat for a spot in the playoffs. One has to wonder what players and fans in Baltimore, Denver, Pittsburgh, Houston, and Miami were thinking as the Colts put forth less than their best team in what was a big game for all of those teams. Maybe some day the Colts will need one of those teams to win a game to enhance their playoff chances and be unhappy to see that team not give its all. It will be interesting to see how the Colts react if/when that happens.

The Colts received a good deal of criticism for this decision. Their own fans were upset, and rightly so. National media reaction was mixed, but Tony Kornheiser and Michael Wilbon perhaps said it best on their ESPN show "Pardon the Interruption". Kornheiser described the Colts as "rolling over in the face of history" and mentioned that fans "didn't get an honest game." Wilbon added, "It goes against everything that we're taught in sports ... There is one thing worse than losing -- not trying." Wilbon summed it up perfectly with a one word description of the Colts' decision, calling it "dishonorable".

The bottom line is that the Colts had a chance at history and didn't care. Peyton Manning did. He was clearly not happy on the sidelines after being pulled from the game. Maybe others did too, but the team decided to rest its players and not go for perfection. It was disappointing, to say the least. It reminded me of the comment from Matt Crossman of *The Sporting News* after the Patriots completed their 16-0 season in 2007. When others wrote and commented that the Patriots' undefeated regular season would mean nothing if they did not win the Super Bowl, Crossman commented, "Some team wins the Super Bowl every year. But no team has ever gone 16-0." The Patriots did, and as a result were, are, and always will be, special. Now the Colts were not and will not be remembered as positively as will that Patriot team. They will always be just another good team in a league that has had many good teams over the years, and very few special ones.

Give me the Patriots any day.

Chapter 45 – Wes Welker is Hurt. What Do We Do Now?

Sunday, January 3, 2010:	1	2	3	4		TOTAL
New England Patriots	7	6	7	7	-	27
Houston Texans	7	6	0	21	-	34

With 9:39 to play in the first quarter of the final game of the 2009 regular season for the New England Patriots, tragedy struck.

If those words are familiar, it is because they are almost exactly the way that Chapter 7, about the Patriots' first game of the 2008 season, began. The only changes from this game to that were the time (9:39 versus 7:27), the year (2009 versus 2008), and the order of the game (final game of the regular season versus first). The other difference was that in 2008 the tragedy was a season-ending injury to Tom Brady, the reigning NFL MVP. In 2009 the tragedy was a season-ending injury to Wes Welker, who many think was the Patriots' team MVP of 2009.

Welker's injury came on a seemingly innocuous play. He had just caught a pass from Brady and planted his leg to make a cut and avoid a potential tackler. Unfortunately, his leg buckled awkwardly and he went down without being hit. It was immediately clear that he had suffered a serious injury. He clutched his knee. The medical team came out, and Tom Brady and other teammates came over to offer words of encouragement. Welker was helped to the sideline and the TV shots showed him distraught on the sidelines, in apparent physical pain from the injury and emotional agony from knowing that it was serious and that his season was over. He was later seen being carted off the field with a towel over his head and with fellow receiver Randy Moss coming over for words of support as he was about to leave.

The other irony is that the Houston player that Welker was trying to avoid was Bernard Pollard, the same player whose hit on Tom Brady had ended Brady's 2009 season. The Patriots should probably try to avoid him as much as possible in the future.

Pollard went on to recover a fumble in the end zone for Houston's second touchdown in this game, and then made a big interception of a Brady pass that led to the winning score. The Patriots should *definitely* try to avoid him in the future.

Yet another irony was that the injury came in a game which was essentially meaningless for the Patriots. They had clinched the

AFC East title and a spot in the playoffs. They could have rested their starters, but chose not to do so. Frankly, I agree with their approach. I disagree with that of the Colts, as noted earlier, where they rested their starters after limited play in the second half when they had a chance for an undefeated season. The fact that this injury happened without contact seems to means that it could have happened at any time, even in practice. It just happened.

The Patriots did make a number of regulars inactive. Vince Wilfork and Ty Warren were allowed to sit out and continue to rehab their injuries. Laurence Maroney and Kevin Faulk were also inactive, allowing Fred Taylor and Sammy Morris to continue to work themselves back into shape after long times away with injuries.

- - -

As has often been the case with Patriot opponents this season, the Houston Texans looked very good early in the game, and then again late, as the Patriot defensive woes continued. Houston took the opening kickoff and had an effortless 76 yard drive to a touchdown. Matt Schaub hit a very wide open Joel Dreessen for a 25 yard touchdown (the closest defender was about 8 yards behind Dreessen).

Welker was hurt on the Partiot's first possession (as was Brady in the 2008 season opener), catching his league-leading 123rd pass of the season. The fact that he could miss two full games and almost all of a third and still catch 123 passes shows how valuable Welker had been to the 2009 team.

Rookie Julian Edelman replaced Welker and did a credible job, catching 10 passes for 103 yards. One of these was a 25 yard catch-and-run on New England's second possession that set New England up at the Houston four yard line. Fred Taylor carried it in for the tying score.

A Brady to Randy Moss pass set up a 51 yard Stephen Gostkowski field goal, and when the Patriots stopped Houston on four downs inside the ten, momentum seemed to be with New England. However, Brian Hoyer came in to replaced Brady with the ball at New England's one yard line, and Fred Taylor fumbled the ball in the end zone. Houston's Bernard Pollard (there he was again) fell on it for a touchdown and a 13-10 Houston lead.

Bernard Pollard was again a key figure on the next drive. He was called for roughing the passer as he threw his shoulder into Brian Hoyer after a pass play. This led to a 43 yard Gostkowski field goal and a 13-13 tie at halftime.

When New England got the ball to start the second half, Tom Brady was surprisingly back in at quarterback. However, the only score in that quarter came on a 91 yard interception return for touchdown by New England's Darius Butler. That put the Patriots ahead 20-13.

An 11 yard run by Fred Taylor in the fourth quarter increased New England's lead to 27-13. That was when the proverbial roof fell in. A pass interference penalty against Darius Butler gave Houston a first and goal and then a TD that cut the lead to 27-20. A New England punt returned for 30 yards to the 34 set up another Texan TD and a 27-27 tie with 4:37 to go.

At this point, the Patriots' chances still looked good. They had plenty of time and Tom Brady back in at quarterback. They got the ball at the 23 but lost five yards on a screen pass. Then Brady was hit as he threw and the ball sailed high. It was intercepted by – who else? – Bernard Pollard, who returned it to the 28 yard line. Four running plays later, the Texans had a touchdown and a 34-27 lead.

When New England got the ball back, Hoyer again came in for Brady, ostensibly to avoid more hard hits on Brady in obvious passing downs. Hoyer moved the team well from their own 34 to Houston's 34, but it was not far enough, as they gave the ball back to the Texans on downs. Houston had the win, and New England finished the season with a loss.

New England's final record for 2009 was 10-6. In a final irony, the 10-6 record was good enough for the AFC East title and a playoff spot, whereas they had missed the playoffs in 2008 with a better record, 11-5. And so it goes.

The Patriots' 10-6 record made them the # 3 seed in the AFC playoffs. Indianapolis was # 1 at 14-2 and San Diego was # 2 at 13-3. The other AFC playoff teams were Cincinnati (10-6), Baltimore (9-7), and the New York Jets (9-7, thanks in part to the Indianapolis debacle). The Patriots would host Baltimore in the opening round of the post-season.

- - -

Meanwhile, in another season-ending game, the Indianapolis Colts continued to display puzzling decision-making. After resting their starters the preceding week shortly after halftime (a) in a game played in a dome in which the weather is controlled, while (b) playing a team with playoff chances, this week they played in Buffalo (a) in snowy weather on a slippery field, and (b) against a team with no playoff chances; despite all of this, the Colts decided to start their regulars. Isn't an injury more likely on a slippery field than in the dome? You would think so. If the Colts were willing to rest their regulars in the dome, why not rest them in worse conditions in Buffalo? Peyton Manning was in the game long enough to throw 18 passes (completing 14), and then the starters were pulled. Buffalo won 30-7 and Indianapolis finished the season 14-2, but why risk the players in a meaningless game when you had already pulled them in a meaningful game? The Colts are a hard team to understand.

- - -

The bostonist.com Sports Redux column the day after the game lamented the injury to Welker. The write-up ended very nicely, saying "We'll leave you with what Benjamin Watson told Peter King, which basically sums it all up: 'The sad part isn't so much the pain of the injury. It's the pain for Wes, if he's not able to play, of not being able to do the thing he loves to do, in the playoffs. He's such a great competitor and valuable guy on the team.' " That is absolutely true.

It was now on to the playoffs and a shot at redemption and reclaimed glory for the Patriots. Without Wes Welker the task would be very, very difficult.

Chapter 46 – Playoffs: Gone in 17 Seconds

Sunday, January 10, 2010	1	2	3	4		TOTAL
Baltimore Ravens	24	0	3	6	-	33
New England Patriots	0	7	7	0	-	14

It was Baltimore that almost ended New England's bid for an undefeated 2007 season. It was Baltimore that took the last AFC Playoff slot in 2008, denying the Patriots a shot at redemption in that year's post-season. It was Baltimore that almost beat New England in Game 4 of the 2009 season. And it was Baltimore that ended New England's 2009 season by thoroughly crushing the Patriots 33-14 in the opening round of the 2009-10 playoffs.

This one was no contest. Baltimore took a 7-0 lead on the very first play of the game, 17 seconds after the game started. The lead stretched to 14-0 less than five minutes into the game, and 24-0 before the end of the first quarter. It was one of those games for which the cliché 'the final score is not indicative of how big a rout this was' applies.

In other words, it could have been worse.

The Patriots went into this game without Wes Welker, but that is not why they lost. They lost because the Ravens thoroughly outplayed them, from the opening kickoff to the final gun. Welker's replacement, Julian Edelman, played well, as did Kevin Faulk, who was expected to take up some of the slack caused by Welker's absence, but that was it. No one else in a Patriot uniform, on the sideline, or in the coach's booth seemed to have had a good game.

The highlight of the game for the Patriots and the fans at Gillette Stadium may have been the appearance of Wes Welker on crutches, joining the other team captains to go out for the opening coin toss. CBS Analyst Phil Simms commented that the Patriots know what Welker meant to the team and wanted to honor him in this way. It was a nice gesture.

Then the game began, unfortunately.

New England won the toss and elected to defer their choice to the second half. That may have been the team's first mistake. The kickoff was returned to the 17 yard line. On Baltimore's first play from scrimmage, running back Ray Rice ran untouched through the middle of the line, cut to his left, and out-raced the New England defense down the left sideline for an 83 yard touchdown run that was much, much too easy. Only 17 seconds into the game, and five minutes into the telecast, there was a feeling that the game was essentially over. As it turned out, the Ravens had taken a lead they would never relinquish.

Things got worse from there. On third down on New England's first possession, Tom Brady went back to pass. Baltimore just used a three man rush, but one of those rushers was Terrell Suggs, who ran around left tackle Matt Light, came up from behind Brady, knocked the ball from his hands, and recovered the fumble at the New England 17 yard line. Once again, a three man rush was able to do what eleven men on the Patriot defense could not do for much of the season -- put pressure on the quarterback. Five plays later Baltimore had a touchdown. With only 4:31 gone in the first quarter, the Baltimore lead was now 14-0.

The New England offense and defense had already been embarrassed, and the special teams would join that parade next, as Baltimore's short kickoff bounced between two Patriots and was almost lost before being fallen on by the Patriots. 'All three phases of the game' are what Belichick usually stresses, and all three phases were currently failing the Patriots.

With New England at the 21, nobody blocked All-Pro Raven linebacker Ray Lewis, leading to an easy sack of Brady and more embarrassment for the Patriot offense. It was three and out, and the special teams failed again, as Baltimore returned the punt 35 yards to the New England 42 yard line. That did not lead to a score, but New England gave the ball back on their next possession as Brady, under pressure again, was intercepted, setting Baltimore up at the 25 yard line. Six plays later, the Ravens had another touchdown, and a 21-0 lead with 3:55 still to go in the first quarter.

Another interception on a Brady pass that bounced off Sam Aiken's hands was run back to the nine yard line and set up a Baltimore field goal and a 24-0 lead in the first quarter. CBS play-by-play commentator Jim Nantz said, in an understatement, "This has to be the longest first quarter ever for New England." He was right. Baltimore's 24-0 lead at the end of the first quarter had them on pace for a 96-0 win. Not really likely, but with the way the first quarter had gone, an epic blowout was not an impossibility.

For a while in the second quarter it looked as if the tide had turned. New England got a break as one of their punts deflected off a Baltimore blocker and was recovered by the Patriots at the Raven 16 yard line. A six yard TD pass from Brady to Edelman cut the deficit to

24-7 with 11:23 to go in the first half. The Patriots then got another opportunity, on a Joe Flacco pass that was deflected by Leigh Bodden and intercepted by Tully Banta-Cain, giving the Patriots the ball at their own 39, but nothing came of that.

Another New England opportunity came on a 28 yard punt return by Edelman, which gave the Patriots the ball at the Raven 44. New England got one first down on a Baltimore off-side, and a pass to Faulk gave them another one, but that was called back by an offensive interference penalty on Randy Moss, who ran just ran over a defender in the middle of the field. It was the first contribution by Moss in this game, and, unfortunately, it was a negative one.

New England was forced to punt, and pinned Baltimore back at their four yard line. With three timeouts left, New England had a chance to edge closer before halftime if they could stop Baltimore and get the ball back with good field position. However, stopping Baltimore was not something the defense could do on this day, even when they knew that Baltimore would just be running the ball. The Ravens did run the ball, and their running attack gained two first downs to close out the first half with that 24-7 lead still intact.

The Patriot woes continued in the third quarter. New England began moving the ball on its second possession, with Brady running the no-huddle offense very effectively. However, another deflection of a Brady pass, this one off Benjamin Watson, led to another interception, ending that drive. Baltimore got a field goal from that, extending their lead to 27-7.

New England got a long kickoff return from Darius Butler to start its next drive at the 47 yard line. This led to a one yard Brady to Edelman touchdown pass, putting New England within two scores at 27-14. However, Baltimore got the ball on its 48 after a short kickoff by Stephen Gostkowski, and drove to yet another touchdown. This one came on a run by Willis McGahee, giving him and Ray Rice each two rushing touchdowns for the day. Baltimore tried a two point conversion to increase the lead to 21 points, but it failed, keeping the score at 33-14.

New England needed three scores to win or tie, and Brady and Edelman tried to get the first, connecting for what looked like one first down on a great second and third effort and stretch by Edelman, but a penalty negated that. Down by 19, Belichick decided to try a field goal to cut the deficit to 16 (meaning that they could tie Baltimore with two TDs and two point conversations), but, almost fittingly for this day, the usually-dependable Gostkowski missed the field goal, and the Patriots' fate was sealed.

The loss to the Ravens ended the season for New England and closed the book on the team's first 50 years. The Ravens had been known for their defense for the last ten years plus, so it was only fitting that they won this game thanks in part to 2 D's:

Defense

Devastating ground game

which led to 2 other D's

Destruction and

Domination

All of which led to another D which is the only way to describe the 2009-10 Patriot season in general, and this game in particular:

Disappointing.

Chapter 47 – 2009-10 Season Wrapup

Unfortunately for Patriot fans, while New England was eliminated in their playoff opener, two of their biggest rivals, the Jets and Colts, worked their way to the AFC Championship game. The Jets had gotten into the playoffs thanks to the Colts and Bengals resting their starters and not really trying to win their games against New York in weeks 16 and 17. Once in the playoffs, the Jets beat up the Bengals again in the first round and then outlasted the perpetually under-achieving Chargers 17-14 to get to the AFC Championship. The Colts beat the Ravens to set up a rematch against the Jets, the very team that they let into the playoffs while simultaneously giving up a chance for an undefeated season (see Chapter 44 for details).

The NFC came down to the Saints and Vikings, but the best game of the playoffs was the first round game between the Cardinals and Packers. It was an old-fashioned shootout, one very fitting for the year that celebrated the AFL's 50th anniversary. Cardinal quarterback Kurt Warner and his Green Bay counterpart, Aaron Rodgers, moved their teams up and down the field at will. It was reminiscent of those old AFL games featuring Darryl Lamonica, Joe Namath, John Hadl and others. This one was a 51-45 overtime thriller. It was won, ironically, not by one of the two offenses, but by the Cardinal defense, which turned an overtime interception return into the game winning touchdown.

- - -

"A month after they opened the playoff door to the Jets by pulling their starters with a 5-point lead in a Week 16 game, the Colts are confronted in the American Football Conference championship game with the monster they helped create."

So wrote Judy Battista in a column in the January 21, 2010 edition of *The New York Times*. She was right. Justice would have had the Jets win the game and the Colts pay the price for their indifference to history and to competitiveness in Week 16.

Justice and the Jets were in the lead 17-6 late in the first half when Peyton Manning led the Colts to a late score just before halftime. After that it was all Colts, as they went on to a 30-17 victory and a berth in the Super Bowl. Justice would have to give way to History which would remember the Colts as just another good team, and not a special one.

The NFC Championship game went to the New Orleans Saints, 31-28 winners in overtime over the Minnesota Vikings. The Vikings could have won, and should have won, but fumbles took away a number of opportunities. Nevertheless, they had a shot with the ball in New Orleans territory and less than a minute to go in the fourth quarter of a 28-28 game. A penalty for too many men in the huddle moved tham back five yards, and then Brett Favre rolled right, and tried to throw left, across the field. The result was a killing interception that ended the Vikings' bid for a possible game-winning field goal. That interception turned out to be Favre's last play of the 2009-10 season, just as an interception was Favre's last play in an overtime loss to the Giants in the NFC Championship game of 2007-08.

- - -

Super Bowl XLIV – New Orleans 31 Indianapolis 17

	1	2	3	4		Total
New Orleans Saints	0	6	10	15	-	31
Indianapolis Colts	10	0	7	0	-	17

Justice prevailed.

In the end, the team that didn't care about history -- didn't care about winning games at the end of the season when they could have gone undefeated -- and didn't care about losing meaningful games, lost the most meaningful game of all. The Indianapolis Colts lost the Super Bowl.

As I wrote previously, the Colts had always been one of my favorite teams -- until they decided to turn their backs on a possible special/undefeated season (see Chapter 44 for details). At that point, I wanted them to lose and definitely did not want them to be champions. The Patriots of 2007-08 went for an undefeated season and fell short, but gave it their best effort every time they set foot onto the field. For them it was a "no guts, no glory" attitude. Despite the loss, they would still have the glory that comes from giving it their all and trying to do something special. Ten years from now, fifteen years from now, their special season will still be a topic of conversation among football fans. For the 2009-10 Colts it was "no guts AND no glory" as they didn't have the guts to even try for football immortality and wound up with no glory anyway. They will not be remembered as special at all. They got what they deserved.

The game was a good one, however. The Saints trailed 10-6 at halftime, and their coach, Sean Payton, made a gutsy call to try for an on-side kick to start the second half. The call worked. The Saints recovered the kick and then drove for a touchdown that helped change momentum. The Colts did strike back with a touchdown of their own to regain the lead at 17-13, but another Saints touchdown engineered by Drew Brees -- who would be voted the game MVP -- put the Saints back into the lead, and a 74 yard interception return by Tracy Porter of a Peyton Manning pass with 3:12 to go clinched the win for New Orleans.

Brees completed 32 passes in 39 attempts for 288 yards. He was outstanding. The 32 completions tied a Super Bowl record held by Tom Brady. The win, which was the icing on the cake of a brilliant four years by Brees in New Orleans, helped Brees move into the class of elite NFL quarterbacks of this era. He and Sean Payton have meant a lot in those four years to the New Orleans region that was still recovering from the tremendous damage inflicted by Hurricane Katrina in 2005, so this win was a feel-good story across America. Moreover, the site of Brees holding his year-old son after the game was great. The boy had on earphones to protect his ears from the extremely loud noise in the stadium, as father and son watched the colorful pieces of confetti flying around the stadium. It was a private moment which was shared by millions, as this father seemed to enjoy his son's company as much as he enjoyed anything about the game. It was great to see.

Thus, while the Patriots quest for redemption fell short, the 2009-10 season still ended with the good guys winning. It was not the good guys that New England fans had hoped that it would be, but if it could not be New England, it couldn't have happened to a better group. The Saints looked like the best team in football when they beat the Patriots in November and they proved themselves to be the best team in football in February. Their win was uplifting for their community, and their sport.

Justice prevailed.

Chapter 48 – Unfinished Business

At what point does a dynasty end?

It is easy sometimes to pinpoint the events that triggered the end of a NFL dynasty. The Packer dynasty in the 1960s ended when a lot of the players got old and Vince Lombardi retired. The burgeoning dynasty in Miami in the early 1970s came apart when Larry Csonka, Paul Warfield, and Jim Kiick defected to the World Football League. The retirements of Joe Montana and John Elway ended the dynastic runs of the San Francisco 49ers of the 1980s and Denver in the 1990s, though Steve Young helped keep things alive for a few more years in San Francisco. The Dallas Cowboys of the 1990s self-imploded and also lost their leader, Jimmy Johnson; they had one more championship under Barry Switzer, but it was really the last vestiges of Johnson's team that won that.

It is not as easy to see when (or, to put an optimistic view on it – if) the Patriot dynasty came to an end. At the end of 2010, the team's 50th season, they still had one of the best quarterbacks and one of the best coaches in NFL history and a nucleus of good players, but things were not the same. If I had to pick an event, it was when the defense could not stop the New York Giants on the last drive in Super Bowl XLII, after Brady had driven the Patriots to a touchdown and the lead and a potential undefeated season. This, following the defense similarly not stopping Indianapolis in the AFC Championship game the preceding year, after Brady had driven the team to another lead, may have been the beginning of the end of the dynasty.

Perhaps a more symbolic event was the crushing loss to New Orleans in the 2009 season. For the first time, the aura of magic and near-invincibility was shattered. New Orleans dominated that game like no other team in the Brady-Belichick era had done previously. The devastating defeat to Baltimore in the team's lone playoff game after that season may have cemented that. The Patriots were not the same. Certainly the perception of them was not the same.

- - -

Had the Patriot defense been able to make those stops against the Colts in 2007 and Giants in the 2008 Super Bowl, one could argue that the Patriots would have won five Super Bowls instead of three in the first decade of the 21st century. Perhaps the dynasty would still even be on-going. But the defense did not hold, the two games ended in losses, and the first chinks in the armor of the Patriots' dynasty began to appear.

These events also have left some fans, including me, with the feeling that the team still has some unfinished business.

Instead of finishing this retrospective on that note, the end of a dynasty, let's look forward instead to the first few years of the next half-century and see what the Patriots can do to reclaim that lost glory and complete that unfinished business that began with that playoff loss to Indianapolis in 2007 and the Super Bowl loss in 2008.

As noted above, the team still has a great coach and one of the best quarterbacks in the history of the game. In one fan's opinion, surrounding them with the following could make a huge, positive difference in returning the team to glory days:

- A pass-rush that could put pressure on the opposing team's quarterback
- A running attack that could better balance the still-strong passing attack
- Experienced offensive and defensive coordinators

These three things could solve what seem to be the team's most glaring problems. A better running attack could give them more options in the red zone and take some of the defensive pressure off Tom Brady. A better pass rush – some might say *any* pass rush – would keep other teams from having so much time to dissect a young defensive backfield. Experienced coordinators could help Bill Belichick make the adjustments at halftime that seemed to be so lacking in 2009.

It would also be nice to see the team improve themselves through the draft, which has not happened in many years. The notion of trading down and stockpiling draft picks may or may not be a good idea (I personally think not), but has not resulted in the team replenishing the roster to overcome the losses of Mike Vrabel, Corey Dillon, Tedy Bruschi, and others. The window of opportunity for Brady is narrowing and the team should be looking not just at the distant future, but also what it can do to win another title (or more) before the end of Brady's career.

Chapter 49 – The Patriots at Age 50

Patriot history over its first 50 years almost reads like that of a person.

The Patriots in their infancy in the 1960s experienced a lot of growing pains. The team's roster included a lot of colorful players who may have been on the edge in terms of professional football. Without the Patriots and the AFL, they may never have gotten a chance. The franchise moved from home to home and never did settle on one home field. Many of the oddest and most memorable events in the team's history happened in that first decade. The player most identified with the Patriots of the 1960s was Gino Cappelletti. Gino may not have made an NFL roster, but he was good enough to be on of the AFL's All-time great players.

The 1970s saw the Patriots settle on a home stadium, rename themselves from Boston to New England (with an intermediate stop as the Bay State Patriots) and begin to become a very competitive team. As the team moved into its late teenage years, with the 1976-78 teams in particular, they fielded teams which were among the best in the franchise's history. Steve Grogan is the player who best exemplifies the Patriots of the 1970s – young, energetic, with a never-quit attitude.

In their 20s, in the decade of the 1980s, there was a good deal of upheaval as the team began to settle and mature. There was one very successful year, 1985, which saw the team reach the Super Bowl for the first time. The team's stability was best personified in the 1980s by John Hannah, a rock-solid offensive guard, who was generally recognized as the best offensive lineman in NFL history.

As the team moved into its 30s, increasingly more stability began to be seen. This was thanks in part to the addition of Bill Parcells, and then the purchase of the team by Robert Kraft. The fans were treated to another Super Bowl appearance, and success appeared to be right around the corner. The face of the franchise for the 1990s was Drew Bledsoe, who brought talent and success to a franchise that sorely needed both.

Success not only came, but it dis so on a grand scale as the team passed the 40 year mark. It became a dynasty. It became a model franchise for others to emulate. It enjoyed enormous success and had built a foundation for future success not only on the field, but in other endeavors (Patriot Place, for example). A lot of that is due to the work of Bob Kraft and Bill Belichick, but there is no player more symbolic of the Patriots in the 21st century than Tom Brady. From an unknown, sixth round draft pick, he became the best player in the league, and one of the best players in league history, just as the Patriots moved from being an NFL doormat to the best team in the league for the decade, and one of the best teams in league history. Brady's hard work, outstanding teamwork, and intelligence paid off in huge success, just as the team's hard work, team-first play, and intelligence paid off in three Super Bowl wins and a near-undefeated season. That team-first attitude was first seen in the team being announced as a team before the 2002 Super Bowl, instead of as individuals, and it can be seen in any Brady press conference.

- - -

Regardless of what happens in the future, the Patriots have sure given us a lot to talk about over the years, laugh about when thinking of the antics of the early days, and celebrate in the strong contending and championship teams of recent years.

The franchise has truly been unique in the annals of American sports history and it has been a pleasure to watch them over the years and share in Patriot Pride. It will be fun to see how the next half-century turns out.

SECTION 5 – The Men Who Made a Difference

Player Interviews

For this book, I interviewed a number of key players from Patriot history to include the players' memories of their time with the Patriots, their most memorable games, their toughest opponents, their thoughts about the 2007 and 2008 seasons, their observations about key games in which they were involved, and their lives and careers since retiring as players.

The players who were interviewed cover the years 1960-2007 and all of the decades of the team's first 50 years. The players interviewed and the years of their Patriot careers are shown below. They are listed in order by the year in which they first joined the Patriots:

Gino Cappelletti	1960 – 1970
Jon Morris	1964 – 1974
Len St. Jean	1964 – 1973
Bob Gladieux	1969 – 1972
Randy Vataha	1971 – 1976
John Hannah	1973 – 1985
John Smith	1974 – 1983
Steve Grogan	1975 – 1990
Tim Fox	1976 – 1981
Troy Brown	1993 – 2007
Drew Bledsoe	1993 – 2001
Lawyer Milloy	1996 – 2002

The interviews are summarized in this section in the order in which they took place, rather than chronologically. This is because, on some occasions, something that was said in one interview was used as a springboard for discussion in a later interview.

John Hannah

Patriot Career: 1973-1985
Position Played: Left Guard
College: Alabama

The August 3, 1981 issue of *Sports Illustrated* magazine had a cover story about Patriot guard John Hannah which was entitled "The Best Offensive Lineman of All Time". Many who saw John Hannah play would have to agree. He was fantastic at his job.

John played his entire career with the Patriots, from his rookie season of 1973 through the first Patriot Super Bowl season of 1985-86. He played in nine Pro Bowls (the NFL All-Star Game) and was named All-Pro as the best left guard in the game for 10 consecutive seasons, 1976-1985. He was inducted into the Pro Football Hall of Fame in 1991 and is one of only two Hall of Fame members who played their entire careers with the Patriots; Andre Tippett is the other. Until Tom Brady came along to lead the Patriots to three Super Bowl wins, John would have finished first in any contest to name the best player in Patriot history. He probably still might in the eyes of some fans.

John's first season with New England was the start of the first really successful era of the team's history. He came to the team in the 1973 draft, the first run by new Coach/GM Chuck Fairbanks. Hannah was the fourth pick of the draft, and was one of three first-round draft picks the Patriots added that season, along with Sam Cunningham and Darryl Stingley.

I had the opportunity to meet with John Hannah at the Patriots' offices on March 18, 2009, and I thoroughly enjoyed the conversation. John was open, honest, and very gracious with his time.

We started by talking about his very successful career at the University of Alabama, where he played for legendary coach Paul "Bear" Bryant, and played in a memorable National Championship game in the 1972 Orange Bowl against a powerful Nebraska Cornhusker team. When I mentioned the game John's first comment was that "we lost badly" (and they did; Nebraska won that game 38-6) but he wished they could have played the night before when they were more ready to play. Alabama got behind quickly due to a kick return for touchdown and never could catch up.

He remembered that Alabama had been 6-4 in his freshman and sophomore years. They went to the wishbone offense for his junior year, and were an undefeated 11-0 in the regular season leading up to that Orange Bowl match-up with Nebraska. John recalled that Alabama just instituted the wishbone all of a sudden one day in practice. They ran the pro set his sophomore year and then one day in practice his junior year, three weeks before the opening game against Southern Cal, as he put it, "Coach Bryant hangs the curtains on all the fences and installs the wishbone. Nobody knew it. We ran the I formation set the day before the game in the Coliseum and then ran the wishbone in the game."

I asked John about his first reaction when he heard that he had been drafted by the Patriots and he candidly replied "I'd never heard of them before." He identified that with college football being so big in Alabama, what he knew about the pro game was mostly the NFL and NFC, and the Dallas Cowboys, and he followed players from the Alabama area who were in the pros, such as Tucker Fredrickson of Auburn who was with the Giants, Green Bay's great quarterback Bart Starr from Alabama, LeRoy Jordan of Alabama and the Cowboys, Ray Perkins from Alabama and the Baltimore Colts, and so on. John's father Herb had also played for Alabama and then with the New York Giants in 1951. He did mention the Jets and Joe Namath, another Alabama alumnus, who led the Jets to the Super Bowl win in 1969, but otherwise the AFL and then AFC teams were not very popular in Alabama.

He remembered joining the team and being "really disappointed" with what he found. He explained that they always had the best of everything at Alabama and Coach Bryant saying "if you can't go first class, don't go at all." What he found with the Patriots was a lot different. The training rooms and locker rooms were smaller or, as John related, "what my wife would call pedestrian" and not what he had been used to having at Alabama or, as he later found out, what other pro players were using. There was no weight room; "You had to join a health club if you wanted to lift weights. You were wondering what you got into" was the way he summed it up.

Despite the accommodations and the sparse crowds attending games at the time, the team did start to have some success early in John's career. They started out 5-0 in 1974, his second season and built up to the playoff team in 1976, which John considers "the greatest team I ever played with". Until the 2001 season, Patriot fans in general felt the same way. That was the team which, as described in earlier chapters, was robbed of a potential playoff win in Oakland by one of the worst officiating performances in football history (see Chapter 3 for details). There were many bad calls, non-calls, etc., that went Oakland's way (or, as John put it, the calls "were not legitimate ... it was unbelievable, frustrating") as the Raiders squeaked out a 21-17 victory and went on to win the Super Bowl.

John told the story about how he, Leon Gray and other Patriot players who went to the Pro Bowl that season were being given a hard time about that playoff game by some of the Raider players when Pittsburgh linebacker Jack Lambert, "who was a pretty outspoken, tough guy told them basically to shut up because everyone in the room knew that they had stolen the game." As a fan who watched that game and felt that way myself, it was gratifying to hear that players from OTHER teams saw it the same way as the Patriots and their fans had seen it.

The following season, 1977, saw the celebrated contract holdout by Hannah and left tackle Leon Gray. John related a very interesting story of how that came to be. He said that during that era it was written in your contract that you could not tell another player what your salary was. At the Pro Bowl after the 1976 season, one of the other offensive linemen who was at the game suggested that instead of doing that, they all write down their salaries, throw them in a hat and they could all see what the salary ranges would be. As a result of all of this, John and Leon found out that other players were making 2 ½ - 3 times as much as they were. They talked to Chuck Fairbanks about this and Fairbanks agreed to look into it. Hannah's agent, Howard Slusher, wanted them both to hold out, but John said he didn't want to do that, that he had faith in Coach Fairbanks, and to let the process continue through training camp through the last exhibition game, but "if they don't sign us then we won't play ... and so that's what happened." Fairbanks had gotten a deal, or so he thought, but when John and Leon went to Chuck Fairbanks' house to sign the new contracts, they found out the owners had backed out and forced Fairbanks to rescind the deals. The players did hold out. The Sullivans filed a grievance against the two players, and ultimately the issue went to arbitration. I asked if they ultimately had gotten the salaries that they wanted and John said "more" and told a very interesting story about the arbitration process. The owners in the arbitration, led by Pittsburgh's Dan Rooney and Wellington Mara of the New York Giants, "saw what they were paying us" and were surprised. They told the players they needed to go back to play in 1977 and they would ensure that after the season they would be paid by the Patriots in a level commensurate with their stature "and if they don't give you a contract that is equivalent to what other players are getting in the league, we are going to force them to trade you to another team." That seemed fair to the players then (as John colorfully put it, "they slapped our wrists but tanned their bottoms"), and it did happen that way. John and Leon played that year and did get paid equitably after that season.

That incident was the start of Chuck Fairbanks becoming disenchanted with the team. It would ultimately lead to Fairbanks leaving after the 1978 season. The next such incident occurred when Darryl Stingley was paralyzed in a 1978 pre-season game (see Chapter 3 for details). I asked John if players realized on the spot how serious the injury to Stingley was. He quietly and somberly said "Yeah, we knew ... I can remember guys actually going into the bathroom and throwing up ... it was a couple of weeks before we even knew that he would live."

Before that game was even played, the Patriots, through Fairbanks, had agreed verbally to a new contract deal with Stingley (an agreement that was "as good as gold" as John said that Fairbanks had told Stingley). However, the owners reneged after the injury. Ultimately, a court decision forced them to pay Stingley. Fairbanks felt he could not maintain the players' trust with incidents like this, and so decided to leave New England. He accepted a job for 1979 with the University of Colorado before the end of the Patriots' season, leading to the brouhaha with him being fired and replaced by two coaches for the final game, then coming back to coach in a playoff game, as related in Chapter 3.

This helped derail what I had thought was going to be a great season for New England in 1978. They had a great running and passing attack, had piled up some big wins during the season, and had a close game against the defending Super Bowl Champion Dallas Cowboys, and seemed on the verge of greatness, but the injury to Stingley before the season and the fiasco surrounding the firing of Fairbanks before the playoffs may have changed things. John Hannah described this team as having "as good an offense as we ever had". He talked about it being Stanley Morgan's first year and that the team had also acquired Harold Jackson, so they had "two guys on the outside who could burn it" to go along with a superior running attack led by Sam Cunningham and Andy Johnson. They also had a quarterback in Steve Grogan who could not only throw well but could also run as well as many running backs. The team lost to Houston in the playoffs and started a downhill slide for the next few years.

Raymond Berry took over as coach in 1985 and led the team to the Super Bowl in what would be John's last season with the team. Berry was a favorite player of mine when he was on the receiving end of all of those passes from Johnny Unitas. I mentioned to John that Berry always seemed to me like a classy guy, which John confirmed, saying "very much so". John commented about how Berry always challenged the players to give 100%. He asked each player to grade themselves, which John did, and he described how one day he graded himself at 76, grading himself down on some plays; he gave as an example a play in which a back was way downfield and you knew as a blocker you would not get into the play, so you may give less of an effort on such a play.

Berry believed that the team could be winners and his attitude apparently grew within the team. John talked about how over the previous three years the players started believing the "negativity of the press" and they didn't believe they were winners. He went on to say that Berry was able "to change that mindset, allow people to regain confidence in their abilities and realize that they were good athletes and were just doing some things wrong, and once we corrected those errors then we could be champions". He credited Steve Grogan with coming in and providing "a real spark, a real fire," praising Grogan's leadership and his ability to adjust on the field. He saw Grogan as a great leader, one whom everyone on the team respected and added, "he probably had more impact than even a coach could have".

The playoffs in 1985 saw the Patriots beating their three biggest rivals – the Jets, Raiders, and Dolphins – on the road in order to get to the Super Bowl. I mentioned the incident that occurred after the Raider game in which Patrick Sullivan, son of Patriot owner Billy Sullivan, got into a fight with Raider defensive tackle Howie Long. John confirmed the incident, adding that Patrick Sullivan had been on the sidelines "where he shouldn't have been in the first place" when the Patriots were backed up inside the 20 and trying to get out. He remembered Sullivan goading Long and calling him names. John was not happy about that since "as a player, you never want to wake up a sleeping dog". The Patriots held on and won the game (as John put it, partly because "Oakland stuck to their passing game, thank goodness" and did not utilize running back Marcus Allen to the extent they could have). As John was walking off the field with Steve Nelson, Mike Haynes, and John's brother Charley (a lineman for the Raiders) they heard the commotion and saw Sullivan and Long in a fight. Charley and Matt Millen went over to help Long and John said that he asked Steve Nelson if they should do something to help Sullivan out and Nelson told him "He got himself into it. Let him get himself out." John confirmed the story, saying "that really happened". He also added that later, when Sullivan was being treated by the medical people in the locker room "sitting on a trunk and they're stitching up his eyes", the players came over to Sullivan and told him "well, Pat, how's it feel to play with the big boys?"

Then it was on to the great Chicago team in the Super Bowl, which elicited a sigh from John. I asked John who he was blocking during the game and he mentioned Dan Hampton, William "Refrigerator" Perry, and Steve McMichael, a player who had been with the Patriots and was traded by Ron Meyer to Chicago, a move that Hannah thought was a big mistake.

This was the first time the Patriots had ever been in the Super Bowl, and John felt "It was great to get there, but the actual experience of the game was awful. I did not enjoy playing in the Super Bowl at all … it was not football, it was way too much Hollywood .... you went up to warm up, then you go back in and sit around for an hour and have to go out and warm up again, and it's a three hour game turned into a five hour game. It just wasn't football. I didn't like that part of the game that wasn't focused on football, it was focused on entertainment." The other disappointment to John was that while Grogan, a team leader whom everybody respected, was ready to play, he wasn't going to start. Lastly, the team abandoned the running attack that had worked so well for them during the season and threw the ball a lot more than they had in the playoffs. In fact, John pointed out the Patriots had only thrown 10 passes in beating Miami. John had hoped that the Patriots would "attack them" with the running game "and get them back on their heels a little", but that was not the plan laid out by the offensive coordinator. The game ended in a 46-10 rout by the Bears.

The Super Bowl was John Hannah's last game. He had surgery on both shoulders and a knee after the season and when he was shown the X-ray of the knee he asked the doctor if he could still play and the doctor told him he could, but he also would run the risk of being crippled early in life. That was enough for John. He told me that he had once been advised by Jim Otto, the great center of the Raiders in the 1960s and 1970s that "if you're hurt, play, but if you see something that's gonna cripple you, don't wind up like me." John also had told his doctors to let him know if that ever looked to be the case. That was now the case, and that was the end of John's career.

- - -

I asked John what his most memorable game was. He said "there are a lot of them, the 1976 game, the game against Miami in 1985, playing Dallas in 1978, especially for me, not only for who we were playing, but that was probably the best game of my career". He also added a funny story about getting kicked out of a game early in his career against Minnesota. It was the second year of his career, 1974. He was blocking Alan Page, and as John describes it, "Head slapping was legal at the time and he wanted to show me what football was all about. They called me for holding after he had head slapped me about a dozen times." Hannah complained about the head slaps and he remembers that the official told him "Shut up, rookie, take care of business yourself." So the next time Page slapped him, "I punched him and they threw me out." John recalled going to the sideline and having

Fairbanks call him "a jackass". That meant that you had screwed up. He said of Fairbanks that "he never yelled. If you were in trouble he just called you a jackass. John added, "if he called you a double jackass you might as well pack your bags, you're gonna be traded." That was the only time in his career that John Hannah was ejected from a game.

I then asked John who his toughest opponent was. He named many and it is a virtual who's who of many of football's great defensive players – Buck Buchanan, Alan Page, Dick Butkus, Randy White, Joe Klecko, Howie Long, Otis Sistrunk, Lyle Alzado, and Ernest Holmes were among the players mentioned.

We then did an exercise in which I would name a former Patriot player and John would say the first thing that came to mind about that player. [This was done with other interviews as well. For ease of reference in these chapters, we'll call this "Player Word Association"].

Steve Grogan – great leader, great fighter

Sam Cunningham – underrated

Leon Gray – worst mistake the Patriots ever made [trading him]

Russ Francis – most gifted athlete I've ever known

Jim Plunkett – mis-used; Patriots ran 4-5 receiver sets and needed to keep a back in to block for him, when he went to San Francisco it was the same thing, but then in Oakland they played in a set that kept backs in so now instead of 2.8 to 3 seconds to throw he had 4 seconds and he was successful [winning two Super Bowls]

Bill Lenkaitis – tenacious; he was the center on a team that broke rushing records

Andy Johnson – I loved blocking for him; he was gifted, but not talented [meant as complimentary] - he didn't have blazing speed or great moves; he had great peripheral vision and knew how to use his blockers - when you're pulling, it's not you who makes the block, it's the back who makes the block, and guides you as you go, on downfield runs he always kept the blocker between him and the defender, other running backs would try to do everything based on speed and they'd outrun you. Other running backs relied on talent. Andy relied on skill and intelligence. He was an unbelievable athlete. He was also one of the best receivers out of the backfield. He was good on the option pass, since he was a quarterback at Georgia. He was a real team guy; kept the team loose.

Craig James – relied on talent; could have been a really good player if he had someone to teach him, unlike Andy Johnson who learned from Mack Herron, a really talented player - and Andy really studied the game from Mack - James had no one to learn from

Red Miller (John's first offensive line coach) – great teacher; got me to a high level; got me fired up

Jim Ringo (offensive line coach) – also a great teacher; showed me techniques; best techniques I've been around; got me over the top

John took the conversation about Red Miller and Jim Ringo to another level by complimenting Chuck Fairbanks on doing two very impressive things: not bringing the college game with him to the pros, and also surrounding himself with "unbelievable" assistant coaches.

- - -

John is very happy with the Patriots these days and is very complimentary to owner Bob Kraft for really setting the stage for the team's success. "Well you know, for any organization that is successful, it starts from the top. You have to have leaders at the top and the strength of where they are today is Bob Kraft."

I then asked him what he thinks of today's game. He does not like it as much. He said that it is "not as good" and when I asked him why he said that it is "based on talent, not heart". Despite that, he was very impressed with how the 2008 Patriots overcame the injuries they had and played hard all year. We agreed that it was a shame that their 11-5 record was not good enough to get them into the playoffs, but John added that you don't always have to win the Super Bowl to have a successful season and he felt that 2008 was very successful for New England.

In response to a question of who from today's team he might have wanted to play with he listed Logan Mankins, Tom Brady, Wes Welker (saying "he inspires me"), Matt Light (though he thinks that with Light's footwork he would play him at right guard), Tedy Bruschi, and, from the recently-retired ranks, Troy Brown.

- - -

For those fans wanting to know how John Hannah is doing today, he says that his health is fine "now that I've lost 50 pounds" though he still has the knee lock up on him on occasion. He has left the Financial Business that he had been in previously, and is now doing business training on team-building and leadership. From what I have seen, John Hannah will be as successful at that as he was great on the football field. It was a real pleasure to talk with him.

Jon Morris

Patriot Career: 1964-1974
Position Played: Center
College: Holy Cross

Jon Morris was an All-Star for seven of his eleven years with the Patriots. He was an AFL All-Star from 1964-1969, and then, after the AFL-NFL merger, was the first Patriot to be selected for the AFC Pro Bowl, being the AFC Pro Bowl Center in 1970. Jon graduated from Holy Cross in 1964 and was a member of the Patriots from 1964-1974, playing 130 games with the team, before finishing his career with the Detroit Lions and Chicago Bears. Many fans consider him to be the best center in the history of both Holy Cross and the Boston/New England Patriots; I am one of those people.

There were two reasons that I was looking forward to talking with Jon. One was to get the perspective of a player who played in the 1960's with the old AFL and 1970s with the merged NFL, and the other was that we are both Holy Cross alumni. When I was able to talk with Jon, on April 2, 2009, I found a third reason – our conversation was great and far-reaching from start to finish, with Jon not only talking about his time with the Patriots, but also sharing some thoughts about Holy Cross and books and authors which we both enjoy.

Jon was drafted from Holy Cross by both the AFL's Boston Patriots and the NFL's powerful Green Bay Packers. The Packers had been NFL Champions in 1961 and 1962 and would go on to championships in 1965, 1966, and 1967 as well. The Patriots had been AFL East Champions in 1963, so there was some hope for them to be successful as well, but they were not the vaunted Packers. As such, I asked Jon why he picked Boston over Green Bay. Jon referenced the Robert Frost poem "The Road Not Taken" and said he has occasionally looked back on his decision and wondered what it would have been like had he decided the other way, pointing out that he would have played in the first two Super Bowls, and the famous Ice Bowl Game in Green Bay (the 1967 Dallas-Green Bay NFL Championship game in frozen Green Bay), but that there was "no doubt that I made the right decision; other than the fact that I would have like to have played for the most famous team of all time, that would have been the only reason to go to Green Bay".

He said his intention in 1964 was to play a little pro football and then do something worthwhile with his life. He also tied that back to his decision about which college to attend, saying that he had been offered the chance to play big-time college football, but he chose to go to Holy Cross "to get an education and then play football for fun". Similarly, he felt after being drafted by the pros that the chances to do something meaningful after playing pro football for a while would be greater in Boston than Green Bay, so, for him, the decision to join the Boston Patriots for his football career was a quality of life decision. Jon did indeed wind up starting a business in the Boston area, Jon Morris and Company, after his retirement. The company has been successful and is still in operation, though Jon himself has moved to South Carolina.

Jon laughingly recalled that he has seen Bill Curry, the center on those Packer teams over the years, and President of the NFL Players' Association when Jon was the Patriots' Player Representative, and has given Curry some good-natured kidding that Jon's deciding to join Boston meant there was a "job opening" for Curry in Green Bay.

Jon's first reactions about the Patriots' organization were similar to those of John Hannah, but at least Jon knew what to expect. Though Jon came from "a small-time football program at Holy Cross, where football was almost a second thought," he said the Patriots were "more of the same … in fact, they were the most minor league operation I have ever been around in my life, looking back on it. They didn't have a clue what they were doing." They did not spend money on things other teams did as a matter of course. The facilities were bad. In fact, Mike Holovak was "doing it with a shoe string, because the Sullivans didn't have any money". For example, they had "no scouting operation". When it came time to do the college draft, they got their information from *Street and Smith's College Football Yearbook*. So even though the team had some success in Jon's first two seasons, they soon dropped off since they were drafting players who couldn't do the job that was expected.

After Mike Holovak left, as Jon remembered, Clive Rush came in as coach and "Things spiraled down from there; it was an absolute nightmare. It was no fun at all." Though Jon was urged to get himself traded, he said that he felt loyalty to the team and often felt, "next year would be better", so he stuck it out. Patriot fans are glad that he did.

"On the positive side," Jon continued, he and his Patriot teammates all felt "the AFL and the Patriots were wonderful experiences. We felt that we were part of building something .. we built this thing up from nothing as players … and that was a tremendous feeling of accomplishment for all of us … I also like to look back on the wonderful players and coaches that I met when I was with the Patriots and all the relationships that we formed .. we were a band of brothers almost and I always enjoyed that."

We then did the Player Word Association, as was done with John Hannah:

Lennie St. Jean – good friend, good teammate, and a wonderful guy to play next to [St. Jean was a guard who would, by nature of the position of course, line up next to the center, Jon Morris]

Tom Neville – Tommy was a good guy, pretty much the same as what I said about Lennie

Babe Parilli – Babe Parilli was a mentor to me; he was a legend when I came in, he played at Kentucky where he was the Sweet Kentucky Babe and he had played in the NFL for years; he was probably 15 years older than me; he took me under his wing and showed me the ropes of pro football;

[Jon told a story about how, in Jon's first season, he came to training camp late since he had played in the College All-Star Game against the Bears.] When Babe and I were coming off the field after losing four straight exhibition games, Babe told me not to worry about it, that "Mike Holovak doesn't care about winning the pre-season games, we'll be okay once the season starts." And we were. We wound up winning ten games that season.

Gino Cappelletti – I knew Gino for a long time, I was the long snapper for Gino on field goals and extra points; Gino was really "The Duke", the sharpest-dressed guy on the team and he was a wonderful guy. [Gino was an analyst for Patriot games but left that to become a special teams coach, and Jon took over Gino's radio duties for about 8 years. Jon told a funny story about a game in Buffalo where, before the game, Gino told Jon that the Patriots had never tried a fake field goal, but they were going to do so that day.] Gino told me, "I'm going to make you look smart. You watch me on the sidelines. When it's field goal time I'm going to raise my hand and wave at you. That means that we are going to fake the field goal. You can look like a smart guy by predicting it in advance." So sure enough the first field goal attempt comes along, I look down and Gino's waving his hand at me. John Carlson was the play-by-play guy and he was a talker and he was going on and on setting up the play and I didn't have a chance to break in. I never got a chance to say anything. And the funny part of the whole thing was that it just didn't work. The fake field goal didn't work. I talked to Gino about it after the game and we laughed about it.

Ron Burton – I have a tremendous respect for Ron Burton, not just for football but for all of the things that he did off the field. He was a real gentleman and really contributed to the community.

Larry Garron – I played with him a lot, he was a good running back

Joe Kapp – I was hoping that you would ask me about Joe Kapp. Joe Kapp arrived at Patriot camp under much media frenzy, after leading the Minnesota Vikings to the Super Bowl the previous season. After his first practice with the Patriots, Joe came into the locker room and looked for me and told me that he [Kapp] had to go do a media session/press conference, but asked me what bar the offensive lineman go to after practice. I told him and he told me to have the players wait for him there and "we're going to sit down and talk". When Kapp showed up he slapped $100 on the bar table, and this was back in the 70's and $100 was worth a lot more, and Joe said "we're not leaving until that $100 is gone. We've got to talk." So we did. I will always remember that. Joe set the room straight that, "This is how it's going to be. I'm in charge here." He's a great guy. I just love Joe Kapp. He was terrific. It was fun being around Joe Kapp.Unfortunately we didn't have anybody on the line who knew how to block very well so he really took a beating that year.

Jim Plunkett – I always liked Jim Plunkett a lot. I thought that he was a terrific quarterback and that he got a bum rap here in New England. He overcame a lot of personal issues. The only problem that I saw with him was in his first couple of years he got sacked a lot, but it wasn't that he had a bad offensive line. Plunkett was a lot like Drew Bledsoe. He had a great arm but he just didn't get rid of the ball. You watch Tom Brady and he gets rid of the ball, that's what quarterbacks need to do. Plunkett would stand back there in the pocket and wait forever and get sacked. But that's water under the dam. He could have been a great quarterback with a little better coaching and a better team around him, and then he did go to the Raiders and won two Super Bowls with them.

John Hannah – I've heard people say that he was the greatest offensive lineman of all time and I second that notion. When he was drafted # 1 out of Alabama we all couldn't wait to see what he was all about because we had heard about him. So he comes to training camp and after the first two days I said to some of the guys "the bar on offensive line play has just been raised". You could tell right away. It was so obvious. He was so much better than anyone else. This guy just knew what he was doing.

Jon recalled good-naturedly that John Hannah was the reason that he (Jon) was traded to Detroit. This had no bad connotation associated with it, but Jon explained that this came from a play in a game with the Chiefs in which Hannah, the left guard, was blocking Kansas City's huge defensive tackle. Buchanan wound up falling on the back of Jon Morris' knee, tearing some ligaments. Jon said he never won his job back after that. He was out for a year with the injury and the next year Bill Lenkaitis took over at center and Jon was traded.

As we continued our conversation, we talked about how the Patriots were good in 1964, almost winning the AFL East, and then they were good again in 1966, almost winning the AFL East and having a chance to play in the first Super Bowl in history. I asked Jon what he remembered most about those experiences. He talked about the Patriots going down to New York to play the Jets in the regular season finale, where a win would give them the AFL Eastern Title. Jon said "Yeah that would have been great to be in the first Super Bowl but it was Joe Namath who knocked us out of it." He said that the team went down to New York "thinking that we were a sure thing. The Jets weren't very good. We were on a roll. We were playing well. We did have a good game offensively, but Namath came into his own that day. He had a superb game. And Matt Snell ran for a couple of hundred yards. It was no contest. We just couldn't believe it. It would have been great to be in the first Super Bowl but it wasn't to be."

Staying with Namath, I asked Jon what the players' reactions were when they heard about the contracts that rookies Joe Namath of Alabama and John Huarte of Notre Dame had signed with the Jets in 1965 ($400,000 for Namath and $200,000 for Huarte, salaries that were unheard of in those days, and were roughly 8-10 times or more the salaries of many players at the time). Jon said that "The first reaction was disbelief, nobody ever thought of making that kind of money. I don't think any of us at the time thought that this was good for all of us, that all salaries would be moving up. The second reaction was that this brought instant credibility to the AFL. That's what we really craved at the time. Then, when we won the Super Bowl, that just took us over the top."

That credibility, and parity with the NFL, really arrived in 1969 when Namath led the Jets to an incredible 16-7 upset over the heavily favored Baltimore Colts in Super Bowl III. When I asked Jon what the AFL players thought of that he said, "We felt like we all played with the Jets" and he talked about how the AFL players all celebrated with Namath and the other Jet players at the Pro Bowl the following week.

The other highy-paid rookie from that 1965 draft was John Huarte, who later played with the Patriots. Jon felt that Huarte was not that good a quarterback, and wondered how he had won the Heisman Trophy since he was small for a quarterback and did not throw well. As it turns out, Huarte did not last long with the Patriots, playing only in 1966 and 1967 and throwing a total of 20 passes (completing 8).

When the AFL-NFL merger finally happened, Jon said that the players had "a tremendous feeling of accomplishment and pride. We had taken this league from the riff-raff that it was back in 1960 to an equal if not superior product to what the NFL had." He went on to say, "The reason for the merger was that the NFL knew that and didn't need that type of competition any more. That was later tempered by the realization that it was all about money and our salaries would eventually be affected." They were until the collective bargain agreement, salary cap, and TV money came into play.

I asked Jon about what NFL team he was interested in playing after the merger and it was the Washington Redskins, which was his favorite team when he was growing up, since he was born and raised in Maryland. Jon recalled a funny story about how his brother, who is seven years younger than Jon, once wrote to George Allen, the coach of the Redskins at the time, asking George to trade for Jon. George wrote Jon's brother a nice letter back, saying that 'We have great admiration for Jon as a center, he's a terrific center and we'd love to have him, but I already have an old center [Len Hauss] on the team and I don't need two of them."

- - -

Jon was with the Patriots when they played in many different places - Fenway Park, BC Alumni Stadium (where I first saw a Patriot game), Harvard Stadium, and Schaeffer Stadium. They even played a home game in Birmingham, Alabama in 1968. I mentioned that that must have been odd to play in so many home parks, and Jon countered with the comment that "there were so many odd things about the Patriots that we didn't think anything of it. It was another odd thing in the long line of odd things the Patriots did." He also remembered that a weird thing about Harvard Stadium was that they couldn't use the locker rooms, so they dressed in a motel and took the bus back and forth in uniform. As Jon put it with a trace of sarcasm, "this was the big leagues, c'mon".

He also recalled the day a fire broke out at BC Stadium during a Patriot exhibition game against the Redskins. Jon said, "It must have been 95 degrees out and nobody wanted to play in the game. Then the fire broke out, and it was in the section where the wives were sitting. They stopped the game and cleared the stands, and the players all wanted to call the game off, but the officials said they didn't know if they could do that, so the game went on." (Everyone was safe, but it was yet one more of the type of odd things that some said could only happen to the Patriots.)

- - -

When asked about the most memorable games in his career, Jon returned to that 1966 season that ended with the loss to the Jets which cost the Patriots a chance to get to the Super Bowl. That Jet loss was one such game. Another was a game earlier in that same season that the Patriots lost on a late interception. He also mentioned a key game with Buffalo earlier that season that the Patriots won, and *Sports Illustrated* had a cover story about it, with the cover a black and white photo of Jim Nance bursting through the Buffalo line. Jon said it was the first time that the Patriots had made the cover of *Sports Illustrated* and said "that was a big thrill for us".

In response to a question about the toughest opponent he faced, Jon said that it was hard to name one guy but he would name a few, and he broke it down to linebackers and defensive tackles. He started with linebackers, since most teams played a 4-3 defense early in his career and he would wind up blocking middle linebackers a lot. He named Mike Curtis, formerly of Baltimore, Nick Buoniconti the former Patriot who then played for Miami where they had "some awful battles", and Kansas City's Willie Lanier. For defensive linemen, he mentioned Bubba Smith as the toughest defensive tackle that he faced after Baltimore switched to the 3-4, and Alan Page of the Minnesota Vikings.

Given the distinction that Jon had made, I asked him to talk more about what the 4-3 versus 3-4 defense meant from a center's standpoint. He pointed out that with the 4-3, NFL centers had to be quick rather than big to get out from the line of scrimmage to block the linebackers, but then they had to bulk up to play against the big nose tackles that the 3-4 defense featured. Jon said that it was hard for him since he wasn't very big and he had to get heavier to battle those nose tackles. He went on to talk about Art Spinney and Joe Bugel, two great offensive line coaches who really taught him pass blocking techniques and Jon felt that he could really pass block well. This meant that the Patriots did not have to double team the nose tackle on passing plays, since Jon could handle him alone, without help. Other teams with smaller centers would have to double team the nose tackle, so this was a big advantage for Jon and his team.

Jon had a lot of respect for both Mike Holovak and Art Spinney. He talked about how Holovak had signed him to a guaranteed two year contract his rookie year, which was unusual for those days. Holovak told Jon that he would be the starting center and he put Jon there as soon as Jon reported to camp from the College All-Star game. Jon said that Holovak "was a man of his word, he did what he said he was going to do." He also said that Holovak later traded for a veteran center. When Jon heard about that tread it made him nervous, but Holovak took Jon aside at breakfast the next day and told him that they traded for the other guy to play tackle and that Jon was the center. Jon says that he'll never forget that, adding "he knew how players think."

With regard to Art Spinney, Jon mentioned that Spinney had played for Baltimore in that historic 1958 championship game that was the first overtime game ever in pro football history, so Jon knew of him and was a big fan of his before he even met him. He says that Spinney also took him under his wing right away. He laughed when he recalled that Spinney sent him back to get a new number when he saw that Jon had been assigned # 53. Spinney told him that that was the number of the previous center, and sent him back to the equipment manager to get a new one, so that's how Jon wound up wearing # 56 for his career. He said that Art showed him techniques, showed him how to pass block. Jon said that "in college you don't know how to pass block. You just bump a guy. But here there are certain techniques to it and he taught me the game. I'll always be grateful for that."

This led me to ask Jon if playing against Penn State, Syracuse, Pitt and other strong college teams (which Holy Cross did at the time that Jon played there; they no longer do) helped in his transition to the pros. Jon said that it did in the sense that when you play for a small time program you get to think that you're not as good a player as those in the big time programs, so playing against Penn State he would play against guys that he would play against in the pros, so that helped from a confidence standpoint. Jon added that then, when he played in the College All-Star game against the Bears, "that solidified it even more" and convinced him that he could compete against NFL players.

- - -

The conversation about Art Spinney also led us to talk about Clive Rush, the Patriot Head Coach who followed Mike Holovak. Jon did not think that Clive Rush was, to put it mildly, a great coach. When I mentioned the story about Rush almost electrocuting himself at a press conference, Jon quipped that that story "fits with his personality". Jon did point out that Rush had some personal problems [Rush had a drinking problem], but that he wasn't a good coach. Jon blames Weeb Ewbank, the Jet Head Coach at the time, for wanting to get rid of Clive Rush from the Jets and foisting Rush onto the Patriots by telling Billy Sullivan that Rush was a great coach, even though Ewbank knew that he was not. Jon pointed out that "The better coach on that team was Buddy Ryan. That's the guy we should have gotten." It is worth pointing out that the stories at that time were that the Patriots were interested in Chuck Noll, an assistant with Baltimore, but when the Jets beat Baltimore in Super Bowl III, the Patriots decided to go with assistant coach Clive Rush of the winning Jets as their new head coach instead of assistant coach Chuck Noll of the losing Colts. One wonders how Patriot history might have been different had the Pats selected Noll, who went on to win four Super Bowls with the Steelers, instead of Rush, who did not do a good job with the Patriots.

Jon went on to say that "Clive just took it from loony tunes into complete chaos. You wouldn't believe some of the stuff that went on." He recalled how one time, when he was the Patriot Offensive Captain and defensive tackle Houston Antwine was Defensive Captain, that Rush approached them and asked them to meet him at 8:00 AM the next morning to discuss how to improve team. As Jon described, when they arrived, "Clive pulls out a bottle of Scotch and three glasses and says 'you guys want to join me?'" Jon pointed out how odd it was for the coach of a team to offer two of his players a drink at eight in the morning, saying "that's when I realized that we were probably going to have some problems here." Though Jon did add one more thing, telling me, "By the way, the drink was pretty good."

It was Rush who created the idea of having 11 black players play defense and giving them the nickname "The Black Power Defense". He wanted some name for the defense to rival the "Doomsday Defense" of the Dallas Cowboys, Minnesota's "Purple People Eaters", and the "Fearsome Foursome" of the LA Rams. Jon says that Rush told the players "I am going to make all of you black guys famous. You're going to get commercials." The commercials that he talked about were for some hair styling gel that was marketed for black men at the time. Jon could not recall the name of the product, but did say that the way that Rush presented the idea "it was almost racist". It sounds it today as well. He also recalled a game at San Diego in which Rush hurt the team's cause greatly by getting two 15 yard penalties for coming far out onto the field to question officials' calls. Jon said of Rush that "We suffered as players from it. [Rush's antics and coaching] We were the laughing stock of the league".

- - -

I asked Jon to look at the 2008 season and what he thought made this Patriot team successful even after the loss of Tom Brady, Rodney Harrison, Adalius Thomas, etc. Jon gave credit to Bill Belichick and pointed out that he had known Belichick when Belichick was an assistant with Detroit and Jon was a player there. Bill was in charge of breaking down films and coaching the Lions' tight ends. Jon commented that, with the Patriots Belichick "took the team from being laughingstocks and now everyone tries to model their organization after the Patriots. It's amazing, almost a state of shock." Jon indicated that he has "tremendous respect for what they have done".

Jon talked about watching the Patriots win their first Super Bowl in 2002. He was in South Carolina then and he and his wife Gail were at a Super Bowl party but left to go home and watch the fourth quarter at home. When Adam Vinatieri kicked that field goal and the Patriots had won, Jon and Gail "just looked at each other in a state of disbelief." Jon added that when the graphic went up on TV that the Patriots had won the Super Bowl, he told Gail "This is a dream. It can't be true." Jon speculated that other Patriot fans felt the same way. Speaking for myself as one of those fans, he was definitely right.

Jon recounted how he caught up with Bob Kraft after that win and congratulated him, and also told him "by the way, it's great for us old guys" as well.

Getting back to 2008, Jon said that he was in Europe when the Patriots opened the season against Kansas City. Jon had a friend check the score and they saw that the Patriots had won, but the story showed that Matt Cassel had helped the Patriots to the win. That's when he learned that Tom Brady had been injured and thought "that's the end of the season" as many of us did, but the team played well and exceeded expectations.

Jon felt that "it wasn't as much fun watching Cassel as it was with Brady, even though they were winning ... I think Brady is the best quarterback I've ever seen ... he's just fabulous". He said that watching the 2007 Patriots with Brady, Welker, and Moss "was the most fun I ever had watching football".

When I followed up by asking Jon what current or former Patriot that he did not play with would he have liked to play with, he responded with one word. That the word was "Brady" should come as no surprise to Patriot fans. He also added that he always likes players like Mike Vrabel and Rodney Harrison "who are leaders in the locker room ... those are the guys that I admire because I'd like to think that is what I was". Based on what other players have said about Jon, he was definitely viewed that way.

- - -

I asked Jon why he retired when he did. He answered succinctly "I was 36 years old. I played 15 years. I couldn't play any more." He did add, however, that he had tried to retire once before, after a couple of years with Detroit, but he was convinced to un-retire and play one more year with the Chicago Bears ("and it was a good year" Jon remembered), but that was it after that year.

Jon said that he sold his fruit brokerage business, Jon Morris and Company, in 2000 and moved south at the request of Gail, his wife of 40 years. Gail was from Oregon and lived with Jon in New England for many years but never liked the cold weather, so they moved to South Carolina in 2002. Jon spends his time playing golf and reading, and has gotten himself involved in local politics. He said that he has been enjoying retirement, and joked that he at least was enjoying it until September 2008 after which, as he told a friend "I've lost 50% of my net worth and didn't even get divorced!"

Jon was an English major at Holy Cross, so he said that he has read a lot of novels, but over the years he felt that his knowledge of history was weak, so he started reading more history and he loves it. We talked about some books and authors, including David Halberstam, a common favorite of both of us. Jon said that he has "read every one of his books" and was amused when I told him that when I first met with the Patriots to discuss this book I was told that my proposal would be a lot more appealing "if it were David Halberstam bringing it to us" and that I was sitting there thinking "yeah, I understand that". Jon said that he has been reading books about the Revolutionary War, the Civil War, and World War II. I asked him if he had read "Team of Rivals" by Doris Kearns Goodwin, which I have read and think is fantastic. Jon also has read that book and said that he has read a lot of her stuff and likes them as well (as do I; she is an excellent writer). At the time that we did the interview for this book he was reading "The Big Rich" about

Texas Oilmen, including H.L. Hunt and Clint Murchison, which he also likes and recommended. I subsequently read it and did indeed like it.

As is clear from the inclusion of historical books in a book about pro football, our conversation covered a wide range of topics, including the Patriots, pro football, Holy Cross and Holy Cross athletics. It was a thoroughly enjoyable discussion with a very nice and interesting man, who just also happens to be one of the greatest Patriot players of all time.

Bob Gladieux

Patriot Career: 1969-1972
Position Played: Running Back and Special Teams
College: Notre Dame

Bob Gladieux had a brief career with the Patriots but left a lasting impact on the team's history. Bob, nicknamed "Harpo" because of his curly blond hair, was drafted in the eighth round of the 1969 draft, the same draft which brought the Patriots wide receiver Ron Sellers in the first round and Carl Garrett in the third.

Before joining the Patriots, Bob had an excellent career at Notre Dame, playing for Coach Ara Parseghian. Bob was involved in what I still believe was the greatest college football game of all time, the 1966 game between undefeated and # 1 ranked Notre Dame (8-0) and undefeated and # 2 ranked Michigan State (9-0), that ended in a 10-10 tie. The two teams were filled with great players, many of whom made All-American teams. Notre Dame had the great sophomore pass-catching combo of quarterback Terry Hanratty and receiver Jim Seymour, excellent running back Nick Eddy, and a defense led by Alan Page, Kevin Hardy, and Jim Lynch. Michigan State had offensive explosiveness in running back Clinton Jones and receiver Gene Washington, and a bruising defense led by Bubba Smith and George Webster. Bob was a sophomore at the time, playing behind Nick Eddy, but started the game when Eddy slipped while stepping off the train in East Lansing, Michigan and injured his shoulder.

Notre Dame also lost Hanratty and starting center George Goeddeke to injury during the game, and were trailing Michigan State 10-0 when Notre Dame started coming back. It was Bob Gladieux, stepping in for Nick Eddy, who scored Notre Dame's only touchdown of the day, on a pass from Coley O'Brien, who had replaced the injured Terry Hanratty. Bob commented that he is remembered more for that play and that game but "they never mention the other 28 touchdowns or the all-purpose yardage record holder etc. etc., but hey I'll take it … it was a heck of a game."

The best comment that I remember from after the game ended in the 10-10 tie was from Michigan State coach Duffy Daugherty, who said that Michigan State and Notre Dame were so good and so evenly matched, that the final college football polls should "rank them alphabetically". It was Gladieux' Notre Dame team that got the nod as National Champions though, since they had gone to East Lansing and battled back to tie the game after suffering those injuries.

I asked Bob what it was like to go from such an outstanding coach as Ara Parseghian to Clive Rush, his first pro coach. Bob first commented on how odd it was "going from a championship program to a franchise that was looking for a foundation, stability, financial solvency .. they were concerned about making payroll". Bob also recalled that, as an Ohio native, he had been heavily recruited for two years by Ohio State Coach Woody Hayes to play for him at Ohio State. He remembered Hayes sitting at Bob's high school basketball games and speaking at football banquets. Bob said he grew up listening to Notre Dame, though, and so he told Hayes Notre Dame was his first choice, but if he was not accepted into the Notre Dame program, he would join Hayes and Ohio State "in a heartbeat". Bob added that he had "the good fortune" to play for Parseghian, who had turned around the fortunes at Notre Dame and had made them a championship contender again after years of mediocrity.

Bob said that he had great admiration for Parseghian and a later Notre Dame Head Coach, Lou Holtz, with whom Bob worked as an assistant in 1986-87. Bob described Parseghian and Holtz as "great coaches ... what great competitors they were ... they just gotta win ... they know what it takes to win and their preparation is just endless ... great organization and commitment to team"

When asked about his most memorable games, Bob talked about both his college and pro careers. His most memorable college games were the 10-10 tie with Michigan State which Bob describes (correctly) as "one of the all-time classics", and another tie, this one 21-21 with Southern Cal in Bob's last college game, a game in which Bob had more rushing yards than Southern Cal's much more celebrated running back, and the Heisman Trophy winner as college football's best player, a player by the name of O.J. Simpson.

As a pro, Bob's most memorable games included a game against the Redskins in which he started in place of the top Patriot running back Jim Nance (even though that made Bob, as he describes it, "a 193 pound fullback", a lot lighter than the pro football norm for fullbacks), and an exhibition game against Atlanta in which he ran for one touchdown and threw for another TD. Bob said that he "had a lot of fun" in the pros, adding, "it was a blast".

There was one other very memorable game in Bob's career we then talked about. It was the game in which he was called down from the stands before the start of the Patriots' opening game against Miami in 1970, after being cut from the team the preceding week, and actually made the tackle on the opening kickoff.

Bob said that this story actually took place over two years. In the first year, Bob felt he had played well in the pre-season and had made the team, and was convinced of that when it was cut-down day and he was not asked to report to the coach, not asked to turn in his playbook, and not told he was cut. Bob said, "I went home tickled to death. I called my family and friends and told them that I made the team." However, he then learned from a TV sports broadcast that he had been cut from the team. The next day he went in to talk to Clive Rush about it. Rush "hemmed and hawed and told me it was a tough decision to make." Rush told Bob he had played well and he could play for the taxi squad (reserve players who practiced with the team during the week but were not on the active roster) if he wanted to, but then, Bob added, "Rush pointed to the phone and told me that he had a player on hold" that would join the squad if Bob did not want to do so. Bob said that he told Clive "I'll play for nothing. I want to be a Patriot." Bob wound up playing for the team that year, and later learned that the Patriots had cut him to save $2,000 in salary had he made the team before the opening game.

A similar thing happened to Bob the next year. Again he felt that he had played well in the exhibition games and again felt that he had made the team since he had not been informed by anyone that he had been cut. This time he learned that he had been cut from reading about it in the paper, commenting cynically, "This is the kind of outfit I'm working with ... that's how they do it here."

After learning that he had been cut, Bob said that he "partied it up. I met a nice young lady and we partied Thursday and I saw her Friday and we partied Friday and I saw her Saturday and we partied Saturday." When he woke up on Sunday he told her "I'm kind of sentimental here. I'm going to the Patriots' game." He said that a friend of his, Jack, picked him up and they went to the game, which was at Harvard Stadium. They didn't have tickets, but Bob said he convinced an usher to let them in by showing him his picture, which was still in the Patriots' program. He recalled that before the game he and Jack had "a tall six-pack of Schlitz and some home made port wine," so Bob was still, shall we say, feeling the effects of his partying as he and his friend went up to their seats.

Meanwhile, down in the Patriots' locker room, they were in a contract dispute with defensive back John Charles and wound up suspending him.

Back up in the stands, Jack had gone below to the concession stand to get them both some hot dogs and beer, when, as Bob related, he heard the PA system say "Bob Gladieux, please report to the Patriot dressing room." Bob quipped that he started "looking up and it's that blue-gray sky and I'm thinking it's the Four Horsemen, and all kinds of things going through my mind," thinking that God might be calling to him (the blue-gray sky comment was a reference to a famous Grantland Rice column about the great Notre Dame backfield of 1927; the column begins "Outlined across a blue gray October sky, the Four Horsemen rode again …").

The PA announcement was repeated so Bob went down to the locker room and they asked him to suit up for the game. Bob said, "All of a sudden, a GE light bulb went off in my head, but it had dollar signs in it. Do it for the money, Bob." Bob said they told him he was activated and he responded, "activated? don't light any matches, man," but he did get ready and went to the sideline. He then heard them call "kickoff team get ready, kickoff team" so he said to himself "oh hell, that's me," so he went out on kick coverage but, given his partying, he was determined to "avoid all contact". The ball was kicked and he started downfield, "bobbing and weaving". He said that he saw the blocking wedge set up in front of him and he "wanted no part of that, so I gave a duck inside to the right and ran around the left side of that wedge and the running back ducked inside to the left and then ran around to the right and I ran into him and made the tackle."

Meanwhile, while this was going on, Jack had returned to the seats with the hot dogs and beer and saw that Bob was gone. He asked the people around him about his friend and they told him, "We saw the guy. He was up. He was down. He was up. He was down. Then he left." Bob said, "Jack says to himself, 'oh, Harpo, where'd you go, man?'" As a result, it greatly surprised Jack to hear the PA system say "tackle made by number 24, Bob Gladieux" on the opening kickoff. He looked down and saw Gladieux coming off the field after the play. It apparently surprised Gladieux that he made that tackle too, given his partying and attempt to avoid contact with any Dolphin player. Bob finished that game (a win over Miami) and played the rest of the year with the Patriots.

- - -

As I had done with John Hannah and Jon Morris, we then did Player Word Association:

Gino Cappelletti – a class act, a pro's pro, so well-respected, a great leader and great teammate

Jon Morris – Jon had great leadership qualities, a good ballplayer, great teammate

Joe Kapp – I had a lot of fun with him, he was a pirate, nobody else you'd rather play for, he was a warrior, he didn't throw the prettiest ball in the world but he just got it done

Jim Plunkett – heck of a competitor, unfortunately had to go through some growing pains there early with the Patriots and didn't have a good surrounding cast, great young man, he needed a little more help

Ron Sellers – did a good job, he was an excellent deep threat, didn't have enough of a supporting cast, so he always got a lot of double coverage until Randy Vataha came onto the team and helped a lot

Carl Garrett – God, what a talent; wish Carl would have put the team first, we could have had a lot more success; he could do so many things; Carl was wrestling once with Jim Nance who was an NCAA wrestling champ and Carl just flipped him over; he was a super talent

Jim Nance – Jim was like a big brother, he would put his arm around me and tell me 'hey hang in there and don't worry so much about that rah rah and win one for the Gipper stuff, just worry about Harpo' and I found out that's the way it kind of worked; Jim was a load, tough to bring down

When I asked Bob about the toughest opponent he had faced in his career, he responded that the toughest team was the Miami Dolphins, and "the man I loved and respected the most was Dick Butkus [the great middle linebacker from the Chicago Bears]. He was my idol." He said that when he was playing the Bears, and the offense would get set, I would "look at my assignment, then I'd look to see where Butkus was … he could make plays from anywhere."

Of the different places that he played as a Patriot, he felt Harvard Stadium was the best, saying "I really like that Stadium … you get the feel of a gladiator in there almost."

We talked briefly about the AFL-NFL merger, and Bob said "that's what I always had trouble with" (the viewed difference between the leagues) since, as he put it, "AFL, NFL ... it was football, pro football ... I just loved to play."

Bob retired from the game and moved to South Bend, Indiana, where he and his wife have owned and operated a travel agency for 20 years. His pro football career was brief, but it certainly was interesting.

Steve Grogan

Patriot Career: 1975-1990
Position Played: Quarterback
College: Kansas State

Before there was Tom Brady, there was Steve Grogan. Grogan was the best quarterback in the first 40 years of the Patriot 50 year history. In fact, perhaps the best way to look at it is that Grogan was the best Patriot quarterback of the 20th century, and Tom Brady has been the best Patriot quarterback of the 21st century.

Before the NFL became more of a passing league than a run-run-pass league, and before Drew Bledsoe and Tom Brady came along in the new offenses to shatter records, Grogan had been the Patriots' all-time career passing leader in many categories. He is still in the top three in most categories, having accumulated 26,886 passing yards by completing 1,879 passes in 3,593 attempts. He threw for 182 touchdowns in his career, a total only surpassed by Tom Brady. In addition, Grogan was not just a passer, but was also feared as a runner, as he rushed for 2,164 yards (4.9 avg.) and 35 touchdowns in his career, numbers unheard of for a quarterback.

Statistics alone, however, do not measure what Steve Grogan meant to the Patriot team. He was an outstanding leader, and was highly respected by his teammates (as can be seen by the interview comments from players such as John Hannah elsewhere in this section). He was a warrior, who would do whatever it took to win a football game. The book *The Good, The Bad, and The Ugly* by Sean Glennon contains two very illuminating quotes about Steve Grogan. One was from Steve's first pro coach, Chuck Fairbanks, who said of Steve in 1976, "his eyes light up when it's time to play." The other was by former teammate Russ Francis, who said Steve "wouldn't acknowledge that anything was remotely impossible, or difficult to do, or dangerous".

This apparently included being as much a runner as any running back, banging repeatedly into the mammoth defenders of the NFL. This was in addition to taking the punishing hits that any quarterback has to take when he drops back to throw. As Steve explained when we talked about this during our interview, "I just tried to play football, I loved to play football and I didn't try to be different because I was a quarterback. I respected those guys that were laying their body on the line every play and if I had to do that a few times a game then that's what I did ... the fans respected me for that and I know that the guys I played with respected me for that. I wasn't the best quarterback in the world, I know that, but I think I was pretty good and I certainly gave it everything I had when I was out there." He certainly did, and it was indeed this kind of work ethic and do-anything attitude that endeared Steve to Patriot fans during his career.

Steve Grogan also played more seasons with the Patriots (16) than any other player in history, which is a testament to his durability and the afore-mentioned work ethic. He was also one of the last NFL quarterbacks who called his own plays, instead of having them sent in from the sidelines or called by an offensive coordinator. This shows the high level of respect that his coaches had for Steve's knowledge of the game. In fact, even when Steve was not the starter, he would be the person calling the plays for the quarterback from the sideline. Coaches clearly valued and trusted his football knowledge and instincts.

Some of this success may have been hard for many to imagine when Steve first joined the Patriots in 1975. The Patriots selected Steve in the fifth round of that draft (Russ Francis was the team's first round pick that year). As Steve recalled, he was "thrilled to be drafted ... I had had some physical problems my senior year and so there was some debate as to whether anybody was going to draft me or not, and I was told that I could go anywhere from the first round to not being drafted at all." As Steve pointed out, this was well before the days where the NFL Draft was a big TV event on ESPN. He just sat around the dorm room and waited to be called, and was relieved when he was finally called by the Patriots after they selected him. He said, "When Chuck Fairbanks called late on the first day of the draft and asked if I was OK with being picked by the Patriots, of course I was thrilled."

I recall that Chuck Fairbanks, the Patriot Coach and GM at the time, was very happy when he saw that Grogan was still available and snapped him up with that pick. However, Steve was not brimming with confidence when he went to mini-camp, saw that he was one of four quarterbacks there, and learned that the team was only going to keep two quarterbacks. One of the four quarterbacks in camp was Jim Plunkett, who had been the top pick in the entire draft in 1971, and had been the Patriot starter in 1972, 1973, and 1974, so it was definite that he would be one of the two. Steve then was competing for the backup spot with veterans Dick Shiner and Neil Graff. Steve said "it did not look good for me and I was just trying to fit in and impress somebody" so he tried to do anything to make the team, saying "I volunteered to play wide receiver in practice, running back in practice, I was kicking a little bit, just trying to do anything and everything to make the roster". Then, as he went on to describe, "Shiner retired during camp, Plunkett got hurt in the last pre-season game, and I was the only quarterback left to be the back up to Neil Graff so they wound up having to keep me ... Graff did not play well in the first few games, he struggled a little bit, so they threw me against the Jets in the fourth quarter at Shea Stadium, I threw a touchdown pass to Russ Francis, and the next day they activated Plunkett and cut Graff, and now I was backing up Plunkett; it was like a whirlwind to me".

Steve then took over as the starting quarterback midway through the season when Plunkett was injured, and the job became his from that point on. Steve said "I went from probably not making the roster to starting for an NFL team in a matter of 10 weeks. It was a dream come true for me. I was able to hang around a lot longer than anyone expected." In fact, as noted above, he stuck around longer than has any Patriot in history – 16 years to be exact.

Steve played so well over the second half of the season that the Patriots decided to trade Jim Plunkett after the season and make Steve their starting quarterback going forward. I asked Steve what his relationship was with Jim Plunkett and Steve recalled, "Jim was a hard guy to get to know, he was very quiet, as was I. He was five years older than me, so we didn't hang out together. It was a pleasant working relationship, but you could kind of sense that he wasn't real happy here." In fact, Steve recalled, "on the plane ride back after the last game of the season, he walked by me on the plane and said 'I hope you have better luck here than I did', which led me to believe that he kind of knew he was on his way out." It seemed a clear sign that even Plunkett could see that the mantle was being passed to Steve as the team's quarterback of the future. Steve felt Jim "was a great quarterback, he just didn't fit in here, and he got beat around, hammered" and we reminisced about how Jim then went to San Francisco and did not do well, but then to the Raiders, where he won two Super Bowls.

The Plunkett trade gave the Patriots a number of draft picks that helped improve the team, and the Patriots indeed did become a contender immediately. In 1976, Steve's second year with the team and first as starter, the team, which had been 3-11 in 1975, suddenly became one of the best teams in the league. "It probably had more talent than any team I played on," recalled Steve. The team finished with an 11-3 record, and made the playoffs. It was the first time that the Patriots had been in the playoffs since 1963. I asked Steve what triggered the turnaround, and he explained that the team had a good "mix of young guys who were really having fun playing the game and older guys like George Webster and Steve Zabel, and Tom Neville was still around at tackle ... they added some maturity, some leadership on how we needed to conduct ourselves in the NFL, so it was a nice blend of veteran and young players, and a great coaching staff and we were doing things that no one expected us to do. It was a fun year."

Steve recalled how he was very cautious in answering questions from his friends and at banquets in Kansas before the season on how the team would do in 1976. This was especially since their first four games were against Baltimore, Pittsburgh, Miami, and Oakland, the four AFC Playoff teams from the previous season. "But we came out 3-1," losing to Baltimore, then beating Miami and the Steelers (the two-time defending Super Bowl Champions) in Pittsburgh, and then drubbing Oakland 48-17 and "it was like, all of a sudden, this is a pretty good football team." The win over Oakland was in fact the only game the Oakland Raiders lost that year, as they went on to win their first Super Bowl.

It was Oakland that the Patriots wound up playing in their first round playoff game. This was the game many feel was stolen from the Patriots by bad officiating. Steve took some of the blame on himself (another sign of a good leader), pointing out, "It was a great battle. I thought we out-played them all day. We just made a couple of foolish mistakes that hurt us." One such mistake was the offense jumping off-sides on a key third down play. Steve blamed himself for that, saying that he changed the snap count from one (which they had been using) to three to try to draw Oakland off-side "and wound up drawing us." Although Steve made sure in the huddle that everyone knew the snap count was three, a lot of the line started driving into their blocks at one, so the Patriots were flagged with a penalty. "If I had it to do all over again", Steve said, "I'd have just lined up and pounded them."

He also recalled a tight end reverse pass that they called toward the end of the first half that did not turn out well. Russ Francis' pass on the play was intercepted, leading to an Oakland score just before halftime. Steve did shake his head remembering the phantom roughing the passer penalty, saying, " that was a bogus call as far as we all were concerned." That call allowed Oakland to go on to score the winning touchdown in the last minute of the game.

He also mentioned how, before the game, the grass was really high and Al Davis had soaked the field, despite a drought in Northern California, making it soggy in an attempt to slow down the faster Patriots. These things, plus other bad calls or hard-to-believe non-calls (as described earlier in the book), made the Raider win a questionable one.

Steve added an interesting story about how, after the game in Oakland, he was waiting to get on the team bus and saw one of the referees, the defensive back judge, whose son had been Steve's backup at Kansas State. Steve started to go over to say hello and ask how his son was doing, but the Oakland police jumped in front of him, thinking that he might have been going over to start a fight with the officials "because of the calls, so it was a crazy finish to what should have been a good football game." (Speaking as a fan, I guess maybe even the Oakland police could tell when a robbery had taken place; it's too bad they didn't have the jurisdiction to arrest the officials for stealing the game from the Patriots). Steve did seem to enjoy my retelling of the story that John Hannah had told me about how at the Pro Bowl mean Pittsburgh linebacker Jack Lambert had told some of the Raider All-Stars who were taunting the Patriot players about that game to "shut up because everyone in the room knew that they had stolen the game."

Steve pointed out, "It would have been a perfect year, because Pittsburgh the next week had only one healthy running back; they were banged up, and then Minnesota in the Super Bowl could never beat anybody," though we were not sure why that was the case with that very good Viking team. In any case, had the Patriots beaten Oakland that day, or as some might say, had that game not been taken away from them, they would have had a great chance to win the Super Bowl. Unfortunately, Oakland did.

I showed Steve the cover of the Sports Illustrated 1977 NFL Season Preview, which had Oakland QB Kenny Stabler on the cover but had a teaser about the story about the predictions that said "Beware of the Patriots". The team wound up missing the playoffs that season, and I asked Steve what happened, and if the celebrated contract holdout by John Hannah and Leon Gray affected the team. Steve admitted it had, saying "yeah, we went from everyone being happy and content and enjoying each other's company to suddenly a couple of guys fighting management" and he felt they were impacted by the holdout.

We then moved on to talking about 1978, which I had thought at the time was going to be a great season for New England. As recounted previously in this section, they had a great running and passing attack, had piled up some big wins during the season, and had a close game against the defending Super Bowl Champion Dallas Cowboys, but a crippling injury to wide receiver Darryl Stingley before the season and a fiasco surrounding the firing of Fairbanks before the playoffs changed things. Steve also added that he had been starting to have some knee problems that year, so he was playing hurt, which also did not help. Nevertheless, the team was going well heading into the season finale when the Fairbanks situation exploded. Steve talked about how owner Billy Sullivan had come into their locker room and told them that "Chuck Fairbanks would not be coaching us any more, and when you are told that, hours before game time, it's distracting." This, was, as Steve acknowledged, the "biggest distraction that we went through". The team lost the season finale to Miami 23-3 and the lost their only playoff game to Houston, 31-14, thus being eliminated from the playoffs. Steve lamented that "We never fully recovered. Things were never the same after that." The record certainly bears that out, as the team began a decline after that season.

I asked Steve about his impressions of Chuck Fairbanks and they were all positive. Steve described Fairbanks as "a great football coach, a great organizer, a great talent evaluator" and said that Fairbanks "had wonderful assistant coaches. Many went on to be head coaches in the NFL." Steve amplified his comment about Fairbanks as a talent evaluator, as seen both by the excellent draft choices that he made, and confirmed by the fact that Bill Parcells brought Fairbanks to Dallas when Parcells became the coach there, to help him evaluate players for the Cowboys.

- - -

We then jumped ahead and talked about the great run the Patriots made in 1985 that got them to the first Super Bowl in the team's history. I commented that Steve was a big reason why the Patriots made the run to the Super Bowl that year and he responded by remembering that starting quarterback Tony Eason had gotten hurt in the sixth game of the season and, as Steve was going in to replace him, Head Coach Raymond Berry told him "I think your best chance to have success is if you call what you are comfortable with". Berry was entrusting the play-calling to Steve Grogan on the field, not to anyone on the sidelines or in the coach's booth. Steve speculated that Berry was comfortable with this since "he had played for Johnny Unitas who called his own plays, so he knew it could be done and that instilled a lot of confidence in me as I went on the field, and I started calling the game and getting input from guys in the huddle and we won the next five."

It was interesting to note that Steve talked about how Berry had played "for" Unitas and not "with" him. It made me think again about how much a successful NFL quarterback has to be a leader, and the most successful ones, such as Unitas, Bart Starr, Roger Staubach, and

Steve Grogan are viewed by their teammates as coaches on the field *for* whom they may be playing. Interesting.

The Patriots won six in a row and nine of their last eleven to finish 11-5 and make the playoffs as a wild card team. They then went on to beat their three most bitter rivals, the Jets, Raiders, and Dolphins, all on the road, to get to the Super Bowl. When I asked about the experience of the Super Bowl, Steve said that he "liked everything about it but the game," which was understandable, since the Patriots were crushed by the powerful Chicago Bears, 46-10.

Unfortunately, Steve had gotten hurt himself along the way, and Eason had once again gone back into the starting QB role for the last few games of the season and playoffs. As the Patriots were preparing for the Super Bowl, Steve was concerned that he and the third-string quarterback, Tom Ramsey, "were probably going to be the only two guys not to see the field and that was killing me because I had waited all that time to get to that point." Steve definitely wanted to play in the Super Bowl, so he said "I was volunteering to cover kicks, block punts, anything to get onto the field."

As it turns out, Steve did get into the game after another injury to Eason, and was one of the Patriots who played well in the loss to the Bears. I asked Steve how difficult it was to prepare for that Bear team and their great defense, and how it felt on the field that day. As John Hannah had said when I talked with him, Steve commented on how surprised the team was that the game plan featured so much passing, since much of their success that year had come from the running game. I added "and turnovers" and Steve agreed (more on that later). One of those turnovers, a fumble by Walter Payton on the Bears' first possession, gave the Patriots the ball deep in Chicago territory. It was a golden opportunity to get an early touchdown, but the Patriots went to the pass immediately. Eason threw three incompletions on three pass attempts, so the Patriots had to settle for a field goal and a 3-0 lead. After that came an avalanche of Chicago points.

When Steve came in to replace the injured Eason, he said that he "had visions of coming in and turning things around" but the Bears kept scoring, and, as Steve remembered, "We got behind so quickly, we had to keep throwing the ball." Against that defense that made things worse, and the rout was underway. Steve finished a respectable 17 for 30 passing for 177 yards and a touchdown in the game, but, as he succinctly put it, for him and for the team, "it was a long afternoon … it was fun to be out there … we did finally score, which was a small accomplishment against that defense … it was a lot of fond memories about that whole experience, but the game is not part of it", but concluded by saying "I'm glad to have experienced it, it was pretty special."

I then asked Steve about Coach Raymond Berry and Steve had great praise for him, "He and Chuck Fairbanks are 1A and 1B in my book ... I really enjoyed playing for Raymond, he's not only a great football coach but a wonderful man. He taught us a lot of life lessons that we have all carried with us ... he had been a great player without the most ability in the world. He became a Hall of Famer by working his tail off, he knew what players had to do, when they needed to do it, and he recognized everybody's different talents."

Steve went back to my comment about the turnovers being a key to that season, saying, "They were a huge part of every win that we had." He gave Raymond Berry credit for making that so. He said that every day in practice Raymond said that he would "blow the whistle and everyone would break out into our individual groups and I'm going to have everybody fall on a fumble and pick up a fumble. We're all looking at each other like 'we know how to do that', but the more we did it every day the more fun it became. You'd see the offensive linemen competing to see who could get up and run with the ball, and it became fun. We did it every day. People think that those fumbles were just happenstance. It happened because we were prepared. We worked on that every day. When the ball was on the ground, everybody on the field knew what to do with it, not just the backs and quarterbacks, and it was a huge part of our success. It was the little things like that that made Raymond Berry a Hall of Famer, and he gave those kind of lessons to us that made us better." This was definitely good insight into the extent of preparation someone like Berry instilled in the team.

He talked about Berry letting him call his own plays when he was out there, and even later, when Eason was the starting quarterback. "He allowed me to call the plays, for Eason, for Doug Flutie when he was there ... he knew I had a talent for doing that ... I got to go to the coaches' meetings a couple of nights a week, and sit in on the game planning ... and really kept me in the game as opposed to most backup quarterbacks who just stand there and listen to the play in their ear and maybe chart, I was reaching the point in my career where I didn't want to do that ... this really kept me in the game and I appreciated that so much."

Talking about being a quarterback who got to call his own plays led Steve to comment about how good it was having players like John Hannah and Stanley Morgan in the huddle that he could rely on, saying, "I could walk into the huddle and say 'John, it's third and three, you think we can run it and get it?' and if he said 'no, not right now' then I'd call a pass play. Or if he said 'yes' I'd ask him 'what's the best run that we got going for us right now?' and he'd look at Pete Brock who was the center and a smart guy next to him and he'd say 'I think this will work' and the rest of the guys would go 'yeah, yeah, that's a good call' so I'd call it and they had a vested interest in making the play work and it kept everybody in the game."

He also talked about how he might "walk up to Stanley Morgan early in the second quarter and ask 'do you think the corner route will work on that guy?' and he might say 'not yet, not yet, I don't have him set up for it' but then in the third quarter he might walk into the huddle and say 'the corner's there now' and I could call it. It was just so much feedback that the coaches couldn't get." Steve added that this was possible since "we had a lot of smart players" on the team. We talked about how that built trust among all the players, and Steve also admitted, "You learn who to listen to and who not to listen to. I didn't always take their suggestions, but it sure was a lot of fun." Hannah and Morgan were ones that he absolutely could listen to and trust.

- - -

This discussion about players was a perfect lead in to our Player Word Association. Jim Plunkett had been first on my list, but we had already spoken about Jim, so we went on to discuss others. Steve's comments about the players were:

Sam Cunningham – a tremendous physical specimen; he looked like a picture of a Greek God: wide shoulders, narrow waist, big strong legs; for a man his size he could really pick them up and lay them down; speed and power - he could run, he was a very good blocker

John Hannah – the most intense football player I was ever around; when he went on the field, practice or game, he was all business, and that's what made him so great; he would never settle for mediocrity; he raised the level of everyone around him

Russ Francis – an interesting character, a tremendous athlete, but somebody that never really worked at it that hard, he just was a naturally gifted athlete. Ran well. Had the softest hands of any big man I ever threw the ball to ... he was a great football player but could have been even greater if he had been a little more serious about it, but he didn't let football consume him; football wasn't important to him

Andy Johnson – multi-talented running back; probably the biggest practical joker in the locker room; he was smart, he understood the game from a lot of different aspects; he could throw it, he could run it, he could block; he could catch the ball as well as any back I ever played with

Craig James – good running back, wasn't as gifted a pass-catcher as Andy Johnson, but he could do a little bit of everything and when we had that running game going in '85, he and Tony Collins together were a great combination

Stanley Morgan – the best receiver I ever played with; tremendous speed, understood how to run routes; he worked hard on learning how to run routes; he could go deep with the best of them, catch the ball over the middle and could outrun people; he was a very smart receiver; we had a great rapport in the huddle

Darryl Stingley – a fun guy to be around, a cutup in the locker room; he enjoyed life, enjoyed having a good time and he was also a very good wide receiver; if he had stayed healthy he would have been one of the all-time better players in Patriot history
[We also talked about the crippling injury which Darryl suffered on a vicious hit by Oakland's Jack Tatum and I asked Steve if he realized at the time how serious the injuries were.] I did not at first, but then when they took him off the field on a stretcher, we knew … it was a devastating thing in the locker room.

Irving Fryar – [I asked Steve if Irving was as crazy as he seemed to most fans, and Steve laughed as he responded] Irving was a little out of control in his early years but then matured … absolutely a tremendous athlete … unbelievable speed and power. Loved to block, he could lay out linebackers like I never saw any other wide receiver … also a great kick return guy; because he was a little immature he got himself into spots that people remember more than what a great football player he was

Tony Eason – a nice kid; he and I got along really well together; the difference between Tony and I was that he didn't have a passion for the game, he had the talent but he didn't have the passion; people would watch my passion for however many years and didn't see the passion from him and I think that hurt him with the fans, New England fans appreciate passion, guys who get down in the dirt and do whatever it takes to win and Tony didn't have that kind of passion

Leon Gray – a very good offensive tackle; real quiet; he was a good tackle and putting him together with John Hannah made them a good tandem to compete with; losing him [when he was traded to Houston] took a bite out of our team and I know it hurt John Hannah badly

Pete Brock – one of the smartest players I played with; he and I had a great rapport; he and I spent a lot of time talking about what would work and what wouldn't work; he had a passion for the game,he played with bad knees, bad shoulders, he would never ask out of a game

Steve Nelson – a tough guy; I watched him dislocate fingers, have a shoulder pop out, and he'd come back two plays later playing again; seeing guys like that, I couldn't allow myself to be a sissy quarterback

- - -

When asked about his most memorable game, Steve said he vividly remembered his first game. It was, as he had talked about earlier, the game in New York which he entered in the fourth quarter and threw a touchdown pass to Russ Francis that helped launch his career. He remembered a play in that game which had the Jet free safety coming in on a blitz, and, he said, "I wasn't prepared for a free safety blitz. I was a rookie. The line opened up, and here came the safety after me and I remember thinking 'what do I do now' so I just kind of stepped to the side and I shoved him and he went right by me and I stood up and I hit the pass."

The other game that he remembered was when Tony Eason was hurt in 1985 and Steve came in and the Patriots came from behind to beat Buffalo and begin the streak that led them to the Super Bowl. Steve remembers it was the first game his son had attended, and the crowd was chanting Grogan's name after the game and "it just gave me a good feeling."

I then asked Steve what play or what game he would like to replay if he could. His reply was right to the point, "I'd like another shot at that '76 Raiders team". He went on to talk about how, when the Patriots beat the Raiders in the 2001-02 playoff game in the snow and with thanks to the tuck rule, people would come up to him and say that he must feel vindicated, but Steve said "the fans may feel vindicated, but those of us that played in that game will never get it back. That should have been the game that launched the dynasty but it just never happened. That would be a game that I'd like to have back."

We then talked about who Steve felt was his toughest opponent. He said "I always played well against the Jets, but when they had Joe Klecko in the middle of their defensive line, he was a force." Steve went on to add, "late in my career, Bruce Smith from Buffalo, you had to know where he was at all times … and we didn't play the Giants all that often so Lawrence Taylor, if we were in the same division I'd have to put him there." Steve recalled that he knew it was time to retire when Bruce Smith sacked him one time and reached his hand out to help Steve up and said "Mr. Grogan, are you okay? … and then he hit me again later … he knocks me down and then calls me mister. I thought I must be getting a little old for this game."

For most fans with whom I talked, Steve was the guy we wanted as QB at that time. Yet it seemed after 1978 that Grogan always had to win the job back, over Matt Cavanaugh, Tony Eason, Doug Flutie, Tom Ramsey, and so on. I asked Steve about that and asked "What were we fans missing?" Steve had the same answer we did: "I don't know", but he added "I may not have been the greatest quarterback that ever came down the pike, but I think I was pretty good and I competed hard."

Steve went on to say that he "threw lot of interceptions" but that the game was different then, saying that it was a run on first down, run on second down, throw on third down offense as opposed to those today that pass all the time. He remembered late in his career he got to play four games in that west coast offense under offensive coordinator Jimmy Raye (the quarterback of the great Michigan State team that Bob Gladieux' Notre Dame team played in that classic 1966 game). Steve asked Raye "What are the reads?" and Raye responded "There are no reads." Steve said "What do you mean?" and Raye told him "I want you to throw to the open guy. I don't care if he's five yards behind the line of scrimmage or 15 yards down the field. If he's open throw him the ball." Steve recounted how he'd always been in a system where "if the safety goes this way you go that way, if the linebacker goes here you go there, so it was a different passing game then than what you see now."

This led me to ask a follow-up of what Steve thinks when he sees the spread formations of today, featuring receivers like Wes Welker, Randy Moss, Troy Brown, and asked if he wished he could play today. He responded, "It would have been fun, but you know what? I liked running the ball personally and I loved it when we could run the ball and just dominate people. There was nothing more fun to me as a quarterback than having a 10 point lead with 8 minutes to go in the game and just take it down and get three yards at a time and just beat the crap out of people. Number 1, the offensive linemen loved doing that it. Number 2 it was just a way to show people that you were more dominant than them. I enjoyed that."

- - -

Our conversation then moved to the Patriots of today, and I asked him what he thought made the 2008 Patriot team successful even after the loss of Tom Brady, Rodney Harrison, Adalius Thomas, etc., when other teams might not have been able to do so. Steve complimented Bill Belichick, saying "They've got a great coach number 1. He recognizes talent. He's another guy, much the same as Chuck Fairbanks, who puts players in a position to be successful. He doesn't ask them to do things that they're not capable of doing. And then he trains them well, [such as] coaches that he's trained to take over when a guy leaves to become a head coach. And he's got really good players: Moss and Welker, they're great. They've got a defense that doesn't give up a lot of points. Everybody knows their role. Kevin Faulk comes in as a third down back and never complains, even though he could go somewhere else and maybe play every down, but he's part of a winner, and happy to succeed. And they all say the right things. I don't know how he gets them all to do that, but he does do a great job of it. He loses Brady and everyone thinks the season is over with and here comes Matt Cassel, a kid who hadn't played a significant game in eight years, and he plays like Tom Brady."

Steve added, "It's been a lot of fun for us old guys to watch them have so much success". Steve also recalled how, as the Patriots were winning their first Super Bowl, over the Rams in 2002, "My wife and I were sitting in the family room watching the game" and when Tebucky Jones picked up that fumble and ran it in (a play later called back due to a holding penalty), "I was sitting there and I turned to my wife and said 'son of a gun, they're going to win' and then they called it back and I was thinking 'old Patriots, here we go again, they're going to get screwed, something's going to happen.'" He wasn't the only one. A lot of fans were thinking that as well. "But then when they won it", Steve continued, "it was really a funny feeling. I was happy but I also had a wave of envy, of jealousy, of 'that could have been us'." I guess once a warrior and competitor, always a warrior and competitor. Bring on those '76 Raiders!

I asked if there was any current or former Patriot with whom Steve did not play but would have liked to have had as a teammate. Steve's first response was Troy Brown, saying "there are guys playing now who could have played in any year. Troy Brown was one of them. He could have played with us. He could have played any time. He was a football player, a smart guy, he could just do a lot of things. He would be fun to play with." He also mentioned Tedy Bruschi, saying "I could see the passion he has for the game, and he's a good kid, he works hard, he's a leader", and Mike Vrabel, about whom he said "another smart guy; I really admired the way that he played the game."

The other player that Steve mentioned was Curtis Martin, saying he was "a great running back".

In continuing his reflection on that question, Steve jokingly added "if they had Stanley Morgan and Randy Moss playing together, I'd still be over there throwing, because between the two of them the ball could go down the field, and that was my forte, the deep throw. I would have had a lot of fun with the two of them."

We talked about some of the odd things that happened with the Patriots during his career, such as the snow plow game in 1982, but Steve recalled that the most unusual thing that happened occurred during training camp one year when "some guy walked onto the field with a bag full of footballs and started kicking field goals. Nobody knew who he was." In those days there was only a rope separating fans from players, "with maybe only one cop out there" so he could easily get in. "We were all watching this guy", Steve remembered, "and pretty soon the security guy started walking toward him and he grabs his bag and balls and runs into the woods and disappeared." He also mentioned "Harold Jackson getting his toe broken in '78 when they tore down the goal posts" as another oddity that "came to mind immediately".

- - -

I suggested to Steve that his many fans who don't live in the area would want to know how he is today and how he spends his time. He responded that he spends a lot of time running his business – Grogan Marciano Sporting Goods – with which he has been involved as an owner for 15 years (the Marciano in the name is former owner Peter Marciano, the brother of one of the greatest boxers of all time, Rocky Marciano). Steve joked, "The Italian barber across the street thought it should be Marciano Grogan but I sent word back that my money was on the table so my name was going first."

Steve also spends his time doing some motivational speaking and some charity work. He said that physically he has been "starting to feel it" the last couple of years, 'it' being the effects of all that pounding a pro quarterback must take and "wondering which hit caused which" of the aches and pains, "but if the phone rang today and they asked me to come back, I'd be there in a flash. There will never be anything as much fun as I had in those sixteen years. There were highs and lows, and I got called names, and booed out of stadiums, but I had success too."

As someone who always was a big fan of Steve Grogan (I have him in my personal Mount Rushmore of favorite NFL quarterbacks, in a foursome with Johnny Unitas, Roger Staubach, and Tom Brady, with Peyton Manning peaking out from behind the rocks, not far behind), it was a special pleasure talking with him. He was a leader and a real competitor then, and he came across the same way now. It would have been great had Steve Grogan been able to win a championship and add that to his long list of NFL accomplishments. He certainly deserved it.

Gino Cappelletti

Patriot Career: 1960-1970
Position Played: Wide Receiver, Placekicker
College: Minnesota

One of the things that made my interview with Gino Cappelletti unique was that we spent some time talking about the areas in Italy from which our ancestors had come (it's something that Italians often do as a matter of course), and Italian food and restaurants. Gino asked me where my family was from and I told him that my father's came from Reggio Calabria and my mother's from just outside of Palermo, Sicily. He kiddingly pointed out "Ah, Calabrese, testa dura" (i.e., thick head). Having been called that many times in my life (don't ask), I could certainly relate to that. Gino's father came from Tuscany, outside of Milan "so he was Milanese" and his mother's family was from the Abbruzzi region. He said that "I had one side of the family wanting to eat pollenta and risotto and my mother's cooking was marinara and tomato."

It was also fitting that my meeting with Gino, Mr. Patriot, took place on Patriots' Day, 2009 (April 20). The Red Sox had beaten Baltimore 12-1 earlier in the day, and later the Bruins would beat Montreal 4-2 to go ahead three games to none in their Opening Round Stanley Cup Playoff Series, and the Celtics would defeat the Chicago Bulls 118-115 on a three-pointer by Ray Allen with 2 seconds to go to tie their Opening Round NBA Playoff Series at a game apiece. But a highlight of the day was spending time that afternoon with Gino Cappelletti, who has been associated with the team since its inception in 1960.

Gino began his career by trying out with the Boston Patriots before their first season. He had graduated from the University of Minnesota, and had played some football while in the Army, and with the Saskatchewan Roughriders in the Canadian Football League, and had a tryout with the Detroit Lions before trying out for the Patriots.

Gino was one of three players who played every game that their team played in the AFL. The other two were George Blanda and Jim Otto, two Oakland Raider greats. Gino has also been an assistant coach with the Patriots, coaching special teams in 1979-1981, and has been a radio analyst with the team for many years, beginning in 1972, and having been doing that for the last 28 years, after his stint as an assistant coach. It was on the field, though, that Gino really made his mark with the team.

Let's start with Gino's statistics. He played in 152 consecutive games, primarily as a wide receiver and placekicker, but also played some defensive back for the team as well. He led the AFL in scoring for five seasons (1961, 1963-66), holds the Patriots' record for most points in a game with 28 (2 touchdowns, 4 field goals, and 4 extra points), most points in a season with 155 in 1964, and is second only to Adam Vinatieri in career points, with 1,130 to Adam's 1,158. His 42 touchdowns rank fifth in team history, and third among receivers. He attempted 343 field goals in his career, more than any other Patriot, and made 176, second only to Vinatieri's 263. He has the Patriot record for most field goals in a game, with 6 (in 6 attempts) against Denver in a 39-10 win on October 4, 1964. Gino even was successful as a defensive back, tying for the team lead in interceptions in 1960, with 4.

Beyond the statistics, Gino was recognized as a key contributor to the Patriots and to the AFL. He was elected as the AFL's Most Valuable Player in 1964, one of only three Patriots selected as MVP in the team's history. He also finished second to Houston's George Blanda, a long-time rival, in the MVP balloting in 1961. He was an AFL All-Star 5 times. He finished as the AFL's all-time scoring leader and with more field goals than any player in AFL history. He was selected as a member of the AFL's all-time team in 1971 and a member of the Patriots' Team of the Century, selected before the 2000 season. His number 20 has been retired by the Patriots, and he was selected as a member of the Patriot Hall of Fame in 1992, in recognition for his years of service and his great career with the Patriots.

If there was any lingering doubt as to why Gino Cappelletti is Mr. Patriot, those last few paragraphs should have dispelled them. He was a great player.

Still, when Gino went to his first Patriot camp in 1960, he wasn't sure if he'd make the team. As he recalled, there were "over 300 players" at that first camp, and the team had a station wagon that made daily trips to Logan Airport at the end of each day, timing it in such a way that they could bring released players to the airport to head home, and pick up new players coming in for tryouts on the same trip. Gino tried everything to make the team, playing defense, doing kicking. He remembered that there was a cut list posted every day after dinner, so some guys couldn't eat because of being nervous about whether their name would be on the list.

I asked Gino how worried he was and he said that "I felt like I was doing okay, but you never knew because sometimes there were surprises." He remembered Lou Saban, the Patriots first coach, as "a terrific guy, and he was a tough guy, and I liked that in a coach. He played football tough and he wanted you to be tough or else you weren't going to be on the team. He wanted tough, very aggressive football players." Gino said that he played defense because he "knew my kicking was strong and I said I've got to find a way stay on this team long enough so that when they start looking for a kicker I'm still here." He talked about how when he had tried out for the Lions he had been there just one week before being cut, and never had a chance to show them his kicking ability. He wanted to have that chance with Boston, so "I played a lot of different positions". Gino went on to relate how Saban "came up to me one day after just about a week of practice ... I was getting heat on my back and one thing you didn't want to do was be in the training room when the coaches are coming in" and have them see you and use that as an excuse to get rid of you, but Saban "came over to me and gave me a slap and said 'keep it up, I like the way you're playing' and boy, I felt ten feet tall."

I also asked Gino to compare what he saw trying out for the Patriots to the Canadian Football League and to the Detroit Lions. Gino was positive about the experience, saying that "the Patriots' situation was such that there was a positive approach from all ends from the get-go ... you felt like this was the big leagues ... I think that gave everybody a sense of pride." He did say, though, that "there seemed to be a lot of unknowns, as far as the makeup of the team ... they were looking for football players so they were looking at just about anybody and everybody."

Needless to say, Gino did make the team and played defensive back and wide receiver and did the placekicking for the team. The team was 5-9 in both its and Gino's first year, then started 2-3 the next year, when Saban was fired and replaced by Mike Holovak, who "turned us right around". Under Holovak the team finished 1961 7-1-1 and then were 9-4-1 in 1962. Gino described Holovak as a good coach who was "very loyal to his players, and when some changes were supposed to be made he stuck with the guys who provided for the franchise in the early years."

The team then made the playoffs for the first time ever in 1963, tying Buffalo for the AFL East title. That sent them to Buffalo for a playoff in very snowy and icy Memorial Stadium for the East title and the right to meet the San Diego Chargers in the AFL Championship game. Gino remembered running back "Ron Burton came off of a serious back injury" to play in that game even though "he had been advised not to play by doctors" and "on the very first play, he got a handoff and he busted it for like 15, 18 yards, and that picked us up big time." Gino kicked four field goals in the game, which he admitted "was tough under those conditions ... I had to run off the field on third down and change my left shoe to put on a sneaker for traction because those cleats that they had those days, not like today, would slide and slip on the ice". Gino also remembered that he caught a few passes that day, but that Larry Garron had a big day and they "rolled on to a 26-8 win". When they came back to Boston, Gino remembered, "the airport was full of East Boston" people ready to greet the team and help celebrate the win.

The 1963 championship game did not work out as well as the Buffalo playoff game, as the Chargers routed the Patriots 51-10. Gino felt that the team had been "sky high" for the Buffalo game, so high that "we could have come home without the plane." Then they came back and went through the practices on Monday and Tuesday and went out to San Diego on Wednesday but never really regained that same intensity. That was one factor in the loss. Another that Gino pointed out was that the Chargers had an extra week to prepare for the game and they knew the Patriots were a blitzing team, so San Diego did a lot of quick pitchouts which allowed their excellent running backs, Keith Lincoln and Paul Lowe, to get around the end and around the blitz and just have to face a safety downfield. So Lincoln had a 67 yard touchdown run in the first quarter, Lowe had a 58 yard touchdown run also in the first quarter, so "when they started rolling, there was just no way that we could catch up", according to Gino.

I have always thought that that San Diego team could have beaten the NFL Champion Bears that year, had there been a Super Bowl, and asked Gino about that. He immediately responded "oh yeah" and added that the early teams that won the AFL, like the 1960 Houston Oilers, could also have done so (Houston would have had to play the Philadelphia Eagles that season had there been a Super Bowl that year).

In the next year, 1964, the Patriots almost won the AFL East again. They finished 10-3-1, but lost the final game to Buffalo at Fenway Park, and so missed the playoffs. Gino, however, had an outstanding season, and was chosen the league's MVP. When asked how it felt to be the MVP, Gino said "it was terrific" but then talked about the difference between "Most Valuable Player" and "Most Outstanding Season". He said in 1964 "everything was falling into place" for him. He had a game-winning field goal with 1 second to go in the game to beat Houston 25-24 in an early November game that he recalled "was a huge win for us to maintain a position to win the

Eastern Division". He scored 155 points, an AFL record that would never be broken. Gino remembered 1964 as a "very exciting year", citing that Houston game and "that 43-43 game with Oakland ... and in Fenway Park we brought everybody to their feet with a lot of games", including that season finale with Buffalo that decided the division. Gino told how the night before that Buffalo game "everything was brown and green and we woke up in the morning and there was like 18 inches of snow on the ground so that kind of changed things in the game plan". Gino remembered that earlier that season he had caught three touchdown passes in a 36-28 win against Buffalo and they were playing man-to-man defense "and we were eating them up". For this game Buffalo switched to a zone, and "we had to change every scheme and with the conditions being what they were, with the ice and slipping and sliding, they were able to do the things that got them touchdowns and their defense just shut us down". Buffalo wound up winning that game 24-14 and went on to beat San Diego for the AFL Championship.

Then, in 1966, the Patriots came into the final game of the season needing a win to face Kansas City for the AFL Championship and the right to play the NFL winner (Green Bay) in the first Super Bowl ever played. The game was a Saturday game in New York against the Jets and the Jets won 38-28, which allowed Buffalo to claim the AFL East title with a win the next day. I asked Gino what he remembered of that season and that game. He described the loss to the Jets by saying "it was all Emerson Boozer and Matt Snell, they did a job on us running the football, and Namath was the quarterback". He then remembered a game against Kansas City earlier in the year which ended in a tie, and said that the team was confident that they could beat the Chiefs in the AFL Championship Game. He also recalled that team owner Billy Sullivan "was having us fitted for blue blazers cause if we were going to the Super Bowl, we were all going to dress collegiate, wearing the same jackets like a lot of college teams do, and Billy was Notre Dame-ish and BC, and they evidently did it. But everything backfired."

After 1966, the team was not as good and had a number of years that were not very successful. We talked about how the team roster was being broken up, with "them getting rid of Babe [Parilli was traded to the Jets], Jimmy Colclough left, Ross O'Hanley ... Mike [Holovak] coached his last game in 1968 ...we all got old together."

In responding to a question about the most memorable game of his playing career, Gino described a 1964 game against Houston, which he won for the team 25-24 with a field goal with one second to go. Gino went on to say that this was his choice because "George

Blanda and I were always having a good competition and good games against each other kicking. He truly was one of the greatest clutch kickers of all time, and I think he perceived me the same way. So that game was such that Houston was moving at the end of the game and went ahead 24-22 with about 16 seconds to go and Blanda kicked about a 12 yard field goal. They are kicking off to us, people started leaving; it looked like the game was over. Before you knew it, we got up to midfield, and then Babe was scrambling and he ran toward the bench and got knocked out of bounds with one second left. So people that were going out were listening to their radios and started coming back into Fenway. That really happened. And I kicked that field goal 44, 41 yards, and that kind of established me as a pretty good player. It was a clutch kick that came at a clutch time for the franchise."

On the flip side, I asked Gino if there was a play or game that he would like to replay, if he could. He mentioned a missed field goal in a 1963 game "in the rain and mud against San Diego at Fenway Park". He said that he had a field goal attempt of about 48 yards in a game that the Patriots wound up losing 7-6. Gino lamented that play saying "I'd like to have that one over", because he "had a lot of pride in my kicking".

At that point, we moved to Player Word Association:

Butch Songin [the Boston Patriots' first quarterback] – a gifted arm; he threw a nice catchable pass, but he just might have been in such a position that he was old when he played with us, we called him grandpa; he helped the Patriots get off the ground

Babe Parilli – a very competitive guy, threw a beautiful pass, he had a strong arm and threw a good touch pass. He was the best holder in football. If I had to single out one player that meant more to my career than any other teammate, it was Babe. He was my quarterback, throwing me the ball. He was my holder, a terrific holder. He made me a better kicker and he made me a better receiver.

Jon Morris – Jon Morris was just great at the center position. He too helped me become a successful kicker, because he was snapping the ball perfectly, and that was not always that usual in those days. It is today because they have specialists. So a lot of times, kickers had trouble with the ball being snapped here, there, and everywhere and by the time the holder holds it and brings it back, puts it on the spot, that's why the kicking percentages were not nearly as great as they are today – bad snaps, bad holds- but Jon was one of a kind for a long time as far as snapping. He was also very effective as a center on running plays and blocking. He was one of the best centers in the league.

Jim Nance – a powerful runner; he had both quickness and power and was a terrific running back

Joe Bellino – a dedicated player; he came out of the Navy and then did his four year stint [on active duty] and may have lost a step in that time, but he came and gave us good heads-up football. He returned kicks for us. He filled in as a receiver. He did a nice job when he was here. He was a good all-around athlete.

Joe Kapp – he came in my last year and was probably the most fiery football player I've ever been around. He was a real leader. He had great leadership abilities. Just to give you an idea of what kind of guy he was, I saw him in a game against the Vikings, his old team, at Harvard Stadium. He threw a pass downfield that was intercepted. Most quarterbacks are just going to stay back and give token resistance, but he took off, outran everybody that is reacting to the interception and made the tackle. And it was a vicious hit. There was just something about Joe Kapp. He played the game one way and that was all out all the time. No question about his toughness.

Jim Plunkett – [though Jim came the year after Gino retired, I asked Gino if he would have liked to have played with him] Yeah, I liked the way Jim threw the ball. He had a nice, high-arching, soft kind of ball. I saw the talent that he had as far as throwing the football, which he displayed in his Super Bowl years with the Raiders [Plunkett won two Super Bowls as a member of the Raiders]. He was a great guy, a pleasant guy, an outstanding football player too.

Bob Gladieux – [laughing at the memory, Gino said that] he was able to give the team a little humor, and we all could use that at times. He was an aggressive player, and he marched to his own drummer. He was going to do things within the limits of team play and everything, but he had some ways doing things a little differently.

Bob Dee, Houston Antwine, Jim Lee Hunt, and Larry
Eisenhauer (Boston's defensive front line in the 1960s)
– We had two of the quickest defensive tackles in the
game in Houston Antwine and Jimmy Hunt. Their forte
was quickness, but yet they also had a good strength
in holding off blockers and rushing the passer like a
good defensive lineman has to do. Larry Eisenhauer
was probably one of the more determined rushers at
getting to the quarterback than anyone that I had ever
seen, and he played a good strong game at defensive
end along with Bob Dee, who was our captain and also
showed a lot of leadership.

Nick Buoniconti – a good linebacker; getting rid of him was the
worst trade since Babe Ruth

I then asked Gino to look at it from the other side, and asked
who his toughest opponent was. Gino mentioned a number of
defensive backs, starting by saying "I always had trouble with George
Byrd, from Buffalo. He was tough. He was tough to turn around or try to
deke him out. He played a pretty tough, solid game at cornerback.
Then some of the safeties: Goose Gonsolin from Denver, Kent
McCloughan from Oakland, Freddy Williamson, Emmitt Thomas, and
Johnny Robinson from Kansas City." Gino also added Nick Buoniconti
who played for Miami after being traded from Boston, saying that he
was "an all-out linebacker; he would fly around and he was a hitter from
the get-go and he could run with the football pretty well" after
interceptions.

In keeping with the discussion about opponents, as I had done
with Jon Morris, a contemporary of Gino at the time, I asked Gino about
his and the other players' reactions when they first heard about the
contract that Joe Namath and John Huarte signed with the Jets in 1965
($400,000 for Namath and $200,000 for Huarte, salaries that were
unheard of in those days). Gino said that "the one with Joe Namath
was a lot about publicity. We weren't sure if that was $400,000 a year,
or for one year, four years, five years, or what, but for some reason the
press was always making it sound like it was $400,000 for one year".
Gino did say that "then again, he was bringing a lot of attraction and a
lot of charisma to the AFL."

About Huarte, who later played for the Patriots, Gino only said,
"He was a little bit of an unknown. He got a contract from the Jets for
$200,000 and those were numbers that were hard to even fathom, so a
lot of us were not even sure what was going on or how much they were
getting, but Joe Namath came through, he backed it up, and he brought

almost like what Tom Brady brings to the current Patriots as a quarterback."

This led to my asking how Gino felt when Namath and the Jets won Super Bowl III in 1969. "OH", Gino quickly and loudly exclaimed, "They made everybody ever connected with the AFL proud. Every AFL-er was pulling for the Jets, but before the game started you had to figure that it was just another loss. Baltimore was 18 point favorites and that was like a lost cause. Then all of a sudden Joe Namath is saying 'we're going to win this game'. Then the Chiefs won it the next year. They just outplayed Minnesota. Both of those teams made all the adversity that this league had gone through worthwhile. They brought a great sense of satisfaction and pride to all of the players of the AFL, especially the long-term ones like myself, Blanda, Hank Stram, that were there from the get-go in 1960."

Since Gino, like Jon Morris, had played in multiple stadiums – Boston University's Nickerson Field, Fenway Park, Boston College's Alumni Stadium (where I first saw a Patriot game), Harvard Stadium, and even a home game in Birmingham, Alabama (as described in the chapter about the 1960s) – I asked if there was one that he preferred. He said "Fenway Park gave us a feeling of 'now, we're professionals'. We played at BU, BC, and those were college stadiums, college atmosphere. We got to Fenway Park and that's when we finally felt professional. We were playing in the city, so we felt that we were part of Boston, along with the Red Sox, Bruins, and Celtics. Walking around in the locker room made us feel like finally we were getting the pro feeling that we should have."

You cannot talk about the old Patriots without bringing up the unusual things that happened with this franchise, and so we did. One that we talked about at length was a play against the Dallas Texans (now the Kansas City Chiefs) in which a fan ran onto the field to deflect a pass and help the Patriots win a game. I asked Gino how this could happen without anyone noticing it. Gino explained that "What happened was that we had just gone ahead of Dallas 28-21 and now Dallas was on the move. Cotton Davidson threw two successive passes to Chris Burford, and Burford got downed at the one yard line, and they called a timeout. As far as the fans were concerned, though, the game was over, so now all the people came running out onto the field, and we're celebrating because we had won the game. However, now the officials told the everyone they had to get off the field because there was still one second to play. What they couldn't do was get everybody back into their seats so they had the fans around the perimeter of the field, they pushed them back, and they were standing there three or four deep. Davidson goes back to pass again, and here comes this guy and he ran into the defensive backfield of the Patriots and just started waving his hands as Davidson was throwing the ball. And don't you know it was the perfect distraction because Burford was there to maybe make the catch. He [the fan] ran out of the back line of the end zone, turned a U-ey [Gino made a U-turn gesture with his hands] to the left and ran back to where he came from. I have it on film. It was hard to see, it was dark, they didn't have the lighting, and you see this guy just do a circle, and it helped us win the game."

Another odd occurrence that we discussed was Clive Rush almost electrocuting himself with a microphone at a press conference. Gino shook his head thinking about Rush and just said, "That was sad. He obviously had a problem with alcohol. But he had a great mind, a great feeling for the game of football, a tactician, a strategist. He helped created that offense for the Jets." It was indeed a sad situation.

I asked Gino why he retired when he did and he said simply, "It was time. The team was no longer the team that I had known. It was part of the reconstruction of the franchise and I wasn't going to be able to help the team in any way at that time."

As noted above, Gino went on to be an assistant coach and long-time radio analyst for the team. Since I had previously asked him about his most memorable game as a player, I also asked him to talk about his most memorable game as a broadcaster. Gino quickly replied, "Ah the snow game, the Oakland game", referring to the playoff game in 2001-02 that involved the famous tuck rule call and two crucial field goals by Adam Vinatieri. Gino said, "I've been a fan of Adam's, I've played golf with him, I got to know him. He was an outstanding placekicker. He proved that. When I saw him line up for that kick, I could relate to that situation. It was 45 yards and the snow was coming down. There was just a question of getting it airborne." I mentioned that I remembered the kick not getting that high and Gino agreed, responding, "That was the kind of kick he had to make in order to go against the snow and against the wind. He had to kick a line drive kick. He hit the ball a little higher in the belly in order to do that. But there is a fine point where you start coming up from the bottom of the ball where you can almost kick a knuckler, but he still got it end over end and it was a low line driving kick and that kick meant everything. It tied the game and then the momentum was big time on the Patriots' side. That kick was as huge as the franchise will ever have."

The kick "enabled them to go to Pittsburgh and do what they did there", as Gino recounted, and ultimately to the Super Bowl in New Orleans against the Rams. I asked Gino what his thoughts were in that Super Bowl when the Rams came back from being down 17-3 to tie it late in the fourth quarter. We talked about the drive that Tom Brady led to the game-winning (make that Super Bowl winning) field goal, and Gino said that "We felt that the Patriots were not playing for overtime." (Interestingly, on TV, the famed analyst John Madden was predicting that the Patriots would take a knee and go into OT.) "Knowing the Patriots and what they were doing," Gino went on, "they knew they just had to get into position. You had an outstanding kicker, you've got an outstanding quarterback who is not going to make a mistake, you've got a Troy Brown who caught that pass going across, and before that J.R. Redmond catching short passes to the left, and they called timeout. That was the next best thing, broadcasting that, after the snow game because that happened here in New England and meant so much to the success of the franchise."

As had been done in other interviews, I asked Gino if there was any current or former Patriot that he did not play with that he would have liked to have had as a teammate. Gino's response was "yeah, Troy Brown. Doug Flutie. Tom Brady of course. These are guys that I admire."

Looking at the 2008 season, I asked Gino what he thought made this Patriot team successful even after the loss of Tom Brady, Rodney Harrison, Adalius Thomas, etc., when other teams might not have been able to do so. Like others interviewed, his immediate answer was "Bill Belichick". Gino lamented that the team had lost three games at home, and he said that the toughest play was that third and 15 that the Jets converted in overtime to help beat the Patriots in Foxboro (the play that I described earlier in this book as the one that I felt was the key play of the season).

We talked about Matt Cassel's season and Cassel as potential MVP. We talked again about Most Valuable versus Most Outstanding, with maybe Peyton Manning being Most Outstanding. Gino felt that it is difficult to determine who is the most valuable for his team. He went on to tell a story about how Joe Kapp refused to accept the MVP award the year (1969) that he was selected for leading the Vikings to the Super Bowl. Gino told how "They had a dinner in Minneapolis. Joe Kapp got up and everybody clapped and cheered and Joe said 'thank you for the recognition, but I cannot accept this. There is no Most Valuable Player on the Minnesota Vikings' and I have to admire that."

Gino was very gracious and we could have gone on talking for hours, but I was aware that his wife was waiting for him, so we ended at this point. It was a great Patriots' Day afternoon spent with a great Patriot player, one of the greatest players in team, AFL, and NFL history.

Troy Brown

Patriot Career: 1993-2007
Position Played: Wide Receiver/Kick Returner (and occasionally
        defensive back)
College: Marshall

Any list or compilation of an all-time Patriots' team would have to include Troy Brown at one position, if not multiple positions.

As a pass receiver, Troy holds the Patriot team record for most career catches, with 557, and for most catches in one game, with 16 against Kansas City in a September game in 2002. He is second to Stanley Morgan in career yards receiving, with 6,366, and is in the top five in receiving yards for one season and receiving yards in one game.

As a kick returner, Troy holds the Patriot team record for most career punt returns, with 270, and most career yards returning punts, with 2,625. An 85 yard punt return for touchdown in 2001 is the second longest in team history, and he has three of the seven highest season punt return average yards. He returned three punts for touchdowns in his career, also a team record.

Troy played more seasons (15) than any Patriot other than Steve Grogan, who played for 16 years. He participated in 20 playoff games, second only to Tedy Bruschi's 22, and in those playoff games caught more passes (58) for more yards (694) than any receiver and returned more punts (33) for more yards (315) than anyone in Patriot playoff history.

Statistics alone, however, don't tell the whole story of why Troy Brown was one of the most beloved players in Patriot history. He always displayed a lot of heart, and a lot of intelligence, on the field, and was willing to do whatever was necessary to help the team win. This included playing defensive back in 2004, when the team's secondary was overcome with injuries. In typical fashion, Troy took to this assignment very well, finishing second on the team with 3 interceptions (Eugene Wilson led the team with four interceptions that season).

He also made a number of key plays that were significant in Patriot history, including:

- a big 23 yard pass reception and run out of bounds on the Patriots' two minute drive in the 2002 Super Bowl to stop the clock and put the Patriots in range for Adam Vinatieri's game-winning field goal that beat the Rams 20-17

- Grabbing a blocked field goal attempt and racing toward a touchdown but then, when caught, lateralling the ball to teammate Antwan Harris to allow Harris to score a big TD against Pittsburgh in the 2001 AFC championship game

- A 55 yard punt return for touchdown against the Steelers in the 2001 AFC championship

- A 27 yard punt return in the snow against Oakland that set up Adam Vinatieri's game-tying field goal

- Agreeing to play defensive back when the Patriot defensive backfield was depleted by injury in 2004, and finishing the year with 3 interceptions

- An 82 yard touchdown reception from Tom Brady in overtime at Miami to give the Pats a dramatic 19-13 win over the Dolphins in 2003

- A defensive strip of the ball to cause a fumble by San Diego's Marlon McCree in the 2006 playoff game at San Diego that helped the Patriots to a big upset win

- - -

With all of this history, it is interesting to note how Troy's career with the Patriots got started, as he described when we met on May 21, 2009 for an interview for this book (Troy had invited me to his house for this interview, which was a pleasant surprise to me, and a very nice thing for him to do). Troy was an eighth round draft pick from Marshall in 1993, the same year that the Patriots drafted Drew Bledsoe with the overall first pick in the draft, and Chris Slade and Vincent Brisby in the second round. I asked Troy what his first reaction was upon hearing that he would become part of the Patriots' organization. Troy smiled and recalled his first reaction was the question: "Where exactly is New England?" He had grown up in South Carolina and went to school at Marshall, so he was not sure where in New England the Patriots played. He remembered flying into Boston and being impressed with the city, but then driving further and further out into the suburbs before getting to Foxboro. He recalled that Foxboro was "nothing like it is today ... no McDonald's, no fast food places, none of that stuff ... it ended up being fine, because after a couple of years I didn't want to deal with that [city] traffic."

Troy's first coach was NFL Legend Bill Parcells, who was in his first year as Patriot Head Coach. When asked what his first impressions of Parcells were, Troy said, "I was familiar with him and his success with the Giants, then he was on television doing the NFL games; I knew that he was a tough-nosed coach." He said that Parcells' first words to him were "you almost cost me a lot of money". Troy went on to explain that his college coach, who had worked with Parcells in the 1970s, had recommended Troy to Bill Parcells, which is why New England picked Troy in the draft. Otherwise they would have had to sign him as a free agent.

As described in earlier chapters, Parcells really started turning things around in New England. Troy remembers that Parcells cleaned house in that first camp, getting rid of veterans such as Eugene Lockhart and "brought in guys that he was familiar with, guys who had played for him with the Giants ... It was an eye-opening situation for me when you saw a guy who had been here and had made a name for himself" getting cut "that put me on pins and needles". That led me to ask Troy how worried he had been about making the team, and he admitted that, "I was very inexperienced in how things worked; I was an eighth round pick, kind of a long shot, so I was kind of worried about it, but I was used to playing a lot, I was used to playing special teams" as well as receiver, and also had played some defensive back at Marshall, so he hoped that his versatility would help him.

Troy added that the Patriots "even had me playing third down back. The biggest problem with that was picking up the blitz, which was the biggest issue with me too, weighing a buck-eighty, but a lot of it was technique. He stuck me in there for a few practices. I actually got run over by Duane Sabb [Patriot linebacker] the first few times that I tried it. I ended up getting a little better at it so they put me there in a game and called some protections that allowed me to release and I actually caught my first two passes out of the backfield." That was also the beginning of a very successful 15 year NFL career.

- - -

Under Parcells, the team improved from 5-11 in his and Troy's first year in 1993 to making the Super Bowl in 1996-97 at 11-5. Troy played some receiver but was mostly in on kick returns then, but unfortunately missed the Super Bowl against Green Bay with a hernia injury. He then really came into his own in 2000 with 83 catches, and had a very successful season in 2001, setting a team record with 101 catches, helping the team go 11-5 again and not only make the Super Bowl but win the Championship in a thrilling game with St. Louis. I asked Troy how things came together for him and for the team that year. Troy remarked that "Our passing game was pretty solid in 2000, my first year really starting as a receiver. I'm going into that season and lost a good friend in Shawn Jefferson", a wide receiver who left the Patriots that season. Then Terry Glenn was suspended for four games to start the 2001 season, so Troy moved up on the depth chart and, as he put it succinctly "I had a good season."

He talked about the team starting that 2001 season slowly, saying, "we go to Cincinnati and lose, then come back here and struggle against the Jets and Drew gets knocked out and we end up losing that game. We came back the next week and kind of got things together. Patten steps up, I step up, and we both started making a lot of plays. Then there was the whole craziness of the season. Drew gets well, so 'Is it going to be Tom? Is it going to be Drew?' We were watching. Bill was monitoring" and ultimately the choice was Tom Brady. Troy said that "Drew did a hell of a job" accepting the role as a backup "and not making it a bigger distraction than it was. He was very, very classy." He also commented about the team that "we had a lot of no-name players, but we worked hard and we made plays" and were able to be very successful doing so. Troy also said that "My thing was just because you don't have the name doesn't mean that you can't play the game. I look back on it now and we had a lot of really good football players on that team that knew how to play the game."

We talked about every step in the playoff run to that first Super Bowl title. Troy said that "going into the playoffs I don't think anybody gave us a chance in hell" of becoming champions. He mentioned how difficult it was in the Oakland game played in that heavy snow storm, remarking that "the toughest thing for me was catching the ball as a punt returner" looking up into those giant snowflakes to find and catch the ball. He remembers that he had "two decent punt returns in that game but I think I fumbled two, but Larry Izzo jumped on them" to prevent them from being turnovers. He also credited fellow wide-out David Patten for making some big catches, including one on his knees, and Jermaine Wiggins making some big catches. Modestly, he did not mention his own big catches or the 27 yard punt return that set up Adam Vinatieri's game-tying field goal, but I'm sure that I'm not the only fan who remembers them.

The overtime win over Oakland sent the Patriots to Pittsburgh for the AFC Championship game against the Steelers. Troy commented that beating the Steelers was "sweet revenge from my childhood. I hated Pittsburgh. I was a Cowboy fan" and the Cowboys suffered a couple of big Super Bowl losses to Pittsburgh over the years. He remembered Bill Belichick "giving us the speech about how they already had their hotels set up" for the Super Bowl. Steeler Coach Bill Cowher and his team seemed to feel that their winning this game was inevitable, so Cowher gave the Steelers the Monday off before the game so that they could make Super Bowl travel arrangements for their families. This kind of arrogance fed the Patriots' motivation. "He fed it to us, and we ate it up" was how Troy happily remembered the team getting psyched by the Steelers pre-supposing the win. Tom Brady was hurt in this game and Drew Bledsoe had to step in at QB. Troy remembered that on the first play Drew scrambled out of bounds and took a hit from Chad Scott similar to the one that knocked him out earlier in the season. The team was wondering if he was reinjured, but Drew got right up and back into the game. Troy laughed when I asked him if he would have been the next option to play quarterback, but it may not have been far from the truth.

The playoff game against the Steelers was one of Troy's best games. He had a super game as a receiver, with 8 catches for 121 yards, and an equally super day on special teams. He had a 55 yard punt return for the Patriots' first score, and then made a lateral on a blocked field goal by Pittsburgh that led to another New England touchdown. On the punt return TD, Troy remembered that the Pittsburgh punter, Josh Miller (who later played with New England) "nailed the first punt; it was about two inches from the sideline, so I didn't catch it. They dropped the flag because somebody had gone downfield too early" so Pittsburgh had to redo the punt. Troy said that the officials inadvertently "put the ball on the wrong hash mark" when setting up for the second kick. They set it up on the right hash mark instead of the left. The first kick had gone out of bounds to the left (Troy's right) since Pittsburgh did not want Troy to catch the punt in the middle of the field. They tried to do so again this time, but now kicking from the other hash mark, the kick did sail into the middle of the field. Troy said "I got my hands on it, and there wasn't a big hole to get through but when I popped through it things opened up" and he was on his way to the touchdown, which "got the scoring started".

I asked Troy about the play on the blocked field goal and he said that

> "this was something that we did in practice, scooping up blocked field goals, for the last two seasons. The situation came up in the AFC championship game. What we practiced we put to work in the game. I scooped it up. I was being tackled. Antwan was running behind me and he was calling. At first I wasn't going to throw it because I didn't know who was around me, Then I realized that it was just the kicker ... Antwan took it to the house and that kind of sealed it up for us."

It was then on to the Super Bowl and the confrontation with 'The Greatest Show on Turf', the St. Louis Rams in New Orleans. Troy remembers that the team found signs welcoming the Steelers in the hotel where the team was staying, and "during the week before the game we had to hear about how we didn't have a chance against the

Rams." Nevertheless, Troy felt that the team was confident going in, having played well against the Rams in a regular season game, "so we knew that we could match up with them … they didn't come in and blow us out like they did everyone else."

The game plan was to be physical with the Rams and the Patriots were that, with key turnovers helping New England take a 17-3 lead into the fourth quarter. The Rams tied it, but the Patriots made a big drive to the game-winning field goal, a drive which included a key catch and run out of bounds by Troy to set up that field goal. Troy remembers that that drive started with him returning the kickoff "and it didn't turn out well. We got the ball only to the 19. They had momentum. It was getting hot inside the dome and they were probably in better shape than we were. I guess Bill's thinking was 'let's just go for it'. We took a couple of short passes to J.R. Redmond …" and other plays (described in Chapter 6), including a big catch by Troy to move them close to field goal range. A couple of plays later Adam Vinatieri hit the field goal that won it.

When asked what his first thoughts were when the Super Bowl ended and his team had won, Troy said "it was probably one of the greatest feelings ... as a kid growing up everybody wants to be a football player and the ultimate goal of being a football player is to win the championship … it was a dream come true." It certainly was for both the team and its fans.

- - -

In 2002, following the Super Bowl win, the Patriots missed the playoffs, though they seemed to be peaking late in the season. I asked Troy what he felt happened in 2002 that kept the team from the playoffs. He responded that it was a couple of factors, "Maybe we were thinking too much about the success we had the year before … we had a couple of injuries, we just could never get it going, we never adjusted to our success." He commented about how every team was motivated to beat them the next year, "I don't think we ever realized that we had to turn our own games up to the next level" to meet those challenges and stay on top.

The Patriots followed that 2002 season by winning the Super Bowl the next two years, beating Carolina 32-29 in 2004 and Philadelphia 24-21 in 2005, and were dominant in both regular seasons, going 14-2 both years and winning an NFL record 21 straight games in a span crossing the two seasons. I asked Troy if the players felt like a dynasty in 2003-04 or felt that they were part of something special, and how that two season success came about. Troy said "I just remember us getting on that roll where we couldn't lose. We bring in Deion Branch. We bring in David Givens ... Daniel Graham. Those guys made a lot of plays. It's hard to find a lot of young guys who could help us as much as those guys did. It was one of those things. We played with a lot of poise. We got back on track and won a lot of ball games".

He said that the Super Bowl game with Carolina in Houston "was like a heavyweight fight, one of those Ali-Joe Frazier fights. It was a slugfest. I remember it being so hot, so uncomfortable. We were covered with sweat. Everybody's jersey was soaking wet ... We were losing defensive backs left and right...... It took us a while to get going [neither team scored in the first quarter] all of a sudden boom, Deion Branch made a big play" and things started. Then again no one scored in the third quarter and then in the fourth quarter, as Troy described, "all of a sudden nobody could stop anybody and then boom, we got a big break when they kicked the ball out of bounds after tying it up and we get the ball on the 40. I make the first catch on that drive. Then I get called for pass interference. We go down and make more plays and here comes Adam."

As was the case in the Super Bowl win over the Rams, it came down to a last second field goal attempt by Adam Vinatieri with the score tied 29-29. Troy said that he had confidence in Vinatieri making the field goal but "you still had to cross your fingers and bow your head" as the teams lined up. The kick was good and New England had another championship.

Against Philadelphia in the Super Bowl the following year, Troy recalls that he "played more defense than offense" after playing some defensive back during the season. He commented that he "was 12 years removed from playing defensive back" while in college at Marshall, but still was able to do it during the regular season and in the Super Bowl. He had three interceptions during the season, as noted above, and he "defended Brandon Stokley", the Eagle receiver, in this game. Troy said, "It was a banged up season for me. I had a bad shoulder, a knee banged up but I made it through all the playoffs just doing my job and that was playing defense and we got to the Super Bowl and I felt like I had done something good, something that I'm not used to doing, and I helped my team get to this point." That was definitely the case.

Another post-season play that we talked about occurred in the 2006 playoff versus San Diego, where Troy made a hit to force a fumble after a Brady interception. Troy described how that play developed, saying, "The play was a little botched up. There was some congestion in there and Tom couldn't really identify anyone so he threw a pick and I thought 'hey we've got to get the ball back'. The guy tried to run it instead of just getting down. I just reached in there and gave it a pull and it came out. I pulled so hard that I fell backward and couldn't get it, but Reche Caldwell was there and he jumped on it. It was switching your mentality from offense to defense right there and we had to come up with something to get the ball back, and it was quick thinking". Troy jokingly added, "Those defensive guys aren't used to carrying the ball anyway." The quick thinking helped seal the Patriot victory. It was yet another heads-up play in a career full of them for Troy.

- - -

In our Player Word Association, Troy commented:

Tom Brady – unbelievably cool under pressure

Drew Bledsoe – one of the best pocket passers you're ever going to see

Adam Vinatieri – clutch

Chris Slade – could have been one heck of a player, but he had some back problems; I wish that he could have been the player that I thought he could be if he didn't have those back problems

Matt Cassel – I think it says a lot about the kind of athlete that he is that he made the team and played so well

Peyton Manning [a big Patriot opponent] Oh, God, just bad nightmares when you're getting ready to play the Colts, thinking about Peyton Manning, but he's a pretty classy guy. He sent me a card when I retired.

- - -

In responding to a question about his most memorable games, Troy mentioned, "That Pittsburgh playoff game was huge." This was the game in 2001-02 where he did so much to contribute to a big New England win. He also added his "first game playing defensive back, against the Rams, in St. Louis" in November, 2004. Troy said, "I played the whole game" at DB against the St. Louis receivers who "were pretty good and pretty fast" and did well, and that "did a world of good for my confidence" in playing that position. He also noted the September 2002 game where he "made 16 catches against Kansas City … I couldn't drop anything that day except the first pass that he threw to me; it was like third an 17 and I dropped it right at the marker, after that I didn't drop another ball all day. It was to the point where Tom was dropping back and just throwing everything in my direction" was how he remembered it. He added that he "ended up getting hurt, with eight minutes to go, and it went into overtime". Who knows how many catches he could have had if he had not had to leave that game at that point.

On the flip side, when asked about the play or games that he would like to replay, if he could, Troy said "there were a few of those, the punt against Miami" (Troy's last game as a Patriot where he was in to receive a punt, got a great ovation from the crowd, and had the ball bounce off of his helmet for a fumble), a fumble on a kickoff return in a game in his rookie season against Detroit where "they picked it up and scored", "a pre-season game in Green Bay where I let a guy take the ball right out of my hands and they ran that back for a touchdown", and a game against Kansas City where "I caught a pass on the sideline and Neil Smith came over and hit me from behind; the ball came out and was lying by my feet. I couldn't reach it, but Max Lane [Patriot offensive lineman] came running around the corner so I just kind of gave a little soccer move with the ball and kicked it up in the air right into Max' hands and he took it to the 2 yard line."

I asked Troy who his toughest opponent was, and he said "I always had a lot of respect for Antoine Winfield when he was with Buffalo. He always played me tough. He always played aggressively. You had to be ready when you caught the ball because he was coming to hit you, and he had a pretty good hit for a guy that was pretty small."

Continuing with the discussion of players, I asked Troy if there was any current or former Patriot that he had not played with that he would have liked to have had as a teammate. He hesitated for a while, because, nicely, he did not want to offend anyone, but finally mentioned Stanley Morgan, "Gino Cappelletti because he could do so many things", Craig James, and former Cowboy great Tony Dorsett (a nice choice and not a surprise from Troy as a former Dallas fan).

We then turned to the three coaches for whom Troy played in his career, Bill Parcells, Pete Carroll, and Bill Belichick. He thought that Carroll was "caught with the wrong football team. We were very young after that Super Bowl, and they got rid of a lot of players who helped us get to that point, but he was a great coach". In comparing Parcells to Belichick, he said that "Parcells was more vocal, more loud, confrontational", and describes Belichick as "one of the brightest minds in football, and one of the greatest people you'd ever want to come across; he was also very knowledgeable about a lot of different things other than football. He is someone that I respect a lot."

- - -

Before we finished our conversation, and as I had done with other retired players, I asked Troy how he was feeling these days and how he spends his time. He said "I feel great, wonderful. My body is feeling great. I spend a lot of time with my kids, a lot of soccer, a lot of basketball, cross-country". I have seen Troy at a number of Celtics' games over the years with his family and he seems to really enjoy being with them, which is great to see. I asked if he was a Celtics' fan and he said that he definitely is.

Troy had came back for a brief time during the 2007 season after starting the season on the physically unable to perform list. He played in just one game, but did get a rousing welcome from the fans when he appeared in that game. He officially retired during the Patriots' bye week in 2008.

During his career, Troy Brown did everything that the Patriots asked of him, and did everything well. That included pass receiving, kickoff and punt returning, playing defensive back, and even being a potential stand-in quarterback. He was a true professional. He was also a clutch performer, as shown numerous times, perhaps most especially with his contributions to Patriot playoff wins and those big catches in the Patriots' first Super Bowl win. Owner Bob Kraft described Brown as "the consummate Patriot". Most fans would whole-heartedly agree.

At his retirement press conference, Troy revealed that he had been offered a contract with the Jets for the 2008 season, but decided that it just wasn't right to play in any uniform other than the Patriot uniform. In his retirement press conference Brown said about retirement that "It's hard. It's tough. ... the only colors that you'll ever see on my back as a football player, the red, white, and blue of the New England Patriots. I'm proud to say that, and thank you guys for all the great memories that you provided."

No, we are the ones that should be thanking him. Clearly, he will be missed. Troy, if you are reading this, thanks for everything that you did on the field, and thanks for doing everything with such class. Enjoy your retirement.

Randy Vataha

Patriot Career: 1971-76
Position Played: Wide Receiver
College: Stanford

Very few NFL players or athletes of any kind can claim the type of success after their playing careers that former Patriot receiver Randy Vataha can.

After a successful playing career with New England (1971-76) and Green Bay (1977), during which he was a member of the Executive Committee of the NFL Players' Association, Randy became one of the founders of the United States Football League (USFL) and was owner of the Boston Breakers team that was part of that league. He served as CEO of Bob Woolf Associates from 1987-1994, negotiating contracts across all four major sports, for sports clients such as Larry Bird and Joe Montana, as well as for show business and music personalities. He has structured business deals, for example one involving the Marriott Hotel chain and Champions Restaurants, and also another involving raising capital and recruiting investors which offered to buy Wang Laboratories out of bankruptcy in 1993; Randy then became an advisor to Wang's new owners. He has won two Emmy Awards for sports broadcasting from the Boston/New England Chapter of the National Academy of Television Arts and Sciences. He is currently the president of Game Plan LLC, a company that specializes in the buying and selling of professional sports teams. In this capacity, Randy was involved in the sale of the Boston Celtics to its current ownership team headed by Wyc Grousbeck and Stephen Pagliuca. In addition, it has been reported that Randy Vataha has the record for highest earnings in a racquetball tournament, reportedly winning $ 59,000 in one such tournament. It is clear that Randy Vataha is a very versatile person who has had success in almost every endeavor with which he has been involved.

The day that we did our interview for this book, June 3, 2009, Randy had just finished finalizing another deal. He graciously went from completing that transaction to doing this interview, and I very much appreciate his taking the time to do so from what is obviously a very busy schedule.

- - -

Randy Vataha was an excellent wide receiver at Stanford University, where his career coincided with that of quarterback Jim Plunkett. Plunkett was College Football's Heisman Trophy winner in 1970, and he and Vataha helped engineer a huge upset of # 1-ranked Ohio State in the 1971 Rose Bowl. Plunkett was the top overall pick of the NFL draft that year, selected by the Patriots. Randy Vataha was picked in the last round (the 17th) by the Los Angeles Rams. Randy indicated that he was happy being selected by the Rams, who played in California, not far from his home. He joked that he thought at the time that "the Rams must have this brilliant scout, a person who could see through no speed, no size, so I couldn't wait to meet him". He remembered seeing in the next day's *Los Angeles Times* newspaper pictures of Jack Youngblood, the team's first round pick, and himself, the Rams' pick in the last round, and then read that "the Rams had a tradition of giving the newest secretary in the office a list for the 17th round and she got to make the pick". He went on to add that if he remembered the article correctly, it reported that she said that "she didn't know any of these guys but liked the name Vataha-ha-ha-ha-ha".

Randy was with the Rams for a good part of the pre-season. He was cut from the team with two games to go, but the Rams then had a pre-season game with the Patriots. After that game, Randy's position coach, Dick Vermiel, later a successful NFL Head Coach, who had recruited him to Stanford when he was on the staff there, was talking with Jim Plunkett and Patriot General Manager Upton Bell, and Randy's name came up. As a result, Upton called Randy and a tryout with the Patriots was arranged. Randy made the team, and was happy to do so, but then pointed out that "New England is sneaky. When you don't get here until September, you think it's a paradise ... never been in any place in November and December like Boston, but I was thrilled" to be on the team, despite the New England winters that he now would be facing.

Plunkett and Vataha had a good rapport, and Randy speculated that he "didn't think I had a chance to make the team, to be honest, without Jim being there, because, for a rookie quarterback learning his way, at least with me he knew what I was going to do in different situations. A good quarterback always has some guys that are on the team from the year before, but a rookie is trying to find his way. So I think the coach, and the GM, and all of them felt that it was a little bit of a help for Jim in making the transition from college to pro to have at least one guy that he was familiar with."

Whatever the reason might have been that allowed Randy to make the team, I believe that talent was definitely a part of it, as he led the team in receptions with 51 and receiving yards with 872 (the next highest totals for the team were 22 and 265 respectively) and he was selected as a wide receiver on the United Press International (UPI) rookie team. I asked Randy what his memories were of that rookie season, and he said "It was like a flash. I was sitting at home applying for graduate school for the winter term, then all of a sudden I got a call from the Patriots, I showed up, I really didn't think I'd really make it, yet they kept me. The next thing I know, we're playing games. It was a real dream to play in the NFL."

Randy had another good season in 1975 with 46 catches, and 720 yards, again leading the team in both categories, but that was Jim Plunkett's last year with New England. In response to my question regarding why he thought that things did not work out as well for Jim in New England as many of us had hoped, Randy responded "Jim got really beat up. Really. He had a lot of injuries. I think Fairbanks came in and was not only rebuilding the team but was rebuilding the whole organization. He put a real emphasis on the running game. Plunkett was playing hurt a good amount of the time. The fans kind of got down on him. I think that was the final blow that turned Jim off on New England. He was never going to live here permanently. He went back when the season was over. I personally think that the clincher was Fairbanks went to Grogan who was a bit of a running quarterback. He liked Jim personally, really respected him, but he didn't know how long Jim could last after the beating he took" and when he found out what he could get in a trade for him with the San Francisco 49ers "they made the deal". Randy summed it up by saying "I think it was a combination of all of those things. I think that Jim was not really comfortable here, he was trying to play hurt, Fairbanks' type of offense was much more directed toward the running game, and then obviously the value that he could bring going back to San Francisco all kind of added up."

The team went 3-11 in that 1975 season, but then went 11-3 in 1976 and made the playoffs. Randy believed that the turnaround was due to a number of factors. "Fairbanks had done a fabulous job of building a fundamentally sound football team, offensively, defensively", he explained, and added "even though Grogan was very young, he did a lot with his legs, our defense played extremely well. A lot of things came together. If you look at Fairbanks' history, he made the Patriots a really solid organization and a solid team. This was a legitimate contender every year."

Getting into the playoffs set up that infamous playoff game in Oakland which the Raiders won with the help of some very questionable officiating, as was described in Chapter 3. I asked Randy about his and the team's reaction to that playoff game and to that officiating, and he indicated that "There was a lot of disbelief. Remember we had beaten Oakland pretty good in the regular season. I really think that we were the better team overall. Everybody always points to the roughing the passer call on Hamilton, but there was one that was just as bad earlier, when we had the ball and were driving … Phil Villapiano literally tackled Russ Francis on a little 5 yard out, right in front of the referee. If you watch the film, Russ is running this little 5 yard out … Grogan just flips it out there. It is halfway to Russ. It is clearly right into his hands, and Villapiano tackles him. There was a referee on the sideline staring at it." and no call was made, though the pass interference was obvious. Randy went on to say, "That was as bad as it gets because that is not a discretionary call. When you watch it, he just tackles him when the ball was halfway to the receiver. And then that call on Hamilton where he tips the ball and then just falls on him [Stabler]. I remember in the locker room complete disbelief that we would have lost the game on that call. When you look at the film later and you look at both of those calls, it was just unbelievable … if there ever was a disappointment, that one game was it."

Turning to happier times, I asked Randy what his most memorable games were as a Patriot, and he named a few. First was a 34-13 win against Miami in Foxboro at the end of his rookie season, "where I caught a touchdown pass and the whole one end of the stadium sang Happy Birthday to Plunk and me. I'll always remember that." (Randy's birthday is December 4, Plunkett's is December 5). Randy also cited "the Oakland game", referencing the playoff game in 1976. Another such game was the last game of the 1971 season, where the Patriots beat the defending Super Bowl Champion Baltimore Colts 21-17 on an 88 yard touchdown pass that he caught late in the game to give his team the win. He also mentioned a 17-14 win over Minnesota in 1974 where he helped set up the winning touchdown with a 55 yard catch that brought the ball to the ten yard line. Randy remembered that "Bob Windsor, the tight end, caught a touchdown pass on the last play of the game and blew his knee out and crawled into the end zone for the winning touchdown" on the last play of the game. He also laughed in mentioning a 52-0 loss to Miami in 1972, the year that the Dolphins went undefeated, saying, "The game wasn't even that close."

When asked if there was any game that he could replay if he could, as was the case with most of the Patriot players of that era, his immediate answer was "I'd certainly like to replay that Oakland game. I think we'd beat them nine out of ten times." I think he's right.

- - -

In our Player Word Association, Randy commented:

Jim Plunkett [beyond what we had already talked about] a great friend

Steve Grogan – I always think of him as just tough

Sam Cunningham – touchdown leaper

John Hannah – drive block; nobody came off the line of scrimmage like him; he was obviously a great offensive lineman, he could pass block, he could pull like crazy, but when he drove block, just straight ahead, he would just knock guys backward five yards

Jon Morris – solid, never made mistakes

Andy Johnson – versatile

Russ Francis – All-World

Bob Gladieux – Harpo; the most unlikely looking running back I've ever seen

Darryl Stingley – oh man, that's a tough one. The first thing that pops into my mind obviously is his injury, but he was just a very smooth receiver, effortless, everything that he did was just so natural.

- - -

When I asked Randy if there was any current or former Patriot that was not his teammate but with whom he would have liked to have had the opportunity to play, he quickly answered "Wes Welker" adding "we didn't do nearly as much out of the slot when I played as the Patriots do [now], but I can see what he is accomplishing in there and what a lot of people don't recognize is how much he helps the other wideouts when he is in that slot. Everybody thinks that everybody is double covering Randy Moss, therefore Welker can do that, but I think if you look at the films, Moss gets a lot of one-on-ones that he wouldn't normally get playing other teams because you just can't leave Welker alone in there."

I also asked him who was his toughest opponent as a player and who was his toughest opponent as a team. Randy responded that "The toughest player was a defensive back with the Buffalo Bills, Robert James. They played bump and run; it was a fist fight right from the start of the game to the end. He'd just come right up to the line of scrimmage and in those days there were very different rules. They could beat you, push you, cut you, do anything until the ball was in the air. Now they can give you one shove in the first five yards and that's it. Miami was always the toughest team to play for us down in Florida." The Patriots in fact went 18 years without a win in Miami, as recounted earlier in the book, so that was easy to understand.

- - -

With just a few minutes remaining in the time that we had, I asked Randy about the successful career that he has had since leaving the playing field, and asked what his proudest memories were of things that he had accomplished. He admitted that "Oh man, that is a hard question", but named a couple of things. He talked about "Bill Lenkaitis and I and a fellow named George Mathews, while we were still playing, started the first kind of Fitness/Racquetball Clubs, we had ten of them around New England. We started that from scratch, an idea that Bill and I had sitting at a kitchen table one morning. To start a business from scratch … we sold that after five years. We were at the very first meeting of the USFL, and were involved in starting up the league, and obviously owning the team in Boston and then moving it down to New Orleans and the Superdome. That was an amazing experience, again starting from scratch and being part of the USFL. There was a great group of owners. That was a great experience. When we sold the team and I came back, I ended up being the CEO at Bob Woolf Associates and we did a lot of high-profile contracts. Started Game Plan with Bob Caporale who was also a partner of the USFL team of ours ... we've had some pretty good fortune. We handled the acquisition of the Celtics, the LA Dodgers acquisition for Frank McCourt. We handled the sale of the St. Louis Blues of the NHL. We were actually the ones that tried to buy the entire NHL when they were in lockout. We offered four and a half billion dollars to buy the whole league. Bain Capital backed us, it was our plan and we actually were invited into the owners' meeting and gave a full presentation ... it's been kind of a dream. As I look back, I don't think I would change anything. Not every business worked out the way you'd like it too. Not every deal is perfect. But I don't think I'd change a thing."

Hearing Randy say, "We've had some pretty good fortune" brings to mind an old adage that I first heard from a fellow Air Force officer many years ago that "Fortune Favors the Bold". Obviously, Randy's abilities, business savvy, and expertise played a huge role in making that luck and in turning these ideas into success. It was a pleasure talking with Randy Vataha for this interview. I wish him continued success going forward, but I certainly don't think that he will need my wishes to make it so. He makes it happen himself.

John Smith

Patriot Career: 1974-1983
Position Played: Kicker

The first American football game that John Smith ever saw was the first one that he played in.

John had played soccer in his native England and was in America running a soccer camp in Pittsfield, Massachusetts during a break "from university in England" where he was studying to be a teacher. One day at Camp Lenox one of the kids at the camp came up to John with a football and asked John to show him how to kick it soccer style since, the boy told him, "there's a guy on the Giants, Gogolak, who kicks soccer style". The player in question was Pete Gogolak, whom the Giants had signed away from the Buffalo Bills years before, thus starting the NFL-AFL wars described earlier in this book. The ball looked to Smith like a rugby ball, with which he was familiar, having also played rugby in England, so he started kicking it.

The boy, whose father was a VP with the Cleveland Browns saw it and told his father about it and that started the process that got this guy into the NFL.

In May of 1973, John got a phone call at his home in Milton-under-Wychwood in the Cotswalds in England. John said that "he got a call on a Tuesday night from this lad" asking him to be at the TWA desk on Thursday morning to come over for a four day tryout with the New England Patriots. John was engaged to be married on June 2, but called his fiancé and said "look, this American lad wants me to go over for tryouts. I'll just go over and eat steaks and come back, and she said 'fine, just be back for the wedding'." So he came over and was brought to Foxboro and he impressed Chuck Fairbanks, the Patriot Head Coach, enough to have him come back for training camp.

Not only was John not familiar with the game of football before that training camp, he had the unusual experience of running out onto the field and making his first kick without wearing a helmet. This happened during the training camp of what would be John's first season with the Patriots, when the Patriots were scrimmaging the Washington Redskins. John described the funny situation saying, "There were three fields there and I was one of several kickers who were there. I was the least experienced. I had never seen a game before, never played the game. I was on the third field away from where they were. Everyone else was watching the scrimmage. I had no clue. I didn't even know what a down was. So I'm over there juggling a soccer ball, and doing my own sprints and warm-ups on my own, thinking they'll never need me." All of a sudden he heard a coach call "John Smith, get over here" and so he raced in and kicked the ball. When he got to the sideline, Chuck Fairbanks asked him "Where is your helmet?" and John realized that he had left it on the practice field. When John told the story I asked him "the key thing is, did you make the field goal?" and John proudly responded, "36 yarder, my first one, right down the middle!"

After that auspicious start, John went on to be one of the best kickers in team history. His 692 points, for example, are third in Patriot history, behind only Adam Vinatieri and Gino Cappelletti.

I asked John what he thought of Chuck Fairbanks, his first NFL coach, and he said "I thought he was a great guy. He was very, very intense, very quiet. He was a great judge of talent. Everybody that he had around him [his assistant coaches] were top people. He delegated. I liked him because when I made the team he would come up to me in pre-season, when there were a couple of kickers there competing with me and he'd come up to me and say 'all right, John, I'm going to cut the kickers. It's your job. Don't let me down. He wouldn't talk to me the rest of the season. When he knew what you could do, he let you do your job."

John contrasted that hands-off, leave-it-to-the experts approach to the very hands-on and less positive style of Ron Meyer, who was John's coach later in his Patriot career, and also Bill Parcells, for whom John did not play, but with whom he was familiar. John started by saying that, after Fairbanks, "I had other coaches who were completely neurotic, who just absolutely couldn't handle the situation that they were in. Every day they had to try to make you uneasy. They tried to keep you on edge. There are two different types of coaches, the negative, the guys who think that their job is to tear you down and then build you back up the way that they want you. Then there's the positive that take your weaknesses and strengths and build on them. And they are builders, and they create opportunities for players to develop." John recalled that Fairbanks' and his assistants' style was the more positive, while he felt that Meyer and Parcells were the opposite.

- - -

Talking about that team under Fairbanks led us to talk about that infamous playoff game in Oakland in 1976. Like the other interviewed players who had talked about that game, John remembered it with a mixture of regret and frustration. His first reaction was "That was quite devastating. We had absolutely crushed them during the season. We had such a great bunch of guys. We were so confident and we had so much talent. We had this belief that we were the best team." Then, he continued, "We went to Oakland and the way that it finished was tough to take. But the other thing was that Russ Francis got absolutely physically beat up on two plays by Phil Villapiano that would have been touchdowns. It was almost like we were in Al Davis' territory and we weren't going to leave it the way that we wanted." He also recalled before the game that the conditions of the field were horribly skewed to favor the Raiders, saying "we get there and the grass is like 6 inches long. Trying to kick the ball was like trying to hit the ball off the tee with a nine iron. The grass was so thick and when we got out there, it hadn't rained in a while, and the doggone field was wet. I'm sure that they watered the field down" to favor the slower Oakland team.

- - -

Not surprisingly, it did not take us long to turn our attention to his field goal in that famous snow plow game in December, 1982, a 3-0 win over the Dolphins. I asked John to take me through how that happened. As John remembered, "in the pre-season I tore a cartilage and had a cartilage operation, so Coach Meyer wanted to put me on injured reserve. He didn't like me from the beginning. He came in and thought he was going to sweep clean the veterans and do it his way. The week before that game he was going to bring me back. He called me and said 'I've got two other kickers and you. You're going to kick from Monday to Thursday, and whoever wins the kicking contest plays against the Miami Dolphins.' I said 'Fine, no problem.' I beat the living daylights out of both of them. Meyer came up to me at the end and says 'you played with their minds, didn't you?' and I said 'Coach, nobody comes in here and takes my job. I told you that I was better than they were. He just didn't like veterans at that time. The guy was a useless football coach."

Then it was on to the game. John describes the conditions as bad, since the day before the game "we had torrential rain and it freezes, so there is ice on the field. About 6:00 in the morning, a Nor'easter comes in. It starts snowing like a son of a gun. We get to the field, now there is snow on top of ice. Early in the game we go down the field for a short field goal. It's only about 20, 30 yards. Ron Meyer can't make a decision whether to run on fourth down or kick a field goal. He takes *forever* to make a decision. I'm on the sideline and all of a sudden he shouts 'field goal'. I run on the field, the holder was Matt Cavanaugh. There is not even a huddle. I'm running toward Matt and he shouts 'Set.' The ball gets sent back, I swing at the ball, and it hits John Hannah in the butt. I just slip up in the air cause I had no chance to clear the snow and land on my butt." John went on,

"My best buddy on the team is Steve Grogan. I come to the sideline and said 'son of a gun, Steve, I had to beat out two kickers this week to make the doggone team, now I miss. I won't even be here next week'. He smiled at me and said 'don't worry, Smitty, I'll get you in range'. Toward the end of the game, he comes up to me in the last few minutes and says 'Smitty, how close do I have to get you?' I said 'Steve, you've got to get me inside the 40, but what I need is a timeout cause I have to dig out the snow and I have to dig out the ice' so he says 'OK, I'll do that.' So he gets me in range, calls a timeout, and we go out. Matt Cavanaugh is clearing out one area with his shoes. I'm clearing out another area, digging out the ice with my shoes, clearing the snow.

All of a sudden the tractor comes out. We had already dug out the areas. The guy comes along and does a little veer. But what he actually did was he brushed snow on Matt where Matt was clearing the area. We had to actually move the spot. I made the kick. We win the game. I run into the locker room, and all of a sudden the tractor driver is the absolute talk of the town. Coach Shula was irate because the guy made this little veer but it wasn't the veer that made it, it was the fact that I was able to have Matt dig out the ice where my standing foot was going to be and I could dig out the ice where I could push off. That was the difference. Not a darn thing to do with the snowplow."

John added that because he had made the kick that won the game, Meyer could not cut him the next week.

- - -

Our Player Word Association led to John's comments about the following players:

Steve Grogan – tough as nails; most intense athlete I've ever met; if he had players around him like the San Francisco 49ers, there would have been no Joe Montana; if you had to go to war and have one guy that you want to pick to be your back: Steve Grogan

Tony Eason – I think I'd still be kicking if he hadn't been drafted. Meyer was absolutely infuriated when Steve Grogan won the job over his draft choice and he was so annoyed, he made Eason hold. Eason had never held in his life, didn't like holding, and he was atrocious at it

John Hannah – intense

Russ Francis – [after a few seconds of thinking] flamboyant

Sam Cunningham – introverted, very quiet; a great talent, an incredible physical athlete; very humble guy

Gino Cappelletti – super guy; his nickname is The Duke and that was appropriate – he was an awesome guy

Adam Vinatieri – I think he's the best kicker ever, great leg, ice in his veins; with the kicks that he has made he's the best kicker that I've seen since I've been over here

Stephen Gostkowski – very good, he has a super leg, he's going to have a very long career; he's very big for a kicker, very strong, very accurate; I think he'll break all the records for the Patriots

The comment about John's troubles with Eason as a holder led me to ask John who was the best holder during his NFL career and John said that it was Mike Patrick, the Patriot punter from 1975-78, about whom John said "great hands, super cool, put the ball down, spun the laces, the guy was the best holder I ever had". John said that "you were better off having a punter" as a holder instead of a quarterback, "because most of the time, a lot of the quarterbacks are prima donnas and don't want to hold."

- - -

When asked about the most memorable games in his career, John mentioned that "the snow plow kick is one that a lot of people remember", but also added a game against the Pittsburgh Steelers in 1976 when "the Steelers were like THE team and I remember playing them in Pittsburgh and we beat them 30-27 on a field goal; that was pretty special, beating Pittsburgh in Pittsburgh, when they still had a lot of those guys" who would win 4 Super Bowls in six years. He also remembered kicking five field goals in a game in San Diego.

Like most players of that era, when I asked if there was a game that John could replay if he could it was "definitely that Oakland game". He went on to add, 'It's funny. There is a little side story. I did British television for 5 years ... one of the stories that we did was interview John Madden [the Oakland coach in that game] about his bus, driving the bus around the country [to broadcast NFL games] ... we went to his hotel and I was interviewing him and I had this list of questions to ask him, and we sat down at a table for a live interview. He puts his hand on the table, and on his hand is that Super Bowl ring. I didn't even look at the questions, I said 'Oh-h, that's the ring that you stole from us, huh?' Oh my God, what an interview that was." I asked if it was good or bad, and John said, "It was awesome. He said 'son of a gun, you Patriots are still fighting over that game? I can't believe it."

- - -

John still spends a lot of his time running soccer camps. He said that he has been doing so for 38 years and "this is my love". He "started the first indoor soccer center in New England in 1988 and just started my first soccer club, called the John Smith Academy" and said that he "really enjoys being out with the kids" teaching them soccer. "I can't really wait to get onto the field. I have never really had a job for a long time. I just play with kids." Good for him, and lucky for those kids to have someone like John to teach him.

Not a bad NFL career (and after) for someone who had never seen a football game before playing in one and who just came over after getting the tryout invitation "to eat some steaks" and then go back to England. I guess that is both Old England and New England blood running through John's veins these days.

Len St. Jean
Patriot Career: 1964-1973

Position Played: Guard
College: Northern Michigan

As was the case with Jon Morris, Len St. Jean was drafted in 1964 by both the Boston Patriots (in the ninth round of the AFL draft) and the powerful Green Bay Packers, who were in the midst of establishing themselves as a pro football dynasty (in the seventeenth round of the NFL draft), "and the Boston Sweepers", Len St. Jean added during our July 2009 interview for this book. The Sweepers were a team in the minor Atlantic Coast Football League which played its games in Everett, MA and New Bedford, MA.

Len had played college ball at Northern Michigan, so the Packers took it for granted that he would stay in the Midwest and sign with them. However, Len said that his coach at Northern Michigan, Frosty Ferzacca, was friends with Mike Holovak, the Head Coach of the Boston Patriots, and that Frosty recommended Len to Mike and the Patriots to Len. In addition, Len, who had played defensive end in college, was told by the Packers that they wanted him to play guard, where he would back up Jerry Kramer and Fuzzy Thurston, two of the NFL's best at that position. Ironically, though Len came to Boston and played defense for two years, he was shifted to guard after that and had his success at that position.

Len didn't know what to expect when he joined the Patriots, explaining that "I had never seen a professional football game in my life. The first one I saw I played in." He did go on to say, "I came in with the mindset that I was going to make the team. After the first week, I saw that it was a family. We were definitely over-achievers, cohesive off the field and on the field. That's a tribute to Mike Holovak. That's the kind of atmosphere that Mike Holovak created."

While Mike Holovak was well respected by Len and the team, that was not the case with Clive Rush, who replaced Holovak as Head Coach. Len remembered Rush as "a nice guy, but as a football coach, I don't think so." Len recalled that the oddities with Rush started in the team's first meeting, where Rush introduced himself and started talking to the players "about health insurance, about life insurance" and everyone was wondering what was going on. Len said that Gino Cappelletti had "one of these laughing things" that you push and the sound of laughing comes out, "and Rush started talking, and Gino did this and everybody started laughing. Clive thought it was great. So the next day we had a meeting and he had it." Clive was using it himself. As I mentioned to Len, and he agreed, this is not what you'd expect from a Head Coach. Certainly, neither of us could imagine Vince Lombardi or any good head coach doing this.

As Len also mentioned, "His practices were unbelievable jokes. Sometimes practices would last an hour and half, sometimes just a half hour." Len also laughed about Rush's 'Black Power Defense' that some other interviewees had mentioned. He remembered Joe Namath bombing passes over it, completing one on a third and 37 that gave the Jets a first down. It was clear that the Black Power Defense was neither a success nor considered a positive in any way by any of the players.

Len also related an amazing story about the Patriots going to Cincinnati for a game during the same weekend that Ohio State, the top ranked team in college football, had a big game scheduled. Rush abandoned his team to attend the game on Saturday, and left an assistant in charge to get the team to Cincinnati, get them set in the hotel, and run the last walkthrough. Len said that Rush, who "used to drink pretty heavily" came in to the team dining room "at 9:45, three sheets to the wind and walks by our table and starts screaming 'Shut up. Shut up. What the hell is wrong with you guys? Don't you know where you're at? This is Paul Brown country. See that centerpiece right there? That's probably bugged.' Everybody's going 'Oh my God'." The players, as Len described it, looked at Rush incredulously.

This got even more incredulous for the players the next day. Len said that "Mike Taliaferro and Gino Cappelletti were his sounding boards. Rush had this idea and yelled 'Mike, Gino, get over here. You know what? I'm going to psych out that Paul Brown. I don't want the team to come out. I want you to stay in the locker room and bring the team out five minutes before the game.' So we said 'That's great. It's cold as hell out there.' The Bengals are out there working out, and Clive went and sat on the bench by himself. Paul Brown was probably saying 'Where the hell are the Patriots? And who's that derelict sitting on the bench?' So five minutes before the game out we come. We take the opening kickoff and take it right down the field, inside the five yard line. It's third down and about six inches, and Clive starts yelling "Gino! Gino! Get in there and kick a field goal.' And Gino says 'It's third down and six inches.' Clive says, 'I don't give a shit. It'll blow his G__D___ mind.' He went berserk. In the meantime we run the play and score." As Len put it, the players were wondering 'What's wrong with this guy?"

Later, Len told the story about how in the same game, Rush sent wide receiver Charley Frazier into the game. As Len recalled, "Here comes Charley into the huddle, sticks his head down, looks around, and turns around and runs right back out of the huddle. We thought that he forgot the play or something. But that is what Clive wanted him to do, so that Paul Brown wouldn't know what we would be doing and think we were confused." The Patriots won the game 25-14, but I have to believe that it was more the case that a veteran team beat a young expansion team and not that these shenanigans by Rush, a not-so-great coach, allowed him to outsmart Paul Brown, one of the great coaches in NFL history.

For Len, the most memorable game of his Patriot career was also the game that he would most like to play over again, if he could. It was the final game of the 1966 season, where the Patriots traveled to Shea Stadium in New York for a Saturday afternoon game against the Jets. If the Patriots won, they would be playing the Kansas City Chiefs for the AFL Championship and the right to play in the first-ever Super Bowl, against the Green Bay Packers. The Patriots lost the game to the Jets 38-28 and thereby lost the AFL East title to Buffalo. It was a heart-breaking defeat for the players. As Len put it, "That game haunts me. I'll never forget it."

Another memorable game for Len was a 1964 game in Boston against Houston, which the Patriots won 25-24 on a last-second field goal by Gino Cappelletti. Len recalled that "The Oilers were ahead of us by two points with 11 seconds to go. It was unbelievable. Babe went back with the ball. Babe was not the fastest guy in the world. He's running and I'm back there with him. He ended up somehow getting knocked out of bounds. I'm sure if that game had been played in Houston, it would have been over. But I looked up and there was one second on the clock. Gino came in and it was kind of a sloppy field but he ended up kicking the field goal." The Patriots won the game.

Len also remembered games against Buffalo in 1973 in which O.J. Simpson ran over and through the Patriots for 250 yards in one game and 219 yards in the other. Simpson, a great player who will now be remembered more for off-the-field events involving the murder of his ex-wife, was on his way to becoming the first player in NFL history to rush for over 2,000 yards in a season, and this in a 14 game schedule. The Patriots certainly helped him with over 20% of those yards coming in those two games.

For Player Word Association, we talked about the following:

Babe Parilli – a great professional, always very well-prepared; he knew the opposition, he knew the defenses; that's what made him great, his knowledge of the game

Gino Cappelletti – class; the ultimate professional; articulate as a speaker; didn't possess great speed or jumping ability but he did it with smarts, he ran precise pass patterns; one of the classiest guys I ever played with; to this day he exudes class

Jon Morris – I'd put him in the same category; not the most physical guy in the world but he was one of the smarter centers; could read defenses; he always got himself into position to make the play; you couldn't fool Jon; we played against a lot of 4-3 defenses, if the linebacker dropped back into coverage, he'd help out and he always had a knack of knowing which guy needed help, which side

Tom Neville – he was the right tackle who played alongside me; fundamentally very sound, made very, very few mistakes; rarely blew his assignment

John Hannah – one of the most intense players I ever played with; his biggest asset was his running and blocking and his pulling ability; he had a knack for knocking defensive backs on their backs; intensity was a big part of his game

Bob Gladieux – oh geez, Harpo; what I remember most about Harpo was that he used to have a dog, Mr. Brown, that he brought everywhere; he was just one of the most likable guys that you'd ever meet; I don't think he ever started but he was a jack of all trades for us, we'd put him in at runner, receiver, kick returner, kick coverage

Jim Nance – for a span of about three years I'd put him in as one the top running backs of all time; when Jim was between 235 and 240 that was his weight; one of the most powerful backs that ever played the game; was an NCAA championship wrestler two years in a row; just one great football player whose downfall was that he had a sweet tooth; one of the nicest people in the world

In response to my question about who his toughest opponent was, Len said, "Jim Dunaway, who played with the Buffalo Bills. I had great battles with him. A guy that I probably worried about the most was Manny Fernandez. He was quick and strong. He was my biggest nemesis." Fernandez, a defensive end for Miami, was the player that both Len and agreed could, and maybe should, have been the MVP of Super Bowl VII for the undefeated Dolphins. Len had some colorful memories of other defensive linemen that he had faced, saying, "One of the truly great defensive tackles was Merlin Olsen. We only played him twice but what made him great was that he was a smart player. You could never fake him out. Mean Joe Greene was a great player but he would line up sideways, so there was only one way for him to go. I just went in there and got position and tried to make him go that way. Billy Ray Smith [Colts] would trash talk, use all kinds of vulgarity. He used to chew tobacco and spit tobacco juice down his face mask. He looked like a crazy person. You don't ever forget playing against him. Ray Jacobs [Bills] could head slap like a boxer. Ernie Ladd [Chargers] was seven feet tall. When you lined up across from him, you'd think that the lights went out."

With regard to what current or former Patriot that he did not play with would he have liked to have had as a teammate, Len immediately responded, "Oh geez yeah, Tom Brady. And Steve Grogan. I would put Grogan in the category of Gino of being a class guy. He was never a loud mouth, but if he said something, you listened. He would definitely be one I would have wanted to play with. If you were ever in a street fight, he's a guy you would want with you." That mirrored almost exactly what others had said about Grogan.

We talked about the AFL-NFL merger, and I asked Len what the players reactions were to the merger, how they felt about the Jets' big upset win in Super Bowl III that gave the AFL credibility, and who he looked forward to playing when the AFL teams started playing NFL teams after the merger. As was the case with the other interviewees who had played in the AFL, the Jets' win was a big moment, as Len said, "When the Jets beat Baltimore, that was one of the greatest feelings of redemption." The AFL had shown that they could compete on equal footing with the top teams of the NFL. Len went on to talk about some of the new challenges that he faced against the NFL's defensive linemen, saying, "Jethro Pugh of Dallas gave me a tough time. He was a big tall guy with long arms. He was unbelievable. We played Alex Karras and the Lions in an exhibition game in Montreal. He came in there and started bad-mouthing us, calling us bush league and everything, but Jon [Morris] and I moved him all over the field. He didn't have much to say after that."

I asked Len how he spends his time now that he is retired and how his health has been since he retired. He replied, "I had both knees replaced right after retirement. I worked for thirty years selling electronic components and retired a year ago last April and now I work my own hours at a referral company. I also run a golf tournament for a scholarship to be awarded to a student at the Ron Burton Training Village in Hubbardston; this is the fourth year that I have run the tournament. The scholarship is for a player who is going to Northern Michigan. It's a full scholarship." He praised both the Village and Burton, his former teammate for whom the Village is named, saying, "The Village emphasizes peace, love, patience, and humility. That was his motto. He never drank, smoked, or that type of thing. And his saying was 'People like nice people.' Ron Burton was probably one of the nicest people that ever walked the face of the earth. I don't think I ever heard him say a bad word about anybody." Ron, the father of Boston TV sports anchor Steve Burton, was a great running back for the Patriots in the 1960s. Len recalled with a smile how to Ron everyone was "Big Guy".

Len left the Patriots after the 1973 season. It was the team's first season under Chuck Fairbanks, and Len said that "I still felt capable of playing, but Chuck Fairbanks had other guys that he wanted to bring in. I went to the WFL and played another two years in that league under Babe Parilli."

This 'Big Guy', Len, still looked to be in good football shape when he and I met. He looked like he could still do a good job of moving defensive linemen all over the field. No offense to Green Bay fans, but I'm glad that he wound up doing that in New England.

Drew Bledsoe

Patriot Career: 1993-2001
Position Played: Quarterback
College: Washington State

Drew Bledsoe has to be included in any list of the most significant people in the history of the New England Patriot franchise. However, that may even be an understatement. He is one of the three people, along with Bill Parcells and Bob Kraft, who should get a lot of the credit for turning the franchise around and making it a strong organization and a regular title contender. Drew is also one of the classiest athletes ever to play in Boston in any sport. This is not only for his play on the field, but also a tribute to the professionalism that he showed in dealing with the good games and bad and highs and lows of being a pro sports figure. He represented himself, his family, and the Patriot organization with a lot of dignity and class. It would be great if the world of sports had more people like him in it.

Before Drew, Parcells, and later Kraft came along, the Patriots were almost an after-thought in the NFL, and often a laughing stock. With Parcells joining the team as coach, after a successful career coaching the New York Giants (including two Super Bowl Championships), the Patriots gained some instant credibility. With the addition of Drew Bledsoe, the Patriots now had a franchise quarterback around which they could build a contending team. When Kraft came along, they added stability and continuity to that mix.

A glance at the record book, and a trip through memories of great games past, shows how important Drew was to the Patriots on the playing field. In his nine years with the team, Drew accumulated more passing yards (29, 657), with more attempts (4,518), and completions (2,544) than anyone in Patriot history. He has the top four entries in the list of most passing yards in a game, all 400+ yard games, including a Patriot record 426 yards in a game against Minnesota in 1994. He holds Patriot and NFL records for most passes and completions in a game (completing 45 of 70 in that same game against Minnesota) and also threw 60 passes (completing 39) in a game against Pittsburgh in 1995. He was a Pro Bowl quarterback four times, including making the Pro Bowl team at age 22, at the time the youngest quarterback ever chosen for that honor.

There was much more to the importance of Drew Bledsoe than mere statistics, however. Drew Bledsoe was the 'face of the franchise' before the phrase 'face of the franchise' had become popular. He joined a team that was a distant fourth in fan interest in the four major sports in Boston. The Red Sox, Bruins, and Celtics were very popular; the Patriots were far from it. A high percentage of Boston fans cared very little about them. In fact, the team almost moved to St. Louis in 1992, but the arrival of Bledsoe and Parcells helped to keep that from happening. Suddenly you could see kids in blue # 11 Patriot jerseys playing in schoolyards and streets as football suddenly 'joined the big time' with the other sports in town.

Also, there was the courage and leadership Drew showed in so many ways. One example was his playing with a broken finger in 1998, and not only playing, but playing well, leading his team to late game victory drives over Miami and Buffalo despite the injury, winning both games with drives of 80+ yards culminated with a winning touchdown pass.

Most significantly, there was the afore-mentioned class that he showed with his work ethic and professionalism throughout his career, perhaps best exemplified by the way he handled having Tom Brady take over his job after Drew suffered a serious injury in 2001. Whereas other athletes of the modern era (for whatever period the modern era may encompass) might have generated controversy and kept themselves in the spotlight as they complained about the situation and created dissension, Drew, as will be described shortly, just 'put on his shoes and went to work' to help Brady and his teammates in any way he could. This endeared him even more to the passionate fans of New England sports who saw him as one of our own.

As one final example, when Drew's career with the Patriots came to an end, and he was traded to Buffalo, he took out a full page ad in the Boston newspapers to thank fans for supporting him during his time with the Patriots. Now *that* is classy.

- - -

Drew started his career with the Patriots as the top overall pick in the college draft. The choice was expected to be either Drew or Notre Dame quarterback Rick Mirer. Most New England fans (I was one) wanted the Patriots to draft Drew and were relieved when they did so. When we spoke for this interview, I asked Drew what his reactions were when he learned he would be coming to New England and what his first impressions were of Bill Parcells. He admitted that "growing up in the Northwest, I was about as far away as I could be from the Patriots and I wasn't that familiar with the Patriots." He said that he knew about players such as Andre Tippett, Steve Grogan, and Hugh Millen (a former University of Washington quarterback), and "was somewhat familiar with Boston as a sports town and how fervent the fans were, but I really had no idea what I was stepping into in terms of how important the sports teams are in Boston and the New England area."

Drew went on to talk about Parcells saying, "My first meeting with Bill was at the scouting combine [before the draft]. I obviously knew Bill, was familiar with his reputation and his past successes. My first meeting with him was pretty enjoyable. He can be somewhat charming when he's trying to be. We sat and visited. Obviously it's an intimidating deal when you're 20 and just coming out of school so I needed to try to impress him to be his first pick. We had a good meeting. We talked a little football, talked a little life, and got to know each other a little bit." He went on to comment that, after being drafted, "coming and playing for Bill as a rookie quarterback, the # 1 draft pick, was an interesting experience. He certainly didn't make things easy on me in practice, which there was a reason for. By the time I put up with all of his grief in practice, when it came time to take the field on Sunday, I was really looking forward to it, because I didn't have to listen to him any more. It was great." That got us both laughing. Parcells apparently rode Drew hard in trying to get him ready for the NFL. Fortunately, Drew was one who thrived on hard work, so he handled this very well.

In fact, things went so well that the team made the playoffs in Drew's second year, as they turned a 5-11 record in 1993, his first season, into a 10-6 record in 1994 and earned a spot in the playoffs as a wildcard team. They wound up losing to Cleveland 20-13 in that game but the game was close (10-10 at halftime, with the New England touchdown coming on a 13 yard pass from Drew) and it was clear the Patriots were a team on the rise.

That improvement reached fruition in 1996 as the team won the AFC East and then went on to the Super Bowl as AFC Champions. I asked Drew to describe the three playoff games that season. The first was a 28-3 win over Pittsburgh in an extremely foggy game at Foxboro Stadium. Drew described this as "one of my all-time favorite games" explaining, "First of all this was the first playoff game in New England in a long time, so obviously the fans were fired up, and we were excited … The fog gave an eerie feeling to the game. It seemed like the fog was almost a roof on the stadium, at least from a noise level standpoint. The stadium was far louder than it had ever been before."

Drew started the game in spectacular fashion, executing a perfect play action fake to Curtis Martin and then throwing a 53 yard completion to Terry Glenn "on the right sideline, over Rod Woodson", the Steelers' great defensive back, on the game's first play. Drew said, "You could almost feel the ground shake, it was so loud," from the noise of the crowd as that play happened. This led to an early touchdown and the Patriots were on their way to victory.

The next game was also at home, and Drew said, "we felt so fortunate to be playing at Foxboro" and they were, thanks to the Jacksonville Jaguars upsetting the top seeded team in the AFC, the Denver Broncos, the preceding week. Drew pointed out that since "the Broncos were so, so dominant that year" (and in fact would go on to win the Super Bowl after the next two seasons), it obviously would have been a very difficult challenge, and "nobody wanted to go play in Denver." Thanks to Jacksonville's win, they didn't have to do so.

The Patriots beat the Jaguars 20-6, scoring an early touchdown after a high snap on a Jaguar punt attempt gave them the ball on the Jaguar four yard line. Then, as they were lining up later for a field goal, Drew recalled that "the lights went out" at Foxboro Stadium (the kind of thing that seemed in line with the previous odd history of the Patriots), and were out for 11 minutes before power was restored. "It was pretty crazy, pretty weird", as Drew remembered. He did not mention, but I will, that he made two big plays to extend the lead to 13-3 at the half, a clutch five yard pass to Ben Coates on a fourth and three at the Jacksonville 45, followed by a long bomb to Shawn Jefferson that got the Patriots inside the five and set up a field goal just before the half.

The win over the Jaguars sent the Patriots to the Super Bowl where they were to face the Green Bay Packers. I asked Drew what it was like to prepare for the Packers and to play in that Super Bowl. He pointed out that "the Packers were so, so good" that year so the Patriots knew they would be in for a tough battle. He said the team "prepared well" for the game, but added, "it is a pretty crazy experience playing in your first Super Bowl. You have all the hype and hoopla leading up to the game, and then when you come out you feel the magnitude of the game." This is similar to what other interviewees have said about the Super Bowl, most notably John Hannah. This was further exacerbated for that 1996-97 Patriot team since a lot of the pre-game media focus went on to Bill Parcells' contract situation. He would leave the team after this season and go on to coach the Jets, and in fact, did not return with the team on the team flight home, which I have never understood and did not think was the right thing for a team leader to do. I asked Drew what the players thought about the controversy and distractions about Parcells before the Super Bowl leading up to his not returning on the team flight and he simply said, "that was disappointing."

The Patriots had a shot at winning the game, as we both agreed, and even took a 14-10 lead early thanks to two touchdown passes by Drew. However, he said that the Packers "were too tough a team for us that day", and "the thing about the Packers that gets lost in all the stories about Brett [Favre] and Desmond Howard was that they had the # 1 defense in the league. Their defense was so, so tough. Reggie White was in his first Super Bowl, going crazy. It was kind of an unfair position to put Max Lane in, where he ended up blocking Reggie one-on-one for a big chunk of the game and with Reggie playing in his first Super Bowl, he was an unstoppable force." However, he summed up the trip to the Super Bowl as "really cool, a really crazy experience being the starting quarterback in a Super Bowl". It was nice to hear how much it meant to him.

- - -

In the interest of time we jumped ahead to 2001 and the Patriots' next Super Bowl season. That was the season in which Drew had been badly injured against the Jets. He suffered a sheared blood vessel in his lung on a powerful hit by linebacker Mo Lewis while scrambling away from a pass rush and trying to get out of bounds on the right sideline. I asked Drew if he knew immediately how badly he was injured. He said, "No. I recognized that I had a concussion and that was why I came out of the game. Then when I went back into the game the next series" it became apparent something was badly wrong. He described a play after the injury in which "We had a very simple little check-with-me audible at the line of scrimmage. It was a running play and it was either going to go to the right or left and I had to make the call at the line of scrimmage. I knew that we were supposed to go to the left with it but I couldn't remember the word that we used to go to the left. I turned around to [fullback] Marc Edwards and said, 'Hey Mark, how do I go left?' and he told me 'Say odd.' so I said 'odd.' Then when I came to the sideline on the next series I grabbed Damon Huard [Patriot backup quarterback] and told him I needed to go over the two minute plays. We have only a handful of two minute plays and they are the same plays that you run from the start of training camp all the way through [the season] so under normal circumstances they were not something that I would want to go over. And so between the two of them, Marc and Damon, they went to the trainer and Charlie [Weis] and Bill [Belichick], and said, 'Hey, he's not all right' so that's when Tommy [Brady] came in.

"Then after the game I was headed for the locker room and Ron O'Neal, our trainer, grabs me and says 'Hey you need to come with me. You don't look very good.' I said 'I'll just go in for team prayer and then I'll come in here' and he said 'No. I think you need to come with me now.' I was just a little woozy but wasn't feeling much pain at that point. But when I got into the locker room, what tipped the team doctor off that there was a problem was that usually when you have a concussion and after a game your pulse will start to slow down pretty dramatically, but instead of slowing down, my pulse started racing pretty rapidly. Then the pain started and it started to hurt inside pretty bad to the point where I couldn't get myself undressed." The staff helped him get undressed, showered, and dressed and then they took him to Mass General Hospital. He couldn't take pain medication that was an anti-coagulant, and he was allergic to others, so "there were no pain-killers to be had, and by the time we got there, there was some pretty excruciating pain."

He went on to say, "They figured a guy my size would probably have 7 or 8 liters of blood total in my body, and when I got there they stuck a tube in my chest and they took 2 liters of blood out of my chest cavity. Then I was bleeding out at the rate of a liter an hour. The doctors at Mass General really stepped up." He indicated that the blood loss he had already suffered and the continuing blood loss rate were both double the criteria for them opening him up but "they elected to wait and allow the wound to start healing itself up while they were recycling my blood ... eventually, after four or five days in the hospital it did stop bleeding and I was able to go home, but it was a pretty touchy situation for a while."

Drew gave a lot of credit to Ron O'Neil, saying, He probably saved my life ... I was dead set on going in for team prayer and heading home. He looked at me and recognized that something wasn't right and said, 'No, you're coming with me.' Had he not done so and allowed me to go home that night I may not be here today." Wow!

- - -

While Drew was recovering, Tom Brady had taken over the starting quarterback role. We talked about that situation and the questions that were circulating when Drew was ready to return about who would be the starter. When the decision was made that it would be Brady, Drew said that it was "pretty frustrating" and explained that he always "thought the job would be there waiting for me" when he recovered "and it wasn't." Drew went on to describe this as "a pretty soul-searching time in my life because I think that anybody who played the game understands that at some point it's going to be over and there's going to be somebody there that's going to step into your job, but at the same time when you put yourself, your blood, sweat, and tears into an organization for eight plus years you feel like you're entitled to a shot. But at that point Tommy had been playing well enough that they didn't feel like they could take him out and I did some soul-searching and spent a long time talking to my wife and my dad and decided to put on my shoes and get to work."

As any Patriot fan can attest, despite his disappointment, Drew handled the situation in an extremely professional and classy way. He did not complain. He did not sulk. He did 'go to work' and did his best to help Tom Brady become a better quarterback and he always got himself prepared to come in if needed. I mentioned to him how much most fans really admired and appreciated him for this and he responded, "I appreciate it. To me it's fairly simple. In life you are always faced with choices and faced with difficult situations and you can look at things and you can determine that there is a right way to handle this and there's a wrong way and it was pretty cut and dried that the right way to do it was to show up and go to work and continue to put the team first and continue to help Tom. It wasn't easy and it wasn't what my knee-jerk reaction was, but it was quite simply just the right way to handle it." This, to me, is an outstanding example of teamwork, and should serve as a role model for athletes everywhere.

Drew did get a chance to play a big role in the AFC Championship Game against Pittsburgh. Drew said that he had "prepared very well" for that game, and added that he "had a feeling more than any other game since this injury happened that I may end up in this game." Sure enough, he did. Tom Brady injured his ankle late in the first half on a late, unnecessary hit by a Pittsburgh tackler and had to leave the game, and for Drew "it was go time again", as he put it, as he came into the game. He said, "For me it felt like something had been snatched way from me and then all of a sudden I'm back in the game. It was a little bit of a surreal experience stepping back on the field again and into the huddle." Drew completed his first pass, a 15 yarder to David Patten, completed his first three passes, and connected with Patten for a touchdown just before halftime that gave the Patriots a 14-3 lead on their way to a 24-17 win. Drew shared one great memory, saying "I remember at the end of that game, the clock's winding down, taking a knee, I remember just kind of being overwhelmed with all that happened. It was pretty emotional. To have all that transpired early in the season and then to have a chance to play and have a chance to win that ball game, it was pretty magical. The other thing that was interesting was that without my knowledge my dad and one of his buddies had just decided that they were going to show up at that game. I didn't know until the night before. We had landed as a team and I got a call from my dad saying 'hey, want to come by the hotel?' and I said 'I didn't even know that you were in town.' I remember when we were standing at the podium after the game, whenever I had a chance to kneel down with the ball at the end of the game I would always keep the ball and walk off the field with it. Generally we would hold on to them or gave them away to friends or family. I had that ball with me as my dad made his way down the field and I saw him and fired that ball at him, and he still has held on to that ball and has it in his trophy case." Thus, his father has the last ball that Drew used in his last game as a Patriot. It's a nice family story and sounds so typical of the class that Drew Bledsoe always displayed.

- - -

I asked Drew what his most memorable game was as a Patriot. He hesitated for a while, saying, "you know, there were so many memorable games" and ultimately singled out three. The first two were the two playoff games with the Steelers, the one in the fog in 1996 and the one just mentioned in which he came off the bench and helped the team to victory. He also mentioned a game that stuck in my memory as well, a game against Minnesota in November, 1994. Drew remembered, "We had really been struggling. We were 3-6 coming into the game and we were in a pretty big hole just before halftime [trailing 20-3]. Parcells had this reputation of playing smash mouth football but he was far more aggressive than that offensively. At halftime he said 'All right, kid, you've got it. We're going two minute.' We went into the two minute offense for the whole second half. We threw it 50 something times after halftime [53 to be exact] and came back and won the game in overtime." It was won on a 14 yard touchdown pass from Drew to Kevin Turner in the left side of the end zone. He added, "I remember distinctly after that pass -- I made a conscious effort when I came out of college ... there were some games that we won in college that I felt like just passed me by and I didn't take a second to really remember what was going on on the field – so I just did that after that play. I made a conscious effort to look around me and soak it all in. The fans were going crazy. The players were rushing onto the field. I kind of took a step back and was able to soak it all in. It was pretty cool."

The main reason that the Patriots won that game (26-20) was Drew's performance. He threw 70 passes in that game (still a team record), 53 of them in the second half, and completed 45, also a team record that still stands. It was a great game to watch as a fan, and, obviously from Drew's comments, a great game in which to have played. It is worth adding that this thrilling come-from-behind win started the Patriots on a seven game winning streak that made their final record 10-6 and put them into the playoffs.

On the flip side, I also asked if there was a game or play that he would like to play over if he could. He joked, "I'm retired now. I don't have to relive the negative stuff." He did point out one game, however. It was the next-to-last game of the 1997 season against (who else) Pittsburgh. It was a Saturday game, nationally televised, and the winner would have a first round bye and home field advantage should the teams meet in the playoffs as it appeared they would. The Patriots were ahead 21-13 and had the ball near midfield with just over two minutes to play, and the Steelers having no timeouts. Drew threw a pass to the right sideline that was intercepted by Pittsburgh linebacker Kevin Henry. The Steelers tied the game and won in overtime and the Patriots wound up going to Pittsburgh for the playoff game and losing there. Drew said, "the interception that late in the game against the Steelers was a heartbreaker", but explained "we really had the game iced. It was just one of those plays. The guy making the interception was playing nose tackle and he was not supposed to drop into coverage on the play. He admitted afterward that he was totally out of position on the play, was not supposed to be where he was. Because he was playing defensive line and was not supposed to be there I just totally didn't see him, didn't expect him to be there. I just dropped back, it was a blitz, and I had to throw it hot to David Meggett and when I threw it, there was Henry right there and catches it. It was a complete and utter shock to me when the ball wound up in his hands ... to have it then go into overtime and not be able to pull it out was pretty disheartening." I was not surprised at this being the play Drew would like to have over as I remember watching that game and being surprised and frustrated at how what looked like a sure victory had turned into defeat. Drew's feeling of shock is completely understandable.

- - -

We then did the Player Word Association exercise that I have done with other interviewees in which I would name a player and ask Drew to say the first thing that comes into his mind about that player:

Ben Coates – tough, fast; maybe with exception of Troy Brown had the best hands of any receiver that I ever played with; he was too strong for the defensive backs, and too fast for linebackers, so they really didn't know what to do with the guy when he was in his prime; Ben, as much as probably just about any of my teammates, was responsible for whatever level of success that I had; if I needed a play and was dropping back and didn't have any other options I would just look at Ben and he would catch it

Curtis Martin – a bit of a surprise; in the first regular season game that we played against the Browns [in Curtis' rookie season] Curtis just exploded; from then on he was a pleasure to watch; there were certain players that as a fellow player you just enjoy watching and I had a great seat to watch Curtis work for the time when we were together. There were times when he would make defenders look silly. I remember a time against the Jets when he made the guys look like little kids because not only could they not tackle him, they couldn't touch him. He was an absolute class act; a *tremendous* football player. Because he was so quiet and understated I think that he maybe doesn't get mentioned as much as he should in the conversation about the best running backs ever, but he certainly deserves to be in that conversation.

Troy Brown – The first day that I showed up for rookie camp in New England I called my Dad after the first practice and mentioned one player by name and it was Troy Brown; he was a guy who absolutely stood out. We had a great relationship for the years that we were together there. I had tremendous faith in Troy as a receiver … and Troy went on to justify that faith and confidence for years to come; he was truly a special player.

Terry Glenn – I love Terry; his relationship with the organization and fans was a bit of a rocky road but Terry is a guy that I have great personal affection for and tremendous respect for as a football player. He was phenomenally gifted, but what people don't recognize or don't know about Terry is that he is and was a phenomenally smart football player – he really knew where to be, when to be there, and I always felt like when Terry was on the field I could count on him to be in the right place at the right time and to be open … fast, smart, great hands, he was THE best wide receiver I ever played with and I played with a lot of them. If he had been able to stay healthy the story on him and his relationship there would be far different.

Lawyer Milloy – one of the toughest football players that I ever played with; he was a guy that always played bigger than he was and played with an attitude that he was not going to let the other team score. It was just a very personal challenge that he put on himself that raised the level of the defense around him; it was very personal that the other team, whoever our opponent was, was not going to score if Lawyer was on the field. That was really his attitude. Some people define a great player as somebody who raises the level of the people around him and Lawyer was one of those guys. If he was on the field the defense was going to play better, and guys individually would play better, than if he were not on the field. He was a tremendous player, a great teammate, a great person, and playing against him on a daily basis in practice made me better.

Tom Brady – Tommy [as Drew called him] - people would probably expect some level of animosity that I would have toward him but I don't. When he arrived as a rookie he was a guy that I immediately liked. He was, is, and continues to conduct himself as a classy person that has a very genuine humility. I was happy to take him under my wing; we had him over to the house for dinner a number of times and he was always great with the kids and with my wife and all of those things, but then as a teammate, watching him in practice, even as a rookie or on the scout team the guys really responded to him. He's got an infectious personality, and when he was on scout team they would have some success against our defense. I'll say this: it's been gratifying to me to watch Tommy's career not only on the field but off the field and the way that he's continually conducted himself while getting all the accolades that he has. I always thought that if somebody needed to take my job he had to be somebody special and he has continued to prove that he is a special player and a very classy person.

After hearing all of this, and particulary the comment about Tom Brady, who, after all, is the man who took Drew's job, my feeling was 'Wow! What great - and very nice - comments.' Drew again and again showed himself to be a class, outstanding person.

Continuing with the discussion of Patriot players, I asked Drew if there was any current or former Patriot that he had not played with that he would have liked to have had as a teammate. The player he mentioned was Irving Fryar, saying, "Irving Fryar was with the Pats the year before I got there. I know that he had a rocky relationship with the Patriots, but having to go play against him when he went to the Dolphins and the career that he put together after that with the Dolphins and then the Eagles, I've always been kind of curious about what that would have been like had he stayed in New England with me. That was kind of intriguing to me."

Drew also made the point of saying that he "got to play with and got to know some of the greats. Playing with Andre Tippett was really a cool experience. He was the grizzled vet when I got there. He really kind of took me under his wing a little bit, even as a linebacker. I got a chance to get to know Steve Grogan very well when I was out there and he's a guy that I have tremendous respect for. Talking with guys who played with him about the way that he approached the game, the toughness he brought to the game was pretty cool."

Our time was running out so I asked Drew how he is feeling now that he is retired and how he spends his time. He answered, "I have transitioned into retirement as well as I could have hoped. When it came time for me to retire I knew it was time. I didn't second guess it. I stepped away from the game and because of that I've been able to really enjoy this next phase of life. I have four young children, from [age] 11 down to 6 and I get to spend a lot of time with them, coaching some of their youth sports teams. I also moved into the business world. We've got a winery in my old hometown of Walla Walla. We're really excited about our first vintage that will be bottled later this month and then released in the spring of 2010. We also have an investment group that we have put together and we are currently working on a project that I am really excited about that has the potential to be both a very successful business and make a positive impact in a pretty significant way on the world. We've got a water purification technology that can clean up the dirtiest water in the world and do it at high volume. We are currently working with the natural gas industry to clean up their waste stream, but the applications for this technology can keep us busy for the next 10 or 15 years and all over the world cleaning up dirty water and supplying a good, clean water stream in places where you wouldn't ordinarily see it." Clearly this sounds like a great idea and something which could be really beneficial world-wide. It is easy to envision Drew being successful at these ventures, given the drive and leadership that he showed during his football career, and given the motivation about these projects that seemed to come through as he was describing them.

Drew said, "I look back with great fondness at my football career. I'm proud of the accomplishments that I had, but at the same time that was a phase in my life and I'm moving on to the next phase now and enjoying that immensely."

As we were finishing our discussion, Drew added "The one thing that I would like to have come across is that, being a 21 year old kid from the wheat fields in Washington State and getting transplanted to Boston and the Northeast, and, as I indicated earlier, it was a bit of a shock to find out just how big a part of people's daily lives the sports teams are in Boston. It just isn't quite the same in the Pacific Northwest. People love their teams and love their college teams but it was a very different level. To come out to New England and be embraced by those fans for nine years was a great experience. I felt extremely fortunate that I was able to play in New England and to experience those fans and to be adopted to a certain extent as one of their own was something that was very flattering and something that I greatly, greatly appreciate, and *miss* to a great extent. It was a really great time in my life."

There were plenty of 'wow' moments that I felt during the interview with Drew, as I listened to him talk about his memories of his teammates, the way that he handled his injury situation in 2001, his reactions in the Minnesota comeback win early in his Patriot career and the AFC Championship game in Pittsburgh late in that career, his new business ventures, and then especially as he made his comments in the preceding paragraph about his relationships with, and feelings about, the fans. He talked about feeling fortunate to play in New England and experience that, but in my opinion, it is we fans in New England who were fortunate to have Drew. He helped save the franchise, was instrumental in turning a whole generation of Red Sox and Celtics fans into Patriot fans as well, gave us many thrills on the field, and showed us how to do it all with dignity and class. Thank you, Drew – it was a great time for us as well.

Lawyer Milloy

Patriot Career: 1996-2002
Position Played: Defensive Back/Safety
College: Washington

Lawyer Milloy's career with the New England Patriots was highlighted by two Super Bowl trips. The first was in his rookie year, 1996, when he quickly established himself as an NFL player, appearing in every game that season and starting the last ten. The second was his next-to-last season in New England, 2001, by which team he was unquestionably a team leader, not just for the defense, but a recognized leader for the whole team. When he was released by the Patriots just before the 2003 season, his departure seriously impacted the whole team, as player after player lamented his loss and complained about the organization and the decision to release him. As noted in Chapter 6, even Tom Brady, who has always been very positive in his praise of the organization, was critical of that decision. The team was definitely affected in its next game and wound up being crushed 31-0, ironically by Lawyer's new team, the Buffalo Bills, where Lawyer would also become a team leader.

- - -

These situations were well in the future when Lawyer finished his college career at the University of Washington, one of the nation's top collegiate programs, and prepared for the 1996 NFL draft. As we talked about this during our interview for this book, Lawyer described the NFL draft process as "nerve-wracking" and explained, "You are at the top in college", and then you are "going to the combine" to try to impress some team into taking you. "I wanted to be in the first round.", Lawyer continued, both for the recognition and that was where the bigger contracts were, but, "I had broken my right foot in my last game, so I could not participate in the combine ... from individual workouts you start to hear what teams want you and where you might go in the draft. From there, I kind of knew where I was going, late first round or early second. I really thought I was going to Kansas City." This was based on his meetings and discussions with the Chiefs. Instead, he went to New England in the second round. The Patriots had drafted wide receiver Terry Glenn with their first pick, and would draft linebacker Tedy Bruschi in the third round, so this draft helped build the Patriot team that would ultimately play in multiple Super Bowls.

However, when I asked Lawyer what his reaction was when he learned that he would be coming to New England, he indicated that he was surprised. He said, "I had sat down with [Bill] Parcells", New England's Head Coach, before the draft, but that the meeting really was a "matter of fact interview. He asked me what I bring to the table and I just told him that I am going to work hard and try to be dependable. That's what I did in college. That's what was instilled in me at the University of Washington ... It was really a quick, short interview." He did not expect the Patriots to draft him, especially since he felt that Kansas City would. He laughingly pointed out that when he heard that it was New England, "I just remember coming into Boston – I had never been to Boston – when they said New England, at first I didn't even know what state I'd be playing in until I actually flew into Boston. I'm an educated guy but when you hear England you just think of London or something. I knew it was New England, but I didn't know if it would be Boston or somewhere else."

When he came to Boston soon after the draft he felt that Boston was a good city, but he was surprised to see that there was still snow on the ground in April, and even more surprised when he was taken to Foxboro Stadium. He found the stadium to be "a downgrade from what I had experienced at the University of Washington." Having seen the U of Washington Stadium, and having been to many games at Foxboro Stadium, I would have to agree. The facilities and amenities for New England's pro football team were indeed less than what college players could enjoy at such schools as Washington, Alabama, Texas, Southern Cal or any of the big programs. Lawyer did go on to add that, despite his first impressions, "It turned out that I ended up in the right situation for me." He and the team did indeed have success immediately and through much of Lawyer's time with New England.

I asked Lawyer about his first reactions to Bill Parcells, whose gruff reputation and biting, sarcastic comments to and about players were well known in NFL circles. Lawyer indicated that he did not have any problems with Bill, and explained that, "Since I came up under Don James [the Head Coach at the University of Washington], I was very workhorse-minded. At Washington you kind of just shut up and did your job and everything else on Saturday was easy. Because of that, it kind of prepared me for a coach like Parcells. Terry Glenn was drafted in the first round. I was the second round pick, so the parade was all for him. I kind of flew under the radar. I was working hard, showed up, never said too much. Terry Glenn got most of the attention." That's for sure. This was the training camp in which Glenn was slow to get started due to injury, and Parcells, when asked at one point by a reporter how Glenn was doing responded that "She's coming along." It was an attempt to motivate Glenn to act like a man and get on the field.

Lawyer recalled that he was doing well in training camp but wasn't sure how Parcells was viewing him. He said that he watched Parcells "trying to break people. It didn't matter if you were a first round pick, or a second round pick. He worked everyone hard to see how you reacted and who he could trust in a war." He said that he saw a lot of people get that treatment and "One day it was my turn." He explained that Parcells "got behind me one day when I was lining up with the second string back then, and I heard him say '36' [referring to Lawyer's number, as Parcells sometimes did with players], and "I just thought 'oh crap, it's my turn' and he said 'you think you're a tough shit' and I didn't say anything. He said 'Well, I'm watching you. Let's see what you've got.' I just turned around to him and nodded my head. In my head I said 'OK I've got to do something. I've got make something happen right now.' That's as long as I had to think about it. The ball was hiked. The running back came through the hole. And I just crushed him. I had a good hit on him. As I was going back, I kind of peeked at Parcells with my peripheral vision and he saw me looking at him and he just nodded his head and walked away, so I said 'whew'." Lawyer knew he had arrived.

The Patriots were very successful in Lawyer's rookie season, finishing 11-5, winning the AFC East, and not only making the playoffs but getting a first round bye. Lawyer felt that he "hit the wall" midway through his rookie season, but noted that he "started every game after the sixth game". He credited fellow defensive back Willie 'Big Play' Clay for helping him in that season, saying "I was lucky to have Willie Clay. He was not the most talented guy but he really knew the game." They were indeed a great duo in the New England defensive backfield. Lawyer explained it that "I'd go in and do the dirty work and he'd sit back and direct the team, get us lined up so we could do our job" since Willie knew where everybody should be and what they should be doing.

The team's first playoff game was with Pittsburgh. That was the game played in that fairly dense fog that hung over Foxboro Stadium, giving the game an "eerie feeling" as Drew Bledsoe described during his interview. Lawyer and the defense played very well, holding the Steelers without a touchdown in a 28-3 win. Lawyer said that "Belichick [at the time the Assistant Head Coach and Defensive Backfield Coach] and Parcells came up with some good defensive schemes. On first and second down we were kind of vanilla. On third and long the defensive backs would fake a blitz and then drop back. I remember that I got an interception," Lawyer recalled.

Jacksonville was New England's next opponent, and the first thing that Lawyer remembered about that game was "That was probably the coldest game in my NFL career. With the wind chill it was like negative 15." Nevertheless, as Lawyer said, "the fans were inspired" by the Patriots hosting an AFC Championship game and with the thought that the team's momentum would carry them into the Super Bowl. Another great game by the defense, again holding their opponent without a touchdown, was the key in New England's 20-6 win that did send them to the Super Bowl against Brett Favre and a very strong Green Bay Packer team.

I asked Lawyer about the preparations for that Super Bowl game and he said, "We practiced so hard ... it was like training camp again. It actually didn't feel like we were going to a Super Bowl because we were working so hard." He went on to talk about the different atmosphere at that game from any other game, as did other players that I had interviewed, saying that the game was different right at the start, explaining that, "You come out, go through the motions, trying to make it a normal game. But I'm sitting there stretching and there is Luther Vandross right next to me. It's a star-studded event, and everyone's eyes are on us, but you try not to think about that kind of stuff." It's certainly a far cry from a December game in ice-cold Buffalo or chilly Foxboro.

The game was close for a while, with the Patriots even taking a 14-10 lead after the first quarter but the Packers went on to a 35-21 victory. Green Bay took the lead for good in the game on an 81 yard touchdown pass in the second quarter from Favre to Antonio Freeman. Lawyer blamed himself for that saying that he had the coverage, adding "I had never really played man-to-man. I got up too close and Brett Favre read that." Favre changed the play to take advantage of it. Willie Clay gave him encouragement, but Lawyer recalled that he was chasing Freeman but "with 20 yards to go I just shut it down and went to the sideline" knowing that he couldn't catch Freeman, and "I didn't want to be part of the celebration. The first person that I saw was Parcells, who kind of looked at me and shook his head." Lawyer went on to add, "I watched the replay [of that game] for the first time last year."

As I had done with Drew Bledsoe, I asked Lawyer about how distracting to the team was the situation with Bill Parcells and all the media attention to his contract situation, and then about Parcells not returning with the team on the team flight home. Lawyer commented, "I think everybody knew the whole year that there was the possibility that he was not going to be our coach the following year, but it kind of shocked everyone because of the way it happened, the stage that we were on, the way that he didn't really address the team, didn't fly back on the plane with us. As a rookie, I didn't understand that, but I heard some things on the plane about Parcells not flying back with us. I didn't say too much."

Parcells went on to coach the arch-rival Jets. After three years under Pete Carroll, the Patriots hired Bill Belichick as their new Head Coach. Bill had been the defensive backfield coach in Lawyer's rookie season, so I asked Lawyer what he thought about Belichick coming in as Head Coach. He responded, "I was happy. I was familiar with him. If anything, I knew that we would be a well prepared team because that's how we were in my rookie year." Lawyer also went on to talk about the fact that "Bob Kraft came and asked me about Bill Belichick before he was hired." This was a nice move, but also unusual as Lawyer pointed out, since Lawyer was a free agent that year. He did have some kind words for Pete Carroll though too, saying, "Pete Carroll put me on the map. He wanted me to be like the 49er defensive backs, like Tim McDonald" and that helped Lawyer develop in his career to the extent that Lawyer "went to my first Pro Bowl under Pete" in 1998.

Lawyer wound up being a four time Pro Bowler during his Patriot career, in 1998, 1999, 2001, and 2002.

After a 5-11 season in 2000, the Patriots took off in 2001 and wound up winning their first Super Bowl. I asked Lawyer what helped turn things around and he said, "The thing that stood out to me the most was Bill bringing in older guys during the off-season, like Roman Phifer and Bryan Cox. He needed a mixture of older guys who knew how he worked, were an extension of him, but still had some years in them, and who could get the ship going in the right direction. We had a very good mix of guys that worked hard together and didn't make mistakes." Lawyer was definitely one of those guys – a veteran leader who did not make mistakes.

Lawyer recalled being injured in the season-opening game against Cincinnati, and getting treatment for the injury on the Tuesday after that game. That was September 11, 2001, and Lawyer said that he was getting treatment for that injury when he heard the news about the terrorist attacks on the United States and the planes flying into the Twin Towers. "That whole morning the trainer and myself kept looking at the monitors, at the TVs with our mouths dropped, thinking about our country and what was going to happen next. It was a day that I'll never forget." It was an awful day, as any American old enough to be aware of what was happening that day can confirm. Lawyer recalled that the games the following Sunday were postponed and then "the next game was a very patriotic day. [Patriot guard Joe] Andruzzi and his brothers came out with the flag [Andruzzi's brother was a New York City fireman]. It wasn't really about football. It was a weird game. It was a moment of healing for our nation. I remember looking across the field at the Jets with a big flag between us and it was like, I really didn't want to go up against fellow Americans. But then the game started and we went back to hitting" and they had to do their jobs.

The game against the Jets was the game in which Drew Bledsoe was seriously injured and Tom Brady came in to replace him and help springboard the team to the Super Bowl. I asked Lawyer what it was like to prepare for that Super Bowl and the high-powered St. Louis Rams' offense that they would be facing. This was the team that had been nicknamed "The Greatest Show on Turf" and which was led by MVP quarterback Kurt Warner, outstanding running back Marshall Faulk and a fleet of speedy and good receivers. Lawyer said, "We were lucky that we had played them during the regular season. It was actually the last game that we lost that season. It was a close game on a Sunday night [24-17]. After the game we said 'hey they are the best team in the world and we played a really good game against them, so why not us' [for winning the championship]. We prepared hard to play them and that in-season game made our preparation that much easier going into the Super Bowl. We decided that when they got the ball we wanted to pound them and make them feel our presence." That is exactly what they did for the first three quarters, taking a 17-3 lead with the defense scoring one touchdown and setting up another.

The Rams, however, came back and tied the score 17-17, with Lawyer recalling that "defensively we were out there [on the field] pretty much the whole game and a little bit of fatigue set in", as they kept working hard to stymie the Ram offense. He went on to say that, after the Rams scored to make it 17-17, "When we sat down, we had a little bit of doubt. I was thinking 'We had played so, so well. This is my second time here and we've already lost one Super Bowl' and I hear above us old guys' voices coming back in my mind saying you might never get a shot again.' I told myself 'My teammates can't see me with any doubt' so I started getting up and telling my teammates 'let's go, we've still got this'." The Patriot offense then began a great drive that led to the game-winning field goal, and Lawyer said, "The offense was out there and the crowd was getting louder. Then Troy Brown made a great catch and I turned around trying to pump everybody up. There was one more big catch by Jermaine Wiggins. That's when we started getting nervous and thinking we had a chance. The kick goes up, through, and I ran onto the field and the first person that I see is Bill Belichick." The picture of Lawyer hugging Belichick with pure joy on both their faces on the field after that win is one that I recall to this day.

Boston had a parade and celebration at City Hall for the Patriots after that win, and one of the highlights of that celebration was Lawyer Milloy and Ty Law dancing on the stage and convincing Bob Kraft to join in. It was fun to see.

- - -

In 2002, following the Super Bowl win, the Patriots missed the playoffs, though they seemed to be peaking late in the season. I asked Lawyer what he felt happened in 2002 that kept the team from the playoffs and he mentioned two things. He said that every team that played them in 2002 was really up for that game, saying that "anyone who wins, you're getting live bullets every week" as other teams are gunning for you (to continue the metaphor). He also said that that 2002 team "made uncharacteristic mistakes. We just weren't good enough."

The Patriots did win the Super Bowl again after the 2003 and 2004 seasons, but by then, unfortunately, Lawyer was no longer with the team, as he was released in a contract dispute. As noted above, Lawyer's teammates were deeply affected by the loss of this acknowledged and well-respected team leader, and it did negatively affect their performance at the beginning of the season. Lawyer helped lead his Buffalo team to a surprising 31-0 upset of New England in the season's opener. He went on to play with the Bills from 2003-2005 and then the Atlanta Falcons from 2006-2009. At the time of our interview (July 2009), Lawyer was a free agent, hoping to play again in the 2009 season and beyond, and he ultimately did sign to play with the Seattle Seahawks in 2009.

- - -

In responding to a question about his most memorable game as a Patriot, Lawyer said "the Super Bowl win – that really summed it all up. It was the most fulfilling because of the stage that we were on and who we were going up against. We were going against Goliath and we won it and we did it our way. It summed up my whole career in New England. The fans there are hard-working, blue collar fans, and they respect a player and team that goes out there and works hard and wins ballgames. That's the kind of team they want to cheer for." That is also why Lawyer was so popular with the fans here. He was exactly that kind of player himself and he helped his team be that way as well.

Conversely, the Super Bowl at the beginning of Lawyer's career featured the play that Lawyer would most like to replay if he could. That was "the Freeman catch for a touchdown in the first Super Bowl. I was a rookie. I did something uncharacteristic for me as far as wanting to cover a guy" and in letting Freeman get behind him for that touchdown. He added, "I wish I could take that back because it was on the biggest stage and it was a big touchdown, and it ultimately didn't give our team a chance to win a championship."

For our version of Player Word Association, we talked about the following players:

> Ty Law – He's my brother. He was the closest person to me that I can think of. Everything that we did was very similar; we were always on the same page. I view him not just as a friend but as a brother. I would do anything for him.

> Tedy Bruschi – heartbeat [of the team]; He had a tremendous amount of spirit and energy, and an unforgettable smile and love for the sport. He was a guy that he earned his way to the spotlight and became a leader of the team.

> Drew Bledsoe – poster boy; outstanding; a guy with an outstanding arm; When I got there he was what Tom Brady is now; he was the face of the franchise. He was the one constant on the team; even if anyone didn't

know where New England was, if they didn't know the colors of the team, they knew that Drew Bledsoe was the quarterback. It was an honor meeting him and playing against him at Washington State when I was at Washington. When we became teammates he kind of took me under his wing, and it was a treat.

Tom Brady – franchise player; All of us are wearing one championship ring, or multiple rings, because of him, because of his greatness, his readiness, and his continuity.

Willie Clay – He was a mentor to me. We were a good mix. He saw a young guy with some potential and wanted to get it out of me.

Troy Brown – dependable; The quarterback could count on him to be in the right position every play in the game.

Adam Vinatieri – money; He was money when we were in a tight game. We had confidence that we had a kicker who could win the game in the end. A lot of times kickers should not get the glory because you set the table for them, but in this situation, with what he did, and the kicks that he had for this organization, he deserves it.

After we talked about these Patriot teammates, I asked Lawyer who his toughest opponent was. He responded, "The person who made me prepare hard was Terrell Davis when he was healthy because I knew that he was going to run hard whether it was a 1 yard run or a 16 yard run." Davis, the former Denver running back was a tough runner for any team to prepare to play. Lawyer also mentioned Curtis Martin, saying "I respected him so much as a teammate on and off the field" and adding that after Martin left New England to play for the Jets he still had that respect for him, adding that they "would line up and both nod to each other and then go collide and I wanted to give him my best every time we went out there. It was a war and then afterward we would give a shake and a hug and ask how we were doing no matter who won or lost."

I asked Lawyer if there was a player that he would have liked to have had as a teammate. Interestingly. Lawyer did not mention any former Patriot or anyone that he did not play with, but someone whose career overlapped with his own for one year at Atlanta, responding "A player that I would like to keep playing with is Matt Ryan. I've seen his approach to the game. I've seen how he makes the people around him better." Ryan was a rookie quarterback with the Falcons in 2008 and had an immediate impact in turning around that franchise. It will be interesting to see how Ryan develops as his career goes forward, especially given these comments from Lawyer.

- - -

As we finished up our interview and after hearing Lawyer's comments about Matt Ryan, I thought that perhaps the best summation of Lawyer's career with the Patriots was given by Drew Bledsoe during his interview: "Some people define a great player as somebody who raises the level of the people around him and Lawyer was one of those guys; if he was on the field the defense was going to play better, and guys individually would play better." Lawyer Milloy was indeed one of those players. We can only wish that his stay with the Patriots could have been longer.

Tim Fox

Patriot Career: 1976-1981
Position Played: Safety
College: Ohio State

The Patriot college draft of 1976 was one of the best in team history. They had three first round picks, and used them to draft three players who would be key contributors to the team for many years. With the 5th, 12th, and 21st overall picks in the draft, the Patriots selected, respectively, defensive back Mike Haynes, center Peter Brock, and safety Tim Fox.

Fox was a hard-hitting safety who had developed his game in a strong Ohio State program under legendary Head Coach Woody Hayes. I asked about his first reaction to learning that he had been drafted by New England and he responded, "I have to be honest with you, I didn't even know where they played … Growing up in Ohio, I didn't really follow professional football that closely. I grew up in Canton, and when you open up the top page of the *Canton Repository*, it is always in the same order, high school sports first, college sports second, and professional sports third." Since Canton is the home of the Pro Football Hal of Fame, that was more than a little surprising.

His first observations about the Patriot organization mirrored the disappointment of some of the other interviewees. It was a step down from Ohio State, not a step up into the pros. This started with Tim's first trip. He remembered, "It was interesting … when I first when up there, I came in for the mini-camp and was picked up at the airport by an elderly gentleman, a friend of Billy Sullivan … he was driving a Volkswagen Beetle and it only has one front seat, the driver's seat, and no passenger seat. I remember asking him why he had only seat and he answered 'I only need one seat.' It wasn't exactly like being picked up in a limo. He took us out past the Stadium and out to the hotel [I won't mention the name for reasons that will be obvious shortly] just south of the stadium, and I will tell you, it was not necessarily what I had expected … I remember it vividly. I came home after the first workout from mini-camp, got into the bed, started getting comfortable, reached my hand up underneath the pillow, and was very pleased to find a used condom under the pillow." It was not exactly a nice welcome to the NFL.

Tim described mini-camp as "pretty intense … I thought that we were going to a hat and shorts workout, but we went at it pretty good, to the point where I broke my wrist trying to break up a pass to Darryl Stingley on the sideline… I was scheduled to play in the College All-Star Game, but because I had broken my wrist the Patriots kept me out of that … they asked me to report to training camp a week early, so I ended up not going to the All-Star Game but coming to a camp that was just absolute misery. They were 3-11 in 1975 and we were without a Collective Bargaining Agreement in 1976. There were no regulations on what teams could and couldn't ask you to do in training camp. So I came into camp and we practiced literally seven days a week, two-a-days, every day of the week … I was shocked by the level of activity in that first training camp. It went on and on and on. We had six pre-season games back then. You literally were in camp for over a month with two-a-days every day. We used to look forward to the pre-season games because there were not two practices that day, there was only one game. So obviously the 3-11 season the year before had an affect on why Fairbanks was working us as hard as he did."

Maybe the hard work did pay off, as the team reversed its 3-11 record in 1975 to 11-3 in Tim's rookie season in 1976, and made the playoffs. The team played Oakland in that memorable game in which the Patriots and their fans felt was only won by Oakland due to one of the worst officiating performances in football history (see Chapter 3 for details). I asked Tim what he remembered of that game and he responded, "We knew that we had matched up pretty well against the Raiders earlier in the year. We were the only team to have beaten them that year. So we certainly weren't intimidated going into the game. We felt pretty good about going in and playing them." He went on to say, "The game was going pretty much the way we had anticipated it going," but then came the bad calls, which included, "it wasn't just the Ray Hamilton play [a roughing the passer penalty], the Russ Francis holding [he was being held by Oakland's Phil Villipiano as he tried to run a pass pattern] that was not called, Francis getting his nose broken with no call … I was just a young and dumb rookie, so I didn't know what to expect ... but by the time the game was over, I really had reservations about the NFL as a whole, because I really feel as though that game was taken from us."

The team wound up missing the playoffs in 1977. I asked Tim what happened, and if the celebrated contract holdout by John Hannah and Leon Gray had affected the team. Tim said, "I don't think there was any question that it did. You can't take the best offensive lineman to ever play the game out of your lineup and then Leon who was a great player in his own right, and expect to be the same team. And you only have to look at the next year when they were both back and they set the all-time record for the most rushing yards by a team to see how much of an impact that could have. "

The next season, 1978, was one which looked for most of the year to be a great season for New England. However, a crippling injury to wide receiver Darryl Stingley before the season and a fiasco surrounding the firing of Fairbanks before the playoffs changed things. I asked Tim if he realized on the spot how serious the injury to Stingley was. He said, "We knew it wasn't good. Any time you see a player laying motionless, you're concerned. Your first assumption is that he's just knocked out, but then when they start immobilizing him, and when they took as long as they took, we knew it was an issue." Tim, however, was unique in saying, "I did not have an issue with the hit. I certainly would have made the same hit. I'm not sure I would have done it in pre-season, but it certainly was within the rules back then." He did add, however, "When he stayed down, the thing that was most frustrating was that, after he stayed down, Tatum and George Atkinson high-fiving each other and laughing and joking about it." Tim, who was known for being a hard-hitting defensive back himself did say, "You have to hit a receiver coming over the middle to make him think twice the next time that he does it." That is definitely part of the game, though Tatum's hit against a defenseless receiver always seemed to me to be both extremely violent and absolutely unnecessary. Tim went on, "The longer we stood there [watching the medical staff tend to a motionless Stingley on the field], the more pissed I was about the whole scenario. When we went back on the field they hit Dave Casper [Oakland's great tight end] with a pass over the middle. Unfortunately he wasn't coming right at me, he was running a turnaround curl route and I hit him as hard as I could possibly hit him. Unfortunately I almost hurt myself, because Casper's so big. I remember going home on the plane, thinking to myself, 'what a stupid game this is. Darryl is in the hospital paralyzed and the first opportunity I got I tried to do the same thing to another guy.' It really made me stop and think about the game on the way home."

The Fairbanks firing was "handled very poorly," as Tim recounted. "He was fired before the last game of the season in Miami. We had co-head coaches for that last game against Miami. I remember that Ron Erhardt gave his pre-game talk, and Hank Bulloch gave his pre-game talk. They were trying to out-do one another. One would have been plenty. Two was overkill. We just wanted to get out of the locker room and we go to leave the locker room and the door's locked. They had kind of like the old padlock on the outside of the door. We couldn't get out." [Stadium officials use that to lock the doors to the locker rooms from the outside when the team leaves the locker room but they did it too early that day, and the team had to wait for someone to come back and unlock it.] A successful coach for a playoff-bound team fired before the team's last game, two head coaches and two pre-game speeches, followed by the team being locked in the locker room and unable to get out onto the field when they wanted to do so – things like this could only happen with the Patriots.

- - -

The team went into the playoffs without Fairbanks, the Head Coach who had helped lead them there. It was the first home playoff game in Patriot history, against the Houston Oilers. Tim was involved in a key play in the game, being called for a late hit to keep a long Oiler drive alive. The play occurred with Houston holding a 7-0 lead, but being backed up on their own one yard line. Momentum seemed to have switched to New England as the Patriots stopped the Oilers on a third down run and looked to have forced the Oilers to punt from deep within their own territory. However, after the whistle, Tim was called for a late hit penalty, which gave the Oilers a first down and allowed them to continue what would be a 99 yard drive to a touchdown and a 14-0 lead. I asked Tim if he wanted to talk about it and he was willing to do so. He started by joking, "I certainly got away with more than my fair share ... They had such a good running game. In my mind, the best way to combat a good running game is to take the shots at the running backs. You can't let them go down without getting hit or they're going to continue to beat you ... I was a physical safety, and was probably far more effective in the running game than in the passing game ... The running back for Houston on that play wasn't Earl Campbell [an outstanding runner for Houston in that era]. It was Tim Wilson ... He was coming in and somebody had hit him and he was still moving, still trying to pick up yardage. When he went down, he landed on his shoulder ... I tried just to dive over the pile caused I'd already started. His upper shoulder was higher off the ground than I thought it was going to be. So when I went over the top, I caught that shoulder. It wasn't a hit at all. It wasn't like I drove him into the ground. Basically I just caught his shoulder and spun him onto his back. I went right over the top and landed on the other side of the pile. It certainly hurt [the Patriots' chances]."

- - -

The team was not as successful after 1978, so we turned our attention to other matters. I asked Tim about his most memorable game as a Patriot and he mentioned two, "the Oakland game for all the wrong reasons," and "my rookie year when we went into Pittsburgh and beat Pittsburgh and they were defending champs. They were the team of the decade ... to me they were THE franchise in the NFL. We thought we had a pretty good team, and when we won that game, it registered for the first time that we could go out and beat anybody in the NFL."

With regard to what game he would like to replay if he could, Tim joked, "You never want to replay your wins," and then looked back at the team's two playoff games during his tenure, admitting, "the Oakland game would be a nice one to have back, and that Houston game would be a nice one to have back too if we were prepared better ... If we had won either one of those games I really feel like we had a shot at going to the Super Bowl."

Tim responded quickly to a question about his toughest opponent, saying, "For us it was always the Dolphins. All six years that I played here it seemed like we would always lose in Miami. We could beat them here but we could never beat them in Miami. We beat Miami every year but 1981 when we couldn't beat anybody. That was a good rivalry. "

- - -

We then went though "Player Word Association", eliciting the following reactions from Tim about his former teammates:

Mike Haynes – he lived with me in my house for our rookie year. He was just a tremendously gifted athlete. He could have played anything.

Steve Nelson – great leader, great competitor

Steve Grogan – both of those could probably go the same for him [great leader, great competitor]; resilient – he took a lot of shots and got up after them.

John Hannah – intense; you didn't want to spend a lot of time with him. I spent six years in New England and probably talked to John Hannah five times. I did not interact a lot with him.

Raymond Clayborn – had the greatest recovery speed I've ever seen in a defensive back. We used to call him 'rubber band man' because a guy would come out of the break and it would be like you stretch a rubber band and then let go of one end of it, and that was how he would get to the guy.

Russ Francis – one of the most gifted athletes I've ever seen, in a super-sized body. He had all the athletic skills that you would find in a guy that was 6 feet, 185 pounds. He just happened to be, what, 6'5" 230. He could run as fast. He was every bit as nimble and had the same dexterity as guys half his size.

Andy Johnson – the best athlete I've ever known, best hand-eye coordination. He could beat you at anything. I don't care if you put a ping-pong paddle, a tennis racket, a racquetball racket, a baseball bat [in his hands], he could beat you at anything.

John Smith – [laughing] probably the most unlikely football player I've ever known

We then talked about his first coach, Chuck Fairbanks. Tim considered Chuck "one of the best coaches I ever had, but not because of his innate knowledge of the game, but his ability to bring excellent coaches together and let them coach. He had really good staffs. He ran the show. He ran the personnel. He ran the front office. He wasn't threatened by good coaches. There are a lot of coaches out there who won't bring a guy on because they don't want someone questioning them, but he was not like that."

We concluded this portion of our session with a question about which current or former Patriot that he did not play with would he have liked to have had as a teammate and played with. He responded, "I would have liked to have played opposite Rodney Harrison. That would have been a lot of fun, with him playing strong safety, me playing free. That would have been dangerous." With those two hard hitters, it might have been. Tim then added, "No offense to Steve Grogan, but it would be great to play with Tom Brady. To have that level of consistency at quarterback. That was at times frustrating with the Patriots. So much of whether we won or lost, when I was with the Patriots, depended on whether Steve had a good or a bad game. Fortunately for us, he had more good games than bad games. But if it was a bad game there wasn't much that we could do to counteract that. When I look at Brady and the consistency that he has it is just incredible. You can make that comparison to anybody"

- - -

Our interview took place at the end of 2009, the week after the Indianapolis Colts had pulled their starters from a game against the Jets, turning a 15-10 lead and a chance for an undefeated season into a 29-15 loss. It dropped the Colts' record to 14-1 (as described in Chapter 44). Since I had been present at two Monday night radio interviews that Tim had done with Upton Bell, and appreciated his insights and observations about the game, I asked him what he thought of the Colts' decision. He admitted, "I know that I'd be very upset if I was a player, and if I was a fan I'd be equally upset, but, having said that, I understand the reasoning behind it." As described in Chapter 44, my opinion – as a fan of the game and of the competition that any sport provides – differs from Tim's reaction. I was incensed by the decision; my reasons are given at the end of that Chapter 44.

Recalling those radio interviews, I remembered a question which I had asked Tim during one of those interviews, and asked it again to get his reaction for this write-up. The question was what would have happened if Tim had been on the field for that David Tyree catch in the 2008 Super Bowl (where Tyree caught the ball against his helmet to keep alive the Giants' game-winning drive). "He wouldn't have caught the ball," Tim confidently replied, "I would have taken him out. I would not have played the ball, I would have played the man."

- - -

Tim went on to play for the San Diego Chargers from 1982-84 and the Los Angeles Rams in 1985-86 before retiring from the NFL. He is currently Sales Director for the New England Region of RR Donnelly in Boston. After one of the radio interviews that Tim did with Upton Bell I learned that Tim had suffered a number of concussions in his career, so I asked about those concussions and his overall health, starting by asking how many concussions he had suffered. Tim replied, "I'm guessing at least 20." When asked about the effects, he said, "I have trouble remembering a lot of things, there are so many things I can't remember it's embarrassing at times. I know I have some issues with the cognitive side of my brain." He went on to recount a story about getting a concussion during a game in college on his birthday one year, going to a party that night and not remembering anything about that party. "They tell me that I had a good time," was all he recalled. He admitted seeing the effects that multiple concussions have had on other players, and wonders what the future holds for him. He also mentioned that he has had one hip replaced, will have to have the other one replaced at some point too, "and a knee and eventually an ankle", he added. Let's hope that Tim's future holds a lot of good times for him to remember.

- - -

I happened to luck into this interview, thanks to meeting Tim at the Upton Bell interviews and enjoying the discussions that he and Upton had. Their conversations flowed very easily and both men had great insights about the game. I enjoyed listening to them both, and learned a lot about the inside view of the game from their discussions. I'm glad to have had a chance to talk in more detail with Tim and to include some of those observations and comments here as well.

Interviews with Media Members

Also interviewed were a number of the members of the media who covered the Patriots over the years.

Dick Cerasuolo

Writer, Worcester Telegram

Dick Cerasuolo was a newspaper writer for the *Worcester Telegram* who covered the Boston/New England Patriots from 1965 through 1999. We met over lunch on April 28, 2009 and talked for about two hours about his memories of covering the team. Dick enjoyed covering the team, and also explained that he had a good relationship with the other members of the press who covered the team, such as Will McDonough and Leigh Montville of the *Boston Globe*, Kevin Mannix of the *Boston Herald*, and others.

This lunch had been set up one Sunday at our church, where I caught up with Dick after Mass and told him that Jon Morris had asked me to pass on a hello for him, since Dick always treated Jon well. We talked briefly that day about the Patriot teams that included Jon, Clive Rush, and other memories of Dick's days with the Patriots. We then set up this lunch so that we would have more time to talk.

I started by asking Dick what the most memorable game was of his time in covering the Patriots. Dick mentioned the 1985 playoff game with the Miami Dolphins that led to the Patriots appearing in the Super Bowl for the first time in the team's history. It was memorable for many reasons: the Patriots getting to the Super Bowl for the first time, the Patriots beating the Dolphins in Miami for the first time in 18 years, and for a conversation that Dick had with Patriots' owner Billy Sullivan. As Dick recalled, that conversation with Billy lasted about 2 ½ hours, "which was par for the course for Billy," during which they talked about Billy selling the team. Dick said that Billy "talked on and on about the subject but never addressed" the reasons for the sale, but Billy kept mentioning Mary, Billy's wife. So Dick caught Mary at lunch and asked her about it, and Mary told him "The simple fact is that we can't afford it, we have to sell it."

Dick also recalled how Billy, who ran the team on a shoestring, used to call him when he was an intern at Northeastern University and ask question about players before the NFL draft and used magazines to get information about players. This is quite a contrast to the extensive pre-draft scouting that is done today.

Another memorable game for Dick was the Patriots' 1976 playoff game with Oakland, "the Ben Drieth game", as he referred to it. This was the game that many feel was stolen from New England by poor officiating by the crew which was led by Drieth (see Chapter 3 for details). Dick felt that "That team was the best team that I covered. They were great. They should have won the Super Bowl". He added a comment that Sam Cunningham should not have been criticized (as he frequently has been) for not making a first down on a key play late in the game. Dick remembers that Cunningham "got nine yards on the first down. He had a bum knee, and a bum rib I think it was, so he ran out of bounds. Now it's second and one and Russ Francis jumps offside, and Leon Gray with him. Then they had to punt." He went on to talk about the phantom roughing the passer call that was a key decision in that game, saying "that pass and that call on Sugar Bear [Hamilton] - it was so bad. It should not have been called. That was a game that will always stick in my head."

I asked Dick if he felt that the 1977 season that followed was impacted by the holdouts of offensive linemen John Hannah and Leon Gray and, like Steve Grogan, Dick did feel that that holdout adversely affected the team that year, as they missed the playoffs entirely.

Dick also mentioned the game that the Patriots won with the help of a fan running onto the field, as recounted also by Gino Cappelletti. As was the case with Gino, Dick mentioned that he had seen and had a film of that play. He remembers the fan bumping into the receiver "right in front of the official and they just didn't call it".

We talked about Bob Gladieux being called down from the stands to make the tackle on the opening kickoff of the season, which Dick not only remembered, but he also added that Bob Gladieux used to buy a seat for his dog on the team plane. "He was a piece of work", as Dick aptly described.

This led us to a discussion about Clive Rush, who was involved in many other of the oddities in Patriot history. Dick recalled how Rush told Jon Morris "anybody can play center in this league" so he benched him "and put somebody else in his place". Dick said, "It lasted two plays. The guy got overwhelmed" and Morris was back in.

Rush also was the coach who employed the "Black Power Defense", with eleven black players playing defense. One flaw with this was that there were not eleven black defensive players on the roster, so he added "five offensive guys" to the defense to get to eleven black defenders. This lasted one play, because, as Dick remembered, "The first time he used it I think it was [Miami's] Larry Csonka ran forever for a touchdown" right through it. That was the end for Rush's special defense.

Dick also described how the Patriots' first choice to replace Mike Holovak was Chuck Noll, the defensive coordinator of the Baltimore Colts, but they went with Clive Rush who had been the offensive coordinator of the Jets, after the Jets had beaten Baltimore in Super Bowl III. Dick talked about how he was in Rush's Patriot office when Rush got his championship ring delivered from the New York Jets. Rush gave Dick the ring and told him "go over there and scratch the window and make sure it's a real diamond". Dick did it, but was concerned about the window, but heard Rush yell "harder, harder". Dick said that he said "but I'll break the glass" and Rush told him "That's what I want you to do."

After his stint with the Patriots, Rush went on to become head coach at Kingspoint "and he was 8-0 and I called him". Dick said that Rush told him during that call that "I'm doing everything here that we wouldn't let me do there, and look at how it's working." Dick went on to add, "He got fired that week for drinking on the bench." Like other players and writers who had been with the team during the Rush years, Dick remembered Rush as a man with a drinking problem that was his undoing. He recalled asking Bake Turner, who had previously been with the Jets and later played with the Patriots, about Rush and Turner told him, "He was the same there. He used to get drunk before the games". It's a shame that a great football mind was wasted with that habit.

I asked Dick how he thought Noll would have done here, and he indicated that he didn't think he'd have had the same success here as he did with Pittsburgh. The reason was simple: players. Dick said "there would have been some civility but I don't think they would have done much better". In Pittsburgh, Noll had Terry Bradshaw, Mean Joe Greene, Franco Harris, Lynn Swann, and other star players. Dick recounted his experience covering a pre-season game with the

Steelers that was held in Louisiana (since Bradshaw had played his college football at Louisiana Tech). Dick said that Bradshaw "showed on one play what he had … he got busted out of the pocket and he was running around. The tight end broke off and Bradshaw started doing this [waving his hands], the cornerback came up, Bradshaw threw the ball for a touchdown". Dick's reaction was "what a quick thinking play …. This guy's a player."

- - -

I asked Dick about his experiences in interviewing the players and coaches - who were the easiest, or most interesting to interview, and who were the toughest. Among the easiest were Steve Grogan, Jon Morris, and Larry Garron. Dick said "Grogan was great. He was honest. He was a likeable guy." Dick noted that Jon Morris was considered one of the team leaders during his playing days (and having spoken to other players from that era, it seemed that they all considered him to be so), "more important in the locker room; people would listen to him, and that was in tough times. He was a class act. He brought a lot to the Patriots." Dick said that fellow reporter "Kevin Mannix made the point that Nance made all those yards, as a straight ahead runner, because he was running behind Jon Morris." Dick said that he has nominated Morris for the Patriot Hall of Fame (Dick is a committee member for that). Here is hoping that Jon Morris gets in. From everything I saw as a fan, and have heard about in these interviews, he would be an excellent choice.

Dick said that among the coaches there were "never many good ones" for interviews. He told one story about interviewing coach John Mazur one time in Mazur's office, and Mazur looked up at the board showing the team's depth chart, and said to Dick, "Look at what they give me. How the hell do you win with that?" Dick said he then went down to the end of the hall to the office of General Manager Upton Bell, who looked at a similar chart in his office and said "look at the players I give him and he can't win!" That's the way it was with those Patriot teams.

I then asked specifically about Bill Parcells, who had the Jekyll-Hyde reputation of having interesting comments in press conferences but also being caustic, to say the least, with some reporters. Dick indicated that he and Parcells had a good relationship, but that "You had to earn it." Dick recalled that when Parcells got the job, he called Phil Simms, who was the primary Giants quarterback when Parcells was coach there, to ask him about Parcells. Dick said that Simms recalled a famous confrontation that he and Parcells had on the sideline during a game that was captured by the TV cameras. Dick said that Simms told him the next day. "Hey, good show, wasn't it?" as a way of telling him to forget about it, it didn't mean anything. Dick said that Phil said that Parcells would do the same with him, "challenge you, and if you back down, it's over". Dick recalled making an error at one time by asking about the condition of the field after three straight home games by the New England Revolution soccer team. Parcells made a biting comment about stupid questions saying, "Is there a penalty for stupidity?" When Dick was informed by the reporter behind him that one Revolution game was on the road, Dick pointed out the error to Parcells and said "I just realized something, and I'll pay the penalty, whatever the stupid fine is." He said Parcells looked at him and kind of smiled, and they were fine after that.

Dick also mentioned that contrary to popular belief, when Parcells joined the Patriots and had the # 1 pick in the college draft, Parcells wanted to draft Notre Dame quarterback Rick Mirer and not Washington State's Drew Bledsoe. It turned out to be then-owner James B. Orthwein who ultimately made the decision to draft Bledsoe. It was a good choice, since Bledsoe became a very good NFL quarterback, and the face of the New England franchise for many years, while Mirer, who was the # 2 pick in the draft by Seattle, did not have any success in the NFL. Dick remembered going to Orthwein and meeting with him and Orthwein's attorney, and telling him "I have a couple of sources that say that Parcells wanted Mirer and you made the decision to take Bledsoe". Dick went on to say that "Orthwein looked at his attorney, the attorney said 'tell him' and Orthwein told him 'Yeah, that was my pick'."

With regard to other coaches, Dick described Mike Holovak positively, commenting on his honesty in dealing with players and the press. He thinks Bill Belichick is "a terrific coach. He does his homework. He knows what's going on. He knows what he wants. He has an eye for people who produce for him." He described Clive Rush as "wacky". Another story that Dick told about Rush illustrated that even further, as Dick remembered an interview that Rush did after a hot day of summer practice. They were in Rush's office, and Rush talked about how hot it was so he stripped naked and sat at his desk with the fan blowing behind him while doing the interview. (I guess there were no concealed plays in the Patriots' repertoire that year.)

Dick talked about some run-ins that he had with players, including one with John Hannah that nearly came to blows. As Dick described it, he had arranged to have a one-on-one interview with Hannah after practice one day. Hannah asked Dick to meet him outside the locker room the next day. Dick waited but Hannah did not show up, so he asked Hannah about it the next day and Hannah said that he was at the other door. Dick pointed out to him that that was a players-only area that to which he did not have access. They agreed to meet again, but when they did, there was also a reporter from *Sports Illustrated* there waiting for John Hannah. Dick said that "Hannah comes out, looks at both of us, goes to get his car, pulls around and goes like this to the guy [makes beckoning gesture], he gets in and they drive off" and left Dick standing there. When Dick confronted Hannah about that the next day, asking John, "Is that what you refer to when you always talk about Southern gentlemen … was that being a Southern gentleman yesterday?" Dick says that Hannah "jumps up and says 'kiss my ass' and everybody starts yelling 'hit him, Hog, hit him' and we bumped. My first thought was 'do I get up when he hits me or do I stay down' [given the difference in size between Hannah and Dick] so he starts pushing me and I pushed him back, because if I backed down from that I could never go into that locker room again so I had to stand my ground. So Bill Lenkaitis jumps up and gets between us, and pushes me away. Hog turns and walks away, but I say 'it ain't over yet' so I head back in. Lenkaitis looks at me [like I'm crazy] and says 'I'm going to let you go'. So I just said something else to Hog and I just walked away. The next day, I'm in a place in Hudson, some discount store, and they had knit caps that said 'Roll Tide' [for Alabama, which was Hannah's alma mater]. So I brought one in and said [to Hannah] 'here, give this to your little boy' and he was all nice. But he was a tough guy to deal with."

He went on to talk about Hannah glowingly, however, saying "He was the best guard I ever saw". He talked about watching John go around end on running plays as pulling guard and "cornerbacks, you'd watch them, they would dive out of his way, because he would just run right over them. He was a great player."

We could not talk about Patriot player interviews without my asking about the Lisa Olson incident. Olson was a reporter for the *Boston Herald* in 1990 who had a number of players expose themselves to her, feeling that she was ogling their naked bodies in the locker room instead of just doing her reporting professionally. Dick recalled that Olson "did not want anything said or written about it", or to have the story to come out at first, but it did, and ultimately led to a lawsuit, for which Dick had to give a deposition. The case ultimately wound up being settled (reportedly with Olson receiving $250,000 from the team) and Dick mentioned that Lisa Olson went on to Australia for a while and then went on to write for Rupert Murdoch in London and for the *New York Daily News*. It was an embarrassing chapter in Patriot history, but luckily it was one of the last before the Parcells and Belichick eras turned the franchise around completely.

- - -

Back to football, I asked Dick what his all-time Patriot team would be, and he went area by area in describing it. For the offensive line, Dick cited

Tom Neville – "he could play and he was a great guy"

John Hannah – "can't do it without Hannah"

Jon Morris – "he was a great center"

Len St. Jean – "he always gave 110%, nobody ever sweat more than him",

Leon Gray – "even though he was only here a short time", and from the current era

Logan Mankins – "he's a horse".

Defensive linemen that Dick mentioned were Jim Lee Hunt and Houston Antwine from that great defensive line of the 1960s. Backing them up at linebacker would be Steve Nelson and Nick Buoniconti in the middle or inside linebackers, and Andre Tippett and Mike Vrabel ("a smart player") as outside linebackers. His choices for defensive backs were Mike Haynes and Raymond Claiborne, and for safeties Rodney Harrison and Fred Marion. I was particularly happy with the choice of Fred Marion who was a favorite of my son Mike and me. Dick described Marion both as one of the nicest players to talk with on the team and of their smartest players. He said that the other defenders would talk about how Marion knew where every player on the defense was supposed to line up on every play and for every formation, and what they were supposed to do. Dick also gave an example of a goal-line play where Marion lined up in the end zone and when the snap occurred, he immediately charged toward the line, and made the play on the receiver that prevented the touchdown. When Dick asked him about this later, Marion said that he remembered that they had run this same play from that same formation in an earlier game. When he saw them lined up that way, it immediately clicked and he knew what they were going to do, so he ran right to it. Sounds like Marion would have been a good player in the Bill Belichick era as well as his own (1982-1991).

Continuing with the list, we turned back to the offense. Dick chose Jim Nance, Andy Johnson, and Curtis Martin for running backs, commenting about how smart a player Johnson was, how powerful a runner Nance was, and how talented a runner, and how nice a guy Martin was. For wide receivers, his choices were Stanley Morgan and Darryl Stingley, though he also mentioned Irving Fryar. I asked Dick his opinion of whether Fryar was as weird as we fans thought from the stories that we heard and read and Dick said that he was. He also talked about how Fryar found religion later in life and became more mature.

That brought us to quarterback and Dick said, "For the time that I was covering the team it was Steve Grogan. He was my favorite player because he gave so much. He was a tough guy. I think he was much better than people always gave him credit for." Dick did add that you would have to add Tom Brady to that mix today.

- - -

By this time the restaurant was empty of everyone except Dick and me and the waitstaff was starting to vacuum and get ready to set up for the dinner crowd. They had been nice enough to let us stay and talk for a while, but we felt that we should get out of their way so we ended our conversation there but continued talking all the way to our cars. We had read Dick's stories in the Worcester Telegram for years, and had seen him at church often, but this was the first time that I had ever had a chance to sit down with Dick and talk about his memories of the Patriots and the NFL. It was well worth the time. I hope that he and I can continue to compare notes about Patriot games and players for years to come.

Bob Lobel

Sports Anchor, WBZ TV,
Radio Talk Show Host

Bob Lobel was a fixture on the Boston Television scene for three decades. He was the Sports Director for WBZ-TV, Channel 4 from 1981 to 2008, after starting as the weekend sports anchor in 1978. He did play-by-play for Patriots pre-season games from 1985-1991 and also covered the Patriots for two NBC national broadcasts in 1985. He was the co-host with Upton Bell of the popular "Calling All Sports" radio talk show on WBZ radio for three years in the mid 1970s. He popularized the use of props such as the "Panic Button" when a local team was going bad (usually it was for a late season swoon by the Red Sox), and the use of catch-phrases such as "Why can't we get players like that?" when a former Boston athlete had a successful night with another team. He was chosen Massachusetts Sportscaster of the Year nine times, and is a legend in Boston broadcasting circles.

I caught up with Bob on May 7, 2009, and we had a very interesting chat about the Patriots and his career in TV and radio.

My first question to Bob was to ask him what his most memorable games were in his years from covering the Patriots as either their broadcaster or in covering sports for WBZ. Bob immediately cited the 1985-1986 team coached by Raymond Berry that won "where they were not supposed to win", winning three playoff games on the road against the Jets, Raiders, and Dolphins (beating the Dolphins in Miami for the first time in 18 years), to get to the 1986 Super Bowl against the Chicago Bears.

Bob also mentioned the 2001-2002 team that won the first Super Bowl in Patriot history, saying that that Super Bowl "right after 9/11 … probably stands out as one of the more remarkable events that we covered, not just the game, but in terms of security and all the things that were going on in the world at the time". Bob said that he and the WBZ crew "had to sleep in the satellite truck because it was inside the compound" the night before the game "to avoid going through security again because it took an hour to get in". They were not forced to do it by Security Forces, but they decided to do it because of the long procedure that had to be followed by anyone coming into the stadium for this game. So, Bob continued, "we were there all day and including all night, and I remember sleeping after putting everything on the air … and I remember having to get up at 5 to do a morning live show back in Boston." Bob recalled sitting in the truck four hours after the game and saying to the others there "They just won the friggin' Super Bowl. I can't believe it. How is that possible, the New England Patriots actually won the Super Bowl?" He added that "Other championships followed, other Super Bowls followed, World Series followed, but this one opened up the championship toy box. The Red Sox winning was one thing, but I have to say that the Patriots winning that Super Bowl was about as big as you can get", given the team's history.

He went on to contrast that with the devastating loss of the Super Bowl to the Giants in February, 2008, and having the potential undefeated season snatched from them in the last seconds, saying "That was about as bad as it can get. That was worse than Buckner or anything that the Red Sox pulled off, in my mind."

This led us to talk about the Patriot success in the 2008 regular season that followed that Super Bowl loss, after the loss of Tom Brady to the knee injury in Game 1 of that season. Bob attributed that success to "a combination of things. First of all, Cassel is a pretty good player. I think you have to start there. He had some adjustments to make, since he hadn't played, and they had some adjustments to make. The Patriots were very smart in handling him. They recognize how important the position of quarterback is, but they also recognize how important the system is that they have in place for whatever quarterback they have. That's where the genius of the coach comes in. They adjust the system to give the quarterback a chance to succeed.

They adjusted their offensive schemes to fit his strengths, much as they did for Tom Brady [when Brady replaced Drew Bledsoe in 2001]. In both cases it worked. It's hard to believe that they were 11-5 and didn't make the playoffs. I know they didn't have the defense to go all the way but it would have been nice to see how far they could have gotten."

I mentioned that I felt that you could make a case for Matt Cassel as MVP in 2008, and Bob agreed, saying "yeah, there is no question. I think you can absolutely make that kind of case." It was nice to hear.

- - -

We then began talking about one of Bob's most famous interviews, that of Terry Glenn in that 2001 season. As described in Chapter 6, Glenn had started the season inactive, having been suspended for four games by the NFL for substance abuse. When he did rejoin the team, he was continually an on-again, off-again distraction, and was later suspended again by the team for his attitude problems.

Bob and Steve Burton had a Sunday night talk show, "Sports Final", on WBZ-TV and did an interview with Glenn during this time, in which Glenn made a complete fool of himself. Bob recalled that Steve Burton had made the arrangements to bring him in, and they "asked him a question about do you want to play here, and he said 'I did.' The follow-up question was 'You did?' He said 'Yeah, I did. d-i-d did." That was a bombshell announcement and it made headlines for days. I asked Bob what he thought when that happened and he answered, 'What did I think? I thought it was a home run. It was like a journalist's dream. I know a good sound bite when I hear it and that is about as good as it gets. And you know, I don't think we baited him. I think he knew what he was doing. He just went on and said what he wanted to say. It was one of those 'wow' moments and you don't get that many 'wow' moments on those kinds of shows, but when you do you've got to be grateful for it."

Another 'wow' show, since it was more than a moment, that Bob made famous was a roundtable interview that he conducted with three all-time great Boston players from three different sports: Ted Williams of the baseball Red Sox, Bobby Orr of the hockey Bruins, and Larry Bird of the basketball Celtics. Bob said "That was special. I was fortunate to have a chance to put that in. At that time there was no pro football player to add to that panel. Of course now Brady would make it automatically." I mentioned that that would be a great Mt. Rushmore of Boston sports, but that you could also add a number of greats like Bill Russell, Bob Cousy, John Havlicek, Carl Yastrzemski, Phil Esposito and others. Bob agreed and said "We wanted to put Russell in there originally, but Russell at that particular time wasn't as amenable to coming back to Boston as he is now."

I asked Bob about other memorable interviews, and whether he had favorite Patriot players to interview. He had a long list, saying "I always loved talking to Vinatieri. We had him in one night to re-enact the snow kick. He was great. I met his father. I thought his father was very gracious. I remember some guys by their families. I always enjoyed Grogan, Tim Fox, Peter Brock, John Hannah. Hannah was about as unique an individual as you can ever find. I always found him fascinating to interview. He was pretty outspoken." About Grogan, Bob said "He was very honest, just a Kansas kid, straight-forward, honest." Bob mentioned how "today players are much more guarded than they used to be. I just think that they have been taught by their agents or management to keep their mouth shut."

Bob also talked about going to Chicago and doing "a three part series with Darryl Stingley in his apartment, which to me was one of the most poignant things that we had done. This was about ten years after the injury. It was remarkable. It was amazing what he was able to accomplish and how he handled certain things. He was always one of my favorites."

Bob continued with his list of favorite interviewees, saying "There was Jon Morris. Morris was great. I loved him. I wish we would have done more with him on television." Bob went on to say, "They always had really smart centers." He cited Morris, Bill Lenkaitis, and Pete Brock as examples, saying, "They really had cerebral centers. The centers for some reason, they seemed to get it. It was fascinating."

- - -

We went on to talk about Patriot owners and coaches. The first that Bob mentioned was former owner Victor Kiam, about whom Bob said "he was a piece of work ... he lashed out at me one day on television and said, 'The day that I make you general manager is the day I sell the team'." Bob contrasted that with the success that the team now has had, since "it all stems from the top ... when you have responsible ownership, and responsible organizations, it is going to translate to winning".

He said that "I loved Parcells. I didn't think a whole lot of Pete Carroll as a pro coach but obviously his college success is remarkable. And the Belichick hiring turned out to be a genius move. I can't imagine even Bob Kraft thinking that it would work out as well as it has. When he hired Belichick he didn't have Tom Brady either, but things happen. Now the window of opportunity between those two, Belichick and Brady, may be closing. You don't know. They won three Super Bowls, maybe they should have won five, and you don't know when they're ever going to get back there." We talked again about the injury to Brady in 2008, and Bob said. "Let's say the same happens again. Let's say that Brady goes down and [Kevin] O'Connell comes in. You know what? O'Connell is more mobile than Cassel, and he was a third round draft pick. Who's to say that O'Connell won't be more successful than Cassel? And who's to say that they wouldn't redo their offense once again with a better defense and go further in the playoffs with O'Connell?"

Staying with coaches, Bob said "I loved Raymond Berry as a coach. I always had a great relationship with him. I totally respected him. I loved his sense of humor. I think that there was mutual thing – he and I connected because I kind of got who he was. A lot of people thought that he was in over his head, but no. You had to get who Raymond Berry was to deal with him. I thought he was one of the best, a great coach."

Parcells was "another guy I loved. He was totally the opposite of Raymond Berry. He was a walking sound bite. He was funny. But he was a tough SOB in a lot of ways. He was one of those guys that you would just never want to cross. He demanded respect. Will McDonough was a huge fan of Parcells, and I have to say that I was too." Bob wondered aloud how history would define Parcells versus Belichick, and I suggested that Parcells may be thought of more like Vince Lombardi, the 'bigger than life' kind of guy, while Belichick would be like Chuck Noll, quiet, efficient and does a great job. Bob thought that was a "legitimate" description, and said that he might ask that question on his radio show and see what other things people have to say.

Bob had some very complimentary things to say about Patrick Sullivan, son of original owner Billy Sullivan. He particularly complimented Pat about what he did after he left the organization, saying that he was "a generous guy with his time ... he understood where he was in life ... he had to build a business" and he did.

"Another interesting guy", Bob went on, "was Ron Meyer. I give him credit for that snow plow game. Shula was apoplectic." Bob confirmed that when the Patriots played in Miami next Shula had a ton of snow brought in and dumped behind the Patriot bench before the game to try to throw the Patriots off of their game.

Speaking of unusual things and players led us to talk about Irving Fryar. Bob talked about how talented a player Fryar was, and said that he "remembered doing a game for NBC where he ran back a punt for a touchdown and that was a highlight for me, but I have to say that as a player he was somewhat undisciplined. He was one of the wide receiver divas. He was a forerunner of that. After he left the game, and as time went on, he straightened things out and I found him an enjoyable guy to be around. He was a terrific athlete and he was a terrific player for them."

Of Drew Bledsoe, Bob remembered "when he first signed, he and his then-girlfriend came in to the studio and we did an interview with him. He was a just like a raw-boned kid. I always felt that he was as professional as he could be, kind of stoic in a way." Bob remembered when Bledsoe took the Patriots to the Super Bowl in New Orleans in 1997, being in a restaurant on Bourbon Street in New Orleans one night before the game, and he saw Beldsoe's father, and the father of Green Bay's quarterback Brett Favre (Green Bay was the team that New England would be playing in that Super Bowl) together having a beer and talking and "We were in the booth right behind them." It was a nice moment.

We talked about other players from that era. Bob felt that "Andre Tippett was a terrific guy. I spent a lot of time with him after he retired. I thought Garon Veris was a great guy, so was Ronnie Lippett … Fred Marion was a very smart player, a good guy." With regard to why Steve Grogan always had to fight for his job, Bob observed that "he wasn't the protypical quarterback. I think that whoever was the coach at the time thought that he could only take them so far. But Grogan had that inner quality, that leadership quality that people responded to, and his fellow players responded to, but for some reason, his coaches may have felt that he didn't have the right touch on the ball, or didn't have the deep ball, but he could do a lot of things. He was never really embraced as the number one guy."

- - -

We then talked about his experience working with Upton Bell on the "Calling All Sports" radio program. I mentioned to Bob that when I had spoken with Upton Bell, Upton had commented about Bob taking him to the edge of the cliff and then bringing him back, and Bob quickly responded "Upton was always willing to go to the edge of the cliff", which made for good radio. Bob added that "Upton did as much for my career as anyone. I was a kid from New Hampshire, and working with him, as a former GM or as the son of a former commissioner, gave me some street cred. He gave me some credibility." He said that "whatever strengths I had always was working with someone else and bouncing ideas of off someone else", and described the radio partnership with Upton Bell as being like "the perfect marriage".

He also brought up the fact that he and Gino Cappelletti did the first broadcast of the Boston Breakers USFL franchise at BU's Nickerson Field. I remembered the team and league, and that the Breakers' quarterback was Johnnie Walton, and Bob remembered that their first game was against the Denver Gold (Who names these teams? Did the fans yell things like 'Let's Go Gold' or 'Hurray, Gold' at their games?). Bob said, "I really enjoyed doing football play-by-play."

As noted previously, Bob used some key props and catch-phrases in his TV broadcasts, such as the Panic Button. He said that he "always liked to use props; you could always play off props, they were sort of like co-hosts, you could always play off of them. The Panic Button was so obvious. You always talk about pushing a panic button. You might as well have one. The key to the Panic Button was never using it too much, using it as little as possible. But then when it came out, it meant something."

As was the case with his relationship with Upton Bell, he always seemed to enjoy working with the other broadcasters, such as Liz Walker and Jack Williams. That also made the TV-4 news fun to watch. Bob said that "I always enjoyed these people."

Now that he is on radio, Bob obviously cannot use props so I asked what he will do instead. In typical confident fashion, Bob said "I'll think of something." It will be interesting to hear what he comes up with.

- - -

While the TV Sports Anchors today are very good, it is too bad that we don't have Bob Lobel on nightly TV any more. Or, to use a variation of one of Bob's favorite catch-phrases, why can't we get broadcasters like that?

Management Interviews

Upton Bell

General Manager, 1971-1972

Upton Bell and his family were significant contributors to the NFL for years before he took on the role of Patriots' General Manager in 1971. Upton's father, Bert Bell, had been the NFL Commissioner from 1946-1959, and before that had been involved in the formation of the Philadelphia Eagles in 1933 and was a co-owner of the Pittsburgh Steelers from 1941-46. Bert Bell died of a heart attack in October, 1959 while watching an Eagles' game at Franklin Field in Philadelphia (where he had played as a quarterback while at the University of Pennsylvania). While tragic, it was probably somewhat comforting for family and friends to realize that he had died while doing something he loved; as Upton put it himself, "What a way to go out." Upton was a junior in college at the time, and after graduation, went to work with the Baltimore Colts, and later became their Director of Player Personnel. Upton stayed in the Baltimore organization from 1960-1971 when he accepted the offer to become General Manager of the Patriots, thereby becoming – at the age of 33 – the youngest General Manager in the league.

During Upton's time with Baltimore the Colts were one of pro football's best teams, featuring such great players as quarterback Johnny Unitas, receiver Raymond Berry, runner/receiver Lenny Moore, offensive tackle Jim Parker, tight end John Mackey, runner Tom Matte, defensive end Gino Marchetti, and others. They regularly were contenders for the championship and had some outstanding seasons, including 12-2 in 1964 and 11-1-2 in 1967 (ironically not even making the playoffs that season), and 13-1 in 1968. They were Super Bowl Champions for the 1970-71 season, Upton's last year with the team.

Upton described his time with the Colts as "the greatest experience I've ever had in sports, and maybe a life-changing experience for many reasons". He talked about the outstanding players, such as those mentioned above, and also added that he "worked with two of the greatest coaches in pro football history, Weeb Ewbank and Don Shula, and I learned a lot from them". He went on to say "I came out of college and worked with a team that basically you may never see again. It was like a family. It was hard work. It was fun." He remembered joining the team as an intern after his junior year of college, after his father died, and on his first day in the Colt locker room Raymond Berry, Hall of Fame receiver and a very classy individual on and off the field, walked over to him and said, "I'm Raymond Berry. Anything that we can do to make your life fine while you are here ... welcome to the Colts." Upton remarked about "Can you imagine this happening today? I'm just a young kid, my father is dead" and here comes one of the NFL's top stars to say something welcoming such as this.

The Colts of those days were known as a close-knit team and a hard-working team, whose players not only were good teammates, but also were involved in the Baltimore-area community. Stories that I have read talked about how players lived in Baltimore neighborhoods and were easily recognizable while walking in those neighborhoods (a far cry from the way things are today). Upton talked about the closeness of the team, citing as an example how "Don Shula would set up activities in the off-season for the coaches and the front office, once a week we all went out to a place, and from nine to noon we all played racquetball, basketball and we all did it together. When we finished, we went back to the office for the afternoon. There was just a great feeling among these people that you will never see again". The sense of <u>team</u> was very strong from the top of the organization, owner Carroll Rosenbloom, on down. Upton summarized his time with the Colts by saying "not everything is perfect in life, but being in Baltimore was like being in the land of Oz. Everyone in town knew everybody, you could go anywhere, eat anywhere, drink anywhere, have fun anywhere, and know that you would be protected."

Coming to the Patriots provided Upton with a sharp contrast to the Colts' organization. The Patriots' history was troubled and Upton was advised by "some of the owners that I knew, or were friends of my father", that the Patriot organization was "not a good place to go", but Upton felt, and some others also told him, that he could turn it around. "The biggest problem", Upton went on to say, "was the ownership situation. There were four or five owners and there was a Board of Directors. I didn't know who was in charge." Ostensibly it would have been primary owner and team president Billy Sullivan, but "because the team had so many factions, many more than Sullivan had their hands in the operation".

With regard to Billy Sullivan, Upton said, "Sullivan and I didn't see eye-to-eye". In particular, as General Manager, Upton had been led to believe, when hired, that among his responsibilities was "the right to hire and fire the head coach". This is very understandable, as that is one of the key responsibilities of a General Manager in any professional sport. This issue became very contentious as the 1971 season wound down (a 6-8 season for the Patriots), as Upton wanted to fire Head Coach John Mazur. However, although he had indicated this would be Bell's decision, Sullivan "publicly reneged on this and said that he would now have to approve it". Upton forced a meeting with the team's Board of Directors to discuss this, and they reached the odd agreement that if the Patriots lost their last game of the season to the World Champion Baltimore Colts (ironically, Upton's old team) by more than two touchdowns, Upton could fire Mazur. Stories and rumors surfaced that this decision by the Board caused Upton to root against his own team during that game (as written in Michael Felger's book "Tales from the Patriot Sideline"), but Upton strongly denies this allegation, pointing out, "even as a child in my father's house, I was taught never to root for or against any sports team publicly." Upton also criticized Felger for "documenting this rumor as fact", adding "that was absolutely wrong, I would not do that." He said that he "wanted the team to win, of course, but wanted the Board to look closely and see that Mazur was not the right man to run the team" going forward. The Patriots won that game 21-17 in dramatic fashion, on a long touchdown pass late in the game from Jim Plunkett to Randy Vataha. The Board decided to keep Mazur for the 1972 season. However, when the team started 1972 by losing seven of their first nine games, the last loss a crushing 52-0 loss to Miami, everyone came to the realization that Mazur was not the right man for the job, as Upton had identified months earlier, and he was replaced on an interim basis by Phil Bengston, who had previously succeeded Vince Lombardi as Green Bay's Head Coach.

I asked Upton who he would have hired as the Patriot Head Coach had he been allowed to replace Mazur. Upton said that his first choice was Howard Schnellenberger, who went on to become a well-respected coach at a number of places, most notably at the University of Miami, where he turned that program around and made it a national power. One wonders if he could have done the same for the Patriots. Other possibilities Upton listed were George Young, who had been an assistant coach in Baltimore and who went on to become the General Manager of the New York Giants, and two great college coaches, Joe Paterno of Penn State and Chuck Fairbanks of Oklahoma. Ironically (it is interesting to note that 'ironically' was often a key word in describing the Patriots of that era), it was Fairbanks who replaced Upton as General Manager after the 1972 season. In fact, Upton said that "Sullivan used my list" when looking for a new Coach and a new GM when Upton was fired at the end of that season. The Patriots sought Paterno first, but he turned down their offer, and Fairbanks ultimately was hired as both Coach and GM.

Upton also mentioned that he "was going to hire Bobby Beathard as Director of Player Personnel". Beathard is a well-respected NFL executive who went on to have success at a number of places in his career (most notably Miami and San Diego). Upton said, "Bobby came here and we did a long interview here ... and when he met Sullivan and some of the people here" he decided not to take the job in New England, and that he told Upton "I'm not sure that is a stable place for me." It was another case of 'what might have been' for the Patriots of that time. Upton recommended Beathard to Don Shula, then Head Coach of Miami. Beathard became Director of Player Personnel for the Dolphins and later became General Manager of the Washington Redskins and San Diego Chargers.

It is also worth noting that under Upton's leadership, the Patriots established a full time scouting system for the organization and joined a scouting combine for the first time. Upton also hired a number of people who helped set the groundwork for the Patriots' and for the League's future. This included:

- Hiring Bucko Kilroy from the Dallas Cowboys as Head Scout. Kilroy later became General Manager of the Patriots
- Hiring Dick Steinberg (Scout) who later became the Personnel Director of the New York Jets, Los Angeles Rams and New Orleans Saints, and later returned to the Patriots in the same capacity
- Hiring Mike Hickey (Scout) who was also later hired as Director of Scouting for the New York Jets
- Hiring Bob Terpening (Scout) who is the Assistant General Manager of the Indianapolis Colts
- Hiring Tom Boisture (Scout) who later was hired as George Young's Director of Player Personnel for the New York Giants during their championship years (author's note: Tom Boisture was also the Head Football Coach at Holy Cross College when I was a student there)
- Hiring Peter Hadhazy as Assistant General Manager; he later became GM of the Cleveland Browns, Commissioner of the USFL and Assistant to Commissioner Pete Rozelle
- Hiring Denny Lynch as Assistant Publicity Director who became Director of Publicity for the Buffalo Bills.

- - -

The 1971 Patriots were the first team to play in Foxboro, after many years of nomadic existence in Boston, playing at BU's Nickerson Field, Harvard Stadium, Fenway Park, and BC's Alumni Stadium. Since the team was moving from Boston to Foxboro, it was decided that the team was more of a regional franchise than just a 'Boston' team, and as such the name should be changed. The first name chosen, before Upton joined the organization, was the Bay State Patriots but Upton said that he wanted it renamed since newspaper headlines about the 'BS' Patriots would not help the team's image. He suggested the name "New England Patriots", and that has been the name of the team since that time.

- - -

Our discussion then turned to players and games during the era in which Upton was GM. His first year was Jim Plunkett's first year with the Patriots, after he had been selected as the overall # 1 pick in the NFL draft. Upton quickly said that he couldn't take credit for drafting Jim Plunkett, since he (Upton) had joined the team after the draft, explaining that the Colts would not let Upton leave for New England until after the draft had taken place.

Upton did say that Plunkett "was beaten up so badly" in his first two years, with multiple sacks and hits while attempting to pass behind an offensive line that was not very strong. Upton said that he "kept trying to bring players in that I thought could help with Plunkett but Mazur wanted to keep the guys that he was familiar with and they were not capable any more because it was a different league and a different time" in terms of quarterback protection. Upton did sign undrafted wide receiver Randy Vataha, who had been Plunkett's teammate at Stanford, and the Plunkett-to-Vataha combination worked very well for the five years that they were together in New England.

Another player that Upton brought in who many thought would be very helpful was running back Duane Thomas, whom Upton acquired in a trade with Dallas. In his first two NFL seasons Thomas, an outstanding running back, had helped the Cowboys reach the Super Bowl in 1971 (losing to Upton's Colts) and then win the Super Bowl in 1972. However, Thomas was involved in a contract dispute with Dallas after the Super Bowl win, which made the Cowboys look to trade him. In talking about that trade, Upton laughed and commented, "It seemed I went from one controversial thing to another." He said that he had scouted Thomas in college and felt that "Duane Thomas was the closest thing that I had ever seen to Jim Brown. He had talent and he was very bright and very aware."

He went on to talk about the trade which sent Patriot running back Carl Garrett to Dallas for Thomas and linebacker Steve Kiner. All three players were later rumored to be players who used drugs, so this made for an odd trade. He felt that Thomas was not only a good running back, but also a good blocker, and would also be a great help in pass protection. He added though that "Mazur never did like the deal" but he went ahead with it anyway since he thought it would help the team.

Upton said that when Thomas got here "I could see that he had a problem … I had a couple of long conversations with him, one famous one out in the middle of the field and one in the office … I told him we would give him a new contract but he had to go and practice". That led to the next problem. Thomas had played in the I formation at Dallas, which had him leaning over with hands on his knees or at his side and he could survey the defense before the play and see where the holes in the defense might be. Mazur wanted him to play in the three point stance with one hand touching the ground. Upton said "you knew the confrontation was coming". He added, "Mazur knew the press was watching and you know how incendiary they could be … so essentially the coach forced my hand and said I don't want the guy here … and this was a way to embarrass him and maybe embarrass me … but I saw that it wasn't going to work" so the trade was rescinded and Garrett was returned to the Patriots, and Thomas to Dallas (he was subsequently traded from Dallas to Washington).

- - -

I asked Upton what his most memorable games were as Patriot GM. He mentioned the Opening Day 20-6 upset of a strong Oakland team in 1971, beating Miami 34-13 in a major upset later in the year with Miami on its way to its first Super Bowl, and beating Baltimore 21-17 on the last day of the season. He also added the early season upset wins over Atlanta and Washington the following year (21-20 and 24-23, respectively), which were 2 of only 3 wins the team had that season.

We went on to talk about the team after he left and particularly the Super Bowl winning team. When the 2001-02 Patriots went on to the Super Bowl, Upton admitted, "I didn't think that they had a chance against the Rams … but I wasn't totally surprised when it happened because I think that Belichick is one of the greatest coaches of all time, [whether people] like his methods or his style or not, and if anyone could devise a defense for the greatest show on turf it would be him. If you look at that defensive team, they were pretty good … their defense pretty much won that game for them."

Upton credits Chuck Fairbanks as being "the original savior of the franchise" and says that the hiring of Bill Parcells "really changed the modus operandi here because not only did he come in here and change the way that they drafted and the things that they did but also that whole coaching staff with Belichick and getting the financial backing from Kraft. It's a shame that Kraft and Parcells couldn't get along because that would have been a great partnership, as it is now with Kraft and Belichick."

- - -

After leaving the Patriots, Upton became involved with the Charlotte Hornets, a team in the newly formed World Football League. When that league folded, the New York Giants were looking for a replacement for their General Manager, Andy Robustelli. Upton was interested in the job, but did not get it. Upton described that he felt he was being bad-mouthed by Billy Sullivan, which contributed to Upton not being hired by the Giants or any other NFL team. Upton said that he "sent a message to Wellington Mara" (the Giant owner), asking him about this, and, although not revealing what Mara said in response, Upton indicated that Mara's response did convince him that Sullivan was indeed doing this. Ironically (there's that word again), the man who got the job as GM of the Giants was George Young, with whom Upton had worked in Baltimore, and the man that Upton wanted to hire as Patriot Coach to replace John Mazur.

- - -

We then talked about his experience working with Bob Lobel on the "Calling All Sports" radio program in the 1970s. It was a very popular show (my wife and I were among its many fans). Upton commented, "if you were to pick a perfect marriage of two people and put them on the radio" it was Bob and Upton. Upton recalled, "we respected our differences … we did things that were unusual like doing a whole thing on the art of motorcycle maintenance. It was not just sports … and there was nothing rehearsed; we both did our own research, we both came to our conclusions" for the show. That helped push the envelope and got good conversations going on between them and with their listeners. He added about Bob that "the greatest thing that he did for me was that he always brought me to the edge of the cliff and then let me come back and that's a real gift" which made for good discussions on the radio. Upton remembered that show as "one of those rare things that would probably never happen again".

- - -

It was really enjoyable talking to Upton, not only for the insights into the role of a General Manager and the inner struggles of the Patriots in the early 1970s, but for the far-reaching discussion that we had on a number of topics, not all of which are included here. I'm sorry that he couldn't have been with the Patriots longer, since it does sound like he could have made a positive difference for the team. As it is, he has also been a positive force on radio as well – he is currently on WCRN 830 AM in the Worcester area – and in the many interviews that he has done, not just with sports figures, but national/political figures, such as the first President Bush (his web site, uptonbell.com has a great interview with Ted Kennedy, for example). It was great talking with him, and I hope to have the opportunity to do so again in the future.

Raymond Berry
Assistant Coach, 1978-1981
Head Coach, mid-1984 - 1989

When I first became a football fan in the 1960s my first favorite team was the Baltimore Colts, and my favorite players were quarterback Johnny Unitas, wide receiver Raymond Berry, and runner/receiver Lenny Moore. It was easy to see that these guys were not only very talented, but worked very hard at being the best that they could be. As noted earlier in the book, Berry and Unitas were famous for staying late after practices to work with each other to improve their timing and feel on pass plays, and that extra work paid off in two championships for the Colts, in 1958 and 1959. The first of those was the famous overtime championship game in 1958, as Unitas completed pass after pass to Berry to drive the Colts down the field to tie the game late in the fourth quarter and win the game in overtime. Berry wound up catching 12 passes for 178 yards in that game as he and Unitas captured the imagination of the country.

Raymond Berry overcame a number of physical issues (e.g., vision problems, one leg being shorter than the other) through a lot of hard work and effort to become a star during his career and a Hall of Famer when that career ended. He was drafted from SMU by the Colts and played his entire 13 year career (1955-1967) with Baltimore. He led the league in pass receptions three times, went to the Pro Bowl six times, and, along with Jerry Rice and Lance Alworth, is considered one of the best receivers of all time. Berry's Baltimore team was one of the best in the league during his playing career, winning those NFL Championships in 1958 and 1959 with 9-3 records each season, and had other outstanding seasons, including 12-2 in 1964, 10-3-1 in 1965, and 11-1-2 in 1967 (ironically not even making the playoffs that season due to a tie-breaker).

Raymond was an Assistant Coach with the Patriots from 1978-1981, first under Chuck Fairbanks and then Ron Erhardt. He became Head Coach of the Patriots in mid-1984 and led the team to the first Super Bowl in the team's history in 1986. In his career as Patriot Head Coach the team was 48-39 in the regular season and 3-2 in the post-season, posting the following records:

1984	4-4	(after taking over from Ron Meyer in mid-season)
1985	11-5	with playoff wins over the Jets, Raiders, and Dolphins, before losing to the Bears in the Super Bowl
1986	11-5	reaching the playoffs where they lost a close game to Denver
1987	8-7	
1988	9-7	

1989   5-11

I had the opportunity to talk with Raymond Berry in May of 2009 about his playing career with the Colts and coaching career with the Patriots, and found him to be everything his former players described him as being, very gracious, very nice, and an easy person with whom to talk.

Raymond described his time in Baltimore as "a great time to be there", saying "We had great leadership. Carroll Rosenbloom was a tremendous owner, and I've learned over the years that it all starts at the top. He hired great coaches. Weeb Ewbank was one of the greatest of all time." I mentioned how Upton Bell had also talked about Baltimore Colt Coaches Ewbank and Don Shula as two of the greatest coaches of all time, and Raymond immediately responded, "That's right. Carroll Rosenbloom was responsible for that. He hired the head guy and that sets the whole tone."

I asked about the Colts' hard-working reputation and Raymond agreed, saying, "It was a team that was very, very serious about its business. We had great chemistry. We got along well together. We had a great mix of humor with some of our players, like Art Donovan, but when it came to football, we were very serious." He also talked about how the Colt players were part of the community in Baltimore, and credited the owner for that, stating, "It was a unique relationship between the fans and the team. I think really that one of the main reasons for that was Carroll Rosenbloom. He reached out to the fans. He created the 'Colt Corral' [a fan group]. He was a people person and it showed in his attitude toward the fans."

Although the choice of Raymond's most memorable game as a player may be obvious (the 1958 overtime Championship Game generally being considered the greatest game of all time), I nevertheless asked him about him most memorable games (plural). The first that he mentioned was that 1958 game saying "without question" that was the most memorable. I mentioned that he was a big contributor to that win with 12 catches and he responded humbly "yeah, it was a big game for me" but then quickly diverted the attention from himself, saying, "It matched the two best defensive teams in pro football. The Giants had finished first in defense and the Colts had finished second. It was a slugging match. It wasn't anything beautiful because these two defenses were so dominant, but the drama of the two minute drive that tied the game with seven seconds on the clock and then there's overtime - which nobody had ever seen overtime and didn't know what it was – it had such drama about it. And then the significance of winning that first championship was just an unbelievable experience." In fact, he described it colorfully as "a mountaintop experience to come off the field after that game as World Champions. There was nothing quite like it that I have ever experienced."

He then added what was another memorable game for the team from earlier that season, a November 30 game against San Francisco, which he described as "a close second" to that 1958 title game. He remembered, "we were behind 27-7 at halftime and came back and won the game 35-27 in the second half in order to win the Western Division Title, which put us in that World Championship Game. The players that were on that '58 team always looked back to that particular game as one of the best games that we ever played". With typical Berry humility he did not mention (but I will) that he was one of the reasons for that comeback, as he accounted for 114 receiving yards to help spur the comeback.

- - -

We then moved on to discuss Raymond's time with the Patriots, first as an Assistant and then as Head Coach. I asked Raymond if he had known Chuck Fairbanks before Fairbanks hired him to be an assistant on his staff, and he said, "I had never met him before. I was on the Cleveland Browns staff and had gotten fired. I was at the Senior Bowl game in Mobile [Alabama] and Chuck Fairbanks talked to me about joining his staff in New England as a receivers coach, and so he offered me the job and I went there." He went on to describe his experience with Fairbanks very positively, saying, "one of the great memories that I have of coaching was being around Chuck Fairbanks, and I was only around him one year ... Chuck Fairbanks was one of the sharpest people that I have ever been around in the coaching business ... he built that Patriot team ... he was responsible for organizing and drafting that team; he was the brains behind that whole organization ... he would hire the best coaches that he could find and he would let them coach ... as a coach he involved his coaches in the draft; it was a great insight ... in four or five years he had built this team from very little until he had a major group of players; had he not gotten into a conflict with Billy Sullivan [see Chapter 3 for details] and if Chuck Fairbanks had stayed there another five years, that would have been a dynasty."

We talked about the fiasco (described in Chapter 3) with Fairbanks being fired from a playoff team before the team's final regular season game, and Raymond described it as "traumatic". He added, "Chuck told me that his understanding with Billy Sullivan was that Chuck would be in total control of the whole operation, and that if there was ever any breech of that, Mr. Sullivan would [void] the whole contract and I would be out of there. When Mr. Sullivan started to influence who Chuck wanted to draft [and other things], Chuck put into effect exactly what he said he was going to do and he walked out of it." It was another of the many cases of 'what might have been' that plagued Patriot history in the 20th century.

As receivers coach, Raymond had a pass-catching corps that included Stanley Morgan, Harold Jackson, Darryl Stingley, Andy Johnson, and Russ Francis among others. I asked about those receivers and Raymond immediately gave the credit to Chuck Fairbanks saying, "he was the one who brought in the receivers; he was a split T coach [in college] and yet he knew how to draft for professional football. That was another tip-off on how brilliant the man was. He didn't know anything about the pro passing game, but he hired people that did and he drafted the pieces to put it together. Those two players were Hall of Fame caliber players – Stanley Morgan and Russ Francis". That Fairbanks brought in Raymond Berry, whom he had not known before, as someone who knew the pro passing game is a testament to the vision and abilities of both men.

Raymond was in his first year as an assistant when Darryl Stingley suffered a hit from Jack Tatum that wound up paralyzing him. Raymond described the vicious hit by Tatum as being "unnecessary". I asked if he realized immediately how severe the injury was and he said he did not, recalling, "I was in the coaching box out in Oakland when that happened. I didn't know that it was as bad as it was. I saw the hit and it was totally unnecessary. It was really a very very sad chapter."

We then turned our attention to a happier chapter, Raymond taking over the head coaching role in 1984 and leading the team to its first Super Bowl in 1985-86. Raymond admitted that he was surprised when the Patriots asked him to be head coach. He had been out of football for a while and just living in Medfield, MA, when Patrick Sullivan came to his home one day and asked him to be the head coach.

I asked Raymond how he turned the team around from being a loser to being in the Super Bowl. He said

"one of the key reasons why the team got turned around, as I look back on it, I had never been a head coach until this time. My dad was a high school football coach in Paris, Texas, and I grew up watching him, being around him, and listening to him. One of his great strengths as a coach was his ability to get a team to play up to their capabilities. He would look at an individual or at a team as a group and if he felt like their talent was at a certain level he would tell them what they were capable of doing. Without my realizing it – I'll use the word 'programmed' - I was basically programmed that way growing up. I played for him and as I look back on my playing experience for him in the years after high school I realized that while playing for him we never thought we were going to lose a game. When I became head coach of the Patriots I was hired with eight games left and I didn't know two thirds of the players. So I walked the sidelines watching this team for eight games and I looked at the film, and I began to realize that this team had everything it needed to be as good as anybody in the league. So I began telling this team what it could do and I don't think they ever really had any idea how good they could be. I think this was one of the greatest, biggest contributions that I made to this football team, bringing them to an awareness of the fact that they were totally under-achieving and they had the ability to play with anybody. So the psychological input was the most important thing I brought to that team. I think they then began to experience what I was talking about, that they could beat people that they didn't think maybe they could beat."

This perfectly mirrors the type of thing that John Hannah and Steve Grogan talked about in the interviews earlier in this section, about what Raymond Berry brought to the players in terms of convincing them that they could be a good team after years of hearing how bad they were.

Beyond that, Raymond continued, "The other thing was the total emphasis on the fundamentals. We had to learn to protect the football and not turn it over. We got very good at doing that. One of the most important fundamentals that I introduced to them was directly right out of high school and my dad. He used to take a break right in the middle of practice, get water and then each player would go to their position coach. The coach would have two or three footballs, and he would roll them out on the ground and make these guys jump on the ball and recover the fumble … I told my team that story and I told them we were going to do it. My defensive coaches took it one step further. They not only had them fall on it .. they had to pick the ball up. All you had to do was look at the record of the games in which we had this playoff run and we may have recovered 12-14 fumbles and lost only one." This fumble exercise was one that Steve Grogan had cited in my interview with him to show how well-organized Berry was and how well he prepared that team for success. Raymond seemed pleased to hear Steve's comments about how it not only was good preparation, but that the players had fun with it.

Raymond remembered a game earlier that season against the Jets, where, as he put it, "we had a big turnover that we got from the Jets when they were inside our ten yard line going in, and I think that in the review of that game and the films of it, the light bulbs started going on, 'we executed this fundamental and it turned the game around' so when we went on the field and fell on the ball it was a different thing" after that.

The playoff wins over the Jets, Raiders, and Dolphins brought the Patriots into the Super Bowl against that powerful Bears team. I asked Raymond what it was like preparing for that great defense and he recalled that earlier in the season the two teams had met and the Bears had won 20-7, with Craig James running for the New England touchdown after catching a short pass. "Other than that we didn't really dent the Bears defense", he said, adding "as we got ready for the Super Bowl, I knew that our run to get there had been an emotional high, and I think we came down to earth … there were a couple of basic reasons why we didn't do any better against the Bears than we did. One was that we did have a letdown after four weeks of emotional highs." He then went on to sum it up perfectly by saying "I think the other key factor was that we put a first grade offense on the field against a PhD defense". This in no way was meant to denigrate his team, as Raymond seemed very proud of that team and that offense, but it does say a lot about the Chicago defense, which, Raymond pointed out, Chicago had "spent seven or eight years putting that defense together" versus the year and a half that he had been with his offense. Raymond talked about the Chicago defensive front seven as being one of the best that he had ever seen, along with the Steel Curtain defense of the great Pittsburgh teams of the 1970s.

- - -

One of the toughest decisions Raymond had to make in that year and others was about his starting quarterback – Tony Eason or Steve Grogan, Doug Flutie or Steve Grogan. I asked Raymond what factored into his decision about the starting quarterback, particularly the Eason-Grogan decision. He told me, "a huge part of our success was when we had both of these guys available. It is a great tribute to Steve Grogan who is a big part of the story. When they fired Ron Meyer and I took over the team in that '84 season, Tony Eason had been installed as the # 1 quarterback, so I did not change anything. We went on to finish that season and in the off-season, I called Steve Grogan and called him in and talked to him. I told him 'You are a starting quarterback and Tony Eason is a starting quarterback too. At this stage of your career, you've been through 10 years of playing and have had a lot of hits on your body, and this is what eventually eliminates quarterbacks. You can be more valuable to our football team at this point coming out of the bullpen. There is another reason for it too. If you're not playing, you're not getting hit, and if you don't get hit, you're going to play longer. You're at the high point of your salary, you're at the end of your playing career, with a few years left, you can extend your career if you're not having to play all the time. I think you will be valuable if you will take that role. We can win with Tony Eason and we can win with you, so it's a good situation.' That is exactly what happened. Then in about our fourth or fifth game Tony Eason gets a shoulder separated", so Grogan was back in at QB.

Raymond continued, "This was one of the more interesting experiences that I had as a head coach. We were playing Buffalo. We were 2-3 at the time, and our offense just wasn't getting on track. Tony Eason gets his shoulder separated. Steve Grogan walks over to me on the sideline during the game and I looked at him and I instinctively made a decision. I said 'Steve, you go in and run the show.' What was behind that was that I came out of a background in which my dad at Paris High School always delegated the play-calling. My dad always gave that to whoever was the smartest player on the team. When I was a senior, he gave that job to me, so I had experience doing it. Then when I was with the Baltimore Colts for 13 years, Coach Weeb Ewbank and Don Shula gave that job of calling plays to Unitas. I was aware of the dynamic that happens whenever a quarterback is doing it. The quarterback is going to start asking the offensive players for information. He would ask Stanley Morgan 'What can you beat this guy on?' or ask John Hannah 'What do you see up there on the line?' As soon as these players knew that Grogan was calling them, their film study and their preparation took on a whole different turn. So we tapped into a dynamic there that I knew was going to happen. I also knew that I had a rare quarterback in Grogan who was the smartest guy on our team, the toughest guy on our team, the best leader, and he was very experienced in using the running game. I knew our best chance of winning was to let him run the show. I saw him do it with Chuck [Fairbanks] and I knew he could do it. We won six straight before he got his knee hurt and Tony came back in and after that I started calling the plays. I took the job over through the Super Bowl."

Raymond went on to say, "The next year in the off-season I called Grogan in and I said 'this play-calling is a heavy burden for a head coach to handle … I think that you can call the plays" even though Tony Eason was still the starter. Raymond recalled that Steve looked at him and said "I've never done that. I've only done it when I was playing", to which Raymond replied "Yeah, I know that, but I think you can do it. When we come to training camp with the rookies I want you to come up there and I want you to go through that week. You'll be on the field and you will be running the offense and calling the plays and get a feel for it." This sounds like a great idea and a great way to develop a smart player into possibly a great coach. Raymond went on to report, "He came to camp and went through all that and said 'yeah, I think I got a feel for this. I'm going to do it.' so in the 1986 season we went 11-5 and Tony had a great year and Grogan called them from the sideline". We agreed that it was surprising and too bad that Grogan was not hired as an assistant. He could have really been very helpful to any team which hired him.

- - -

In the days following the Patriots' Super Bowl loss to the Bears, there were stories published in *The Boston Globe* about rampant drug use among Patriot players. Raymond has been given a lot of credit from a number of sources not only for working hard to eliminate this as a problem with the team, but also for going above and beyond his coaching duties and helping players deal with and get rid of their personal problems with drugs. I asked Raymond if he was willing to talk about this, and to his credit he was willing and was very open about it.

He said that he first learned about the problem at the end of the 1984 season, saying that head coaches are privy to a lot of information that others, including other coaches, are not. He said that he "resolved that this is going to stop" and cited three reasons why he felt so strongly about this, explaining "Number one is the integrity of the National Football League. The second reason is that if you have an entire coaching staff, an entire organization, and 95% of your players are busting their butts trying to win, the head coach's responsibility is to make darn sure that we don't have any saboteurs on board. The third reason is that I didn't go for standing by and seeing young men destroy their lives."

He said that he "started looking around at what tools I had to make it stop and I found out I didn't have hardly any because nobody was dealing with it". As a result, he decided to start "in the off-season of '85 talking to players one-on-on; I spent the whole off-season flying places and bringing them in, and I talked to them about why we were going to stop this drug use … what we were going to do to stop it, and that I was not going to tolerate it... and I talked to them about Big Daddy Lipscomb [a former Baltimore Colt who died in the 1960s from an overdose of heroin] … and I told them about a player with the Detroit Lions [where Berry was an Assistant Coach in the 1970s] who almost lost his life from cocaine". He indicated that he wanted all of the players to agree to start doing voluntary drug testing beginning when the players reported to training camp.

I found all of this to be utterly fantastic. Not only was Raymond Berry great as a player and great as a coach, but he was also great as a human being. This kind of thing is almost unheard of. It is hard to imagine baseball dealing with its problems this way, for example, or the baseball union allowing any team to do this kind of thing, but Raymond drove for it. He ultimately didn't institute it because he wanted 100% of the players to agree and he said "all but one or two went along with it", so he did not do it. However, it did have the effect of causing some players to quit and Raymond said "I do know that when we came to camp that year we were the cleanest team, no question about that."

Raymond said that at a reunion of that time a few years ago arranged by Mr. Kraft, two players came up to him and told him "Coach, you saved my life". That is one of those 'wow' moments that you don't always get in life, and it shows that Raymond Berry was not just a great coach, but may have been an even better leader of men.

- - -

The way that the players reacted to him in this case made me read for Raymond some of the very positive comments I had gotten about him from other interviewees (see the interviews above for details, for example, the comments of John Hannah and Steve Grogan). I asked what his reaction was to those comments and he responded that he was "very satisfied ... it makes you feel good ... it's great to have that kind of feedback ... particularly years later as players live lives and reflect on things, things come into better focus and I think for them to be saying things like that is very encouraging to me". In my opinion, it also says a lot about Raymond Berry the man.

I then asked him if there was anything that he wanted to say about those players, and he said, "The number one fundamental to me, if you want to be a great coach, there's a simple formula, get great players." He went on to recall how he was out of coaching, living in Medfield, working for his brother-in-law, when Pat Sullivan came over to his house "on a Wednesday night in October" and asked him to be Head Coach. I asked if he was surprised and he answered, "surprise was a small word, that's for sure" that didn't begin to tell how floored Raymond was with this offer. Having smart, hard-working players like Hannah and Grogan may have made the decision to coach, and his coaching experience, a lot easier for him.

- - -

We talked about the current Patriots and I asked if he followed them and he said "The Patriots are the number one team that I root for and I keep up with them close and really enjoy doing that. Bill Belichick is at another level from most coaches. I don't know how to describe Bill Belichick other than to say he's outstanding."

He attributes much of their success in 2008 to Belichick, and said that it was interesting that I brought up that 2008 season and how successful the Patriots were after the injury to Brady, because it reminded him of Don Shula handling the loss of Johnny Unitas and

Gary Cuozzo one year, and having running back Tom Matte (who had been a quarterback at Ohio State) take over as quarterback. He said that "Shula comes into the meeting room on Monday and says 'OK, this is our plan. We are going to shift Matte to quarterback. Defense, your job is to shut them out. Lou [Michaels, their kicker] we are going to get you close enough to kick field goals. That's the way we're going to go about approaching things. It was one of the most powerful leadership acts that I have ever witnessed, and it was pure Don Shula. He wasn't concerned about the odds. He already had a plan about how we were going to go win." It worked, as that Colt team went 10-3-1, tied mighty Green Bay for the Western Division title, and lost a playoff with Green Bay on a controversial field goal in overtime.

Raymond tied that to the 2008 Patriots, saying "You're looking at Belichick, so many years later, in a little better situation" since he had a backup quarterback. We talked about Matt Cassel and my observation that you could make a case for Cassel as the NFL's MVP in 2008, the same way Earl Morrall was MVP in 1968, a second year in which the Baltimore Colts lost their great quarterback, Johnny Unitas, to injury. He said "I think that's true. I don't think anyone would blink an eye at that." It was nice to have a Hall of Fame football player agree with my assessment.

- - -

As I had done with retired players, I asked Raymond how he was feeling these days and how he spends his time. He said "I've got great health and energy, and I'm on the go all the time. I have a busy life … I've got four grandchildren right over the back fence and they walk right through and come over here every day" which he greatly enjoys.

I asked if there was anything that he wanted to add and he said "When I think about that team, I feel real gratitude to the Sullivan family for letting me come to the team at the time that I did and to help those players. There have been two or three times in my life where the formula has been that I was in the right place at the right time with the right people. That certainly happened with the Baltimore Colt experience. And it certainly happened with the New England Patriots."

- - -

In my opinion, Raymond Berry was the right guy in the right place at the right time for the Patriots as well.

Well before I spoke with Raymond – in fact, well before I even knew that there was a *chance* that I could speak with him or any of these interviewees - I wrote the chapter in this book that is entitled "The Class of Raymond Berry". Everything that I have heard about, read about, and experienced directly with Raymond has led me to believe that "classy" may be one very good way to describe him. With his tremendous work ethic as a player and coach, with his treatment of players and the way he proactively helped to clean out the drug problems some of the players had, with the way he almost always deflected praise that was coming his way to giving credit to someone else instead, Raymond Berry came across as a truly remarkable individual.

Raymond Berry and Johnny Unitas were two of my first favorite football players when I was growing up, and it is extremely pleasing to find that the person that I admired so much on the playing field was such a great person off the field as well.

My mother-in-law, Helen, used to have a way of looking at people, especially celebrities, and trying to determine if they were a good person by considering if you would want to have them living next door to you. This always struck me as a good, positive way to judge people by a person who was a really good person herself. It strikes me that she would have enjoyed having Raymond Berry as a neighbor. I know that I would.

Not Interviewed, Just Profiled

Tom Brady

Patriot Career: 2000 – present
Position Played: Quarterback
College: Michigan

While I was able to interview a number of key players and difference makers from Patriot history, I was unfortunately not able to do so with Tom Brady, though I did contact the agency that represents him to try to arrange to do so. Although it was disappointing, it was also understandable, given the demands on his time, his fame, and his busy schedule. However, we will include a profile of Tom Brady here, since no list of Patriot difference makers would be complete without Tom Brady.

Tom Brady is, quite simply, the most significant person in the history of the New England Patriots. You could make a case for the owner, Bob Kraft, the Head Coach, Bill Belichick, or even previous owners, coaches, and players such as Billy Sullivan, Gino Cappelletti, Steve Grogan, John Hannah, or Bill Parcells, but the greatest successes that the Patriots have had have come since Tom Brady was established as the starting quarterback.

Every Boston sport has its iconic figure – Ted Williams for the Red Sox, Bobby Orr for the Bruins, and a myriad of choices for the Boston Celtics: Bill Russell, Larry Bird, Bob Cousy, John Havlicek, Red Auerbach, and others. These are the individuals that people think of when they hear the team name. It's also true of other teams in football and other sports: the Chicago Bulls and Michael Jordan, the Cleveland Browns and Jim Brown, the Denver Broncos and John Elway, the 49ers and Joe Montana, for example. The Patriots never really had such a player until Tom Brady. In fact, as Bob Lobel mentioned during his interview for this book, when he did his famous show in which he did a roundtable interview with Ted Williams, Bobby Orr, and Larry Bird, "At that time there was no pro football player to add to that panel. Of course now Brady would make it automatically."

Tom Brady had a good career at the University of Michigan, but, for some reason, was overshadowed during his time there by two other quarterbacks, Brian Griese and Drew Henson. Henson was heavily recruited by Michigan and heavily hyped by Michigan PR and the national press, and was practically anointed as the Michigan starter, but Brady proved to be the better player.

When he finished his Michigan career, Brady was drafted by the New England Patriots, but, surprisingly, he lasted until the sixth round of the draft before he was picked. New England's pick in the first six rounds that year were:

Round	Overall Pick #	Player	College	Position
1	16	(Pick was traded to New York Jets)		
2	46	Adrian Klemm	Hawaii	Offensive Tackle
3	76	J.R.Redmond	Arizona	Running Back
4	127	Greg Robinson-Randall	Michigan State	Offensive Tackle
5a	141	Dave Stachelski	Boise State	Tight End
5b	161	Jeff Marriott	Missouri	Defensive Tackle
6a	187	Antwan Harris	Virginia	Defensive Back
6b	**199**	**Tom Brady**	**Michigan**	**Quarterback**
6c	201	David Nugent	Purdue	Defensive Tackle

Quarterbacks taken by other teams before New England selected Tom Brady included Chad Pennington in the first round by the Jets, Giovanni Carmazzi in the third round by the 49ers, and Tee Martin in the fifth round by the Steelers. Of these, only Pennington has had any success in the NFL, and none approaching that of Brady.

As recounted in an earlier chapter, Nick Cafardo told a story in his book, "The Impossible Team", of how shortly after Brady was drafted, in April 2000, he and owner Bob Kraft passed each other in the stairs at the New England practice facility. Brady, carrying a pizza, introduced himself to Kraft. As they started back, Brady reportedly turned and said "Mr. Kraft, I'm the best decision your organization ever made." He was absolutely right.

When Tom reported to training camp, he found that he was fourth on the quarterback depth chart. Drew Bledsoe, the starter, was a former Pro Bowl quarterback, the holder of many franchise records, and the face of the franchise in advertising and for the media. Between Drew and Tom were veteran Damon Huard and young Michael Bishop. Bishop had become somewhat of a media darling and fan favorite, and many expected him to be the person who could ultimately replace Drew Bledsoe, when Bledsoe retired or left the team.

However, he had impressed the Patriot staff with his hard work and willingness to do anything to help the team. He was especially good at being the scout team quarterback, running the opposition's offense against the Patriots' defense in the practice week preceding games.

In his book "The Education of a Coach", David Halberstam wrote the following about Brady's dedication:

> "Brady ... became even more determined to turn himself into a quality NFL quarterback. No one, he decided, was going to work harder ... here was Brady during his off-hours behaving as if there were no off-hours; he was always sitting in a small room, studying film, comparing it with the playbook, which he had already mastered. He did it in an interesting way ... some players might have done it noisily, to show how hard they were working ... but Brady ... was doing it as a private thing ... as quietly as possible, sneaking into a tiny office and burying himself in front of the film.
>
> Then when everyone else was gone for the day, he would go out and practice, using some of the receivers from the taxi squad ... He was not just telling the receivers, let's run a down and out, or a square in, but he was calling plays ... as if the players were in a pressurized, game-time situation. He would use the playbook terminology and call the requisite play ... so he could understand it in a game situation, in case he was ever sent in."

In addition, Brady kept working out in the weight room and kept building up and strengthening his body. He was one of the hardest working members of the team. In fact, as has often been reported, the Patriots had a parking spot reserved close to the locker room that was awarded to the player who was looked at as the hardest-working; for years, the person who regularly had that spot was Tom Brady. Think of it, it was a quarterback, not an offensive lineman or defensive player, but a quarterback. That is a great testament to the tremendous work ethic that has characterized Tom Brady's career.

By the beginning of his second pro season, 2001, Brady had moved ahead of Huard and Bishop to be the primary backup behind Drew Bledsoe. He may not have had the strongest throwing arm at the time (though he now probably has one of the strongest in the game), but he was smart. He understood the game, he had mastered the playbook as Halberstam pointed out, he could make good reads on the field, and he did not make mistakes. All of this added up to success when he had to step in to the starting QB role.

Brady was thrust into this role on September 23, 2001, after a brutal injury to Patriot starter Drew Bledsoe in a game against the Jets (details of that injury can be found in the Bledsoe interview). Brady came into the game to replace Bledsoe, having thrown exactly three passes, completing one, in his NFL career up to that point.

The Patriots lost that game to the Jets to fall to 0-2 for the season, but won the next week in Brady's first start as a pro. It was a big 44-13 win over the Indianapolis Colts and their superstar quarterback Peyton Manning. Brady provided an error-free performance as the starting QB, hitting 13 of 23 passes for 168 yards with no turnovers.

As the season progressed, Brady and the Patriots began a roll that would take them to the Super Bowl. Two weeks after the win over the Colts, the Brady legend began to be created, as he led the team to a thrilling 29-26 comeback win in overtime against San Diego. The Patriots were trailing 26-16 8:38 to go, when Brady led them on a 69 yard, 15 play drive to a field goal by Adam Vinatieri, followed by another drive to the tying score on a touchdown pass by Brady with only 40 seconds left in regulation. The Pats won on an Adam Vinatieri field goal in overtime.

When Bledsoe was healed he expected to get back into the lineup, but Head Coach Bill Belichick decided to stay with Brady. He felt that the team was playing better under Brady than they had been under Bledsoe, and also liked Brady's outstanding leadership qualities and work ethic.

When Belichick made this decision, the Patriots were 5-5. They would not lose another game all season, as they won their last six regular season games to finish 11-5 and win the AFC East, and then won all three of their playoff games to win the Super Bowl for the first time in the team's history.

The first playoff game in that run has become one of the most famous games in NFL history. "The Tuck Rule Game". The game was played in Foxboro, against the Oakland Raiders, on a Saturday night, during a major snowstorm. The Raiders had a 13-3 lead going into the fourth quarter, when the Patriots decided to go with a no huddle offense, and put the game in Brady's hands. Tom led the team on a long drive that resulted in touchdown, getting the score himself by scrambling on a busted pass play for six yards and the TD. Brady dove into the snowy end zone, got up, and emphatically spiked the ball in triumph, falling down as he did so and bouncing up happily. As I mentioned in the write-up of this game in Chapter 6, I will never forget that look of joy and almost-boyish enthusiasm on his face as he did this.

The Patriots then got the ball with time remaining for one last drive to tie or win the game. Brady dropped back to throw and was blitzed by Oakland defensive back Charles Woodson. Brady's arm came forward to throw but as he did, he noticed the defender coming in. He brought the ball down to his waist and tried to cover it with his left hand, but Woodson stripped the ball from his hands, and Oakland recovered the fumble.

However, referee Walt Coleman went over to review the replay and what he saw made him overturn the fumble call. Since Brady's arm had been going forward, it was, by rule, an incomplete pass. The Patriots still had the ball. Brady marched the team down, and with 27 seconds to go in the game, Adam Vinatieri made a difficult 45 yard field goal to tie the game.

The Patriots got the ball first in overtime and Brady once again marched them down the field beautifully, completing his first six passes, and driving the team 61 yards in 15 plays to a winning 23 yard field goal by Vinatieri. As described in Chapter 6, despite playing in horrible weather conditions, Brady was fantastic. He was 32 of 52 passing for 312 yards and led his team on three clutch drives for three scores and the win. He and Adam Vinatieri really started building their reputations as outstanding clutch performers in this game.

Brady was injured in the AFC Championship Game in Pittsburgh the next week, but Drew Bledsoe came in and helped the team to a win that sent them to the Super Bowl against the powerful St. Louis Rams. Brady was back in for that game, but it was the defense that helped give the Patriots a 17-3 lead after three quarters. The

Rams came back to tie the game 17-17, but this is when the Brady legend jumped up another few notches.

The Patriots took over after the Ram kickoff at their own 17 yard line, with only 1:21 left in the game and no timeouts remaining. The conventional wisdom was that New England should just have Brady 'take a knee' and have the clock run out, sending the Super Bowl into overtime. Esteemed TV analyst John Madden even stated that that is what he expected the Patriots to do. However, Bill Belichick was concerned that the Rams had momentum and he decided to go for it. *Sports Illustrated* later quoted Belichick as saying "With a quarterback like Brady, going for the win is not that dangerous, because he is not going to make a mistake." That is supreme confidence.

Brady was surprised at the decision, but excited.

Then he executed the drive perfectly. He dropped back three times and three times completed drop-off passes to J.R. Redmond for 5 yards, 8 yards, 11 yards, and two first downs. On a second and ten on the New England 41 Brady hit Troy Brown over the middle and Brown gained 23 yards to the St. Louis 36 and ran out of bounds to stop the clock. Another Brady completion, this one to Jerome Wiggins, got the ball down to the 30. As written in Chapter 6,

> With time running down, Brady coolly brought the team to the line of scrimmage and spiked the ball, stopping the clock with 7 seconds left in regulation. How cool was Brady? He nonchalantly caught the ball as it was bouncing back down after the spike and handed it to the referee.

> After watching Brady's execution on this drive, announcer John Madden, who had earlier felt that the Patriots should play for overtime, said "What Tom Brady just did gives me goose bumps." It was another indication that the Patriots had something really special with this young quarterback.

Adam Vinatieri came in, made the field goal, and the New England Patriots were Champions of the World.

Tom Brady was named the Most Valuable Player in the game and was now an overnight sensation. His cool, calm demeanor, burning intensity, and great clutch play had made him a star. That star would only shine brighter as the years went on.

The 2002 season started well, with a 30-14 win over Pittsburgh on Monday night, September 9, in the first regular season game at the new Gillette Stadium. A very confident Tom Brady directed the no-huddle offense brilliantly, keeping the Steeler defense off-balance and wrapping this one up early. However, as many of the interviewees noted, the team was not the same that year and other teams were ready for them, so the Patriots wound up 9-7 and missed the playoffs.

The Patriots were dominant in 2003 and 2004, but had to overcome a rocky start to do so. They had gone undefeated in the 2003 pre-season games, and looked very strong in doing so. Then Lawyer Milloy, a well-respected team leader, was cut from the team's roster just before the 2003 opener. The news of Milloy's release was received very bitterly by the team, and even, Tom Brady, normally very positive about the organization, was critical of that decision. The Patriots opened the season with a 31-0 blowout loss to the Buffalo Bills, Milloy's new team.

As noted in Chapter 6, after going 2-2 in their first four games, the Patriots went off on a winning streak unparalleled in NFL history. They won their next 15 games that season, including the Super Bowl, and the first six games of their next season. The 21 straight wins was an all-time NFL record. The Patriots were unquestionably the best team in football.

Within that winning streak were a couple of very notable games. One was a thrilling 19-13 overtime win in Miami, won on an 82 yeard touchdown pass in overtime from Tom to Troy Brown. Another was a Monday night game against the Broncos in Denver, where the Patriots came back from a 24-23 deficit with less than 3:00 to go. The Patriots had been backed up to their own 1 yard line and had to punt. The win was set up by the Patriots taking a safety instead of punting deep in their own territory and forcing the Broncos to punt on their ensuing possession. When New England got the ball back, Tom marched them down the field and got the game-winning TD on an 18 yard pass to David Givens, perfectly thrown into Givens' hands in the left side of the end zone.

New England rolled into the playoffs with a 14-2 record and won their two playoff games to head into the Super Bowl against the Carolina Panthers. It was another tight Super Bowl that would be decided by three points, and by more clutch fourth quarter heroics from Tom Brady and Adam Vinatieri. Tom led the Patriots on two dramatic drives in the last seven minutes of the game and once again set up Vinatieri for the game-winning field goal. Tom played a marvelous game, going 32 for 48 for 354 and 3 touchdowns, and, as a result, was the Super Bowl MVP for the second time.

The Patriots' winning ways continued into the 2004 season, as the team won its first six games to extend its NFL record winning streak to 21 games, before losing to Pittsburgh. New England finished 14-2 for the second consecutive year, and defeated Indianapolis and

Pittsburgh (a nice revenge win) to get to their second consecutive Super Bowl and third in four years. They would be facing a very strong Philadelphia team.

The game was tied 14-14 in the fourth quarter, when Tom, as calm and determined as ever, led his team on a 9 play 66 yard drive, that put them in the lead, and then, on their next possession, completed a highlight reel play, a 19 yard completion over the middle to Deion Branch with Branch making an acrobatic catch over the back of the Philly defender. That set up a field goal by Adam Vinatieri that pushed the New England lead to 24-14. They would hold on for a 24-21 victory. The Patriots were now Super Bowl champions for the third time in four years, only the second team in history to have accomplished that feat. They were the NFL's first dynasty of the 21st century.

Tom could have easily been chosen for his third Super Bowl MVP as he had another great day, completing 23 of 33 passes for 236 yards, 2 touchdowns and no interceptions. However, the choice went to Patriot receiver Deion Branch, and it was well deserved, as Branch had an equally great day, with 11 catches for 133 yards. Either choice was a good one.

Tom Brady was named Sportsman of the Year by *Sports Illustrated* in its end of year issue. With that honor, Brady joined such sports greats as Tiger Woods, Stan Musial, Bill Russell, Bobby Orr, Chris Evert, Jack Nicklaus, Cal Ripken Jr., and Joe Montana. As written earlier in this book,

> Although he had won two Super Bowl MVP awards and was one of the most popular players in all of sports, Brady was still a down-to-earth guy who was acknowledged as one of the hardest working members of the team. He personified the classy style of the Patriots. Perhaps the highest praise that Brady ever received came a couple of years later from his normally stoic coach, Bill Belichick. When Belichick was recruiting free agent wide receiver Jabar Gaffney to the team in 2006, he explained the Patriot team-first approach and overall Patriot style to Gaffney. He explained that everything revolves around the team, not individual statistics or glory. He described a scenario where no one takes credit, and everyone is part of the whole team effort. He concluded his comments to Gaffney by stating "Just listen to Tom." It would be hard to find any higher praise than that which is conveyed in those four words from Belichick about his hard-working star whose only goal is team success.

- - -

The Patriots went into the 2005 season hoping to become the first team ever to win three consecutive Super Bowls. However, it was not meant to be. Brady had to carry the team on his shoulders quite a bit in the 2005 season, as injuries kept mounting up on the team. The Patriots got two wins, over Pittsburgh and Atlanta, thanks in both games to late drives by Tom Brady that led to game-winning field goals by Adam Vinatieri.

The Patriots made the playoffs and won their first game, raising their post-season record to an almost unbelievable 10-0 in the Brady-Belichick era. Unfortunately, they lost the next playoff game, against Denver. The Patriots committed an uncharacteristic five turnovers in this game. The biggest came was an interception thrown by Tom Brady on a Patriot drive late in the third quarter. The Patriots were trailing 10-6 at the time, but had driven down to the Denver five yard line and were poised to take the lead. However, as Tom went back to pass, Denver came in with a blitz and Tom's pass to his right was picked off by Denver's Champ Bailey, who raced the ball back to the New England one yard line. The play turned the game around, gave the momentum back to Denver, and the Broncos rode it to a 27-13 win that eliminated the Patriots from the playoffs.

New England had a solid year in 2006, finishing with a 12-4 record. The Patriots beat the Jets 37-16 in their first playoff game, and then Tom Brady and Troy Brown led them to a stirring come-from-behind 24-21 win over San Diego with 11 points in the last eight minutes of the game. A beautifully thrown 49 yard completion to Reche Caldwell set up what would prove to be the game-winning field goal.

This win then sent the Patriots to Indianapolis for the AFC Championship Game, and, at first, this game had the makings of a New England rout and another big win for Brady and the Patriots over Manning and the Colts. New England jumped off to an early 21-3 lead, but the Colts came back to tie it 21-21 early in the third quarter. As described earlier,

> What followed next was alternating heroics by two fantastic quarterbacks, Tom Brady and Peyton Manning.

> Brady threw a 6 yard TD pass to Jabar Gaffney to make it 28-21 Patriots.

> Manning then drove Indianapolis to … a touchdown … and the game was again tied, 28-28.

> A field goal by New England, one by Indianapolis, and another by New England (a 43 yard field goal by Gostkowski after a

nice drive engineered by Tom Brady) gave the Patriots a 34-31 lead with under 4:00 to go. In the biggest play of the game, however, a Brady pass to the right to a wide open wide receiver, Reche Caldwell, was dropped. It would have been a sure first down and perhaps a drive that would have resulted in a touchdown. Instead the Pats had to settle for a field goal.

After two punts, Indianapolis had the ball on their own 20 yard line, with 2:17 to go in the game. The Colts needed to go 80 yards to score a touchdown and win the game ... But the defense could not hold. Indianapolis drove for the touchdown ... now the Colts led 38-34.

There was still one minute to play in the game ... Brady started moving New England down the field, getting them to the Indianapolis 45 with 24 seconds to go, when a pass over the middle intended for Benjamin Watson was intercepted by Marlin Jackson. The Patriots' last chance had been thwarted. It would be Indianapolis going to the Super Bowl.

It was a disappointing loss for the Patriots, but a great win for the Colts and for Peyton Manning. Manning and Brady have been universally recognized as the two best players in the game. Their rivalry was a friendly one, and they even collaborated on getting the NFL to change its procedures regarding the preparation and use of game balls, changing it to a way that gave the quarterbacks a better feel for the balls that would be used during a game. When quarterbacks and classy players such as Tom and Peyton make a request, the NFL listens.

The 2007 season was a dream season for the Patriots and for Tom. The addition of wide receivers Randy Moss and Wes Welker allowed Tom to have one of the best seasons an NFL quarterback has ever had. He threw for an NFL record 50 touchdown passes. Tom and Randy Moss combined for 23 of those touchdowns, the most ever by any passer-receiver combination. Tom had only eight interceptions, making his touchdown-to-interception differential an NFL record 42. He had a record 12 games with three or more touchdown passes. The season and Tom exploits are recounted in great detail in Chapter 6, so won't be repeated here, but suffice to say that it was indeed one of the greatest seasons in NFL history.

Similarly, the trials and tribulations of Tom's injury-plagued 2008 season, and his comeback in 2009 are chronicled earlier in this book, and won't be repeated here, but we'll close with a reverse "Player Word Association", showing the quotes about Tom made by some of the people who were interviewed, and others who have worked with him.

Troy Brown said of Tom that he is "unbelievably cool under pressure".

Lawyer Milloy called Tom a "franchise player" and added, succinctly, "All of us are wearing one championship ring, or multiple rings, because of him, because of his greatness, his readiness, and his continuity."

Drew Bledsoe felt that people would have expected that he would have some animosity toward Tom, since, after all, Tom is the player who took his job, but he told me that he did not. He said of Tom that "It's been gratifying to me to watch Tommy's career not only on the field but off the field and the way that he's continually conducted himself while getting all the accolades that he has." What he said after that remains one of the most memorable comments in the set of interviews that I did for the book: "I always thought that if somebody needed to take my job he had to be somebody special and he has continued to prove that he is a special player and a very classy person."

Jon Morris commented that he thinks "Brady is the best quarterback I've ever seen ... he's just fabulous." He and many of the others interviewed who did not play with Brady named him as one player that they wish they had had a chance to play with, when that question came up in the interview.

We'll close with quotes from two people who were not interviewed for this book (though I tried).

The September 14, 2009 issue of The Sporting News had a four page feature on Kansas City Chief quarterback Matt Cassel. Matt was Brady's backup for three years and then took over in 2008 when Tom was injured. Dennis Dillon, who authored the article, points out. "If you have to be an understudy, Tom Brady is the one to study under. Brady's fingers are clearly on Cassel's development." In the article, Matt is quoted as saying of Tom,

> "When you come in as a rookie, you're just hoping one of the veterans will take an interest in you, and he did that in such an amazing way, welcoming me with open arms. Any questions I had, he was helpful. Then I got to watch him study and prepare and work out throughout the course of a week. It taught me how to be a professional and taught me kind of like the menu of what you need to do to be successful as a quarterback in the NFL."

We'll leave the last word on Tom Brady for the man who has been his coach during Tom's 10 years with the New England Patriots, Bill Belichick. At a press conference after the Patriots' game in London, England on October 25, 2009, In his post-game press conference, Bill Belichick talked about the game and talked about some of the things that he had done in England. Visiting Churchill's war bunkers was a highlight for him, "something that I'm sure I'll remember," said the coach. Then one of the questioners mentioned, "You haven't touched upon Tom Brady very much," and said something inaudible to us about Brady being comfortable in the offense. Belichick's reply was almost effusive in praising Brady:

> "Tom's comfortable running our offense. He's been doing it for nine years. Tom's a guy that just works hard and every week he's such a positive player on our football team, both for himself, our team, and the younger players, particularly in a week like this with Sam [Aiken], Brandon [Tate], and even Matt Slater jumping in there and taking a few plays.

> "Nobody prepares harder than Tom. Nobody works harder than Tom. And all the success that he gets on the field he really deserves, because he puts so much into it and he gives so much of himself for this football team.

> "He's a great leader. He's a great worker. And I'm glad he's our quarterback. There's nobody I'd rather have than Tom Brady."

Me too.

APPENDICES

Vin Femia Patriot Pride

Appendix A – Bibliography

Books

Cafardo, Nick, *The Impossible Team*, Triumph Books, 2002.

Curran, Bob, *The $ 400,000 Quarterback, or: The League that Came In From the Cold,* Signet Books, The New American Library, 1969.

Donaldson, Jim, *Stadium Stories: New England Patriots*, Pequot Press, 2005.

Felger, Michael, *Tales from the Patriots Sideline*, Sports Publishing L.L.C., 2006.

Halberstam, David, *The Education of a Coach*, Hyperion, 2005.

Holley, Michael, *Patriot Reign*, HarperCollins, 2004.

Horrigan, Jack and Rathet, Mike, *The Other League*, Follett Publishing Company, 1970.

Izenberg, Jerry, *No Medals for Trying*, Ballantine Books, 1990.

Parcells, Bill with Coplon, Jeff, *Finding a Way to Win*, Doubleday 1995.

Price, Christopher, *The Blueprint*, Thomas Dunne Books, 2007.

Magazines

Sports Illustrated, Time Inc. – various issues

The Sporting News, American City Business Journals, Inc. – various issues

Internet Web Sites

Femia, Michael, Sports Redux column in www.boston.com – various postings

Wikipedia, on-line encyclopedia – various postings

Sports Media Publications

2008 New England Patriots Media Guide,
2008 NFL Record & Fact Book,Time, Inc. 2008

Appendix B – Relevant NFL Rules

The following provide more of a description of some of the NFL rules and procedures that have played a part in Patriot history.

The Tuck Rule

(from description found in the book "The Blueprint" by Christopher Price of NFL Rule 3, Section 21, Article 2, Note 2.)

"When a Team A player is holding the ball to pass it forward, any intentional forward movement of the passer's arm starts a forward pass, even if the player loses possession of the ball as he is attempting to tuck it back toward his body."

Rules/Provisions Related to In-game Filming

(as listed in the on-line encyclopedia, Wikipedia.)

"Page 105 of the 2007 NFL *Game Operations Manual* states, 'No video recording devices of any kind are permitted to be in use in the coaches' booth, on the field, or in the locker room during the game...All video shooting locations must be enclosed on all sides with a roof overhead.' ... In a September 2006 memorandum sent out by NFL Vice President of Football Operations ... all teams were told that 'videotaping of any type, including but not limited to taping of an opponent's offensive or defensive signals, is prohibited on the sidelines, in the coaches' booth, in the locker room, or at any other locations accessible to club staff members during the game.' "

Computing Quarterback Rating

(as listed in the on-line encyclopedia, Wikipedia.)

The NFL's current passer rating (also known as quarterback rating) system was conceived by Pro Football Hall of Fame's retired vice president Don Smith in 1973. The system is a sliding scale design, where outstanding performances meet diminishing returns faster than sub-par ones. The best passer rating that a quarterback can obtain is 158.3, while the worst is 0. ... Passer rating is determined by four statistical components, each of which is computed as a number between zero and 2.375. The benchmarks for these statistics are based on historical averages. If any of the raw components are beyond the limits of zero or 2.375, the component is set to limiting value of zero or 2.375 as the case may be.

- The component for completion percentage, C, is calculated as $((Comp/Att)*100-30)/20$
- The component for yards per attempt, Y, is calculated as $(.25 * ((yds/att) -3))$
- The component for touchdowns per attempt, T, is calculated as $(TD/Att) * 20$
- The component for interceptions per attempt, I, is calculated as $2.375 - ((Int/Att) * 25$

The four components are then added, divided by 6, and multiplied by 100. Thus, the formula for passer rating is
$((max(min(C,2.375),0)+max(min(Y,2.375),0)+max(min(T,2.375),0)+ max(min(I,2.375),0))/ 6) * 100$

Since each component of passer rating can be at most 2.375, the maximum passer rating is
$((4 * 2.375) / 6) * 100$, or 158.3

Appendix C – Miscellaneous Lists

In my previous book, "The Possible Dream", I mentioned that many a Red Sox fan has spent time making lists as a way of remembering both happy times and disappointments. Here are some lists for Patriot fans who may have the same mentality.

All-Time Patriot Teams (in one fan's opinion)

The following is a subjective look at the all-time Patriot teams, the best at each position in my opinion, since 1960. There are two lists, the All-Time Team, and Honorable Mentions at each position.

	All-Time Team	**Honorable Mention**
QB	Tom Brady	Steve Grogan, Drew Bledsoe
RB	Jim Nance	Sam Cunningham,Craig James
RB	Curtis Martin	Corey Dillon, Andy Johnson
WR	Troy Brown	Stanley Morgan
WR	Wes Welker	Gino Cappelletti
T	Leon Gray	Matt Light
G	John Hannah	Logan Mankins
C	Jon Morris	Dan Koppen, Pete Brock
G	Len St. Jean	Billy Neighbors, Sam Adams
T	Bruce Armstrong	Tom Neville
TE	Ben Coates	Russ Francis
K	Adam Vinatieri	John Smith
DE	Bob Dee	Julius Adams
DT	Houston Antwine	Richard Seymour
DT	Jim Lee Hunt	Vince Wilfork
DE	Larry Eisenhauer	Willie McGinest
OLB	Mike Vrabel	Chris Slade
MLB	Steve Nelson	Nick Buoniconti, Tedy Bruschi
OLB	Andre Tippett	Roman Phifer
DB	Mike Haynes	Raymond Clayborn
DB	Ty Law	Assante Samuel
S	Tim Fox	Fred Marion
S	Lawyer Milloy	Rodney Harrison
P	Rich Camarillo	Tom Tupa
KR	Kevin Faulk	Dave Meggett
Spec Tms	Larry Izzo	Mosi Tatupu
Coach	Bill Belichick	Bill Parcells, Raymond Berry

Patriots on all three championship teams (2001, 2003, 2004)

Tom Brady	QB	Richard Seymour	DL
Troy Brown	WR	Willie McGinest	LB/DL
Matt Light	OL	Mike Vrabel	LB
Joe Andruzzi	OL	Tedy Bruschi	LB
Stephen Neal	OL	Ty Law	DB
Kevin Faulk	WR/RB	Roman Phifer	LB
David Patten	WR	Ted Johnson	LB
Lonie Paxton	Long Snapper	Larry Izzo	Special Teams
Adrian Klemm	OL	Matt Chatham	LB
Patrick Pass	RB	Je'Rod Cherry	S
Adam Vinatieri	K		

Teams Winning Consecutive Championships

Chicago	1940-41	Green Bay	1961-62	Houston	1960-61 AFL
Philadelphia	1948-49	Green Bay	1965-67	Buffalo	1964-65 AFL
Detroit	1952-53	Miami	1972-73		
Cleveland	1954-55	Pittsburgh	1974-75		
Baltimore	1958-59	Pittsburgh	1978-79		
		San Francisco	1988-89		
		Dallas	1992-93		
		Denver	1997-98		
		New England	2003-04		

Most Super Bowls Won as of 2010

Pittsburgh	6
Dallas	5
San Francisco	5
Green Bay	3
New England	3
NY Giants	3
Oakland/LA	3
Washington	3

Top Post-Season Won-Lost Records as of 2010

	W	L	
Pittsburgh	31	19	.620
Green Bay	25	16	.610
New England	21	14	.600
San Francisco	25	17	.595
Oakland/LA	25	18	.581
Washington	23	17	.575
Dallas	33	25	.569

New England's NFL Record 21 game winning streak
(October 5, 2003–October 24, 2004)

1.	Titans	38-30	
2.	Giants	17-6	
3.	Dolphins	19-13	
4.	Browns	9-3	
5.	Broncos	30-26	
6.	Cowboys	12-0	
7.	Texans	23-20	
8.	Colts	38-34	
9.	Dolphins	12-0	
10.	Jaguars	27-13	
11.	Jets	21-16	
12.	Bills	31-0	
13.	Titans	17-14	Playoffs
14.	Colts	24-14	AFC Championship
15.	Panthers	32-29	Super Bowl
16.	Colts	27-24	
17.	Cardinals	23-12	
18.	Bills	31-17	
19.	Dolphins	24-10	
20.	Seahawks	30-20	
21.	Jets	13-7	

New England's Record 21 game regular season winning streak
(December 17, 2006 – September 14, 2008)

1.	Texans	40-7	
2.	Jaguars	24-21	
3.	Titans	40-23	
4.	Jets	38-14	Part of 16-0 regular season
5.	Chargers	38-14	Part of 16-0 regular season
6.	Bills	38-7	Part of 16-0 regular season
7.	Bengals	34-13	Part of 16-0 regular season
8.	Browns	34-17	Part of 16-0 regular season
9.	Cowboys	48-27	Part of 16-0 regular season
10.	Dolphins	49-28	Part of 16-0 regular season
11.	Redskins	52-7	Part of 16-0 regular season
12.	Colts	24-20	Part of 16-0 regular season
13.	Bills	56-10	Part of 16-0 regular season
14.	Eagles	31-28	Part of 16-0 regular season
15.	Ravens	27-24	Part of 16-0 regular season
16.	Steelers	34-13	Part of 16-0 regular season
17.	Jets	20-10	Part of 16-0 regular season
18.	Dolphins	28-7	Part of 16-0 regular season
19.	Giants	38-35	Part of 16-0 regular season
20.	Chiefs	17-10	
21.	Jets	19-10	

New England's Primary Coaches, QB's, and W-L records

Year	Coach	QB	W-L
1960	Lou Saban	Butch Songin	5-9
1961	"	"	9-4-1
1962	Mike Holovak	Babe Parilli	9-4-1
1963	"	"	7-6-1
1964	"	"	10-3-1
1965	"	"	4-8-2
1966	"	"	8-4-2
1967	"	"	3-10-1
1968	"	Tom Sherman	4-10
1969	Clive Rush	Mike Taliaferro	4-10
1970	"	Joe Kapp	2-12
1971	John Mazur	Jim Plunkett	6-8
1972	"	"	3-11
1973	Chuck Fairbanks	"	5-9
1974	"	"	7-7
1975	"	Steve Grogan	3-11
1976	"	"	11-3
1977	"	"	9-5
1978	"	"	11-5
1979	Ron Erhardt	"	9-7
1980	"	"	10-6
1981	"	"	2-14
1982	Ron Meyer	"	5-4
1983	"	"	8-8
1984	"	Tony Eason	9-7
1985	Raymond Berry	"	11-5
1986	"	"	11-5
1987	"	Steve Grogan	8-7
1988	"	Doug Flutie	9-7
1989	"	Steve Grogan	5-11
1990	Rod Rust	Marc Wilson	1-15
1991	Dick MacPherson	Hugh Millen	6-10
1992	"	"	2-14
1993	Bill Parcells	Drew Bledsoe	5-11
1994	"	"	10-6
1995	"	"	6-10
1996	"	"	11-5
1997	Pete Carroll	"	10-6
1998	"	"	9-7
1999	"	"	8-8
2000	Bill Belichick	"	5-11
2001	"	Tom Brady	11-5
2002	"	"	9-7
2003	"	"	14-2
2004	"	"	14-2
2005	"	"	10-6
2006	"	"	12-4
2007	"	"	16-0
2008	"	Matt Cassel	11-5
2009	"	Tom Brady	10-6

Super Bowl Champions

Year	Winner	Loser	Score
1967	Green Bay Packers	Kansas City Chiefs	35-10
1968	Green Bay Packers	Oakland Raiders	33-14
1969	New York Jets	Baltimore Colts	16-7
1970	Kansas City Chiefs	Minnesota Vikings	23-7
1971	Baltimore Colts	Dallas Cowboys	16-13
1972	Dallas Cowboys	Miami Dolphins	24-3
1973	Miami Dolphins	Washington Redskins	14-7
1974	Miami Dolphins	Minnesota Vikings	24-7
1975	Pittsburgh Steelers	Minnesota Vikings	16-6
1976	Pittsburgh Steelers	Dallas Cowboys	21-17
1977	Oakland Raiders	Minnesota Vikings	32-14
1978	Dallas Cowboys	Denver Broncos	27-10
1979	Pittsburgh Steelers	Dallas Cowboys	35-31
1980	Pittsburgh Steelers	Los Angeles Rams	31-19
1981	Oakland Raiders	Philadelphia Eagles	27-10
1982	San Francisco 49ers	Cincinnati Bengals	26-21
1983	Washington Redskins	Miami Dolphins	27-17
1984	Los Angeles Raiders	Washington Redskins	38-9
1985	San Francisco 49ers	Miami Dolphins	38-16
1986	Chicago Bears	New England Patriots	46-10
1987	New York Giants	Denver Broncos	39-20
1988	Washington Redskins	Denver Broncos	42-10
1989	San Fraancisco 49ers	Cincinnati Bengals	20-16
1990	San Francisco 49ers	Denver Broncos	55-10
1991	New York Giants	Buffalo Bills	20-19
1992	Washington Redskins	Buffalo Bills	37-24
1993	Dallas Cowboys	Buffalo Bills	52-17
1994	Dallas Cowboys	Buffalo Bills	30-13
1995	San Francisco 49ers	San Diego Chargers	49-26
1996	Dallas Cowboys	Pittsburgh Steelers	27-17
1997	Green Bay Packers	New England Patriots	35-21
1998	Denver Broncos	Green Bay Packers	31-24
1999	Denver Broncos	Atlanta Falcons	34-19
2000	St. Louis Rams	Tennessee Titans	23-16
2001	Baltimore Ravens	New York Giants	34-7
2002	New England Patriots	St. Louis Rams	20-17
2003	Tampa Bay Buccaneers	Oakland Raiders	48-21
2004	New England Patriots	Carolina Panthers	32-29
2005	New England Patriots	Philadelphia Eagles	24-21
2006	Pittsburgh Steelers	Seattle Seahawks	21-10
2007	Indianapolis Colts	Chicago Bears	29-17
2008	New York Giants	New England Patriots	17-14
2009	Pittsburgh Steelers	Arizona Cardinals	27-23
2010	New Orleans Saints	Indianapolis Colts	31-17

AFL Champions

Year	Winner	Loser	Score	
1960	Houston Oilers	Los Angeles Chargers	24-16	
1961	Houston Oilers	San Diego Chargers	10-3	
1962	Dallas Texans	Houston Oilers	20-17	(OT)
1963	San Diego Chargers	Boston Patriots	51-10	
1964	Buffalo Bills	San Diego Chargers	20-7	
1965	Buffalo Bills	San Diego Chargers	23-0	
1966	Kansas City Chiefs	Buffalo Bills	31-7	
1967	Oakland Raiders	Houston Oilers	40-7	
1968	New York Jets	Oakland Raiders	27-23	
1969	Kansas City Chiefs	Oakland Raiders	17-7	

Patriot #1 overall picks in NFL Draft

1964	Jack Concannon	QB	Boston College	(AFL)
1971	Jim Plunkett	QB	Stanford	
1982	Kenneth Sims	DL	Texas	
1984	Irving Fryar	WR	Nebraska	
1993	Drew Bledsoe	QB	Washington State	

Patriots selected as AFL/NFL Most Valuable Player

1964	Gino Cappelletti	(AFL)
1966	Jim Nance	(AFL)
2007	Tom Brady	

Patriot Home Fields

1960-62	Boston University Field	
1963-68	Fenway Park	
1969	Boston College Alumni Field	
1970	Harvard Stadium	
1971-82	Schaefer Stadium	*
1983-89	Sullivan Stadium	*
1990-2001	Foxboro Stadium	*
2002-present	Gillette Stadium	

* - same field, different name

Top Ten Most Significant Players in Patriot History (in my opinion)

1. Tom Brady
2. Steve Grogan
3. Adam Vinatieri
4. Drew Bledsoe
5. John Hannah
6. Jim Plunkett
7. Mike Haynes
8. Tedy Bruschi
9. Mike Vrabel
10. Jim Nance

Top Ten Most Significant Games in Patriot History (in my opinion)

1. February 3, 2002 Patriots 20 Rams 17 – Patriots win Super Bowl for first time in team history
2. January 19, 2001 Patriots 16 Raiders 13 – Patriots defeat Oakland in playoff game played in a blizzard, thanks to tuck rule and to the great clutch play of Brady and Vinatieri
3. December 18, 1976 Raiders 24 Patriots 21 – Raiders win playoff game with help of dubious officiating
4. February 1, 2004 Patriots 32 Panthers 29 – Patriots win Super Bowl for second time
5. February 6, 2005 – Patriots 24 Eagles 21 – Patriots win second consecutive Super Bowl and become only second team in NFL history to win three Super Bowls in a four year span
6. January 12, 1986 Patriots 31 Dolphins 14 – Patriots win for first time in Orange Bowl since 1967 (18 years), to win first AFC Championship
7. February 3, 2008 Giants 17 Patriots 14 – Giants upset Patriots to prevent New England from completing a perfect 19-0 season
8. December 29, 2007 Patriots 38 Giants 35 – Patriots defeat Giants to finish the first 16-0 season in NFL history; Tom Brady throws NFL record 50th touchdown pass and Randy Moss catches NFL record 23rd touchdown pass of season
9. September 23, 2001 Jets 10 Patriots 3 – First game after 9/11 terrorist attacks on U.S. Bledsoe injury paves way for Tom Brady to step in as the Patriot's new starting quarterback
10. September 9, 1960 Broncos 13 Patriots 10 – First regular season game in franchise history is first AFL game ever played

All-Time NFL Team 1960-present (in one fan's opinion)

QB	Johnny Unitas, Colts	DL	David "Deacon" Jones, Rams
RB	Jim Brown, Browns		Bob Lilly, Cowboys
RB	Emmitt Smith, Cowboys		Mean Joe Greene, Steelers
WR	Jerry Rice, 49ers		Alan Page, Vikings
WR	Raymond Berry, Colts	OLB	Lawrence Taylor, Giants
TE	Dave Casper, Raiders		Chuck Howley, Cowboys
T	Jim Parker, Colts	MLB	Dick Butkus, Bears
	Ron Mix, Chargers	DB	Dick "Night Train" Lane, Lions
G	John Hannah, Patriots		Willie Wood, Packers
	Gene Upshaw, Raiders	SS	Charlie Waters, Cowboys
C	Jim Otto, Raiders	FS	Jake Scott, Dolphins
K	Adam Vinatieri, Patriots	P	Ray Guy Raiders

Coach   Vince Lombardi, Packers

Patriots in the post-season

Season
1963	at Buffalo	W	26-8	(one game playoff for AFL East)
	at San Diego	L	10-51	(AFL Championship)
1976	at Oakland	L	21-24	
1978	Houston	L	14-31	
1982	at Miami	L	13-28	
1985	at NY Jets	W	26-14	
	at LA Raiders	W	27-20	
	at Miami	W	31-14	
*	Chicago	L	10-46	(1986 Super Bowl)
1986	at Denver	L	17-22	
1995	at Cleveland	L	13-20	
1996	Pittsburgh	W	28-3	
	Jacksonville	W	20-6	
*	Green Bay	L	21-35	(1997 Super Bowl)
1997	Miami	W	17-3	
	at Pittsburgh	L	6-7	
1998	at Jacksonville	L	10-25	
2001	Oakland	W	16-13	(Overtime)
	at Pittsburgh	W	24-17	
*	St. Louis	W	20-17	(2002 Super Bowl)
2003	Tennessee	W	17-14	
	Indianapolis	W	24-14	
*	Carolina	W	32-29	(2004 Super Bowl)
2004	Indianapolis	W	20-3	
	at Pittsburgh	W	41-27	
*	Philadelphia	W	24-21	(2005 Super Bowl)
2005	Jacksonville	W	28-3	
	at Denver	L	13-27	
2006	NY Jets	W	37-16	
	at San Diego	W	24-21	
	at Indianapolis	L	34-38	
2007	Jacksonville	W	31-20	
	San Diego	W	21-12	
*	NY Giants	L	14-17	(2008 Super Bowl)
2009	Baltimore	L	14-33	

The Patriots have an overall post-season record of 21-14

Top Quarterbacks, Running Backs, 1960-present

1.	Johnny Unitas	Jim Brown
2.	Joe Montana	Emmitt Smith
3.	Peyton Manning	Walter Payton
4.	Tom Brady	Barry Sanders
5.	Roger Staubach	Franco Harris
6.	Bart Starr	Larry Csonka
7.	Terry Bradshaw	Eric Dickerson
8.	Dan Marino	Gale Sayers
9.	Joe Namath	O.J. Simpson
10.	John Elway	Jim Taylor

Boston and New England Pro Football Franchises

1925-31	Providence Steam Roller	
1929	Boston Bulldogs	
1932	Boston Braves	*
1933-36	Boston Redskins	*
1944-48	Boston Yanks	
1960-1970	Boston Patriots	
1971-present	New England Patriots	

There was also a Boston Shamrocks team that played in an older AFL circa 1936 and a Boston Breakers team that played in the USFL in the 1980s. There have also been other teams in minor leagues such as the Hartford Charter Oaks in the 1960s. The above are those that were part of the NFL or its predecessor leagues, or the AFL which merged with the NFL in 1970.

* The 1932 team called the Boston Braves was owned by George Preston Marshall and played at Braves Field. When they moved to Fenway Park the following season, they were renamed the Redskins. Marshall moved the team to Washington in 1937, where they have remained since as the Washington Redskins. (Note: the Redskins won the NFL Championship in their first season in Washington, beating the Chicago Bears 28-21.)

Appendix D – Adventures in Interviewing

The section on Difference Makers which has the interviews with players, team management, and media members is mostly meant to contain their memories of their years with the Patriots (most memorable games, toughest opponents, how they remember teammates, and so on). My comments about those key games and all can be found in the earlier part of the book. However, friends who have read some of the interviews have told me that readers might be interested in some of my experiences in doing these interviews, so I have chosen to include those here, in an appendix to the book, so as not to get in the way of readers enjoying the interviews with the men who made the history.

This project started during the week of September 7, 2008. It was the week after the season-ending injury to Tom Brady in the first game of that season. I awoke during the middle of the night with the thought that a book about how the Patriots overcame the loss of the Super Bowl in February and the loss of Tom Brady to injury in September could be interesting to Patriot and football fans. I soon realized that the Patriots were about to enter their 50th season as a franchise, and decided to expand the book to include the team's history over those 50 years.

A few weeks later, I decided that I wanted to include interviews with Patriot players and management who helped create the history, and so, on October 21, 2008, I sent a letter to Bob Kraft, Jonathan Kraft, and Stacey James (Patriot VP of Media Relations) to begin the process of trying to make that happen. When I received no response, I tried e-mails on November 3, 15, and December 2. When I received no response, I made phone calls on December 4, 16, 17, 31, and January 2 and 5. I ultimately was invited in to meet with Stacey James, which I did on January 8, 2009.

Mr. James was very accommodating, though he did try to dissuade me from this project. He talked about the numerous similar requests that they get. He mentioned that this would be a lot more interesting if it were David Halberstam coming in with this proposal, which, putting aside the fact that unfortunately Mr. Halberstam, a great writer, is dead, I completely understood. Frankly, if David Halberstam were writing this, I'd be more interested in reading it myself. He also mentioned that more people would be reading the *Boston Globe* the next day than would read my book. I agreed but mentioned that they would throw away the Globe, but keep my book and might refer to it again from time to time, as I do with books that I have. He did finally agree to consider the proposal, and to talk to others in the Patriot office about it and get back to me in a week, and I left some materials with him to help in those discussions. He did mention that, if this happened at all, I would be more likely to get to talk with former players than current players, since there were more demands on current players' time.

After not hearing back, I followed up a few more times by e-mail and phone, and finally heard back from Stacey James on February 25 (interestingly, it was four months after my original request), that they would do it, and asked me to send a list of former players that I would like to interview, and that Donna Spigarolo, the Patriots' Alumni Coordinator would see what she could set up.

I responded with a list of eight players that I believed lived in the local area, and who represented time across the five decades that are covered in the book: Steve Grogan, Steve Nelson, Troy Brown, Gino Cappelletti, Jon Morris (we are both alumni of Holy Cross, which I thought might make this more appealing to him), Bob Gladieux (related to some of the stories in the book), Doug Flutie, and Scott Zolak. I also added that it would be great to interview the four Hall of Famers who had played with the Patriots, John Hannah, Andre Tippett, Nick Buoniconti, and Mike Haynes.

Donna Spigarolo did a great job in setting up these first interviews. She called me on March 16 to let me know that she was in the process of setting them up, but that John Hannah would be in town on the 18th and asked if I could meet him then, which I did. I was a little apprehensive going into the meeting, since John Hannah had a reputation for being surly with some people. I had prepared well for the meeting (as I would like to believe that I did for every interview) and had a bunch of questions, but found early on that that John was absolutely fantastic doing this, very open and honest and willing to share his memories, so we had a great conversation.

The ball was now rolling and the other interviews followed. Six were set up by Donna. Others were set up by my directly contacting players (e.g., Drew Bledsoe) or their agents (e.g., Lawyer Milloy), or through friends or other contacts (e.g., John Smith and Bob Lobel), and others being set up thanks to previous interviews (e.g., through Bob Lobel I was able to contact Upton Bell, through Upton Bell I was able to contact Raymond Berry, Randy Vataha, and Len St. Jean).

One of the most interesting scenarios occurred during my interview with Troy Brown, which was arranged through the Patriots, and through Troy's personal assistant, Barbara Rizzo. Troy was kind enough to invite me do the interview at his house. As we were doing the interview at his dining room table, the doorbell rang, and Barbara went to answer it. She came back and said that it was a police officer and that he needed to speak to both of us. When we got to the door, he told us that they had gotten a report of a car driving by Troy's house and of an unfamiliar car parked in Troy's driveway. He asked if that car was mine and what I was doing there, and I explained the interview. He then turned and asked Troy, "Is everything OK?" and Troy said "Yes." However, the police officer then leaned in closer to him and asked, "Are you sure that everything is OK, Troy?" Troy told him that everything was fine and so he left. Later, as I was driving home, I thought that was weird and nice. Weird that it happened, but sort of nice, I guess, that the police in Troy's town are so interested in protecting him and making sure that he is not dealing with a stalker, an over-exuberant fan, or some other sort of uninvited guest.

The interview with Drew Bledsoe was set up thanks to his mother, Barbara. I had written Drew a letter asking for the interview, and followed up a few days later with a phone call, only to find his voicemail box full. It was still full in subsequent tries over the next few days, so I sent another letter to tell Drew about his voicemail box being full. I tried calling again a few times over the next few days, only to find the same situation. So I called his parents' number to let them know so that they could tell Drew. I talked with his mother who was very nice and she asked me to send her an e-mail about this and she would forward it to Drew and he could decide whether to do the interview or not, so I did send her an e-mail. After a few more tries over a few days that found the voicemail box still full. So I sent her another message saying that I still hadn't heard whether he would do the interview or not but wanted to let her know that the problem with Drew's voicemail still existed. I told her that I wouldn't bother her again about this but wanted to let her know about the mailbox so that she could tell him. She wrote back to say that I wasn't bothering her, that she would forward this message to Drew and while it was still his decision whether or not to do the interview she added that she "will ask him to be the polite guy he was raised to be and give you a response." A couple of days later I got an e-mail from Drew asking if there was a time that we could talk. Thank you, Mrs. Bledsoe.

By the way, we did the interview and Drew was great - very nice, very open, and he had some great things to say including a lot of 'wow' moments, as you probably have already seen in that interview write-up, such as his great comments about Tom Brady and in describing the work with which he is now involved.

My interview with Len St. Jean was also at his house. It should have been a 57 minute ride from my house to his, according to Mapquest and Google Maps, but these applications cannot account for the completely frustrating Mass Pike. An accident at the intersection of the Pike and Route 128 backed traffic up to Framingham, so what should have taken me those 57 minutes, took me about 120 minutes instead. It is a real chore to drive on the Mass Pike these days. There is almost always a bottleneck. The only thing worse in New England is the interchange between Route 91 North and Route 84 East in Hartford. It never used to be a problem, but now, some misguided, ill-planning, non-thinking road planner decided that the exchange between these two major, heavily traveled highways should be a single lane up a hill. It is terrible. There are frequently long lines and cars zipping in from multiple lanes to try to get as far into the queue as they can. Whoever designed that should be forced to drive up that interchange and dodge those merging cars at the end of every holiday weekend. It would be worse than the famed Chinese Water Torture, but it would be well-deserved.

After I did get to Len St. Jean's house, the interview went well. However, when it was time to leave, Len and his dog came out when I did, and the dog decided to play a game with Len where it would run around to one side of my car, wait for him to come around to that side, and then would run to the other side and wait. I was in my car but did not want to back up and hit the dog. After a few rounds of this canine hide-and-seek, Len suggested that I turn off my car. I did and a few yells by Len got the dog to run into the house and I was able to take off. I got home in just about an hour, but it was a long day.

The interview with Lawyer Milloy was done by phone, and it was fun to hear him interact with his kids while it was being done. I realized that this was happening when the answer to one of my questions was "You have your shoes on the wrong feet." Even though we do not have video phones, I knew that it was not me that he was addressing, though I did check my own feet, just to be sure.

My biggest disappointment in arranging for the interviews was not being able to do an interview with Tom Brady, who is obviously one of the most significant difference-makers in Patriots' history. However, I want to acknowledge and thank Shantal Lamelas, Director of Client Relations for the agency that represents Tom, for discussing my proposal within the agency, and trying to make this happen. It wound up that they could not fit this into Tom's schedule, which was no surprise, given his schedule and popularity, and the fact that 2009 was the year of his wedding, rehab from injury, and birth of his second son. It was also nice to get her comment about how they appreciated the professionalism of the proposal that I had sent in this regard, and my response. I in turn appreciated that they took the time to discuss and consider this and get back to me.

On the flip side, while the representatives for Tom Brady did consider this and respond for Brady, who is one of the most popular athletes on the planet, this was unfortunately not always the case. For example, I spoke with the agent for Doug Flutie and she asked for a proposal but then never got back to me (despite many phone and e-mail follow-ups by me). Neither did Rodney Harrison, Jim Plunkett, Kevin Faulk, Fred Smerlas, Steve Nelson, or the contact person for Charlie Weis at Notre Dame. I realize that I am no David Halberstam, but a quick 'no, not interested', 'no thank you', 'won't be able to do it', or even a simple 'no' would have been nice. It made me appreciate the comment from Barbara Bledsoe even more.

The agents and/or team reps for Deion Branch, Adam Vinatieri, Willie McGinest, Andre Tippett, Wes Welker, Mike Vrabel, and Matt Cassel were also contacted and did respond, although, for various reasons we could not get the interviews scheduled.

I also had tried to include a section of interviews with "The Noble Opposition". To that end, I contacted the agents for John Madden, Tony Dungy, and Tim Brown. I was interested in John Madden since he was the Head Coach of the Oakland team that played the Patriots in that epic 1976 playoff game and since he has broadcast many Patriot games over the years. One of these was their first Super Bowl win when he said of Tom Brady's last minute drive to the winning field goal, "What Tom Brady just did gives me goose bumps." I was interested in Dungy both to talk about the many thrilling games that his Indianapolis Colts played against the Patriots from 2002 to 2008, and to talk about the good works that he has been doing since leaving pro football. I was hoping to talk to Tim Brown about his career at Notre Dame and Oakland and his observations about the snowy "Tuck Rule" game in 2001. I never heard back from Tim Brown's agent, but I did hear back from the agents for Coach Madden and Coach Dungy, but we could not get the interviews scheduled. Nevertheless, I do appreciate their trying to do so.

For those people whom I did get to interview, I offered them a chance to ask that something not be included if they said something that they would rather not see in print, and, in many cases, offered them the opportunity to read the interview before it was published to see if there is anything that they would have liked not to have included. A few took me up on that, and I was glad to oblige.

To sum up, it was a fantastic experience getting to talk with these men and share their memories. My thanks go to one and all for their willingness to do so. I hope that you readers have also enjoyed reliving some of those moments and seeing what those moments meant to the men who were directly involved.

Appendix E – Information About IMEC

The International Medical Equipment Collaborative (IMEC) is a non-profit, volunteer-based organization whose mission is to provide doctors in developing countries with quality medical equipment to improve health care for the poor.

For the past 14 years, IMEC has worked with over sixty other humanitarian organizations to revitalize hundreds of existing, impoverished hospitals with donated surplus medical equipment and supplies that are organized into complete medical departments, delivering them to over seventy countries around the world.

IMEC has provided tools for doctors in Kenya, sent hospital equipment to Vietnam, delivered hospital furniture to Nicaragua, and brought medical supplies to Uzbekistan.

At the core of the service that IMEC offers is its system of Complete Medical Suites. IMEC assembles and ships donated medical equipment and supplies into function-focused suites, based on providing all the equipment needed to turn an empty room into a fully functional department of a working hospital. Complete Medical Suites — nursery, exam room, delivery, operating room, radiology, laboratory, etc.— include furniture and linens as well as medical equipment and tools, all cleaned, repaired and fully operational. Over years of service, IMEC has developed this system into an efficient and effective process for improving health care in impoverished hospitals worldwide.

Portions of the proceeds from the sale of this book are being donated to IMEC.

For additional information about IMEC or how you can make additional contributions directly to IMEC, you may contact IMEC America at:

International Medical Equipment Collaborative
1600 Osgood Street
North Andover, MA 01845
(phone) 978-557-5510
(email) imec@imecamerica.org

Appendix F – Information About the ALS Association

The ALS Association Massachusetts Chapter, Inc. (ALSA-MA Chapter) is a non-profit organization that serves people with Amyotrophic Lateral Sclerosis (ALS), commonly known as Lou Gehrig's disease.

ALS is a progressive and ultimately fatal disease of the neurological system. There is no cure. It causes patients to lose all muscular and nerve control, so the muscles weaken and waste away. It ultimately leads to paralysis. ALS manifests itself first in different ways such as falling, losing control of extremities, difficulty in speaking or swallowing, and fatigue. Eventually all bodily control is lost and failure of lungs or heart will lead to death. Having had an uncle die from this disease, I know the effects of the disease and know that it is very debilitating.

The ALS Association Massachusetts Chapter provides services for people with ALS, including free durable medical equipment, transportation, respite grants for home health care, financial and legal referrals to patients, education for their families and caregivers, support groups for patients' families, funding for research, and so on. The Association builds hope and enhances quality of life while aggressively searching for new treatments and a cure.

It also advocates for patient and caregiver rights by hosting an annual ALS Advocacy Day on Beacon Hill at the State level and participating in a nationwide effort at the Federal level. It pools research funds with other network chapters, making the ALS Association the largest funding source for ALS research in the world.

Portions of the proceeds from the sale of this book are being donated to the ALS Association.

For additional information about the ALS Association or how you can help or make additional contributions, you may contact

The ALS Association
320 Norwood Park S., 2nd Floor
Norwood, MA 02062
(phone) 781-255-8884 or toll free 888-CURE-ALS
(e-mail) info@als-ma.org

ACKNOWLEDGEMENTS

Thanks go to a lot of people for their help with the book and for their encouragement with this writing effort. Specifically, thanks to:

My late father, Frank Femia, who introduced me to football many years ago and helped make me a fan of the game. He was such a football fan that his friend, Ed Grimes, gave him a football for me on the day I was born. It was a white football with the autograph of Otto Graham, the great quarterback of the Cleveland Browns. That football was thrown around so much in the backyard that the seams split and I was throwing it for a while with the inside rubber showing -- though even with it like that, I could still hit my favorite targets with it: the bush in the front yard and right between the branches of the giant white birch tree in our back yard.

Thanks to my father I came to appreciate listening to football on the radio and watching it on TV, and I can remember laying on the floor, listening to radio broadcasts of such games as the Green Bay-Philadelphia championship in 1960, the Southern Cal-Wisconsin Rose Bowl game in 1963, numerous Notre Dame games in Ara Parseghian's first year as coach in 1964, and a number of Patriot games in the early 1960's. As the years went by, I always enjoyed watching NFL games with him on Sundays, and was glad when I was old enough to talk semi-intelligently about football with him.

Christine Femia, my daughter, for doing a great job of editing the book and providing excellent comments about what was written and how it was presented. Her comments and suggestions about potential titles as we were riding to the bus station in Hartford in September 2008 are also much appreciated. As she wrote when we had identified a number of potential titles and I asked her to write them down, it was "the result of two great brains, brainstorming".

Michael Femia, my son, for providing feedback and information about some of the games that we watched together in that great 2007-08 season, and some great pictures. Thanks also for all the phone calls after both thrilling victories and heart-breaking defeats.

Marjorie Femia, my wife, Steve and Debbie Femia, my son and daughter-in-law, for their willingness to listen to progress reports on the book patiently, and for their help with the pictures for this book.

Fred and Pat Link, and Randy and Pat Cumming, for their continued interest in, and encouragement about, the book, and their willingness both to listen patiently to my stories about the book, and to ask frequently about what was happening with the writing and publication. Their interest throughout this process was very encouraging and much appreciated.

Jean Setne and Mark Lancisi for doing a great job of editing the book and providing their comments and feedback.

Lisa and Gary Eklund for allowing me to use tickets to a couple of games in 2009 that they could not attend themselves. This enabled me to add a number of pictures to this book.

Tom Mulligan, my classmate at Holy Cross and my lifelong friend, for all of the e-mail exchanges over the years, and his interest in, questions about, and comments concerning the interviews that I was doing as they were going on, and for his patience in listening to and reading my comments and opinions.

Rick Kenny, my roommate at Holy Cross and my lifelong friend, a former high school football player in New Jersey, for helping me learn to appreciate offensive and defensive line play, especially as we watched such great players as Bob Lilly and David 'Deacon' Jones on TV and played snow football with other friends up on the hill at Holy Cross where the Hart Center is now.

Stacey James, New England Patriots' Vice President of Media Relations and Donna Spigarolo, New England Patriots' Alumni Coordinator, for their help in arranging interviews with John Hannah, Jon Morris, Bob Gladieux, Steve Grogan, Gino Cappelletti, and Troy Brown.

The Patriot players, management personnel, and media representatives who agreed to do the interviews for this book and who were so open and honest in their comments: John Hannah, Jon Morris, Bob Gladieux, Steve Grogan, Gino Cappelletti, Dick Cerasuolo, Bob Lobel, Upton Bell, Raymond Berry, Troy Brown, Randy Vataha, John Smith, Len St. Jean, Tim Fox, Drew Bledsoe, and Lawyer Milloy. Thanks also to those who provided pictures for this book: Jon Morris, Bob Gladieux, Gino Cappelletti, Len St. Jean, Upton Bell, Raymond Berry, Randy Vataha, and Drew Bledsoe.

Upton Bell, not only for doing the interview for this book about his time as General Manager of the team, but also for his continued interest in the book, and his help in putting me in contact with some of the other contributors who were interviewed: Raymond Berry, Randy Vataha, and Len St. Jean.

Barbara Bledsoe, mother of Drew Bledsoe, for her assistance in contacting Drew Bledsoe and helping to make the interview with Drew for this book happen.

Barbara Rizzo, Assistant to Troy Brown, for helping to set up the interview with Troy.

Caitlin Reddinger and Larry Kennan of the NFL Players' Association offices for providing contact info for the agents of some of the other interviewees.

Beth Dutton, a Troy Brown fan and former work colleague at Data General and Netezza, for her comments about the Troy Brown interview write-up.

Brian Khung, a former Netezza work colleague, for his comments about the Steve Grogan interview.

Paul Marino, a former Data General work colleague, for putting me in contact with John Smith for the interview with him.

Victoria Welch, for many of the great pictures that she took and which have been included in this book.

Len Lazure, Photo Editor of the Worcester Telegram & Gazette, for arranging for me to view, select, and use pictures from the Telegram archives for this book.

Trish Murphy, Licensing Manager, for ZUMA Press, Inc., for arranging for me to use pictures from *The Sporting News* for this book.

JoAnne O'Neill for providing pictures of Upton Bell, Steve Grogan, me, and others, and for always thinking of us for Upton's radio shows and events.

The Kansas City Chiefs for providing me with pictures of Matt Cassel and Mike Vrabel to use within the book, and for their patience in trying to arrange interviews with those former Patriots.

Jason Chayut and Chris Heroux of Sportstars, Inc. for providing the pictures of Deion Branch to use within the book.

Erica Levine, who handles Public Relations for the firm that represents Lawyer Milloy, for her help in arranging the interview with Lawyer.

And thanks to the players, owners, coaches, and staff of the Boston/New England Patriots for providing five decades of material for this book, and thanks especially for many unforgettable seasons (1963, 1976, 1978, 1985, 2001, 2003, 2004, that great 2007 season, and the fascinating 2008 and 2009 seasons that followed it).

ABOUT THE AUTHOR

This is Vin Femia's second book. His first, *The Possible Dream*, published in 2005, describes the reasons why the Red Sox had not won a World Series in so many years, and what they did in 2004 to finally achieve that goal. Vin donated a portion of all proceeds received from that book to a charity, the ALS Association, which helps patients with Lou Gehrig's disease and provides assistance to their families. *The Possible Dream* was # 2 on the Worcester County Best Seller list for two consecutive weeks in 2005, and, as a result, he was able to make a significant donation to that charity.

Vin has been in the Computer Software Industry for 35+ years, having started his post-Air Force career at Data General. He is currently working at EMC. At the time of the writing of this book, Vin was semi-retired after having served as Vice President of Engineering at such companies as Netezza Corporation and Concentric Data Systems. He has been in the industry since graduating magna cum laude from Holy Cross College in Worcester, MA.

Vin has been a life-long sports fan, having spent many hours listening to games on the radio and watching on TV while growing up in Connecticut. He has an excellent memory, which is not always the best attribute for a long-suffering Boston fan to have (since memories of some crushing last minute defeats never then fade). Friends and fans often call on him to answer questions or provide background information on the game.

Vin lives in Massachusetts with his wife Marjorie, who has heard his observations and opinions about sports for many years, and is probably happy to share them with Patriot and football fans everywhere and not have to listen to them all herself.